Formulation, Implementation, and Control of Competitive Strategy

Formulation, Implementation, and Control of Competitive Strategy

Ninth Edition

John A. Pearce II
College of Commerce and Finance
Villanova University

Richard B. Robinson, Jr.
Moore School of Business
University of South Carolina

McGraw-Hill Irwin

Boston   Burr Ridge, IL   Dubuque, IA   Madison, WI   New York   San Francisco   St. Louis
Bangkok   Bogotá   Caracas   Kuala Lumpur   Lisbon   London   Madrid   Mexico City
Milan   Montreal   New Delhi   Santiago   Seoul   Singapore   Sydney   Taipei   Toronto

The McGraw·Hill Companies

McGraw-Hill
Irwin

FORMULATION, IMPLEMENTATION, AND CONTROL OF COMPETITIVE STRATEGY
Published by McGraw-Hill/Irwin, a business unit of The McGraw-Hill Companies, Inc., 1221 Avenue of the Americas, New York, NY, 10020.
Copyright © 2005, 2003, 2000, 1997, 1994, 1991, 1988, 1985, 1982 by The McGraw-Hill Companies, Inc. All rights reserved. No part of this publication may be reproduced or distributed in any form or by any means, or stored in a database or retrieval system, without the prior written consent of The McGraw-Hill Companies, Inc., including, but not limited to, in any network or other electronic storage or transmission, or broadcast for distance learning.
Some ancillaries, including electronic and print components, may not be available to customers outside the United States.
This book is printed on acid-free paper.

domestic   1 2 3 4 5 6 7 8 9 0 DOW/DOW 0 9 8 7 6 5 4
international 1 2 3 4 5 6 7 8 9 0 DOW/DOW 0 9 8 7 6 5 4

ISBN 0-07-294688-1

Vice president and editor-in-chief: *Robin J. Zwettler*
Editorial director: *John E. Biernat*
Senior sponsoring editor: *Andy Winston*
Development editor: *Natalie Ruffatto*
Marketing manager: *Lisa Nicks*
Lead producer, Media technology: *Victoria Parker*
Project manager: *Marlena Pechan*
Senior production supervisor: *Sesha Bolisetty*
Freelance design coordinator: *Kami Carter*
Supplement producer: *Matthew Perry*
Senior digital content specialist: *Brian Nacik*
Cover design: *Kiera Pohl*
Typeface: *10/12 Times New Roman*
Compositor: *Carlisle Communications, Ltd.*
Printer: *R. R. Donnelley*

Library of Congress Cataloging-in-Publication Data
Pearce, John A.
  Formulation, implementation, and control of competitive strategy / John A. Pearce II,
  Richard B. Robinson, Jr.—9th ed.
      p. cm.
    Includes index.
      ISBN 0-07-294688-1 (alk. paper)
    1. Strategic planning. 2. Strategic planning—Case studies. I. Robinson, Richard B.
  (Richard Braden), 1947-II. Title.
  HD30.28.P3385 2005
  658.4'01–dc22
                                                                2003065112
INTERNATIONAL EDITION ISBN 0-07-111174-3
Copyright © 2005. Exclusive rights by The McGraw-Hill Companies, Inc. for manufacture and export. This book cannot be re-exported from the country to which it is sold by McGraw-Hill. The International Edition is not available in North America.

www.mhhe.com

To Mary Frances and Jack Pearce
Mattie and Frank Fletcher

Preface

This ninth edition of *Formulation, Implementation, and Control of Competitive Strategy* is both the culmination of work by many people and a major revision designed to accommodate the needs of strategy students in the twenty-first century. These are exciting times and they are reflected on the many new developments in this book and the accompanying McGraw-Hill supplements. This preface describes what we have done to make the ninth edition uniquely effective in preparing students for strategic decisions in tomorrow's fast-paced global business arena. It also allows us the opportunity to recognize many outstanding contributors.

The ninth edition of *Formulation, Implementation, and Control of Competitive Strategy* is divided into 11 chapters that provide a thorough, state-of-the-art treatment of the critical business skills needed to plan and manage strategic activities. Each chapter has been filled with new, current real-world examples to illustrate concepts in companies that students recognize and regularly read about in the news around the world. Strategic ramifications of topics like executive compensation, E-commerce, the Internet, entrepreneurship, ethics, continuous improvement, virtual organization, cultural diversity, outsourcing, strategic alliances, and global competition can be found across several chapters. While the text continues a solid academic connection, students will find the text material to be practical, skills oriented, and relevant to their jobs.

We are excited and honored to be selected by *BusinessWeek* as its exclusive partner among strategic management textbooks. We were thrilled to have unlimited access to the world's best business publication to create examples, illustration modules, and various cases. The result is an extensively enhanced text and cases benefiting from hundreds of contemporary examples and illustrations provided by *BusinessWeek* writers worldwide. You will see *BusinessWeek*'s impact on our discussion case feature, our Strategy in Action modules, and our website. Of course, we are also pleased with several hundred examples blended into the text material, which came from recent issues of *BusinessWeek* or www.businessweek.com.

AN OVERVIEW OF OUR TEXT MATERIAL

The ninth edition uses a model of the strategic management process as the basis for the organization of the text material. Previous adopters have identified this model as a key distinctive competence for our text because it offers a logical flow, distinct elements, and an easy-to-understand guide to strategic management. The model has been modestly refined to reflect strategic analysis at different organizational levels as well as the importance of internal analysis in the strategic management process. The model and subsequent structure provide a student-friendly approach to the study of strategic management.

The first chapter provides an overview of the strategic management process and explains what students will find as they use this book. The remaining 10 chapters cover each part of the strategic management process and techniques that aid strategic analysis, decision making, implementation, and control. The literature and research in the strategic management area have developed at a rapid pace in recent years in both the academic and business press. This ninth edition includes several upgrades designed to incorporate major developments from both these sources. While we include cutting-edge concepts, we emphasize straight-forward, logical, and simple presentation so that students can grasp these new ideas without additional reading. The following are a few of the revisions that deserve particular note:

Sarbanes-Oxley Act of 2002

Following the Enron bankruptcy and the wrongdoings of Worldcom executives, Washington lawmakers passed the Sarbanes-Oxley Act of 2002, which requires certifications for financial statements, new corporate regulations, disclosure requirements, and penalties for failure to comply. Chapter 2 provides in-depth coverage of the Act, including discussions of the provisions restricting the corporate control of executives, accounting firms, auditing committees, and attorneys. Also discussed is the change of the governance structure of American corporations, including the heightened role of corporate internal auditors who now routinely deal directly with top corporate officials.

Expanded Coverage of Social Responsibility

The ninth edition expands on its market-leading coverage of social responsibility. Principal perspectives are presented. A continuum of social responsibilities is discussed to help students differentiate among economic, legal, ethical, and discretionary social responsibilities. Arguments for and against social responsibility are explained. Numerous examples, drawn from recent headlines, appear in this section.

A New Section on Management Ethics

Central to the belief that companies should be operated in a socially responsive way for the benefit of all stakeholders is the belief that managers will behave in an ethical manner. Thus, planners often adopt a philosophical approach that can provide the basis for the consistency they seek. The utilitarian, moral rights, and social justice approaches are presented and explained in this new edition.

The Value Disciplines

A new approach to generic strategy centers on delivering superior customer value through one of three value disciplines: operational excellence, customer intimacy, or product leadership. Companies that specialize in one of these disciplines, while simultaneously meeting industry standards in the other two, gain a sustainable lead in their markets. Chapter 6 provides details on these approaches with several examples of successful company experiences.

Agency Theory

Of the recent approaches to corporate governance and strategic management, probably none has had a greater impact on managerial thinking than agency theory. While the breadth and measurement of its usefulness continue to be hotly debated, students of strategic management need to understand the role of agency in our free enterprise, capitalistic system. This edition presents agency theory in a coherent and practical manner. We believe that it arms students with a cutting-edge approach to increasing their understanding of the priorities of executive decision making and strategic control.

Resource-Based View of the Firm

One of the most significant conceptual frameworks to systematize and "measure" a firm's strategic capabilities is the resource-based view (RBV) of the firm. The RBV has received major academic and business press attention during the last decade helping to shape its value as a conceptual tool by adding rigor during the internal analysis and strategic analysis phases of the strategic management process. This edition provides a revised treatment of this concept in Chapter 5. We present the RBV in a logical and practical manner as a central underpinning of sound strategic analysis. Students will find several useful examples and a straightforward treatment of different types of "assets" and organizational capabilities culminating in the ability to determine when these resources create competitive advantage. They will see different ways to answer the question "what makes a resource valuable?" and be able to determine when that resource creates a competitive advantage in a systematic, disciplined, creative manner.

Value Chain Analysis

Outsourcing is becoming a standard business practice in every facet of business operations. This trend enhances the usefulness of the value chain approach in strategic analysis. We have simplified our treatment of this useful conceptual framework and added several contemporary examples to enable students to quickly incorporate the value chain perspective into their strategic thinking process.

Executive Compensation

While our text has led the field in providing a practice-oriented approach to strategic management, we have redoubled our efforts to treat topics with an emphasis on application. Our revised section on executive compensation in Chapter 9 is a clear example. You will find an extended discussion of executive bonus options that provides a comparison of the relative merits of the five most popular approaches, to include the current debate on the use, or overuse, of stock options and the need to accurately account for their true cost.

Balanced Scoreboard

A recent evolution in the motivation that underpins strategic management is reflected in the adoption of the Balanced Scoreboard approach to corporate performance evaluation. While the maximization of shareholder wealth retains the top spot in executive priorities, the guideline is now widely accepted that strategic initiatives must produce favorable outcomes over a range of stakeholder objectives. We try to help our readers gain an appreciation for this perspective in our ninth edition.

Bankruptcy

Many times revisions in this book are driven by changes in business trends. Nowhere is that more evident than in our discussion of company bankruptcy. In the 1980s bankruptcy was treated as a last option that precluded any future for the firm. In the first decade of the 2000s the view has dramatically changed. Bankruptcy has been elevated to the status of a strategic option, and executives need to be well versed in its potentials and limitations, as you will see in Chapter 6.

Strategic Analysis and Choice

We have divided the discussion of strategic analysis and choice into two chapters. Chapter 7 examines the single business setting. Chapter 8 looks at the multibusiness company and the diversification decision. We have provided extensive new coverage of the decision to diversify or not in Chapter 8. In addition to historical reviews of the portfolio and core competency approaches and their deficiencies, we include comprehensive ways to evaluate the role of the corporate parent in adding value, if any, beyond the sum of its businesses. And the concept of "patching," with its identification of "strategy as simple rules" to thrive in turbulent markets receives extensive coverage in this edition. The pages of *BusinessWeek* have helped us add numerous outstanding examples to these two chapters from business writers around the world. Samsung, Apple, Disney, Quanta, Hewlett-Packard, Delta, and Ryanair are just a few of the names students will quickly recognize in coverage that illustrates and helps them more easily understand how strategic analysis is conducted and choices made.

Strategy Implementation

Chapter 9 focuses on reward systems, short-term objectives, and empowerment mechanisms as part of strategy implementation. Doing so allows students to move quickly into strategy implementation considerations from an executive perspective. At the same time we include in this edition an appendix containing approximately ten pages discussing various functional area tactics necessary to implement business strategy. Doing so serves as a convenient review of functional courses leading up to the capstone strategy class for instructors that prefer to do so.

Structuring an Effective Organization

Chapter 10 provides a new perspective on the issue of organizational structure as a central mechanism for strategy implementation, particularly in larger companies. It explores three fundamental driving forces on contemporary organizational structure—globalization, the Internet, and speed. From this beginning, it covers research by academics and prominent business analysts to identify guidelines relevant to matching structure to strategy in the twenty-first century. Six contemporary guidelines to structuring an effective organization are explored in depth, providing students with useful conceptual tools to take into their postgraduation companies and contribute to specific structural challenges. A concise appendix is provided to Chapter 10 detailing the pros and cons of different basic organizational structures. It is included there rather than in the chapter to increase the readability and contemporary focus of the chapter material.

Organizational Leadership

Chapter 10 has added coverage of outsourcing, virtual organizations, and the recruitment/development process as key contemporary considerations in building effective management teams. How to get and keep top management talent is an issue of critical importance examined in this new edition. The role that leadership and organizational culture has played in the impressive turnaround at P&G is explored in detail in the discussion case.

Strategic Control and Continuous Improvement

Chapter 11 offers a major revision in our treatment of these topics. First, a reduced and concise treatment of four broad strategic controls used in the formulation and implementation phases of strategic management are discussed and illustrated. Second, the link between quality/continuous improvement initiatives and the strategic management process receive new, in-depth treatment in this chapter. ISO9004 and Six Sigma are examined as contemporary approaches to the continuous improvement of a company's value chain and a mechanism to guide strategic control. The experiences of several well-known companies in adopting these tools help illustrate their value in a comprehensive strategic management commitment. Finally, the increasingly popular use of the balanced scoreboard approach is explored in this chapter because of its value in supporting strategic control and continuous improvement.

OUR STRATEGIC ALLIANCE WITH *BUSINESSWEEK*

Thanks to the leadership at McGraw-Hill and *BusinessWeek,* we have completed a strategic alliance of our own that benefits every professor and student who uses this book. Our book is *BusinessWeek*'s exclusive partner among strategic management textbooks in the collegiate market. We have long felt *BusinessWeek* to be the unquestionable leader among business periodicals for its coverage of strategic issues in businesses, industries, and economies worldwide. Personal surveys of collegiate faculty teaching strategic management confirmed our intuition: While there are many outstanding business magazines and new publications, none match the consistent quality found in *BusinessWeek* for the coverage of corporate strategies, case stories, and topics of interest to students and professors of strategic management.

Through this partnership, we get unconditional access to *BusinessWeek* material for this book and the use of their cutting-edge stories and topical coverage. From our point of view, this is a unique four-way win-win; teachers, students, authors, and *BusinessWeek* all stand to gain in many ways. The most direct way you can see the impact of the *BusinessWeek* alliance is in the discussion cases and Strategy in Action modules.

Strategy in Action Modules

Another pedagogical feature we pioneered, Strategy in Action modules, has become standard in most strategy books. Our strategic alliance with *BusinessWeek* lets us once again pioneer an innovation. We have drawn on the work of *BusinessWeek* field correspondents worldwide to fill over 60 new *BusinessWeek* Strategy in Action modules with short, hard-hitting current illustrations of key chapter topics. We are the only strategy book to have *BusinessWeek*–derived illustration modules, and we are energized by the excitement, interest, and practical illustration value our students tell us they provide.

OUR WEBSITE

A substantial website has been designed to aid your use of this book. It includes areas accessible only to instructors and areas specifically designed to assist students. The instructor section includes downloadable supplements, which keep your work area less cluttered and let you quickly obtain information. *BusinessWeek* provides access to the article archives through the instructor website. The site offers an elaborate array of linkages to company websites and other sources that you might find useful in your course preparation. The student resources section of the website provides interactive discussion groups where students and groups using the book may interact with other students around the world doing the same thing. Students are provided company and related business periodical (and other) website linkages to aid and expedite their case research and preparation efforts. Practice quizzes and tests are provided to help students prepare for tests on the text material and attempt to lower their anxiety in that regard. Access to *BusinessWeek* articles that update the cases and key illustration modules in the book are provided. We expect students will find the website useful and interesting. Please visit us at www.mhhe.com/pearce9e.

SUPPLEMENTS

Components of our teaching package include a revised, comprehensive instructor's manual, test bank, PowerPoint presentation, and a computerized test bank. These are all available to qualified adopters of the text.

Professors can also choose between two simulation games as a possible package with this text: The International Business Management Decision Simulation (McDonald/Neelankavil), or the Business Strategy Game (Thompson/Stappenbeck).

- The International Business Management Decision Simulation is also a Windows-based simulation that provides an international business analysis and plan simulation allowing students to create multinational business plans and compete with other student groups. Fifteen countries representing three regions of the world along with four product categories are included in the simulation. Students assess business plans by using the financial reports contained in the simulation.

- The Business Strategy Game provides an exercise to help students understand how the functional pieces of a business fit together. Students will work with the numbers, explore options, and try to unite production, marketing, finance, and human resource decisions into a coherent strategy.

ACKNOWLEDGMENTS

We have benefited from the help of many people in the evolution of this project over nine editions. Students, adopters, colleagues, reviewers, and business contacts have provided hundreds of insightful comments, suggestions, and contributions that have progressively enhanced this book and its supplements. We are indebted to the researchers and practicing managers who have accelerated the development of the literature on strategic management.

We are particularly indebted to the talented case researchers who have produced the cases used in this book, as well as to case researchers dedicated to the revitalization of case research as an important academic endeavor. First-class case research is a major avenue through which top strategic management scholars should be recognized.

The development of this book through nine editions has benefited from the generous commitments of time, energy, and ideas from the following colleagues. The valuable ideas, recommendations, and support from these outstanding scholars, teachers, and practitioners have added quality to this book (we apologize if affiliations have changed):

Mary Ackenhusen
INSEAD

Bill Boulton
Auburn University

A. J. Almaney
DePaul University

Charles Boyd
Southwest Missouri State University

James Almeida
Fairleigh Dickinson University

Jeff Bracker
University of Louisville

B. Alpert
San Francisco State University

Dorothy Brawley
Kennesaw State College

Alan Amason
University of Georgia

James W. Bronson
Washington State University

Sonny Aries
University of Toledo

Eric Brown
George Mason University

Katherine A. Auer
The Pennsylvania State University

Robert F. Bruner
INSEAD

Amy Vernberg Beekman
University of Tampa

William Burr
University of Oregon

Patricia Bilafer
Bentley College

Gene E. Burton
California State University–Fresno

Robert Earl Bolick
Metropolitan State University

Edgar T. Busch
Western Kentucky University

Charles M. Byles
Virginia Commonwealth University

Jim Callahan
University of LaVerne

James W. Camerius
Northern Michigan University

Richard Castaldi
San Francisco State University

Gary J. Castogiovanni
Louisiana State University

Jafor Chowdbury
University of Scranton

James J. Chrisman
University of Calgary

Neil Churchill
INSEAD

J. Carl Clamp
University of South Carolina

Earl D. Cooper
Florida Institute of Technology

Louis Coraggio
Troy State University

Jeff Covin
Indiana University

John P. Cragin
Oklahoma Baptist University

Larry Cummings
Northwestern University

Peter Davis
University of Memphis

William Davis
Auburn University

Julio DeCastro
University of Colorado

Kim DeDee
University of Wisconsin

Philippe Demigne
INSEAD

D. Keith Denton
Southwest Missouri State University

F. Derakhshan
California State University–San Bernardino

Brook Dobni
University of Saskatchewan

Mark Dollinger
Indiana University

Jean–Christopher Donck
INSEAD

Max E. Douglas
Indiana State University

Yves Doz
INSEAD

Julie Driscoll
Bentley College

Derrick Dsouza
University of North Texas

Thomas J. Dudley
Pepperdine University

John Dunkelberg
Wake Forest University

Soumitra Dutta
INSEAD

Harold Dyck
California State University

Norbert Esser
Central Wesleyan College

Forest D. Etheredge
Aurora University

Liam Fahey
Babson College

Mary Fandel
Bentley College

Mark Fiegener
University of Washington–Tacoma

Calvin D. Fowler
Embry-Riddle Aeronautical University

Debbie Francis
Jacksonville State University

Elizabeth Freeman
Southern Methodist University

Mahmound A. Gaballa
Mansfield University

Donna M. Gallo
Boston College

Diane Garsombke
Brenau University

Betsy Gatewood
Indiana University

Bertrand George
INSEAD

Michael Geringer
Southern Methodist University

Manton C. Gibbs
Indiana University of Pennsylvania

Nicholas A. Glaskowsky, Jr.
University of Miami

Tom Goho
Wake Forest University

Jon Goodman
University of Southern California

Pradeep Gopalakrishna
Hofstra University

R. H. Gordon
Hofstra University

Barbara Gottfried
Bentley College

Peter Goulet
University of Northern Iowa

Walter E. Greene
University of Texas–Pan American

Sue Greenfeld
California State University–San Bernardino

David W. Grigsby
Clemson University

Daniel E. Hallock
St. Edward's University

Don Hambrick
Pennsylvania State University

Barry Hand
Indiana State University

Jean M. Hanebury
Texas A&M University

Karen Hare
Bentley College

Earl Harper
Grand Valley State University

Samuel Hazen
Tarleton State University

W. Harvey Hegarty
Indiana University

Edward A. Hegner
California State University–Sacramento

Marilyn M. Helms
Dalton State College

Lanny Herron
University of Baltimore

D. Higginbothan
University of Missouri

Roger Higgs
Western Carolina University

William H. Hinkle
Johns Hopkins University

Charles T. Hofer
University of Georgia

Alan N. Hoffman
Bentley College

Richard Hoffman
Salisbury University

Eileen Hogan
Kutztown University

Phyllis G. Holland
Valdosta State University

Gary L. Holman
St. Martin's College

Don Hopkins
Temple University

Cecil Horst
Keller Graduate School of Management

Mel Horwitch
Theseus

Henry F. House
Auburn University–Montgomery

William C. House
University of Arkansas–Fayetteville

Frank Hoy
University of Texas–El Paso

Warren Huckabay
Sammamish, WA

Eugene H. Hunt
Virginia Commonwealth University

Tammy G. Hunt
University of North Carolina–Wilmington

John W. Huonker
University of Arizona

Stephen R. Jenner
California State University

Shailendra Jha
Wilfrid Laurier University–Ontario

C. Boyd Johnson
California State University–Fresno

Troy Jones
University of Central Florida

Jon Kalinowski
Mankato State University

Al Kayloe
Lake Erie College

Michael J. Keefe
Southwest Texas State University

Kay Keels
Brenau University

James A. Kidney
Southern Connecticut State University

John D. King
Embry-Riddle Aeronautical University

Raymond M. Kinnunen
Northeastern University

John B. Knauff
University of St. Thomas

Rose Knotts
University of North Texas

Dan Kopp
Southwest Missouri State University

Michael Koshuta
Valparaiso University

Jeffrey A. Krug
The University of Illinois

Myroslaw Kyj
Widener University of Pennsylvania

Dick LaBarre
Ferris State University

Joseph Lampel
City University–London

Ryan Lancaster
The University of Phoenix

Sharon Ungar Lane
Bentley College

Roland Larose
Bentley College

Anne T. Lawrence
San Jose State University

Joseph Leonard
Miami University–Ohio

Robert Letovsky
Saint Michael's College

Michael Levy
INSEAD

Benjamin Litt
Lehigh University

Frank S. Lockwood
Western Carolina University

John Logan
University of South Carolina

Sandra Logan
Newberry College

Jean M. Lundin
Lake Superior State University

Rodney H. Mabry
Clemson University

Donald C. Malm
University of Missouri–St. Louis

Charles C. Manz
University of Massachusetts

John Maurer
Wayne State University

Denise Mazur
Aquinas College

Edward McClelland
Roanoke College

Bob McDonald
Central Wesleyan College

Patricia P. McDougall
Indiana University

S. Mehta
San Jose State University

Ralph Melaragno
Pepperdine University

Richard Merner
University of Delaware

Linda Merrill
Bentley College

Timothy Mescon
Kennesaw State College

Philip C. Micka
Park College

Bill J. Middlebrook
Southwest Texas State University

Robert Mockler
St. John's University

James F. Molly, Jr.
Northeastern University

Cynthia Montgomery
Harvard University

W. Kent Moore
Valdosta State University

Jaideep Motwani
Grand Valley State University

Karen Mullen
Bentley College

Gary W. Muller
Hofstra University

Terry Muson
Northern Montana College

Daniel Muzyka
INSEAD

Stephanie Newell
Eastern Michigan University

Michael E. Nix
Trinity College of Vermont

Kenneth Olm
University of Texas–Austin

Benjamin M. Oviatt
Georgia State University

Joseph Paolillo
University of Mississippi

Gerald Parker
St. Louis University

Paul J. Patinka
University of Colorado

James W. Pearce
Western Carolina University

Michael W. Pitts
Virginia Commonwealth University

Douglas Polley
St. Cloud State University

Carlos de Pommes
Theseus

Valerie J. Porciello
Bentley College

Mark S. Poulous
St. Edward's University

John B. Pratt
Saint Joseph's College

Oliver Ray Price
West Coast University

John Primus
Golden Gate University

Norris Rath
Shepard College

Paula Rechner
California State University–Fresno

Richard Reed
Washington State University

J. Bruce Regan
University of St. Thomas

H. Lee Remmers
INSEAD

F. A. Ricci
Georgetown University

Keith Robbins
Winthrop University

Gary Roberts
Kennesaw State College

Lloyd E. Roberts
Mississippi College

John K. Ross III
Southwest Texas State University

George C. Rubenson
Salisbury State University

Alison Rude
Bentley College

Les Rue
Georgia State University

Carol Rugg
Bentley College

J. A. Ruslyk
Memphis State University

Ronald J. Salazar
Human Skills Management, LLC

Bill Sandberg
University of South Carolina

Uri Savoray
INSEAD

Jack Scarborough
Barry University

Paul J. Schlachter
Florida International University

David Schweiger
University of South Carolina

John Seeger
Bentley College

Martin Shapiro
Iona College

Arthur Sharplin
McNeese State University

Frank M. Shipper
Salisbury State University

Rodney C. Shrader
University of Illinois

Lois Shufeldt
Southwest Missouri State University

Bonnie Silvieria
Bentley College

F. Bruce Simmons III
The University of Akron

Mark Simon
Oakland University

Michael Skipton
Memorial University

Fred Smith
Western Illinois University

Scott Snell
Michigan State University

Coral R. Snodgrass
Canisius College

Rudolph P. Snowadzky
University of Maine

Neil Snyder
University of Virginia

Melvin J. Stanford
Mankato State University

Romuald A. Stone
DeVry University

Warren S. Stone
Virginia Commonwealth University

Ram Subramanian
Grand Valley State University

Paul M. Swiercz
George Washington University

Robert L. Swinth
Montana State University

Chris Taubman
INSEAD

Russell Teasley
University of South Carolina

James Teboul
INSEAD

George H. Tompson
University of Tampa

Melanie Trevino
University of Texas–El Paso

Howard Tu
University of Memphis

Craig Tunwall
Empire State College

Elaine M. Tweedy
University of Scranton

Arieh A. Ullmann
Binghamton University

P. Veglahn
James Madison University

George Vozikis
University of Tulsa

William Waddell
California State University–Los Angeles

Bill Warren
College of William and Mary

Kirby Warren
Columbia University

Steven J. Warren
Rutgers University

Michael White
University of Tulsa

Randy White
Auburn University

Sam E. White
Portland State University

Frank Winfrey
Lyon College

Joseph Wolfe
Experiential Adventures

Robley Wood
Virginia Commonwealth University

Edward D. Writh, Jr.
Florida Institute of Technology

John Young
University of New Mexico

S. David Young
INSEAD

Jan Zahrly
Old Dominion University

Alan Zeiber
Portland State University

We are affiliated with two separate universities, both of which provide environments that deserve thanks. As the Endowed Chair of the College of Commerce and Finance at Villanova University, Jack is able to combine his scholarly and teaching activities with his coauthorship of this text. He is grateful to Villanova University and his colleagues for the support and encouragement they provide.

Richard appreciates the support provided within the Moore School of Business by Mr. Dean Kress. Mr. Kress provides multifaceted assistance on projects, classes, and research that leverages the scope of what can be accomplished each year. Moore School colleagues in the management department along with Dean Joel Smith and Program Director Brian Klaas provide encouragement while staff members Cheryl Fowler, Susie Gorsage, and Carol Lucas provide logistical support for which Richard is grateful.

Leadership from Irwin/McGraw-Hill deserves our utmost thanks and appreciation. Gerald Saykes got us started and continues his support. Andy Winston's editorial leadership has enhanced our quality and success. Editorial and production assistance from Natalie Ruffatto helped this to become a much better book. The Irwin/McGraw-Hill field organization deserves particular recognition and thanks for the success of this project.

We also want to thank *BusinessWeek,* which is proving to be an excellent strategic partner.

We hope that you will find our book and ancillaries all that you expect. We welcome your ideas and recommendations about our material. Please contact us at the following addresses:

Dr. John A. Pearce II
College of Commerce and Finance
Villanova University
Villanova, PA 19085-1678
610-519-4332
john.pearce@villanova.edu

Dr. Richard Robinson
Moore School of Business
University of South Carolina
Columbia, SC 29205
803-777-5961
Robinson@sc.edu.

We wish you the utmost success in teaching and studying strategic management.

Jack Pearce and Richard Robinson

About the Authors

John A. Pearce II, Ph.D., holds the Endowed Chair in Strategic Management and Entrepreneurship at Villanova University. In 2004, he was the Distinguished Visiting Professor at ITAM in Mexico City. Previously, Professor Pearce was the Eakin Endowed Chair in Strategic Management at George Mason University and a State of Virginia Eminent Scholar. He received the 1994 Fulbright U.S. Professional Award, which he served at INTAN in Malaysia. Dr. Pearce has taught at Penn State University, West Virginia University, the University of Malta as the Fulbright Senior Professor in International Management, and at the University of South Carolina where he was Director of Ph.D. Programs in Strategic Management. He received a Ph.D. degree in Business Administration and Strategic Management from the Pennsylvania State University.

Professor Pearce is coauthor of 36 books and has authored more than 250 articles and refereed professional papers. The articles have appeared in journals that include *Academy of Management Executive, Academy of Management Journal, Academy of Management Review, Business Horizons, California Management Review, Journal of Applied Psychology, Journal of Business Venturing, Long Range Planning, Organizational Dynamics, Sloan Management Review,* and *Strategic Management Journal.* Several of these publications have resulted from Professor Pearce's work as a principal on research projects funded for more than $2 million. He is a widely recognized expert in the field of strategic management, with special accomplishments in the areas of strategic planning and management, including strategy formulation, implementation, and control, mission statement development, environmental assessment, industry analysis, and tools for strategy evaluation and selection.

Professor Pearce is the recipient of several awards in recognition of his accomplishments in teaching, research, scholarship, and professional service, including three Outstanding Paper Awards from the Academy of Management and the 2003 Villanova University Outstanding Faculty Research Award. A frequent leader of executive development programs and an active consultant to business and industry, Dr. Pearce's client list includes domestic and multinational firms engaged in manufacturing and service industries.

Richard B. Robinson, Jr., Ph.D., is the Business Partnership Foundation Fellow in Strategic Management and Entrepreneurship in the Moore School of Business, University of South Carolina. He also serves as Director of the Faber Entrepreneurship Center at USC and Assistant Director of the Center for Manufacturing and Technology in USC's College of Engineering and Information Technology. Dr. Robinson received his Ph.D. in Business Administration from the University of Georgia. He graduated from Georgia Tech in Industrial Management.

Professor Robinson has coauthored over 30 books addressing strategic management and entrepreneurship issues that students and managers use worldwide. He has authored over 300 articles, professional papers, and case studies that have been published in major journals including the *Academy of Management Journal, Academy of Management Review, Strategic Management Journal, Academy of Entrepreneurship Journal,* and the *Journal of Business Venturing.*

Dr. Robinson has previously held executive positions with companies in the pulp and paper, hazardous waste, building products, lodging, and restaurant industries. He currently serves as a director or adviser to entrepreneurial companies that are global leaders in niche markets in the log home, building products, animation, and computer chip thermal management industries. Dr. Robinson also supervises over 50 student teams each year that undertake field consulting projects and internships with entrepreneurial companies worldwide.

Brief Contents

Contents

Chapter 11
Strategic Control and Continuous
Improvement   365

Part One

Overview of Strategic Management

The first chapter of this book introduces strategic management, the set of decisions and actions that result in the design and activation of strategies to achieve the objectives of an organization. The chapter provides an overview of the nature, benefits, and terminology of and the need for strategic management. Subsequent chapters provide greater detail.

The first major section of Chapter 1, "The Nature and Value of Strategic Management," emphasizes the practical value and benefits of strategic management for a firm. It also distinguishes between a firm's strategic decisions and its other planning tasks.

The section stresses the key point that strategic management activities are undertaken at three levels: corporate, business, and functional. The distinctive characteristics of strategic decision making at each of these levels affect the impact of activities at these levels on company operations. Other topics dealt with in this section are the value of formality in strategic management and the alignment of strategy makers in strategy formulation and implementation. The section concludes with a review of the planning research on business, which demonstrates that the use of strategic management processes yields financial and behavioral benefits that justify their costs.

The second major section of Chapter 1 presents a model of the strategic management process. The model, which will serve as an outline for the remainder of the text, describes approaches currently used by strategic planners. Its individual components are carefully defined and explained, as is the process for integrating them into the strategic management process. The section ends with a discussion of the model's practical limitations and the advisability of tailoring the recommendations made to actual business situations.

Chapter **One**

Strategic Management

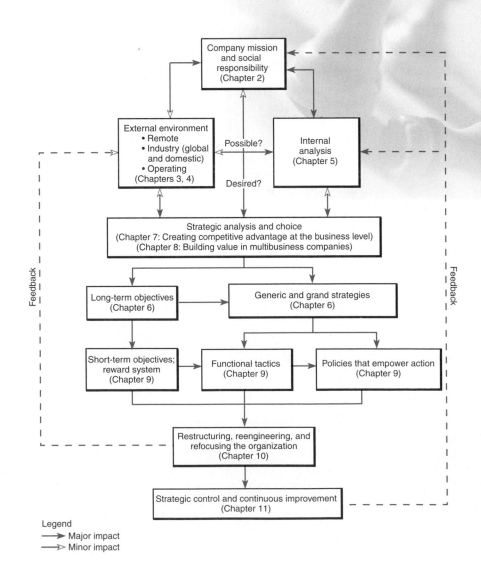

```
                    ┌──────────────────────┐
                    │   Company mission     │
                    │   and social          │
                    │   responsibility      │
                    │   (Chapter 2)         │
                    └──────────────────────┘

┌──────────────────────┐                    ┌──────────────────────┐
│ External environment  │   Possible?        │   Internal            │
│  • Remote             │                    │   analysis            │
│  • Industry (global   │                    │   (Chapter 5)         │
│    and domestic)      │                    │                       │
│  • Operating          │   Desired?         │                       │
│  (Chapters 3, 4)      │                    │                       │
└──────────────────────┘                    └──────────────────────┘

        ┌──────────────────────────────────────────────────────────┐
        │   Strategic analysis and choice                            │
        │   (Chapter 7: Creating competitive advantage at the        │
        │    business level)                                         │
        │   (Chapter 8: Building value in multibusiness companies)   │
        └──────────────────────────────────────────────────────────┘

┌──────────────────────┐        ┌──────────────────────────────┐
│ Long-term objectives  │───────▶│ Generic and grand strategies  │
│ (Chapter 6)           │        │ (Chapter 6)                   │
└──────────────────────┘        └──────────────────────────────┘

┌──────────────────────┐  ┌──────────────────┐  ┌──────────────────────────┐
│ Short-term objectives;│  │ Functional tactics│  │ Policies that empower     │
│ reward system         │  │ (Chapter 9)       │  │ action                    │
│ (Chapter 9)           │  │                   │  │ (Chapter 9)               │
└──────────────────────┘  └──────────────────┘  └──────────────────────────┘

              ┌──────────────────────────────────────┐
              │ Restructuring, reengineering, and     │
              │ refocusing the organization           │
              │ (Chapter 10)                          │
              └──────────────────────────────────────┘

              ┌──────────────────────────────────────┐
              │ Strategic control and continuous      │
              │ improvement (Chapter 11)              │
              └──────────────────────────────────────┘
```

Feedback

Feedback

Legend
——▶ Major impact
——▷ Minor impact

THE NATURE AND VALUE OF STRATEGIC MANAGEMENT

Managing activities internal to the firm is only part of the modern executive's responsibilities. The modern executive also must respond to the challenges posed by the firm's immediate and remote external environments. The immediate external environment includes competitors, suppliers, increasingly scarce resources, government agencies and their ever more numerous regulations, and customers whose preferences often shift inexplicably. The remote external environment comprises economic and social conditions, political priorities, and technological developments, all of which must be anticipated, monitored, assessed, and incorporated into the executive's decision making. However, the executive often is compelled to subordinate the demands of the firm's internal activities and external environment to the multiple and often inconsistent requirements of its stakeholders: owners, top managers, employees, communities, customers, and country. To deal effectively with everything that affects the growth and profitability of a firm, executives employ management processes that they feel will position it optimally in its competitive environment by maximizing the anticipation of environmental changes and of unexpected internal and competitive demands.

Broad-scope, large-scale management processes became dramatically more sophisticated after World War II. These processes responded to increases in the size and number of competing firms; to the expanded role of government as a buyer, seller, regulator, and competitor in the free enterprise system; and to greater business involvement in international trade. Perhaps the most significant improvement in management processes came in the 1970s, when "long-range planning," "new venture management," "planning, programming, budgeting," and "business policy" were blended. At the same time, increased emphasis was placed on environmental forecasting and external considerations in formulating and implementing plans. This all-encompassing approach is known as strategic management.

Strategic management is defined as the set of decisions and actions that result in the formulation and implementation of plans designed to achieve a company's objectives. It comprises nine critical tasks:

1. Formulate the company's mission, including broad statements about its purpose, philosophy, and goals.

2. Conduct an analysis that reflects the company's internal conditions and capabilities.

3. Assess the company's external environment, including both the competitive and the general contextual factors.

4. Analyze the company's options by matching its resources with the external environment.

5. Identify the most desirable options by evaluating each option in light of the company's mission.

6. Select a set of long-term objectives and grand strategies that will achieve the most desirable options.

7. Develop annual objectives and short-term strategies that are compatible with the selected set of long-term objectives and grand strategies.

8. Implement the strategic choices by means of budgeted resource allocations in which the matching of tasks, people, structures, technologies, and reward systems is emphasized.

9. Evaluate the success of the strategic process as an input for future decision making.

As these nine tasks indicate, strategic management involves the planning, directing, organizing, and controlling of a company's strategy-related decisions and actions. By *strategy*, managers mean their large-scale, future-oriented plans for interacting with the competitive environment to achieve company objectives. A strategy is a company's game plan. Although that plan does not precisely detail all future deployments (of people, finances, and material), it does provide a framework for managerial decisions. A strategy reflects a company's awareness of how, when, and where it should compete; against whom it should compete; and for what purposes it should compete.

Dimensions of Strategic Decisions

What decisions facing a business are strategic and therefore deserve strategic management attention? Typically, strategic issues have the following dimensions.

Strategic Issues Require Top-Management Decisions Since strategic decisions overarch several areas of a firm's operations, they require top-management involvement. Usually only top management has the perspective needed to understand the broad implications of such decisions and the power to authorize the necessary resource allocations. As top manager of Volvo GM Heavy Truck Corporation, Karl-Erling Trogen, president, wanted to push the company closer to the customer by overarching operations with service and customer relations empowering the workforce closest to the customer with greater knowledge and authority. This strategy called for a major commitment to the parts and service end of the business where customer relations was first priority. Trogen's philosophy was to so empower the workforce that more operating questions were handled on the line where workers worked directly with customers. He believed that the corporate headquarters should be more focused on strategic issues, such as engineering, production, quality, and marketing.

Strategic Issues Require Large Amounts of the Firm's Resources Strategic decisions involve substantial allocations of people, physical assets, or moneys that either must be redirected from internal sources or secured from outside the firm. They also commit the firm to actions over an extended period. For these reasons, they require substantial resources. Whirlpool Corporation's "Quality Express" product delivery program exemplified a strategy that required a strong financial and personnel commitment from the company. The plan was to deliver products to customers when, where, and how they wanted them. This proprietary service uses contract logistics strategy to deliver Whirlpool, Kitchen Aid, Roper, and Estate brand appliances to 90 percent of the company's dealer and builder customers within 24 hours and to the other 10 percent within 48 hours. In highly competitive service-oriented businesses, achieving and maintaining customer satisfaction frequently involve a commitment from every facet of the organization.

Strategic Issues Often Affect the Firm's Long-Term Prosperity Strategic decisions ostensibly commit the firm for a long time, typically five years; however, the impact of such decisions often lasts much longer. Once a firm has committed itself to a particular strategy, its image and competitive advantages usually are tied to that strategy. Firms become known in certain markets, for certain products, with certain technologies. They would jeopardize their previous gains if they shifted from these markets, products, or technologies by adopting a radically different strategy. Thus, strategic decisions have enduring effects on firms—for better or worse. Exhibit 1–1, Strategy in Action, provides an example of a problem that can arise. Commerce One created an alliance with SAP in 1999 to improve its position in the e-marketplace for B2B business. After taking three years to ready its e-portals, Commerce One and SAP were ready to take on the market in 2002. Unfortunately, the market changed. The "foolproof strategy" got to the market too late and the alliance failed.

BusinessWeek Commerce One's (CMRC) breakthrough came in the old-economy bastion of Detroit. In October of 1999, General Motors (GM) procurement chief Harold R. Kutner staged a bake-off between Commerce One and software giant Oracle for the right to power GM's e-marketplace. The car maker set harsh terms. It wanted stock in the tech companies, and it wouldn't pay for software or services. Oracle refused to play by those rules.

At first, Commerce One's CEO Mark Hoffman also recoiled. But while taking a shower at home in California a day after hearing GM's ultimatum, he realized that running its trading exchange could set Commerce One up for huge transaction fees. He decided it was worth the gamble, so he agreed to negotiate on those terms. They struck a deal.

The GM deal set off a business bonanza that made Commerce One the fastest-growing Nasdaq company—ever. It signed up dozens of e-marketplaces, from aerospace to wood products. And at the peak, customers even competed with one another to land it as their supplier. After logging just $33.6 million in sales in 1999, Commerce One racked up $401 million in 2000, and was on a pace to double that in 2001.

Even while Commerce One was riding high, Hoffman fretted. At a brainstorming session at the Walnut Creek Marriott in January 2000, he worried about a new alliance between Ariba, IBM, and supply-chain software maker i2 Technologies (ITWO). Commerce One needed a strong partner that would lend it credence in giant corporations that were more comfortable buying software from the likes of IBM. SAP, the king of corporate software, looked like the best choice.

Hoffman called SAP Co-CEO Hasso Plattner. By June the two companies had a deal. They would combine their engineering teams to deliver a new set of products and then unleash their sales teams on corporate America. No two technology companies had ever tried to combine forces so thoroughly—short of merging. The coupling brought Commerce One instant credibility and nearly $500 million in cash.

By the end of 2000, Commerce One's fortunes were soaring. The company boasted 567 customers and 157 e-marketplaces. Everybody there got a taste of riches. Rank-and-file employees saw their stock options grow to be worth hundreds of thousands of dollars. Top salespeople became ridiculously wealthy. And customers and partners shared in the bounty.

The problem was, it didn't get any better than that. In the first quarter of 2001, demand began to taper off. Revenues of $170 million were down 10 percent from the previous quarter. What went wrong? A bunch of things. Some of the early e-marketplaces took many months to get going, partly because of problems with the technology but mainly because the industry consortiums that formed the e-marketplaces had trouble getting coordinated.

Then the slow economy put the brakes on all kinds of technology spending. "People were buying vision in 2000. When the new products from Commerce One and SAP were ready to conquer the world in early 2001, the world had changed. E-marketplace software was no longer in demand.

The team eventually retooled the products to handle private e-marketplaces, where individual corporations would interact with their suppliers. But that fell flat too. And so did Commerce One's revenues, dropping to $101.25 million in the second quarter of 2001—roughly half of their peak.

By then, Commerce One's fate was totally entangled with SAP. The U.S. company had spent a year focusing its 400 engineers on combining its technology with SAP's e-commerce applications. Commerce One had bet everything on the SAP relationship and had let its e-procurement software slip. It wasn't competitive anymore as a stand-alone company. So when Plattner proposed merger talks during an August 10, 2001, lunch at SAP's Silicon Valley offices, Hoffman put aside his dreams of building an independent software powerhouse and said yes.

Undoing the SAP relationship practically ruined Commerce One. The deal fell through a couple of weeks after the September 11 terror attacks. Plattner, who had forged the alliance with Hoffman and was loath to give up on it, got a back-channel call from a board member. "They pre-preempted it. They asked me not to spend any more money on Commerce One," says Plattner.

Breaking up was extremely hard to do. The companies' products were thoroughly integrated with one another, and they were pushing a single e-marketplace package. Because most major corporations already had relationships with SAP, many of the new deals were written as addenda to existing SAP contracts. Now, though they maintained a marketing partnership, most of their relationship had to be unwound.

At the same time, SAP started warning corporations that they had better play it safe and buy technology from big, stable suppliers—undercutting Commerce One. Hoffman had learned the hard way to avoid intertangling alliances.

Source: Excerpted from Steve Hamm, Online Extra. "From Hot to Scorched at Commerce One," *BusinessWeek,* February 3, 2003.

BusinessWeek The hearty appetite for fancy German metal has Toyota Motor Co. (TM) spooked. "Higher-priced sedans are a traditional base of strength for Toyota," says Yasuhiko Fukatsu, managing director for domestic luxury sales. "But BMW and Mercedes-Benz are doing a better job attracting younger buyers." Toyota also is increasingly worried about a resurgent Nissan Motor Co. (NSANY), which is staging a comeback in the sedan niche.

Toyota's answer: Run its rivals off the road. To do so, it is unleashing on Japan a dozen-plus new or improved vehicles. Besides updating such midrange standbys as the Camry, Toyota is bulking up on eye-candy luxury models, most of which sell for $30,000 to $60,000. Among them: fully loaded versions of the muscular and decidedly BMW-ish Verossa, the remodeled Lexus ES 300 (known in Japan as the Windom), and a Mercedes-like sedan called the Brevis. Toyota is even debating marketing cars at home under the Lexus badge, which now exists only overseas.

Aging customers are a problem for Toyota everywhere, but nowhere more than in Japan. Most of the folks buying such luxury Toyota sedans as the best-selling Crown are graying executives who started out with entry-level Toyotas in the 1950s and 1960s. By contrast, upwardly mobile Japanese wouldn't be caught dead in a Crown, a $30,000 sedan often used as a taxi. Consider Shunsuke Kurita, a 46-year-old interior designer who drives a black 1999 BMW 318i. "It's a status symbol more than anything else, but I figure a BMW has better resale value than domestic cars," he says. "Toyota sedans have a fuddy-duddy image."

Still, why all the fuss? After all, foreign imports account for less than 10 percent of the Japanese auto market. Well, what worries Toyota is that up-and-coming Japanese drivers will develop the kind of loyalty to their German imports that their parents had to Toyota. Were that to happen, Toyota could lose out on future sales to drivers now in their late thirties and early forties.

Source: Extracted from C. Dawson, "Toyota: Taking on BMW," *BusinessWeek*, July 30, 2001.

Exhibit 1–2, Global Strategy in Action, is a *BusinessWeek* excerpt that provides an excellent example of a firm's strategy tied to its image and competitive advantage. For years, Toyota had a successful strategy of marketing its sedans in Japan. With this strategy came an image, a car for an older customer, and a competitive advantage, a traditional base for Toyota. The strategy was effective, but as its customer base grew older its strategy remained unchanged. A younger customer market saw the image as unattractive and began to seek out other manufacturers. Toyota's strategic task in foreign markets is to formulate and implement a strategy that will reignite interest in its image.

Strategic Issues Are Future Oriented Strategic decisions are based on what managers forecast, rather than on what they know. In such decisions, emphasis is placed on the development of projections that will enable the firm to select the most promising strategic options. In the turbulent and competitive free enterprise environment, a firm will succeed only if it takes a proactive (anticipatory) stance toward change.

Strategic Issues Usually Have Multifunctional or Multibusiness Consequences Strategic decisions have complex implications for most areas of the firm. Decisions about such matters as customer mix, competitive emphasis, or organizational structure necessarily involve a number of the firm's strategic business units (SBUs), divisions, or program units. All of these areas will be affected by allocations or reallocations of responsibilities and resources that result from these decisions.

Strategic Issues Require Considering the Firm's External Environment All business firms exist in an open system. They affect and are affected by external conditions that are largely beyond their control. Therefore, to successfully position a firm in competitive situations, its strategic managers must look beyond its operations. They must consider what relevant others (e.g., competitors, customers, suppliers, creditors, government, and labor) are likely to do.

Three Levels of Strategy

The decision-making hierarchy of a firm typically contains three levels. At the top of this hierarchy is the corporate level, composed principally of a board of directors and the chief executive and administrative officers. They are responsible for the firm's financial performance and for the achievement of nonfinancial goals, such as enhancing the firm's image and fulfilling its social responsibilities. To a large extent, attitudes at the corporate level reflect the concerns of stockholders and society at large. In a multibusiness firm, corporate-level executives determine the businesses in which the firm should be involved. They also set objectives and formulate strategies that span the activities and functional areas of these businesses. Corporate-level strategic managers attempt to exploit their firm's distinctive competencies by adopting a portfolio approach to the management of its businesses and by developing long-term plans, typically for a five-year period. A key corporate strategy of Airborne Express's operations involved direct sale to high-volume corporate accounts and developing an expansive network in the international arena. Instead of setting up operations overseas, Airborne's long-term strategy was to form direct associations with national companies within foreign countries to expand and diversify their operations.

Another example of the portfolio approach involved a plan by state-owned Saudi Arabian Oil to spend $1.4 billion to build and operate an oil refinery in Korea with its partner, Ssangyong. To implement their program, the Saudis embarked on a new "cut-out-the-middleman" strategy to reduce the role of international oil companies in the processing and selling of Saudi crude oil.

In the middle of the decision-making hierarchy is the business level, composed principally of business and corporate managers. These managers must translate the statements of direction and intent generated at the corporate level into concrete objectives and strategies for individual business divisions, or SBUs. In essence, business-level strategic managers determine how the firm will compete in the selected product-market arena. They strive to identify and secure the most promising market segment within that arena. This segment is the piece of the total market that the firm can claim and defend because of its competitive advantages.

At the bottom of the decision-making hierarchy is the functional level, composed principally of managers of product, geographic, and functional areas. They develop annual objectives and short-term strategies in such areas as production, operations, research and development, finance and accounting, marketing, and human relations. However, their principal responsibility is to implement or execute the firm's strategic plans. Whereas corporate- and business-level managers center their attention on "doing the right things," managers at the functional level center their attention on "doing things right." Thus, they address such issues as the efficiency and effectiveness of production and marketing systems, the quality of customer service, and the success of particular products and services in increasing the firm's market shares.

Exhibit 1–3 depicts the three levels of strategic management as structured in practice. In alternative 1, the firm is engaged in only one business and the corporate- and business-level responsibilities are concentrated in a single group of directors, officers, and managers. This is the organizational format of most small businesses.

Alternative 2, the classical corporate structure, comprises three fully operative levels: the corporate level, the business level, and the functional level. The approach taken throughout this text assumes the use of alternative 2. Moreover, whenever appropriate, topics are

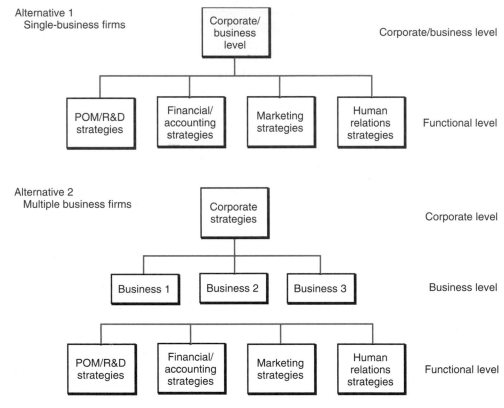

EXHIBIT 1–3
Alternative Strategic Management Structures

covered from the perspective of each level of strategic management. In this way, the text presents a comprehensive discussion of the strategic management process.

Characteristics of Strategic Management Decisions

The characteristics of strategic management decisions vary with the level of strategic activity considered. As shown in Exhibit 1–4, decisions at the corporate level tend to be more value oriented, more conceptual, and less concrete than decisions at the business or functional level. For example, at Alcoa, the world's largest aluminum maker, chairman Paul O'Neill made Alcoa one of the nation's most centralized organizations by imposing a dramatic management reorganization that wiped out two layers of management. He found that this effort not only reduced costs but also enabled him to be closer to the front-line operations managers. Corporate-level decisions are often characterized by greater risk, cost, and profit potential; greater need for flexibility; and longer time horizons. Such decisions include the choice of businesses, dividend policies, sources of long-term financing, and priorities for growth.

Functional-level decisions implement the overall strategy formulated at the corporate and business levels. They involve action-oriented operational issues and are relatively short range and low risk. Functional-level decisions incur only modest costs, because they depend on available resources. They usually are adaptable to ongoing activities and, therefore, can be implemented with minimal cooperation. For example, the corporate headquarters of Sears, Roebuck & Company spent $60 million to automate 6,900 clerical jobs by installing 28,000 computerized cash registers at its 868 stores in the United States. Though this move eliminated many functional-level jobs, top management believed that reducing annual operating expenses by at least $50 million was crucial to competitive survival.

EXHIBIT 1–4   **Hierarchy of Objectives and Strategies**

Ends (What is to be achieved?)	Means (How is it to be achieved?)	Strategic Decision Makers			
		Board of Directors	Corporate Managers	Business Managers	Functional Managers
Mission, including goals and philosophy		✓✓	✓✓	✓	
Long-term objectives	Grand strategy	✓	✓✓	✓✓	
Annual objectives	Short-term strategies and policies		✓	✓✓	✓✓

Note: ✓✓ indicates a principal responsibility; ✓ indicates a secondary responsibility.

Because functional-level decisions are relatively concrete and quantifiable, they receive critical attention and analysis even though their comparative profit potential is low. Common functional-level decisions include decisions on generic versus brandname labeling, basic versus applied research and development (R&D), high versus low inventory levels, general-purpose versus specific-purpose production equipment, and close versus loose supervision.

Business-level decisions help bridge decisions at the corporate and functional levels. Such decisions are less costly, risky, and potentially profitable than corporate-level decisions, but they are more costly, risky, and potentially profitable than functional-level decisions. Common business-level decisions include decisions on plant location, marketing segmentation and geographic coverage, and distribution channels.

Formality in Strategic Management

The formality of strategic management systems varies widely among companies. *Formality* refers to the degree to which participants, responsibilities, authority, and discretion in decision making are specified. It is an important consideration in the study of strategic management, because greater formality is usually positively correlated with the cost, comprehensiveness, accuracy, and success of planning.

A number of forces determine how much formality is needed in strategic management. The size of the organization, its predominant management styles, the complexity of its environment, its production process, its problems, and the purpose of its planning system all play a part in determining the appropriate degree of formality.

In particular, formality is associated with the size of the firm and with its stage of development. Methods of evaluating strategic success also are linked to formality. Some firms, especially smaller ones, follow an *entrepreneurial* mode. They are basically under the control of a single individual, and they produce a limited number of products or services. In such firms, strategic evaluation is informal, intuitive, and limited. Very large firms, on the other hand, make strategic evaluation part of a comprehensive, formal planning system, an approach that Henry Mintzberg called the *planning mode*. Mintzberg also identified a third mode (the *adaptive mode*), which he associated with medium-sized firms in relatively stable environments.[1] For firms that follow the adaptive mode, the identification and evaluation of alternative strategies are closely related to existing strategy. It is not unusual to find different modes within the same organization. For example, Exxon might follow an entrepreneurial mode in developing and evaluating the strategy of its solar subsidiary but follow a planning mode in the rest of the company.

[1] H. Mintzberg, "Strategy Making in Three Modes," *California Management Review* 16, no. 2 (1973), pp. 44–53.

The Strategy Makers

The ideal strategic management team includes decision makers from all three company levels (the corporate, business, and functional)—for example, the chief executive officer (CEO), the product managers, and the heads of functional areas. In addition, the team obtains input from company planning staffs, when they exist, and from lower-level managers and supervisors. The latter provide data for strategic decision making and then implement strategies.

Because strategic decisions have a tremendous impact on a company and require large commitments of company resources, top managers must give final approval for strategic action. Exhibit 1.4 aligns levels of strategic decision makers with the kinds of objectives and strategies for which they are typically responsible.

Planning departments, often headed by a corporate vice president for planning, are common in large corporations. Medium-sized firms often employ at least one full-time staff member to spearhead strategic data-collection efforts. Even in small firms or less progressive larger firms, strategic planning often is spearheaded by an officer or by a group of officers designated as a planning committee.

Precisely what are managers' responsibilities in the strategic planning process at the corporate and business levels? Top management shoulders broad responsibility for all the major elements of strategic planning and management. It develops the major portions of the strategic plan and reviews, and it evaluates and counsels on all other portions. General managers at the business level typically have principal responsibilities for developing environmental analysis and forecasting, establishing business objectives, and developing business plans prepared by staff groups.

A firm's president or CEO characteristically plays a dominant role in the strategic planning process. In many ways, this situation is desirable. The CEO's principal duty often is defined as giving long-term direction to the firm, and the CEO is ultimately responsible for the firm's success and, therefore, for the success of its strategy. In addition, CEOs are typically strong-willed, company-oriented individuals with high self-esteem. They often resist delegating authority to formulate or approve strategic decisions.

However, when the dominance of the CEO approaches autocracy, the effectiveness of the firm's strategic planning and management processes is likely to be diminished. For this reason, establishing a strategic management system implies that the CEO will allow managers at all levels to participate in the strategic posture of the company.

In implementing a company's strategy, the CEO must have an appreciation for the power and responsibility of the board, while retaining the power to lead the company with the guidance of informed directors. The interaction between the CEO and board is key to any corporation's strategy. Empowerment of nonmanagerial employees has been a recent trend across major management teams. Exhibit 1–5, Strategy in Action, presents one example. In 2003, IBM replaced its 92-year-old executive board structure with three, newly created management teams: strategy, operations, and technology. Each team combined top executives, managers, and engineers going down six levels in some cases. This new team structure was responsible for guiding the creation of IBM's strategy and for helping to implement the strategies once they were authorized.

Benefits of Strategic Management

Using the strategic management approach, managers at all levels of the firm interact in planning and implementing. As a result, the behavioral consequences of strategic management are similar to those of participative decision making. Therefore, an accurate assessment of the impact of strategy formulation on organizational performance requires not only financial evaluation criteria but also nonfinancial evaluation criteria—measures of

BusinessWeek IBM CEO Samuel J. Palmisano took aim at a bastion of power and privilege at Big Blue, the 92-year-old executive management committee. For generations, this 12-person body presiding over IBM's strategy and initiatives represented the inner sanctum for every aspiring Big Blue executive. The CEO hit the send button on an e-mail to 300 senior managers announcing that this venerable committee was finished. Palmisano instead would work directly, with three teams he had put in place in 2002—they comprised people from all over the company who brought the best ideas to the table. The old committee, with its monthly meetings, just slowed things down.

Palmisano asked his team to draw up a project as epochal as the mainframe. The team cobbled together a vision of systems that altered the very nature of how technology was delivered. They unveiled "e-business on demand."

In 2002 before Palmisano disbanded the executive management committee, he had put in place his management teams for the future. He created three of them: strategy, operations, and technology. Instead of picking only high-level executives for each team, Palmisano selected managers and engineers most familiar with the issues.

For IBM to come up with a broad array of on-demand technologies in a hurry, the whole company had to work smoothly from one far-flung cubicle to another. That meant bringing researchers in touch not only with product developers, but also with consultants and even customers. Only by reaching across these old boundaries did IBM find out what customers were clamoring for—and produce it fast.

Source: Excerpted from Ante Spencer, "The New Blue," *Business Week*, March 17, 2003, pp. 80–88.

behavior-based effects. In fact, promoting positive behavioral consequences also enables the firm to achieve its financial goals. However, regardless of the profitability of strategic plans, several behavioral effects of strategic management improve the firm's welfare:

1. Strategy formulation activities enhance the firm's ability to prevent problems. Managers who encourage subordinates' attention to planning are aided in their monitoring and forecasting responsibilities by subordinates who are aware of the needs of strategic planning.

2. Group-based strategic decisions are likely to be drawn from the best available alternatives. The strategic management process results in better decisions because group interaction generates a greater variety of strategies and because forecasts based on the specialized perspectives of group members improve the screening of options.

3. The involvement of employees in strategy formulation improves their understanding of the productivity-reward relationship in every strategic plan and, thus, heightens their motivation.

4. Gaps and overlaps in activities among individuals and groups are reduced as participation in strategy formulation clarifies differences in roles.

5. Resistance to change is reduced. Though the participants in strategy formulation may be no more pleased with their own decisions than they would be with authoritarian decisions, their greater awareness of the parameters that limit the available options makes them more likely to accept those decisions.

Risks of Strategic Management

Managers must be trained to guard against three types of unintended negative consequences of involvement in strategy formulation.

First, the time that managers spend on the strategic management process may have a negative impact on operational responsibilities. Managers must be trained to minimize that impact by scheduling their duties to allow the necessary time for strategic activities.

Second, if the formulators of strategy are not intimately involved in its implementation, they may shirk their individual responsibility for the decisions reached. Thus, strategic managers must be trained to limit their promises to performance that the decision makers and their subordinates can deliver.

Third, strategic managers must be trained to anticipate and respond to the disappointment of participating subordinates over unattained expectations. Subordinates may expect their involvement in even minor phases of total strategy formulation to result in both acceptance of their proposals and an increase in their rewards, or they may expect a solicitation of their input on selected issues to extend to other areas of decision making.

Sensitizing managers to these possible negative consequences and preparing them with effective means of minimizing such consequences will greatly enhance the potential of strategic planning.

THE STRATEGIC MANAGEMENT PROCESS

Businesses vary in the processes they use to formulate and direct their strategic management activities. Sophisticated planners, such as General Electric, Procter & Gamble, and IBM, have developed more detailed processes than less-formal planners of similar size. Small businesses that rely on the strategy formulation skills and limited time of an entrepreneur typically exhibit more basic planning concerns than those of larger firms in their industries. Understandably, firms with multiple products, markets, or technologies tend to use more complex strategic management systems. However, despite differences in detail and the degree of formalization, the basic components of the models used to analyze strategic management operations are very similar.

Because of the similarity among the general models of the strategic management process, it is possible to develop an eclectic model representative of the foremost thought in the strategic management area. This model is shown in Exhibit 1–6. It serves three major functions. First, it depicts the sequence and the relationships of the major components of the strategic management process. Second, it is the outline for this book. This chapter provides a general overview of the strategic management process, and the major components of the model will be the principal theme of subsequent chapters. Notice that the chapters of the text that discuss each of the strategic management process components are shown in each block. Finally, the model offers one approach for analyzing the case studies in this text and thus helps the analyst develop strategy formulation skills.

Components of the Strategic Management Model

This section will define and briefly describe the key components of the strategic management model. Each of these components will receive much greater attention in a later chapter. The intention here is simply to introduce them.

Company Mission

The mission of a company is the unique purpose that sets it apart from other companies of its type and identifies the scope of its operations. In short, the mission describes the company's product, market, and technological areas of emphasis in a way that reflects the values and priorities of the strategic decision makers. For example, Lee Hun-Hee, the new chairman of the Samsung Group, revamped the company mission by stamping his own

EXHIBIT 1–6   **Strategic Management Model**

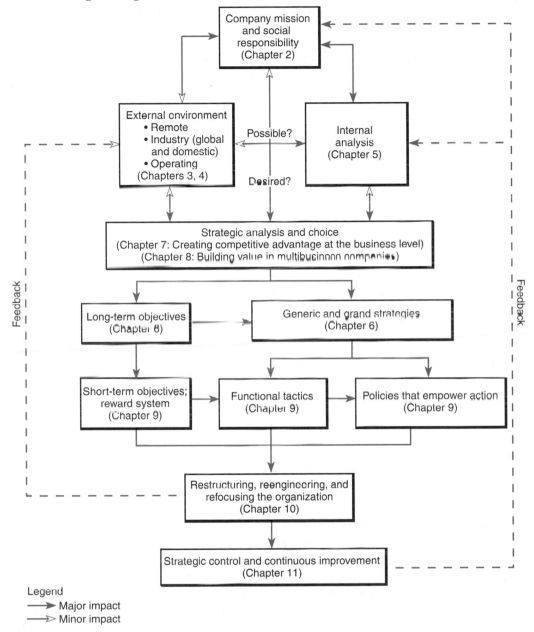

Legend
→ Major impact
⇾ Minor impact

brand of management on Samsung. Immediately, Samsung separated Chonju Paper Manufacturing and Shinsegae Department Store from other operations. This corporate act of
downscaling reflected a revised management philosophy that favored specialization,
thereby changing the direction and scope of the organization.

Social responsibility is a critical consideration for a company's strategic decision makers since the mission statement must express how the company intends to contribute to the
societies that sustain it. A firm needs to set social responsibility aspirations for itself, just
as it does in other areas of corporate performance.

Internal Analysis

The company analyzes the quantity and quality of the company's financial, human, and physical resources. It also assesses the strengths and weaknesses of the company's management and organizational structure. Finally, it contrasts the company's past successes and traditional concerns with the company's current capabilities in an attempt to identify the company's future capabilities.

External Environment

A firm's external environment consists of all the conditions and forces that affect its strategic options and define its competitive situation. The strategic management model shows the external environment as three interactive segments: the remote, industry, and operating environments.

Strategic Analysis and Choice

Simultaneous assessment of the external environment and the company profile enables a firm to identify a range of possibly attractive interactive opportunities. These opportunities are *possible* avenues for investment. However, they must be screened through the criterion of the company mission to generate a set of possible and *desired* opportunities. This screening process results in the selection of options from which a *strategic choice* is made. The process is meant to provide the combination of long-term objectives and generic and grand strategies that optimally position the firm in its external environment to achieve the company mission.

Strategic analysis and choice in single or dominant product/service businesses center around identifying strategies that are most effective at building sustainable competitive advantage based on key value chain activities and capabilities—core competencies of the firm. Multibusiness companies find their managers focused on the question of which combination of businesses maximizes shareholder value as the guiding theme during their strategic analysis and choice.

Long-Term Objectives

The results that an organization seeks over a multiyear period are its *long-term objectives.* Such objectives typically involve some or all of the following areas: profitability, return on investment, competitive position, technological leadership, productivity, employee relations, public responsibility, and employee development.

Generic and Grand Strategies

Many businesses explicitly and all implicitly adopt one or more *generic strategies* characterizing their competitive orientation in the marketplace. Low cost, differentiation, or focus strategies define the three fundamental options. Enlightened managers seek to create ways their firm possesses both low cost and differentiation competitive advantages as part of their overall generic strategy. They usually combine these capabilities with a comprehensive, general plan of major actions through which their firm intends to achieve its long-term objectives in a dynamic environment. Called the *grand strategy,* this statement of means indicates how the objectives are to be achieved. Although every grand strategy is, in fact, a unique package of long-term strategies, 14 basic approaches can be identified: concentration, market development, product development, innovation, horizontal integration, vertical integration, joint venture, strategic alliances, consortia, concentric diversification, conglomerate diversification, turnaround, divestiture, and liquidation.

Each of these grand strategies will be covered in detail in Chapter 6.

Action Plans and Short-Term Objectives

Action plans translate generic and grand strategies into "action" by incorporating four elements. First, they identify specific functional *tactics and actions* to be undertaken in the next week, month, or quarter as part of the business's effort to build competitive advantage. The second element is a clear time frame for completion. Third, action plans create accountability by identifying who is responsible for each "action" in the plan. Fourth, each "action" in an action plan has one or more specific, immediate objectives that are identified as outcomes that action should generate.

Functional Tactics

Within the general framework created by the business's generic and grand strategies, each business function needs to identify and undertake activities unique to the function that help build a sustainable competitive advantage. Managers in each business function develop tactics that delineate the functional activities undertaken in their part of the business and usually include them as a core part of their action plan. *Functional tactics* are detailed statements of the "means" or activities that will be used to achieve short-term objectives and establish competitive advantage.

Policies That Empower Action

Speed is a critical necessity for success in today's competitive, global marketplace. One way to enhance speed and responsiveness is to force/allow decisions to be made whenever possible at the lowest level in organizations. *Policies* are broad, precedent-setting decisions that guide or substitute for repetitive or time-sensitive managerial decision making. Creating policies that guide and "preauthorize" the thinking, decisions, and actions of operating managers and their subordinates in implementing the business's strategy is essential for establishing and controlling the ongoing operating process of the firm in a manner consistent with the firm's strategic objectives. Policies often increase managerial effectiveness by standardizing routine decisions and empowering or expanding the discretion of managers and subordinates in implementing business strategies.

The following are examples of the nature and diversity of company policies:

A requirement that managers have purchase requests for items costing more than $5,000 cosigned by the controller.

The minimum equity position required for all new McDonald's franchises.

The standard formula used to calculate return on investment for the 43 strategic business units of General Electric.

A decision that Sears service and repair employees have the right to waive repair charges to appliance customers they feel have been poorly served by their Sears appliance.

Restructuring, Reengineering, and Refocusing the Organization

Until this point in the strategic management process, managers have maintained a decidedly market-oriented focus as they formulate strategies and begin implementation through action plans and functional tactics. Now the process takes an internal focus—getting the work of the business done efficiently and effectively so as to make the strategy successful. What is the best way to organize ourselves to accomplish the mission? Where should leadership come from? What values should guide our daily activities—what should the organization and its people be like? How can we shape rewards to encourage appropriate action? The intense competition in the global marketplace has made this tradition "internally focused" set of questions—how the activities within their business are conducted—recast themselves with unprecedented attentiveness to the marketplace. *Downsizing, restructuring,* and *reengineering* are terms that reflect the critical stage in strategy implementation wherein managers attempt to recast their organization. The company's structure, leadership, culture, and reward systems may all be changed to ensure cost competitiveness and quality demanded by unique requirements of its strategies.

The elements of the strategic management process are evident in the recent activities at GM, as seen in Exhibit 1–7, Strategy in Action. In 2003, GM undertook to create a strategy

Strategy in Action
Rick Wagoner's Game Plan

Exhibit 1–7

BusinessWeek A day after General Motors Corp. (GM) announced that it had lifted operating earnings 30 percent in a stagnant car market, Standard & Poor's downgraded the auto maker's debt with no warning. Surprised investors rushed to sell, and the stock dropped 8 percent. Credit analysts pointed to GM's $76 billion pension fund, which they estimated at the time to be underfunded by as much as $23 billion. GM would have had to plow in billions of dollars for years to keep the fund flush, they said.

GM finished 2002, with an operating profit of $3.9 billion, nearly double what it earned in 2001, on 5 percent higher sales of $186.2 billion. GM clearly led the rest of the U.S. big three car companies, reflecting real operational improvements. After GM lost a staggering $30 billion during a single three-year stretch in the early '90s, Wagoner and Chairman John F. "Jack" Smith Jr. forced GM back to basics. They slashed costs, cut payroll, and overhauled aging plants. Once he took over the corner office in May 2000, CEO Wagoner pulled the efficiency collar even tighter. Then GM ranked close to Honda Motor Co. (HMC) and Toyota Motor Corp. (TM) in productivity and made strides in quality. GM also recaptured leadership of the truck business from rival Ford Motor Co. (F), a coup that made the company billions. In 2000, GM increased its share of the U.S. market, to 28.3 percent from 28.1 percent.

But as good as those moves were, they paled next to the problems of GM's weak car brands and gargantuan pension payments. Even worse for GM was the buildup of lavish health and retirement benefits for workers that it agreed to in fatter days as a way to buy peace with the United Auto Workers. The company said the gap between its pension funding and future liabilities was $19.3 billion. That meant GM had to pump as much as $4 billion into the fund from 2003 to 2004. Providing health care to former and current workers would drain an additional $5 billion per year. The pension costs alone would have cut projected 2003 net income from $4.2 billion to $2.8 billion. Those huge legacy costs explained why Wagoner kept the heat on his competition with the zero percent financing deals he unleashed after September 11, 2001.

That made Wagoner's imperative clear: He had to keep up cash flow to cover those costs until they started to shrink. At the same time, he continued to rack up improvements in quality, efficiency, design, and brand appeal.

Walking around GM's sprawling headquarters complex, you realized that against all odds, Wagoner was making real progress in energizing GM's torpid culture. He broke with GM tradition by recruiting two respected outsiders for key positions—Robert A. Lutz as head of product development and John Devine as vice-chairman and chief financial officer. And he had given them extraordinary leeway to fix the company's problems. Since giving the swaggering Lutz rule over product development, Wagoner spiked the design-by-committee system and cut the time it took to develop a new car to 20 months from nearly four years. GM used to have different studios for each division working on car designs that would get passed on to marketing, then engineering, then manufacturing. Lutz had one committee to cover the entire process.

It was a testament to Wagoner's ability to cut costs that GM managed to nearly double margins in North America in 2002, to 2.6 percent of sales. Thanks to efficiency gains, GM was now one of the leanest car builders, with variable costs—labor, parts, outsourced production, and so on—amounting to 62 percent of revenues, according to UBS Warburg. That put it ahead of Ford and Chrysler (DCX) at 68 percent, and it was not far behind leaders Toyota and Honda at 60 percent.

Wagoner also streamlined GM's factories. GM became the most productive domestic auto maker, having cut the time it takes to assemble a vehicle from an average of 32 hours in 1998 to 26 hours in 2001, according to Harbour & Associates. That compared with 27 for Ford, almost 31 at DaimlerChrysler, 22.5 at Toyota, and 17.9 at Nissan. A big factor was expanding parts shared across vehicles. The new Chevy Malibu, for instance, used the same platform and many of the same parts as the Saab 9-3 sedan. . . . GM's plants were also more flexible—each of seven full-size pickup and SUV plants could make any of the vehicles designed on that platform.

The cars rolling off GM's assembly lines were undeniably better built than they used to be. Once ranked below the industry average, GM trailed only Honda and Toyota in J.D. Power & Associates Inc.'s initial quality survey.

Source: Excerpted from Kathleen Kenurin and David Welch, "Rick Wagoner's Game Plan," *BusinessWeek,* February 10, 2003, pp. 52–60.

to lower costs, increase efficiency, improve designs, and increase brand appeal. These improvements were needed to keep cash flows up to cover rising pension costs. For GM to accomplish this new strategy it had to improve operations. New executives were brought in to lead product development and financial controls. To break down the bureaucratic boundaries, a committee was created that included employees from the major functional areas, and it was given the assignment to reduce the time needed to develop a new-concept vehicle.

Strategy in Action
Can Yahoo! Make the Bounce Last?

Exhibit 1–8

BusinessWeek Following a $93 million loss in 2001, Terry S. Semel had led Yahoo! Inc. (YHOO) back with positive earnings in 2002. Then he predicted that in 2003 the Internet giant would best its previous records in annual sales and profits—both set in 2000, at the height of the tech boom. With Yahoo's stock still down about 20 percent, Semel convinced the market that he built a long-term growth engine that would have justified Yahoo's $10.6 billion market valuation. Semel got his chance when he presented his strategy in crucial new markets, particularly forayed into broadband access and the Internet search market.

Bulking up the broadband business, with its stable monthly subscriber fees, was Semel's most important task. True, Yahoo's five-month-old partnership with SBC Communications Inc. (SBC) to sell broadband access was by most accounts a success. The business garnered Yahoo at least $7 million in sales in the fourth quarter of 2002, with an additional $70 million expected in 2003, according to analysts.

With Yahoo capable of reaching only one-third of the country through its SBC alliance, Yahoo needed to find a way to reach the rest. Yahoo rolled out a "bring-your-own-broadband" service. Subscribers paid a monthly fee to use a souped-up Yahoo gateway, regardless of what broadband provider they used. Yahoo sold its service for about $5 a month, compared with $9.95 and $14.95 for Microsoft Corp.'s (MSFT) MSN and AOL, respectively.

Yahoo relied on blitz marketing and the low price to win customers. Yahoo needed to bolster its premium content and services. Less than 1 percent of Yahoo's visitors paid for services such as jumbo-size e-mail accounts or Yahoo's personal-ad listings. With even loyal Yahoo users reluctant to shell out for extras, it was harder to convince non-Yahoo users, who already frequent other portals.

Yahoo proved it could compete in the Internet search market, where it ranked No. 3 behind MSN and Google. In 2002, revenues from ads on its search-results pages boomed from next to nothing to over $100 million. In 2003, Yahoo tinkered with its search pages to squeeze in more ads. For that to matter, Yahoo solidified its standing as a premier search destination. The portal had long used search technology from other providers, such as Inktomi Corp. (INKT) and Google. But when Google emerged as a serious rival, Yahoo acquired Inktomi for $235 million and evicted Google as its search-technology source.

To succeed, Yahoo had to grab market share back from Google. The popular site snared 4 percent more search traffic than Yahoo in December of 2002, according to comScore Media Metrix. Proving that Inktomi's search technology rivaled Google's was more a branding challenge than a technological one.

Source: Excerpted from Ben Elgin, "Can Yahoo Make the Bounce Last?" *BusinessWeek*, February 17, 2003, p. 41.

Strategic Control and Continuous Improvement

Strategic control is concerned with tracking a strategy as it is being implemented, detecting problems or changes in its underlying premises, and making necessary adjustments. In contrast to postaction control, strategic control seeks to guide action on behalf of the generic and grand strategies as they are taking place and when the end results are still several years away. The rapid, accelerating change of the global marketplace of the last 10 years has made continuous improvement another aspect of strategic control in many organizations. *Continuous improvement* provides a way for managers to provide a form of strategic control that allows their organization to respond more proactively and timely to rapid developments in hundreds of areas that influence a business's success.

In 2002–2003, Yahoo's strategy was to move into the broadband and Internet search markets, as discussed in Exhibit 1–8, Strategy in Action. However, even in its early implementation stages the strategy required revisions. Yahoo had formed an alliance with SBC to provide the broadband service, but SBC had such limited capabilities that Yahoo had to find new ways to reach users. Yahoo also needed to continuously improve its new Internet search market, given competitors' upgrades and rapidly rising customer expectations. Additionally, for Yahoo to increase its market share, it needed to continually improve its branding, rather than rely largely on its technological capabilities.

Strategic Management as a Process

A *process* is the flow of information through interrelated stages of analysis toward the achievement of an aim. Thus, the strategic management model in Exhibit 1–6 depicts a process. In the strategic management process, the flow of information involves historical, current, and forecast data on the operations and environment of the business. Managers evaluate these data in light of the values and priorities of influential individuals and groups—often called *stakeholders*—that are vitally interested in the actions of the business. The interrelated stages of the process are the 11 components discussed in the previous section. Finally, the aim of the process is the formulation and implementation of strategies that work, achieving the company's long-term mission and near-term objectives.

Viewing strategic management as a process has several important implications. First, a change in any component will affect several or all of the other components. Most of the arrows in the model point two ways, suggesting that the flow of information usually is reciprocal. For example, forces in the external environment may influence the nature of a company's mission, and the company may in turn affect the external environment and heighten competition in its realm of operation. A specific example is a power company that is persuaded, in part by governmental incentives, to include a commitment to the development of energy alternatives in its mission statement. The company then might promise to extend its R&D efforts in the area of coal liquefaction. The external environment has affected the company's mission, and the revised mission signals a competitive condition in the environment.

A second implication of viewing strategic management as a process is that strategy formulation and implementation are sequential. The process begins with development or reevaluation of the company mission. This step is associated with, but essentially followed by, development of a company profile and assessment of the external environment. Then follow, in order, strategic choice, definition of long-term objectives, design of the grand strategy, definition of short-term objectives, design of operating strategies, institutionalization of the strategy, and review and evaluation.

The apparent rigidity of the process, however, must be qualified.

First, a firm's strategic posture may have to be reevaluated in response to changes in any of the principal factors that determine or affect its performance. Entry by a major new competitor, the death of a prominent board member, replacement of the chief executive officer, and a downturn in market responsiveness are among the thousands of changes that can prompt reassessment of a firm's strategic plan. However, no matter where the need for a reassessment originates, the strategic management process begins with the mission statement.

Second, not every component of the strategic management process deserves equal attention each time planning activity takes place. Firms in an extremely stable environment may find that an in-depth assessment is not required every five years. Companies often are satisfied with their original mission statements even after a decade of operation and spend only a minimal amount of time addressing this subject. In addition, while formal strategic planning may be undertaken only every five years, objectives and strategies usually are updated each year, and rigorous reassessment of the initial stages of strategic planning rarely is undertaken at these times.

A third implication of viewing strategic management as a process is the necessity of feedback from institutionalization, review, and evaluation to the early stages of the process. *Feedback* can be defined as the collection of postimplementation results to enhance future decision making. Therefore, as indicated in Exhibit 1–6, strategic managers should assess the impact of implemented strategies on external environments. Thus, future planning can reflect any changes precipitated by strategic actions. Strategic managers also should analyze the impact of strategies on the possible need for modifications in the company mission.

A fourth implication of viewing strategic management as a process is the need to regard it as a dynamic system. The term *dynamic* characterizes the constantly changing conditions that affect interrelated and interdependent strategic activities. Managers should recognize that the components of the strategic process are constantly evolving but that formal planning artificially freezes those components, much as an action photograph freezes the movement of a swimmer. Since change is continuous, the dynamic strategic planning process must be monitored constantly for significant shifts in any of its components as a precaution against implementing an obsolete strategy.

Changes in the Process

The strategic management process undergoes continual assessment and subtle updating. Although the elements of the basic strategic management model rarely change, the relative emphasis that each element receives will vary with the decision makers who use the model and with the environments of their companies.

A recent study describes general trends in strategic management, summarizing the responses of over 200 corporate executives. This update shows there has been an increasing companywide emphasis on and appreciation for the value of strategic management activities. It also provides evidence that practicing managers have given increasing attention to the need for frequent and widespread involvement in the formulation and implementation phases of the strategic management process. Finally, it indicates that, as managers and their firms gain knowledge, experience, skill, and understanding in how to design and manage their planning activities, they become better able to avoid the potential negative consequences of instituting a vigorous strategic management process.

Summary

Strategic management is the set of decisions and actions that result in the formulation and implementation of plans designed to achieve a company's objectives. Because it involves long-term, future-oriented, complex decision making and requires considerable resources, top-management participation is essential.

Strategic management is a three-tier process involving corporate-, business-, and functional-level planners, and support personnel. At each progressively lower level, strategic activities were shown to be more specific, narrow, short term, and action oriented, with lower risks but fewer opportunities for dramatic impact.

The strategic management model presented in this chapter will serve as the structure for understanding and integrating all the major phases of strategy formulation and implementation. The chapter provided a summary account of these phases, each of which is given extensive individual attention in subsequent chapters.

The chapter stressed that the strategic management process centers on the belief that a firm's mission can be best achieved through a systematic and comprehensive assessment of both its internal capabilities and its external environment. Subsequent evaluation of the firm's opportunities leads, in turn, to the choice of long-term objectives and grand strategies and, ultimately, to annual objectives and operating strategies, which must be implemented, monitored, and controlled.

Questions for Discussion

1. Find a recent copy of *BusinessWeek* and read the "Corporate Strategies" section. Was the main decision discussed strategic? At what level in the organization was the key decision made?

2. In what ways do you think the subject matter in this strategic management–business policy course will differ from that of previous courses you have taken?

3. After graduation, you are not likely to move directly to a top-level management position. In fact, few members of your class will ever reach the top-management level. Why, then, is it important for all business majors to study the field of strategic management?

4. Do you expect outstanding performance in this course to require a great deal of memorization? Why or why not?

5. You undoubtedly have read about individuals who seemingly have given singled-handed direction to their corporations. Is a participative strategic management approach likely to stifle or suppress the contributions of such individuals?

6. Think about the courses you have taken in functional areas, such as marketing, finance, production, personnel, and accounting. What is the importance of each of these areas to the strategic planning process?

7. Discuss with practicing business managers the strategic management models used in their firms. What are the similarities and differences between these models and the one in the text?

8. In what ways do you believe the strategic planning approach of not-for-profit organizations would differ from that of profit-oriented organizations?

9. How do you explain the success of firms that do not use a formal strategic planning process?

10. Think about your postgraduation job search as a strategic decision. How would the strategic management model be helpful to you in identifying and securing the most promising position?

Chapter 1 Discussion Case

Kraft's Global Strategy: Can Kraft Be a Big Cheese Abroad?

1 When Aussies stroll down the aisles of their local supermarket, what catches their eyes are snacks from Unilever (UL) and Nestlé (NSRGY). Kraft Macaroni & Cheese and Oscar Mayer hot dogs, on the other hand, are hard to find and far from first choice. "They would be classified as a slow-moving line," says Terry Walters, the owner of an IGA store in Cairns, Queensland, about the classic American macaroni-and-cheese dinner. As for hot dogs: "We have the meat pie."

2 Kraft may be ubiquitous in U.S. grocery stores, but overseas it's a far different picture. Kraft isn't one of Walters' top five food suppliers, ranking below even H. J. Heinz Co. (HNZ), despite its ownership of Australia's famed Vegemite spread. Only 27 percent of its total revenues come from overseas, versus 44 percent for Heinz, more than 50 percent for McDonald's Corp. (MCD), and more than 80 percent for Coca-Cola Co. (KO)

3 That will have to change. As Kraft embarks on a giant initial public offering, expected in mid-June, its challenge is to once again become a growth company. Widely admired for the astute management of its brand lineup, Kraft's nevertheless stuck in a slow-growth industry in the United States. Smart marketing and methodical cost cutting helped it boost earnings 14.1 percent last year, but Kraft's sales actually dipped slightly, to $26.53 billion. In fact, Kraft's annual sales have dropped 16.2 percent since 1994. The company took a big step toward building revenues in December with its $19.2 billion purchase of Nabisco Group Holdings Corp. (NGH-U), whose cookie and cracker brands are growing faster than Kraft's top brands.

4 That deal should boost Kraft's sales to an expected $35.05 billion this year. But analysts say that if Kraft is to spark long-term growth, it must do a better job of tapping foreign consumers. Kraft acknowledged as much when it announced that once the IPO is completed, Betsy D. Holden, CEO of Kraft Foods North America, would share the chief executive office with Roger K. Deromedi, a 13-year Kraft veteran who has been president and CEO of Kraft Foods International Inc. for the past two years. The company declined to comment or make top executives available to *Busi-*

nessWeek, citing the quiet period before the IPO, as did parent Philip Morris Cos. (MO).

5 AMERICAN ICONS. The largest food company in North America by far, Kraft has dominated U.S. grocery-store shelves for decades. Its powerhouse brands are American icons: Philadelphia Cream Cheese, Oreo cookies, Tang, Jell-O, Kool-Aid, Life Savers, Planters peanuts, Lunchables prepackaged meals for kids. Its portfolio comprises a remarkable 61 brands with more than $100 million in sales last year. Supermarket consultants say it would be nearly impossible to run a U.S. grocery store without its products.

6 But these aren't the best of times, even for strong supermarket brands. Shopper loyalty has waned as the grocery chains' in-house brands compete for shelf space, and big brands such as Kraft's tend to be mature. Take salad dressing. Even though Kraft is the market leader, "there's Kraft, there's Wish-Bone, there's Hellmann's," says John P. Mahar, operations director at the Green Hills Farms supermarket in Syracuse, N.Y. "If we have Wish-Bone on sale, shoppers pick up Wish-Bone. They don't care. The majority of Kraft's brands are just another commodity."

7 TOBACCO TAINT. Boosting sales will become even more urgent once Kraft has outside shareholders to answer to. Cigarette maker Philip Morris, which has owned Kraft since 1988, is putting 16.1 percent of the company on the market in an offering that could raise as much as $8.4 billion. That would be the second-largest IPO on record, behind only AT&T Wireless Group's $10.5 billion stock market debut last year. Philip Morris will remain firmly in control, but its goal is to realize more of Kraft's value by distancing the business from the tobacco taint that has held Philip Morris' stock price down.

8 The first concern for investors might be whether Kraft's co-CEO structure can work. Deromedi, 47, and Holden, 45, who started at Kraft as an assistant product manager in 1982, will both report to Geoffrey Bible, chairman of Philip Morris. Analysts wonder how long the arrangement will last, citing a long list of prominent companies, from DaimlerChrysler to Citigroup, where co-CEO setups fizzled. "The co-CEO structure calls into question if this is truly an independent company," says Goldman, Sachs & Co. analyst Romitha

S. Mally. "At the end of the day, it will be the chairman and the board, which is controlled by Philip Morris, who will be the ultimate decision makers for Kraft."

9   In this case, though, the co-CEOs have well-defined management areas. Another plus: Their personalities seem to complement each other. James J. Drury, vice-chairman of Spencer Stuart, an executive-search firm in Chicago, describes Deromedi, who holds a math degree, as "more focused on problem solving and more likely to make tough decisions in complex situations." Holden, he says, is creative, charismatic, and more people-oriented: "She's more the one to take into consideration how a business situation may impact people."

10   A top task for the new CEOs will be figuring out how to expand outside North America. Overseas, Kraft faces a lineup of tough global competitors—Unilever, Nestlé, Groupe Danone—that were quicker to break into fast-growing markets in Asia, Latin America, and Eastern Europe. Unilever and Nestlé, for example, each get 32 percent of their sales in developing countries. Western Europe, Kraft's strongest international market, is almost as saturated as the United States. Even in Great Britain, Kraft is only the eighth-largest food company. "A truly global organization would have a quarter to one-third of their business in North America, not three-quarters," says Adrian Richardson, global consumer and retail-sector head at BT Funds Management, a large money manager in Sydney.

11   FORTRESS. One problem is that Kraft's strength, convenience products, doesn't go over well in emerging markets, where scarce shopping dollars are concentrated on necessities. Unilever, for example, sells staples in India such as rice with added protein and salt with iodine. Kraft, on the other hand, has only a tiny presence there. But Kraft plans to jump-start sales in emerging markets by introducing additional snack, beverage, cheese, and other brands in countries where it already has a presence. It also plans to enter countries where it has no operations and to make acquisitions, especially in snacks and beverages, according to its filings with the Securities & Exchange Commission. Richardson believes Kraft could make up to three significant acquisitions in the next few years to beef up its offshore operations: "If

they just build, build, build [new plants], they won't meaningfully move the dial," he says. For Kraft, "the U.S. domestic base is an absolute fortress that provides a very good cash cow" with which to go shopping. "They're not too late."

12   Close to home, Kraft is getting a much-needed shot of adrenaline from the Nabisco purchase. Last year, Kraft's sales dipped 1 percent, versus. gains of 7.3 percent at General Mills Inc. (GIS) and 6.3 percent at Hershey Foods Corp. (HSY) Many older Kraft products are in aging categories with flat or declining volumes, such as cereal and traditional store-bought coffee. But with Nabisco, Kraft picked up faster-growing product lines such as Chips Ahoy! cookies and Ritz crackers that will fuel earnings growth. Overnight, Kraft moved from a 6 percent to a 20 percent market share in crackers and cookies, a category that's expanding at more than twice the rate of the food-industry average. Goldman's Mally expects Kraft sales to rise 3.5 percent in each of the next three years, just ahead of the industry average. And with the cost savings it expects to squeeze from Nabisco, Kraft estimates that its earnings will grow at an above-average 18 percent to 22 percent annually over the same period.

13   That additional growth will be needed to cover the cost of the Nabisco deal. The newly public Kraft will carry an $18.5 billion debt load, even after using the offering proceeds to pay off a portion of the $11 billion it borrowed through Philip Morris to buy Nabisco. Next year, $7 billion of this debt comes due, and Kraft won't be able to meet that payment, according to its prospectus. But it says it plans to use its good credit rating to refinance.

14   Kraft has long been a leader in product development—in 1989 it launched the novel Lunchables line that's now a $750 million-a-year product. Innovations like that put Kraft on top of the U.S. food industry. Now investors will be counting on Deromedi and Holden to sprinkle some of that magic overseas.

Source: Julie Forster and Becky Gaylord, "Can Kraft Be a Big Cheese Abroad? It needs more global clout to offset a mature U.S. market," *BusinessWeek*, June 4, 2001.

Part **Two**

Strategy Formulation

Strategy formulation guides executives in defining the business their firm is in, the ends it seeks, and the means it will use to accomplish those ends. The approach of strategy formulation is an improvement over that of traditional long-range planning. As discussed in the next eight chapters—about developing a firm's competitive plan of action—strategy formulation combines a future-oriented perspective with concern for the firm's internal and external environments.

The strategy formulation process begins with definition of the company mission, as discussed in Chapter 2. In this chapter, the purpose of business is defined to reflect the values of a wide variety of interested parties. Social responsibility is discussed as a critical consideration for a company's strategic decision makers since the mission statement must express how the company intends to contribute to the societies that sustain it. Central to the idea that companies should be operated in socially responsible ways is the belief that managers will behave in an ethical manner. Management ethics are discussed in this chapter with special attention to the utilitarian, moral rights, and social justice approaches.

Chapter 3 deals with the principal factors in a firm's external environment that strategic managers must assess so they can anticipate and take advantage of future business conditions. It emphasizes the importance to a firm's planning activities of factors in the firm's remote, industry, and operating environments. A key theme of the chapter is the problem of deciding whether to accept environmental constraints or to maneuver around them.

Chapter 4 describes the key differences in strategic planning and implementation among domestic, multinational, and global firms. It gives special attention to the new vision that a firm must communicate in a revised company mission when it multinationalizes.

Chapter 5 shows how firms evaluate their company's strengths and weaknesses to produce an internal analysis. Strategic managers use such profiles to target competitive advantages they can emphasize and competitive disadvantages they should correct or minimize.

Chapter 6 examines the types of long-range objectives strategic managers set and specifies the qualities these objectives must have to provide a basis for direction and evaluation. The chapter also examines the generic and grand strategies that firms use to achieve long-range objectives.

Comprehensive approaches to the evaluation of strategic opportunities and to the final strategic decision are the focus of Chapter 7. The chapter shows how a firm's strategic options can be compared in a way that allows selection of the best available option. It also discusses how a company can create competitive advantages for each of its businesses.

Chapter 8 extends the attention on strategic analysis and choice by showing how managers can build value in multibusiness companies.

Chapter **Two**

Defining the Company's Mission and Social Responsibility

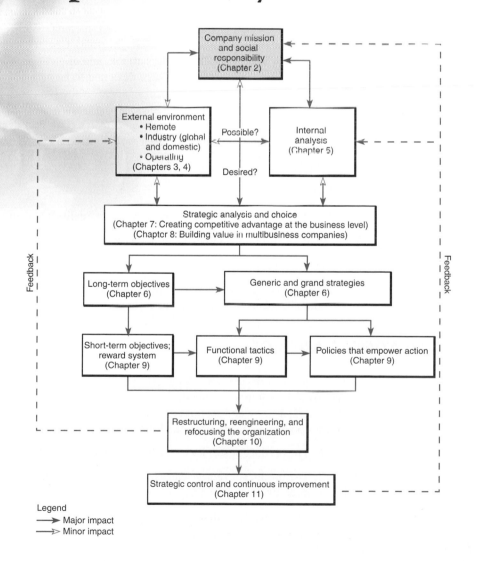

Company mission and social responsibility (Chapter 2)

External environment
• Remote
• Industry (global and domestic)
• Operating
(Chapters 3, 4)

Possible?

Desired?

Internal analysis (Chapter 5)

Strategic analysis and choice
(Chapter 7: Creating competitive advantage at the business level)
(Chapter 8: Building value in multibusiness companies)

Long-term objectives (Chapter 6)

Generic and grand strategies (Chapter 6)

Short-term objectives; reward system (Chapter 9)

Functional tactics (Chapter 9)

Policies that empower action (Chapter 9)

Restructuring, reengineering, and refocusing the organization (Chapter 10)

Strategic control and continuous improvement (Chapter 11)

Feedback

Feedback

Legend
⟶ Major impact
⟶ Minor impact

WHAT IS A COMPANY MISSION?

Whether a firm is developing a new business or reformulating direction for an ongoing business, it must determine the basic goals and philosophies that will shape its strategic posture. This fundamental purpose that sets a firm apart from other firms of its type and identifies the scope of its operations in product and market terms is defined as the company mission. As discussed in Chapter 1, the company mission is a broadly framed but enduring statement of a firm's intent. It embodies the business philosophy of the firm's strategic decision makers, implies the image the firm seeks to project, reflects the firm's self-concept, and indicates the firm's principal product or service areas and the primary customer needs the firm will attempt to satisfy. In short, it describes the firm's product, market, and technological areas of emphasis, and it does so in a way that reflects the values and priorities of the firm's strategic decision makers. An excellent example is the company mission statement of Nicor, Inc., shown in Exhibit 2–1, Strategy in Action.

The Need for an Explicit Mission

No external body requires that the company mission be defined, and the process of defining it is time-consuming and tedious. Moreover, it contains broadly outlined or implied objectives and strategies rather than specific directives. Characteristically, it is a statement, not of measurable targets but of attitude, outlook, and orientation.

The mission statement is a message designed to be inclusive of the expectations of all stakeholders for the company's performance over the long run. The executives and board who prepare the mission statement attempt to provide a unifying purpose for the company that will provide a basis for strategic objective setting and decision making. In general terms, the mission statement addresses the following questions:

Why is this firm in business?

What are our economic goals?

What is our operating philosophy in terms of quality, company image, and self-concept?

What are our core competencies and competitive advantages?

What customers do and can we serve?

How do we view our responsibilities to stockholders, employees, communities, environment, social issues, and competitors?

FORMULATING A MISSION

The process of defining the company mission for a specific business can perhaps be best understood by thinking about the business at its inception. The typical business begins with the beliefs, desires, and aspirations of a single entrepreneur. Such an owner-manager's sense of mission usually is based on the following fundamental beliefs:

1. The product or service of the business can provide benefits at least equal to its price.

2. The product or service can satisfy a customer need of specific market segments that is currently not being met adequately.

3. The technology that is to be used in production will provide a cost- and quality-competitive product or service.

PREAMBLE

We, the management of Nicor, Inc., here set forth our belief as to the purpose for which the company is established and the principles under which it should operate. We pledge our effort to the accomplishment of these purposes within these principles.

BASIC PURPOSE

The basic purpose of Nicor, Inc., is to perpetuate an investor-owned company engaging in various phases of the energy business, striving for balance among those phases so as to render needed satisfactory products and services and earn optimum, long-range profits.

WHAT WE DO

The principal business of the company, through its utility subsidiary, is the provision of energy through a pipe system to meet the needs of ultimate consumers. To accomplish its basic purpose, and to ensure its strength, the company will engage in other energy-related activities, directly or through subsidiaries or in participation with other persons, corporations, firms, or entities.

All activities of the company shall be consistent with its responsibilities to investors, customers, employees, and the public and its concern for the optimum development and utilization of natural resources and for environmental needs.

WHERE WE DO IT

The company's operations shall be primarily in the United States, but no self-imposed or regulatory geographical limitations are placed upon the acquisition, development, processing, transportation, or storage of energy resources, or upon other energy-related ventures in which the company may engage. The company will engage in such activities in any location where, after careful review, it has determined that such activity is in the best interest of its stockholders.

Utility service will be offered in the territory of the company's utility subsidiary to the best of its ability, in accordance with the requirements of regulatory agencies and pursuant to the subsidiary's purposes and principles.

4. With hard work and the support of others, the business can not only survive but also grow and be profitable.

5. The management philosophy of the business will result in a favorable public image and will provide financial and psychological rewards for those who are willing to invest their labor and money in helping the business to succeed.

6. The entrepreneur's self-concept of the business can be communicated to and adopted by employees and stockholders.

As the business grows or is forced by competitive pressures to alter its product, market, or technology, redefining the company mission may be necessary. If so, the revised mission statement will contain the same components as the original. It will state the basic type of product or service to be offered, the primary markets or customer groups to be served; the technology to be used in production or delivery; the firm's fundamental concern for survival through growth and profitability; the firm's managerial philosophy; the public image the firm seeks; and the self-concept those affiliated with the firm should have of it. This chapter will discuss in detail these components. The examples shown in Exhibit 2–2 provide insights into how some major corporations handle them.

Basic Product or Service; Primary Market; Principal Technology

Three indispensable components of the mission statement are specification of the basic product or service, specification of the primary market, and specification of the principal technology for production or delivery. These components are discussed under one heading because only in combination do they describe the company's business activity. A good example of the three components is to be found in the business plan of ITT Barton, a division of ITT. Under the heading of business mission and area served, the following information is presented:

Strategy in Action
Identifying Mission Statement Components: A Compilation
of Excerpts from Actual Corporate Mission Statements

Exhibit 2–2

1. Customer-market	We believe our first responsibility is to the doctors, nurses, and patients, to mothers and all others who use our products and services. (Johnson & Johnson)
	To anticipate and meet market needs of farmers, ranchers, and rural communities within North America. (CENEX)
2. Product-service	AMAX's principal products are molybdenum, coal, iron ore, copper, lead, zinc, petroleum and natural gas, potash, phosphates, nickel, tungsten, silver, gold, and magnesium. (AMAX)
3. Geographic domain	We are dedicated to total success of Corning Glass Works as a worldwide competitor. (Corning Glass)
4. Technology	Control Data is in the business of applying microelectronics and computer technology in two general areas: computer-related hardware and computing-enhancing services, which include computation, information, education, and finance. (Control Data)
	The common technology in these areas relates to discrete particle coatings. (NASHUA)
5. Concern for survival	In this respect, the company will conduct its operation prudently, and will provide the profits and growth which will assure Hoover's ultimate success. (Hoover Universal)
6. Philosophy	We are committed to improve health care throughout the world. (Baxter Travenol)
	We believe human development to be the worthiest of the goals of civilization and independence to be the superior condition for nurturing growth in the capabilities of people. (Sun Company)
7. Self-concept	Hoover Universal is a diversified, multi-industry corporation with strong manufacturing capabilities, entrepreneurial policies, and individual business unit autonomy. (Hoover Universal)
8. Concern for public image	We are responsible to the communities in which we live and work and to the world community as well. (Johnson & Johnson)
	Also, we must be responsive to the broader concerns of the public, including especially the general desire for improvement in the quality of life, equal opportunity for all, and the constructive use of natural resources. (Sun Company)

The unit's mission is to serve industry and government with quality instruments used for the primary measurement, analysis, and local control of fluid flow, level, pressure, temperature, and fluid properties. This instrumentation includes flow meters, electronic readouts, indicators, recorders, switches, liquid level systems, analytical instruments such as titrators, integrators, controllers, transmitters, and various instruments for the measurement of fluid properties (density, viscosity, gravity) used for processing variable sensing, data collecting, control, and transmission. The unit's mission includes fundamental loop-closing control and display devices, when economically justified, but excludes broadline central control room instrumentation, systems design, and turnkey responsibility.

Markets served include instrumentation for oil and gas production, gas transportation, chemical and petrochemical processing, cryogenics, power generation, aerospace, government, and marine, as well as other instrument and equipment manufacturers.

In only 129 words, this segment of the mission statement clearly indicates to all readers—from company employees to casual observers—the basic products, primary markets, and principal technologies of ITT Barton.

Often the most referenced public statement of a company's selected products and markets appears in "silver bullet" form in the mission statement; for example, "Dayton-Hudson Corporation is a diversified retailing company whose business is to serve the American consumer through the retailing of fashion-oriented quality merchandise." Such an abstract of company direction is particularly helpful to outsiders who value condensed overviews.

Company Goals: Survival, Growth, Profitability

Three economic goals guide the strategic direction of almost every business organization. Whether or not the mission statement explicitly states these goals, it reflects the firm's intention to secure *survival* through *growth* and *profitability.*

A firm that is unable to survive will be incapable of satisfying the aims of any of its stakeholders. Unfortunately, the goal of survival, like the goals of growth and profitability, often is taken for granted to such an extent that it is neglected as a principal criterion in strategic decision making. When this happens, the firm may focus on short-term aims at the expense of the long run. Concerns for expediency, a quick fix, or a bargain may displace the assessment of long-term impact. Too often, the result is near-term economic failure owing to a lack of resource synergy and sound business practice. For example, Consolidated Foods, maker of Shasta soft drinks and L'eggs hosiery, sought growth through the acquisition of bargain businesses. However, the erratic sales patterns of its diverse holdings forced it to divest itself of more than four dozen companies. This process cost Consolidated Foods millions of dollars and hampered its growth.

Profitability is the mainstay goal of a business organization. No matter how profit is measured or defined, profit over the long term is the clearest indication of a firm's ability to satisfy the principal claims and desires of employees and stockholders. The key phrase here is "over the long term." Obviously, basing decisions on a short-term concern for profitability would lead to a strategic myopia. Overlooking the enduring concerns of customers, suppliers, creditors, ecologists, and regulatory agents may produce profit in the short term, but, over time, the financial consequences are likely to be detrimental.

The following excerpt from the Hewlett-Packard statement of mission ably expresses the importance of an orientation toward long-term profit:

> To achieve sufficient profit to finance our company growth and to provide the resources we need to achieve our other corporate objectives.
>
> In our economic system, the profit we generate from our operation is the ultimate source of the funds we need to prosper and grow. It is the one absolutely essential measure of our corporate performance over the long term. Only if we continue to meet our profit objective can we achieve our other corporate objectives.

A firm's growth is tied inextricably to its survival and profitability. In this context, the meaning of growth must be broadly defined. Although product impact market studies (PIMS) have shown that growth in market share is correlated with profitability, other important forms of growth do exist. Growth in the number of markets served, in the variety of products offered, and in the technologies that are used to provide goods or services frequently lead to improvements in a firm's competitive ability. Growth means change, and proactive change is essential in a dynamic business environment.

AOL's strategy provides an example, as shown in Exhibit 2–3, Strategy in Action. In 2003, some analysts believed that AOL Time Warner should change to a survival strategy because of the amount of debt that it was carrying. They believed that AOL should try to reduce debt and regain some market share that it had lost over the previous year. AOL did decide to reduce its $7 billion debt by the end of 2004, but not simply to survive. AOL was trying to position itself for the acquisition of either Adelphia or Cablevision. AOL felt that if it could acquire one of these two companies or possibly both, it could increase its footprint in the market. AOL believed that growth for its company would have to come from the Cable TV market and that the only way to grow was to serve more markets. Luckily, AOL's top competitor, Comcast, was in the same debt position as AOL and could not immediately preempt the acquisitions.

Hewlett-Packard's mission statement provides another excellent example of corporate regard for growth:

> Objective: To let our growth be limited only by our profits and our ability to develop and produce technical products that satisfy real customer needs.

BusinessWeek   AOL Time Warner Chief Executive Parsons stressed once again his goal of reducing AOL Time Warner's (AOL) total debt to $20 billion by the end of 2004, versus the $27 billion it had in January 2003. Everybody assumed that his primary aim was to adopt a more financially conservative approach to managing AOL Time Warner. That would have made sense, considering that its debt rating was lingering dangerously close to junk-bond grade, that the financial performance of its America Online division was still flagging, and that its damaged credibility with investors left its stock trading in the $10 to $12 range, far below its 52-week high of $27.44.

Parsons' debt-reduction plan was an effort to clear the decks for another AOL acquisition. While he did intend to improve the company's soundness and its stock price, industry analysts said he also wanted to make a run for the nation's number five cable operator, Adelphia Cable in Coudersport, Pa., which entered Chapter 11 bankruptcy after members of the controlling Rigas family were charged with looting their company of more than $2 billion. Alternatively, Time Warner Cable may have been interested in acquiring Cablevision (CVC), the number six operator, whose Long Island (NY) systems were contiguous with Time Warner Cable's New York City market. Both Time Warner Cable and Comcast (CMCSA), the nation's number one cable company, were salivating over Adelphia's 5.3 million subscribers. But Comcast was also too debt-laden to make an offer, and that bought Parsons a little time to clean up AOL's balance sheet and perhaps make the first move as early as a year from now.

Parsons was in the camp of media execs who believed that cable is likely, eventually, to dominate the distribution of nearly all digital media to homes. Locking up as many local cable monopolies as possible would have helped AOL distribute its TV programming, movies, music, and Internet services.

Source: Extracted from David Shook, "Will Cable be AOL's Lifeline?" *BusinessWeek Online,* March 10, 2003.

We do not believe that large size is important for its own sake; however, for at least two basic reasons, continuous growth is essential for us to achieve our other objectives.

In the first place, we serve a rapidly growing and expanding segment of our technological society. To remain static would be to lose ground. We cannot maintain a position of strength and leadership in our field without growth.

In the second place, growth is important in order to attract and hold high-caliber people. These individuals will align their future only with a company that offers them considerable opportunity for personal progress. Opportunities are greater and more challenging in a growing company.

The issue of growth raises a concern about the definition of the company mission. How can a firm's product, market, and technology be specified sufficiently to provide direction without precluding the exercise of unanticipated strategic options? How can a firm so define its mission that it can consider opportunistic diversification while maintaining the parameters that guide its growth decision? Perhaps such questions are best addressed when a firm's mission statement outlines the conditions under which the firm might depart from ongoing operations. General Electric Company's extensive global mission provided the foundation for its GE Appliances (GEA) in Louisville, Kentucky. GEA did not see consumer preferences in the world market becoming Americanized. Instead, its expansion goals allowed for flexibility in examining the unique characteristics of individual foreign markets and tailoring strategies to fit them.

The growth philosophy of Dayton-Hudson also embodies this approach:

The stability and quality of the corporation's financial performance will be developed through the profitable execution of our existing businesses, as well as through the acquisition or development of new businesses. Our growth priorities, in order, are as follows:

1. Development of the profitable market preeminence of existing companies in existing markets through new store development or new strategies within existing stores.
2. Expansion of our companies to feasible new markets.

We, the Saturn Team, in concert with the UAW and General Motors, believe that meeting the needs of customers, Saturn members, suppliers, dealers, and neighbors is fundamental to fulfilling our mission.

To meet our customer's needs . . .

- our products and services must be world leaders in value and satisfaction.

To meet our members' needs, we . . .

- will create a sense of belonging in an environment of mutual trust, respect, and dignity;

- believe that all people want to be involved in decisions that affect them, care about their jobs and each other, take pride in themselves and in their contributions, and want to share in the success of their efforts;

- will develop the tools, training, and education for each member, recognizing individual skills and knowledge;

- believe that creative, motivated, responsible team members who understand that change is critical to success are Saturn's most important asset.

To meet our suppliers' and dealers' needs, we . . .

- will strive to create real partnerships with them;

- will be open and fair in our dealings, reflecting trust, respect, and their importance to Saturn;

- want dealers and suppliers to feel ownerships in Saturn's mission and philosophy as their own.

To meet the needs of our neighbors, the communities in which we live and operate, we . . .

- will be good citizens, protect the environment, and conserve natural resources;

- will seek to cooperate with government at all levels and strive to be sensitive, open, and candid in all our public statements.

3. Acquisition of other retailing companies that are strategically and financially compatible with Dayton-Hudson.
4. Internal development of new retailing strategies.

Capital allocations to fund the expansion of existing Dayton-Hudson operating companies will be based on each company's return on investment (ROI), in relationship to its ROI objective and its consistency in earnings growth and on the ability of its management to perform up to the forecasts contained in its capital requests. Expansion via acquisition or new venture will occur when the opportunity promises an acceptable rate of long-term growth and profitability, an acceptable degree of risk, and compatibility with Dayton-Hudson's long-term strategy.

Company Philosophy

The statement of a company's philosophy, often called the *company creed,* usually accompanies or appears within the mission statement. It reflects or specifies the basic beliefs, values, aspirations, and philosophical priorities to which strategic decision makers are committed in managing the company. Fortunately, the philosophies vary little from one firm to another. Owners and managers implicitly accept a general, unwritten, yet pervasive code of behavior that governs business actions and permits them to be largely self-regulated. Unfortunately, statements of company philosophy are often so similar and so platitudinous that they read more like public relations handouts than the commitment to values they are meant to be.

Saturn's statement of philosophy, presented in Exhibit 2–4, Strategy in Action, indicates the company's clearly defined initiatives for satisfying the needs of its customers, employees, suppliers, and dealers.

Despite the similarity of these statements, the intentions of the strategic managers in developing them do not warrant cynicism. Company executives attempt to provide a

The corporation will:

Set standards for return on investment (ROI) and earnings growth.

Approve strategic plans.

Allocate capital.

Approve goals.

Monitor, measure, and audit results.

Reward performance.

Allocate management resources.

The operating companies will be accorded the freedom and responsibility:

To manage their own business.

To develop strategic plans and goals that will optimize their growth.

To develop an organization that can ensure consistency of results and optimum growth.

To operate their businesses consistent with the corporation's statement of philosophy.

The corporate staff will provide only those services that are:

Essential to the protection of the corporation.

Needed for the growth of the corporation.

Wanted by operating companies and that provide a significant advantage in quality or cost.

The corporation will insist on:

Uniform accounting practices by type of business.

Prompt disclosure of operating results.

A systematic approach to training and developing people.

Adherence to appropriately high standards of business conduct and civic responsibility in accordance with the corporation's statement of philosophy.

distinctive and accurate picture of the firm's managerial outlook. One such statement of company philosophy is that of Dayton-Hudson Corporation. As Exhibit 2–5, Strategy in Action, shows, Dayton-Hudson's board of directors and executives have established especially clear directions for company decision making and action.

Perhaps most noteworthy in the Dayton-Hudson statement is its delineation of responsibility at both the corporate and business levels. In many ways, the statement could serve as a prototype for the three-tier approach to strategic management. This approach implies that the mission statement must address strategic concerns at the corporate, business, and functional levels of the organization. Dayton-Hudson's management philosophy does this by balancing operating autonomy and flexibility on the one hand with corporate input and direction on the other.

As seen in Exhibit 2–6, Global Strategy in Action, the philosophy of Nissan Motor Manufacturing is expressed by the company's People Principles and Key Corporate Principles. These principles form the basis of the way the company operates on a daily basis. They address the principal concepts used in meeting the company's established goals. Nissan focuses on the distinction between the role of the individual and the corporation. In this way, employees can link their productivity and success to the productivity and success of the company. Given these principles, the company is able to concentrate on the issues most important to its survival, growth, and profitability.

Strategy in Action Exhibit 2–7 provides an example of how General Motors uses a statement of company philosophy to clarify its environmental principles.

Public Image

Both present and potential customers attribute certain qualities to particular businesses. Gerber and Johnson & Johnson make safe products; Cross Pen makes high-quality writing instruments;

Global Strategy in Action
Principles of Nissan Motor Manufacturing (UK) Ltd.

Exhibit 2–6

	People Principles **(All Other Objectives Can Only Be Achieved by People)**
Selection	Hire the highest caliber people; look for technical capabilities and emphasize attitude.
Responsibility	Maximize the responsibility; staff by devolving decision making.
Teamwork	Recognize and encourage individual contributions, with everyone working toward the same objectives.
Flexibility	Expand the role of the individual: multiskilled, no job description, generic job titles.
Kaizen	Continuously seek 100.1 percent improvements; give "ownership of change."
Communications	"Every day, face to face."
Training	Establish individual "continuous development programs."
Supervisors	Regard as "the professionals at managing the production process"; give them much responsibility normally assumed by individual departments; make them the genuine leaders of their teams.
Single status	Treat everyone as a "first class" citizen; eliminate all illogical differences.
Trade unionism	Establish single union agreement with AEU emphasizing the common objective for a successful enterprise.

	Key Corporate Principles
Quality	Building profitably the highest quality car sold in Europe.
Customers	Achieve target of no. 1 customer satisfaction in Europe.
Volume	Always achieve required volume.
New products	Deliver on time, at required quality, within cost.
Suppliers	Establish long-term relationship with single-source suppliers; aim for zero defects and just-in-time delivery; apply Nissan principles to suppliers.
Production	Use "most appropriate" technology; develop predictable "best method" of doing job; build in quality.
Engineering	Design "quality" and "ease of working" into the product and facilities; establish "simultaneous engineering" to reduce development time.

Étienne Aigner makes stylish but affordable leather products; Corvettes are power machines; and Izod Lacoste stands for the preppy look. Thus, mission statements should reflect the public's expectations, since this makes achievement of the firm's goals more likely. Gerber's mission statement should not open the possibility for diversification into pesticides, and Cross Pen's should not open the possibility for diversification into $0.59 brand-name disposables.

On the other hand, a negative public image often prompts firms to reemphasize the beneficial aspects of their mission. For example, in response to what it saw as a disturbing trend in public opinion, Dow Chemical undertook an aggressive promotional campaign to fortify its credibility, particularly among "employees and those who live and work in [their] plant communities." Dow described its approach in its annual report:

> All around the world today, Dow people are speaking up. People who care deeply about their company, what it stands for, and how it is viewed by others. People who are immensely proud of their company's performance, yet realistic enough to realize it is the public's perception of that performance that counts in the long run.

As a responsible corporate citizen, General Motors is dedicated to protecting human health, natural resources, and the global environment. This dedication reaches further than compliance with the law to encompass the integration of sound environmental practices into our business decisions.

The following environmental principles provide guidance to General Motors personnel worldwide in the conduct of their daily business practices:

1. We are committed to actions to restore and preserve the environment.

2. We are committed to reducing waste and pollutants, conserving resources, and recycling materials at every stage of the product life cycle.

3. We will continue to participate actively in educating the public regarding environmental conservation.

4. We will continue to pursue vigorously the development and implementation of technologies for minimizing pollutant emissions.

5. We will continue to work with all governmental entities for the development of technically sound and financially responsible environmental laws and regulations.

6. We will continually assess the impact of our plants and products on the environment and the communities in which we live and operate with a goal of continuous improvement.

Firms seldom address the question of their public image in an intermittent fashion. Although public agitation often stimulates greater attention to this question, firms are concerned about their public image even in the absence of such agitation. The following excerpt from the mission statement of Intel Corporation is an example of this attitude:

> We are sensitive to our *image with our customers and the business community*. Commitments to customers are considered sacred, and we are upset with ourselves when we do not meet our commitments. We strive to demonstrate to the business world on a continuing basis that we are credible in describing the state of the corporation, and that we are well organized and in complete control of all things that determine the numbers.

Exhibit 2–8, Strategy in Action, presents a marketing translation of the essence of the mission statements of six high-end shoe companies. The impressive feature of the exhibit is that it shows dramatically how closely competing firms can incorporate subtle, yet meaningful, differences into their mission statements.

Company Self-Concept

A major determinant of a firm's success is the extent to which the firm can relate functionally to its external environment. To achieve its proper place in a competitive situation, the firm realistically must evaluate its competitive strengths and weaknesses. This idea—that the firm must know itself—is the essence of the company self-concept. The idea is not commonly integrated into theories of strategic management; its importance for individuals has been recognized since ancient times.

Both individuals and firms have a crucial need to know themselves. The ability of either to survive in a dynamic and highly competitive environment would be severely limited if they did not understand their impact on others or of others on them.

In some senses, then, firms take on personalities of their own. Much behavior in firms is organizationally based; that is, a firm acts on its members in other ways than their individual interactions. Thus, firms are entities whose personality transcends the personalities of their members. As such, they can set decision-making parameters based on aims different and distinct from the aims of their members. These organizational considerations have pervasive effects.

Ordinarily, descriptions of the company self-concept per se do not appear in mission statements. Yet such statements often provide strong impressions of the company self-

Allen-Edmonds

Allen-Edmonds provides high-quality shoes for the affluent consumer who appreciates a well-made, finely crafted, stylish dress shoe.

Bally

Bally shoes set you apart. They are the perfect shoe to complement your lifestyle. Bally shoes project an image of European style and elegance that ensures one is not just dressed, but well dressed.

Bostonian

Bostonian shoes are for those successful individuals who are well-traveled, on the "go" and want a stylish dress shoe that can keep up with their variety of needs and activities. With Bostonian, you know you will always be well dressed whatever the situation.

Cole-Hahn

Cole-Hahn offers a line of contemporary shoes for the man who wants to go his own way. They are shoes for the urban, upscale, stylish man who wants to project an image of being one step ahead.

Florsheim

Florsheim shoes are the affordable classic men's dress shoes for those who want to experience the comfort and style of a solid dress shoe.

Johnston & Murphy

Johnston & Murphy is the quintessential business shoe for those affluent individuals who know and demand the best.

Source: "Thinking on Your Feet, the Johnston & Murphy Guerrilla Marketing Competition" (Johnston & Murphy, # GENLSCO Company).

concept. For example, ARCO's environment, health, and safety (EHS) managers were adamant about emphasizing the company's position on safety and environmental performance as a part of the mission statement. The challenges facing the ARCO EHS managers included dealing with concerned environmental groups and a public that has become environmentally aware. They hoped to motivate employees toward safer behavior while reducing emissions and waste. They saw this as a reflection of the company's positive self-image.

The following excerpts from the Intel Corporation mission statement describe the corporate persona that its top management seeks to foster:

Management is self-critical. The leaders must be capable of recognizing and accepting their mistakes and learning from them.

Open (constructive) confrontation is encouraged at all levels of the corporation and is viewed as a method of problem solving and conflict resolution.

Decision by consensus is the rule. Decisions once made are supported. Position in the organization is not the basis for quality of ideas.

A highly communicative, open management is part of the style.

Management must be ethical. Managing by telling the truth and treating all employees equitably has established credibility that is ethical.

We strive to provide an opportunity for rapid development.

Intel is a results-oriented company. The focus is on substance versus form, quality versus quantity.

We believe in the principle that hard work, high productivity is something to be proud of.

The concept of assumed responsibility is accepted. (If a task needs to be done, assume you have the responsibility to get it done.)

Commitments are long term. If career problems occur at some point, reassignment is a better alternative than termination.

We desire to have all employees involved and participative in their relationship with Intel.

Newest Trends in Mission Components

Recently, three issues have become so prominent in the strategic planning for organizations that they are increasingly becoming integral parts in the development and revisions of mission statements: sensitivity to consumer wants, concern for quality, and statements of company vision.

Customers

"The customer is our top priority" is a slogan that would be claimed by the majority of businesses in the United States and abroad. For companies including Caterpillar Tractor, General Electric, and Johnson & Johnson this means analyzing consumer needs before as well as after a sale. The bonus plan at Xerox allows for a 40 percent annual bonus, based on high customer reviews of the service that they receive, and a 20 percent penalty if the feedback is especially bad. For these firms and many others, the overriding concern for the company has become consumer satisfaction.

In addition many U.S. firms maintain extensive product safety programs to help ensure consumer satisfaction. RCA, Sears, and 3M boast of such programs. Other firms including Calgon Corporation, Amoco, Mobil Oil, Whirlpool, and Zenith provide toll-free telephone lines to answer customer concerns and complaints.

The focus on customer satisfaction is demonstrated by retailer J. C. Penney in this excerpt from its statement of philosophy: "The Penney Idea is (1) To serve the public as nearly as we can to its complete satisfaction; (2) To expect for the service we render a fair remuneration, and not all the profit the traffic will bear; (3) To do all in our power to pack the customer's dollar full of value, quality, and satisfaction."

A focus on customer satisfaction causes managers to realize the importance of providing quality customer service. Strong customer service initiatives have led some firms to gain competitive advantages in the marketplace. Hence, many corporations have made the customer service initiative a key component of their corporate mission.

Quality

"Quality is job one!" is a rallying point not only for Ford Motor Corporation but for many resurging U.S. businesses as well. Two U.S. management experts fostered a worldwide emphasis on quality in manufacturing. W. Edwards Deming and J. M. Juran's messages were first embraced by Japanese managers, whose quality consciousness led to global dominance in several industries including automobile, TV, audio equipment, and electronic components manufacturing. Deming summarizes his approach in 14 now well-known points:

1. Create constancy of purpose.

2. Adopt the new philosophy.

3. Cease dependence on mass inspection to achieve quality.

4. End the practice of awarding business on price tag alone. Instead, minimize total cost, often accomplished by working with a single supplier.

5. Improve constantly the system of production and service.

6. Institute training on the job.

7. Institute leadership.

8. Drive out fear.

9. Break down barriers between departments.

10. Eliminate slogans, exhortations, and numerical targets.

11. Eliminate work standards (quotas) and management by objective.

12. Remove barriers that rob workers, engineers, and managers of their right to pride of workmanship.

CADILLAC

The Mission of the Cadillac Motor Company is to engineer, produce, and market the world's finest automobiles known for uncompromised levels of distinctiveness, comfort, convenience, and refined performance. Through its people, who are its strength, Cadillac will continuously improve the quality of its products and services to meet or exceed customer expectations and succeed as a profitable business.

MOTOROLA

Dedication to quality is a way of life at our company, so much so that it goes far beyond rhetorical slogans. Our ongoing program is one of continued improvement out for change, refinement, and even revolution in our pursuit of quality excellence.

It is the objective of Motorola, Inc., to produce and provide products and services of the highest quality. In its activities, Motorola will pursue goals aimed at the achievement of quality excellence. These results will be derived from the dedicated efforts of each employee in conjunction with supportive participation from management at all levels of the corporation.

ZYTEC

Zytec is a company that competes on value; is market driven; provides superior quality and service, builds strong relationship with its customers; and provides technical excellence in its products.

13. Institute a vigorous program of education and self-improvement.

14. Put everyone in the company to work to accomplish the transformation.

Firms in the United States responded aggressively. The new philosophy is that quality should be the norm. For example, Motorola's production goal is 60 or fewer defects per every billion components that it manufactures.

Exhibit 2–9, Strategy in Action, presents the integration of the quality initiative into the mission statements of three corporations. The emphasis on quality has received added emphasis in many corporate philosophies since the Congress created the Malcolm Baldrige Quality Award in 1987. Each year up to two Baldrige Awards can be given in three categories of a company's operations: manufacturing, services, and small businesses.

Vision Statement

Whereas the mission statement expresses an answer to the question "What business are we in?" a company *vision statement* is sometimes developed to express the aspirations of the executive leadership. A vision statement presents the firm's strategic intent that focuses the energies and resources of the company on achieving a desirable future. However, in actual practice, the mission and vision statement are frequently combined into a single statement. When they are separated, the vision statement is often a single sentence, designed to be memorable. For example:

Federal Express: "Our vision is to change the way we all connect with each other in the New Network Economy."

Lexmark: "Customers for Life."

Microsoft: "A computer on every desk, and in every home, running on Microsoft software."

An Exemplary Mission Statement

When BB&T merged with Southern Bank, the Board of Directors and officers undertook the creation of a comprehensive mission statement that was designed to include most of the topics that we discussed in this chapter. In 2003, the company updated its statement and mailed the resulting booklet to its shareholders and other interested parties. The foreword to the document expresses the greatest values of such a public pronouncement and was signed by BB&T's Chairman and CEO, John A. Allison:

> In a rapidly changing and unpredictable world, individuals and organizations need a clear set of fundamental principals to guide their actions. At BB&T we know the content of our business will, and should, experience constant change. Change is necessary for progress. However, the context, our fundamental principles, is unchanging because these principles are based on basic truths.
>
> BB&T is a mission-driven organization with a clearly defined set of values. We encourage our employees to have a strong sense of purpose, a high level of self-esteem and the capacity to think clearly and logically.
>
> We believe that competitive advantage is largely in the minds of our employees as represented by their capacity to turn rational ideas into action towards the accomplishment of our mission.

Appendix 2 presents BB&T's Vision, Mission, and Purpose Statement in its entirety. It also includes detailed expressions of the company's values and views on the role of emotions, management style, the management concept, attributes of an outstanding employee, the importance of positive attitude, obligations to its employees, virtues of an outstanding credit culture, achieving the company goal, the nature of a "world standard" revenue-driven sales organization, the nature of a "world standard" client service community bank, the company's commitment to education and learning, and its passions.

BOARDS OF DIRECTORS

Who is responsible for determining the firm's mission? Who is responsible for acquiring and allocating resources so the firm can thoughtfully develop and implement a strategic plan? Who is responsible for monitoring the firm's success in the competitive marketplace to determine whether that plan was well designed and activated? The answer to all of these questions is strategic decision makers. As you saw in Exhibit 1–3, most organizations have multiple levels of strategic decision makers; typically, the larger the firm, the more levels it will have. The strategic managers at the highest level are responsible for decisions that affect the entire firm, commit the firm and its resources for the longest periods, and declare the firm's sense of values. In other words, this group of strategic managers is responsible for overseeing the creation and accomplishment of the company mission. The term that describes the group is *board of directors*.

In overseeing the management of a firm, the board of directors operates as the representatives of the firm's stockholders. Elected by the stockholders, the board has these major responsibilities:

1. To establish and update the company mission.

2. To elect the company's top officers, the foremost of whom is the CEO.

3. To establish the compensation levels of the top officers, including their salaries and bonuses.

4. To determine the amount and timing of the dividends paid to stockholders.

5. To set broad company policy on such matters as labor–management relations, product or service lines of business, and employee benefit packages.

6. To set company objectives and to authorize managers to implement the long-term strategies that the top officers and the board have found agreeable.

7. To mandate company compliance with legal and ethical dictates.

In the current business environment, boards of directors are accepting the challenge of shareholders and other stakeholders to become active in establishing the strategic initiatives of the companies that they serve.

This chapter considers the board of directors because the board's greatest impact on the behavior of a firm results from its determination of the company mission. The philosophy espoused in the mission statement sets the tone by which the firm and all of its employees will be judged. As logical extensions of the mission statement, the firm's objectives and strategies embody the board's view of proper business demeanor. Through its appointment of top executives and its decisions about their compensation, the board reveals its priorities for organizational achievement.

SARBANES-OXLEY ACT OF 2002

Following a string of alleged wrongdoings by corporate executives in 2000 to 2002, and the subsequent failures of their firms, Washington lawmakers proposed more than 50 policies to reassure investors. None of the resulting bills were able to pass both houses of Congress until the Banking Committee Chairman Paul Sarbanes (D-MD) proposed legislation to establish new auditing and accounting standards. The bill was called the Public Company Accounting Reform and Investor Protection Act of 2002. Later the name was changed to Sarbanes-Oxley Act of 2002.

On July 30, 2002, President George Bush signed the Sarbanes-Oxley Act into law. This revolutionary act applies to public companies with securities registered under Section 12 of the Securities Act of 1934, and those required to file reports under Section 15(d) of the Exchange Act. Sarbanes-Oxley includes required certifications for financial statements, new corporate regulations, disclosure requirements, and penalties for failure to comply.

The Sarbanes-Oxley Act states that the CEO and CFO must certify every report containing the company's financial statements. The certification acknowledges that the CEO or CFO has reviewed the report. Among the review, the officer must attest that the information does not include untrue statements or necessary omitted information. Furthermore, based on the officer's knowledge, the report is a reliable source of the company's financial condition and result of operations for the period represented. The certification also makes the officers responsible for establishing and maintaining internal controls such that they are aware of any material information relating to the company. The officers must also evaluate the effectiveness of the internal controls within 90 days of the release of the report and present their conclusions of the effectiveness of the controls. Also, the officers must disclose any fraudulent material, deficiencies in the reporting of the financial reports, or problems with the internal control to the company's auditors and auditing committee. Finally, the officers must indicate any changes to the internal controls or factors that could affect them.

The Sarbanes-Oxley Act includes provisions restricting the corporate control of executives, accounting firms, auditing committees, and attorneys. With regard to executives, the Act bans personal loans. A company can no longer directly or indirectly issue, extend, or maintain a personal loan to any director or executive officer. Executive officers and directors are not permitted to purchase, to sell, to acquire, or to transfer any equity security during any pension fund blackout period. Executives are required to notify fund participants of any blackout period and the reasons for the blackout period. The SEC will provide the company's executives with a code of ethics for the company to adopt. Failure to meet the code must be disclosed to the SEC.

The Act limits some and issues new duties of the registered public accounting firms that conduct the audits of the financial statements. Accounting firms are prohibited from performing bookkeeping or other accounting services related to the financial statements, designing or implementing financial systems, appraising, internal auditing, brokering banking services, or providing legal services unrelated to the audit. All critical accounting policies and alternative

The following outline presents the major elements of the Sarbanes-Oxley Act of 2002.

Corporate Responsibility

- The CEO and CFO of each company are required to submit a report, based on their knowledge, to the SEC certifying the company's financial statements are fair representations of the financial condition without false statements or omissions.

- The CEO and CFO must reimburse the company for any bonuses or equity-based incentives received for the last 12-month period if the company is required to restate its financial statements due to material noncompliance with any financial reporting requirement that resulted from misconduct.

- Directors and executive officers are prohibited from trading a company's 401(k) plan, profit sharing plan, or retirement plan during any blackout period. The plan administrators are required to notify the plan participants and beneficiaries with notice of all blackout periods, reasons for the blackout period, and a statement that the participant or beneficiary should evaluate their investment even though they are unable to direct or diversify their accounts during the blackout.

- No company may make, extend, modify, or renew any personal loans to its executives or directors. Limited exceptions are for loans made in the course of the company's business, on market terms, for home improvement and home loans, consumer credit, or extension of credit.

Increased Disclosure

- Each annual and quarterly financial report filed with the SEC must disclose all material off-balance-sheet transactions, arrangements, and obligations that may affect the current or future financial condition of the company or its operations.

- Companies must present pro forma financial information with the SEC in a manner that is not misleading and must be reconciled with the company's financial condition and with generally accepted accounting principles (GAAP).

- Each company is required to disclose whether they have adopted a code of ethics for its senior financial officers. If not, the company must explain the reasons. Any change or waiver of the code of ethics must be disclosed.

- Each annual report must contain a statement of management's responsibility for establishing and maintaining an internal control structure and procedures for financial reporting. The report must also include an assessment of the effectiveness of the internal control procedures.

- The Form 4 will be provided within two business days after the execution date of the trading of a company's securities by directors and executive officers. The SEC may extend this deadline if it determines the two-day period is not feasible.

- The company must disclose information concerning changes in financial conditions or operations "on a rapid and current basis," in plain English.

The SEC must review the financial statements of each reporting company no less than once every three years.

Audit Committees

- The audit committee must be composed entirely of independent directors. Committee members are not permitted to accept any fees from the company, cannot control 5 percent or more of the voting of the company, nor be an officer, director, partner, or employee of the company.

treatments of financial information within GAAP, and written communication between the accounting firm and the company's management must be reported to the audit committee.

The Act defines the composition of the audit committee and specifies its responsibilities. The members of the audit committee must be members of the company's board of directors. At least one member of the committee should be classified as a "financial expert." The audit committee is directly responsible for the work of any accounting firm employed by the company, and the accounting firm must report directly to the audit committee. The audit committee must create procedures for employee complaints or concerns over accounting or auditing matters. Upon discovery of unlawful acts by the company, the audit committee must report and be supervised in its investigation by a Public Company Accounting Oversight Board.

The Act includes rules for attorney conduct. If a company's attorneys find evidence of securities violations, they are required to report the matter to the chief legal counsel or CEO. If there is not an appropriate response, the attorneys must report the information to the audit committee or the board of directors.

- The audit committee must have the authority to engage the outside auditing firm.

- The audit committee must establish procedures for the treatment of complaints regarding accounting controls or auditing matters. They are responsible for employee complaints concerning questionable accounting and auditing.

- The audit committee must disclose whether at least one of the committee members is a "financial expert." If not, the committee must explain why not.

New Crimes and Increased Criminal Penalties

- Tampering with records with intent to impede or influence any federal investigation or bankruptcy will be punishable by a fine and/or prison sentence up to 20 years.

- Failure by an accountant to maintain all auditing papers for five years after the end of the fiscal period will be punishable by a fine and/or up to 10-year prison sentence.

- Knowingly executing, or attempting to execute, a scheme to defraud investors will be punishable by a fine and/or prison sentence of up to 25 years.

- Willfully certifying a report that does not comply with the law can be punishable with a fine up to $5,000,000 and/or a prison sentence up to 20 years.

New Civil Cause of Action and Increased Enforcement Powers

- Protection will be provided to whistle-blowers who provide information or assist in an investigation by law enforcement, congressional committee, or employee supervisor.

- Bankruptcy cannot be used to avoid liability from securities laws violations.

- Investors are able to file a civil action for fraud up to two years after discovery of the facts and five years after the occurrence of fraud.

- The SEC can receive a restraining order prohibiting payments to insiders during an investigation.

- The SEC can prevent individuals from holding an officer's or director's position in a public company as a result of violation of the securities law.

Auditor Independence

- All audit services must be preapproved by the audit committee and must be disclosed to investors.

- The lead audit or reviewing audit partner from the auditing accounting firm must change at least once every five fiscal years.

- The registered accounting firms must report to the audit committee all accounting policies and practices used, alternative uses of the financial information within GAAP that has been discussed with management, and written communications between the accounting firm and management.

- An auditing firm is prohibited from auditing a company if the company's CEO or CFO was employed by the auditing firm within the past year.

A Public Company Accounting Oversight Board is established by the SEC to oversee the audits of public companies. The Board will register public accounting firms, establish audit standards, inspect registered accounting firms, and discipline violators of the rules. No person can take part in an audit if not employed by a registered public accounting firm.

Other sections of the Sarbanes-Oxley Act stipulate disclosure periods for financial operations and reporting. Relevant information relating to changes in the financial condition or operations of a company must be immediately reported in plain English. Off-balance sheet transactions, correcting adjustments, and pro-forma information must be presented in the annual and quarterly financial reports. The information must not contain any untrue statements, must not omit material facts, and must meet GAAP standards.

Stricter penalties have been issued for violations of the Sarbanes-Oxley Act. If a company must restate its financial statements due to noncompliance, the CEO and CFO must relinquish any bonus or incentive-based compensation or realized profits from the sale of securities during the 12-month period following the filing with the SEC. Other securities fraud, such as destruction or falsification of records, results in fines and prison sentences up to 25 years.

More details on the Sarbanes-Oxley Act of 2002 are provided in Exhibit 2–10, Strategy in Action.

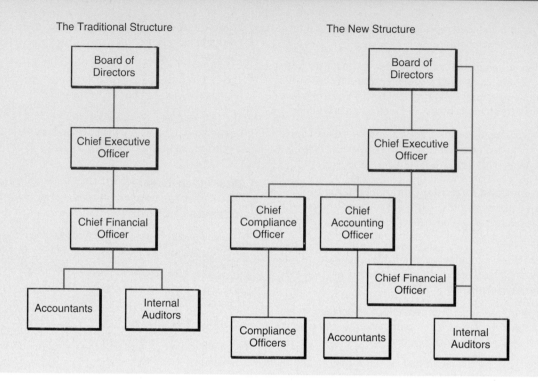

The Traditional Structure

The New Structure

The New Corporate Governance Structure

A major consequence of the 2000–2002 accounting scandals was the Sarbanes-Oxley Act of 2002, and a major consequence of Sarbanes-Oxley has been the restructuring of the governance structure of American corporations. The most significant change in the restructuring is the heightened role of corporate internal auditors, as depicted in Strategy in Action 2–11. Auditors have traditionally been viewed as performing a necessary but perfunctory function, namely to probe corporate financial records for unintentional or illicit misrepresentations. Although a majority of U.S. corporations have longstanding traditions of reporting that their auditors operated independently of CFO approval and that they had direct access to the board, in practice, the auditors' work usually traveled through the organization's hierarchical chain of command.

In the past, internal auditors reviewed financial reports generated by other corporate accountants. The auditors considered professional accounting and financial practices, as well as relevant aspects of corporate law, and then presented their findings to the chief financial officer (CFO). Historically, the CFO reviewed the audits and determined the financial data and information that was to be presented to top management, directors, and investors of the company.

However, because Sarbanes-Oxley requires that CEOs and audit committees sign-off on financial results, auditors now routinely deal directly with top corporate officials, as shown in the new structure in Strategy in Action 2-11. Approximately 75% of senior corporate auditors now report directly to the Board of Directors' audit committee. Additionally, to eliminate the potential for accounting problems, companies are establishing direct lines of communication between top managers and the board and auditors that inform the CFO but that are not dependent on CFO approval or authorization.

The new structure also provides the CEO information provided directly by the company's chief compliance and chief accounting officers. Consequently, the CFO, who is responsible for ultimately approving all company payments, is not empowered to be the sole provider of data for financial evaluations by the CEO and board.

AGENCY THEORY

Whenever there is a separation of the owners (principals) and the managers (agents) of a firm, the potential exists for the wishes of the owners to be ignored. This fact, and the recognition that agents are expensive, established the basis for a set of complex but helpful ideas known as *agency theory*. Whenever owners (or managers) delegate decision-making authority to others, an agency relationship exists between the two parties. Agency relationships, such as those between stockholders and managers, can be very effective as long as managers make investment decisions in ways that are consistent with stockholders' interests. However, when the interests of managers diverge from those of owners, then managers' decisions are more likely to reflect the managers' preferences than the owners' preferences.

In general, owners seek stock value maximization. When managers hold important blocks of company stock, they too prefer strategies that result in stock appreciation. However, when managers better resemble "hired hands" than owner-partners, they often prefer strategies that increase their personal payoffs rather than those of shareholders. Such behavior can result in decreased stock performance (as when high executive bonuses reduce corporate earnings) and in strategic decisions that point the firm in the direction of outcomes that are suboptimal from a stockholder's perspective.

If, as agency theory argues, self-interested managers act in ways that increase their own welfare at the expense of the gain of corporate stockholders, then owners who delegate decision-making authority to their agents will incur both the loss of potential gain that would have resulted from owner-optimal strategies and/or the costs of monitoring and control systems that are designed to minimize the consequences of such self-centered management decisions. In combination, the cost of agency problems and the cost of actions taken to minimize agency problems, are called *agency costs*. These costs can often be identified by their direct benefit for the agents and their negative present value. Agency costs are found when there are differing self-interests between shareholders and managers, superiors and subordinates, or managers of competing departments or branch offices.

How Agency Problems Occur

Because owners have access to only a relatively small portion of the information that is available to executives about the performance of the firm and cannot afford to monitor every executive decision or action, executives are often free to pursue their own interests.[1] This condition is known as the *moral hazard problem* or *shirking*.[2]

As a result of moral hazards, executives may design strategies that provide the greatest possible benefits for themselves, with the welfare of the organization being given only secondary consideration. For example, executives may presell products at year-end to trigger their annual bonuses even though the deep discounts that they must offer will threaten the price stability of their products for the upcoming year. Similarly, unchecked

---

[1] Substitute the terms *managers* for *owners* and *subordinates* for *executives* for another example of agency theory in operation.
[2] Shirking is described as "self-interest combined with guile."

executives may advance their own self-interests by slacking on the job, altering forecasts to maximize their performance bonuses; unrealistically assessing acquisition targets' outlooks in order to increase the probability of increasing organizational size through their acquisition; or manipulating personnel records to keep or acquire key company personnel.

The second major reason that agency costs are incurred is known as *adverse selection.* This refers to the limited ability that stockholders have to precisely determine the competencies and priorities of executives at the time that they are hired. Because principals cannot initially verify an executive's appropriateness as an agent of the owners, unanticipated problems of nonoverlapping priorities between owners and agents are likely to occur.

The most popular solution to moral dilemma and adverse selection problems is for owners to attempt to more closely align their own best interests with those of their agents through the use of executive bonus plans.[3] Foremost among these approaches are stock option plans, which enable executives to benefit directly from the appreciation of the company's stock just as other stockholders do. In most instances, executive bonus plans are unabashed attempts to align the interests of owners and executives and to thereby induce executives to support strategies that increase stockholder wealth. While such schemes are unlikely to eliminate self-interest as a major criterion in executive decision making, they help to reduce the costs associated with moral dilemmas and adverse selections.

Problems That Can Result from Agency

From a strategic management perspective there are five different kinds of problems that can arise because of the agency relationship between corporate stockholders and their company's executives:

1. Executives pursue growth in company size rather than in earnings. Shareholders generally want to maximize earnings, because earnings growth yields stock appreciation. However, because managers are typically more heavily compensated for increases in firm size than for earnings growth, they may recommend strategies that yield company growth such as mergers and acquisitions.

In addition, managers' stature in the business community is commonly associated with company size. Managers gain prominence by directing the growth of an organization, and they benefit in the forms of career advancement and job mobility that are associated with increases in company size.

Finally, executives need an enlarging set of advancement opportunities for subordinates whom they wish to motivate with nonfinancial inducements. Acquisitions can provide the needed positions.

2. Executives attempt to diversify their corporate risk. Whereas stockholders can vary their investment risks through management of their individual stock portfolios, managers' careers and stock incentives are tied to the performance of a single corporation, albeit the one that employs them. Consequently, executives are tempted to diversify their corporation's operation, businesses, and product lines to moderate the risk incurred in any single venture. While this approach serves the executives' personal agendas, it compromises the "pure play" quality of their firm as an investment. In other words, diversifying a corporation reduces the beta associated with the firm's return, which is an undesirable outcome for many stockholders.

3. Executives avoid risk. Even when, or perhaps especially when, executives are willing to restrict the diversification of their companies, they are tempted to minimize the risk that they face. Executives are often fired for failure, but rarely for mediocre corporate per-

[3] An in-depth discussion of executive bonus compensation is provided in Chapter 9.

formance. Therefore, executives may avoid desirable levels of risk, if they anticipate little reward and opt for conservative strategies that minimize the risk of company failure. If they do, executives will rarely support plans for innovation, diversification, and rapid growth.

However, from an investor's perspective, risk taking is desirable when it is systematic. In other words, when investors can reasonably expect that their company will generate higher long-term returns from assuming greater risk, they may wish to pursue the greater payoff, especially when the company is positioned to perform better than its competitors that face the same nominal risks. Obviously, the agency relationship creates a problem—should executives prioritize their job security or the company's financial returns to stockholders?

4. Managers act to optimize their personal payoffs. If executives can gain more from an annual performance bonus by achieving objective 1 than from stock appreciation resulting from the achievement of objective 2, then owners must anticipate that the executives will target objective 1 as their priority, even though objective 2 is clearly in the best interest of the shareholders. Similarly, executives may pursue a range of expensive perquisites that have a net negative effect on shareholder returns. Elegant corner offices, corporate jets, large staffs, golf club memberships, extravagant retirement programs, and limousines for executive benefit are rarely good investments for stockholders.

5. Executives act to protect their status. When their companies expand, executives want to ensure that their knowledge, experience, and skills remain relevant and central to the strategic direction of the corporation. They favor doing more of what they already do well. In contrast, investors may prefer revolutionary advancement to incremental improvement. For example, when confronted with Amazon.com, competitor Barnes & Noble initiated a joint venture website with Bertelsmann. In addition, Barnes & Noble used vertical integration with the nation's largest book distributor, which supplies 60 percent of Amazon's books. This type of revolutionary strategy is most likely to occur when executives are given assurances that they will not make themselves obsolete within the changing company that they create.

Solutions to the Agency Problem

In addition to defining an agent's responsibilities in a contract and including elements like bonus incentives that help align executives' and owners' interests, principals can take several other actions to minimize agency problems. The first is for the owners to pay executives a premium for their service. This premium helps executives to see their loyalty to the stockholders as the key to achieving their personal financial targets.

A second solution to agency problems is for executives to receive backloaded compensation. This means that executives are paid a handsome premium for superior future performance. Strategic actions taken in year one, which are to have an impact in year three, become the basis for executive bonuses in year three. This lag time between action and bonus more realistically rewards executives for the consequences of their decision making, ties the executive to the company for the long term, and properly focuses strategic management activities on the future.

Finally, creating teams of executives across different units of a corporation can help to focus performance measures on organizational rather than personal goals. Through the use of executive teams, owner interests often receive the priority that they deserve.

THE STAKEHOLDER APPROACH TO SOCIAL RESPONSIBILITY

In defining or redefining the company mission, strategic managers must recognize the legitimate rights of the firm's claimants. These include not only stockholders and employees but also outsiders affected by the firm's actions. Such outsiders commonly include customers, suppliers, governments, unions, competitors, local communities, and the general public. Each of these interest groups has justifiable reasons for expecting (and often for demanding) that the firm satisfy their claims in a responsible manner. In general, stockholders claim appropriate returns on their investment; employees seek broadly defined job satisfactions; customers want what they pay for; suppliers seek dependable buyers; governments want adherence to legislation; unions seek benefits for their members; competitors want fair competition; local communities want the firm to be a responsible citizen; and the general public expects the firm's existence to improve the quality of life.

According to a survey of 2,361 directors in 291 of the largest southeastern U.S. companies:

1. Directors perceived the existence of distinct stakeholder groups.

2. Directors have high stakeholder orientations.

3. Directors view some stakeholders differently, depending on their occupation (CEO directors versus non-CEO directors) and type (inside versus outside directors).

The study also found that the perceived stakeholders were, in the order of their importance, customers and government, stockholders, employees, and society. The results clearly indicated that boards of directors no longer believe that the stockholder is the only constituency to whom they are responsible.

However, when a firm attempts to incorporate the interests of these groups into its mission statement, broad generalizations are insufficient. These steps need to be taken:

1. Identification of the stakeholders.

2. Understanding the stakeholders' specific claims vis-à-vis the firm.

3. Reconciliation of these claims and assignment of priorities to them.

4. Coordination of the claims with other elements of the company mission.

Identification The left-hand column of Exhibit 2–12 lists the commonly encountered stakeholder groups, to which the executive officer group often is added. Obviously, though, every business faces a slightly different set of stakeholder groups, which vary in number, size, influence, and importance. In defining the company, strategic managers must identify all of the stakeholder groups and weigh their relative rights and their relative ability to affect the firm's success.

Understanding The concerns of the principal stakeholder groups tend to center on the general claims listed in the right-hand column of Exhibit 2–12. However, strategic decision makers should understand the specific demands of each group. They then will be better able to initiate actions that satisfy these demands.

Reconciliation and Priorities Unfortunately, the claims of various stakeholder groups often conflict. For example, the claims of governments and the general public tend to limit profitability, which is the central claim of most creditors and stockholders. Thus, claims must be reconciled in a mission statement that resolves the competing, conflicting, and contradicting claims of stakeholders. For objectives and strategies to be internally consistent and precisely focused, the statement must display a single-minded, though multidimensional, approach to the firm's aims.

There are hundreds, if not thousands, of claims on any firm—high wages, pure air, job security, product quality, community service, taxes, occupational health and safety regulations, equal employment opportunity regulations, product variety, wide markets, career opportunities, company growth, investment security, high ROI, and many, many more. Although most, perhaps all, of these claims may be desirable ends, they cannot

EXHIBIT 2–12
A Stakeholder View of Company Responsibility

Source: William R. King and David I. Cleland, *Strategic Planning and Policy.* © 1978 by Litton Educational Publishing, Inc., p. 153. Reprinted by permission of Van Nostrand Reinhold Company.

Stakeholder	Nature of the Claim
Stockholders	Participation in distribution of profits, additional stock offerings, assets on liquidation; vote of stock; inspection of company books; transfer of stock; election of board of directors; and such additional rights as have been established in the contract with the corporation.
Creditors	Legal proportion of interest payments due and return of principal from the investment. Security of pledged assets; relative priority in event of liquidation. Management and owner prerogatives if certain conditions exist with the company (such as default of interest payments).
Employees	Economic, social, and psychological satisfaction in the place of employment. Freedom from arbitrary and capricious behavior on the part of company officials. Share in fringe benefits, freedom to join union and participate in collective bargaining, individual freedom in offering up their services through an employment contract. Adequate working conditions.
Customers	Service provided with the product; technical data to use the product; suitable warranties; spare parts to support the product during use; R&D leading to product improvement; facilitation of credit.
Suppliers	Continuing source of business; timely consummation of trade credit obligations; professional relationship in contracting for, purchasing, and receiving goods and services.
Governments	Taxes (income, property, and so on); adherence to the letter and intent of public policy dealing with the requirements of fair and free competition; discharge of legal obligations of businesspeople (and business organizations); adherence to antitrust laws.
Unions	Recognition as the negotiating agent for employees. Opportunity to perpetuate the union as a participant in the business organization.
Competitors	Observation of the norms for competitive conduct established by society and the industry. Business statesmanship on the part of peers.
Local communities	Place of productive and healthful employment in the community. Participation of company officials in community affairs, provision of regular employment, fair play, reasonable portion of purchases made in the local community, interest in and support of local government, support of cultural and charitable projects.
The general public	Participation in and contribution to society as a whole; creative communications between governmental and business units designed for reciprocal understanding; assumption of fair proportion of the burden of government and society. Fair price for products and advancement of the state-of-the-art technology that the product line involves.

be pursued with equal emphasis. They must be assigned priorities in accordance with the relative emphasis that the firm will give them. That emphasis is reflected in the criteria that the firm uses in its strategic decision making; in the firm's allocation of its human, financial, and physical resources; and in the firm's long-term objectives and strategies.

EXHIBIT 2–13
Inputs to the Development of the Company Mission

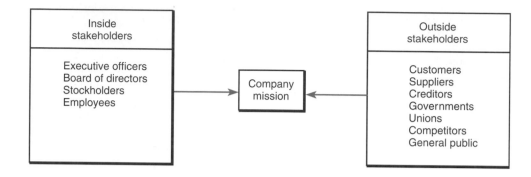

Coordination with Other Elements   The demands of stakeholder groups constitute only one principal set of inputs to the company mission. The other principal sets are the managerial operating philosophy and the determinants of the product-market offering. Those determinants constitute a reality test that the accepted claims must pass. The key question is: How can the firm satisfy its claimants and at the same time optimize its economic success in the marketplace?

The Dynamics of Social Responsibility

As indicated in Exhibit 2–13, the various stakeholders of a firm can be divided into inside stakeholders and outside stakeholders. The insiders are the individuals or groups that are stockholders or employees of the firm. The outsiders are all the other individuals or groups that the firm's actions affect. The extremely large and often amorphous set of outsiders makes the general claim that the firm be socially responsible.

Perhaps the thorniest issues faced in defining a company mission are those that pertain to responsibility. The stakeholder approach offers the clearest perspective on such issues. Broadly stated, outsiders often demand that insiders' claims be subordinated to the greater good of the society; that is, to the greater good of outsiders. They believe that such issues as pollution, the disposal of solid and liquid wastes, and the conservation of natural resources should be principal considerations in strategic decision making. Also broadly stated, insiders tend to believe that the competing claims of outsiders should be balanced against one another in a way that protects the company mission. For example, they tend to believe that the need of consumers for a product should be balanced against the water pollution resulting from its production if the firm cannot eliminate that pollution entirely and still remain profitable. Some insiders also argue that the claims of society, as expressed in government regulation, provide tax money that can be used to eliminate water pollution and the like if the general public wants this to be done.

The issues are numerous, complex, and contingent on specific situations. Thus, rigid rules of business conduct cannot deal with them. Each firm *regardless of size* must decide how to meet its perceived social responsibility. While large, well-capitalized companies may have easy access to environmental consultants, this is not an affordable strategy for smaller companies. However, the experience of many small businesses demonstrates that it is feasible to accomplish significant pollution prevention and waste reduction without big expenditures and without hiring consultants. Once a problem area has been identified, a company's line employees frequently can develop a solution. Other important pollution prevention strategies include changing the materials used or redesigning how operations are bid out. Making pollution prevention a social responsibility can be beneficial to smaller companies. Publicly traded firms also can benefit directly from socially responsible strategies.

Global Strategy in Action
Occidental Petroleum Accepts Corporate Social Responsibility

Exhibit 2–14

BusinessWeek In Colombia, Los Angeles–based Occidental Petroleum Corp. is clearing the land for an exploratory oil well to be drilled. The government believes the land holds more than half of Colombia's oil reserves and has contracted Occidental to find it. The nature-worshiping U'wa adamantly oppose the exploration. But Occidental emphatically denies that the U'wa will be affected either. The company has held dozens of meetings with community groups and says it is trying to meet all their concerns. Occidental has spent some $140,000 on educational, environmental, agricultural, and basic infrastructure projects in communities closest to the project.

The plight of indigenous groups is penetrating the boardrooms of multinationals, which are being forced to respond as never before to protect their reputations and brand names. Nowhere are the issues more contentious than in investments, such as Occidental's, that involve extracting natural resources in developing nations. Many of these projects have long been marred by corruption, military atrocities, ecological damage, and social upheaval.

Activists and environmental groups have put heavy pressure on multinationals, governments of developing nations, and the World Bank—which funds many such projects—to show there are humane, eco-friendly, and equitable ways to drill and mine in poor nations. On top of this, oil and mining companies now have to answer to institutional investors. And they must meet increasingly stringent environmental and social standards to get financial backing and political-risk guarantees from the World Bank for overseas projects.

The result is shaping up as a new era of corporate responsibility. Multinationals are hiring human-rights advisers, drafting and enforcing codes of conduct, appointing outside monitors, and improving operating practices. They are developing global standards of conduct, such as procedures for security of their installations. They are putting local people on boards of directors and urging government ministers and generals to adhere to international human-rights standards, lest their misdeeds reflect poorly on the investors, too.

Source: An excerpt from P. Raeburn and S. Prasso, "Whose Globe?," *BusinessWeek*, November 6, 2000.

Different approaches adopted by different firms reflect differences in competitive position, industry, country, environmental and ecological pressures, and a host of other factors. In other words, they will reflect both situational factors and differing priorities in the acknowledgment of claims. Obviously, winning the loyalty of the growing legions of consumers will require new marketing strategies and new alliances in the twenty-first century. Many marketers already have discovered these new marketing realities by adopting strategies called the "*4 E's*": (1) make it easy for the consumer to be green, (2) empower consumers with solutions, (3) enlist the support of the consumer, and (4) establish credibility with all publics and help to avoid a backlash.

As presented in Exhibit 2–14, Global Strategy in Action, Occidental Petroleum faces issues of corporate social responsibility in addressing the needs of the many stakeholders involved in the firm's oil exploration in developing countries. The article outlines the many parties that have potential to be impacted by the company's endeavors, including local inhabitants and government, environmental groups, and institutional investors. The article also describes how multinational corporations are acting to benefit the local communities, to restructure their organizations, and to implement codes of conduct to address the needs of the many stakeholders.

British Petroleum's CEO, John Browne, faces the social responsibility questions asked of all leaders of global firms. Global Strategy in Action Exhibit 2–15 presents Browne's view that for his global company to thrive, so must the communities in which his company does business.

Despite differences in their approaches, most American firms now try to assure outsiders that they attempt to conduct business in a socially responsible manner. Many firms, including Abt Associates, Dow Chemical, Eastern Gas and Fuel Associates, Exxon, and the Bank of America, conduct and publish annual social audits. Such audits attempt to evaluate a firm

BusinessWeek Making globalization work humanely is quickly becoming the dominant issue of our time. From Boston to Bangkok, trade, investment, and information technology are exploding across borders and overwhelming governments' ability to provide social safety nets and public services to cushion the impact on people. A political backlash is building in Asia, Europe, and Latin America. Although international corporations cannot shoulder all the *responsibility*, no challenge is more central to global management than finding a balance between the relentless pressure for short-term profits and broader social *responsibilities*.

What's a chief executive to do? To what degree should companies take on the *responsibility* heretofore shouldered by governments? To what degree can they? One chief executive, John Browne of British Petroleum Co., has a clear philosophy and strategy. Browne believes that for BP to thrive, so must the communities in which it does business. To make that happen, Browne has insisted that the economic and social health of the villages, towns, and cities in which BP does business be a matter of central concern to the company's *board* of directors. He has also made social investment for the long term an important variable in compensating BP employees around the world.

AMBITIOUS GOALS

What to do and how to do it is left to local BP business units. But regular reviews of their activities are held by regional executives. In such areas as job training for local employees and building schools, ambitious goals are set, and performance is measured against them. Involved in the process along with BP

employees and *board* directors are local residents whose views are regularly surveyed.

BP's community investments are extensive. In Vietnam, the company is providing computer-based technology to control the damage from recurrent flooding. In Turkey, BP recently financed the replanting of a forest around the Black Sea that had been destroyed by fire. In Zambia, it has supplied 200 solar-powered refrigerators to help doctors store antimalaria vaccines. In South Africa, it has supported the development of small business in urban areas such as Soweto. In Colombia, it is turning its own waste material into bricks for local homebuilding.

In addition, accidents in the workplace, noxious emissions, and oil spills are subject to monitoring and quantification. Ernst & Young verifies company recordkeeping. There is constant pressure to eliminate accidents.

NOT CHARITY

So far, the strategy has not impaired BP's bottom line. To the contrary. "These efforts have nothing to do with charity," says Browne, "and everything to do with our long-term self-interest. I see no trade-off between the short term and the long. Twenty years is just 80 quarters. And our shareholders want performance today, and tomorrow, and the day after."

Corporations would do well to take a page out of Browne's playbook: think long-term, invest heavily in the communities that you do business in, be obsessive about achieving profits, and fully integrate social *responsibility* into your policies on governance and compensation.

Source: Jeffrey E. Garten, "Globalism Doesn't Have to Be Cruel," *BusinessWeek*, February 9, 1998.

from the perspective of social responsibility. Private consultants often conduct them for the firm and offer minimally biased evaluations on what are inherently highly subjective issues.

A CONTINUUM OF SOCIAL RESPONSIBILITIES

To better understand the nature and range of social responsibilities for which they must plan, strategic managers can use a continuum that encompasses four types of social commitment: economic, legal, ethical, and discretionary social responsibilities.

Economic responsibilities are the most basic social responsibilities of business. As we have noted, some economists see these as the only legitimate social responsibility of business. Living up to their economic responsibilities requires managers to maximize profits whenever possible. The essential responsibility of business is assumed to be providing goods and services to society at a reasonable cost. In discharging that economic responsibility, the company also emerges as socially responsible by providing productive jobs for its workforce, and tax payments for its local, state, and federal governments.

Legal responsibilities reflect the firm's obligations to comply with the laws that regulate business activities. The consumer and environmental movements focused increased public attention on the need for social responsibility in business by lobbying for laws that govern business in the areas of pollution control and consumer safety. The intent of consumer legislation has been to correct the "balance of power" between buyers and sellers in the marketplace. Among the most important laws are the Federal Fair Packaging and Labeling Act that regulates labeling procedures for business, the Truth in Lending Act that regulates the extension of credit to individuals, and the Consumer Product Safety Act that protects consumers against unreasonable risks of injury in the use of consumer products.

The environmental movement has had a similar impact on the regulation of business. This movement achieved stricter enforcement of existing environmental protections and it spurred the passage of new, more comprehensive laws such as the National Environmental Policy Act which is devoted to preserving the United State's ecological balance and making environmental protection a federal policy goal. It requires environmental impact studies whenever new construction may threaten an existing ecosystem, and it established the Council on Environmental Quality to guide business development. Another product of the environmental movement was the creation of the federal Environmental Protection Agency which interprets and administers the environmental protection policies of the U.S. government.

Clearly, these legal responsibilities are supplemental to the requirement that businesses and their employees comply fully with the general civil and criminal laws that apply to all individuals and institutions in the country. Yet, strangely, individual failures to adhere to the law have recently produced some of the greatest scandals in the history of American free enterprise. Strategy in Action Exhibit 2–16 presents an overview of seven of these cases that involved executives from Adelphia Communications, Arthur Andersen, Global Crossing, ImClone Systems, Merrill Lynch, WorldCom, and Xerox.

Ethical responsibilities reflect the company's notion of right or proper business behavior. Ethical responsibilities are obligations that transcend legal requirements. Firms are expected, but not required, to behave ethically. Some actions that are legal might be considered unethical. For example, the manufacture and distribution of cigarettes is legal. But in light of the often-lethal consequences of smoking, many consider the continued sale of cigarettes to be unethical. The topic of management ethics receives additional attention later in this chapter.

Discretionary responsibilities are those that are voluntarily assumed by a business organization. They include public relations activities, good citizenship, and full corporate social responsibility. Through public relations activities, managers attempt to enhance the image of their companies, products, and services by supporting worthy causes. This form of discretionary responsibility has a self-serving dimension. Companies that adopt the good citizenship approach actively support ongoing charities, public-service advertising campaigns, or issues in the public interest. A commitment to full corporate responsibility requires strategic managers to attack social problems with the same zeal in which they attack business problems. For example, teams in the National Football League provide time off for players and other employees afflicted with drug or alcohol addictions who agree to enter rehabilitation programs.

It is important to remember that the categories on the continuum of social responsibility overlap, creating gray areas where societal expectations on organizational behavior are difficult to categorize. In considering the overlaps among various demands for social responsibility, however, managers should keep in mind that in the view of the general public, economic and legal responsibilities are required, ethical responsibility is expected, and discretionary responsibility is desired.

Adelphia Communications

On July 24, 2002, John Rigas, the 77-year-old founder of the country's sixth largest cable television operator was arrested, along with two of his sons, and accused of looting the now bankrupt company. Several other former Adelphia executives were also arrested. The SEC brought a civil suit against the company for allegedly fraudulently excluding billions of dollars in liabilities from its financial statements, falsifying statistics, inflating its earnings to meet Wall Street's expectations and concealing "rampant self-dealing by the Rigas family." The family, which founded Adelphia in 1952, gave up control of the firm in May, and on June 25 the company filed for bankruptcy protection. The company was delisted by Nasdaq in June 2002.

Arthur Andersen

On June 15, 2002, a Texas jury found the accounting firm guilty of obstructing justice for its role in shredding financial documents related to its former client Enron. Andersen, founded in 1913, had already been largely destroyed after admitting that it sped up the shredding of Enron documents following the launch of an SEC investigation. Andersen fired David Duncan, who led its Houston office saying he was responsible for shredding the Enron documents. Duncan admitted to obstruction of justice, turned state's evidence, and testified on behalf of the government.

Global Crossing

The SEC and the FBI are probing the five-year-old telecom company Global Crossing regarding alleged swaps of network capacity with other telecommunications firms to inflate revenue. The company ran into trouble by betting that it could borrow billions of dollars to build a fiber-optic infrastructure that would be in strong demand by corporations. Because others made the same bet, there was a glut of fiber optic and prices plunged, leaving Global Crossing with massive debts. It filed for bankruptcy on January 28, 2002. Chairman Gary Winnick, who founded Global Crossing in 1997, cashed out $734 million in stock before the company collapsed. Global Crossing was delisted from NYSE in January 2002.

ImClone Systems

The biotech firm is being investigated by a congressional committee that is seeking to find out if ImClone correctly informed investors that the Food and Drug Administration had declined to accept for review its key experimental cancer drug, Erbitux. Former CEO Samuel Waksal pled guilty in June 2003 to insider trading charges related to Erbitux and was sentenced to seven years in prison. Also, Federal investigators filed charges against home decorating diva Martha Stewart for using insider information on the cancer drug when she sold 4,000 ImClone shares one day before the FDA initially said it would reject the drug.

Merrill Lynch

On May 21, 2002, Merrill Lynch agreed to pay $100 million to settle New York Attorney General Eliot Spitzer's charges that the nation's largest securities firm knowingly peddled Internet stocks to investors to generate lucrative investment banking fees. Internal memos written by Merrill's feted Internet analyst Henry Blodgett revealed that company analysts thought little of the Web stocks that they urged investors to buy. Merrill agreed to strengthen firewalls between its research and investment-banking divisions, ensuring advice given to investors is not influenced by efforts to win underwriting fees.

WorldCom

The nation's second largest telecom company filed for the nation's biggest ever bankruptcy on July 21, 2002. WorldCom's demise accelerated on June 25, 2002, when it admitted it hid $3.85 billion in expenses, allowing it to post net income of $1.38 billion in 2001, instead of a loss. The company fired its CFO Scott Sullivan and on June 28 began cutting 17,000 jobs, over 20 percent of its workforce. CEO Bernie Ebbers resigned in April amid questions about $408 million of personal loans he received from the company to cover losses he incurred in buying its shares. WorldCom was delisted from Nasdaq in July 2002.

Xerox

Xerox said on June 28, 2002 that it would restate five years of financial results to reclassify more than $6 billion in revenues. In April, the company settled SEC charges that it used "accounting tricks" to defraud investors, agreeing to pay a $10 million fine. The firm admitted no wrongdoing. Xerox manufactures imaging products, such as copiers, printers, fax machines, and scanners.

*This section was derived in its entirety from "A guide to corporate scandals," MSNBC, www.msnbc.com/news/corpscandal front.

Corporate Social Responsibility and Profitability

Few trends could so thoroughly undermine the very foundations of our free society as the acceptance by corporate officials of a social responsibility other than to make as much money for their stockholders as possible.

Milton Friedman, Capitalism and Freedom, 1962

In the four decades since Milton Friedman wrote these words, the issue of *corporate social responsibility* (CSR)—the idea that business has a duty to serve society as well as the financial interest of stockholders—has remained a highly contentious one. Yet managers recognize that deciding to what extent to embrace CSR is an important strategic decision.

There are three principal reasons why managers should be concerned about the socially responsible behavior of their firms. First, a company's right to exist depends on its responsiveness to the external environment. Second, federal, state, and local governments threaten increased regulation if business does not evolve to meet changing social standards. Third, a responsive corporate social policy may enhance a firm's long-term viability. Underscoring the importance of these factors to the firm is the implicit belief that long-run profit maximization is inexorably linked to CSR.

The Debate

Should a company behave in a socially responsible manner? Coming down on one side of the question are those who, like Friedman, believe that a business bears a responsibility only for the financial well-being of its stockholders. Implicit in this statement is the idea that corporate actions motivated by anything other than shareholder wealth maximization threatens that well-being. On the other side, proponents of CSR assert that business does not function in a vacuum; it exists to serve, depends upon its environment, cannot be separated from it, and therefore has a responsibility to ensure its well-being. The environment is represented not only by stockholders/owners and employees, but also by such external stakeholders as customers, unions, suppliers, competitors, government agencies, local communities, and society in general.

The second argument for CSR suggests that stockholders' interests may transcend the financial. Many stockholders expect more from the companies in which they invest than simple appreciation in the economic value of the firm.

The third argument in favor of CSR is that the best way for a company to maximize shareholder wealth is to act in a socially responsible manner. It suggests that when a company behaves responsibly, benefits accrue directly to the bottom line. It also implies that when a company does not behave responsibly, the company and its shareholders suffer financially.

Exhibit 2–17, Strategy in Action, presents an argument that eBay is acting in a socially irresponsible manner by allowing, and profiting from, the sale of "murderabilia" on their website. eBay's lack of prevention is perceived by some critics as "morally reprehensible" and socially irresponsible. Since there are no laws against this type of sale on the Internet, it is not illegal. However, corporate social responsibility is an element of strategic decision making that eBay cannot ignore. If websites are not responsive to society, they increase the odds that people will turn to legislation to discipline corporate behavior.

CSR and the Bottom Line

The goal of every firm is to maintain viability through long-run profitability. Until all costs and benefits are accounted for, however, profits may not be claimed. In the case of CSR, costs and benefits are both economic and social. While economic costs and benefits are easily quantifiable, social costs and benefits are not. Managers therefore risk subordinating social consequences to other performance results that can be more straightforwardly measured.

BusinessWeek Serial killer Angel Resendez-Ramirez smiles as he sits behind bulletproof glass on Death Row in a maximum-security prison. He has admitted to murdering 12 women across the U.S., yet he jokes and revels in his fame. Locks of his hair and shavings from the calloused on his feet have been sold on Internet auction site eBay for $9.99 a pop. He gets a cut from dealers each time a little piece of him is sold. Tom Konvicka's mother was one of the victims. When Resendez-Ramirez was caught and locked up, Konvicka remembers feeling relief that his mom's murderer was being brought to justice. Now, he's disgusted. Serial killers shouldn't profit from their murders. Their victims are dead and gone and they're still here and making a profit on what they've done.

In Texas, as in most other states, there's nothing to prevent criminals from selling "murderabilia" on the Internet. eBay and other sites don't prevent it, either. In fact, there's little to discourage the sale of a whole range of questionable items online. As the Internet has grown in popularity, it's a ready-made market connecting individuals with a vast audience of potential buyers—all protected by a cloak of semi-anonymity and the hands-off policies of Web auction sites. That wide-open flea market has produced a cornucopia of items for sale that are in bad taste or unethical.

A growing chorus of ethicists, lawmakers, consumer groups, and Internet activists say something needs to be done—either stepped-up monitoring by auction sites themselves, or statutes that police the Netways. By refusing to take responsibility for what is sold on their site, they're cashing in on an overall lack of social accountability the Internet offers. While the sale of murderabilia is not illegal, it's morally reprehensible.

Problem is, when it comes to the Web, it's sometimes difficult to tell what's illegal, what ought to be illegal, and what's just in bad taste. It's clearly against the law to sell things such as endangered species and certain kinds of firearms. But how do you prevent minors from buying alcohol and pornography in a realm where nobody knows their age? Selling body organs online isn't necessarily a crime, but a doctor who participates could breach professional ethics. And how do you prevent the trafficking in items like neo-Nazi paraphernalia that are illegal in some places but not in others?

Given all the confusion, society's first line of defense could be auction site operators—but they're having none of it. eBay has a laissez-faire attitude about what is sold on the site. The company claims it's all part of eBay's philosophy of building a community based on trust. However, by not screening items, eBay skirts potential liability and high monitoring costs.

Now that Net auctions have become such a magnet for potentially dicey items, some states and federal agencies are stepping up their efforts to stop abuses. FBI's Internet Fraud Complaint Center gets more than 1,000 complaints of online auction fraud each month—most of them involving eBay traffic. Agents have begun turning some of these cases over to local law enforcement authorities. In October, state elections officials in Illinois and New York temporarily shut down Voteauction.com, an Internet site where Americans could sell their votes to the highest bidder. Authorities say they are keeping close watch and will nab all who accept money for their votes—and the people who pay them—charging them with violating state and federal election laws. The very nature of the Web makes the unthinkable more possible. Absent the Internet, many people might not have been exposed to the opportunity to revel in Nazi items or bloody murder photos, or be offered an easy chance to buy them without fear of social backlash. eBay is a magnet for people who previously didn't have many outlets because you're immediately linked up to millions of people.

The Web amplifies ethical dilemmas, too. Consider MedicineOnline.com, a site that connects plastic surgery doctors and patients on the Net. The site asks doctors to provide info about their education and experience—including their history of malpractice suits—but takes no responsibility for the veracity of that information. By contrast, a regular hospital is legally bound to take responsibility for the credentials and services of doctors who practice there. That's eBay's answer, too: Since it does not sell anything itself, it's not responsible for what is sold on the site. eBay asks sellers to report any breach of guidelines—in other words, to police the site themselves.

For now, eBay plans to continue to rely on its guidelines—and on its community of members—to blow the whistle on anything beyond the pale. However, with creeps and criminals like Resendez-Ramirez virtually on the loose, eBay's self-monitoring system may not be enough.

Source: An excerpt from Marcia Stepanek, "Making a Killing Online," *BusinessWeek*, November 20, 2000.

The dynamic between CSR and success (profit) is complex. While one concept is clearly not mutually exclusive of the other, it is also clear that neither is a prerequisite of the other. Rather than viewing these two concepts as competing, it may be better to view CSR as a component in the decision-making process of business that must determine, among other objectives, how to maximize profits.

Attempts to undertake a cost-benefit analysis of CSR have not been very successful. The process is complicated by several factors. First, some CSR activities incur no dollar costs at all. For example, Second Harvest, the largest nongovernment, charitable food distributor in the nation, accepts donations from food manufacturers and food retailers of surplus food that would otherwise be thrown out due to overruns, warehouse damage, or labeling errors. In 10 years, Second Harvest has distributed more than 2 billion pounds of food. Gifts in Kind America is an organization that enables companies to reduce unsold or obsolete inventory by matching a corporation's donated products with a charity's or other nonprofit organization's needs. In addition, a tax break is realized by the company. In the past, corporate donations have included 130,000 pairs of shoes from Nike, 10,000 pairs of gloves from Aris Isotoner, and 480 computer systems from Apple Computer.

In addition, philanthropic activities of a corporation, which have been a traditional mainstay of CSR, are undertaken at a discounted cost to the firm since they are often tax deductible. The benefits of corporate philanthropy can be enormous as is shown by the many national social welfare causes that have been spurred by corporate giving. A few of these causes are described in Exhibit 2–18. While such acts of benevolence often help establish a general perception of the involved companies within society, some philanthropic acts bring specific credit to the firm.

Second, socially responsible behavior does not come at a prohibitive cost. One needs only to look at the problems of A. H. Robbins Company (Dalkon Shield), Beech-Nut Corporation (apple juice), Drexel Burnham (insider trading), and Exxon (*Valdez*) for stark answers on the "cost" of social responsibility (or its absence) in the business environment.

Third, socially responsible practices may create savings and, as a result, increase profits. SET Laboratories uses popcorn to ship software rather than polystyrene peanuts. It is environmentally safer and costs 60 percent less to use. Corporations that offer part-time and adjustable work schedules have realized that this can lead to reduced absenteeism, greater productivity and increased morale. DuPont opted for more flexible schedules for its employees after a survey revealed 50 percent of women and 25 percent of men considered working for another employer with more flexibility for family concerns.

Proponents argue that CSR costs are more than offset in the long run by an improved company image and increased community goodwill. These intangible assets can prove valuable in a crisis, as Johnson & Johnson discovered with the Tylenol cyanide scare in 1982. Because it had established a solid reputation as a socially responsible company before the incident, the public readily accepted the company's assurances of public safety. Consequently, financial damage to Johnson & Johnson was minimized, despite the company's $100 million voluntary recall of potentially tainted capsules. CSR may also head off new regulation, preventing increased compliance costs. It may even attract investors who are themselves socially responsible. Proponents believe that for these reasons, socially responsible behavior increases the financial value of the firm in the long run. The mission statement of Johnson & Johnson is provided as Exhibit 2–19, Strategy in Action.

Performance   To explore the relationship between socially responsible behavior and financial performance, an important question must first be answered: How do managers measure the financial impact of corporate social performance?

Now that U.S. companies are adopting strategic philanthropy, they are assuming an activist stance on social issues. As a result, many causes, including the following, have become national movements.

HUNGER

Before the new approach to corporate philanthropy, the foundations of food companies gave cash donations to antihunger organizations. But when the ranks of the hungry increased tenfold in the 1980s, contributions managers in companies such as General Mills, Grand Metropolitan, Kraft General Foods, and Sara Lee decided to play a larger role *and* establish a rallying point around which disparate units of their companies could come together. Marketers arranged for a portion of product sales to be donated to antihunger programs, human resources staffs deployed volunteers, operating units provided free food, and CEOs joined the board of Chicago-based Second Harvest, the food industry's antihunger voice. As a result of those efforts, a complex infrastructure of food banks and soup kitchens was developed.

COMMUNITY AND ECONOMIC DEVELOPMENT

Major banks such as Bank of America, Chase Manhattan, Citicorp, Morgan Guaranty, and Wells Fargo explored how philanthropy could be tied to marketing, human resources, government affairs, investment, and even trust management. Their business managers were concerned about the Community Reinvestment Act, which requires lenders to be responsive to low-income communities. Philanthropy managers point out that by going beyond the CRA requirements, they develop positive relationships with regulators while scoring public relations points. For example, at least 60 banks in the United States have created community development corporations to assist run-down neighborhoods.

LITERACY

The effort to increase literacy in the United States is the favorite cause of the communications industry. Print media companies such as McGraw-Hill, Prentice Hall, the *Los Angeles Times,* the *Washington Post,* and the *New York Times* are trying to halt the drop in readership, and broadcasters and cable companies are compensating for their role in the decline of literacy. Those companies have mobilized their marketing, human resources, and lobbying power to establish workplace literacy programs. While human resources budgets fund such programs, philanthropy dollars go mostly to volunteer organizations.

SCHOOL REFORM

About 15 percent of the country's cash gifts go to school reform, and a recent study estimated that at least one-third of U.S. school districts have partnership programs with business. The next step toward reform, promoted by the Business Roundtable, is for companies to mobilize their lobbying power at the state level to press for the overhaul of state educational agencies.

AIDS

AIDS is a top cause for insurance companies, who want to reduce claims; pharmaceutical companies, who want public support for the commercialization of AIDS drugs; and design-related companies, who want to support the large number of gays in their work force. Those industries put the first big money into AIDS prevention measures, and they've helped turn the American Foundation for AIDS Research into an advocate for more and better research by the National Institutes of Health.

ENVIRONMENTALISM

Environmental support varies across industries. In high-tech companies, environmentalism is largely a human resources issue because it's the favorite cause of many employees. Among the makers of outdoor apparel, environmentalism is largely a marketing issue, so companies donate a portion of the purchase price to environmental nonprofits. In industries that pollute or extract natural resources, environmentalism is often a government affairs matter.

Critics of CSR believe that companies that behave in a socially responsible manner, and portfolios comprising these companies' securities, should perform more poorly financially than those that do not. The costs of CSR outweigh the benefits for individual firms, they suggest. In addition, traditional portfolio theory holds that investors minimize risk and maximize return by being able to choose from an infinite universe of investment opportunities. Portfolios based on social criteria should suffer, critics argue, because they are by definition restrictive in nature. This restriction should increase portfolio risk and reduce portfolio return.

"We believe our first responsibility is to the doctors, nurses and patients, to mothers and fathers and all others who use our products and services. In meeting their needs everything we do must be of high quality. We must constantly strive to reduce our costs in order to maintain reasonable prices. Customers' orders must be serviced promptly and accurately. Our suppliers and distributors must have an opportunity to make a fair profit.

We are responsible to our employees, the men and women who work with us throughout the world. Everyone must be considered as an individual. We must respect their dignity and recognize their merit. They must have a sense of security in their jobs. Compensation must be fair and adequate, and working conditions clean, orderly and safe. Employees must feel free to make suggestions and complaints. There must be equal opportunity for employment, development and advancement for those qualified. We must provide competent management, and their actions must be just and ethical.

We are responsible to the communities in which we live and work and to the world community as well. We must be good citizens—support good works and charities and bear our fair share of taxes. We must encourage civic improvements and better health and education. We must maintain in good order the property we are privileged to use, protecting the environment and natural resources.

Our final responsibility is to our stockholders. Business must make a sound profit. We must experiment with new ideas. Research must be carried on, innovative programs developed and mistakes paid for. New equipment must be purchased, new facilities provided and new products launched. Reserves must be created to provide for adverse times. When we operate according to these principles, the stockholders should realize a fair return."

Several research studies have attempted to determine the relationship between corporate social performance and financial performance. Taken together, these studies fail to establish the nature of the relationship between social and financial performance. There are a number of possible explanations for the findings. One possibility is that there is no meaningful correlation between social and financial performance. A second possibility is that the benefits of CSR are offset by its negative consequences for the firm, thus producing a nondetectable net financial effect. Other explanations include methodological weaknesses and/or insufficient conceptual models or operational definitions used in the studies. However, among experts, a sense remains that a relationship between CSR and the bottom line does exist, although the exact nature of that relationship is unclear.

CSR Today

A survey of 2,737 senior U.S. managers revealed that 92 percent believed that business should take primary responsibility for, or an active role in, solving environmental problems; 84 percent believed business should do the same for educational concerns.[4] Despite the uncertain impact of CSR on the corporate bottom line, CSR has become a priority with American business. Why? In addition to a commonsense belief that companies should be able to "do well by doing good," at least three broad trends are driving businesses to adopt CSR frameworks: the resurgence of environmentalism, increasing buyer power, and the globalization of business.

The Resurgence of Environmentalism In March 1989, the Exxon *Valdez* ran aground in Prince William Sound, spilling 11 million gallons of oil, polluting miles of ocean and shore, and helping to revive worldwide concern for the ecological environment. Six months after the *Valdez* incident, the Coalition for Environmentally Responsible Economies (CERES) was

[4] Rosabeth Moss Kanter, "Transcending Business Boundaries: 12,000 World Managers View Change," *Harvard Business Review* 69, no. 3 (May–June 1991), pp. 151–64.

formed to establish new goals for environmentally responsible corporate behavior. The group drafted the CERES Principles to "establish an environmental ethic with criteria by which investors and others can assess the environmental performance of companies. Companies that sign these Principles pledge to go voluntarily beyond the requirements of the law."

Increasing Buyer Power   The rise of the consumer movement has meant that buyers—consumers and investors—are increasingly flexing their economic muscle. Consumers are becoming more interested in buying products from socially responsible companies. Organizations such as the Council on Economic Priorities (CEP) help consumers make more informed buying decisions through such publications as *Shopping for a Better World,* which provides social performance information on 191 companies making more than 2,000 consumer products. CEP also sponsors the annual Corporate Conscience Awards, which recognize socially responsible companies. One example of consumer power at work is the effective outcry over the deaths of dolphins in tuna fishermen's nets.

Investors represent a second type of influential consumer. There has been a dramatic increase in the number of people interested in supporting socially responsible companies through their investments. Membership in the Social Investment Forum, a trade association serving social investing professionals, has been growing at a rate of about 50 percent annually. As baby boomers achieve their own financial success, the social investing movement has continued its rapid growth.

While social investing wields relatively low power as an individual private act (selling one's shares of Exxon does not affect the company), it can be very powerful as a collective public act. When investors vote their shares in behalf of pro-CSR issues, companies may be pressured to change their social behavior. The South African divestiture movement is one example of how effective this pressure can be.

The Vermont National Bank has added a Socially Responsible Banking Fund to its product line. Investors can designate any of their interest-bearing accounts with a $500 minimum balance to be used by the fund. This fund then lends these monies for purposes such as low-income housing, the environment, education, farming, or small business development. Although it has had a "humble" beginning of approximately 800 people investing about $11 million, the bank has attracted out-of-state depositors and is growing faster than expected.

Social investors comprise both individuals and institutions. Much of the impetus for social investing originated with religious organizations that wanted their investments to mirror their beliefs. At present, the ranks of social investors have expanded to include educational institutions and large pension funds.

Large-scale social investing can be broken down into the two broad areas of guideline portfolio investing and shareholder activism. Guideline portfolio investing is the largest and fastest-growing segment of social investing. Individual and institutional guideline portfolio investors use ethical guidelines as screens to identify possible investments in stocks, bonds, and mutual funds. The investment instruments that survive the social screens are then layered over the investor's financial screens to create the investor's universe of possible investments.

Screens may be negative (e.g., excluding all tobacco companies) or they may combine negative and positive elements (e.g., eliminating companies with bad labor records while seeking out companies with good ones). Most investors rely on screens created by investment firms such as Kinder, Lydenberg Domini & Co. or by industry groups such as the Council on Economic Priorities. In addition to ecology, employee relations, and community development, corporations may be screened on their association with "sin" products (alcohol, tobacco, gambling), defense/weapons production, and nuclear power.

In contrast to guideline portfolio investors, who passively indicate their approval or disapproval of a company's social behavior by simply including or excluding it from their portfolios, shareholder activists seek to directly influence corporate social behavior. Shareholder activists invest in a corporation hoping to improve specific aspects of the company's social performance, typically by seeking a dialogue with upper management. If this and successive actions fail to achieve the desired results, shareholder activists may introduce proxy resolutions to be voted upon at the corporation's annual meeting. The goal of these resolutions is to achieve change by gaining public exposure for the issue at hand. While the number of shareholder activists is relatively small, they are by no means small in achievement: Shareholder activists, led by such groups as the Interfaith Center on Corporate Responsibility, were the driving force behind the South African divestiture movement. Currently, there are more than 35 socially screened mutual funds available in the United States alone.

The Globalization of Business   Management issues, including CSR, have become more complex as companies increasingly transcend national borders: It is difficult enough to come to a consensus on what constitutes socially responsible behavior within one culture, let alone determine common ethical values across cultures. In addition to different cultural views, the high barriers facing international CSR include differing corporate disclosure practices, inconsistent financial data and reporting methods, and the lack of CSR research organizations within countries. Despite these problems, CSR is growing abroad. The United Kingdom has 30 ethical mutual funds and Canada offers 6 socially responsible funds.

CSR's Effect on the Mission Statement

The mission statement not only identifies what product or service a company produces, how it produces it, and what market it serves, it also embodies what the company believes. As such, it is essential that the mission statement recognize the legitimate claims of its external stakeholders, which may include creditors, customers, suppliers, government, unions, competitors, local communities, and elements of the general public. This stakeholder approach has become widely accepted by U.S. business. For example, a survey of directors in 291 of the largest southeastern U.S. companies found that directors had high stakeholder orientations. Customers, government, stockholders, employees, and society, in that order, were the stakeholders these directors perceived as most important.

In developing mission statements, managers must identify all stakeholder groups and weigh their relative rights and abilities to affect the firm's success. Some companies are proactive in their approach to CSR, making it an integral part of their raison d'être (e.g., Ben & Jerry's ice cream); others are reactive, adopting socially responsible behavior only when they must (e.g., Exxon after the *Valdez* incident).

Social Audit

A *social audit* attempts to measure a company's actual social performance against the social objectives it has set for itself. A social audit may be conducted by the company itself. However, one conducted by an outside consultant who will impose minimal biases may prove more beneficial to the firm. As with a financial audit, an outside auditor brings credibility to the evaluation. This credibility is essential if management is to take the results seriously and if the general public is to believe the company's public relations pronouncements.

Careful, accurate monitoring and evaluation of a company's CSR actions are important not only because the company wants to be sure it is implementing CSR policy as planned, but also because CSR actions by their nature are open to intense public scrutiny. To make sure it is making good on its CSR promises, a company may conduct a social audit of its performance.

Once the social audit is complete, it may be distributed internally or both internally and externally, depending on the firm's goals and situation. Some firms include a section in their annual report devoted to social responsibility activities; others publish a separate periodic report on their social responsiveness. Companies publishing separate social audits include General Motors, Bank of America, Atlantic Richfield, Control Data, and Aetna Life and Casualty Company. Nearly all Fortune 500 corporations disclose social performance information in their annual reports.

Large firms are not the only companies employing the social audit. Boutique ice cream maker Ben & Jerry's, a CSR pioneer, publishes a social audit in its annual report. The audit, conducted by an outside consultant, scores company performance in such areas as employee benefits, plant safety, ecology, community involvement, and customer service. The report is published unedited.

The social audit may be used for more than simply monitoring and evaluating firm social performance. Managers also use social audits to scan the external environment, determine firm vulnerabilities, and institutionalize CSR within the firm. In addition, companies themselves are not the only ones who conduct social audits; public interest groups and the media watch companies who claim to be socially responsible very closely to see if they practice what they preach. These organizations include consumer groups and socially responsible investing firms that construct their own guidelines for evaluating companies.

The Body Shop learned what can happen when a company's behavior falls short of its espoused mission and objectives. The 20-year-old manufacturer and retailer of naturally based hair and skin products had cultivated a socially responsible corporate image based on a reputation for socially responsible behavior. In late 1994, however, *Business Ethics* magazine published an exposé claiming that the company did not "walk the talk." It accused the Body Shop of using nonrenewable petrochemicals in its products, recycling far less than it claimed, using ingredients tested on animals, and making threats against investigative journalists. The Body Shop's contradictions were noteworthy because Anita Roddick, the company's founder, made CSR a centerpiece of the company's strategy.[5]

MANAGEMENT ETHICS

The Nature of Ethics in Business

Central to the belief that companies should be operated in a socially responsive way for the benefit of all stakeholders is the belief that managers will behave in an ethical manner. The term *ethics* refers to the moral principles that govern the actions of an individual or a group. Of course, the values of one individual, group, or society may be at odds with the values of another individual, group, or society. Ethical standards, therefore, reflect not a universally accepted code, but rather the end product of a process of defining and clarifying the nature and content of human interaction.

[5] Jon Entine, "Shattered Image," *Business Ethics* 8, no. 5 (September/October 1994), pp. 23–28.

Strategy in Action
Enron: Running on Empty

Exhibit 2–20

BusinessWeek The fall of mighty Enron Corp. (ENE)—once one of the most valuable companies in America—was a collapse of mind-boggling proportions. In 2001, Enron had $101 billion in revenues, a stock-market capitalization of $63 billion, and a chairman who was a high-profile confidant of President Bush. Yet in a sickeningly swift spiral, the powerful energy trading company tumbled to the brink of bankruptcy in late November 2001—the victim of a botched expansion attempt, an accounting scandal, and the overweening ambition of its once widely admired top executives.

The end came quickly because Enron had overextended itself—and because investors and customers lost faith in its secretive and complex financial maneuvers. With legions of traders working out of a Houston skyscraper, the company put together trades so exotic that they mystified many Wall Street veterans. Under Chairman Kenneth L Lay— who pressed the administration to embrace a controversial policy of electricity deregulation—and former CEO Jeffrey K. Skilling, Enron had become largely a trading operation, dubbed by some the Goldman, Sachs & Co. of the energy business.

Enron's success depended on maintaining the trust of customers that it would make good on its dealings in the market. But that trust evaporated in recent weeks as it shocked the market with changes to its nearly incomprehensible financial statements. "If you are running a trading operation, you have to be like Caesar's wife, beyond reproach. Unfortunately, the company didn't realize it," says a senior Enron employee who asked not to be identified.

The fall of Enron—to 61 cents a share on Nov. 28, 2001— has already wiped out more than 99 percent of its stock-market value. Some $3.5 billion of its bonds are trading at just a quarter of their face value. Banks that lent billions to Enron will have to fight for a share in bankruptcy court. Enron's biggest lenders are J. P. Morgan Chase & Co. and Citigroup, which together have an estimated $1.6 billion in exposure. Of that, $900 million is unsecured, according to sources. Other losers: Enron's customers, who traded everything from electricity, gas, and metals to telecom bandwidth, credit insurance, and weather derivatives.

Already the once-arrogant Enron has become vulture meat. In addition to clamoring creditors, it faces class actions by shareholders and employees, whose pensions were heavily invested in Enron stock. That raises questions about how much value is left in the company, which will probably be dismembered and sold off in parts.

Since creditors had time to shield themselves, it doesn't appear that the implosion of Enron will drag down any other big players. "The Wall Street firms have had plenty of time to unwind whatever exposure they may have had," says Richard Strauss of Goldman Sachs. "What they may still have remaining is either collateralized or hedged."

Who's to blame? Perhaps the biggest culprit was arrogance, which has caused Enron to be compared to past self-proclaimed masters of the universe such as Drexel Burnham Lambert Inc. in the 1980s and Long-Term Capital Management in the 1990s. Many fingers are pointing at Skilling, the longtime Enron financial engineer who took over as CEO in February and then resigned with little explanation in August, shortly before the company hit the skids. Also facing the music are Lay and Andrew S. Fastow, who was ousted as chief financial officer on Oct. 24, 2001. Fastow put together several partnerships that were intended to streamline Enron's balance sheet by taking on certain assets and liabilities. That created a conflict of interest for Fastow, who made over $30 million from his partnerships.

The most poignant aspect of Enron's failure is the damage to its own employees. "People have had their total savings disappear," says William Miller, business manager of the International Brotherhood of Electrical Workers union local in Portland, Ore., which represents employees of Enron's Portland General Electric Co. subsidiary. "Some lives have been pretty well destroyed." Enron flew high, but when it fell, it fell hard.

Source: Excerpted from Peter Coy, Emily Thornton, Stephanie Anderson Forest, and Christopher Palmeri, "Enron: Running on Empty," *BusinessWeek*, December 10, 2001, p. 80.

Unfortunately, the public's perception of the ethics of corporate executives in America is near its all-time low. A major cause is a spate of corporate scandals prompted by self-serving, and often criminal executive action that resulted in the loss of stakeholder investments and employee jobs. The most notorious of these cases was the failure of the Enron Corporation, as described in Strategy in Action Exhibit 2–20.

However, even when groups agree on what constitutes human welfare in a given case, the means they choose to achieve this welfare may differ. Therefore, ethics also involve acting to attain human goals. For example, many people would agree that health is a value worth seeking—that is, health enhances human welfare. But what if the means deemed necessary to attain this value for some include the denial or risk of health for others, as is commonly an issue faced by pharmaceutical manufacturers? During production of some drugs, employees are sometimes subjected to great risk of personal injury and infection. For example, if contacted or inhaled, the mercury used in making thermometers and blood pressure equipment can cause heavy metal poisoning. If inhaled, ethylene oxide used to sterilize medical equipment before it is shipped to doctors can cause fetal abnormalities and miscarriages. Even penicillin, if inhaled during its manufacturing process, can cause acute anaphylaxis or shock. Thus, although the goal of customer health might be widely accepted, the means (involving jeopardy to production employees) may not be.

Approaches to Questions of Ethics

Managers report that the most critical quality of ethical decision making is consistency. Thus, they often try to adopt a philosophical approach that can provide the basis for the consistency they seek. There are three fundamental ethical approaches for executives to consider: the utilitarian approach, the moral rights approach, and the social justice approach.

Managers who adopt the *utilitarian approach* judge the effects of a particular action on the people directly involved, in terms of what provides the greatest good for the greatest number of people. The utilitarian approach focuses on actions, rather than on the motives behind the actions. Potentially positive results are weighed against potentially negative results. If the former outweigh the latter, the manager taking the utilitarian approach is likely to proceed with the action. That some people might be adversely affected by the action is accepted as inevitable. For example, the Council on Environmental Quality conducts cost-benefit analysis when selecting air pollution standards under the Clean Air Act, thereby acknowledging that some pollution must be accepted.

Managers who subscribe to the *moral rights approach* judge whether decisions and actions are in keeping with the maintenance of fundamental individual and group rights and privileges. The moral rights approach (also referred to as deontology) includes the rights of human beings to life and safety, a standard of truthfulness, privacy, freedom to express one's conscience, freedom of speech, and private property.

Managers who take the *social justice approach* judge how consistent actions are with equity, fairness, and impartiality in the distribution of rewards and costs among individuals and groups. These ideas stem from two principles known as the liberty principle and the difference principle. The liberty principle states that individuals have certain basic liberties compatible with similar liberties by other people. The difference principle holds that social and economic inequities must be addressed to achieve a more equitable distribution of goods and services.

In addition to these defining principles, three implementing principles are essential to the social justice approach. According to the distributive-justice principle, individuals should not be treated differently on the basis of arbitrary characteristics, such as race, sex, religion or national origin. This familiar principle is embodied in the Civil Rights Act. The fairness principle means that employees must be expected to engage in cooperative activities according to the rules of the company, assuming that the company rules are deemed fair. The most obvious example is that, in order to further the mutual interests of the company, themselves, and other workers, employees must accept limits on their freedom to be absent from work. The natural-duty principle points up a number of general obligations, including the duty to help others who are in need or danger, the duty not to cause unnecessary suffering, and the duty to comply with the just rules of an institution.

Summary

Defining the company mission is one of the most often slighted tasks in strategic management. Emphasizing the operational aspects of long-range management activities comes much more easily for most executives. But the critical role of the mission statement repeatedly is demonstrated by failing firms whose short-run actions have been at odds with their long-run purposes.

The principal value of the mission statement is its specification of the firm's ultimate aims. A firm gains a heightened sense of purpose when its board of directors and its top executives address these issues: "What business are we in?" "What customers do we serve?" "Why does this organization exist?" However, the potential contribution of the company mission can be undermined if platitudes or ambiguous generalizations are accepted in response to these questions. It is not enough to say that Lever Brothers is in the business of "making anything that cleans anything" or that Polaroid is committed to businesses that deal with "the interaction of light and matter." Only if a firm clearly articulates its long-term intentions can its goals serve as a basis for shared expectations, planning, and performance evaluation.

A mission statement that is developed from this perspective provides managers with a unity of direction transcending individual, parochial, and temporary needs. It promotes a sense of shared expectations among all levels and generations of employees. It consolidates values over time and across individuals and interest groups. It projects a sense of worth and intent that can be identified and assimilated by outside stakeholders, that is, customers, suppliers, competitors, local committees, and the general public. Finally, it asserts the firm's commitment to responsible action in symbiosis with the preservation and protection of the essential claims of insider stakeholders' survival, growth, and profitability.

Questions for Discussion

1. Reread Nicor, Inc.'s mission statement in Exhibit 2–1, Strategy in Action. List five insights into Nicor that you feel you gained from knowing its mission.

2. Locate the mission statement of a company not mentioned in the chapter. Where did you find it? Was it presented as a consolidated statement, or were you forced to assemble it yourself from various publications of the firm? How many of the mission statement elements outlined in this chapter were discussed or revealed in the statement you found?

3. Prepare a two-page typewritten mission statement for your school of business or for a firm selected by your instructor.

4. List five potentially vulnerable areas of a firm without a stated company mission.

5. Define the term *social responsibility*. Find an example of a company action that was legal but not socially responsible. Defend your example on the basis of your definition.

6. Name five potentially valuable indicators of a firm's social responsibility and describe how company performance in each could be measured.

7. Do you think a business organization in today's society benefits by defining a socially responsible role for itself? Why or why not?

8. Which of the three basic philosophies of social responsibility would you find most appealing as the chief executive of a large corporation? Explain.

9. Do you think society's expectations for corporate social responsibility will change in the next decade? Explain.

10. How much should social responsibility be considered in evaluating an organization's overall performance?

11. Is it necessary that an action be voluntary to be termed socially responsible? Explain.

12. Do you think an organization should adhere to different philosophies of corporate responsibility when confronted with different issues, or should its philosophy always remain the same? Explain.

13. After reviewing arguments for and against social responsibility, which side do you find more compelling? Why?

14. Describe yourself as a stakeholder in a company. What kind of stakeholder role do you play now? What kind of stakeholder roles do you expect to play in the future?

15. What sets the affirmative philosophy apart from the stakeholder philosophy of social responsibility? In what areas do the two philosophies overlap?

16. Cite examples of both ethical and unethical behavior drawn from your knowledge of current business events.

17. How would you describe the contemporary state of business ethics?

18. How can business self-interest also serve social interests?

Chapter 2 Discussion Case

Inside a Chinese Sweatshop

BusinessWeek

1 Liu Zhang (not his real name) was apprehensive about taking a job at the Chun Si Enterprise Handbag Factory in Zhongshan, a booming city in Guangdong Province in southern China, where thousands of factories churn out goods for Western companies. Chun Si, which made Kathie Lee Gifford handbags sold by Wal-Mart Stores Inc. as well as handbags sold by Kansas-based Payless ShoeSource Inc., advertised decent working conditions and a fair salary. But word among migrant workers in the area was that managers there demanded long hours of their workers and sometimes hit them. Still, Liu, a 32-year-old former farmer and construction worker from far-off Henan province, was desperate for work. A factory job would give him living quarters and the temporary-residence permit internal migrants need to avoid being locked up by police in special detention centers. So in late August 1999, he signed up.

2 Liu quickly realized that the factory was even worse than its reputation. Chun Si, owned by Chun Kwan, a Macau businessman, charged workers $15 a month for food and lodging in a crowded dorm—a crushing sum given the $22 Liu cleared his first month. What's more, the factory gave Liu an expired temporary-resident permit; and in return, Liu had to hand over his personal identification card. This left him a virtual captive. Only the local police near the factory knew that Chun Si issued expired cards, Liu says, so workers risked arrest if they ventured out of the immediate neighborhood.

3 HALF A CENT. Liu also found that Chun Si's 900 workers were locked in the walled factory compound for all but a total of 60 minutes a day for meals. Guards regularly punched and hit workers for talking back to managers or even for walking too fast, he says. And they fined them up to $1 for infractions such as taking too long in the bathroom. Liu left the factory for good in December, after he and about 60 other workers descended on the local labor office to protest Chun Si's latest offenses: requiring cash payments for dinner and a phony factory it set up to dupe Wal-Mart's auditors. In his pocket was a total of $6 for three months of 90-hour weeks—an average of about one-half cent an hour. "Workers there face a life of fines and beating," says Liu. Chun Kwan couldn't be reached, but his daughter, Selina Chun, one of the factory managers, says "this is not true,

none of this." She concedes that Chun Si did not pay overtime but says few other factories do, either. In a face-to-face interview in August, she also admitted that workers have tried to sue Chun Si.

4 Liu's Dickensian tale stands in stark contrast to the reassurances that Wal-Mart, Payless, and other U.S. companies give American consumers that their goods aren't produced under sweatshop conditions. Since 1992, Wal-Mart has required its suppliers to sign a code of basic labor standards. After exposés in the mid–1990s of abuses in factories making Kathie Lee products, which the chain carries, Wal-Mart and Kathie Lee both began hiring outside auditing firms to inspect supplier factories to ensure their compliance with the code. Many other companies that produce or sell goods made in low-wage countries do similar self-policing, from Toys 'R' Us to Nike and Gap. While no company suggests that its auditing systems are perfect, most say they catch major abuses and either force suppliers to fix them or yank production.

5 What happened at Chun Si suggests that these auditing systems can miss serious problems—and that self-policing allows companies to avoid painful public revelations about them. Allegations about Chun Si first surfaced this May in a report by the National Labor Committee (NLC), a small anti-sweatshop group in New York that in 1997 exposed Kathie Lee's connection to labor violations in Central America. For several months, Wal-Mart repeatedly denied any connection to Chun Si. Wal-Mart and Kathie Lee even went so far as to pass out a press release when the report came out dismissing it as "lies" and insisting that they never had "any relationship with a company or factory by this name anywhere in the world."

6 But in mid-September, after a three-month *Business-Week* investigation that involved a visit to the factory, tracking down ex-Chun Si workers, and obtaining copies of records they had smuggled out of the factory, Wal-Mart conceded that it had produced the Kathie Lee bags there until December, 1999. Wal-Mart Vice-President of Corporate Affairs Jay Allen now says that Wal-Mart denied using Chun Si because it was "defensive" about the sweatshop issue.

7 Wal-Mart Director of Corporate Compliance Denise Fenton says its auditors, Pricewaterhouse

Coopers LLP (PWC) and Cal Safety Compliance Corp., had inspected Chun Si five times in 1999 and found that the factory didn't pay the legal overtime rate and had required excessive work hours. Because the factory didn't fix the problems, she says, Wal-Mart stopped making Kathie Lee bags there. Kathie Lee, who licenses her name to Wal-Mart, which handles production, concurred with the chain's action at Chun Si, says her lawyer Richard Hofstetter. Payless also stopped production there after an investigation, a spokesman says.

8   Still, the auditors failed to uncover many of the egregious conditions in the factory despite interviews with dozens of workers, concedes Fenton. Charges NLC Executive Director Charles Kernaghan: "The real issue here is why anyone should believe their audits."

9   A SECOND LOOK. And it's not just Wal-Mart. The NLC's report, entitled Made in China, detailed labor abuses in a dozen factories producing for household-name U.S. companies (www.nlcnet.org). After it came out, bootmaker Timberland Co. asked its auditors to revisit its plant, also in Zhongshan. They found that the factory hadn't fixed most of the violations cited the first time, despite repeated assurances to Timberland that it had. Similarly, in mid-September, Social Accountability International (SAI), a New York group that started a factory monitoring system last year, revoked its certification of a Chinese factory that makes shoes for New Balance Athletic Shoe Inc. after auditors reinspected the plant following the NLC report. "The auditors found that indeed there were many violations they had not picked up the first time," says SAI President Alice Tepper Marlin.

10   Because such efforts to reassure consumers have proven so unsatisfactory, a handful of companies, including Nike Inc. and Reebok International Ltd.—so far, the companies most tarnished by anti-sweatshop activists—have concluded that self-policing isn't enough. They—along with Kathie Lee—helped form the Fair Labor Assn., created in 1998 after a White House-sponsored initiative. The FLA now has a dozen members and is setting up an independent monitoring system that includes human rights groups.

11   Wal-Mart and many other companies, though, reject such efforts, saying they don't want to tell critics or rivals where their products are made. Yet without independent inspections, such companies leave themselves open to critics' accusations that self-policing doesn't work. "The big retailers, such as Wal-Mart, drive the market today, yet . . . they're not committed to changing the way they do business," says Michael Posner, head of New York-based Lawyers Committee for Human Rights and an FLA board member. Wal-Mart's Allen says that after three years of talks, the company may soon set up independent monitoring with the Interfaith Center on Corporate Responsibility, a religious group in New York City.

12   Certainly, what happened at Chun Si illustrates the inadequacy of many labor-auditing systems in place today. Wal-Mart uses nine auditing firms, including PWC. Like other big accounting firms, PWC has a booming labor-auditing business inspecting many of the thousands of factories making toys and clothes made by Wal-Mart and other companies. After Kathie Lee's drubbing by sweatshop critics, she hired Cal Safety, a Los Angeles-based labor-auditing firm, to do separate audits of the factories that produce the clothing and accessories bearing her name. According to Wal-Mart's Fenton, Cal Safety inspected the factory four times from March to December of last year, and PWC inspected it once, in September. The auditors found that Chun Si had numerous problems, including overtime violations and excessively long hours, says Fenton.

13   But otherwise, concedes Fenton, the audits missed most of the more serious abuses listed in the NLC report and confirmed by *BusinessWeek,* including beatings and confiscated identity papers. (Wal-Mart declined to allow *BusinessWeek* to talk in detail to Cal Safety or PWC, citing confidentiality agreements. Randal H. Rankin, head of PWC's labor practices unit, insists his audit did catch many of the abuses found by the NLC, though he wouldn't provide specifics, also citing Wal-Mart's confidentiality agreement. Cal Safety President Carol Pender says her firm caught some, though not all, of the abuses.)

14   All the while, evidence was piling up at the local labor office in Zhongshan. There, officials received a constant stream of worker complaints—several a month since the factory opened 10 years ago, says Mr. Chen, the head of the local labor office, who declined to give his full name. "Since they opened their factory, the complaints never stopped," he says. Officials would call or go to the factory once a month or so to mediate disputes, but new complaints kept arising, he says. Neither Wal-Mart's nor Kathie Lee's auditors discovered this history.

15   Chun Si also tried to hoodwink the auditors, according to the workers *BusinessWeek* interviewed. After Cal Safety's initial inspection in March, 1999,

Wal-Mart (through its U.S. supplier, which placed the order with the factory) insisted that Chun Si remedy the violations or it would pull the contract. Cal Safety found little improvement when it returned in June, as did PWC in September.

16   DOUBLE STANDARD. Chun Si then took drastic steps, apparently in an effort to pass the final audit upon which its contract depended. In early November, management gave a facelift to the two attached five-story factory buildings, painting walls, cleaning workshops, even putting high-quality toilet paper in the dank bathrooms, according to Liu and Pang Yinguang (also not his real name), another worker employed there at the time whom *Business-Week* interviewed in mid-September. Management then split the factory into two groups. The first, with about 200 workers, was assigned to work on the fixed-up second floor, while the remaining 700 or so worked on the fourth floor, leaving the other floors largely vacant. Managers announced that those on the fourth floor were no longer working for Chun Si but for a new factory they called Yecheng. Workers signed new labor contracts with Yecheng, whose name went up outside the fourth floor.

17   The reality soon became clear. Workers on the fourth floor, including Liu and Pang, were still laboring under the old egregious conditions—illegally low pay, 14-hour days, exorbitant fees for meals—and still making the same Kathie Lee handbags. "It felt like being in prison," says Pang, 22. But those on the second floor now received the local minimum wage of $55 a month and no longer had to do mandatory overtime. A new sign went up in the cafeteria used by workers on all floors explaining that the factory was a Wal-Mart supplier and should live up to certain labor standards. Liu says there was even a phone number workers could call with problems: 1-800-WM-ETHIC. "When we saw the Wal-Mart statement, we felt very excited and happy because we thought that now there was a possibility to improve our conditions," says Liu.

18   LAST STRAW. Instead, they got worse. On Nov. 28, a second notice went up stating that starting on Dec. 10,

all workers would be required to pay cash for dinner rather than just have money subtracted from their paychecks as before, say Liu and Pang. With up to 80 percent of workers already skipping breakfast to save money, the upper-floor employees were aghast, says Liu. "If we had left the factory then, we wouldn't have had even enough money for a bus ticket home," he says. "But if we stayed, we knew we wouldn't have enough money to eat."

19   A group of workers, including Liu and Pang, met around a small pond on the factory grounds on one of the following evenings. They knew that workers had fruitlessly complained before to the local labor office. So they decided on a plan to smuggle out documents to prove Chun Si's illegal fees and subminimum wages. On Dec. 1, 58 workers overcame their fears of retaliation and marched out the factory gates, down to the labor office.

20   Faced with the throng of workers, local labor officials visited Chun Si and forced the factory to immediately pay the workers and return the illegally collected fees. But the officials also told these workers they would have to give up their jobs at Chun Si. Days later, some 40 labor officials returned, ordered Chun Si to properly register or shut down the so-called Yecheng factory, and fined the company about $8,500. Shortly after the blow-up, Wal-Mart ended production at Chun Si.

21   Kernaghan and other labor activists concede that Chun Si is an extreme example of working conditions in China today. Yet many experts think most factories in China producing for Western companies routinely break China's labor laws. Some Western companies' monitoring efforts do catch and fix some of these problems. But unless companies and governments alike take more serious steps, labor watchdogs will give little credence to company claims that they're doing the best they can.

Source: Dexter Roberts and Aaron Bernstein, "A Life of Fines and Beating: Wal-Mart's self-policing in the Chun Si factory was a disaster. What kind of monitoring system works?" *BusinessWeek,* October 2, 2000.

Appendix 2

BB&T Vision, Mission, and Purpose

BB&T VISION

To create the best financial institution possible: *"The Best of The Best."*

BB&T MISSION

To make the world a better place to live by: helping our clients achieve economic success and financial security; creating a place where our employees can learn, grow and be fulfilled in their work; making the communities in which we work better places to be; and thereby: optimizing the long-term return to our shareholders, while providing a safe and sound investment.

BB&T PURPOSE

Our ultimate purpose is to create superior long-term economic rewards for our shareholders.

This purpose is defined by the free market and is as it should be. Our shareholders provide the capital that is necessary to make our business possible. They take the risk if the business is unsuccessful. They have the right to receive economic rewards for the risk which they have undertaken.

However, our purpose, to create superior long-term economic rewards for our shareholders, can only be accomplished by providing excellent service to our clients, as our clients are our source of revenues.

To have excellent client relations, we must have outstanding employees to serve our clients. To attract and retain outstanding employees, we must reward them financially and create an environment where they can learn and grow.

Our economic results are significantly impacted by the success of our communities. The community's "quality of life" impacts its ability to attract industry for growth.

Therefore, we manage our business in a long-term context, as an integrated whole, with the ultimate objective of rewarding the shareholders for their investment, while realizing that the cause of this result is quality client service. Excellent service will be delivered by motivated employees working as an integrated team. These results will be impacted by our capacity to contribute to the growth and well-being of the communities we serve.

VALUES

"Excellence is an art won by training and habituation. We are what we repeatedly do. Excellence then is not an act, but a habit."—Aristotle

The great Greek philosophers saw values as guides to excellence in thinking and action. In this context, values are standards which we strive to achieve. Values are practical habits that enable us as individuals to live, be successful and achieve happiness. For BB&T, our values enable us to achieve our mission and corporate purpose.

To be useful, values must be consciously held and be consistent (noncontradictory). Many people have conflicting values which prevent them from acting with clarity and self-confidence.

There are 10 primary values at BB&T. These values are consistent with one another and are integrated. To fully act on one of these values, you must also act consistently with the other values. Our focus on values grows from our belief that ideas matter and that an individual's character is of critical significance.

Values are important at BB&T!

1. REALITY (FACT-BASED)

What is, is. If we want to be better, we must act within the context of reality (the facts). Businesses and individuals often make serious mistakes by making decisions based on what they "wish was so," or based on theories which are disconnected from reality. The foundation for quality decision making is a careful understanding of the facts.

There is a fundamental difference between the laws of nature (reality), which are immutable, and the man-made. The law of gravity is the law of gravity. The existence of the law of gravity does not mean man can not create an airplane. However, an airplane must be created within the context of the law of gravity. At BB&T, we believe in being "reality grounded."

2. REASON (OBJECTIVITY)

Mankind has a specific means of survival, which is his ability to think, i.e., his capacity to reason logically from the facts of reality as presented to his five senses. A lion has claws to hunt. A deer has swiftness to avoid the hunter. Man has his ability to think. There is only one "natural resource"—the human mind.

Clear thinking is not automatic. It requires intellectual discipline and begins with sound premises based on observed facts. You must be able to draw general conclusions in a rational manner from specific examples (induction) and be able to apply general principles to the solution of specific problems (deduction). You must be able to think in an integrated way, thereby avoiding logical contradictions.

We cannot all be geniuses, but each of us can develop the mental habits which ensure that when making decisions we carefully examine the facts and think logically without contradiction in deriving a conclusion. We must learn to think in terms of what is essential, i.e., about what is important. Our goal is to objectively make the best decision to accomplish our purpose.

Rational thinking is a learned skill which requires mental focus and a fundamental commitment to consistently improving the clarity of our mental processes. At BB&T, we are looking for people who are committed to constantly improving their ability to reason.

3. INDEPENDENT THINKING

All employees are challenged to use their individual minds to their optimum to make rational decisions. In this context, each of us is *responsible* for what we do and who we are. In addition, creativity is strongly encouraged and only possible with independent thought.

We learn a great deal from each other. Teamwork is important at BB&T (as will be discussed later). However, each of us thinks alone. Our minds are not physically connected. In this regard, each of us must be willing to make an independent judgment of the facts based on our capacity to think logically. Just because the "crowd" says it is so, does not make it so.

In this context, each of us is responsible for our own actions. Each of us is responsible for our personal success or failure, i.e., it is not the bank's fault if someone does not achieve his objectives.

All human progress by definition is based on creativity, because creativity is the source of positive change. Creativity is only possible to an independent thinker. Creativity is not about just doing something different. It is about doing something better. To be better, the new method/process must be judged by its impact on the whole organization, and as to whether it contributes to the accomplishment of our mission.

There is an infinite opportunity for each of us to do whatever we do better. A significant aspect of the self-fulfillment which work can provide comes from creative thought and action.

4. PRODUCTIVITY

We are committed to being producers of wealth and well-being by taking the actions necessary to accomplish our mission. The tangible evidence of our productivity is that we have rationally allocated capital through our lending and investment process, and that we have provided needed services to our clients in an efficient manner resulting in superior profitability.

Profitability is a measure of the differences in the economic value of the products/services we produce and the cost of producing these products/services. In a long-term context and in a free market, the bigger the profit, the better. This is true not only from our shareholders' perspective (which would be enough justification), but also in terms of the impact of our work on society as a whole. Healthy profits represent productive work. At BB&T we are looking for people who want to create, to produce, and who are thereby committed to turning their thoughts into actions that improve economic well-being.

5. HONESTY

Being honest is simply being consistent with reality. To be dishonest is to be in conflict with reality, which is therefore self-defeating. A primary reason that individuals fail is because they become disconnected from reality, pretending that facts are other than they are.

To be honest does not require that we know everything. Knowledge is always contextual and man is not omniscient. However, we must be responsible for saying what we mean and meaning what we say.

6. INTEGRITY

Because we have developed our principles logically, based on reality, we will always act consistently with our principles. Regardless of the short-term benefits, acting inconsistently with our principles is to our long-term detriment. We do not, therefore, believe in compromising our principles in any situation.

Principles provide carefully thought-out concepts which will lead to our long-term success and happiness. Violating our principles will always lead to failure. BB&T is an organization of the highest integrity.

7. JUSTICE (FAIRNESS)

Individuals should be evaluated and rewarded objectively (for better or worse) based on their contributions toward accomplishing our mission and adherence to our values. Those who contribute the most should receive the most.

The single most significant way in which employees evaluate their managers is in determining whether the manager is just. Employees become extremely unhappy (and rightly so) when they perceive that a person who is not contributing is overrewarded or a strong contributor is underrewarded.

If we do not reward those who contribute the most, they will leave and our organization will be less successful. Even more important, if there is no reward for superior performance, the average person will not be motivated to maximize his productivity.

We must evaluate whether the food we eat is healthy, the clothes we wear attractive, the car we drive functional, etc., and we must also evaluate whether relationships with other people are good for us or not.

In evaluating other people, it is critical that we judge based on essentials. At BB&T we do not discriminate based on nonessentials such as race, sex, nationality, etc. We do discriminate based on competency, performance and character. We consciously reject egalitarianism and collectivism. Individuals must be judged individually based on their personal merits, not their membership in any group.

8. PRIDE

Pride is the psychological reward we earn from living by our values, i.e., from being just, honest, having integrity, being an independent thinker, being productive and rational.

Aristotle believed that "earned" pride (not arrogance) was the highest of virtues, because it presupposed all the others. Striving for earned pride simply reinforces the importance of having high moral values.

Each of us must perform our work in a manner as to be able to be justly proud of what we have accomplished. BB&T must be the kind of organization with which each employee and client can be proud to be associated.

9. SELF-ESTEEM (SELF-MOTIVATION)

We expect our employees to earn positive self-esteem from doing their work well. We expect and want our employees to act in their rational, long-term self-interest. We want employees who have strong personal goals and who expect to be able to accomplish their goals within the context of our mission.

A necessary attribute for self-esteem is self-motivation. We have a strong work ethic. We believe that you receive from your work in proportion to how much you contribute. If you do not want to work hard, work somewhere else.

While there are many trade-offs in the content of life, you need to be clear that BB&T is the best place, all things considered, for you to work to accomplish your long-term goals. When you know this, you can be more productive and happy.

10. TEAMWORK/MUTUAL SUPPORTIVENESS

While independent thought and strong personal goals are critically important, our work is accomplished within teams. Each of us must consistently act to achieve the agreed-upon objectives of the team, with respect for our fellow employees, while acting in a mutually supportive manner.

Our work at BB&T is so complex that it requires an integrated effort among many people to accomplish important tasks. While we are looking for self-motivated and independent thinking individuals, these individuals must recognize that almost nothing at BB&T can be accomplished without the help of their team members. One of the responsibilities of leadership in our organization is to ensure that each individual is rewarded based on their contribution to the success of the total team. We need outstanding individuals working together to create an outstanding team.

Our values are held consciously and are logically consistent. To fully execute on any one value, you must act consistently with all 10 values. At BB&T values are practical and important

THE ROLE OF EMOTIONS

Often people believe that making logical decisions means that we should be unemotional and that emotions are thereby unimportant. In fact, emotions are important. However, the real issue is how rational are our emotions. Emotions are mental habits which are often developed as children. Emotions give us automatic responses to people and events; these responses can either be very useful or destructive indicators. Emotions as such are not means of decision or of knowledge; the issue is: How were your emotions formed? The real question is: Are we happy when we should be happy, and unhappy when we should be unhappy, or are we unhappy when we should be happy?

Emotions are learned behaviors. The goal is to "train up" our emotions so that our emotions objectively reinforce the best decisions and behaviors toward our long-term success and happiness. Just because someone is unemotional does not mean that they are logical.

CONCEPTS THAT DESCRIBE BB&T

1. CLIENT-DRIVEN

"World class" client service organization.

Our clients are our partners.

Our goal is to create win/win relationships.

"You can tell we want your business."

"It is easy to do business with BB&T."

"Respect the individual, value the relationship."

We will absolutely never, ever, take advantage of anyone, nor do we want to do business with those who would take advantage of us. Our clients are long-term partners and should be treated accordingly. One of the attributes of partnerships is that both partners must keep their agreements. We keep our agreements. When our partners fail to keep their agreements, they are terminating the partnership.

There are an infinite number of opportunities where we can get better together, where we can help our clients achieve their financial goals and where our client will enable us to make a profit in doing so.

2. QUALITY ORIENTED

Quality must be built into the process.

In every aspect of our business we want to execute and deliver quality. It is easier and less expensive to do things correctly than to fix what has been done incorrectly.

3. EFFICIENT

"Waste not, want not."

Design efficiency into the system.

4. GROWING BOTH OUR BUSINESS AND OUR PEOPLE

Grow or die.

Life requires constant, focused thought and actions towards one's goals.

5. CONTINUOUS IMPROVEMENT

Everything can be done better.

Fundamental commitment to innovation.

Every employee should constantly use their reasoning ability to do whatever they do better every day. All managers of systems/processes should constantly search for better methods to solve problems and serve the client.

6. OBJECTIVE DECISION MAKING

Fact-Based and rational

BB&T MANAGEMENT STYLE

Participative

Team Oriented

Fact-Based

Rational

Objective

Our management process, by intention, is designed to be participative and team oriented. We work hard to create consensus. When people are involved in the decision process, better information is available to make decisions. The participant's understanding of the decision is greater and, therefore, execution is better.

However, there is a risk in participative decision making: the decision process can become a popularity contest. Therefore, our decision process is disciplined. Our decisions will be made based on the facts using reason. The best objective decision will be the one which is enacted.

Therefore, it does not matter who you know, who your friends are, etc.; it matters whether you can offer the best objective solution to accomplishing the goal or solving the problem at hand.

BB&T MANAGEMENT CONCEPT

Hire excellent people

Train them well

Give them an appropriate level of authority and responsibility

Expect a high level of achievement

Reward their performance

Our concept is to operate a highly autonomous, entrepreneurial organization. In order to execute this concept, we must have extremely competent individuals who are "masters" of BB&T's philosophy and who are "masters" in their field of technical expertise.

By having individuals who are "masters" in their field, we can afford to have less costly control systems and be more responsive in meeting the needs of our clients.

ATTRIBUTES OF AN OUTSTANDING BB&T EMPLOYEE

Purpose

Rationality

Self-Esteem

Consistent with our values, successful individuals at BB&T have a sense of purpose for their lives, i.e., they believe that their lives matter and that they can accomplish something meaningful through their work. We are looking for people who are rational and have a high level of personal self-esteem. People with a strong personal self-esteem get along better with others, because they are at peace with themselves.

BB&T POSITIVE ATTITUDE

Since we build on the facts of reality and our ability to reason, we are capable of achieving both success and happiness.

We do not believe that "realism" means pessimism. On the contrary, precisely because our goals are based on and consistent with reality, we fully expect to accomplish them.

BB&T'S OBLIGATIONS TO ITS EMPLOYEES

We will do our best to:

Compensate employees fairly in relation to internal equity and market-comparable pay practices—performance-based compensation.

Provide a comprehensive and market-competitive benefit program.

Create a place where employees can learn and grow—to become more productive workers and better people.

Train employees so they are competent to do the work asked of them. (Never ask anyone to do anything they are not trained to do.)

Evaluate and recognize performance objectively, fairly and consistently based on the individual's contribution to the accomplishment of our mission and adherence to our values.

Treat each employee as an individual with dignity and respect.

VIRTUES OF AN OUTSTANDING CREDIT CULTURE

Just as individuals need a set of values (virtues) to guide their actions, systems should be designed to have a set of attributes which optimize their performance towards our goals. In this regard, our credit culture has seven fundamental virtues:

1. Provides fundamental insight to help clients achieve their economic goals and solve their financial problems: We are in the high-quality financial advice business.
2. Responsive: The client deserves an answer as quickly as possible, even when the answer is no.
3. Flexible (Creative): We are committed to finding better ways to meet the client's financial needs.
4. Reliable: Our clients are selected as long-term partners and treated accordingly. BB&T must continue to earn the right to be known as the most reliable bank.
5. Manages risk within agreed-upon limits: Clients do not want to fail financially, and the bank does not want a bad loan.
6. Ensures an appropriate economic return to the bank for risk taken: The higher the risk, the higher the return. The lower the risk, the lower the return. This is an expression of justice.
7. Creates a "premium" for service delivery: The concept is to provide superior value to the client through outstanding service quality. A rational client will fairly compensate us when we provide sound financial advice, are responsive, creative and reliable, because these attributes are of economic value to the client.

STRATEGIC OBJECTIVES

Create a high performance financial institution that can survive and prosper in a rapidly changing, highly competitive, globally integrated environment.

ACHIEVING OUR GOAL

The key to maximizing our probability of being both independent and prosperous over the long term is to create a superior earnings per share (EPS) growth rate without sacrificing the fundamental quality and long-term competitiveness of our business and without taking unreasonable risk.

While being fundamentally efficient is critical, the "easy" way to rapid EPS growth is to artifically cut cost. However, not investing for the future is long-term suicide, as it destroys our capability to compete.

The intelligent process to achieve superior EPS growth is to grow revenues by providing (and selling) superior quality service while systematically enhancing our margins, improving our efficiency, expanding our profitable product offerings and creating more effective distribution channels.

THE "WORLD STANDARD" REVENUE-DRIVEN SALES ORGANIZATION

At BB&T, selling is about identifying our clients' legitimate financial needs and finding a way to help the client achieve economic goals by providing the right products and services.

Effective selling requires a disciplined approach in which the BB&T employee asks the client about financial goals and problems and has a complete understanding of how our products can help the client achieve objectives and solve financial problems.

It also requires exceptional execution by support staffs and product managers, since service and sales are fundamentally connected and creativity is required in product design and development.

"WORLD STANDARD" CLIENT SERVICE COMMUNITY BANKS

BB&T operates as a series of "Community Banks." The "Community Bank" concept is the foundation for local decision making and the basis for responsive, reliable and empathetic client service.

By putting decision making closer to the client, all local factors can be considered, and we can ensure that the client is being treated as an individual.

To operate in this decentralized decision-making fashion, we must have highly trained employees who understand BB&T's philosophy and are "masters" of their areas of responsibility.

COMMITMENT TO EDUCATION/LEARNING

Competitive advantage is in the minds of our employees. We are committed to making substantial investments in employee education to create a "knowledge-based learning organization" founded on the premise that knowledge (understanding), properly applied, is the source of superior performance.

We believe in systematized learning founded on Aristotle's concept that "excellence is an art won by training and habituation." We attempt to train our employees with the best knowledge/methods in their fields and to habituate those behaviors through consistent management reinforcement. The goal is for each employee to be a "master" of his or her role, whether it be a computer operator, teller, lender, financial consultant or any other job responsibility.

OUR PASSIONS

To create the best financial institution possible.

To consistently provide the client with better value through rational innovation and productivity improvement.

At BB&T we have two powerful passions. Our fundamental passion is our Vision: To Create The Best Financial Institution Possible—The "World Standard"—The "Best of the Best." We believe that the best can be objectively evaluated by rational performance standards in relation to the accomplishment of our mission.

To be the best of the best, we must constantly find ways to deliver better value to our clients in a highly profitable manner. This requires us to keep our minds focused at all times on innovative ways to enhance our productivity.

Chapter **Three**

The External Environment

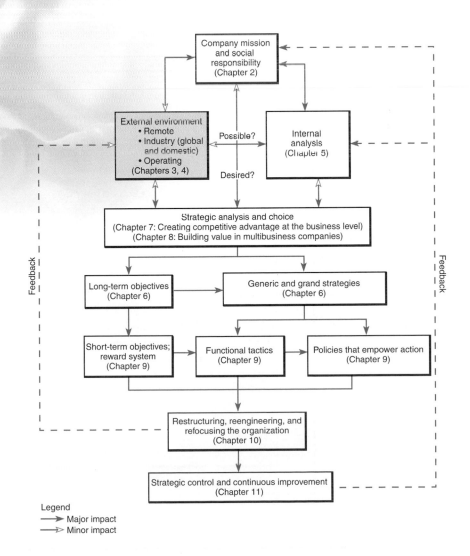

Company mission and social responsibility
(Chapter 2)

External environment
• Remote
• Industry (global and domestic)
• Operating
(Chapters 3, 4)

Possible?

Desired?

Internal analysis
(Chapter 5)

Strategic analysis and choice
(Chapter 7: Creating competitive advantage at the business level)
(Chapter 8: Building value in multibusiness companies)

Long-term objectives
(Chapter 6)

Generic and grand strategies
(Chapter 6)

Short-term objectives; reward system
(Chapter 9)

Functional tactics
(Chapter 9)

Policies that empower action
(Chapter 9)

Restructuring, reengineering, and refocusing the organization
(Chapter 10)

Strategic control and continuous improvement
(Chapter 11)

Feedback

Feedback

Legend
⟶ Major impact
⤍ Minor impact

A host of external factors influence a firm's choice of direction and action and, ultimately, its organizational structure and internal processes. These factors, which constitute the *external environment,* can be divided into three interrelated subcategories: factors in the *remote* environment, factors in the *industry* environment, and factors in the *operating* environment. This chapter describes the complex necessities involved in formulating strategies that optimize a firm's market opportunities. Exhibit 3–1 suggests the interrelationship between the firm and its remote, its industry, and its operating environments. In combination, these factors form the basis of the opportunities and threats that a firm faces in its competitive environment.

EXHIBIT 3–1
The Firm's External Environment

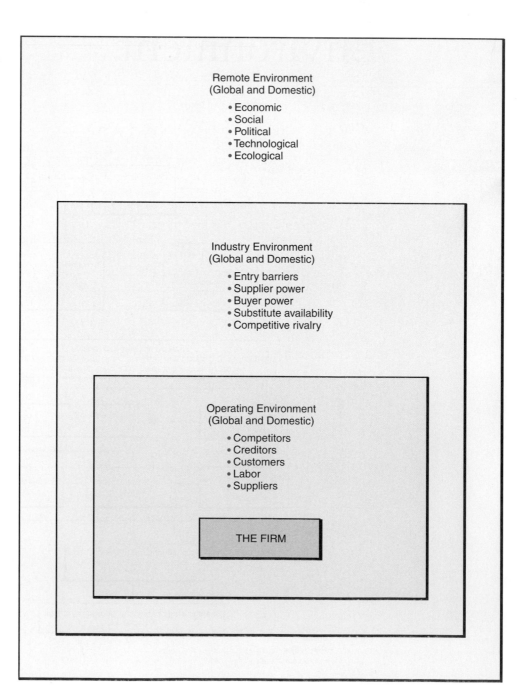

Remote Environment
(Global and Domestic)

• Economic
• Social
• Political
• Technological
• Ecological

Industry Environment
(Global and Domestic)

• Entry barriers
• Supplier power
• Buyer power
• Substitute availability
• Competitive rivalry

Operating Environment
(Global and Domestic)

• Competitors
• Creditors
• Customers
• Labor
• Suppliers

THE FIRM

REMOTE ENVIRONMENT

The remote environment comprises factors that originate beyond, and usually irrespective of, any single firm's operating situation: (1) economic, (2) social, (3) political, (4) technological, and (5) ecological factors. That environment presents firms with opportunities, threats, and constraints, but rarely does a single firm exert any meaningful reciprocal influence. For example, when the economy slows and construction starts to decrease, an individual contractor is likely to suffer a decline in business, but that contractor's efforts in stimulating local construction activities would be unable to reverse the overall decrease in construction starts. The trade agreements that resulted from improved relations between the United States and China and the United States and Russia are examples of political factors that impact individual firms. The agreements provided individual U.S. manufacturers with opportunities to broaden their international operations.

Economic Factors

Economic factors concern the nature and direction of the economy in which a firm operates. Because consumption patterns are affected by the relative affluence of various market segments, each firm must consider economic trends in the segments that affect its industry. On both the national and international level, managers must consider the general availability of credit, the level of disposable income, and the propensity of people to spend. Prime interest rates, inflation rates, and trends in the growth of the gross national product are other economic factors they should monitor.

For example, in 2003, the depressed economy was hitting Crown Cork & Seal Co. especially hard because it had $2 billion in debt due in the year and no way to raise the money to pay it. The down market had caused its stock price to be too low to raise cash as it normally would. Therefore, Crown Cork managers turned to issuing bonds to refinance its debt. With the slow market, investors were taking advantage of such bonds because they could safely gain higher returns over stocks. Not only were investors getting a deal, but Crown Cork and other companies were seeing the lowest interest rates on bonds in years and by issuing bonds could reorganize their balance sheets. For more details on this example, read Exhibit 3–2, Strategy in Action

The emergence of new international power brokers has changed the focus of economic environmental forecasting. Among the most prominent of these power brokers are the European Economic Community (EEC, or Common Market), the Organization of Petroleum Exporting Countries (OPEC), and coalitions of developing countries.

The EEC, whose members include most of the West European countries, eliminated quotas and established a tariff-free trade area for industrial products among its members. By fostering intra-European economic cooperation, it has helped its member countries compete more effectively in non-European international markets.

Social Factors

The social factors that affect a firm involve the beliefs, values, attitudes, opinions, and lifestyles of persons in the firm's external environment, as developed from cultural, ecological, demographic, religious, educational, and ethnic conditioning. As social attitudes change, so too does the demand for various types of clothing, books, leisure activities, and so on. Like other forces in the remote external environment, social forces are dynamic, with constant change resulting from the efforts of individuals to satisfy their desires and needs by controlling and adapting to environmental factors. Teresa Iglesias-Soloman hopes to benefit from social changes with *Ninos,* a children's catalog written in both English and Spanish. The catalog features books, videos, and Spanish cultural offerings for English-speaking children who

BusinessWeek The sluggish economy was hitting Crown Cork & Seal Co. (CCK) hard. More than half of its $4 billion in debt was coming due in the year, but its low share price ruled out raising money by issuing more stock. The Philadelphia company already had raised the prices of the aluminum cans it makes for everything from soda to aerosol, and spun off a top business, but that was far from enough. Then it found a way out.

On Feb. 11, 2003, Crown issued $2.1 billion in 8- and 10-year bonds in the country's biggest junk-bond deal in three years. Investors snapped up the debt, which carries rates from 9 1/2 percent to 10 7/8 percent, giving the company some badly needed breathing room.

Corporate America was issuing debt faster in 2003 than a tapped-out sailor on shore leave. The bond bonanza might top 2001's record $738 billion. General Electric Co. (GE) issued $5 billion in 10-year bonds on Jan. 21, 2003. Goldman Sachs Group (GS), J. P. Morgan Chase (JPM), Citigroup (C), and other investment banks have raised $38 billion in bonds for themselves, versus $23 billion in 2002.

Despite their rush to issue bonds, companies aren't digging themselves much deeper into debt. Most of the proceeds are earmarked for refinancing their old debt. And companies are seizing a chance to retool their balance sheets by locking in the lowest interest rates in years: For example, top-quality five-year bonds now pay 1.4 percentage points less than they did a year ago. Other companies are replacing short-term debt with long-term financing that may cost more—a top-rated 30-year bond will pay roughly 2.45 points more than a five-year bond—but protects them against rate increases that would jack up their future borrowing costs.

A lot more than routine refinancing is taking place. Indeed, many chief executives now consider restructuring their debt a critical mission, especially as investors increasingly scrutinize companies' credit profiles in the wake of fiascos such as Enron Corp. and WorldCom Inc. As a result, says Thomas J. Gahan, head of corporate finance in the United States for Deutsche Bank, "Debt has gone from being a commodity product to a strategic tool for management."

Many of the companies rolling over their debt would rather be reducing it, but they can't get cash any other way. Hiving off unwanted businesses won't work because buyers won't come out of hiding until the sour economic climate improves. And with stock markets still in the doldrums, most companies don't want to sell new shares at giveaway prices.

The bear market was spurring investors to look for higher returns with relative safety. That fed the huge demand for bonds, and in turn made it much easier for companies to sell them. For companies that are saddled with debt from big mergers, refinancing with longer maturities buys them time to strengthen their balance sheets.

The stubbornly high level of corporate debt means that companies may have an even tougher time paying it down if the economy doesn't pick up. Already, debt makes up 76.5 percent of the net assets of nonfarm, nonfinancial corporations, versus 70 percent in 1999. Meanwhile, ratings agency Moody's Investors Service is downgrading five investment-grade companies for every one it raises.

The strains are beginning to show as companies try to sidestep a possible financing crunch by, for example, slowing down capital investments. "Corporations have little choice but to use their cash flow to pay back debt rather than increase capital expenditure," says David Bowers, chief global investment strategist at Merrill Lynch. "They are being run to generate cash instead of growth."

Many bankers, however, are optimistic. They believe that when the economy and stock market revive eventually, companies will decide it's time to clean up their balance sheets for real by issuing equity. "There will be a lot of business for investment bankers," predicts Marcel Ospel, chairman of UBS.

Source: Excerpted from Diane Brady and Emily Thornton, "Why Business Is Crazy for Debt," *BusinessWeek,* March 10, 2003, pp. 64–65.

---

want to learn Spanish and for Spanish-speaking children who want to learn English. *Ninos'* target market includes middle-to-upper-income Hispanic parents, consumers, educators, bilingual schools, libraries, and purchasing agents. Iglesias-Solomon has reason to be optimistic about the future of *Ninos,* because the Hispanic population is growing five times faster than the general U.S. population and ranks as the nation's largest minority.

One of the most profound social changes in recent years has been the entry of large numbers of women into the labor market. This has not only affected the hiring and compensation policies and the resource capabilities of their employers; it has also created or greatly expanded the demand for a wide range of products and services necessitated by their absence from the home. Firms that anticipated or reacted quickly to this social change offered such products and services as convenience foods, microwave ovens, and day care centers.

A second profound social change has been the accelerating interest of consumers and employees in quality-of-life issues. Evidence of this change is seen in recent contract negotiations. In addition to the traditional demand for increased salaries, worker demands such benefits as sabbaticals, flexible hours or four-day workweeks, lump-sum vacation plans, and opportunities for advanced training.

A third profound social change has been the shift in the age distribution of the population. Changing social values and a growing acceptance of improved birth control methods are expected to raise the mean age of the U.S. population, which was 27.9 in 1970, and 34.9 in the year 2000. This trend will have an increasingly unfavorable impact on most producers of predominantly youth-oriented goods and will necessitate a shift in their long-range marketing strategies. Producers of hair and skin care preparations already have begun to adjust their research and development to reflect anticipated changes in demand.

A consequence of the changing age distribution of the population has been a sharp increase in the demands made by a growing number of senior citizens. Constrained by fixed incomes, these citizens have demanded that arbitrary and rigid policies on retirement age be modified and have successfully lobbied for tax exemptions and increases in Social Security benefits. Such changes have significantly altered the opportunity-risk equations of many firms—often to the benefit of firms that anticipated the changes.

Cutting across these issues is concern for individual health. The fast food industry has been the target of a great deal of public concern, as discussed in Exhibit 3–3, Strategy in Action. In 2002, a great deal of popular press attention was directed toward Americans' concern over the relationship between obesity and health. McDonalds was caught in the middle of this new social concern because its menu consisted principally of high-calorie, artery clogging foods. Health experts blamed the fast food industry for the rise in obesity, claiming that companies like McDonalds created an environment that encouraged overeating and discouraged physical activity. Specifically, McDonalds had taken advantage of the fact that kids and adults were watching more TV, by targeting certain program slots to increase sales. For McDonalds and others in the industry to maintain revenues, it now appeared that they were going to have to change their strategies and successfully market new, healthier products.

Translating social change into forecasts of business effects is a difficult process, at best. Nevertheless, informed estimates of the impact of such alterations as geographic shifts in populations and changing work values, ethical standards, and religious orientation can only help a strategizing firm in its attempts to prosper.

Political Factors

The direction and stability of political factors are a major consideration for managers on formulating company strategy. Political factors define the legal and regulatory parameters within which firms must operate. Political constraints are placed on firms through fair-trade decisions, antitrust laws, tax programs, minimum wage legislation, pollution and pricing policies, administrative jawboning, and many other actions aimed at protecting employees, consumers, the general public, and the environment. Since such laws and regulations are most commonly restrictive, they tend to reduce the potential profits of firms. However, some political actions are designed to benefit and protect firms. Such actions include patent laws, government subsidies, and product research grants. Thus, political factors either may limit or benefit the firms they influence. For example, in a pair of surprising decisions in 2003, the FCC ruled that local phone companies had to continue to lease their lines to the long-distance carriers at what the locals said was below cost. At the same time, the FCC ruled that the local companies were not required to

BusinessWeek McDonalds' sales were stagnant. The company's earnings had declined for six consecutive quarters. And 2001 was the company's worst year ever for profits. The company's sagging profits might have been a sign of the nation's growing concern about nutrition: Americans were getting fatter at an alarming rate, and some of them were worried enough, perhaps, to skip those trips to the Golden Arches.

Obesity was, by far, the nation's leading health problem. A growing number of health experts said this alarming rise in obesity was the consequence of an unhealthy environment that encouraged overeating and discouraged physical activity. High-calorie, artery-clogging foods were cheap and plentiful. Healthy foods could sometimes be hard to find. And children were surrounded by increasing amounts of junk-food advertising. The food industry spent an estimated $33 billion a year on ads and promotions. "When you have $33 billion of marketing aimed at you, challenging you to eat more at all times, it's difficult not to eat too much," said Marion Nestle, chair of the nutrition and food studies department at New York University and author of *Food Politics*, published in 2002.

The idea that obesity was partly the consequence of an unhealthy environment was a relatively new one—but its time had arrived. And the surest sign the antiobesity campaign was starting to work was the wave of new health programs from food makers. Many companies—from PepsiCo Inc. (PEP), with its Get Active, Stay Active program, to McDonald's, with its just-announced yogurt and sweetened-fruit menu for kids—were rushing to show their concern for the nation's health.

To understand the rise in obesity, it was useful to look at the economics of food. The U.S. food industry produced enough to supply each of us with 3,800 calories a day. That was one-third more than what most men needed and nearly doubled the needs of most women. Supply exceeded demand. Prices fell. And Americans ate more. With the exception of a spike during the oil shock in the 1970s, food prices have dropped by an average of 0.2 percent a year since World War II, according to the Bureau of Labor Statistics. At the same time, the average American's food intake, which was 1,826 calories a day in the late 1970s, rose nearly 10 percent to 2,002, by the mid-1990s.

According to the Agriculture Dept., muffins that weighed an average of 1.5 ounces in 1957 averaged half a pound each in 2002. Fast-food hamburgers had swollen from an ounce of meat to six ounces or more. An eight-ounce bottle of soda was now a monstrous one-quart tumbler. And the original order of McDonald's fries, at 200 calories, paled next to today's 610-calorie super-size fries.

Television was just as crucial a factor in the rise of obesity in children, critics said. In 1987, an average of 225 commercials was shown during Saturday morning cartoon hours. By the mid-1990s, that had jumped to 997, NYU's Nestle said. Roughly two-thirds of those commercials promoted "foods of dubious nutritional value," Nestle said—presweetened cereals, candy, and fast foods.

Solving the obesity epidemic was, on one level, quite easy. To make that happen, however, the environment in which Americans live and eat must be changed. Changing the environment could have sharply cut America's health costs. And if it was done by shifting to healthier foods, it did not have to cripple the industry. That was a lesson McDonald's, Coke, Pepsi, and others may have started to learn.

Source: Excerpted from Diane Brady, Dean Foust, Julie Forster, and Paul Raeburn, "Why We're So Fat," *Business Week*, October 21, 2002, pp. 112–113.

---

lease their broadband lines to the national carriers. These decisions were good and bad for the local companies because although they would lose money by leasing to the long-distance carriers, they could regain some of that loss with their broadband services that did not have to be leased.

As discussed in Exhibit 3–4, Strategy in Action, the decisions did not mean that the local carriers had to remove existing lines and replace them with broadband lines. Instead, the local carriers would have to run two networks to areas where they want to incorporate broadband because the long-distance carriers had a right to the conventional lines as ruled in the decision. These regulations caused the local carriers to alter their strategies. For example, they often chose to reduce capital investments on new broadband lines because they had to maintain old lines as well. The reduction in capital investments was used to offset the losses they incurred in subsidizing their current lines to the long-distance carriers.

BusinessWeek When the Federal Communications Commission began to debate a revamp of deregulation policy, the FCC ruled that local phone companies must continue to lease their networks to long-distance rivals, such as AT&T (T) and WorldCom Inc., at steeply discounted rates. For local carriers, the decision was a huge setback: They complained they would have to continue selling capacity for less than their costs. The FCC had opened the door for states to weigh in with their own rules on local competition. Increased competition in the local market will benefit consumers.

Consumers should have done well, since the price of local phone service would have likely continued to fall. As carriers battle for their loyalty, customers may have also benefited from new services, such as the combination of wireless and traditional phone service under one phone number. And competition from cable and wireless rivals would have also forced the Bells to continue to invest in their networks, resulting in faster home Internet connections.

Just as no-holds-barred competition led to a debilitating price war in long distance, local carriers could have been destabilized. The economics of the local and long-distance markets were very different. The capital investment required to build a local phone system was five or six times higher than the capital costs of long-distance phone service, because local carriers must have extended their networks all the way into the homes and offices of their customers.

Rival broadband providers and consumer advocates were furious because the FCC ruled that the Bells did not have to lease their DSL lines. Still, the Bells said their victory in broadband was not as clear as it seemed. In markets where they built next-generation fiber networks, state regulators were denying the Bells permission to rip out old slow-speed copper connections to homes and offices because those wires were still serving competitors. That could have forced the Bells to operate two networks.

The FCC ruling did not help telecom-equipment makers Lucent Technologies Inc. (LU) and Nortel Networks Ltd. (NT), which were struggling to return to profitability. It did nothing to encourage new entrants in the local phone market to buy their own telephone switches, which directed traffic across the network.

Source: Excerpted from Roger Crockett, Charles Haddad, and Steve Rosenbush, "Telecom: What Hath the FCC Wrought?" *Business Week*, March 10, 2003, pp. 38–39.

As described in Exhibit 3–5, Global Strategy in Action, the direction and stability of political factors are a major consideration when evaluating the remote environment. Specifically, the article addresses the fact that the legal basis of piracy is political. Microsoft's performance in the Chinese market is greatly affected by the lack of legal enforcement of piracy and also by the policies of the Chinese government. Likewise, the government's actions in support of its competitor, Linux, have limited Microsoft's ability to penetrate the Chinese market.

Political activity also has a significant impact on two governmental functions that influence the remote environment of firms: the supplier function and the customer function.

Supplier Function

Government decisions regarding the accessibility of private businesses to government-owned natural resources and national stockpiles of agricultural products will affect profoundly the viability of the strategies of some firms.

Customer Function

Government demand for products and services can create, sustain, enhance, or eliminate many market opportunities. For example, in the same way that the Kennedy administration's emphasis on landing a man on the moon spawned a demand for thousands of new products; the Carter administration's emphasis on developing synthetic fuels created a demand for new skills, technologies, and products; the Reagan administration's strategic defense initiative (the "Star Wars" defense) sharply accelerated the development of laser technologies; Clinton's federal block grants to the states for welfare reform led to office rental and lease opportunities; and the war against terrorism during the Bush administration created enormous investment in aviation.

BusinessWeek One box that solves two problems. That was Microsoft's hope for Venus, a $240–$360 gadget running Windows CE software that turns Chinese TV sets into Internet appliances. Venus would solve two problems by making it both easier and cheaper for Chinese consumers to access the Web. Venus was the key to penetrating China, because it would make Windows nearly ubiquitous in living rooms from Shenzhen to Shanghai.

Fast-forward to late 2000: Venus seems more like one box containing two disasters. Of the three main Chinese companies that signed up to sell Venus boxes, two have pulled them from the market. Only Legend Computer is still selling the units in China—and it ships most of its supply to Southeast Asia. Why has Venus fizzled? Zhang blames both a lack of online content and the relatively high cost of Internet access. But others say Microsoft misjudged the willingness of Chinese to buy what is essentially low-rent technology. And with PCs selling for as little as $600, there isn't much reason to buy Venus.

The Venus project is not the only misfire in Microsoft's China strategy. Microsoft continues to battle software pirates, a poor image with Chinese authorities and consumers, and a growing threat from local rivals offering inexpensive Linux-based service. Microsoft won't release its China revenues, but analysts say they're probably under $100 million this year—less than the company makes in Hong Kong. "We are much smaller than we expected," says Microsoft General Manager Jack Gao.

Increasingly, Microsoft must contend with companies offering Linux, the open-source operating system. The threat is perhaps more political than anything else. Beijing likes to set one foreign company against another—as it has done with Boeing and Airbus. By playing up the potential of Linux, the government may be telling Microsoft that it had better play by its rules.

But Microsoft faces no greater competitor than the thieves who have elevated software piracy to a fine art. Last year, overall sales of computer hardware in China topped $18 billion. But software sales were a measly $2.1 billion. In other countries, the ratio is closer to even. Blame the shortfall on the pirates. Because of all the counterfeiting, Microsoft sold only 2 million licensed copies of its software in China during the year ending in June.

Chinese aren't ready to give up on counterfeit versions of Windows either. "We have a lot of users," says Jack Gao ruefully. "But we don't have a lot of customers." With Beijing intent on developing a local software industry, he says, cracking down on the pirates is in China's interest, too. That will take time. For now, a more humble Microsoft will have to keep trying to win friends in the emerging market it values most.

Source: An excerpt from B. Einhorn and A. Webb, "Microsoft Misfires in China," *BusinessWeek,* December 18, 2000.

Technological Factors

The fourth set of factors in the remote environment involves technological change. To avoid obsolescence and promote innovation, a firm must be aware of technological changes that might influence its industry. Creative technological adaptations can suggest possibilities for new products, for improvements in existing products, or in manufacturing and marketing techniques.

A technological breakthrough can have a sudden and dramatic effect on a firm's environment. It may spawn sophisticated new markets and products or significantly shorten the anticipated life of a manufacturing facility. Thus, all firms, and most particularly those in turbulent growth industries, must strive for an understanding both of the existing technological advances and the probable future advances that can affect their products and services. This quasi-science of attempting to foresee advancements and estimate their impact on an organization's operations is known as *technological forecasting*.

Technological forecasting can help protect and improve the profitability of firms in growing industries. It alerts strategic managers to both impending challenges and promising opportunities. As examples: (1) advances in xerography were a key to Xerox's success but caused major difficulties for carbon paper manufacturers, and (2) the perfection of transistors changed the nature of competition in the radio and television industry, helping such giants as RCA while seriously weakening smaller firms whose resource commitments required that they continue to base their products on vacuum tubes.

The key to beneficial forecasting of technological advancement lies in accurately predicting future technological capabilities and their probable impacts. A comprehensive analysis of the effect of technological change involves study of the expected impact of new technologies on the remote environment, on the competitive business situation, and on the business-society interface. In recent years, forecasting in the last area has warranted particular attention. For example, as a consequence of increased concern over the environment, firms must carefully investigate the probable effect of technological advances on quality-of-life factors, such as ecology and public safety.

For example, by combining the powers of Internet technologies with the capability of downloading music in a digital format, Bertelsmann has found a creative technological adaptation for distributing music online to millions of consumers whenever or wherever they might be. Bertelsmann, AOL Time Warner, and EMI formed a joint venture called Musicnet. The ease and wide availability of Internet technologies is increasing the marketplace for online e-tailers. Bertelsmann's response to the shifts in technological factors enables it to distribute music more rapidly through Musicnet to a growing consumer base.

Ecological Factors

The most prominent factor in the remote environment is often the reciprocal relationship between business and the ecology. The term *ecology* refers to the relationships among human beings and other living things and the air, soil, and water that support them. Threats to our life-supporting ecology caused principally by human activities in an industrial society are commonly referred to as *pollution*. Specific concerns include global warming, loss of habitat and biodiversity, as well as air, water, and land pollution.

The global climate has been changing for ages; however, it is now evident that humanity's activities are accelerating this tremendously. A change in atmospheric radiation, due in part to ozone depletion, causes global warming. Solar radiation that is normally absorbed into the atmosphere reaches the earth's surface, heating the soil, water, and air.

Another area of great importance is the loss of habitat and biodiversity. Ecologists agree that the extinction of important flora and fauna is occurring at a rapid rate and if this pace is continued, could constitute a global extinction on the scale of those found in fossil records. The earth's life forms depend on a well-functioning ecosystem. In addition, immeasurable advances in disease treatment can be attributed to research involving substances found in plants. As species become extinct, the life support system is irreparably harmed. The primary cause of extinction on this scale is a disturbance of natural habitat. For example, current data suggest that the earth's primary tropical forests, a prime source of oxygen and potential plant "cure," could be destroyed in only five decades.

Air pollution is created by dust particles and gaseous discharges that contaminate the air. Acid rain, or rain contaminated by sulfur dioxide, which can destroy aquatic and plant life, is believed to result from coal-burning factories in 70 percent of all cases. A health-threatening "thermal blanket" is created when the atmosphere traps carbon dioxide emitted from smokestacks in factories burning fossil fuels. This "greenhouse effect" can have disastrous consequences, making the climate unpredictable and raising temperatures.

Water pollution occurs principally when industrial toxic wastes are dumped or leak into the nation's waterways. Since fewer than 50 percent of all municipal sewer systems are in compliance with Environmental Protection Agency requirements for water safety, contaminated waters represent a substantial present threat to public welfare. Efforts to keep

BusinessWeek Outdoor clothing company Patagonia Inc. has worked hard to be one of the greenest businesses around. It was the first apparel maker to sell synthetic fleece sweaters and warm-up pants made from recycled soda bottles. Last year, it switched to organic cotton for shirts and trousers—and ate half of the 20 percent markup that organic production added to the garments' cost. Its glossy catalog, printed on recycled paper that is 50 percent chlorine-free, uses pictures of adventurers in wild places to promote environmental causes.

But Patagonia still has a troubled conscience. In a surprisingly public mea culpa, the company's fall catalog opens with a letter to customers that is a stark critique of Patagonia's reliance on waterproof coatings such as Gore-Tex, which contains chemical toxins, and bright dyes based on strip-mined metals. It is only by using such "dirty" manufacturing processes, the company confesses, that it can offer the "bombproof" outdoor gear and striking colors that customers love. As the letter laments: "The production of our clothing takes a significant toll on the earth."

Turns out it's not easy being green. Patagonia and a handful of other companies that have made protection of the environment a central tenet of their businesses are running into a new wave of polluting problems that require tougher trade-offs than those of the past. Whether it's Ben & Jerry's Home-made coping with massive amounts of high-fat dairy waste, Stonyfield Farm searching for an affordable way to convert to organic fruit for its yogurt, or Orvis, the fishing-gear maker, trying to build a new headquarters that won't threaten bear habitats, green pioneers are struggling for ways to balance *environmental principles* with profit goals.

None are backing off their commitment to the environment. Instead, the greenest companies are testing the limits of what can be done cleanly. "We want it all," Yvon Chouinard, Patagonia's president, told a meeting of the company's suppliers last year. "The best quality and the lowest environmental impact." But it's getting tougher to push the green envelope without compromising business goals. "Our whole system of commerce is not designed to be ecologically sustainable," says Matthew Arnold, director of Washington-based Management Institute for Environment & Business. "These guys are showing the limits of the system to respond."

And customers have made it clear that quality comes first, even if it means passing up the chance to have less impact on the environment. Patagonia surveys show that just 20 percent of its customers buy from the company because they believe in its environmental mission.

Source: Paul C. Judge in Boston, "It's Not Easy Being Green," *BusinessWeek,* November 24, 1997.

from contaminating the water supply are a major challenge to even the most conscientious of manufacturing firms. As described in Exhibit 3–6, Strategy in Action, highly reputed "green" supporter Patagonia has judged itself to be guilty of water pollution.

The Patagonia story is especially interesting because of the "green" fervor with which the company pursues its manufacturing objectives. It provides some details on the difficulties that Patagonia faces in its attempts to do what many ecological activists believe should be a national mandate for all corporations.

Land pollution is caused by the need to dispose of ever-increasing amounts of waste. Routine, everyday packaging is a major contributor to this problem. Land pollution is more dauntingly caused by the disposal of industrial toxic wastes in underground sites. With approximately 90 percent of the annual U.S. output of 500 million metric tons of hazardous industrial wastes being placed in underground dumps, it is evident that land pollution and its resulting endangerment of the ecology have become a major item on the political agenda.

As a major contributor to ecological pollution, business now is being held responsible for eliminating the toxic by-products of its current manufacturing processes and for cleaning up the environmental damage that it did previously. Increasingly, managers are being required by the government or are being expected by the public to incorporate ecological concerns into their decision making. For example, between 1975 and 1992, 3M cut its pollution in half by reformulating products, modifying processes, redesigning production equipment, and recycling by-products. Similarly, steel companies and public utilities have invested billions of dollars in costlier but cleaner-burning fuels and pollution control equipment. The automobile industry has been required to install expensive emission controls in cars. The gasoline industry has been forced to formulate new low-lead and no-lead products. And thousands of companies have found it necessary to direct their R&D resources into the search for ecologically superior products, such as Sears's phosphate-free laundry detergent and Pepsi-Cola's biodegradable plastic soft-drink bottle.

Environmental legislation impacts corporate strategies worldwide. Many companies fear the consequences of highly restrictive and costly environmental regulations. However, some manufacturers view these new controls as an opportunity, capturing markets with products that help customers satisfy their own regulatory standards. Other manufacturers contend that the costs of environmental spending inhibit the growth and productivity of their operations.

Despite cleanup efforts to date, the job of protecting the ecology will continue to be a top strategic priority—usually because corporate stockholders and executives choose it, increasingly because the public and the government require it. As evidenced by Exhibit 3–7, the government has made numerous interventions into the conduct of business for the purpose of bettering the ecology.

Benefits of Eco-Efficiency

Many of the world's largest corporations are realizing that business activities must no longer ignore environmental concerns. Every activity is linked to thousands of other transactions and their environmental impact; therefore, corporate environmental responsibility must be taken seriously and environmental policy must be implemented to ensure a comprehensive organizational strategy. Because of increases in government regulations and consumer environmental concerns, the implementation of environmental policy has become a point of competitive advantage. Therefore, the rational goal of business should be to limit its impact on the environment, thus ensuring long-run benefits to both the firm and society. To neglect this responsibility is to ensure the demise of both the firm and our ecosystem.

Stephen Schmidheiny, chairman of the Business Council for Sustainable Development, has coined the term *eco-efficiency* to describe corporations that produce more-useful goods and services while continuously reducing resource consumption and pollution. He cites a number of reasons for corporations to implement environmental policy: customers demand cleaner products, environmental regulations are increasingly more stringent, employees prefer to work for environmentally conscious firms, and financing is more readily available for eco-efficient firms. In addition, the government provides incentives for environmentally responsible companies.

Setting priorities, developing corporate standards, controlling property acquisition and use to preserve habitats, implementing energy-conserving activities, and redesigning products (e.g., minimizing packaging) are a number of measures the firm can implement to enhance an eco-efficient strategy. One of the most important steps a firm can take in achieving a competitive position with regard to the eco-efficient strategy is to fully capitalize on technological developments as a method of gaining efficiency.

Four key characteristics of eco-efficient corporations are:

- Eco-efficient firms are proactive, not reactive. Policy is initiated and promoted by business because it is in their own interests and the interest of their customers, not because it is imposed by one or more external forces.

- Eco-efficiency is designed in, not added on. This characteristic implies that the optimization of eco-efficiency requires every business effort regarding the product and process to internalize the strategy.

EXHIBIT 3–7
Federal Ecological Legislation

Centerpiece Legislation:

National Environmental Policy Act, 1969   Established Environmental Protection Agency; consolidated federal environmental activities under it. Established Council on Environmental Quality to advise president on environmental policy and to review environmental impact statements.

Air Pollution:

Clean Air Act, 1963   Authorized assistance to state and local governments in formulating control programs. Authorized limited federal action in correcting specific pollution problems.

Clean Air Act, Amendments (Motor Vehicle Air Pollution Control Act), 1965
Authorized federal standards for auto exhaust emission. Standards first set for 1968 models.

Air Quality Act, 1967   Authorized federal government to establish air quality control regions and to set maximum permissible pollution levels. Required states and localities to carry out approved control programs or else give way to federal controls.

Clean Air Act Amendments, 1970   Authorized EPA to establish nationwide air pollution standards and to limit the discharge of six principal pollutants into the lower atmosphere. Authorized citizens to take legal action to require EPA to implement its standards against undiscovered offenders.

Clean Air Act Amendments, 1977   Postponed auto emission requirements. Required use of scrubbers in new coal-fired power plants. Directed EPA to establish a system to prevent deterioration of air quality in clean areas.

Solid Waste Pollution:

Solid Waste Disposal Act, 1965   Authorized research and assistance to state and local control programs.

Resource Recovery Act, 1970   Subsidized construction of pilot recycling plants; authorized development of nationwide control programs.

Resource Conservation and Recovery Act, 1976   Directed EPA to regulate hazardous waste management, from generation through disposal.

Surface Mining and Reclamation Act, 1976   Controlled strip mining and restoration of reclaimed land.

Water Pollution:

Refuse Act, 1899   Prohibited dumping of debris into navigable waters without a permit. Extended by court decision to industrial discharges.

Federal Water Pollution Control Act, 1956   Authorized grants to states for water pollution control. Gave federal government limited authority to correct specific pollution problems.

Water Quality Act, 1965   Provided for adoption of water quality standards by states, subject to federal approval.

Water Quality Improvement Act, 1970   Provided for federal cleanup of oil spills. Strengthened federal authority over water pollution control.

Federal Water Pollution Control Act Amendments, 1972   Authorized EPA to set water quality and effluent standards; provided for enforcement and research.

Safe Drinking Water Act, 1974   Set standards for drinking water quality.

Clean Water Act, 1977   Ordered control of toxic pollutants by 1984 with best available technology economically feasible.

- Flexibility is imperative for eco-efficient strategy implementation. Continuous attention must be paid to technological innovation and market evolution.

- Eco-efficiency is encompassing, not insular. In the modern global business environment, efforts must cross not only industrial sectors but national and cultural boundaries as well.

ECONOMIC ENVIRONMENT

Level of economic development
Population
Gross national product
Per capita income
Literacy level
Social infrastructure
Natural resources
Climate
Membership in regional economic blocs (EU, NAFTA, LAFTA)
Monetary and fiscal policies
Wage and salary levels
Nature of competition
Currency convertibility
Inflation
Taxation system
Interest rates

LEGAL ENVIRONMENT

Legal tradition
Effectiveness of legal system
Treaties with foreign nations

Patent trademark laws
Laws affecting business firms

POLITICAL SYSTEM

Form of government
Political ideology
Stability of government
Strength of opposition parties and groups
Social unrest
Political strife and insurgency
Governmental attitude towards foreign firms
Foreign policy

CULTURAL ENVIRONMENT

Customs, norms, values, beliefs
Language
Attitudes
Motivations
Social institutions
Status symbols
Religious beliefs

Source: Arvind V. Phatak, *International Management* (Cincinnati, OH: South-Western College Publishing, 1997), p. 6.

INTERNATIONAL ENVIRONMENT

Monitoring the international environment, perhaps better thought of as the international dimension of the global environment, involves assessing each nondomestic market on the same factors that are used in a domestic assessment. While the importance of factors will differ, the same set of considerations can be used for each country. For example, Exhibit 3–8, Global Strategy in Action, lists economic, political, legal, and social factors used to assess international environments. However, there is one complication to this process, namely, that the interplay among international markets must be considered. For example, in recent years, conflicts in the Middle East have made collaborative business strategies among firms in traditionally antagonistic countries especially difficult to implement.

INDUSTRY ENVIRONMENT

Harvard professor Michael E. Porter propelled the concept of industry environment into the foreground of strategic thought and business planning. The cornerstone of his work first appeared in the *Harvard Business Review,* in which Porter explains the five forces that shape competition in an industry. His well-defined analytic framework helps strategic managers to link remote factors to their effects on a firm's operating environment.

With the special permission of Professor Porter and the *Harvard Business Review,* we present in this section of the chapter the major portion of his seminal article on the industry environment and its impact on strategic management.[1]

OVERVIEW

The nature and degree of competition in an industry hinge on five forces: the threat of new entrants, the bargaining power of customers, the bargaining power of suppliers, the threat of substitute products or services (where applicable), and the jockeying among current contestants. To establish a strategic agenda for dealing with these contending currents and to grow despite them, a company must understand how they work in its industry and how they affect the company in its particular situation. This chapter will detail how these forces operate and suggest ways of adjusting to them, and, where possible, of taking advantage of opportunities that they create.

HOW COMPETITIVE FORCES SHAPE STRATEGY

The essence of strategy formulation is coping with competition. Yet it is easy to view competition too narrowly and too pessimistically. While one sometimes hears executives complaining to the contrary, intense competition in an industry is neither coincidence nor bad luck.

Moreover, in the fight for market share, competition is not manifested only in the other players. Rather, competition in an industry is rooted in its underlying economics, and competitive forces exist that go well beyond the established combatants in a particular industry. Customers, suppliers, potential entrants, and substitute products are all competitors that may be more or less prominent or active depending on the industry.

The state of competition in an industry depends on five basic forces, which are diagrammed in Exhibit 3–9. The collective strength of these forces determines the ultimate profit potential of an industry. It ranges from intense in industries like tires, metal cans, and steel, where no company earns spectacular returns on investment, to mild in industries like oil-field services and equipment, soft drinks, and toiletries, where there is room for quite high returns.

In the economists' "perfectly competitive" industry, jockeying for position is unbridled and entry to the industry very easy. This kind of industry structure, of course, offers the worst prospect for long-run profitability. The weaker the forces collectively, however, the greater the opportunity for superior performance.

Whatever their collective strength, the corporate strategist's goal is to find a position in the industry where his or her company can best defend itself against these forces or can influence them in its favor. The collective strength of the forces may be painfully apparent to all the antagonists; but to cope with them, the strategist must delve below the surface and analyze the sources of competition. For example, what makes the industry vulnerable to entry? What determines the bargaining power of suppliers?

Knowledge of these underlying sources of competitive pressure provides the groundwork for a strategic agenda of action. They highlight the critical strengths and weaknesses of the company, animate the positioning of the company in its industry, clarify

---

[1] M. E. Porter, "How Competitive Forces Shape Strategy," *Harvard Business Review,* March–April 1979, pp. 137–45.

EXHIBIT 3–9 **Forces Driving Industry Competition**

Entry barriers

Economies of scale
Proprietary product differences
Brand identity
Switching costs
Capital requirements
Access to distribution
Absolute cost advantages
　Proprietary curve
　Access to necessary inputs
　Proprietary low-cost product design
Government policy
Expected retaliation

Rivalry Determinants

Industry growth
Fixed (or storage) costs/value added
Intermittent overcapacity
Product differences
Brand identity
Switching costs
Concentration and balance
Informational complexity
Diversity of competitors
Corporate stakes
Exit barriers

New Entrants

Threat of New Entrants

Industry Competitors

Intensity of Rivalry

Bargaining Power of Suppliers

Suppliers

Bargaining Power of Buyers

Buyers

Threat of Substitutes

Substitutes

Determinants of Supplier Power

Differentiation of Inputs
Switching costs of suppliers and firms
　in the industry
Presence of substitute inputs
Supplier concentration
Importance of volume to supplier
Cost relative to total purchases in
　the industry
Impact of inputs on cost or differentiation
Threat of forward integration relative to
　threat of backward integration by firms
　in the industry

Determinants of Substitution Threat

Relative price
　performance
　of substitutes
Switching costs
Buyer propensity
　to substitute

Determinants of Buyer Power

Bargaining Leverage	Price Sensitivity
Buyer concentration	Price/total purchases
versus firm concentration	Product differences
Buyer volume	Brand identity
Buyer switching costs	Impact on quality/
relative to firm	performance
switching costs	Buyer profits
Buyer information	Decision makers'
Ability to backward	incentives
integrate	
Substitute products	
Pull-through	

the areas where strategic changes may yield the greatest payoff, and highlight the places where industry trends promise to hold the greatest significance as either opportunities or threats.

Understanding these sources also proves to be of help in considering areas for diversification.

CONTENDING FORCES

The strongest competitive force or forces determine the profitability of an industry and so are of greatest importance in strategy formulation. For example, even a company with a strong position in an industry unthreatened by potential entrants will earn low returns if it faces a superior or a lower-cost substitute product—as the leading manufacturers of vacuum tubes and coffee percolators have learned to their sorrow. In such a situation, coping with the substitute product becomes the number one strategic priority.

Different forces take on prominence, of course, in shaping competition in each industry. In the oceangoing tanker industry, the key force is probably the buyers (the major oil companies), while in tires it is powerful OEM buyers coupled with tough competitors. In the steel industry the key forces are foreign competitors and substitute materials.

Every industry has an underlying structure, or a set of fundamental economic and technical characteristics, that gives rise to these competitive forces. The strategist, wanting to position his or her company to cope best with its industry environment or to influence that environment in the company's favor, must learn what makes the environment tick.

This view of competition pertains equally to industries dealing in services and to those selling products. To avoid monotony, I refer to both products and services as *products*. The same general principles apply to all types of business.

A few characteristics are critical to the strength of each competitive force. They will be discussed in this section.

Threat of Entry

New entrants to an industry bring new capacity, the desire to gain market share, and often substantial resources. Companies diversifying through acquisition into the industry from other markets often leverage their resources to cause a shake-up, as Philip Morris did with Miller beer.

The seriousness of the threat of entry depends on the barriers present and on the reaction from existing competitors that the entrant can expect. If barriers to entry are high and a newcomer can expect sharp retaliation from the entrenched competitors, he or she obviously will not pose a serious threat of entering.

There are six major sources of barriers to entry:

Economies of Scale

These economies deter entry by forcing the aspirant either to come in on a large scale or to accept a cost disadvantage. Scale economies in production, research, marketing, and service are probably the key barriers to entry in the mainframe computer industry, as Xerox and GE sadly discovered. Economies of scale also can act as hurdles in distribution, utilization of the sales force, financing, and nearly any other part of a business.

Product Differentiation

Brand identification creates a barrier by forcing entrants to spend heavily to overcome customer loyalty. Advertising, customer service, being first in the industry, and product differences are among the factors fostering brand identification. It is perhaps the most important entry barrier in soft drinks, over-the-counter drugs, cosmetics, investment banking, and public accounting. To create high fences around their business, brewers couple brand identification with economies of scale in production, distribution, and marketing.

Capital Requirements

The need to invest large financial resources in order to compete creates a barrier to entry, particularly if the capital is required for unrecoverable expenditures in up-front advertising or R&D. Capital is necessary not only for fixed facilities but also for customer credit, inventories, and absorbing start-up losses. While major corporations have the financial resources to invade almost any industry, the huge capital requirements in certain fields, such as computer manufacturing and mineral extraction, limit the pool of likely entrants.

Cost Disadvantages Independent of Size

Entrenched companies may have cost advantages not available to potential rivals, no matter what their size and attainable economies of scale. These advantages can stem from the effects of the learning curve (and of its first cousin, the experience curve), proprietary tech-

In recent years, the experience curve has become widely discussed as a key element of industry structure. According to this concept, unit costs in many manufacturing industries (some dogmatic adherents say in all manufacturing industries) as well as in some service industries decline with "experience," or a particular company's cumulative volume of production. (The experience curve, which encompasses many factors, is a broader concept than the better-known learning curve, which refers to the efficiency achieved over time by workers through much repetition.)

The causes of the decline in unit costs are a combination of elements, including economies of scale, the learning curve for labor, and capita-labor substitution. The cost decline creates a barrier to entry because new competitors with no "experience" face higher costs than established ones, particularly the producer with the largest market share, and have difficulty catching up with the entrenched competitors.

Adherents of the experience curve concept stress the importance of achieving market leadership to maximize this barrier to entry, and they recommend aggressive action to achieve it, such as price cutting in anticipation of falling costs in order to build volume. For the combatant that cannot achieve a healthy market share, the prescription is usually, "Get out."

Is the experience curve an entry barrier on which strategies should be built? The answer is: not in every industry. In fact, in some industries, building a strategy on the experience curve can be potentially disastrous. That costs decline with experience in some industries is not news to corporate executives. The significance of the experience curve for strategy depends on what factors are causing the decline.

A new entrant may well be more efficient than the more experienced competitors: if it has built the newest plant, it will face no disadvantage in having to catch up. The strategic prescription, "You must have the largest, most efficient plant," is a lot different from "You must produce the greatest cumulative output of the item to get your costs down."

Whether a drop in costs with cumulative (not absolute) volume erects an entry barrier also depends on the sources of the decline. If costs go down because of technical advances known generally in the industry or because of the development of improved equipment that can be copied or purchased from equipment suppliers, the experience curve is not an entry barrier at all—in fact, new or less-experienced competitors may actually enjoy a cost advantage over the leaders. Free of the legacy of heavy past investments, the newcomer or less-experienced competitor can purchase or copy the newest and lowest-cost equipment and technology.

If, however, experience can be kept proprietary, the leaders will maintain a cost advantage. But new entrants may require less experience to reduce their costs than the leaders needed. All this suggests that the experience curve can be a shaky entry barrier on which to build a strategy.

While space does not permit a complete treatment here, I want to mention a few other crucial elements in determining the appropriateness of a strategy built on the entry barrier provided by the experience curve:

The height of the barrier depends on how important costs are to competition compared with other areas like marketing, selling, and innovation.

The barrier can be nullified by product or process innovations leading to a substantially new technology and, thereby, creating an entirely new experience curve. New entrants can leapfrog the industry leaders and alight on the new experience curve, to which those leaders may be poorly positioned to jump.

If more than one strong company is building its strategy on the experience curve, the consequences can be nearly fatal. By the time only one rival is left pursuing such a strategy, industry growth may have stopped and the prospects of reaping the spoils of victory may long since have evaporated.

nology, access to the best raw materials sources, assets purchased at preinflation prices, government subsidies, or favorable locations. Sometimes cost advantages are enforceable legally, as they are through patents. (For analysis of the much-discussed experience curve as a barrier to entry, see Exhibit 3–10, Strategy in Action.)

Access to Distribution Channels

The new boy or girl on the block must, of course, secure distribution of his or her product or service. A new food product, for example, must displace others from the supermarket shelf via price breaks, promotions, intense selling efforts, or some other means. The more limited the wholesale or retail channels are and the more that existing competitors have these tied up, obviously the tougher that entry into the industry will be. Sometimes this barrier is so high that, to surmount it, a new contestant must create its own distribution channels, as Timex did in the watch industry in the 1950s.

Government Policy

The government can limit or even foreclose entry to industries, with such controls as license requirements and limits on access to raw materials. Regulated industries like trucking, liquor retailing, and freight forwarding are noticeable examples; more subtle government restrictions operate in fields like ski-area development and coal mining. The government also can play a major indirect role by affecting entry barriers through such controls as air and water pollution standards and safety regulations.

The potential rival's expectations about the reaction of existing competitors also will influence its decision on whether to enter. The company is likely to have second thoughts if incumbents have previously lashed out at new entrants, or if:

The incumbents possess substantial resources to fight back, including excess cash and unused borrowing power, productive capacity, or clout with distribution channels and customers.

The incumbents seem likely to cut prices because of a desire to keep market shares or because of industrywide excess capacity.

Industry growth is slow, affecting its ability to absorb the new arrival and probably causing the financial performance of all the parties involved to decline.

Powerful Suppliers

Suppliers can exert bargaining power on participants in an industry by raising prices or reducing the quality of purchased goods and services. Powerful suppliers, thereby, can squeeze profitability out of an industry unable to recover cost increases in its own prices. By raising their prices, soft-drink concentrate producers have contributed to the erosion of profitability of bottling companies because the bottlers—facing intense competition from powdered mixes, fruit drinks, and other beverages—have limited freedom to raise their prices accordingly.

The power of each important supplier (or buyer) group depends on a number of characteristics of its market situation and on the relative importance of its sales or purchases to the industry compared with its overall business.

A *supplier* group is powerful if:

1. It is dominated by a few companies and is more concentrated than the industry it sells.

2. Its product is unique or at least differentiated, or if it has built-up switching costs. Switching costs are fixed costs that buyers face in changing suppliers. These arise because, among other things, a buyer's product specifications tie it to particular suppliers, it has invested heavily in specialized ancillary equipment or in learning how to operate a supplier's equipment (as in computer software), or its production lines are connected to the supplier's manufacturing facilities (as in some manufacturing of beverage containers).

3. It is not obliged to contend with other products for sale to the industry. For instance, the competition between the steel companies and the aluminum companies to sell to the can industry checks the power of each supplier.

4. It poses a credible threat of integrating forward into the industry's business. This provides a check against the industry's ability to improve the terms on which it purchases.

5. The industry is not an important customer of the supplier group. If the industry is an important customer, suppliers' fortunes will be tied closely to the industry, and they will want to protect the industry through reasonable pricing and assistance in activities like R&D and lobbying.

Powerful Buyers

Customers likewise can force down prices, demand higher quality or more service, and play competitors off against each other—all at the expense of industry profits.

A *buyer* group is powerful if:

1. It is concentrated or purchases in large volumes. Large-volume buyers are particularly potent forces if heavy fixed costs characterize the industry—as they do in metal containers, corn refining, and bulk chemicals, for example—which raise the stakes to keep capacity filled.

2. The products it purchases from the industry are standard or undifferentiated. The buyers, sure that they always can find alternative suppliers, may play one company against another, as they do in aluminum extrusion.

3. The products it purchases from the industry form a component of its product and represent a significant fraction of its cost. The buyers are likely to shop for a favorable price and purchase selectively. Where the product sold by the industry in question is a small fraction of buyers' costs, buyers are usually much less price sensitive.

4. It earns low profits, which create great incentive to lower its purchasing costs. Highly profitable buyers, however, are generally less price sensitive (i.e., of course, if the item does not represent a large fraction of their costs).

5. The industry's product is unimportant to the quality of the buyers' products or services. Where the quality of the buyers' products is very much affected by the industry's product, buyers are generally less price sensitive. Industries in which this situation exists include oil-field equipment, where a malfunction can lead to large losses and enclosures for electronic medical and test instruments, where the quality of the enclosure can influence the user's impression about the quality of the equipment inside.

6. The industry's product does not save the buyer money. Where the industry's product or service can pay for itself many times over, the buyer is rarely price sensitive; rather, he or she is interested in quality. This is true in services like investment banking and public accounting, where errors in judgment can be costly and embarrassing, and in businesses like the mapping of oil wells, where an accurate survey can save thousands of dollars in drilling costs.

7. The buyers pose a credible threat of integrating backward to make the industry's product. The Big Three auto producers and major buyers of cars often have used the threat of self-manufacture as a bargaining lever. But sometimes an industry so engenders a threat to buyers that its members may integrate forward.

Most of these sources of buyer power can be attributed to consumers as a group as well as to industrial and commercial buyers; only a modification of the frame of reference is necessary. Consumers tend to be more price sensitive if they are purchasing products that are undifferentiated, expensive relative to their incomes, and of a sort where quality is not particularly important.

The buying power of retailers is determined by the same rules, with one important addition. Retailers can gain significant bargaining power over manufacturers when they can influence consumers' purchasing decisions, as they do in audio components, jewelry, appliances, sporting goods, and other goods.

Substitute Products

By placing a ceiling on the prices it can charge, substitute products or services limit the potential of an industry. Unless it can upgrade the quality of the product or differentiate it somehow (as via marketing), the industry will suffer in earnings and possibly in growth.

Manifestly, the more attractive the price-performance trade-off offered by substitute products, the firmer the lid placed on the industry's profit potential. Sugar producers confronted with the large-scale commercialization of high-fructose corn syrup, a sugar substitute, learned this lesson.

Substitutes not only limit profits in normal times but also reduce the bonanza an industry can reap in boom times. The producers of fiberglass insulation enjoyed unprecedented demand as a result of high energy costs and severe winter weather. But the industry's ability to raise prices was tempered by the plethora of insulation substitutes, including cellulose, rock wool, and Styrofoam. These substitutes are bound to become an even stronger force once the current round of plant additions by fiberglass insulation producers has boosted capacity enough to meet demand (and then some).

Substitute products that deserve the most attention strategically are those that (*a*) are subject to trends improving their price-performance trade-off with the industry's product or (*b*) are produced by industries earning high profits. Substitutes often come rapidly into play if some development increases competition in their industries and causes price reduction or performance improvement.

Jockeying for Position

Rivalry among existing competitors takes the familiar form of jockeying for position—using tactics like price competition, product introduction, and advertising slug fests. This type of intense rivalry is related to the presence of a number of factors:

1. Competitors are numerous or are roughly equal in size and power. In many U.S. industries in recent years, foreign contenders, of course, have become part of the competitive picture.

2. Industry growth is slow, precipitating fights for market share that involve expansion-minded members.

3. The product or service lacks differentiation or switching costs, which lock in buyers and protect one combatant from raids on its customers by another.

4. Fixed costs are high or the product is perishable, creating strong temptation to cut prices. Many basic materials businesses, like paper and aluminum, suffer from this problem when demand slackens.

5. Capacity normally is augmented in large increments. Such additions, as in the chlorine and vinyl chloride businesses, disrupt the industry's supply-demand balance and often lead to periods of overcapacity and price cutting.

6. Exit barriers are high. Exit barriers, like very specialized assets or management's loyalty to a particular business, keep companies competing even though they may be earning low or even negative returns on investment. Excess capacity remains functioning, and the profitability of the healthy competitors suffers as the sick ones hang on. If the entire industry suffers from overcapacity, it may seek government help—particularly if foreign competition is present.

7. The rivals are diverse in strategies, origins, and "personalities." They have different ideas about how to compete and continually run head-on into each other in the process.

As an industry matures, its growth rate changes, resulting in declining profits and (often) a shakeout. In the booming recreational vehicle industry of the early 1970s, nearly every producer did well; but slow growth since then has eliminated the high returns, except for the strongest members, not to mention many of the weaker companies. The same profit story has been played out in industry after industry—snowmobiles, aerosol packaging, and sports equipment are just a few examples.

An acquisition can introduce a very different personality to an industry, as has been the case with Black & Decker's takeover of McCullough, the producer of chain saws. Technological innovation can boost the level of fixed costs in the production process, as it did in the shift from batch to continuous-line photo finishing in the 1960s.

While a company must live with many of these factors—because they are built into the industry economics—it may have some latitude for improving matters through strategic shifts. For example, it may try to raise buyers' switching costs or increase product differentiation. A focus on selling efforts in the fastest-growing segments of the industry or on market areas with the lowest fixed costs can reduce the impact of industry rivalry. If it is feasible, a company can try to avoid confrontation with competitors having high exit barriers and, thus, can sidestep involvement in bitter price cutting.

INDUSTRY ANALYSIS AND COMPETITIVE ANALYSIS

Designing viable strategies for a firm requires a thorough understanding of the firm's industry and competition. The firm's executives need to address four questions: (1) What are the boundaries of the industry? (2) What is the structure of the industry? (3) Which firms are our competitors? (4) What are the major determinants of competition? The answers to these questions provide a basis for thinking about the appropriate strategies that are open to the firm.

Industry Boundaries

An industry is a collection of firms that offer similar products or services. By "similar products," we mean products that customers perceive to be substitutable for one another. Consider, for example, the brands of personal computers (PCs) that are now being marketed. The firms that produce these PCs, such as AT&T, IBM, Apple, and Compaq, form the nucleus of the microcomputer industry.

Suppose a firm competes in the microcomputer industry. Where do the boundaries of this industry begin and end? Does the industry include desktops? Laptops? These are the kinds of questions that executives face in defining industry boundaries.

Why is a definition of industry boundaries important? First, it helps executives determine the arena in which their firm is competing. A firm competing in the microcomputer industry participates in an environment very different from that of the broader electronics business. The microcomputer industry comprises several related product families, including personal computers, inexpensive computers for home use, and workstations. The unifying characteristic of these product families is the use of a central processing unit (CPU) in a microchip. On the other hand, the electronics industry is far more extensive; it includes computers, radios, supercomputers, superconductors, and many other products.

The microcomputer and electronics industries differ in their volume of sales, their scope (some would consider microcomputers a segment of the electronics industry), their rate of growth, and their competitive makeup. The dominant issues faced by the two industries also are different. Witness, for example, the raging public debate being waged on the future of the "high-definition TV." U.S. policy makers are attempting to ensure domestic control of that segment of the electronics industry. They also are considering ways to stimulate "cutting-edge" research in superconductivity. These efforts are likely to spur innovation and stimulate progress in the electronics industry.

Second, a definition of industry boundaries focuses attention on the firm's competitors. Defining industry boundaries enables the firm to identify its competitors and producers of substitute products. This is critically important to the firm's design of its competitive strategy.

Third, a definition of industry boundaries helps executives determine key factors for success. Survival in the premier segment of the microcomputer industry requires skills that are considerably different from those required in the lower end of the industry. Firms that compete in the premier segment need to be on the cutting edge of technological development and to provide extensive customer support and education. On the other hand, firms that compete in the lower end need to excel in imitating the products introduced by the premier segment, to focus on customer convenience, and to maintain operational efficiency that permits them to charge the lowest market price. Defining industry boundaries enables executives to ask these questions: Do we have the skills it takes to succeed here? If not, what must we do to develop these skills?

Finally, a definition of industry boundaries gives executives another basis on which to evaluate their firm's goals. Executives use that definition to forecast demand for their firm's products and services. Armed with that forecast, they can determine whether those goals are realistic.

Problems in Defining Industry Boundaries

Defining industry boundaries requires both caution and imagination. Caution is necessary because there are no precise rules for this task and because a poor definition will lead to poor planning. Imagination is necessary because industries are dynamic—in every industry, important changes are under way in such key factors as competition, technology, and consumer demand.

Defining industry boundaries is a very difficult task. The difficulty stems from three sources:

1. The evolution of industries over time creates new opportunities and threats. Compare the financial services industry as we know it today with that of the 1990s, and then try to imagine how different the industry will be in the year 2020.

2. Industrial evolution creates industries within industries. The electronics industry of the 1960s has been transformed into many "industries"—TV sets, transistor radios, micro- and macrocomputers, supercomputers, superconductors, and so on. Such transformation allows some firms to specialize and others to compete in different, related industries.

3. Industries are becoming global in scope. Consider the civilian aircraft manufacturing industry. For nearly three decades, U.S. firms dominated world production in that industry. But small and large competitors were challenging their dominance by 1990. At that time, Airbus Industries (a consortium of European firms) and Brazilian, Korean, and Japanese firms were actively competing in the industry.

Developing a Realistic Industry Definition

Given the difficulties outlined above, how do executives draw accurate boundaries for an industry? The starting point is a definition of the industry in global terms; that is, in terms that consider the industry's international components as well as its domestic components.

Having developed a preliminary concept of the industry (e.g., computers), executives flesh out its current components. This can be done by defining its product segments. Executives need to select the scope of their firm's potential market from among these related but distinct areas.

To understand the makeup of the industry, executives adopt a longitudinal perspective. They examine the emergence and evolution of product families. Why did these product families arise? How and why did they change? The answers to such questions provide executives with clues about the factors that drive competition in the industry.

Executives also examine the companies that offer different product families, the overlapping or distinctiveness of customer segments, and the rate of substitutability among product families.

To realistically define their industry, executives need to examine five issues:

1. Which part of the industry corresponds to our firm's goals?

2. What are the key ingredients of success in that part of the industry?

3. Does our firm have the skills needed to compete in that part of the industry? If not, can we build those skills?

4. Will the skills enable us to seize emerging opportunities and deal with future threats?

5. Is our definition of the industry flexible enough to allow necessary adjustments to our business concept as the industry grows?

Industry Structure

Defining an industry's boundaries is incomplete without an understanding of its structural attributes. *Structural attributes* are the enduring characteristics that give an industry its distinctive character. Consider the cable television and financial services industries. Both industries are competitive, and both are important for our quality of life. But these industries have very different requirements for success. To succeed in the cable television industry, firms require vertical integration, which helps them lower their operating costs and ensures their access to quality programs; technological innovation, to enlarge the scope of their services and deliver them in new ways; and extensive marketing, using appropriate segmentation techniques to locate potentially viable niches. To succeed in the financial services industry, firms need to meet very different requirements, among which are extensive orientation of customers and an extensive capital base.

How can we explain such variations among industries? The answer lies in examining the four variables that industry comprises: (1) concentration, (2) economies of scale, (3) product differentiation, and (4) barriers to entry.

Concentration

This variable refers to the extent to which industry sales are dominated by only a few firms. In a highly concentrated industry (i.e., an industry whose sales are dominated by a handful of companies), the intensity of competition declines over time. High concentration serves as a barrier to entry into an industry, because it enables the firms that hold large market shares to achieve significant economies of scale (e.g., savings in production costs due to increased production quantities) and, thus, to lower their prices to stymie attempts of new firms to enter the market.

The U.S. aircraft manufacturing industry is highly concentrated. Its concentration ratio—the percent of market share held by the top four firms in the industry—is 67 percent. Competition in the industry has not been vigorous. Firms in the industry have been able to deter entry through proprietary technologies and the formation of strategic alliances (e.g., joint ventures).

Economies of Scale

This variable refers to the savings that companies within an industry achieve due to increased volume. Simply put, when the volume of production increases, the long-range average cost of a unit produced will decline.

Economies of scale result from technological and nontechnological sources. The technological sources are a higher level of mechanization or automation and a greater up-to-dateness of plant and facilities. The nontechnological sources include better managerial coordination of production functions and processes, long-term contractual agreements with suppliers, and enhanced employee performance arising from specialization.

Economies of scale are an important determinant of the intensity of competition in an industry. Firms that enjoy such economies can charge lower prices than their competitors. They also can create barriers to entry by reducing their prices temporarily or permanently to deter new firms from entering the industry.

Product Differentiation

This variable refers to the extent to which customers perceive products or services offered by firms in the industry as different.

The differentiation of products can be real or perceived. The differentiation between Apple's Macintosh and IBM's PS/2 Personal Computer was a prime example of real differentiation. These products differed significantly in their technology and performance. Similarly, the civilian aircraft models produced by Boeing differed markedly from those produced by Airbus. The differences resulted from the use of different design principles and different construction technologies. For example, the newer Airbus planes followed the principle of "fly by wire," whereas Boeing planes utilized the laws of hydraulics. Thus, in Boeing planes, wings were activated by mechanical handling of different parts of the plane, whereas in the Airbus planes, this was done almost automatically.

Perceived differentiation results from the way in which firms position their products and from their success in persuading customers that their products differ significantly from competing products. Marketing strategies provide the vehicles through which this is done. Witness, for example, the extensive advertising campaigns of the automakers, each of which attempts to convey an image of distinctiveness. BMW ads highlight the excellent engineering of the BMW and its symbolic value as a sign of achievement. Some automakers focus on roominess and durability, which are desirable attributes for the family segment of the automobile market.

Real and perceived differentiations often intensify competition among existing firms. On the other hand, successful differentiation poses a competitive disadvantage for firms that attempt to enter an industry.

Barriers to Entry

As Porter noted earlier in this chapter, barriers to entry are the obstacles that a firm must overcome to enter an industry. The barriers can be tangible or intangible. The tangible barriers include capital requirements, technological know-how, resources, and the laws regulating entry into an industry. The intangible barriers include the reputation of existing firms, the loyalty of consumers to existing brands, and access to the managerial skills required for successful operation in an industry.

Entry barriers both increase and reflect the level of concentration, economies of scale, and product differentiation in an industry, and such increases make it more difficult for new firms to enter the industry. Therefore, when high barriers exist in an industry, competition in that industry declines over time.

In summary, analysis of concentration, economies of scale, product differentiation, and barriers to entry in an industry enable a firm's executives to understand the forces that determine competition in an industry and set the stage for identifying the firm's competitors and how they position themselves in the marketplace.

Industry regulations are a key element of industry structure and can constitute a significant barrier to entry for corporations. Escalating regulatory standards costs have been a serious concern for corporations for years. As legislative bodies continue their stronghold on corporate activities, businesses feel the impact on their bottom line. In-house counsel departments have been perhaps the most significant additions to corporate structure in the past decade. Legal fees have skyrocketed and managers have learned the hard way about the importance of adhering to regulatory standards.

Competitive Analysis

How to Identify Competitors

In identifying their firm's current and potential competitors, executives consider several important variables:

1. How do other firms define the scope of their market? The more similar the definitions of firms, the more likely the firms will view each other as competitors.

2. How similar are the benefits the customers derive from the products and services that other firms offer? The more similar the benefits of products or services, the higher the level of substitutability between them. High substitutability levels force firms to compete fiercely for customers.

3. How committed are other firms to the industry? Although this question may appear to be far removed from the identification of competitors, it is in fact one of the most important questions that competitive analysis must address, because it sheds light on the long-term intentions and goals. To size up the commitment of potential competitors to the industry, reliable intelligence data are needed. Such data may relate to potential resource commitments (e.g., planned facility expansions).

Common Mistakes in Identifying Competitors

Identifying competitors is a milestone in the development of strategy. But it is a process laden with uncertainty and risk, a process in which executives sometimes make costly mistakes. Examples of these mistakes are:

1. Overemphasizing current and known competitors while giving inadequate attention to potential entrants.

2. Overemphasizing large competitors while ignoring small competitors.

3. Overlooking potential international competitors.

4. Assuming that competitors will continue to behave in the same way they have behaved in the past.

5. Misreading signals that may indicate a shift in the focus of competitors or a refinement of their present strategies or tactics.

6. Overemphasizing competitors' financial resources, market position, and strategies while ignoring their intangible assets, such as a top-management team.

7. Assuming that all of the firms in the industry are subject to the same constraints or are open to the same opportunities.

8. Believing that the purpose of strategy is to outsmart the competition, rather than to satisfy customer needs and expectations.

OPERATING ENVIRONMENT

The operating environment, also called the *competitive* or *task environment,* comprises factors in the competitive situation that affect a firm's success in acquiring needed resources or in profitably marketing its goods and services. Among the most important of these factors are the firm's competitive position, the composition of its customers, its reputation among suppliers and creditors, and its ability to attract capable employees. The operating environment is typically much more subject to the firm's influence or control than the remote environment. Thus, firms can be much more proactive (as opposed to reactive) in dealing with the operating environment than in dealing with the remote environment.

Competitive Position

Assessing its competitive position improves a firm's chances of designing strategies that optimize its environmental opportunities. Development of competitor profiles enables a firm to more accurately forecast both its short- and long-term growth and its profit potentials. Although the exact criteria used in constructing a competitor's profile are largely determined by situational factors, the following criteria are often included:

1. Market share.

2. Breadth of product line.

3. Effectiveness of sales distribution.

4. Proprietary and key-account advantages.

5. Price competitiveness.

6. Advertising and promotion effectiveness.

7. Location and age of facility.

8. Capacity and productivity.

9. Experience.

10. Raw materials costs.

11. Financial position.

12. Relative product quality.

13. R&D advantages position.

14. Caliber of personnel.

15. General images.

16. Customer profile.

17. Patents and copyrights.

18. Union relations.

EXHIBIT 3–11
Competitor Profile

Key Success Factors	Weight	Rating*	Weighted Score
Market share	0.30	4	1.20
Price competitiveness	0.20	3	0.60
Facilities location	0.20	5	1.00
Raw materials costs	0.10	3	0.30
Caliber of personnel	0.20	1	0.20
	1.00†		3.30

*The rating scale suggested is as follows: very strong competitive position (5 points), strong (4), average (3), weak (2), very weak (1).
†The total of the weights must always equal 1.00.

19. Technological position.

20. Community reputation.

Once appropriate criteria have been selected, they are weighted to reflect their importance to a firm's success. Then the competitor being evaluated is rated on the criteria, the ratings are multiplied by the weight, and the weighted scores are summed to yield a numerical profile of the competitor, as shown in Exhibit 3–11.

This type of competitor profile is limited by the subjectivity of its criteria selection, weighting, and evaluation approaches. Nevertheless, the process of developing such profiles is of considerable help to a firm in defining its perception of its competitive position. Moreover, comparing the firm's profile with those of its competitors can aid its managers in identifying factors that might make the competitors vulnerable to the strategies the firm might choose to implement.

Customer Profiles

Perhaps the most vulnerable result of analyzing the operating environment is the understanding of a firm's customers that this provides. Developing a profile of a firm's present and prospective customers improves the ability of its managers to plan strategic operations, to anticipate changes in the size of markets, and to reallocate resources so as to support forecast shifts in demand patterns. The traditional approach to segmenting customers is based on customer profiles constructed from geographic, demographic, psychographic, and buyer behavior information.

Enterprising companies have quickly learned the importance of identifying target segments. In recent years, market research has increased tremendously as companies realize the benefits of demographic and psychographic segmentation. Research by American Express showed that competitors were stealing a prime segment of the company's business, affluent business travelers. AMEX's competing companies, including Visa and Mastercard, began offering high-spending business travelers frequent flier programs and other rewards including discounts on new cars. In turn, AMEX began to invest heavily in rewards programs, while also focusing on its strongest capabilities, assets, and competitive advantage. Unlike most credit card companies, AMEX cannot rely on charging interest to make money because its customers pay in full each month. Therefore, the company charges higher transaction fees to its merchants. In this way, increases in spending by AMEX customers who pay off their balances each month are more profitable to AMEX than to competing credit card companies.

Assessing consumer behavior is a key element in the process of satisfying your target market needs. Many firms lose market share as a result of assumptions made about target segments. Market research and industry surveys can help to reduce a firm's chances of relying on illusive assumptions. Firms most vulnerable are those that have had success with one or more products in the marketplace and as a result try to base consumer behavior on past data and trends.

Geographic

It is important to define the geographic area from which customers do or could come. Almost every product or service has some quality that makes it variably attractive to buyers from different locations. Obviously, a Wisconsin manufacturer of snow skis should think twice about investing in a wholesale distribution center in South Carolina. On the other hand, advertising in the *Milwaukee Sun-Times* could significantly expand the geographically defined customer market of a major Myrtle Beach hotel in South Carolina.

Demographic

Demographic variables most commonly are used to differentiate groups of present or potential customers. Demographic information (e.g., information on sex, age, marital status, income, and occupation) is comparatively easy to collect, quantify, and use in strategic forecasting, and such information is the minimum basis for a customer profile.

Psychographic

Personality and lifestyle variables often are better predictors of customer purchasing behavior than geographic or demographic variables. In such situations, a psychographic study is an important component of the customer profile. Advertising campaigns by soft-drink producers—Pepsi-Cola ("the Pepsi generation"), Coca-Cola ("the real thing"), and 7UP ("America's turning 7UP")—reflect strategic management's attention to the psychographic characteristics of their largest customer segment—physically active, group-oriented nonprofessionals.

Buyer Behavior

Buyer behavior data also can be a component of the customer profile. Such data are used to explain or predict some aspect of customer behavior with regard to a product or service. Information on buyer behavior (e.g., usage rate, benefits sought, and brand loyalty) can provide significant aid in the design of more accurate and profitable strategies. A second approach to identifying customer groups is by segmenting industrial markets, as shown in Exhibit 3–12.

Suppliers

Dependable relationships between a firm and its suppliers are essential to the firm's long-term survival and growth. A firm regularly relies on its suppliers for financial support, services, materials, and equipment. In addition, it occasionally is forced to make special requests for such favors as quick delivery, liberal credit terms, or broken-lot orders. Particularly at such times, it is essential for a firm to have had an ongoing relationship with its suppliers.

In the assessment of a firm's relationships with its suppliers, several factors, other than the strength of that relationship, should be considered. With regard to its competitive position with its suppliers, the firm should address the following questions:

Are the suppliers' prices competitive? Do the suppliers offer attractive quantity discounts?

How costly are their shipping charges? Are the suppliers competitive in terms of production standards?

EXHIBIT 3–12
Major Segmentation Variables for Industrial Markets

Source: Adapted from Thomas V. Bonoma and Benson P. Shapiro, *Segmenting the Industrial Market* (Lexington, MA: Lexington Books, 1983).

Demographic

Industry: Which industries that buy this product should we focus on?
Company size: What size companies should we focus on?
Location: What geographical areas should we focus on?

Operating Variables

Technology: What customer technologies should we focus on?
User-nonuser status: Should we focus on heavy, medium, light users or nonusers?
Customer capabilities: Should we focus on customers needing many services or few services?

Purchasing Approaches

Purchasing-function organization: Should we focus on companies with highly centralized or decentralized purchasing organizations?
Power structure: Should we focus on companies that are engineering dominated? Financially dominated? Other ways dominated?
Nature of existing relationships: Should we focus on companies with which we have strong existing relationships or simply go after the most desirable companies?
General purchase policies: Should we focus on companies that prefer leasing? Service contracts? Systems purchases? Sealed bidding?
Purchasing criteria: Should we focus on companies that are seeking quality? Service? Price?

Situational Factors

Urgency: Should we focus on companies that need quick and sudden delivery or service?
Specific application: Should we focus on certain applications of our product, rather than all applications?
Size of order: Should we focus on large or small orders?

Perfect Characteristics

Buyer-seller similarity: Should we focus on companies whose people and values are similar to ours?
Attitudes toward risk: Should we focus on risk-taking or risk-avoiding customers?
Loyalty: Should we focus on companies that show high loyalty to their suppliers?

In terms of deficiency rates, are the suppliers' abilities, reputations, and services competitive?

Are the suppliers reciprocally dependent on the firm?

Creditors

Because the quantity, quality, price, and accessibility of financial, human, and material resources are rarely ideal, assessment of suppliers and creditors is critical to an accurate evaluation of a firm's operating environment. With regard to its competitive position with its creditors, among the most important questions that the firm should address are the following:

Do the creditors fairly value and willingly accept the firm's stock as collateral?

Do the creditors perceive the firm as having an acceptable record of past payment?

A strong working capital position? Little or no leverage?

Are the creditors' loan terms compatible with the firm's profitability objectives?

Are the creditors able to extend the necessary lines of credit?

The answers to these and related questions help a firm forecast the availability of the resources it will need to implement and sustain its competitive strategies.

Human Resources: Nature of the Labor Market

A firm's ability to attract and hold capable employees is essential to its success. However, a firm's personnel recruitment and selection alternatives often are influenced by the nature of its operating environment. A firm's access to needed personnel is affected primarily by three factors: the firm's reputation as an employer, local employment rates, and the ready availability of people with the needed skills.

Reputation

A firm's reputation within its operating environment is a major element of its ability to satisfy its personnel needs. A firm is more likely to attract and retain valuable employees if it is seen as permanent in the community, competitive in its compensation package, and concerned with the welfare of its employees, and if it is respected for its product or service and appreciated for its overall contribution to the general welfare.

Employment Rates

The readily available supply of skilled and experienced personnel may vary considerably with the stage of a community's growth. A new manufacturing firm would find it far more difficult to obtain skilled employees in a vigorous industrialized community than in an economically depressed community in which similar firms had recently cut back operations.

Availability

The skills of some people are so specialized that relocation may be necessary to secure the jobs and the compensation that those skills commonly command. People with such skills include oil drillers, chefs, technical specialists, and industry executives. A firm that seeks to hire such a person is said to have broad labor market boundaries; that is, the geographic area within which the firm might reasonably expect to attract qualified candidates is quite large. On the other hand, people with more common skills are less likely to relocate from a considerable distance to achieve modest economic or career advancements. Thus, the labor market boundaries are fairly limited for such occupational groups as unskilled laborers, clerical personnel, and retail clerks.

EMPHASIS ON ENVIRONMENTAL FACTORS

This chapter has described the remote, industry, and operating environments as encompassing five components each. While that description is generally accurate, it may give the false impression that the components are easily identified, mutually exclusive, and equally applicable in all situations. In fact, the forces in the external environment are so dynamic and interactive that the impact of any single element cannot be wholly disassociated from the impact of other elements. For example, are increases in OPEC oil prices the result of economic, political, social, or technological changes? Or are a manufacturer's surprisingly good relations with suppliers a result of competitors', customers', or creditors' activities or of the supplier's own activities? The answer to both questions is probably that a number of forces in the external environment have combined to create the situation. Such is the case in most studies of the environment.

Strategic managers are frequently frustrated in their attempts to anticipate the environments changing influences. Different external elements affect different strategies at different times and with varying strengths. The only certainty is that the impact of the remote and operating environments will be uncertain until a strategy is implemented. This leads many managers, particularly in less-powerful or smaller firms to minimize long-term planning, which requires a commitment of resources. Instead, they favor allowing managers to adapt to new pressures from the environment. While such a decision has considerable merit for many firms, there is an associated trade-off, namely that absence of a strong resource and psychological commitment to a proactive strategy effectively bars a firm from assuming a leadership role in its competitive environment.

There is yet another difficulty in assessing the probable impact of remote, industry, and operating environments on the effectiveness of alternative strategies. Assessment of this kind involves collecting information that can be analyzed to disclose predictable effects. Except in rare instances, however, it is virtually impossible for any single firm to anticipate the consequences of a change in the environment; for example, what is the precise effect on alternative strategies of a 2 percent increase in the national inflation rate, a 1 percent decrease in statewide unemployment, or the entry of a new competitor in a regional market?

Still, assessing the potential impact of changes in the external environment offers a real advantage. It enables decision makers to narrow the range of the available options and to eliminate options that are clearly inconsistent with the forecast opportunities. Environmental assessment seldom identifies the best strategy, but it generally leads to the elimination of all but the most promising options.

Exhibit 3–13 provides a set of key strategic forecasting issues for each level of environmental assessment—remote, industry, and operating. While the issues that are presented are not inclusive of all of the questions that are important, they provide an excellent set of questions with which to begin. Appendix 3, Sources for Environmental Forecasting, is provided to help identify valuable sources of data and information from which answers and subsequent forecasts can be constructed. It lists governmental and private marketplace intelligence that can be used by a firm to gain a foothold in undertaking a strategic assessment of any level of the competitive environment.

Summary

A firm's external environment consists of three interrelated sets of factors that play a principal role in determining the opportunities, threats, and constraints that the firm faces. The remote environment comprises factors originating beyond, and usually irrespective of, any single firm's operating situation—economic, social, political, technological, and ecological factors. Factors that more directly influence a firm's prospects originate in the environment of its industry, including entry barriers, competitor rivalry, the availability of substitutes, and the bargaining power of buyers and suppliers. The operating environment comprises factors that influence a firm's immediate competitive situation—competitive position, customer profiles, suppliers, creditors, and the labor market. These three sets of factors provide many of the challenges that a particular firm faces in its attempts to attract or acquire needed resources and to profitably market its goods and services. Environmental assessment is more complicated for multinational corporations (MNCs) than for domestic firms because multinationals must evaluate several environments simultaneously.

Thus, the design of business strategies is based on the conviction that a firm able to anticipate future business conditions will improve its performance and profitability. Despite the uncertainty and dynamic nature of the business environment, an assessment process that narrows, even if it does not precisely define, future expectations is of substantial value to strategic managers.

EXHIBIT 3–13
Strategic Forecasting Issues

Key Issues in the Remote Environment Economy

What are the probable future directions of the economies in the firm's regional, national, and international market? What changes in economic growth, inflation, interest rates, capital availability, credit availability, and consumer purchasing power can be expected? What income differences can be expected between the wealthy upper middle class, the working class, and the underclass in various regions? What shifts in relative demand for different categories of goods and services can be expected?

Society and demographics

What effects will changes in social values and attitudes regarding childbearing, marriage, lifestyle, work, ethics, sex roles, racial equality, education, retirement, pollution, and energy have on the firm's development? What effects will population changes have on major social and political expectations—at home and abroad? What constraints or opportunities will develop? What pressure groups will increase in power?

Ecology

What natural or pollution-caused disasters threaten the firm's employees, customers, or facilities? How rigorously will existing environment legislature be enforced? What new federal, state, and local laws will affect the firm, and in what ways?

Politics

What changes in government policy can be expected with regard to industry cooperation, antitrust activities, foreign trade, taxation, depreciation, environmental protection, deregulation, defense, foreign trade barriers, and other important parameters? What success will a new administration have in achieving its stated goals? What effect will that success have on the firm? Will specific international climates be hostile or favorable? Is there a tendency toward instability, corruption, or violence? What is the level of political risk in each foreign market? What other political or legal constraints or supports can be expected in international business (e.g., trade barriers, equity requirements, nationalism, patent protection)?

Technology

What is the current state of the art? How will it change? What pertinent new products or services are likely to become technically feasible in the foreseeable future? What future impact can be expected from technological breakthroughs in related product areas? How will those breakthroughs interface with the other remote considerations, such as economic issues, social values, public safety, regulations, and court interpretations?

Key Issues in the Industry Environment

New entrants

Will new technologies or market demands enable competitors to minimize the impact of traditional economies of scale in the industry? Will consumers accept our claims of product or service differentiation? Will potential new entrants be able to match the capital requirements that currently exist? How permanent are the cost disadvantages (independent of size) in our industry? Will conditions change so that all competitors have equal access to marketing channels? Is government policy toward competition in our industry likely to change?

Bargaining power of suppliers

How stable are the size and composition of our supplier group? Are any suppliers likely to attempt forward integration into our business level? How dependent will our suppliers be in the future? Are substitute suppliers likely to become available? Could we become our own supplier?

Exhibit 3–13
(continued)

Substitute products or services

Are new substitutes likely? Will they be price competitive? Could we fight off substitutes by price competition? By advertising to sharpen product differentiation? What actions could we take to reduce the potential for having alternative products seen as legitimate substitutes?

Bargaining power of buyers

Can we break free of overcommitment to a few large buyers? How would our buyers react to attempts by us to differentiate our products? What possibilities exist that our buyers might vertically integrate backward? Should we consider forward integration? How can we make the value of our components greater in the products of our buyers?

Rivalry among existing firms

Are major competitors likely to undo the established balance of power in our industry? Is growth in our industry slowing such that competition will become fiercer? What excess capacity exists in our industry? How capable are our major competitors of withstanding intensified price competition? How unique are the objectives and strategies of our major competitors?

Key Issues in the Operating Environment

Competitive position

What strategic moves are expected by existing rivals—inside and outside the United States? What competitive advantage is necessary in selected foreign markets? What will be our competitors' priorities and ability to change? Is the behavior of our competitors predictable?

Customer profiles and market changes

What will our customer regard as needed value? Is marketing research done, or do managers talk to each other to discover what the customer wants? Which customer needs are not being met by existing products? Why? Are R&D activities under way to develop means for fulfilling these needs? What is the status of these activities? What marketing and distribution channels should we use? What do demographic and population changes portend for the size and sales potential of our market? What new market segments or products might develop as a result of these changes? What will be the buying power of our customer groups?

Supplier relationships

What is the likelihood of major cost increases because of dwindling supplies of a needed natural resource? Will sources of supply, especially of energy, be reliable? Are there reasons to expect major changes in the cost or availability of inputs as a result of money, people, or subassembly problems? Which suppliers can be expected to respond to emergency requests?

Creditors

What lines of credit are available to help finance our growth? What changes may occur in our creditworthiness? Are creditors likely to feel comfortable with our strategic plan and performance? What is the stock market likely to feel about our firm? What flexibility would our creditors show toward us during a downturn? Do we have sufficient cash reserves to protect our creditors and our credit rating?

Labor market

Are potential employees with desired skills and abilities available in the geographic areas in which our facilities are located? Are colleges and vocational-technical schools that can aid in meeting our training needs located near our plant or store sites? Are labor relations in our industry conducive to meeting our expanding needs for employees? Are workers whose skills we need shifting toward or away from the geographic location of our facilities?

Questions for Discussion

1. Briefly describe two important recent changes in the remote environment of U.S. business in each of the following areas:
   a. Economic.
   b. Social.
   c. Political.
   d. Technological.
   e. Ecological.

2. Describe two major environmental changes that you expect to have a major impact on the whole-sale food industry in the next 10 years.

3. Develop a competitor profile for your college and for the college geographically closest to yours. Next, prepare a brief strategic plan to improve the competitive position of the weaker of the two colleges.

4. Assume the invention of a competitively priced synthetic fuel that could supply 25 percent of U.S. energy needs within 20 years. In what major ways might this change the external environment of U.S. business?

5. With your instructor's help, identify a local firm that has enjoyed great growth in recent years. To what degree and in what ways do you think this firm's success resulted from taking advantage of favorable conditions in its remote, industry, and operating environments?

6. Choose a specific industry and, relying solely on your impressions, evaluate the impact of the five forces that drive competition in that industry.

7. Choose an industry in which you would like to compete. Use the five-forces method of analysis to explain why you find that industry attractive.

8. Many firms neglect industry analysis. When does this hurt them? When does it not?

9. The model below depicts industry analysis as a funnel that focuses on remote-factor analysis to better understand the impact of factors in the operating environment. Do you find this model satisfactory? If not, how would you improve it?

10. Who in a firm should be responsible for industry analysis? Assume that the firm does not have a strategic planning department.

Chapter 3 Discussion Case

McDonald's Hamburger Hell

BusinessWeek

1 Richard Steinig remembers beaming as if he had won the lottery. There he was, all of 27 when he became a junior partner with a McDonald's Corp. (MCD) franchisee in 1973, just a year after starting as a $115-a-week manager trainee in Miami. "It was an incredible feeling," says Steinig. His two stores each generated $80,000 in annual sales, and he pocketed more than 15 percent of that as profit. Not bad at a time when the minimum wage was still under $2 an hour and a McDonald's hamburger and fries set you back less than a dollar, even with a regular Coke.

2 Fast-forward 30 years. Franchise owner Steinig's four restaurants average annual sales of $1.56 million, but his face is creased with worry. Instead of living the American Dream, Steinig says he's barely scraping by. Sales haven't budged since 1999, but costs keep rising. So when McDonald's began advertising its $1 menu featuring the Big N' Tasty burger, Steinig rebelled. The popular item cost him $1.07 to make—so he sells it for $2.25 unless a customer asks for the $1 promotion price. No wonder profit margins are no more than half of what they were when he started out. "We have become our worst enemy," Steinig says.

3 Welcome to Hamburger Hell. For decades, McDonald's was a juggernaut. It gave millions of Americans their first jobs while changing the way a nation ate. It rose from a single outlet in a nondescript Chicago suburb to become an American icon. But today, McDonald's is a reeling giant that teeters from one mess to another.

4 Consider the events of just the past three months: On Dec. 5, after watching McDonald's stock slide 60 percent in three years, the board ousted chief executive Jack M. Greenberg, 60. His tenure was marked by the introduction of 40 new menu items, none of which caught on big, and the purchase of a handful of nonburger chains, none of which were rolled out widely enough to make much difference. Indeed, his critics say that by trying so many different things—and executing them poorly—Greenberg let the burger business deteriorate. Consumer surveys show that service and quality now lag far behind those of rivals.

5 The company's solution was to bring back retired vice-chairman James R. Cantalupo, 59, who had overseen McDonald's successful international expansion in the '80s and '90s. Unfortunately, seven weeks later, the company reported the first quarterly loss in its 47-year history. Then it revealed that January sales at outlets open at least a year skidded 2.4 percent, after sliding 2.1 percent in 2002.

6 Can Cantalupo reverse the long slide at McDonald's? When he and his new team lay out their plan to analysts in early April, they are expected to concentrate on getting the basics of service and quality right, in part by reinstituting a tough "up or out" grading system that will kick out underperforming franchises. "We have to rebuild the foundation. It's fruitless to add growth if the foundation is weak," says Cantalupo. He gives himself 18 months to do that with help from Australian-bred chief operating officer, Charles Bell, 42, whom Cantalupo has designated his successor, and Mats Lederhausen, a 39-year-old Swede in charge of global strategy.

7 But the problems at McDonald's go way beyond cleaning up restaurants and freshening the menu. The chain is being squeezed by long-term trends that threaten to leave it marginalized. It faces a rapidly fragmenting market, where America's recent immigrants have made once-exotic foods like sushi and burritos everyday options, and quick meals of all sorts can be found in supermarkets, convenience stores, even vending machines. One of the fastest-growing restaurant categories is the "fast-casual" segment—those places with slightly more expensive menus, such as Cosi, a sandwich shop, or Quizno's, a gourmet sub sandwich chain, where customers find the food healthier and better-tasting. As Lederhausen succinctly puts it: "We are clearly living through the death of the mass market."

8 If so, it may well mark the end of McDonald's long run as a growth company. Cantalupo seemed to acknowledge as much when he slashed sales growth estimates in the near term to only 2 percent annually, down from 15 percent. No one at Oak Brook (Ill.) headquarters blames the strong dollar or mad cow disease anymore for the company's problems—a big change from the Greenberg era. Perhaps most telling is that the chain plans to add only 250 new outlets in the United States this year, 40 percent fewer than in 2002. Sales in Europe rose only 1 percent, and the chain this year will add only 200 units to the 6,070 it has there—30 percent fewer new openings than last year. Meanwhile, it is closing 176 of its 2,800 stores in Japan because of the economic doldrums there.

9   Up until a few years ago, franchises clamored to jump on board. But last year, in an exodus that was unheard of in Mickey D's heyday, 126 franchises left the system, with 68, representing 169 restaurants, forced out for poor performance. The others left seeking greener pastures. The company buys back franchises if they cannot be sold, so forcing out a franchisee is not cheap. McDonald's took a pretax charge of $292 million last quarter to close 719 restaurants—200 in 2002 and the rest expected this year.

10   For their part, investors have already accepted that the growth days are over. Those who remain will happily settle for steady dividends. Last Oct. 22, when McDonald's announced a 1 cent hike in its annual dividend, to 23 1/2 cents, its stock rose 9 percent, to $18.95—even though the company said third-quarter profits would decline. It was the biggest one-day gain for McDonald's on the New York Stock Exchange in at least two years. Today, though, the stock is near an eight-year low of $13.50, off 48 percent in the past year. One of the few money managers willing to give McDonald's a chance, Wendell L. Perkins at Johnson Asset Management in Racine, Wis., says: "McDonald's needs to understand that it is a different company from 10 years ago and increase its dividend to return some of that cash flow to shareholders to reflect its mature market position."

11   The company has the cash to boost shareholder payouts. It recently canceled an expensive stock buyback program. Cantalupo won praise on Wall Street for killing an expensive revamp of the company's technology that would have cost $1 billion. But if increasing the dividend would make Wall Street happy, it would raise problems with its 2,461 franchises. That would be essentially an admission that McDonald's is giving up on the kind of growth for which they signed up.

12   Already, franchises who see the chain as stuck in a rut are jumping ship to faster-growing rivals. Paul Saber, a McDonald's franchisee for 17 years, sold his 14 restaurants back to the company in 2000 when he realized that eating habits were shifting away from McDonald's burgers to fresher, better-tasting food. So he moved to rival Panera Bread Co., a fast-growing national bakery cafe chain. "The McDonald's-type fast food isn't relevant to today's consumer," says Saber, who will open 15 Paneras in San Diego.

13   In the past, owner-operators were McDonald's evangelists. Prospective franchises were once so eager to get into the two-year training program that they would wait in line for hours when applications were handed out at the chain's offices around the country.

But there aren't any lines today, and many existing franchises feel alienated. They have seen their margins dip to a paltry 4 percent, from 15 percent at the peak. Richard Adams, a former franchisee and a food consultant, claims that as many as 20 franchises are currently leaving McDonald's every month. Why? "Because it's so hard to survive these days," he says.

14   One of the biggest sore points for franchises is the top-down manner in which Greenberg and other past CEOs attempted to fix pricing and menu problems. Many owner-operators still grumble over the $18,000 to $100,000 they had to spend in the late 1990s to install company-mandated "Made for You" kitchen upgrades in each restaurant. The new kitchens were supposed to speed up orders and accommodate new menu items. But in the end, they actually slowed service. Reggie Webb, who operates 11 McDonald's restaurants in Los Angeles, says his sales have dipped by an average of $50,000 at each of his outlets over the past 15 years. "From my perspective, I am working harder than ever and making less than I ever had on an average-store basis," says Webb. He'll have to open his wallet again if McDonald's includes his units in the next 200 restaurants it selects for refurbishing. Franchises pay 70 percent of that $150,000 cost.

15   Franchises also beef about McDonald's addiction to discounting. When McDonald's cut prices in a 1997 price war, sales fell over the next four months. The lesson should have been obvious. "Pulling hard on the price lever is dangerous. It risks cheapening the brand," says Sam Rovit, a partner at Chicago consultant Bain & Co. Yet Cantalupo is sticking with the $1 menu program introduced last year. "We like to wear out our competitors with our price," he says. Burger King and Wendy's International Inc. admit that the tactic is squeezing their sales. But in the five months since its debut, the $1 menu has done nothing to improve McDonald's results.

16   As a last resort, McDonald's is getting rid of the weakest franchises. Continuous growth can no longer bail out underperformers, so Cantalupo is enforcing a "tough love" program that Greenberg reinstated last year after the company gave it up in 1990. Owners that flunk the rating and inspection system will get a chance to clean up their act. But if they don't improve, they'll be booted.

17   The decline in McDonald's once-vaunted service and quality can be traced to its expansion of the 1990s, when headquarters stopped grading franchises for cleanliness, speed, and service. Training declined as restaurants fought for workers in a tight

labor market. That led to a falloff in kitchen and counter skills—according to a 2002 survey by Columbus (Ohio) market researcher Global Growth Group, McDonald's came in third in average service time behind Wendy's and sandwich shop Chick-fil-A Inc. Wendy's took an average 127 seconds to place and fill an order, versus 151 seconds at Chick-fil-A and 163 at McDonald's. That may not seem like much, but Greenberg has said that saving six seconds at a drive-through brings a 1 percent increase in sales.

18   Trouble is, it's tough to sell franchisees on a new quality gauge at the same time the company is asking them to do everything from offering cheap burgers to shouldering renovation costs. Franchising works best when a market is expanding and owners can be rewarded for meeting incentives. In the past, franchises who beat McDonald's national sales average were typically rewarded with the chance to open or buy more stores. The largest franchisees now operate upwards of 50 stores. But with falling sales, those incentives don't cut it. "Any company today has to be very vigilant about their business model and willing to break it, even if it's successful, to make sure they stay on top of the changing trends," says Alan Feldman, CEO of Midas Inc., who was COO for domestic operations at McDonald's until January, 2002. "You can't just go on cloning your business into the future."

19   By the late 1990s, it was clear that the system was losing traction. New menu items like the low-fat McLean Deluxe and Arch Deluxe burgers, meant to appeal to adults, bombed. Nonburger offerings did no better, often because of poor planning. Consultant Michael Seid, who manages a franchise consulting firm in West Hartford, Conn., points out that McDonald's offered a pizza that didn't fit through the drive-through window and salad shakers that were packed so tightly that dressing couldn't flow through them. By 1998, McDonald's posted its first-ever decline in annual earnings and then-CEO Michael R. Quinlan was out, replaced by Greenberg, a 16-year McDonald's veteran.

20   Greenberg won points for braking the chain's runaway U.S. expansion. He also broadened its portfolio, acquiring Chipotle Mexican Grill and Boston Market Corp. But he was unable to focus on the new ventures while also improving quality, getting the new kitchens rolled out, and developing new menu items. Says Los Angeles franchisee Webb: "We would have been better off trying fewer things and making them work." Greenberg was unable to reverse skidding sales and profits, and after last year's disastrous

fourth quarter, he offered his resignation at the Dec. 5 board meeting. There were no angry words from directors. But there were no objections, either.

21   Insiders say Cantalupo, who had retired only a year earlier, was the only candidate seriously considered to take over, despite shareholder sentiment for an outsider. The board felt that it needed someone who knew the company and could move quickly. Cantalupo has chosen to work with younger McDonald's executives, whom he feels will bring energy and fresh ideas to the table. Bell, formerly president of McDonald's Europe, became a store manager in his native Australia at 19 and rose through the ranks. There, he launched a coffeehouse concept called McCafe, which is now being introduced around the globe. He later achieved success in France, where he abandoned McDonald's cookie-cutter orange-and-yellow stores for individualized ones that offer local fare like the ham-and-cheese Croque McDo.

22   The second top executive Cantalupo has recruited is a bona fide outsider—at least by company standards. Lederhausen holds an MBA from the Stockholm School of Economics and worked with Boston Consulting Group Inc. for two years. However, he jokes that he grew up in a french-fry vat because his father introduced McDonald's to Sweden in 1973. Lederhausen is in charge of growth and menu development.

23   Getting the recipe right will be tougher now that consumers have tasted better burgers. While McDonald's says it may start toasting its buns longer to get the flavor right, rivals go even further. Industry experts point to 160-store In-N-Out, a profitable California burger chain. Its burgers are grilled when ordered—no heat lamps to warm up precooked food. Today, In-N-Out is rated No. 1 by fast-food consumers tracked by consultant Sandelman & Associates Inc. in San Diego. "The burger category has great strength," adds David C. Novak, chairman and CEO of Yum! Brands Inc. (YUM), parent of KFC and Taco Bell. "That's America's food. People love hamburgers."

24   McDonald's best hope to recapture that love might be to turn to its most innovative franchisees. Take Irwin Kruger in New York, who recently opened a 17,000-square-foot showcase unit in Times Square with video monitors showing movie trailers, brick walls, theatrical lighting—and strong profits. "We're slated to have sales of over $5 million this year and profits exceeding 10 percent," says Kruger. Rejuvenated marketing would help, too: McDonald's called its top ad agencies

together in February to draw up a plan that would go beyond the ubiquitous Disney movie tie-ins.

25   It will take nothing short of a marketing miracle, though, to return McDonald's to its youthful vigor. "They are at a critical juncture and what they do today will shape whether they just fade away or recapture some of the magic and greatness again," says Robert S. Goldin, executive vice-president at food consultant Technomic Inc. As McDonald's settles into middle age, Cantalupo and his team may have to settle for stable and reliable.

Source: Pallavi Gogoi and Michael Arndt, "McDonald's Hamburger Hell," *BusinessWeek Online,* March 3, 2003.

Appendix 3

Sources for Environmental Forecasting

REMOTE AND INDUSTRY ENVIRONMENTS

A. Economic considerations:
1. *Predicasts* (most complete and up-to-date review of forecasts).
2. National Bureau of Economic Research.
3. *Handbook of Basic Economic Statistics.*
4. *Statistical Abstract of the United States* (also includes industrial, social, and political statistics).
5. Publications by Department of Commerce agencies:
    a. Office of Business Economics (e.g., *Survey of Business*).
    b. Bureau of Economic Analysis (e.g., *Business Conditions Digest*).
    c. Bureau of the Census (e.g., *Survey of Manufacturers* and various reports on population, housing, and industries).
    d. Business and Defense Services Administration (e.g., *United States Industrial Outlook*).
6. Securities and Exchange Commission (various quarterly reports on plant and equipment, financial reports, working capital of corporations).
7. The Conference Board.
8. *Survey of Buying Power.*
9. *Marketing Economic Guide.*
10. *Industrial Arts Index.*
11. U.S. and national chambers of commerce.
12. American Manufacturers Association.
13. *Federal Reserve Bulletin.*
14. *Economic Indicators,* annual report.
15. *Kiplinger Newsletter.*
16. International economic sources:
    a. *Worldcasts.*
    b. Master key index for business international publications.
    c. Department of Commerce.
        (1) Overseas business reports.
        (2) Industry and Trade Administration.
        (3) Bureau of the Census—*Guide to Foreign Trade Statistics.*
17. *Business Periodicals Index.*
B. Social considerations:
1. Public opinion polls.
2. Surveys such as *Social Indicators and Social Reporting,* the annals of the American Academy of Political and Social Sciences.
3. Current controls: Social and behavioral sciences.
4. Abstract services and indexes for articles in sociological, psychological, and political journals.
5. Indexes for *The Wall Street Journal, New York Times,* and other newspapers.

6. Bureau of the Census reports on population, housing, manufacturers, selected services, construction, retail trade, wholesale trade, and enterprise statistics.
7. Various reports from such groups as the Brookings Institution and the Ford Foundation.
8. World Bank Atlas (population growth and GNP data).
9. World Bank–World Development Report.

C. Political considerations:
1. *Public Affairs Information Services Bulletin.*
2. CIS Index (Congressional Information Index).
3. Business periodicals.
4. Funk & Scott (regulations by product breakdown).
5. Weekly compilation of presidential documents.
6. *Monthly Catalog of Government Publications.*
7. *Federal Register* (daily announcements of pending regulations).
8. *Code of Federal Regulations* (final listing of regulations).
9. Business International Master Key Index (regulations, tariffs).
10. Various state publications.
11. Various information services (Bureau of National Affairs, Commerce Clearing House, Prentice Hall).

D. Technological considerations:
1. *Applied Science and Technology Index.*
2. *Statistical Abstract of the United States.*
3. Scientific and Technical Information Service.
4. University reports, congressional reports.
5. Department of Defense and military purchasing publishers.
6. Trade journals and industrial reports.
7. Industry contacts, professional meetings.
8. Computer-assisted information searches.
9. National Science Foundation annual report.
10. *Research and Development Directory* patent records.

E. Industry considerations:
1. *Concentration Ratios in Manufacturing* (Bureau of the Census).
2. *Input-Output Survey* (productivity ratios).
3. *Monthly Labor Review* (productivity ratios).
4. *Quarterly Failure Report* (Dun & Bradstreet).
5. *Federal Reserve Bulletin* (capacity utilization).
6. *Report on Industrial Concentration and Product Diversification in the 1,000 Largest Manufacturing Companies* (Federal Trade Commission).
7. Industry trade publications.
8. Bureau of Economic Analysis, Department of Commerce (specialization ratios).

INDUSTRY AND OPERATING ENVIRONMENTS

A. Competition and supplier considerations:
1. Target Group Index.
2. U.S. Industrial Outlook.
3. Robert Morris annual statement studies.
4. Troy, Leo Almanac of Business & Industrial Financial Ratios.
5. Census of Enterprise Statistics.

6. Securities and Exchange Commission (10-K reports).
7. Annual reports of specific companies.
8. *Fortune 500 Directory, The Wall Street Journal, Barron's, Forbes, Dun's Review.*
9. Investment services and directories: Moody's, Dun & Bradstreet, Standard & Poor's, Starch Marketing, Funk & Scott Index.
10. Trade association surveys.
11. Industry surveys.
12. Market research surveys.
13. *Country Business Patterns.*
14. *Country and City Data Book.*
15. Industry contacts, professional meetings, salespeople.
16. *NFIB Quarterly Economic Report for Small Business.*

B. Customer profile:

1. *Statistical Abstract of the United States,* first source of statistics.
2. *Statistical Sources* by Paul Wasserman (a subject guide to data—both domestic and international).
3. *American Statistics Index* (Congressional Information Service Guide to statistical publications of U.S. government—monthly).
4. Office to the Department of Commerce:
   a. Bureau of the Census reports on population, housing, and industries.
   b. *U.S. Census of Manufacturers* (statistics by industry, area, and products).
   c. *Survey of Current Business* (analysis of business trends, especially February and July issues).
5. Market research studies (*A Basic Bibliography on Market Review,* compiled by Robert Ferber et al., American Marketing Association).
6. *Current Sources of Marketing Information: A Bibliography of Primary Marketing Data* by Gunther & Goldstein, AMA.
7. *Guide to Consumer Markets,* The Conference Board (provides statistical information with demographic, social, and economic data—annual).
8. *Survey of Buying Power.*
9. *Predicasts* (abstracts of publishing forecasts of all industries, detailed products, and end-use data).
10. *Predicasts Basebook* (historical data from 1960 to present, covering subjects ranging from population and GNP to specific products and services; series are coded by Standard Industrial Classifications).
11. *Market Guide* (individual market surveys of over 1,500 U.S. and Canadian cities; includes population, location, trade areas, banks, principal industries, colleges and universities, department and chain stores, newspapers, retail outlets, and sales).
12. *Country and City Data Book* (includes bank deposits, birth and death rates, business firms, education, employment, income of families, manufacturers, population, savings, and wholesale and retail trade).
13. *Yearbook of International Trade Statistics* (UN).
14. *Yearbook of National Accounts Statistics* (UN).
15. *Statistical Yearbook* (UN—covers population, national income, agricultural and industrial production, energy, external trade, and transport).
16. *Statistics of (Continents): Sources for Market Research* (includes separate books on Africa, America, Europe).

C. Key natural resources:
1. *Minerals Yearbook, Geological Survey* (Bureau of Mines, Department of the Interior).
2. *Agricultural Abstract* (Department of Agriculture).
3. Statistics of electric utilities and gas pipeline companies (Federal Power Commission).
4. Publications of various institutions: American Petroleum Institute, Atomic Energy Commission, Coal Mining Institute of America, American Steel Institute, and Brookings Institution.

Chapter **Four**

The Global Environment: Strategic Considerations for Multinational Firms

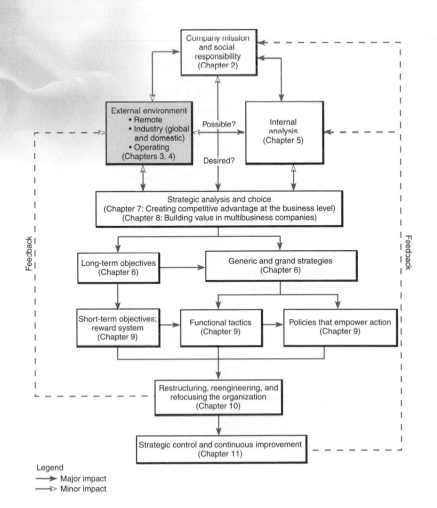

Company mission
and social
responsibility
(Chapter 2)

External environment
• Remote
• Industry (global
and domestic)
• Operating
(Chapters 3, 4)

Possible?

Internal
analysis
(Chapter 5)

Desired?

Strategic analysis and choice
(Chapter 7: Creating competitive advantage at the business level)
(Chapter 8: Building value in multibusiness companies)

Long-term objectives
(Chapter 6)

Generic and grand strategies
(Chapter 6)

Short-term objectives;
reward system
(Chapter 9)

Functional tactics
(Chapter 9)

Policies that empower action
(Chapter 9)

Restructuring, reengineering, and
refocusing the organization
(Chapter 10)

Strategic control and continuous improvement
(Chapter 11)

Feedback

Feedback

Legend
→ Major impact
⇢ Minor impact

Special complications confront a firm involved in the globalization of its operations. *Globalization* refers to the strategy of approaching worldwide markets with standardized products. Such markets are most commonly created by end consumers that prefer lower-priced, standardized products over higher-priced, customized products and by global corporations that use their worldwide operations to compete in local markets. Global corporations headquartered in one country with subsidiaries in other countries experience difficulties that are understandably associated with operating in several distinctly different competitive arenas.

Awareness of the strategic opportunities faced by global corporations and of the threats posed to them is important to planners in almost every domestic U.S. industry. Among corporations headquartered in the United States that receive more than 50 percent of their annual profits from foreign operations are Citicorp, Coca-Cola, Exxon, Gillette, IBM, Otis Elevator, and Texas Instruments. In fact, the 100 largest U.S. globals earn an average of 37 percent of their operating profits abroad. Equally impressive is the impact of foreign-based globals that operate in the United States. Their "direct foreign investment" in the United States now exceeds $90 billion, with Japanese, German, and French firms leading the way.

Understanding the myriad and sometimes subtle nuances of competing in global markets or against global corporations is rapidly becoming a required competence of strategic managers. For example, experts in the advertising community contend that Korean companies only recently recognized the importance of making their names known abroad. In the 1980s, there was very little advertising of Korean brands, and the country had very few recognizable brands abroad. Korean companies tended to emphasize sales and production more than marketing. The opening of the Korean advertising market in the 1990s indicated that Korean firms had acquired a new appreciation for the strategic competencies that are needed to compete globally and created an influx of global firms like Saatchi and Saatchi, J. W. Thompson, Ogilvy and Mather, and Bozell. Many of them established joint ventures or partnerships with Korean agencies. An excellent example of such a strategic approach to globalization by Philip Morris's KGFI is described in Exhibit 4–1, Global Strategy in Action. The opportunities for corporate growth often seem brightest in global markets. Exhibit 4–2 reports on the growth in national shares of the world's outputs and growth in national economies to the year 2020. While the United States had a commanding lead in the size of its economy in 1992, it was caught by China in the year 2000 and will be far surpassed by 2020. Overall, in less than 20 years, rich industrial countries will be overshadowed by developing countries in their produced share of the world's output.

Because the growth in the number of global firms continues to overshadow other changes in the competitive environment, this section will focus on the nature, outlook, and operations of global corporations.

DEVELOPMENT OF A GLOBAL CORPORATION

The evolution of a global corporation often entails progressively involved strategy levels. The first level, which often entails export-import activity, has minimal effect on the existing management orientation or on existing product lines. The second level, which can involve foreign licensing and technology transfer, requires little change in management or operation. The third level typically is characterized by direct investment in overseas operations, including manufacturing plants. This level requires large capital outlays and the development of global management skills. Although the domestic operations of a firm at this level continue to dominate its policy, such a firm is commonly categorized as a true multinational corporation (MNC). The

Outside of its core Western markets, Kraft General Foods International's (KGFI) food products have a growing presence in one of the most dynamic business environments in the world—the Asia-Pacific region. Its operations there are expanding rapidly, often aided by links with local manufacturers and distributors.

Japan and Korea are important examples. In both countries, local alliances can be crucial to market entry and success. Realizing this fact in the early 1970s, General Foods established joint ventures in both Japan and Korea. These joint ventures, combined with Kraft General Foods International's (KGFI) stand alone operations, generate more than $1 billion in revenues. In the aggregate, their combined food operations in Japan and Korea are larger than many Fortune 500 companies.

Whereas soluble coffee accounts for just over 25 percent of the coffee consumed in U.S. homes, it fills over 70 percent of the cups consumed in the homes of convenience-minded Japan. Additionally, Japan is the origin of a unique form of packaged coffee—liquid—and a unique channel of distribution—vending machines. Japanese consumers have purchased packaged liquid coffee for years, and it amounts to a $5 billion category. Some 2 million vending machines dispense 9 billion cans of liquid coffee annually—an average of 75 cans per person.

Japan offers a culturally unique distribution channel for coffee products—the gift-set market. Many Japanese exchange specially packaged food or beverage assortments at least twice a year to commemorate holidays as well as special personal or business occasions. The gift-set business has helped Maxim products reinforce their quality image; it also will be a launching pad and support vehicle for Carte Noire coffees.

Outside the Ajinomoto General Foods joint venture, KGFI is developing a freestanding food business under the name Kraft Japan. It is building a cheese business with imported Philadelphia Brand cream cheese, the leading cream cheese in the Tokyo metropolitan market, as well as locally manufactured and licensed Kraft Milk Farm cheese slices. The cheese market is expected to grow approximately 5 percent per year. This is a rapid growth rate for a large food category. In addition to cheese, KGFI also imports Oscar Mayer prepared meats and Jacobs Suchard chocolates.

KGFI's joint venture in Korea, Doug Suh Foods Corporation, is one of the top 10 food companies in the country. Doug Suh manufactures coffees and cereals and has its own distribution network. One of Doug Suh's other businesses in Korea, Post Cereals, is also a strong number two, with a 42 percent category share.

Korea's $400 million coffee market is the fastest-growing major coffee market in the world, expanding at an average annual rate of 14 percent. Growing with the market, Maxim and Maxwell soluble coffees, in both traditional "agglomerate" and freeze-dried forms, account for more than 70 percent of the country's soluble coffee sales. The strength of these brands also brings the company a strong number one position in coffee mix, a mixture of soluble coffee, creamer, and sugar. In addition, its Frima brand leads the market in the nondairy creamer segment.

Beyond Japan and Korea, KGFI is targeting many other countries for geographic expansion. In Indonesia, for instance, KGFI has established a rapidly growing cheese business through a licensee and introduced other KGFI products. In Taiwan, the joint venture company, PremierFoods Corporation, holds a 34 percent share of the soluble coffee market and is aggressively developing a Kraft cheese and Jacobs Suchard import business. KGFI Philippines, a wholly owned subsidiary, has a leading position in the cheese and powdered soft-drink markets in its country. In the People's Republic of China, the company produces and markets Maxwell House coffees and Tang powdered soft drinks through two successful and rapidly growing joint ventures.

---

most involved strategy level is characterized by a substantial increase in foreign investment, with foreign assets comprising a significant portion of total assets. At this level, the firm begins to emerge as a global enterprise with global approaches to production, sales, finance, and control.

Some firms downplay their global nature (to never appear distracted from their domestic operations), whereas others highlight it. For example, General Electric's formal statement of mission and business philosophy includes the following commitment:

> To carry out a diversified, growing, and profitable worldwide manufacturing business in
> electrical apparatus, appliances, and supplies, and in related materials, products, systems,
> and services for industry, commerce, agriculture, government, the community, and the home.

A similar global orientation is evident at IBM, which operates in 125 countries, conducts business in 30 languages and more than 100 currencies, and has 23 major manufacturing facilities in 14 countries.

EXHIBIT 4–2   **Projected Economic Growth**

Source: World Bank, *Global Economic Prospects and the Developing Countries.*

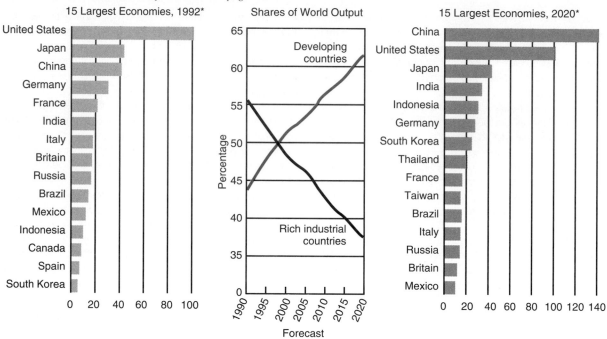

* United States = 100;
Other countries = percentage of U.S.'s GDP

WHY FIRMS GLOBALIZE

The technological advantage once enjoyed by the United States has declined dramatically during the past 30 years. In the late 1950s, over 80 percent of the world's major technological innovations were first introduced in the United States. By 1990, the figure had declined to less than 50 percent. In contrast, France is making impressive advances in electric traction, nuclear power, and aviation. Germany leads in chemicals and pharmaceuticals, precision and heavy machinery, heavy electrical goods, metallurgy, and surface transport equipment. Japan leads in optics, solid-state physics, engineering, chemistry, and process metallurgy. Eastern Europe and the former Soviet Union, the so-called COMECON (Council for Mutual Economic Assistance) countries, generate 30 percent of annual worldwide patent applications. However, the United States has regained some of its lost technological advantage. Through globalization, U.S. firms often can reap benefits from industries and technologies developed abroad. Even a relatively small service firm that possesses a distinct competitive advantage can capitalize on large overseas operations.

As discussed in Exhibit 4–3, Global Strategy in Action, Diebold Inc. once operated solely in the United States, selling ATM machines, bank vaults, and security systems to financial institutions. However, with the U.S. market saturated, Diebold needed to expand internationally to continue its growth. The firm's globalization efforts led to both the development of new technologies in emerging markets and opportunistic entry into entirely new industries that significantly improved Diebold's sales.

In many situations, global development makes sense as a competitive weapon. Direct penetration of foreign markets can drain vital cash flows from a foreign competitor's domestic operations. The resulting lost opportunities, reduced income, and limited production can impair the competitor's ability to invade U.S. markets. A case in point is IBM's move to

BusinessWeek For most of its 142-year history, Diebold Inc. never worried much about global strategy. As a premier name in bank vaults—and then automated teller machines and security systems—the company focused on U.S. financial institutions, content to let partners hawk what they could abroad. But in 1998, with the U.S. ATM market saturated, Diebold decided it had to be more ambitious. Since then, Diebold has taken off. Sales of security devices, software, and services surged 38 percent in 2000, to $1.74 billion, led by a 146 percent jump in overseas sales, to $729 million. The momentum continued in 2001. International sales have gone from 22 percent of the total to 40 percent in just two years, and should soon overtake North America.

The ventures overseas have taken Diebold into whole new directions. In China, where it now has half of the fast-growing ATM market, it also is helping the giant International Commercial Bank of China design its self-service branches and data network. In Brazil, Diebold owns and manages a network of 5,000 ATMs—as well as surveillance cameras—for a state-owned bank. In Colombia, it's handling bill collection for a power utility. In Taiwan, where most consumers still prefer to pay bills in cash, Diebold is about to introduce ATMs that both accept and count stacks of up to 100 currency notes and weed out counterfeits. And in South Africa, its ATMs for the techno-illiterate scan fingerprints for identification.

Diebold found it could serve much broader needs in emerging markets than in the United States. Across Latin America, consumers use banks to pay everything from utility bills to taxes. So Diebold ATMs handle these services, 24 hours a day. In Argentina, where filing taxes is a nightmare, citizens now can fill out returns on a PC, store them on a disk, and have their disks scanned on one of 5,000 special Diebold terminals, most of them at banks. Diebold also is landing new contracts across Latin America to manage bank ATM networks.

The $240 million acquisition of Brazil's Procom also gave Diebold an entree into an entirely new line: It landed a huge contract to supply electronic voting machines for Brazil's presidential election last year. Now Diebold is getting into the voting-machine business in the United States, where it expects demand to surge in the wake of the controversial Presidential contest in Florida. Globalization, it seems, can even unveil new opportunities at home.

Source: Excerpt from M. Arndt, P. Engardio, and J. Goodman, "Diebold," *BusinessWeek* (3746), p. 138, August 27, 2001.

---

establish a position of strength in the Japanese mainframe computer industry before two key competitors, Fiyitsue and Hitachi, could dominate it. Once IBM had achieved a substantial share of the Japanese market, it worked to deny its Japanese competitors the vital cash and production experience they needed to invade the U.S. market.

Firms that operate principally in the domestic environment have an important decision to make with regard to their globalization: Should they act before being forced to do so by competitive pressures or after? Should they: (1) be proactive by entering global markets in advance of other firms and thereby enjoy the first-mover advantages often accruing to risk-taker firms that introduce new products or services; or (2) be reactive by taking the more conservative approach and following other companies into global markets once customer demand has been proven and the high costs of new-product or new-service introductions have been absorbed by competitors? Although the answers to these questions are determined by the specifics of the company and the context, the issues raised in Exhibit 4–4 are helpful to strategic decision makers faced with the dilemma.

Strategic Orientations of Global Firms

Multinational corporations typically display one of four orientations toward their overseas activities. They have a certain set of beliefs about how the management of foreign operations should be handled. A company with an *ethnocentric orientation* believes that the values and priorities of the parent organization should guide the strategic decision making of all its operations. If a corporation has a *polycentric orientation,* then the culture of the country in which a strategy is to be implemented is allowed to dominate the decision-making process. In contrast, a *regiocentric orientation* exists when the parent attempts to blend its own predispositions with those of the region under consideration, thereby arriving at a region-sensitive compromise. Finally, a corporation with a *geocentric orientation* adopts a global systems approach to strategic decision making, thereby emphasizing global integration.

EXHIBIT 4–4
Reasons for Going Global

Source: Betty Jane Punnett and David A. Ricks, *International Business* (Boston: PWS-Kent, 1992), pp. 249–50.

Proactive	
Advantage/Opportunity	**Explanation of Action**
Additional resources	Various inputs—including natural resources, technologies, skilled personnel, and materials—may be obtained more readily outside the home country.
Lowered costs	Various costs—including labor, materials, transportation, and financing—may be lower outside the home country.
Incentives	Various incentives may be available from the host government or the home government to encourage foreign investment in specific locations.
New, expanded markets	New and different markets may be available outside the home country; excess resources—including management, skills, machinery, and money—can be utilized in foreign locations.
Exploitation of firm-specific advantages	Technologies, brands, and recognized names can all provide opportunities in foreign locations.
Taxes	Differing corporate tax rates and tax systems in different locations provide opportunities for companies to maximize their after-tax worldwide profits.
Economies of scale	National markets may be too small to support efficient production, while sales from several combined allow for larger-scale production.
Synergy	Operations in more than one national environment provide opportunities to combine benefits from one location with another, which is impossible without both of them.
Power and prestige	The image of being international may increase a company's power and prestige and improve its domestic sales and relations with various stakeholder groups.
Protect home market through offense in competitor's home	A strong offense in a competitor's market can put pressure on the competitor that results in a pull-back from foreign activities to protect itself at home.

Reactive	
Outside Occurrence	**Explanation of Reaction**
Trade barriers	Tariffs, quotas, buy-local policies, and other restrictive trade practices can make exports to foreign markets less attractive; local operations in foreign locations thus become attractive.
International customers	If a company's customer base becomes international, and the company wants to continue to serve it, then local operations in foreign locations may be necessary.
International competition	If a company's competitors become international, and the company wants to remain competitive, foreign operations may be necessary.
Regulations	Regulations and restrictions imposed by the home government may increase the cost of operating at home; it may be possible to avoid these costs by establishing foreign operations.
Chance	Chance occurrence results in a company deciding to enter foreign locations.

EXHIBIT 4–5   Orientation of a Global Firm

	Orientation of the Firm			
	Ethnocentric	**Polycentric**	**Regiocentric**	**Geocentric**
Mission	Profitability (viability)	Public acceptance (legitimacy)	Both profitability and public acceptance (viability and legitimacy)	Same as regiocentric
Governance	Top-down	Bottom-up (each subsidiary decides on local objectives)	Mutually negotiated between region and its subsidiaries	Mutually negotiated at all levels of the corporation
Strategy	Global integration	National responsiveness	Regional integration and national responsiveness	Global integration and national responsiveness
Structure	Hierarchical product divisions	Hierarchical area divisions, with autonomous national units	Product and regional organization tied through a matrix	A network of organizations (including some stakeholders and competitor organizations)
Culture	Home country	Host country	Regional	Global
Technology	Mass production	Batch production	Flexible manufacturing	Flexible manufacturing
Marketing	Product development determined primarily by the needs of home-country customers	Local product development based on local needs	Standardize within region but not across regions	Global product, with local variations
Finance	Repatriation of profits to home country	Retention of profits in host country	Redistribution within region	Redistribution globally
Personnel practices	People of home country developed for key positions everywhere in the world	People of local nationality developed for key positions in their own country	Regional people developed for key positions anywhere in the region	Best people everywhere in the world developed for key positions everywhere in the world

Source: Adapted from Balaji S. Chakravarthy and Howard V. Perlmutter, "Strategic Planning for a Global Business," *Columbia Journal of World Business,* Summer 1985, pp. 5–6. Copyright 1985, Columbia Journal of World Business. Used with permission.

American firms often adopt a regiocentric orientation for pursing strategies in Europe. U.S. e-tailers have attempted to blend their own corporate structure and expertise with that of European corporations. For example, Amazon has been able to leverage its experience in the United States while developing regionally and culturally specific strategies overseas. By purchasing European franchises that have had regional success, E*Trade is pursuing a foreign strategy in which they insert their European units into corporate structure. This strategy requires the combination and use of culturally different management styles and involves major challenges for upper management.

Exhibit 4–5 shows the impacts of each of the four orientations on key activities of the firm. It is clear from the figure that the strategic orientation of a global firm plays a major role in determining the locus of control and corporate priorities of the firm's decision makers.

AT THE START OF GLOBALIZATION

External and internal assessments are conducted before a firm enters global markets. For example, Japanese investors conduct extensive assessments and analyses before selecting a U.S. site for a Japanese-owned firm. They prefer states with strong markets, low unionization rates, and low taxes. In addition, Japanese manufacturing plants prefer counties characterized by manufacturing conglomeration; low unemployment and poverty rates; and concentrations of educated, productive workers.

External assessment involves careful examination of critical features of the global environment, particular attention being paid to the status of the host nations in such areas as economic progress, political control, and nationalism. Expansion of industrial facilities, favorable balances of payments, and improvements in technological capabilities over the past decade are gauges of the host nation's economic progress. Political status can be gauged by the host nation's power in and impact on global affairs.

Internal assessment involves identification of the basic strengths of a firm's operations. These strengths are particularly important in global operations, because they are often the characteristics of a firm that the host nation values most and, thus, offer significant bargaining leverage. The firm's resource strengths and global capabilities must be analyzed. The resources that should be analyzed include, in particular, technical and managerial skills, capital, labor, and raw materials. The global capabilities that should be analyzed include the firm's product delivery and financial management systems.

A firm that gives serious consideration to internal and external assessment is Business International Corporation, which recommends that seven broad categories of factors be considered. As shown in Exhibit 4–6, Global Strategy in Action, these categories include economic, political, geographic, labor, tax, capital source, and business factors.

COMPLEXITY OF THE GLOBAL ENVIRONMENT

By 2003, Coke was finally achieving a goal that it had set a decade earlier when it went to India. That goal was to take the market away from Pepsi and local beverage companies. However, when it arrived, Coke found that the Indian market was extremely complex and smaller than it had estimated. As described in Exhibit 4–7, Global Strategy-in-Action, Coke also encountered cultural problems, in part because the chief of Coke India was an expatriate. The key to overcoming this cultural problem was promoting an Indian to operations chief. Coke also changed its marketing strategy by pushing their "Thums Up" products, a local brand owned by Coke. Then, they began to focus their efforts on creating new products for rural areas and lowering the prices of their existing products to increase sales. Once Coke had new products in the market, they focused on a new advertising campaign to better relate to Indian consumers.

Coke's experience highlights the fact that global strategic planning is more complex than purely domestic planning. There are at least five factors that contribute to this increase in complexity:

1. Globals face multiple political, economic, legal, social, and cultural environments as well as various rates of changes within each of them.

2. Interactions between the national and foreign environments are complex, because of national sovereignty issues and widely differing economic and social conditions.

3. Geographic separation, cultural and national differences, and variations in business practices all tend to make communication and control efforts between headquarters and the overseas affiliates difficult.

4. Globals face extreme competition, because of differences in industry structures.

The following considerations were drawn from an 88-point checklist developed by Business International Corporation.

Economic factors:

1. Size of GNP and projected rate of growth.

2. Foreign exchange position.

3. Size of market for the firm's products; rate of growth.

Political factors:

4. Form and stability of government.

5. Attitude toward private and foreign investment by government, customers, and competition.

6. Degree of antiforeign discrimination.

Geographic factors:

7. Proximity of site to export markets.

8. Availability of local raw materials.

9. Availability of power, water, gas.

Labor factors:

10. Availability of managerial, technical, and office personnel able to speak the language of the parent company.

11. Degree of skill and discipline at all levels.

12. Degree and nature of labor voice in management.

Tax factors:

13. Tax-rate trends.

14. Joint tax treaties with home country and others.

15. Availability of tariff protection.

Capital source factors:

16. Cost of local borrowing.

17. Modern banking systems.

18. Government credit aids to new businesses.

Business factors:

19. State of marketing and distribution system.

20. Normal profit margins in the firm's industry.

21. Competitive situation in the firm's industry: do cartels exist?

5. Globals are restricted in their selection of competitive strategies by various regional blocs and economic integrations, such as the European Economic Community, the European Free Trade Area, and the Latin American Free Trade Area.

CONTROL PROBLEMS OF THE GLOBAL FIRM

An inherent complicating factor for many global firms is that their financial policies typically are designed to further the goals of the parent company and pay minimal attention to the goals of the host countries. This built-in bias creates conflict between the different parts of the global firm, between the whole firm and its home and host countries, and between the home country and host country themselves. The conflict is accentuated by the use of various schemes to shift earnings from one country to another in order to avoid taxes, minimize risk, or achieve other objectives.

Moreover, different financial environments make normal standards of company behavior concerning the disposition of earnings, sources of finance, and the structure of capital more problematic. Thus, it becomes increasingly difficult to measure the performance of international divisions.

In addition, important differences in measurement and control systems often exist. Fundamental to the concept of planning is a well-conceived, future-oriented approach to decision making that is based on accepted procedures and methods of analysis. Consistent

BusinessWeek Despite having billion-plus consumers, a growing middle class, and a hot climate, India had not been a successful market for the beverage giant Coca-Cola Co. Though various Coke products possessed more than half the market, the flagship brand, Coca Cola, remained a distant third, with an estimated market share of 16.5 percent, far behind arch rival Pepsi-Cola's 23.5 percent. Almost as embarrassing, number two was Thums Up, a sweeter local cola that Coke acquired in 1993, then proceeded to neglect.

In 1993—15 years after being thrown out by India's socialist government—Coke stormed back into the country with big plans to wrest control from Pepsi and the local beverage marketers that had risen up in its absence. Instead, the company spent years on the defensive after overestimating the size of the market, misreading consumers, and battling with the government. And Coke India has been hurt by a revolving door in the executive suite. In 10 years, it has had five expatriate heads.

Coke planned to sell 49 percent of its Indian bottler, Hindustan Coca-Cola Beverages, for $41 million. The sale was not the domestic stock listing that some in New Delhi had sought. Instead, the shares will be sold in a private placement with institutional investors and employees. But it put to rest a thorny issue that had chilled relations with the government, which wanted Indians to have a substantial ownership stake in Coke's local operation. Better yet, Indians appeared to be developing a taste for Coke products: The Company's overall sales in India jumped 24 percent, to $940 million.

India, with soft-drink consumption of just seven 8-ounce (250 milliliters) servings per capita annually, held more potential for growth than just about any other market on earth. Determined to consolidate its position and boost growth, Coke cut prices on all of its beverages by an aggressive 15 percent to 25 percent, forcing Pepsi to follow suit.

Key to Coke's battle plans was operations chief Sanjeev Gupta. Gupta's first step: revitalizing Thums Up, which led the market in 1993 with more than 60 percent of carbonated beverage sales but had slipped to just 15 percent by 1998. After Atlanta (Coca Cola's headquarters) gave the green light to pushing local brands as much as Coca-Cola, the 41-year-old Gupta spent $3.5 million to beef up advertising and distribution for Thums Up. Within a year, he built it into India's number two soda. Then Gupta—a veteran of marketing juggernaut Hindustan Lever Ltd.—persuaded Atlanta to revamp pricing and advertising for Coca-Cola. In 2001, he launched a new size, a 200-ml. bottle that sold for 10 cents and was aimed at rural areas and lower-income urban markets. Then, he dropped the price of a 300-ml. bottle to 17 cents from 24 cents. The price cuts were key to boosting sales and the little bottle was a big hit. In 2002, after years of lackluster ad campaigns, Gupta's team settled on an advertising strategy that caught the imagination of Indians. Breaking with Coke tradition, he hired a celebrity spokesman, Bollywood movie star Amir Khan.

The changes were paying Coke dividends. Execs at Coca-Cola India said the company was no longer losing money. "We have turned a corner," said N. Sridhar, Coke India's finance director. "This will release our energies to concentrate on building market share." Now, Coke planned on investing $150 million more to expand its bottling and distribution network. That would make India Coke's second-largest Asian investment after China.

Source: Excerpted from Manjeet Kripalani and Mark L. Clifford, "Finally Coke Gets It Right In India," *Business Week,* February 10, 2003, p. 47.

approaches to planning throughout a firm are needed for effective review and evaluation by corporate headquarters. In the global firm, planning is complicated by differences in national attitudes toward work measurement, and by differences in government requirements about disclosure of information.

Although such problems are an aspect of the global environment, rather than a consequence of poor management, they are often most effectively reduced through increased attention to strategic planning. Such planning will aid in coordinating and integrating the firm's direction, objectives, and policies around the world. It enables the firm to anticipate and prepare for change. It facilitates the creation of programs to deal with worldwide development. Finally, it helps the management of overseas affiliates become more actively involved in setting goals and in developing means to more effectively utilize the firm's total resources.

An example of the need for coordination in global ventures and evidence that firms can successfully plan for global collaboration (e.g., through rationalized production) is the Ford Escort (Europe), the best-selling automobile in the world, which has a component manufacturing network that consists of plants in 15 countries.

GLOBAL STRATEGIC PLANNING

It should be evident from the previous sections that the strategic decisions of a firm competing in the global marketplace become increasingly complex. In such a firm, managers cannot view global operations as a set of independent decisions. These managers are faced with trade-off decisions in which multiple products, country environments, resource sourcing options, corporate and subsidiary capabilities, and strategic options must be considered.

A recent trend toward increased activism of stakeholders has added to the complexity of strategic planning for the global firm. *Stakeholder activism* refers to demands placed on the global firm by the foreign environments in which it operates, principally by foreign governments. This section provides a basic framework for the analysis of strategic decisions in this complex setting.

Multidomestic Industries and Global Industries

Multidomestic Industries

International industries can be ranked along a continuum that ranges from multidomestic to global.

A multidomestic industry is one in which competition is essentially segmented from country to country. Thus, even if global corporations are in the industry, competition in one country is independent of competition in other countries. Examples of such industries include retailing, insurance, and consumer finance.

In a multidomestic industry, a global corporation's subsidiaries should be managed as distinct entities; that is, each subsidiary should be rather autonomous, having the authority to make independent decisions in response to local market conditions. Thus, the global strategy of such an industry is the sum of the strategies developed by subsidiaries operating in different countries. The primary difference between a domestic firm and a global firm competing in a multidomestic industry is that the latter makes decisions related to the countries in which it competes and to how it conducts business abroad.

Factors that increase the degree to which an industry is multidomestic include:[1]

The need for customized products to meet the tastes or preferences of local customers.

Fragmentation of the industry, with many competitors in each national market.

A lack of economies of scale in the functional activities of firms in the industry.

Distribution channels unique to each country.

A low technological dependence of subsidiaries on R&D provided by the global firm.

Global Industries

A global industry is one in which competition crosses national borders. In fact, it occurs on a worldwide basis. In a global industry, a firm's strategic moves in one country can be significantly affected by its competitive position in another country. The very rapidly expanding list of global industries includes commercial aircraft, automobiles, mainframe computers, and electronic consumer equipment. Many authorities are convinced that almost

---

[1] Y. Doz and C. K. Prahalad, "Patterns of Strategic Control within Multinational Corporations," *Journal of International Business Studies,* Fall 1984, pp. 55–72.

all product-oriented industries soon will be global. As a result, strategic management planning must be global for at least six reasons:

1. *The increased scope of the global management task.* Growth in the size and complexity of global firms made management virtually impossible without a coordinated plan of action detailing what is expected of whom during a given period. The common practice of management by exception is impossible without such a plan.

2. *The increased globalization of firms.* Three aspects of global business make global planning necessary: (1) differences among the environmental forces in different countries, (2) greater distances, and (3) the interrelationships of global operations.

3. *The information explosion.* It has been estimated that the world's stock of knowledge is doubling every 10 years. Without the aid of a formal plan, executives can no longer know all that they must know to solve the complex problems they face. A global planning process provides an ordered means for assembling, analyzing, and distilling the information required for sound decisions.

4. *The increase in global competition.* Because of the rapid increase in global competition, firms must constantly adjust to changing conditions or lose markets to competitors. The increase in global competition also spurs managements to search for methods of increasing efficiency and economy.

5. *The rapid development of technology.* Rapid technological development has shortened product life cycles. Strategic management planning is necessary to ensure the replacement of products that are moving into the maturity stage, with fewer sales and declining profits. Planning gives management greater control of all aspects of new product introduction.

6. *Strategic management planning breeds managerial confidence.* Like the motorist with a road map, managers with a plan for reaching their objectives know where they are going. Such a plan breeds confidence, because it spells out every step along the way and assigns responsibility for every task. The plan simplifies the managerial job.

A firm in a global industry must maximize its capabilities through a worldwide strategy. Such a strategy necessitates a high degree of centralized decision making in corporate headquarters so as to permit trade-off decisions across subsidiaries.

Among the factors that make for the creation of a global industry are:

Economies of scale in the functional activities of firms in the industry.

A high level of R&D expenditures on products that require more than one market to recover development costs.

The presence in the industry of predominantly global firms that expect consistency of products and services across markets.

The presence of homogeneous product needs across markets, which reduces the requirement of customizing the product for each market. The presence of a small group of global competitors.

A low level of trade regulation and of regulation regarding foreign direction investment.[2]

---

[2] G. Harvel and C. K. Prahalad, "Managing Strategic Responsibility in the MNC," *Strategic Management Journal,* October–December 1983, pp. 341–51.

EXHIBIT 4–8
Factors That Drive Global Companies

Source: Robert N. Lussier, Robert W. Baeder, and Joel Corman, "Measuring Global Practices: Global Strategic Planning through Company Situational Analysis," p. 57. Reprinted from *Business Horizons*, September–October 1994. Copyright 1994 by the Foundation for the School of Business at Indiana University. Used with permission.

1. Global Management Team

Possesses global vision and culture.
Includes foreign nationals.
Leaves management of subsidiaries to foreign nationals.
Frequently travels internationally.
Has cross-cultural training.

2. Global Strategy

Implement strategy as opposed to independent country strategies.
Develop significant cross-country alliances.
Select country targets strategically rather than opportunistically.
Perform business functions where most efficient—no home-country bias.
Emphasize participation in the triad—North America, Europe, and Japan.

3. Global Operations and Products

Use common core operating processes worldwide to ensure quantity and uniformity.
Product globally to obtain best cost and market advantage.

4. Global Technology and R&D

Design global products but take regional differences into account.
Manage development work centrally but carry out globally.
Do not duplicate R&D and product development; gain economies of scale.

5. Global Financing

Finance globally to obtain lowest cost.
Hedge when necessary to protect currency risk.
Price in local currencies.
List shares on foreign exchanges.

6. Global Marketing

Market global products but provide regional discretion if economies of scale are not affected.
Develop global brands.
Use core global marketing practices and themes.
Simultaneously introduce new global products worldwide.

Six factors that drive the success of global companies are listed in Exhibit 4–8. They address key aspects of globalizing a business's operations and provide a framework within which companies can effectively pursue the global marketplace.

The Global Challenge

Although industries can be characterized as global or multidomestic, few "pure" cases of either type exist. A global firm competing in a global industry must be responsive, to some degree, to local market conditions. Similarly, a global firm competing in a multidomestic industry cannot totally ignore opportunities to utilize intracorporate resources in competitive positioning. Thus, each global firm must decide which of its corporate functional activities should be performed where and what degree of coordination should exist among them.

Location and Coordination of functional activities

Typical functional activities of a firm include purchases of input resources, operations, research and development, marketing and sales, and after-sales service. A multinational corporation has a wide range of possible location options for each of these activities and must

EXHIBIT 4–9
Location and Coordination Issues of Functional Activities

Source: Copyright © 1986, by The Regents of the University of California. Reprinted from the California Management Review, Vol. 28, No. 2. By permission of The Regents.

Functional Activity	Location Issues	Coordination Issues
Operations	Location of production facilities for components.	Networking of international plants.
Marketing	Product line selection. Country (market) selection.	Commonality of brand name worldwide. Coordination of sales to multinational accounts. Similarity of channels and product positioning worldwide. Coordination of pricing in different countries.
Service	Location of service organization.	Similarity of service standards and procedures worldwide.
Research and development	Number and location of R&D centers.	Interchange among dispersed R&D centers. Developing products responsive to market needs in many countries. Sequence of product introductions around the world.
Purchasing	Location of the purchasing function.	Managing suppliers located in different countries. Transferring market knowledge. Coordinating purchases of common items.

decide which sets of activities will be performed in how many and which locations. A multinational corporation may have each location perform each activity, or it may center an activity in one location to serve the organization worldwide. For example, research and development centered in one facility may serve the entire organization.

A multinational corporation also must determine the degree to which functional activities are to be coordinated across locations. Such coordination can be extremely low, allowing each location to perform each activity autonomously, or extremely high, tightly linking the functional activities of different locations. Coca-Cola tightly links its R&D and marketing functions worldwide to offer a standardized brand name, concentrate formula, market positioning, and advertising theme. However, its operations function is more autonomous, with the artificial sweetener and packaging differing across locations.

Location and Coordination Issues

Exhibit 4–9 presents some of the issues related to the critical dimensions of location and coordination in multinational strategic planning. It also shows the functional activities that the firm performs with regard to each of these dimensions. For example, in connection with the service function, a firm must decide where to perform after-sale service and whether to standardize such service.

How a particular firm should address location and coordination issues depends on the nature of its industry and on the type of international strategy that the firm is pursuing. As discussed earlier, an industry can be ranked along a continuum that ranges between multidomestic at one extreme and global at the other. Little coordination of functional

The Model

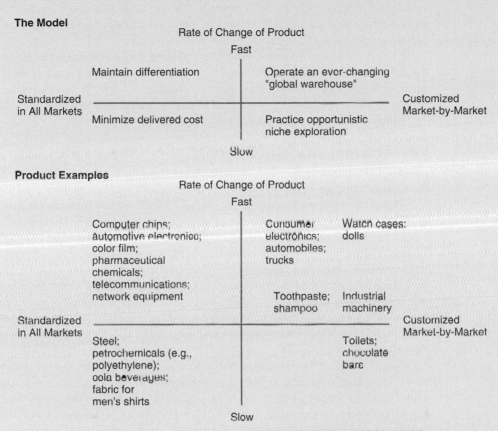

Rate of Change of Product

Fast

Maintain differentiation	Operate an ever-changing "global warehouse"

Standardized in All Markets ————————————————————— Customized Market-by-Market

Minimize delivered cost	Practice opportunistic niche exploration

Slow

Product Examples

Rate of Change of Product

Fast

Computer chips; automotive electronics; color film; pharmaceutical chemicals; telecommunications; network equipment

Consumer electronics; automobiles; trucks

Watch cases; dolls

Toothpaste; shampoo

Industrial machinery

Standardized in All Markets ————————————————————— Customized Market-by-Market

Steel; petrochemicals (e.g., polyethylene); cola beverages; fabric for men's shirts

Toilets; chocolate bars

Slow

Source: Lawrence H. Wortzel, *1989 International Business Resource Book* (Strategic Direction Publishers, 1989).

activities across countries may be necessary in a multidomestic industry, since competition occurs within each country in such an industry. However, as its industry becomes increasingly global, a firm must begin to coordinate an increasing number of functional activities to effectively compete across countries.

Going global impacts every aspect of a company's operations and structure. As firms redefine themselves as global competitors, workforces are becoming increasingly diversified. The most significant challenge for firms, therefore, is the ability to adjust to a workforce of varied cultures and lifestyles and the capacity to incorporate cultural differences to the benefit of the company's mission.

Market Requirements and Product Characteristics

Businesses have discovered that being successful in foreign markets often demands much more than simply shipping their well-received domestic products overseas. Firms must assess two key dimensions of customer demand: customers' acceptance of standardized products and the rate of product innovation desired. As shown in the top figure of Exhibit 4–10, Global Strategy in Action, all markets can be arrayed along a continuum from markets in which products are standardized to markets in which products must be customized for customers from market to market. Standardized products in all markets include color film and petrochemicals, while dolls and toilets are good examples of customized products.

Similarly, products can be arrayed along a continuum from products that are not subject to frequent product innovations to products that are often upgraded. Products with a fast rate of change include computer chips and industrial machinery, while steel and chocolate bars are products that fit in the slow rate of change category.

The bottom figure of Exhibit 4–10 shows that the two dimensions can be combined to enable companies to simultaneously assess both customer need for product standardization and rate of product innovation. The examples listed demonstrate the usefulness of the model in helping firms to determine the degree of customization that they must be willing to accept to become engaged in transnational operations.

International Strategy Options

Exhibit 4–11 presents the basic multinational strategy options that have been derived from a consideration of the location and coordination dimensions. Low coordination and geographic dispersion of functional activities are implied if a firm is operating in a multidomestic industry and has chosen a country-centered strategy. This allows each subsidiary to closely monitor the local market conditions it faces and to respond freely to these conditions.

High coordination and geographic concentration of functional activities result from the choice of a pure global strategy. Although some functional activities, such as after-sale service, may need to be located in each market, tight control of those activities is necessary to ensure standardized performance worldwide. For example, IBM expects the same high level of marketing support and service for all of its customers, regardless of their location.

Two other strategy options are shown in Exhibit 4–11. High foreign investment with extensive coordination among subsidiaries would describe the choice of remaining at a particular growth stage, such as that of an exporter. An export-based strategy with decentralized marketing would describe the choice of moving toward globalization, which a multinational firm might make.

EXHIBIT 4–11
International Strategy Options

Source: Copyright © 1986, by The Regents of the University of California. Reprinted from the California Management Review, Vol. 28, No. 2. By permission of The Regents.

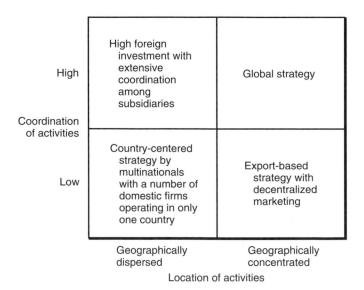

COMPETITIVE STRATEGIES FOR FIRMS IN FOREIGN MARKETS

Strategies for firms that are attempting to move toward globalization can be categorized by the degree of complexity of each foreign market being considered and by the diversity in a company's product line (see Exhibit 4–12). *Complexity* refers to the number of critical success factors that are required to prosper in a given competitive arena. When a firm must consider many such factors, the requirements of success increase in complexity. *Diversity,* the second variable, refers to the breadth of a firm's business lines. When a company offers many product lines, diversity is high.

Together, the complexity and diversity dimensions form a continuum of possible strategic choices. Combining these two dimensions highlights many possible actions.

Niche Market Exporting

The primary niche market approach for the company that wants to export is to modify select product performance or measurement characteristics to meet special foreign demands. Combining product criteria from both the U.S. and the foreign markets can be slow and tedious. There are, however, a number of expansion techniques that provide the U.S. firm with the know-how to exploit opportunities in the new environment. For example, copying product innovations in countries where patent protection is not emphasized and utilizing nonequity contractual arrangements with a foreign partner can assist in rapid product innovation. N. V. Philips and various Japanese competitors, such as Sony and Matsushita, now are working together for common global product standards within their markets. Siemens, with a centralized R&D in electronics, also has been very successful with this approach.

As described in Exhibit 4–13, Global Strategy in Action, the Taiwanese company, Gigabyte, researched the U.S. market and found that a sizable number of computer buyers wanted a PC that could complete the basic tasks provided by domestic desktops, but that would be considerably smaller. Gigabyte decided to serve this niche market by exporting their mini-PCs into the United States with a price tag of $200 to $300. This price was considerably less than the closest U.S. manufacturer, Dell, whose minicomputer was still larger and cost $766.

EXHIBIT 4–12
International
Strategy Options

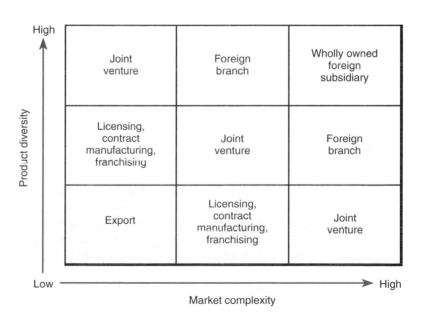

BusinessWeek Gigabyte rolled out its first mini-PC, a no-frills computer for word processing, accessing the Web, and playing CD-ROMs and DVDs. It could not be upgraded, but the price was right. Depending on features, the mini-PC sold for between $200 and $300, said Alonzo Cardenas, vice-president for marketing and business development at Gigabyte-USA. That was a lot less than the $1,100 for a typical consumer desktop, and it came at a time when many buyers were no longer entranced by fancy bells and whistles.

What lots of customers wanted was a smaller box. As the mini-PC name suggested, the box containing the processor occupied 30 percent less space than a standard desktop. Saving space also appealed to consumers, who have shown a willingness to pay extra for smaller PCs that boasted all the features of high-end models but could fit on the VCR shelf of their entertainment centers. That was an opportunity for Gigabyte and other newcomers.

By some accounts, the market for smaller PCs exploded. In the United States alone, sales growth had been up as much as 50 percent a month. It had been estimated that by 2008, mini-models should account for more than 50 percent of all desktops sold. That would be a huge market considering that 75 percent of the 128 million PCs shipped worldwide in 2001 were desktops, according to market consultancy Gartner Dataquest.

Major manufacturers started to notice. Dell, which held 25 percent of the corporate desktop market, introduced its most diminutive desktop, the OptiPlex SX260. About 50 percent smaller than its predecessor (but still bigger than Gigabyte's model), it weighed eight pounds and could be mounted vertically or horizontally. Unlike the Taiwanese makers, Dell had retained PC-level power. The downside was that Dell's cheapest mini-PC still cost a not-so-mini $766. Still, prices on the biggest players' mini-PCs and Media Centers remained high compared with what newcomers like Gigabyte were charging.

Source: Extracted from Olga Kharif, "Can Mini-PC's Mean Maxi Profits?" *BusinessWeek Online,* January 23, 2003.

Exporting usually requires minimal capital investment. The organization maintains its quality control standards over production processes and finished goods inventory, and risk to the survival of the firm is typically minimal. Additionally, the U.S. Commerce Department through its Export Now Program and related government agencies lowers the risks to smaller companies by providing export information and marketing advice.

Licensing/Contract Manufacturing

Establishing a contractual arrangement is the next step for U.S. companies that want to venture beyond exporting but are not ready for an equity position on foreign soil. Licensing involves the transfer of some industrial property right from the U.S. licensor to a motivated licensee. Most tend to be patents, trademarks, or technical know-how that are granted to the licensee for a specified time in return for a royalty and for avoiding tariffs or import quotas. Bell South and U.S. West, with various marketing and service competitive advantages valuable to Europe, have extended a number of licenses to create personal computer networks in the United Kingdom.

Another licensing strategy open to U.S. firms is to contract the manufacturing of its product line to a foreign company to exploit local comparative advantages in technology, materials, or labor.

U.S. firms that use either licensing option will benefit from lowering the risk of entry into the foreign markets. Clearly, alliances of this type are not for everyone. They are used best in companies large enough to have a combination of international strategic activities and for firms with standardized products in narrow margin industries.

Two major problems exist with licensing. One is the possibility that the foreign partner will gain the experience and evolve into a major competitor after the contract expires. The experience of some U.S. electronics firms with Japanese companies shows that licensees gain the potential to become powerful rivals. The other potential problem stems from the control that the licensor forfeits on production, marketing, and general distribution of its products. This loss of control minimizes a company's degrees of freedom as it reevaluates its future options.

Franchising

A special form of licensing is franchising, which allows the franchisee to sell a highly publicized product or service, using the parent's brand name or trademark, carefully developed procedures, and marketing strategies. In exchange, the franchisee pays a fee to the parent company, typically based on the volume of sales of the franchisor in its defined market area. The franchise is operated by the local investor who must adhere to the strict policies of the parent.

Franchising is so popular that an estimated 500 U.S. businesses now franchise to over 50,000 local owners in foreign countries. Among the most active franchisees are Avis, Burger King, Canada Dry, Coca-Cola, Hilton, Kentucky Fried Chicken, Manpower, Marriott, Midas, Muzak, Pepsi, and Service Master. However, the acknowledged global champion of franchising is McDonald's, which has 70 percent of its company-owned stores as franchisees in foreign nations.

Joint Ventures

As the multinational strategies of U.S. firms mature, most will include some form of joint venture (JV) with a target nation firm. AT&T followed this option in its strategy to produce its own personal computer by entering into several joint ventures with European producers to acquire the required technology and position itself for European expansion. Because JVs begin with a mutually agreeable pooling of capital, production or marketing equipment, patents, trademarks, or management expertise, they offer more permanent cooperative relationships than export or contract manufacturing.

Compared with full ownership of the foreign entity, JVs provide a variety of benefits to each partner. U.S. firms without the managerial or financial assets to make a profitable independent impact on the integrated foreign markets can share management tasks and cash requirements often at exchange rates that favor the dollar. The coordination of manufacturing and marketing allows ready access to new markets, intelligence data, and reciprocal flows of technical information.

For example, Siemens, the German electronics firm, has a wide range of strategic alliances throughout Europe to share technology and research developments. For years, Siemens grew by acquisitions, but now, to support its horizontal expansion objectives, it is engaged in joint ventures with companies like Groupe Bull of France, International Computers of Britain, General Electric Company of Britain, IBM, Intel, Philips, and Rolm. Another example is Airbus Industries, which produces wide-body passenger planes for the world market as a direct result of JVs among many companies in Britain, France, Spain, and Germany.

JVs speed up the efforts of U.S. firms to integrate into the political, corporate, and cultural infrastructure of the foreign environment, often with a lower financial commitment than acquiring a foreign subsidiary. General Electric's (GE) 3 percent share in the European lighting market was very weak and below expectations. Significant increases in competition throughout many of their American markets by the European giant, Philips Lighting, forced GE to retaliate by expanding in Europe. GE's first strategy was an attempted joint venture with the Siemens lighting subsidiary, Osram, and with the British electronics firm, Thorn EMI. Negotiations failed over control issues. When recent events in Eastern Europe opened the opportunity for a JV with the Hungarian lighting manufacturer, Tungsram, which was receiving 70 percent of revenues from the West, GE capitalized on it.

Although joint ventures can address many of the requirements of complex markets and diverse product lines, U.S. firms considering either equity- or nonequity-based JVs face many challenges. For example, making full use of the native firm's comparative advantage may involve managerial relationships where no single authority exists to make strategic decisions or solve conflicts. Additionally, dealing with host-company management requires the disclosure of proprietary information and the potential loss of control over production and marketing quality standards. Addressing such challenges with well-defined covenants agreeable to all parties is difficult. Equally important is the compatibility of partners and their enduring commitments to mutually supportive goals. Without this compatibility and commitment, a joint venture is critically endangered.

Foreign Branching

A foreign branch is an extension of the company in its foreign market—a separately located strategic business unit directly responsible for fulfilling the operational duties assigned to it by corporate management, including sales, customer service, and physical distribution. Host countries may require that the branch be "domesticated", that is, have some local managers in middle and upper-level positions. The branch most likely will be outside any U.S. legal jurisdiction, liabilities may not be restricted to the assets of the given branch, and business licenses for operations may be of short duration, requiring the company to renew them during changing business regulations.

Wholly Owned Subsidiaries

Wholly owned foreign subsidiaries are considered by companies that are willing and able to make the highest investment commitment to the foreign market. These companies insist on full ownership for reasons of control and managerial efficiency. Policy decisions about local product lines, expansion, profits, and dividends typically remain with the U.S. senior managers.

Fully owned subsidiaries can be started either from scratch or by acquiring established firms in the host country. U.S. firms can benefit significantly if the acquired company has complementary product lines or an established distribution or service network.

U.S. firms seeking to improve their competitive postures through a foreign subsidiary face a number of risks to their normal mode of operations. First, if the high capital investment is to be rewarded, managers must attain extensive knowledge of the market, the host nation's language, and its business culture. Second, the host country expects both a long-term commitment from the U.S. enterprise and a portion of their nationals to be employed in positions of management or operations. Fortunately, hiring or training foreign managers for leadership positions is commonly a good policy, since they are close to both the market and contacts. This is especially important for smaller firms when markets are regional. Third, changing standards mandated by foreign regulations may eliminate a company's protected market niche. Product design and worker protection liabilities also may extend back to the home office.

The strategies shown in Exhibit 4–12 are not exhaustive. For example, a firm may engage in any number of joint ventures while maintaining an export business. Additionally, there are a number of other strategies that a firm should consider before deciding on its long-term approach to foreign markets. These will be discussed in detail in Chapter 6 under the topic of grand strategies. However, the strategies discussed in this chapter provide the most popular starting points for planning the globalization of a firm.

Summary

To understand the strategic planning options available to a corporation, its managers need to recognize that different types of industry-based competition exist. Specifically, they must identify the position of their industry along the global versus multidomestic continuum and then consider the implications of that position for their firm.

The differences between global and multidomestic industries about the location and coordination of functional corporate activities necessitate differences in strategic emphasis. As an industry becomes global, managers of firms within that industry must increase the coordination and concentration of functional activities.

Appendix 4 at the end of this chapter lists many components of the environment with which global corporations must contend. This list is useful in understanding the issues that confront global corporations and in evaluating the thoroughness of global corporation strategies.

As a starting point for global expansion, the firm's mission statement needs to be reviewed and revised. As global operations fundamentally alter the direction and strategic capabilities of a firm, its mission statement, if originally developed from a domestic perspective, must be globalized.

The globalized mission statement provides the firm with a unity of direction that transcends the divergent perspectives of geographically dispersed managers. It provides a basis for strategic decisions in situations where strategic alternatives may appear to conflict. It promotes corporate values and commitments that extend beyond single cultures and satisfies the demands of the firm's internal and external claimants in different countries. Finally, it ensures the survival of the global corporation by asserting the global corporation's legitimacy with respect to support coalitions in a variety of operating environments.

Movement of a firm toward globalization often follows a systematic pattern of development. Commonly, businesses begin their foreign nation involvements progressively through niche market exporting, license-contract manufacturing, franchising, joint ventures, foreign branching, and foreign subsidiaries.

Questions for Discussion	1. How does environmental analysis at the domestic level differ from global analysis?
	2. Which factors complicate environmental analysis at the global level? Which factors are making such analysis easier?
	3. Do you agree with the suggestion that soon all industries will need to evaluate global environments?
	4. Which industries operate almost devoid of global competition? Which inherent immunities do they enjoy?

Chapter 4 Discussion Case

BusinessWeek

Planet Starbucks:
To Keep up the Growth, It Must Go Global Quickly

1   The Starbucks coffee shop on Sixth Avenue and Pine Street in downtown Seattle sits serene and orderly, as unremarkable as any other in the chain bought 15 years ago by entrepreneur Howard Schultz. A little less than three years ago, however, the quiet storefront made front pages around the world. During the World Trade Organization talks in November, 1999, protesters flooded Seattle's streets, and among their targets was Starbucks, a symbol, to them, of free-market capitalism run amok, another multinational out to blanket the earth. Amid the crowds of protesters and riot police were black-masked anarchists who trashed the store, leaving its windows smashed and its tasteful green-and-white decor smelling of tear gas instead of espresso. Says an angry Schultz: "It's hurtful. I think people are ill-informed. It's very difficult to protest against a can of Coke, a bottle of Pepsi, or a can of Folgers. Starbucks is both this ubiquitous brand and a place where you can go and break a window. You can't break a can of Coke."

2   The store was quickly repaired, and the protesters have scattered to other cities. Yet cup by cup, Starbucks really is caffeinating the world, its green-and-white emblem beckoning to consumers on three continents. In 1999, Starbucks Corp. had 281 stores abroad. Today, it has about 1,200—and it's still in the early stages of a plan to colonize the globe. If the protesters were wrong in their tactics, they weren't wrong about Starbucks' ambitions. They were just early.

3   The story of how Schultz & Co. transformed a pedestrian commodity into an up-scale consumer accessory has a fairy-tale quality. Starbucks has grown from 17 coffee shops in Seattle 15 years ago to 5,689 outlets in 28 countries. Sales have climbed an average of 20 percent annually since the company went public 10 years ago, to $2.6 billion in 2001, while profits bounded ahead an average of 30 percent per year, hitting $181.2 million last year. And the momentum continues. In the first three quarters of this fiscal year, sales climbed 24 percent, year to year, to $2.4 billion, while profits, excluding onetime charges and capital gains, rose 25 percent, to $159.5 million.

4   Moreover, the Starbucks name and image connect with millions of consumers around the globe. It was one of the fastest-growing brands in a *BusinessWeek* survey of the to100 global brands published Aug. 5. At a time when one corporate star after another has crashed to earth, brought down by revelations of earnings misstatements, executive greed, or worse, Starbucks hasn't faltered: The company confidently predicts up to 25 percent annual sales and earnings growth this year. On Wall Street, Starbucks is the last great growth story. Its stock, including four splits, has soared more than 2,200 percent over the past decade, surpassing Wal-Mart, General Electric, PepsiCo, Coca-Cola, Microsoft, and IBM in total return. Now at $21, it is hovering near its all-time high of $23 in July, before the overall market drop.

5   And after a slowdown last fall and winter, when consumers seemed to draw inward after September 11, Starbucks is rocketing ahead once again. Sales in stores open at least 13 months grew by 6 percent in the 43 weeks through July 28, and the company predicts monthly same-store sales gains as high as 7 percent through the end of this fiscal year. That's below the 9 percent growth rate in 2000, but investors seem encouraged. "We're going to see a lot more growth," says Jerome A. Castellini, president of Chicago-based CastleArk Management, which controls about 300,000 Starbucks shares. "The stock is on a run."

6   But how long can that run last? Already, Schultz's team is hard-pressed to grind out new profits in a home market that is quickly becoming saturated. Amazingly, with 4,247 stores scattered across the U.S. and Canada, there are still eight states in the U.S. with no Starbucks stores. Frappuccino-free cities include Butte, Mont., and Fargo, N. D. But big cities, affluent suburbs, and shopping malls are full to the brim. In coffee-crazed Seattle, there is a Starbucks outlet for every 9,400 people, and the company considers that the upper limit of coffee-shop saturation. In Manhattan's 24 square miles, Starbucks has 124 cafés, with four more on the way this year. That's one for every 12,000 people—meaning that there could be room for even more stores. Given such concentration, it is likely to take annual

same-store sales increases of 10 percent or more if the company is going to match its historic overall sales growth. That, as they might say at Starbucks, is a tall order to fill.

7   Indeed, the crowding of so many stores so close together has become a national joke, eliciting quips such as this headline in *The Onion,* a satirical publication: "A New Starbucks Opens in Rest-room of Existing Starbucks." And even the company admits that while its practice of blanketing an area with stores helps achieve market dominance, it can cut sales at existing outlets. "We probably self-cannibalize our stores at a rate of 30 percent a year," Schultz says. Adds Lehman Brothers Inc. analyst Mitchell Speiser: "Starbucks is at a defining point in its growth. It's reaching a level that makes it harder and harder to grow, just due to the law of large numbers."

8   To duplicate the staggering returns of its first decade, Starbucks has no choice but to export its concept aggressively. Indeed, some analysts give Starbucks only two years at most before it saturates the U.S. market. The chain now operates 1,200 international outlets, from Beijing to Bristol. That leaves plenty of room to grow. Indeed, about 400 of its planned 1,200 new stores this year will be built overseas, representing a 35 percent increase in its foreign base. Starbucks expects to double the number of its stores worldwide, to 10,000 in three years. During the past 12 months, the chain has opened stores in Vienna, Zurich, Madrid, Berlin, and even in far-off Jakarta. Athens comes next. And within the next year, Starbucks plans to move into Mexico and Puerto Rico. But global expansion poses huge risks for Starbucks. For one thing, it makes less money on each overseas store because most of them are operated with local partners. While that makes it easier to start up on foreign turf, it reduces the company's share of the profits to only 20 percent to 50 percent.

9   Moreover Starbucks must cope with some predictable challenges of becoming a mature company in the U.S. After riding the wave of successful baby boomers through the '90s, the company faces an ominously hostile reception from its future consumers, the twenty- or thirtysomethings of Generation X. Not only are the activists among them turned off by the power and image of the well-known brand, but many others say that Starbucks' latte-sipping sophisticates and piped-in Kenny G music are a real turn-off. They don't feel wanted in a place that sells designer coffee at $3 a cup.

10   Even the thirst of loyalists for high-price coffee can't be taken for granted. Starbucks' growth over the past decade coincided with a remarkable surge in the economy. Consumer spending has continued strong in the downturn, but if that changes, those $3 lattes might be an easy place for people on a budget to cut back. Starbucks executives insist that won't happen, pointing out that even in the weeks following the terrorist attacks, same-store comparisons stayed positive while those of other retailers skidded.

11   Starbucks also faces slumping morale and employee burnout among its store managers and its once cheery army of *baristas.* Stock options for part-timers in the restaurant business was a Starbucks innovation that once commanded awe and respect from its employees. But now, though employees are still paid better than comparable workers elsewhere about $7 per hour—many regard the job as just another fast-food gig. Dissatisfaction over odd hours and low pay is affecting the quality of the normally sterling service and even the coffee itself, say some customers and employees. Frustrated store managers among the company's roughly 470 California stores sued Starbucks in 2001 for allegedly refusing to pay legally mandated overtime. Starbucks settled the suit for $18 million this past April, shaving $0.03 per share off an otherwise strong second quarter.

12   However, the heart of the complaint—feeling overworked and underappreciated—doesn't seem to be going away.

To be sure, Starbucks has a lot going for it as it confronts the challenge of maintaining its growth. Nearly free of debt, it fuels expansion with internal cash flow. And Starbucks can maintain a tight grip on its image because stores are company-owned: There are no franchisees to get sloppy about running things. By relying on mystique and word-of-mouth, whether here or overseas, the company saves a bundle on marketing costs. Starbucks spends just $30 million annually on advertising, or roughly 1 percent of revenues, usually just for new flavors of coffee drinks in the summer and product launches, such as its new in-store Web service. Most consumer companies its size shell out upwards of $300 million per year. Moreover, unlike a McDonald's or a Gap Inc., two other retailers that rapidly grew in the U.S., Starbucks has no nationwide competitor.

Starbucks also has a well-seasoned management team. Schultz, 49, stepped down as chief executive in 2000 to become chairman and chief global strategist. Orin Smith, 60, the company's numbers-cruncher, is now CEO and in charge of day-to-day operations. The head of North American operations is Howard Behar, 57, a retailing expert who returned last September, two years after retiring. The management trio is known as H₂O, for Howard, Howard, and Orin.

13   Schultz remains the heart and soul of the operation. Raised in a Brooklyn public-housing project, he found his way to Starbucks, a tiny chain of Seattle coffee shops, as a marketing executive in the early '80s. The name came about when the original owners looked to Seattle history for inspiration and chose the moniker of an old mining camp: Starbo. Further refinement led to Starbucks, after the first mate in *Moby-Dick,* which they felt evoked the seafaring romance of the early coffee traders (hence the mermaid logo). Schultz got the idea for the modern Starbucks format while visiting a Milan coffee bar. He bought out his bosses in 1987 and began expanding. Today, Schultz has a net worth of about $700 million, including $400 million of company stock.

14   Starbucks has come light years from those humble beginnings, but Schultz and his team still think there's room to grow in the U.S.—even in communities where the chain already has dozens of stores. Clustering stores increases total revenue and market share, Smith argues, even when individual stores poach on each other's sales. The strategy works, he says, because of Starbucks' size. It is large enough to absorb losses at existing stores as new ones open up, and soon overall sales grow beyond what they would have with just one store. Meanwhile, it's cheaper to deliver to and manage stores located close together. And by clustering, Starbucks can quickly dominate a local market.

15   The company is still capable of designing and opening a store in 16 weeks or less and recouping the initial investment in three years. The stores may be oases of tranquility, but management's expansion tactics are something else. Take what critics call its "predatory real estate" strategy—paying more than market-rate rents to keep competitors out of a location. David C. Schomer, owner of Espresso Vivace in Seattle's hip Capitol Hill neighborhood, says Starbucks approached his landlord and offered to pay nearly double the rate to put a coffee shop in the same building. The landlord stuck with Schomer, who says: "It's a little disconcerting to know that someone is willing to pay twice the going rate." Another time, Starbucks and Tully's Coffee Corp., a Seattle-based coffee chain, were competing for a space in the city. Starbucks got the lease but vacated the premises before the term was up. Still, rather than let Tully's

get the space, Starbucks decided to pay the rent on the empty store so its competitor could not move in. Schultz makes no apologies for the hardball tactics. "The real estate business in America is a very, very tough game," he says. "It's not for the faint of heart."

16   Still, the company's strategy could backfire. Not only will neighborhood activists and local businesses increasingly resent the tactics, but customers could also grow annoyed over having fewer choices. Moreover, analysts contend that Starbucks can maintain about 15 percent square-footage growth in the U.S.— equivalent to 550 new stores—for only about two more years. After that, it will have to depend on overseas growth to maintain annual 20 percent revenue growth.

17   Starbucks was hoping to make up much of that growth with more sales of food and other noncoffee items, but has stumbled somewhat. In the late '90s, Schultz thought that offering $8 sandwiches, desserts, and CDS in his stores and selling packaged coffee in supermarkets would significantly boost sales. The specialty business now accounts for about 16 percent of sales, but growth has been less than expected. A healthy 19 percent this year, it's still far below the 38 percent growth rate of fiscal 2000. That suggests that while coffee can command high prices in a slump, food—at least at Starbucks—cannot. One of Behar's most important goals is to improve that record. For instance, the company now has a test program of serving hot breakfasts in 20 Seattle stores and may move to expand supermarket sales of whole beans.

18   What's more important for the bottom line, though, is that Starbucks has proven to be highly innovative in the way it sells its main course: coffee. In 800 locations it has installed automatic espresso machines to speed up service. And in November, it began offering prepaid Starbucks cards, priced from $5 to $500, which clerks swipe through a reader to deduct a sale. That, says the company, cuts transaction times in half. Starbucks has sold $70 million of the cards.

19   In early August, Starbucks launched Starbucks Express, its boldest experiment yet, which blends java, Web technology, and faster service. At about 60 stores in the Denver area, customers can pre-order and prepay for beverages and pastries via phone or on the Starbucks Express Web site. They just make the call or click the mouse before arriving at the store, and their beverage will be waiting—with their name printed on the cup. The company will decide in January on a national launch.

20   And Starbucks is bent on even more fundamental store changes. On Aug. 21, it announced expansion of a high-speed wireless Internet service to about 1,200 Starbucks locations in North America and Europe. Partners in the project—which Starbucks calls the world's largest Wi-Fi network—include Mobile International, a wireless subsidiary of Deutsche Telekom, and Hewlett-Packard. Customers sit in a store and check e-mail, surf the Web, or download multimedia presentations without looking for connections or tripping over cords. They start with 24 hours of free wireless broadband before choosing from a variety of monthly subscription plans.

21   Starbucks executives hope such innovations will help surmount their toughest challenge in the home market: attracting the next generation of customers. Younger coffee drinkers already feel uncomfortable in the stores. The company knows that because it once had a group of twentysomethings hypnotized for a market study. When their defenses were down, out came the bad news. "They either can't afford to buy coffee at Starbucks, or the only peers they see are those working behind the counter," says Mark Barden, who conducted the research for the Hal Riney & Partners ad agency (now part of Publicis Worldwide) in San Francisco. One of the recurring themes the hypnosis brought out was a sense that "people like me aren't welcome here except to serve the yuppies," he says. Then there are those who just find the whole Starbucks scene a bit pretentious. Katie Kelleher, 22, a Chicago paralegal, is put off by Starbucks' Italian terminology of *grande* and *venti* for coffee sizes. She goes to Dunkin' Donuts, saying: "Small, medium, and large is fine for me."

22   As it expands, Starbucks faces another big risk: that of becoming a far less special place for its employees. For a company modeled around enthusiastic service, that could have dire consequences for both image and sales. During its growth spurt of the mid- to late 1990s, Starbucks had the lowest employee turnover rate of any restaurant or fast-food company, largely thanks to its then unheard-of policy of giving health insurance and modest stock options to part-timers making barely more than minimum wage.

23   Such perks are no longer enough to keep all the workers happy. Starbucks' pay doesn't come close to matching the workload it requires, complain some staff. Says Carrie Shay, a former store manager in West Hollywood, Calif.: "If I were making a decent living, I'd still be there." Shay, one of the plaintiffs in the suit against the company says she earned $32,000 a year to run a store with 10 to 15 part-time employees. She hired employees, managed their schedules, and monitored the store's weekly profit-and-loss statement. But she was also expected to put in significant time behind the counter and had to sign an affidavit pledging to work up to 20 hours of overtime a week without extra pay—a requirement the company has dropped since the settlement. Smith says that Starbucks offers better pay, benefits, and training than comparable companies, while it encourages promotions from within.

24   For sure, employee discontent is far from the image Starbucks wants to project of relaxed workers cheerfully making cappuccinos. But perhaps it is inevitable. The business model calls for lots of low-wage workers. And the more people who are hired as Starbucks expands, the less they are apt to feel connected to the original mission of high service—bantering with customers and treating them like family. Robert J. Thompson, a professor of popular culture at Syracuse University, says of Starbucks: "It's turning out to be one of the great twenty-first century American success stories—complete with all the ambiguities."

25   Overseas, though, the whole Starbucks package seems new and, to many young people, still very cool. In Vienna, where Starbucks had a gala opening for its first Austrian store last December, Helmut Spudich, a business editor for the paper *Der Standard,* predicted that Starbucks would attract a younger crowd than the established cafés. "The coffeehouses in Vienna are nice, but they are old. Starbucks is considered hip," he says.

26   But if Starbucks can count on its youth appeal to win a welcome in new markets, such enthusiasm cannot be counted on indefinitely. In Japan, the company beat even its own bullish expectations, growing to 368 stores after opening its first in Tokyo in 1996. Affluent young Japanese women like Anna Kato, a 22-year-old Toyota Motor Corp. worker, loved the place. "I don't care if it costs more, as long as it tastes sweet," she says, sitting in the world's busiest Starbucks, in Tokyo's Shibuya district. Yet same-store sales growth has fallen in the past 10 months in Japan, Starbucks' top foreign market, as rivals offer similar fare. Add to that the depressed economy, and Starbucks Japan seems to be losing steam. Although it forecasts a 30 percent gain in net profit, to $8 million, for the year started in April, on record sales of $516 million, same-store sales are down 14 percent for the year ended in June. Meanwhile in England, Starbucks' second-biggest overseas market, with 310

stores, imitators are popping up left and right to steal market share.

27   Entering other big markets may be tougher yet. The French seem to be ready for Starbucks' sweeter taste, says Philippe Bloch, cofounder of Columbus Café, a Starbucks-like chain. But he wonders if the company can profitably cope with France's arcane regulations and generous labor benefits. And in Italy, the epicenter of European coffee culture, the notion that the locals will abandon their own 200,000 coffee bars en masse for Starbucks strikes many as ludicrous. For one, Italian coffee bars prosper by serving food as well as coffee, an area where Starbucks still struggles. Also, Italian coffee is cheaper than U.S. java and, say Italian purists, much better. Americans pay about $1.50 for an espresso. In northern Italy, the price is 67¢; in the south, just 55¢. Schultz insists that Starbucks will eventually come to Italy. It'll have a lot to prove when it does. Carlo Petrini, founder of the antiglobalization movement Slow Food, sniffs that Starbucks' "substances served in styrofoam" won't cut it. The cups are paper, of course. But the skepticism is real.

28   As Starbucks spreads out, Schultz will have to be increasingly sensitive to those cultural challenges. In December, for instance, he flew to Israel to meet with Foreign Secretary Shimon Peres and other Israeli officials to discuss the Middle East crisis. He won't divulge the nature of his discussions. But subsequently, at a Seattle synagogue, Schultz let the Palestinians have it. With Starbucks outlets already in Kuwait, Lebanon, Oman, Qatar, and Saudi Arabia, he created a mild uproar among Palestinian supporters. Schultz quickly backpedaled, saying that his words were taken out of context and asserting that he is "pro-peace" for both sides.

29   There are plenty more minefields ahead. So far, the Seattle coffee company has compiled an envious record of growth. But the giddy buzz of that initial expansion is wearing off. Now, Starbucks is waking up to the grande challenges faced by any corporation bent on becoming a global powerhouse.

By Stanley Holmes in Seattle, with Drake Bennett in Paris, Kate Carlisle in Rome, and Chester Dawson in Tokyo, with bureau reports.

Source: Drake Bennett, Kate Carlisle, Chester Dawson, and Stanley Holmes, "Planet Starbucks; To Keep Up Growth it Must Go Global Quickly," *BusinessWeek,* September 9, 2002.

Appendix **4**

Components of the Multinational Environment

Multinational firms must operate within an environment that has numerous components. These components include:

1. Government, laws, regulations, and policies of home country (United States, for example).
   a. Monetary and fiscal policies and their effect on price trends, interest rates, economic growth, and stability.
   b. Balance-of-payments policies.
      1. Mandatory controls on direct investment.
      2. Interest equalization tax and other policies.
   c. Commercial policies, especially tariffs, quantitative import restrictions, and voluntary import controls.
   d. Export controls and other restrictions on trade.
   e. Tax policies and their impact on overseas business.
   f. Antitrust regulations, their administration, and their impact on international business.
   g. Investment guarantees, investment surveys, and other programs to encourage private investments in less-developed countries.
   h. Export-import and government export expansion programs.
   i. Other changes in government policy that affect international business.
2. Key political and legal parameters in foreign countries and their projection.
   a. Type of political and economic system, political philosophy, national ideology.
   b. Major political parties, their philosophies, and their policies.
   c. Stability of the government.
      1. Changes in political parties.
      2. Changes in governments.
   d. Assessment of nationalism and its possible impact on political environment and legislation.
   e. Assessment of political vulnerability.
      1. Possibilities of expropriation.
      2. Unfavorable and discriminatory national legislation and tax laws.
      3. Labor laws and problems.
   f. Favorable political aspects.
      1. Tax and other concessions to encourage foreign investments.
      2. Credit and other guarantees.
   g. Differences in legal system and commercial law.
   h. Jurisdiction in legal disputes.
   i. Antitrust laws and rules of competition.
   j. Arbitration clauses and their enforcement.
   k. Protection of patents, trademarks, brand names, and other industrial property rights.
3. Key economic parameters and their projection.
   a. Population and its distribution by age groups, density, annual percentage increase, percentage of working age, percentage of total in agriculture, and percentage in urban centers.
   b. Level of economic development and industrialization.
   c. Gross national product, gross domestic product, or national income in real terms and also on a per capita basis in recent years and projections over future planning period.

  d. Distribution of personal income.

  e. Measures of price stability and inflation, wholesale price index, consumer price index, other price indexes.

  f. Supply of labor, wage rates.

  g. Balance-of-payments equilibrium or disequilibrium, level of international monetary reserves, and balance-of-payments policies.

  h. Trends in exchange rates, currency stability, evaluation of possibility of depreciation of currency.

  i. Tariffs, quantitative restrictions, export controls, border taxes, exchange controls, state trading, and other entry barriers to foreign trade.

  j. Monetary, fiscal, and tax policies.

  k. Exchange controls and other restrictions on capital movements, repatriation of capital, and remission of earnings.

4. Business system and structure.

  a. Prevailing business philosophy: mixed capitalism, planned economy, state socialism.

  b. Major types of industry and economic activities.

  c. Numbers, size, and types of firms, including legal forms of business.

  d. Organization: proprietorships, partnerships, limited companies, corporations, cooperatives, state enterprises.

  e. Local ownership patterns: public and privately held corporations, family-owned enterprises.

  f. Domestic and foreign patterns of ownership in major industries.

  g. Business managers available: their education, training, experience, career patterns, attitudes, and reputations.

  h. Business associations and chambers of commerce and their influence.

  i. Business codes, both formal and informal.

  j. Marketing institutions: distributors, agents, wholesalers, retailers, advertising agencies, advertising media, marketing research, and other consultants.

  k. Financial and other business institutions: commercial and investment banks, other financial institutions, capital markets, money markets, foreign exchange dealers, insurance firms, engineering companies.

  l. Managerial processes and practices with respect to planning, administration, operations, accounting, budgeting, and control.

5. Social and cultural parameters and their projections.

  a. Literacy and educational levels.

  b. Business, economic, technical, and other specialized education available.

  c. Language and cultural characteristics.

  d. Class structure and mobility.

  e. Religious, racial, and national characteristics.

  f. Degree of urbanization and rural-urban shifts.

  g. Strength of nationalistic sentiment.

  h. Rate of social change.

  i. Impact of nationalism on social and institutional change.

Chapter **Five**

Internal Analysis

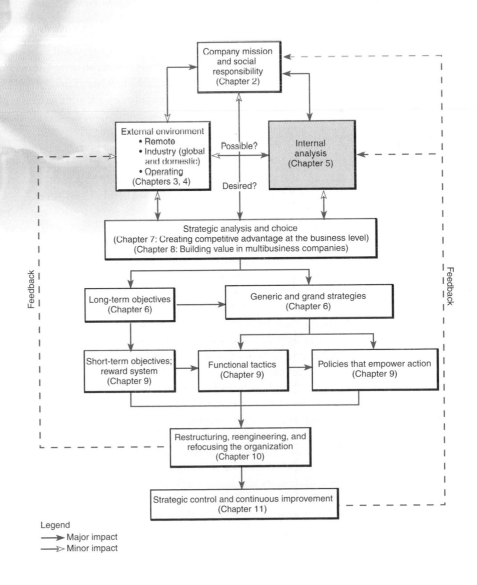

Legend
→ Major impact
⇒ Minor impact

Three ingredients are critical to the success of a strategy. First, the strategy must be *consistent* with conditions in the competitive environment. Specifically, it must take advantage of existing or projected opportunities and minimize the impact of major threats. Second, the strategy must place *realistic* requirements on the firm's resources. In other words, the firm's pursuit of market opportunities must be based not only on the existence of external opportunities but also on competitive advantages that arise from the firm's key resources. Finally, the strategy must be *carefully executed.* The focus of this chapter is on the second ingredient: *realistic analysis of the firm's resources.*

Managers often do this subjectively, based on intuition and "gut feel." Years of seasoned industry experience positions managers to make sound subjective judgments. But just as often, or more often, this may not be the case. In fast-changing environments, reliance on past experiences can cause management myopia or a tendency to accept the status quo and disregard signals that change is needed. And with managers new to strategic decision making, subjective decisions are particularly suspect. A lack of experience is easily replaced by emotion, narrow functional expertise, and the opinions of others creating the foundation on which newer managers build strategic recommendations. So it is that new managers' subjective assessments often come back to haunt them.

Strategy in Action Exhibit 5–1 helps us understand this "subjective" tendency among both new and experienced managers. It looks at what happened a few years ago at Navistar when CEO John R. Horne admonished his management team to join him in buying their rapidly deteriorating (in price) stock as a sign to Wall Street that they had confidence in their company. Most managers declined, as their subjective sense of the company's situation and resources was quite negative. Some were reported to have even shorted the stock. The CEO acted virtually alone based on his view that several Navistar resources provided potential competitive advantages. Two years later, Navistar stock was up 400 percent. Subjective assessment had probably been holding the company back. It undoubtedly hit hard in the pocketbooks of several key managers that saw their own stock as an unwise investment.

Internal analysis has received increased attention in recent years as being a critical underpinning to effective strategic management. Indeed many managers and writers have adopted a new perspective on understanding firm success based on how well the firm uses its internal resources—the *resource-based view* (RBV) of the firm. This chapter will start with a look at the RBV to provide a useful vocabulary for identifying and examining internal *resources.* The recent recession has seen insightful managers return to the notion of examining their business as a chain of activities that add value by creating the products or services they sell. Associated with this perspective is a powerful concept for introducing rigor and objectivity into internal analysis, the *value chain,* which this chapter will examine in great detail.

Next the chapter looks at ways managers achieve greater objectivity and rigor as they analyze their company's resources and value chain activities. Managers often start their internal analysis with questions like: "How well is the current strategy working? What is our current situation? Or what are our strengths and weaknesses?" Traditional *SWOT analysis* is then presented because it remains an approach that managers frequently use to answer these questions. Finally, objectivity and realism are enhanced when managers use meaningful standards for comparison regardless of the particular analytical framework they employ in internal analysis. We conclude this chapter by examining how managers do this using *past performance, stages of industry evolution, comparison with competitors* or other *"benchmarks,"* industry norms, and traditional *financial analysis.*

BusinessWeek As it moved toward a new century, things looked bleak for Navistar International Corp. After decades of crippling labor problems and manufacturing snafus, the $6.4 billion Chicago truck and engine maker had suffered another steep earnings slide last year. Then, in a showdown with United Auto Workers members over costs, CEO John R. Horne had been forced to scrap the company's latest truck introduction. Disheartened investors let the stock drop to $9 a share, just 50¢ above its low.

That's when Horne called his 30 top executives into his office to make a personal plea. Looking for a show of faith in the company, he implored all of them to spend their own money to buy as many shares of Navistar stock as they could. Horne knew it was a lot to ask. Over the previous 10 years, the company—once known as International Harvester—had tallied the worst total return to shareholders of all publicly traded U.S. companies. But he was convinced that if his managers bought, Wall Street would see that as a sign that Navistar's fortunes were turning.

Management's reply was a unanimous no. Many felt that Navistar's shares might drop as low as 6, and all 30 backed away. So Horne bit the bullet alone, buying as much as he could for cash and also turning his 401(k) account entirely into Navistar stock. "I couldn't force them because it was their money," he says. "I laugh at them some now."

All the way to the bank, he might add. By late 2001, Navistar's stock hit 40, a blazing 350 percent return to shareholders.

What Horne—a 34-year veteran who became president in 1991 and CEO in 1995—convinced himself about was the presence of key resources that were on the verge of becoming distinctive competencies, and key strengths, at Navistar.

TANGIBLE ASSET: CLEANEST BURNING DIESEL ENGINE

Navistar's diesel engine business was the first to be worked over. Horne immediately cut the number of engines in production to two, down from 70 in the mid-80s, for example. And by 1994, with Navistar's balance sheet improving, he introduced a new engine.

Navistar's offering, still the cleanest burning model on the market, quickly attracted major truck manufacturers such as Ford Motor Co. Ford puts the engine in vans and pickups and recently on its hot Expedition sport utility vehicle. Thanks largely to this model, Navistar's share of the diesel engine market rose from 25 percent in 1990 to 44 percent in 1998. That's one big reason operating results climbed from a $355 million loss in 1993 to a $349 million profit for the fiscal year ended October 2000.

TANGIBLE ASSET: EXCESS TRUCK AND ENGINE MANUFACTURING CAPACITY

Horne began a wide-ranging overhaul of Navistar's remaining truck and engine manufacturing lines. He started by drastically slicing the number of products Navistar made. Assembly was rationalized too. While Navistar plants used to build multiple trucks for several different markets, today each one specializes in one type of truck with fewer models.

Tackling problems in Navistar's truck and tractor division proved far tougher. Two years ago, for example, Horne laid out a plan to introduce a new generation of trucks. By simplifying the design of components, Horne hoped to bring out a series of truck and trailer models with interchangeable designs and standardized parts, thus cutting costs while reducing errors on the assembly line. Horne's goal: to reduce the 19 heavy-duty and medium truck designs in his main Springfield (Illinois) plant to one or two.

ORGANIZATIONAL CAPABILITY: IMPROVED UNION RELATIONS

Before he got that far, Horne ran smack into the problem that has dogged Navistar for more than a decade: He needed significant concessions from the UAW, which represents almost 80 percent of Navistar's truck workers. Horne demanded a wage freeze until 2002 and the flexibility to consolidate production. He took a direct approach. "I showed them the books," he says. "They knew survival of the plants depended on the changes."

Union leaders may have known it, but U.S. union members weren't convinced. They rejected the contract outright. Convinced that he could never achieve his profitability goals without the changes, Horne cancelled the new trucks. He took a $35 million charge and made clear his next step would be to look abroad for lower labor costs. By August 1997, the workers folded their cards and approved the plan. Horne's tough stance has paid off. He quickly revived plans for the new truck. And since the new labor contract and other manufacturing changes went into effect last fall, productivity at U.S. plants has already risen 15 percent.

ORGANIZATIONAL CAPABILITY: NEW PRODUCT DEVELOPMENT PROCESS

Just as important, Horne got Navistar working on new models again for the first time in years. Having brought out few new products during Navistar's long slide, most of the company's models were aging. But to make sure the new products pay off, Horne also introduced tight financial discipline: Today, new projects only win the nod if they can earn a 17.5 percent return on equity and a 15 percent return on assets through a

(continued)

business cycle and be available in 2 years or less. *Popular Science* recognized Navistar's revolutionary camless engine technology as "Best of What's New in 2002."

INTANGIBLE ASSET: A VISIONARY LEADER WITH STRONG LEADERSHIP SKILLS

"Horne did a magnificent job," said David Pedowitz, director of research at New York's David J. Greene & Co. brokerage firm, the largest outside investor with a 5 percent stake. "For the first time since the breakup of International Harvester, they're in a position to be a world-class competitor."

In the meantime, Horne continued to spread his penny-pinching gospel. Indeed, though a big basketball fan, he would not buy courtside seats to see his favorite competitor, Washington Wizards' Michael Jordan, in Jordan's final season. When Horne went to a home game, it was always as a guest. He had other things to do with the fortune he's made in Navistar stock. Like reinvest.

Source: "Navistar: Gunning the Engines," *BusinessWeek,* February 2, 1998; "Diesels Are the New Thing—Again," *BusinessWeek,* November 13, 2000, and "Up from the Scrap Heap," *Business Week,* July 21, 2003.

RESOURCE-BASED VIEW OF THE FIRM

Coca-Cola versus Pepsi is a competitive situation virtually all of us recognize. Stock analysts look at the two and frequently conclude that Coke is the clear leader. They cite Coke's superiority in tangible assets (warehouses, bottling facilities, computerization, cash, etc.) and intangible assets (reputation, brand name awareness, tight competitive culture, global business system, etc.). They also mention that Coke leads Pepsi in several capabilities to make use of these assets effectively—managing distribution globally, influencing retailer shelf space allocation, managing franchise bottler relations, marketing savvy, investing in bottling infrastructure, and speed of decision making to take quick advantage of changing global conditions are just a few that are frequently mentioned. The combination of capabilities and assets, most analysts conclude, creates several competencies that give Coke several competitive advantages over Pepsi that are durable and not easily imitated.

The Coke-Pepsi situation provides a useful illustration for understanding several concepts central to the resource-based view (RBV) of the firm. The RBV's underlying premise is that firms differ in fundamental ways because each firm possesses a unique "bundle" of resources—tangible and intangible assets and organizational capabilities to make use of those assets. Each firm develops competencies from these resources and, when developed especially well, these become the source of the firm's competitive advantages. Coke's decision to buy out weak bottling franchisees and regularly invest in or own newer bottling locations worldwide has given Coke a competitive advantage analysts estimate Pepsi will take at least 10 years or longer to match. Coke's strategy for the last 15 years was based in part on the identification of this resource and the development of it into a distinctive competence—a sustained competitive advantage. The RBV is a useful starting point for understanding internal analysis. Let's look at the basic concepts underlying the RBV.

Three Basic Resources: Tangible Assets, Intangible Assets, and Organizational Capabilities

Executives charting the strategy of their businesses historically concentrated their thinking on the notion of a "core competence." Basically, a core competence was seen as a capability or skill running through a firm's businesses that once identified, nurtured, and deployed throughout the firm became the basis for lasting competitive advantage. Executives, enthusiastic about the notion that their job as strategists was to identify and leverage core competencies, encountered difficulty applying the concept because of the generality of its level of analysis. The RBV emerged as a way to make the core competency concept more focused and measurable—creating a more meaningful internal analysis. Central to the RBV's ability to do this is its notion of three basic types of resources that together create the building blocks for distinctive competencies. They are defined below and illustrated in Exhibit 5–2.

Tangible assets are the easiest to identify and are often found on a firm's balance sheet. They include production facilities, raw materials, financial resources, real estate, and computers. Tangible assets are the physical and financial means a company uses to provide value to its customers.

Intangible assets are things like brand names, company reputation, organizational morale, technical knowledge, patents and trademarks, and accumulated experience within an organization. While they are not assets that you can touch or see, they are very often critical in creating competitive advantage.

Organizational capabilities are not specific "inputs" like tangible or intangible assets; rather, they are the skills—the ability and ways of combining assets, people, and processes—that a company uses to transform inputs into outputs. Dell Computer built its first 10 years of unprecedented growth by creating an organization capable of the speedy and inexpensive manufacture and delivery of custom-built PCs. Gateway and Micron have attempted to copy Dell for most of that time but remain far behind Dell's diverse organizational capabilities. Dell subsequently revolutionized its own "system" using the Internet to automate and customize service, creating a whole new level of organizational capability that combines assets, people, and processes throughout and beyond their organization. Concerning this organizational capability, Michael Dell recently said: "Anyone who tries to go direct now will find it very difficult—like trying to jump over the Grand Canyon." Finely developed capabilities, such as Dell's Internet-based customer-friendly system, can be a source of sustained competitive advantage. They enable a firm to take the same input factors as rivals (like Gateway and Micron) and convert them into products and services, either with greater efficiency in the process or greater quality in the output or both.

What Makes a Resource Valuable?

Once managers begin to identify their firm's resources, they face the challenge of determining which of those resources represent strengths or weaknesses—which resources generate core competencies that are sources of sustained competitive advantage. This has been a complex task for managers attempting to conduct a meaningful internal analysis. The RBV has addressed this by setting forth some key guidelines that help determine what constitutes a valuable asset, capability, or competence—that is, what makes a resource valuable.

1. **Competitive superiority: Does the resource help fulfill a customer's need better than those of the firm's competitors?** Two restaurants offer similar food, at similar prices, but one has a location much more convenient to downtown offices than the other. The tangible asset, location, helps fulfill daytime workers' lunch eating needs better than its competitor, resulting in greater profitability and sales volume for the conveniently located restaurant. Wal-Mart redefined discount retailing and outperformed the industry in profitability by 4.5 percent of sales—a 200 percent improvement. Four resources—store locations, brand recognition, employee loyalty, and sophisticated

EXHIBIT 5–2

Examples of Different Resources

Source: R. M. Grant, *Contemporary Strategy Analysis* (Oxford: Blackwell, 2001), p. 140.

Tangible Assets	Intangible Assets	Organizational Capabilities
Hampton Inn's reservation system	Budweiser's brand name	Dell Computer's customer service P & G's management training program
Ford Motor Company's cash reserves	Dell Computer's reputation	Wal-Mart's purchasing and inbound logistics
Georgia Pacific's land holdings	Nike's advertising with LeBron James	Sony's product-development processes
Virgin Airlines' plane fleet	Katie Couric as NBC's "Today" host	Coke's global distribution coordination
Coca-Cola's Coke formula	IBM's management team Wal-Mart's culture	3M's innovation process

Classifying and Assessing the Firm's Resources

Resource	Relevant Characteristics	Key Indicators
Tangible Resources Financial Resources	The firm's borrowing capacity and its internal funds generation determine its resilience and capacity for investment.	• Debt/equity ratio • Operating cash flow/free cash flow • Credit rating
Physical Resources	Physical resources constrain the firm's set of production possibilities and impact its cost position. Key characteristics include: • The size, location, technical sophistication, and flexibility of plant and equipment • Location and alternative uses for land and buildings • Reserves of raw materials	• Market values of fixed assets • Vintage of capital equipment • Scale of plants • Flexibility of fixed assets
Intangible Resources Technological Resources	Intellectual property: patent portfolio, copyright, trade secrets Resources for innovation: research facilities, technical and scientific employees	• Number and significance of patents • Revenue from licensing patents and copyrights • R&D staff as a percent of total employment • Number and location of research facilities
Reputation	Reputation with customers through the ownership of brands and trademarks; established relationships with customers; the reputation of the firm's products and services for quality and reliability. The reputation of the company with suppliers (including component suppliers, banks and financiers, employees and potential employees), with government and government agencies, and with the community.	• Brand recognition • Brand equity • Percent of repeat buying • Objective measures of comparative product performance (e.g., Consumers' Association ratings, J. D. Power ratings) • Surveys of corporate reputation (e.g., *BusinessWeek*)

EXHIBIT 5–3
Wal-Mart's Resource-Based Competitive Advantage

Source: Pankaj Ghemawat, "Wal-Mart Stores' Discount Operations," Harvard Business School case number 9–387–018.

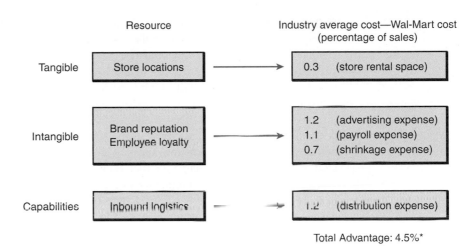

	Resource	Industry average cost—Wal-Mart cost (percentage of sales)
Tangible	Store locations	0.3 (store rental space)
Intangible	Brand reputation Employee loyalty	1.2 (advertising expense) 1.1 (payroll expense) 0.7 (shrinkage expense)
Capabilities	Inbound logistics	1.2 (distribution expense)

Total Advantage: 4.5%*

*Wal-Mart's cost advantage as a percent of sales. Each percentage point advantage is worth $500 million in net income to Wal-Mart.

inbound logistics—allowed Wal-Mart to fulfill customer needs much better and more cost effectively than Kmart and other discount retailers, as shown in Exhibit 5–3. In both of these examples, *it is important to recognize that only resources that contributed to competitive superiority were valuable.* At the same time, other resources such as the restaurant's menu and specific products or parking space at Wal-Mart were essential to doing business but contributed little to competitive advantage because they did not distinguish how the firm fulfilled customer needs.

2. **Resource scarcity: Is the resource in short supply?** When it is, it is more valuable. When a firm possesses a resource and few if any others do, and it is central to fulfilling customers' needs, then it becomes a distinctive competence for the firm. The real way resource scarcity contributes value is when it can be sustained over time. To really answer this very basic question we must explore the following questions.

3. **Inimitability: Is the resource easily copied or acquired?** A resource that competitors can readily copy can only generate temporary value. It cannot generate a long-term competitive advantage. When Wendy's first emerged, it was the only major hamburger chain with a drive-through window. This unique organizational capability was part of a "bundle" of resources that allowed Wendy's to provide unique value to its target customers, young adults seeking convenient food service. But once this resource, or organizational capability, proved valuable to fast-food customers, every fast-food chain copied the feature. Then Wendy's continued success was built on other resources that generated other distinctive competencies.

Inimitability doesn't last forever, as the Wendy's example illustrates. Competitors will match or better any resource as soon as they can. It should be obvious, then, that the firm's ability to forestall this eventuality is very important. The RBV identifies four characteristics, called *isolating mechanisms,* that make resources difficult to imitate:

- **Physically unique resources** are virtually impossible to imitate. A one-of-a-kind real estate location, mineral rights, and patents are examples of resources that cannot be imitated. Disney's Mickey Mouse copyright or Winter Park, Colorado's Iron Horse resort possess physical uniqueness. While many strategists claim that resources are physically unique, this is seldom true. Rather, other characteristics are typically what make most resources difficult to imitate.

- **Path-dependent resources** are very difficult to imitate because of the difficult "path" another firm must follow to create the resource. These are resources that cannot be instantaneously acquired but rather must be created over time in a manner that is frequently very expensive and always difficult to accelerate. When Michael Dell said that "anyone who tries to go direct now will find it very difficult—like trying to jump over the Grand Canyon" (see page 151), he was asserting that Dell's system of selling customized PCs direct via the Internet and Dell's unmatched customer service is in effect a path-dependent organizational capability. It would take any competitor years to develop the expertise, infrastructure, reputation, and capabilities necessary to compete effectively with Dell. Coca-Cola's brand name, Gerber Baby Food's reputation for quality, and Steinway's expertise in piano manufacture would take competitors many years and millions of dollars to match. Consumers' many years of experience drinking Coke or using Gerber or playing a Steinway would also need to be matched.

- **Causal ambiguity** is a third way resources can be very difficult to imitate. This refers to situations where it is difficult for competitors to understand exactly how a firm has created the advantage it enjoys. Competitors can't figure out exactly what the uniquely valuable resource is, or how resources are combined to create the competitive advantage. Causally ambiguous resources are often organizational capabilities that arise from subtle combinations of tangible and intangible assets and culture, processes, and organizational attributes the firm possesses. Southwest Airlines has regularly faced competition from major and regional airlines, with some like United and Continental eschewing their traditional approach and attempting to compete by using their own version of the Southwest approach—same planes, routes, gate procedures, number of attendants, and so on. They have yet to succeed. The most difficult thing to replicate is Southwest's "personality," or culture of fun, family, and frugal yet focused services and attitude. Just how that works is hard for United and Continental to figure out.

- **Economic deterrence** is a fourth source of inimitability. This usually involves large capital investments in capacity to provide products or services in a given market that are scale sensitive. It occurs when a competitor understands the resource that provides a competitive advantage and may even have the capacity to imitate, but chooses not to because of the limited market size that realistically would not support two players the size of the first mover.

While we may be inclined to think of a resource's inimitability as a yes-or-no situation, inimitability is more accurately measured on a continuum that reflects difficulty and time. Exhibit 5–4 illustrates such a continuum. Some resources may have multiple imitation deterrents. For example, 3M's reputation for innovativeness may involve path dependencies and causal ambiguity.

4. **Appropriability: Who actually gets the profit created by a resource?** Warren Buffet is known worldwide as one of the most successful investors of the last 25 years. One of his legendary investments was the Walt Disney Company, which he once said he liked "because the Mouse does not have an agent."[1] What he was really saying was that Disney owned the Mickey Mouse copyright, and all profits from that valuable resource went directly to Disney. Other competitors in the "entertainment" industry generated similar profits from their competing offerings, for example, movies, but they often "captured" substantially less of those profits because of the amounts that had to be paid to well-known actors or directors or other entertainment contributors seen as the real creators of the movie's value.

[1]*The Harbus,* March 25, 1996, p. 12.

EXHIBIT 5–4
Resource
Inimitability

Source: Cynthia A. Montgomery, "Resources: The Essence of Corporate Advantage," Harvard Business School Case N1–792–064.

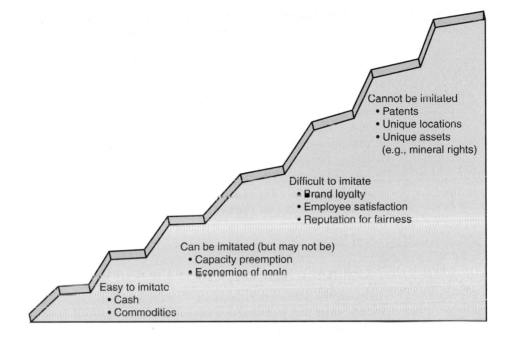

Cannot be imitated
• Patents
• Unique locations
• Unique assets
  (e.g., mineral rights)

Difficult to imitate
• Brand loyalty
• Employee satisfaction
• Reputation for fairness

Can be imitated (but may not be)
• Capacity preemption
• Economies of scale

Easy to imitate
• Cash
• Commodities

Sports teams, investment services, and consulting businesses are other examples of companies that generate sizable profits based on resources (key people, skills, contacts, for example) that are not inextricably linked to the company and therefore do not allow the company to easily capture the profits. Superstar sports players can move from one team to another, or command excessively high salaries, and this circumstance could arise in other personal services business situations. It could also occur when one firm joint ventures with another, sharing resources and capabilities and the profits that result. Sometimes restaurants or lodging facilities that are franchisees of a national organization are frustrated by the fees they pay the franchisor each month and decide to leave the organization and go "independent." They often find, to their dismay, that the business declines significantly. The value of the franchise name, reservation system, and brand recognition is critical in generating the profits of the business.

Bottom line: resources that one develops and controls—where ownership of the resource and its role in value creation is obvious—are more valuable than resources that can be easily bought, sold, or moved from one firm to another. And it is the presence of resources and capabilities that are not easily sold, bought, or moved that create sustained competitive advantage.

5. **Durability: How rapidly will the resource depreciate?** The slower a resource depreciates, the more valuable it is. Tangible assets, like commodities or capital, can have their depletion measured. Intangible resources, like brand names or organizational capabilities, present a much more difficult depreciation challenge. The Coca-Cola brand has continued to appreciate, whereas technical know-how in various computer technologies depreciates rapidly. In the increasingly hypercompetitive global economy of the twenty-first century, distinctive competencies and competitive advantages can fade quickly, making the notion of durability a critical test of the value of key resources and capabilities. Some believe that this reality makes well-articulated visions and associated cultures within organizations potentially the most important contributor to long-term survival.[2]

[2]James C. Collins, *Good to Great: Why Some Companies Make the Leap . . . and Others Don't* (New York: HarperCollins, 2001).

6. **Substitutability: Are other alternatives available?** We discussed the threat of substitute products in Chapter 3 as part of the five forces model for examining industry profitability. This basic idea can be taken further and used to gauge the value of particular resources. DeLite's of America was once a hot IPO as a new fast-food restaurant chain focused exclusively on selling lite food   salads, lean sandwiches, and so on. The basic idea was to offer, in a fast-food format, food low in calories and saturated fat. Investors were very excited about this concept because of the high-calorie, high-fat content of the foods offered by virtually every existing chain. Unfortunately for these investors, several key fast-food players, like Wendy's and later McDonald's, Burger King, and Hardees, adapted their operations to offer salad bars or premade salads and other "lean" sandwich offerings without disrupting their more well known fare. With little change and adaptation of their existing facility and operational resources, these chains quickly created alternatives to DeLite's offerings and the initial excitement about those offerings faded. DeLite's was driven out of business by substitute resources and capabilities rather than substitute products.

Using the Resource-Based View in Internal Analysis

To use the RBV in internal analysis, a firm must first identify and evaluate its resources to find those that provide the basis for future competitive advantage. This process involves defining the various resources the firm possesses, and examining them based on the above discussion to gauge which resources truly have strategic value. Four final guidelines have proven helpful in this undertaking:

- *Disaggregate resources*—break them down into more specific competencies—rather than stay with broad categorizations. Saying that Domino's Pizza has better marketing skills than Pizza Hut conveys little information. But dividing that into subcategories such as advertising that, in turn, can be divided into national advertising, local promotions, and couponing allows for a more measurable assessment. Exhibit 5–5 provides a useful illustration of this at Whitbread's Restaurant.

- *Utilize a functional perspective.* Looking at different functional areas of the firm, disaggregating tangible and intangible assets as well as organizational capabilities that are present, can begin to uncover important value-building resources and activities that deserve further analysis. Exhibit 5–6 lists a variety of functional area resources and activities that deserve consideration.

- *Look at organizational processes* and combinations of resources and not only at isolated assets or capabilities. While disaggregation is critical, you must also take a creative, gestalt look at what competencies the firm possesses or has the potential to possess that might generate competitive advantage.

- *Use the value chain approach* to uncover organizational capabilities, activities, and processes that are valuable potential sources of competitive advantage. Value chain analysis is discussed starting on page 159.

Although the RBV enables a systematic assessment of internal resources, it is important to stress that a meaningful analysis of those resources best takes place in the context of the firm's competitive environment. Possessing valuable resources will not generate commensurate profits unless resources are applied in an effective product market strategy; they must be deployed in an optimum way and align related activities for the firm to pursue its chosen sources of competitive advantage. Traditional strategy formulation—externally positioning a firm to capitalize on its strengths and opportuni-

EXHIBIT 5–5

Disaggregating Whitbread Restaurant's Customer Service Resource

Source: Andrew Campbell and Kathleen Sommers-Luchs, *Core Competency-Based Strategy* (London: International Thomson, 1997).

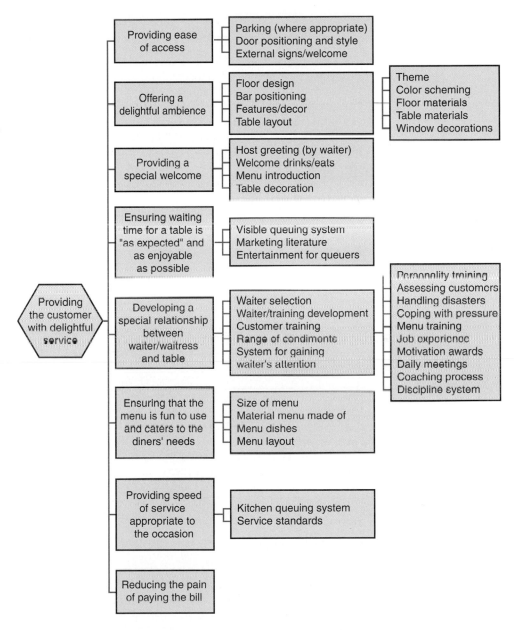

ties and to minimize its threats and weaknesses—remains essential to realizing the competitive advantage envisioned from an RBV of the firm.[3] A subsequent section examines this traditional approach, often called *SWOT analysis,* as a conceptual framework that applies input from the RBV in conducting a sound internal analysis. Before doing so, it is important to understand a second way to look at a firm's capabilities—as components in a value chain of activities.

[3]Jay B. Barney and Asli M. Arikan, "The Resource-Based View: Origins and Implications," in *Handbook of Strategic Management,* Michael A. Hitt, R. Edward Freeman, and Jeffrey S. Harrison, editors (Oxford, UK: Blackwell Publishers, 2001).

EXHIBIT 5–6
Key Resources across
Functional Areas

Marketing

Firm's products-services: breadth of product line.
Concentration of sales in a few products or to a few customers.
Ability to gather needed information about markets.
Market share or submarket shares.
Product-service mix and expansion potential: life cycle of key products; profit-sales balance in product-service.
Channels of distribution: number, coverage, and control.
Effective sales organization: knowledge of customer needs.
Internet usage.
Product-service image, reputation, and quality.
Imaginativeness, efficiency, and effectiveness of sales promotion and advertising.
Pricing strategy and pricing flexibility.
Procedures for digesting market feedback and developing new products, services, or markets.
After-sale service and follow-up.
Goodwill—brand loyalty.

Financial and Accounting

Ability to raise short-term capital.
Ability to raise long-term capital; debt-equity.
Corporate-level resources (multibusiness firm).
Cost of capital relative to that of industry and competitors.
Tax considerations.
Relations with owners, investors, and stockholders.
Leverage position; capacity to utilize alternative financial strategies, such as lease or sale and leaseback.
Cost of entry and barriers to entry.
Price-earnings ratio.
Working capital; flexibility of capital structure.
Effective cost control; ability to reduce cost.
Financial size.
Efficiency and effectiveness of accounting system for cost, budget, and profit planning.

Production, Operations, Technical

Raw materials' cost and availability, supplier relationships.
Inventory control systems; inventory turnover.
Location of facilities; layout and utilization of facilities.
Economies of scale.
Technical efficiency of facilities and utilization of capacity.
Effectiveness of subcontracting use.
Degree of vertical integration; value added and profit margin.
Efficiency and cost-benefit of equipment.
Effectiveness of operation control procedures: design, scheduling, purchasing, quality control, and efficiency.
Costs and technological competencies relative to those of industry and competitors.
Research and development—technology—innovation.
Patents, trademarks, and similar legal protection.

Personnel

Management personnel.
Employees' skill and morale.
Labor relations costs compared with those of industry and competitors.
Efficiency and effectiveness of personnel policies.

EXHIBIT 5–6
(continued)

Personnel *(continued)*

Effectiveness of incentives used to motivate performance.
Ability to level peaks and valleys of employment.
Employee turnover and absenteeism.
Specialized skills.
Experience.

Quality Management

Relationship with suppliers, customers.
Internal practices to enhance quality of products and services.
Procedures for monitoring quality.

Information Systems

Timeliness and accuracy of information about sales, operations, cash, and suppliers.
Relevance of information for tactical decisions.
Information to manage quality issues: customer service.
Ability of people to use the information that is provided.
Linkages to suppliers and customers.

Organization and General Management

Organizational structure.
Firm's image and prestige.
Firm's record in achieving objectives.
Organization of communication system.
Overall organizational control system (effectiveness and utilization).
Organizational climate; organizational culture.
Use of systematic procedures and techniques in decision making
Top-management skill, capabilities, and interest
Strategic planning system.
Intraorganizational synergy (multibusiness firms).

VALUE CHAIN ANALYSIS

The term *value chain* describes a way of looking at a business as a chain of activities that transform inputs into outputs that customers value. Customer value derives from three basic sources: activities that differentiate the product, activities that lower its cost, and activities that meet the customer's need quickly. *Value chain analysis* (VCA) attempts to understand how a business creates customer value by examining the contributions of different activities within the business to that value.

VCA takes a process point of view: It divides (sometimes called disaggregates) the business into sets of activities that occur *within the business,* starting with the inputs a firm receives and finishing with the firm's products (or services) and after-sales service to customers. VCA attempts to look at its costs across the series of activities the business performs to determine where low-cost advantages or cost disadvantages exist. It looks at the attributes of each of these different activities to determine in what ways each activity that occurs between purchasing inputs and after-sales service helps differentiate the company's products and services. Proponents of VCA believe it allows managers to better identify their firm's strengths and weaknesses by looking at the business as a process—a chain of activities—of what actually happens in the business rather than simply looking at it based on arbitrary organizational dividing lines or historical accounting protocol.

Exhibit 5–7 shows a typical value chain framework. It divides activities within the firm into two broad categories: primary activities and support activities. *Primary activities*

EXHIBIT 5–7
The Value Chain

Source: Based on Michael Porter, On Competition, 1998, Harvard Business School Press.

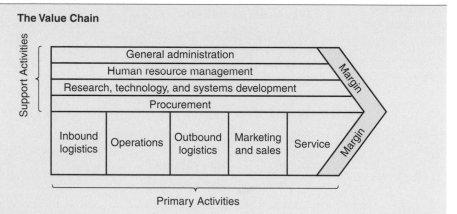

The Value Chain

Primary Activities

- **Inbound Logistics**—Activities, costs, and assets associated with obtaining fuel, energy, raw materials, parts components, merchandise, and consumable items from vendors; receiving, storing, and disseminating inputs from suppliers; inspection; and inventory management.
- **Operations**—Activities, costs, and assets associated with converting inputs into final product form (production, assembly, packaging, equipment maintenance, facilities, operations, quality assurance, environmental protection).
- **Outbound Logistics**—Activities, costs, and assets dealing with physically distributing the product to buyers (finished goods warehousing, order processing, order picking and packing, shipping, delivery vehicle operations).
- **Marketing and Sales**—Activities, costs, and assets related to sales force efforts, advertising and promotion, market research and planning, and dealer/distributor support.
- **Service**—Activities, costs, and assets associated with providing assistance to buyers, such as installation, spare parts delivery, maintenance and repair, technical assistance, buyer inquiries, and complaints.

Support Activities

- **General Administration**—Activities, costs, and assets relating to general management, accounting and finance, legal and regulatory affairs, safety and security, management information systems, and other "overhead" functions.
- **Human Resources Management**—Activities, costs, and assets associated with the recruitment, hiring, training, development, and compensation of all types of personnel; labor relations activities; development of knowledge-based skills.
- **Research, Technology, and Systems Development**—Activities, costs, and assets relating to product R&D, process R&D, process design improvement, equipment design, computer software development, telecommunications systems, computer-assisted design and engineering, new database capabilities, and development of computerized support systems.
- **Procurement**—Activities, costs, and assets associated with purchasing and providing raw materials, supplies, services, and outsourcing necessary to support the firm and its activities. Sometimes this activity is assigned as part of a firm's inbound logistic purchasing activities.

(sometimes called *line* functions) are those involved in the physical creation of the product, marketing and transfer to the buyer, and after-sale support. *Support activities* (sometimes called *staff* or *overhead* functions) assist the firm as a whole by providing infrastructure or inputs that allow the primary activities to take place on an ongoing basis. The value chain includes a *profit margin* since a markup above the cost of providing a firm's value-adding

BusinessWeek Founder Fred Smith and executives running companies controlled by FedEx say they are planning a monumental shift in the FedEx mission. They are accelerating plans to focus on information systems that track and coordinate packages. They are seeking to "morph" themselves from being a transportation company into an information company.

FedEx already has one of the most heavily used websites on the Internet. Company management claims to have 1,500 in-house programmers writing more software code than almost any other non-software company. To complement package delivery, FedEx designs and operates high-tech warehouses and distribution systems for big manufacturers and retailers around the world. For almost two decades, FedEx has been investing massive amounts to develop software and create a giant digital network. FedEx has built corporate technology campuses around the world, and its electronic systems are directly linked via the Internet or otherwise to over 1 million customers worldwide. That system now allows FedEx to track packages on an hourly basis, but it also allows FedEx to predict future flow of goods and then rapidly refigure the information and logistical network to handle those flows.

"Moving an item from point A to point B is no longer a big deal," say James Barksdale, CEO of Netscape and early architect of FedEx's information strategies. "Having the information about that item, and where it is, and the best way to use it. . . . That is value. The companies that will be big winners will be the ones who can best maximize the value of these information systems." Where FedEx's value has long been built on giant airplanes and big trucks, founder Smith sees a time when it will be built on information, computers, and the allure of the FedEx brand name.

If it works, FedEx's value chain will shrink in areas involved with inbound and outbound operations—taking off and landing on the tarmac—and will expand in areas involved with zapping around the pristine and pilot-tree world of cyberspace to manage a client's supply chain and its distribution network.

Source: "UPS vs. FedEx: Ground Wars," *BusinessWeek*, May 21, 2001.

activities is normally part of the price paid by the buyer—creating value that exceeds cost so as to generate a return for the effort.[4]

Judgment is required across individual firms and different industries because what may be seen as a support activity in one firm or industry may be a primary activity in another. Computer operations might typically be seen as infrastructure support, for example, but may be seen as a primary activity in airlines, newspapers, or banks. Exhibit 5–8, Strategy in Action, describes how Federal Express reconceptualized its company using a value chain analysis that ultimately saw its information support become its primary activity and source of customer value.

Conducting a Value Chain Analysis

Identify Activities

The initial step in value chain analysis is to divide a company's operations into specific activities or business processes, usually grouping them similarly to the primary and support activity categories shown in Exhibit 5–7. Within each category, a firm typically performs a number of discrete activities that may represent key strengths or weaknesses. Service activities, for example, may include such discrete activities as installation, repair, parts distribution, and upgrading—any of which could be a major source of competitive advantage or disadvantage. The manager's challenge at this point is to be very detailed attempting to "disaggregate" what actually goes on into numerous distinct, analyzable activities rather than settling for a broad, general categorization.

Allocate Costs

The next step is to attempt to attach costs to each discrete activity. Each activity in the value chain incurs costs and ties up time and assets. Value chain analysis requires managers to

---

[4]Different "value chain" or value activities may become the focus of value chain analysis. For example, companies using Hammer's *Reengineering the Corporation* might use (1) order procurement, (2) order fulfillment, (3) customer service, (4) product design, and (5) strategic planning plus support activities.

EXHIBIT 5–9

The Difference between Traditional Cost Accounting and Activity-Based Cost Accounting

Traditional Cost Accounting in a Purchasing Department		Activity-Based Cost Accounting in the Same Purchasing Department for its "Procurement" Activities	
Wages and salaries	$175,000	Evaluate supplier capabilities	$ 67,875
Employee benefits	57,500	Process purchase orders	41,050
Supplies	3,250	Expedite supplier deliveries	11,750
Travel	1,200	Expedite internal processing	7,920
Depreciation	8,500	Check quality of items purchased	47,150
Other fixed charges	62,000	Check incoming deliveries against purchase orders	24,225
Miscellaneous operating expenses	12,625	Resolve problems	55,000
	$320,075	Internal administration	65,105
			$320,075

assign costs and assets to each activity, thereby providing a very different way of viewing costs than traditional cost accounting methods would produce. Exhibit 5–9 helps illustrate this distinction. Both approaches in Exhibit 5–9 tell us that the purchasing department (procurement activities) cost $320,075. The traditional method lets us see that payroll expenses are 73 percent [(175 + 57.5)/320] of our costs with "other fixed charges" the second largest cost, 19 percent [62/320] of the total procurement costs. VCA proponents would argue that the benefit of this information is limited. Their argument might be the following:

> With this information we could compare our procurement costs to key competitors, budgets, or industry averages, and conclude that we are better, worse, or equal. We could then ascertain that our "people" costs and "other fixed charges" cost are advantages, disadvantages, or "in line" with competitors. Managers could then argue to cut people, add people, or debate fixed overhead charges. However, they would get lost in what is really a budgetary debate without ever examining what it is those people do in accomplishing the procurement function, what value that provides, and how cost effective each activity is.

VCA proponents hold that the activity-based VCA approach would provide a more meaningful analysis of the procurement function's costs and consequent value-added. The activity-based side of Exhibit 5–9 shows that approximately 21 percent of the procurement cost or value-added involves evaluating supplier capabilities. A rather sizable cost, 20 percent, involves internal administration, with an additional 17 percent spent resolving problems and almost 15 percent spent on quality control efforts. VCA advocates see this information as being much more useful than traditional cost accounting information, especially when compared to the cost information of key competitors or other "benchmark" companies. VCA supporters might assert the following argument that the benefit of this activity-based information is substantial:

> Rather than analyzing just "people" and "other charges," we are now looking at meaningful categorizations of the work that procurement actually does. We see, for example, that a key value-added activity (and cost) involves "evaluating supplier capabilities." The amount spent on "internal administration" and "resolving problems" seems high, and may indicate a weakness or area for improvement if the other activities' costs are in line and outcomes favorable. The bottom line is that this approach lets us look at what we actually "do" in the business—the specific activities—to create customer value, and that in turn allows more specific internal analysis than traditional, accounting-based cost categories.

Recognize the Difficulty in Activity-Based Cost Accounting   It is important to note that existing financial management and accounting systems in many firms are not set up to easily provide activity-based cost breakdowns. Likewise, in virtually all firms, the information requirements to support activity-based cost accounting can create redundant work because of the financial reporting requirements that may force firms to retain the traditional approach for financial statement purposes. The time and energy to change to an activity-based approach can be formidable, and still typically involves arbitrary cost allocation decisions trying to allocate selected asset or people costs across multiple activities in which they are involved. Challenges dealing with a cost-based use of VCA have not deterred use of the framework to identify sources of differentiation. Indeed, conducting a VCA to analyze competitive advantages that differentiate the firm is compatible with the RBV's examination of intangible assets and capabilities as sources of distinctive competence.

Identify the Activities That Differentiate the Firm

Scrutinizing a firm's value chain may not only reveal cost advantages or disadvantages, it may also bring attention to several sources of differentiation advantage relative to competitors. Dell Computer considers its Internet-based after-sales service (activities) to be far superior to any competitor's. Dell knows it has cost advantage because of the time and expense replicating this activity would take. But Dell considers it an even more important source of value to the customer because of the importance customers place on this activity, which differentiates Dell from many similarly priced competitors. Likewise Federal Express, as we noted earlier, considers its information management skills to have become the core competence and essence of the company because of the value these skills allow FedEx to provide its customers and the importance they in turn place on such skills. Exhibit 5–10 suggests some factors for assessing primary and support activities' differentiation and contribution.

Examine the Value Chain

Once the value chain has been documented, managers need to identify the activities that are critical to buyer satisfaction and market success. It is those activities that deserve major scrutiny in an internal analysis. Three considerations are essential at this stage in the value chain analysis. First, the company's basic mission needs to influence managers' choice of the activities they examine in detail. If the company is focused on being a low-cost provider, then management attention to lower costs should be very visible; and missions built around commitment to differentiation should find managers spending more on activities that are differentiation cornerstones. Retailer Wal-Mart focuses intensely on costs related to inbound logistics, advertising, and loyalty to build its competitive advantage (see Exhibit 5–3), while Nordstrom builds its distinct position in retailing by emphasizing sales and support activities on which they spend twice the retail industry average. The application of value chain analysis to explore Volkswagen's strategic situation in 2003–2004 is described in Exhibit 5–11, Strategy in Action.

Second, the nature of value chains and the relative importance of the activities within them vary by industry. Lodging firms like Holiday Inn's major costs and concerns involve operational activities—it provides its service instantaneously at each location—and marketing activities, while having minimal concern for outbound logistics. Yet for a distributor, such as the food distributor PYA, inbound and outbound logistics are the most critical area. Major retailers like Wal-Mart have built value advantages focusing on purchasing and inbound logistics while the most successful personal computer companies have built via sales, outbound logistics, and service through the mail order process.

Third, the relative importance of value activities can vary by a company's position in a broader value system that includes the value chains of its upstream suppliers and downstream customers or partners involved in providing products or services to end users. A producer of roofing shingles depends heavily on the downstream activities of wholesale distributors and building supply retailers to reach roofing contractors and do-it-yourselfers.

EXHIBIT 5–10   Possible Factors for Assessing Sources of Differentiation in Primary and Support Activities

Source: Based on Michael Porter, On Competition, 1998, Harvard Business School Press.

Support Activities

- Capability to identify new-product market opportunities and potential environmental threats
- Quality of the strategic planning system to achieve corporate objectives
- Coordination and integration of all value chain activities among organizational subunits
- Ability to obtain relatively low-cost funds for capital expenditures and working capital
- Level of information systems support in making strategic and routine decisions
- Timely and accurate management information on general and competitive environments
- Relationships with public policymakers and interest groups
- Public image and corporate citizenship

General Administration

- Effectiveness of procedures for recruiting, training, and promoting all levels of employees
- Appropriateness of reward systems for motivating and challenging employees
- A work environment that minimizes absenteeism and keeps turnover at desirable levels
- Relations with trade unions
- Active participation by managers and technical personnel in professional organizations
- Levels of employee motivation and job satisfaction

Human Resource Management

- Success of research and development activities in leading to product and process innovations
- Quality of working relationships between R&D personnel and other departments
- Timeliness of technology development activities in meeting critical deadlines
- Quality of laboratories and other facilities
- Qualification and experience of laboratory technicians and scientists
- Ability of work environment to encourage creativity and innovation

Technology Development

- Development of alternate sources for inputs to minimize dependence on a single supplier
- Procurement of raw materials (1) on a timely basis, (2) at lowest possible cost, (3) at acceptable levels of quality
- Procedures for procurement of plant, machinery, and buildings
- Development of criteria for lease-versus-purchase decisions
- Good, long-term relationships with reliable suppliers

Procurement

Profit Margin

Inbound Logistics	Operations	Outbound Logistics	Marketing and Sales	Service
- Soundness of material and inventory control systems - Efficiency of raw material warehousing activities	- Productivity of equipment compared to that of key competitors - Appropriate automation of production processes - Effectiveness of production control systems to improve quality and reduce costs - Efficiency of plant layout and work-flow design	- Timeliness and efficiency of delivery of finished goods and services - Efficiency of finished goods warehousing activities	- Effectiveness of market research to identify customer segments and needs - Innovation in sales promotion and advertising - Evaluation of alternate distribution channels - Motivation and competence of sales force - Development of an image of quality and a favorable reputation - Extent of brand loyalty among customers - Extent of market dominance within the market segment or overall market	- Means to solicit customer input for product improvements - Promptness of attention to customer complaints - Appropriateness of warranty and guarantee policies - Quality of customer education and training - Ability to provide replacement parts and repair services

Profit Margin

Primary Activities

BusinessWeek Volkswagen CEO Ferdinand Piëch had every reason to feel satisfied. The Austrian engineer and scion of one of Europe's most noted automotive dynasties was less than a year from retirement as chief of the German carmaker. As he looked back, Piëch could boast of one of the great turnarounds in automotive history. Since taking the top job at the Wolfsburg headquarters in 1993, his engineering brilliance had helped resurrect Volkswagen quality and turn models such as the Golf and Passat into all-time best-sellers. Piëch's relaunch of the Beetle cemented VW's hold in the U.S. market. Only VW had successfully revived a communist-era carmaker, Skoda of the Czech Republic. In 2001, as the global car industry lurched through a stressful year, VW saw profits grow above 2000 levels, when they more than doubled, to $1.8 billion, on sales of $76 billion.

Yet Piëch was stressed. Value chain analysis suggested two key value activities had driven his success—product development and operations. It also suggested that two other activities were becoming serious potential drains on the value chain and value he had so meticulously driven—human resource management and marketing and sales.

PRODUCT DEVELOPMENT

Piëch was driven. Unlike many other auto chiefs, he called the shots on product design and engineering. And if you worked for Dr. Piëch, you had better get it right. In Wolfsburg, executives joked that PEP, the acronym for the product development process *(Produktentwicklungsprozess)* really stands for *Piëch entscheidet persönlich—Piëch* decides himself. And he did so fast. He is said to have sketched out the Audi's all-wheel-drive system on the back of an envelope.

Without question, those achievements have been considerable. Volkswagen's four main brands—VW, Audi, Seat, and Skoda—have taken 19 percent of the European auto market, a gain of some three points in eight years, mostly at the expense of General Motors Corp. and Ford. Not bad for a company that eight years ago suffered from quality problems and a paucity of hit models. In South America, VW vehicles account for one-quarter of car sales, and in China, one-half. The top VW brands in the United States are the Jetta, Passat, and the new Beetle, a remake of the humble bug so beloved of 60s youth. Part of VW success lies in its quirky features. At night, the dashboard instruments the driver looks at, such as the speedometer and clock, light up in red, while those the driver touches, such as the radio, are backlit in blue. "It gives the vehicle some soul, which many of VW's competitors lack horribly," says Wes Brown, a consultant at Nextrend Inc., a Thousand Oaks (Calif.) auto-research firm.

OPERATIONS

When Piëch wasn't drawing up the plans, he was examining them with a gimlet eye. No screaming, of course: That was not the way for Piëch, an Austrian blueblood. One former transmission-plant manager said Piëch would tour the factory quietly, reviewing production data sheets and zeroing in instantly on any numbers suggesting something was amiss in the manufacturing process. "He's the only person whose very presence on the floor would make my stomach begin to hurt," says this manager.

Terrifying, yet inspiring. Under Piëch's tutelage, VW sweated the small stuff. Check this out, says one rival exec. On VW models, the gap between body panels—say between the front fender and wheel panel—had been cut to 1 millimeter. That puts them in a league with the industry's best.

HUMAN RESOURCE MANAGEMENT

In 1993, to buy labor peace, Piëch cut the workweek at VW's German plants from 35 hours to 28.8. That saved 30,000 jobs. But now VW workers can make upwards of $34 an hour. Piëch tried to push through a plan to lower the base wages of new German workers and link them to output instead of hours as this story was published. If this doesn't succeed, VW threatens to put new projects in places such as the Czech Republic, where wages are less than one-third German levels. Cutting such a deal is turning into a hard slog. The unions concede they need to be more flexible. But they are resisting management's demands to increase the workweek to more than 40 hours during peak production without paying overtime.

And investors frustrated with a low stock-PE ratio cannot expect a swift boost to the stock price. The government of Lower Saxony, the biggest investor, worries more about jobs than shareholder value. Five of VW's seven German factories are located in Lower Saxony, and they're among the least productive in Europe. According to World Markets Research Center in London, production at the Wolfsburg plant runs at 46 cars per worker per year, compared with 101 at Nissan Motor Co.'s British factory in Sunderland.

MARKETING AND SALES

VW also had gaps in its product lineup. It had nothing to offer in the category of compact minivans—the scaled-down versions of minivans that are popular in Europe. A sport utility vehicle was not scheduled to come out until 2003. "We're [also] missing some niche models—sports car, roadster, another convertible," said Jürgen Lehmann, manager of the Autohaus Moltke dealership in Stuttgart. VW had to sort out these issues while the competition gets tougher.

Bottomline, VW's value chain presents interesting challenges for Piëch's successor, Bernd Pischetsrieder. He inherited extraordinary strengths in product development and manufacturing operations. But for all of the success of the last decade, and an impressive market presence worldwide, he faces emerging value chain weaknesses in human resource management cost considerations and product line gaps in marketing and sales.

Source: "Volkswagen," *BusinessWeek,* July 23, 2001; "VW Needs a Jump," *BusinessWeek;* May 12, 2003.

Maytag manufactures its own appliances, sells them through independent distributors, and provides warranty service to the buyer. Sears outsources the manufacture of its appliances while it promotes its brand name—Kenmore—and handles all sales and service.

As these examples suggest, it is important that managers take into account their level of vertical integration when comparing their cost structure for activities on their value chain to those of key competitors. Comparing a fully integrated rival with a partially integrated one requires adjusting for the scope of activities performed to achieve meaningful comparison. It also suggests the need for examining costs associated with activities provided by upstream or downstream companies; these activities ultimately determine comparable, final costs to end users. Said another way, one company's comparative cost disadvantage (or advantage) may emanate more from activities undertaken by upstream or downstream "partners" than from activities under the direct control of that company—therefore suggesting less of a relative advantage or disadvantage within the company's direct value chain.

Value Chain Activities as Strengths or Weaknesses

The final basic consideration when applying value chain analysis is the need to have a meaningful comparison to use when evaluating a value activity as a strength or weakness. Similarly, the RBV identifies resources and competencies that become the basis for a sustained competitive advantage based on whether they provide the company with key strengths or weaknesses to shape strategic action. To do so requires a SWOT analysis which we now explore.

SWOT ANALYSIS

SWOT is an acronym for the internal Strengths and Weaknesses of a firm and the environmental Opportunities and Threats facing that firm. SWOT analysis is a widely used technique through which managers create a quick overview of a company's strategic situation. It is based on the assumption that an effective strategy derives from a sound "fit" between a firm's internal resources (strengths and weaknesses) and its external situation (opportunities and threats). A good fit maximizes a firm's strengths and opportunities and minimizes its weaknesses and threats. Accurately applied, this simple assumption has powerful implications for the design of a successful strategy.

Environmental and industry analysis in Chapters 3 and 4 provides the information needed to identify opportunities and threats in a firm's environment, the first fundamental focus in SWOT analysis.

Opportunities

An *opportunity* is a major favorable situation in a firm's environment. Key trends are one source of opportunities. Identification of a previously overlooked market segment, changes in competitive or regulatory circumstances, technological changes, and improved buyer or supplier relationships could represent opportunities for the firm.

Threats

A *threat* is a major unfavorable situation in a firm's environment. Threats are key impediments to the firm's current or desired position. The entrance of new competitors, slow market growth, increased bargaining power of key buyers or suppliers, technological changes, and new or revised regulations could represent threats to a firm's success.

Understanding the key opportunities and threats facing a firm helps its managers identify realistic options from which to choose an appropriate strategy and clarifies the most effective niche for the firm. The second fundamental focus in SWOT analysis is the identification of internal strengths and weaknesses.

Strengths

A *strength* is a resource advantage relative to competitors and the needs of the markets a firm serves or expects to serve. It is a *distinctive competence* when it gives the firm a comparative advantage in the marketplace. Strengths arise from the resources and competencies available to the firm.

Weaknesses

A *weakness* is a limitation or deficiency in one or more resources or competencies relative to competitors that impedes a firm's effective performance.

The sheer size and level of Microsoft's user base have proven to be a key strength on which it built its aggressive entry into Internet services. Limited financial capacity was a weakness recognized by Southwest Airlines, which charted a selective route expansion strategy to build the best profit record in a deregulated airline industry.

SWOT analysis can be used in many ways to aid strategic analysis. The most common way is to use it as a logical framework guiding systematic discussion of a firm's resources and the basic alternatives that emerge from this resource-based view. What one manager sees as an opportunity, another may see as a potential threat. Likewise, a strength to one manager may be a weakness to another. Different assessments may reflect underlying power considerations within the firm or differing factual perspectives. Systematic analysis of these issues facilitates objective internal analysis.

The diagram in Exhibit 5–12 illustrates how SWOT analysis builds on the results of an RBV of a firm to aid strategic analysis. Key external opportunities and threats are systematically

EXHIBIT 5–12
SWOT Analysis Diagram

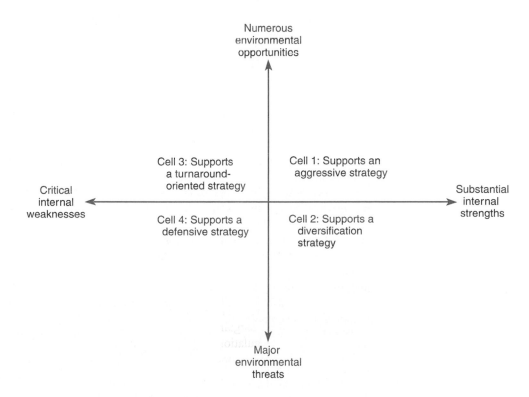

compared with internal resources and competencies—that is, strengths and weaknesses—in a structured approach. The objective is identification of one of four distinct patterns in the match between a firm's internal resources and external situation. Cell 1 is the most favorable situation; the firm faces several environmental opportunities and has numerous strengths that encourage pursuit of those opportunities. This situation suggests growth-oriented strategies to exploit the favorable match. America OnLine's intensive market development strategy in the online services market is the result of a favorable match of its strong technical expertise, early entry, and reputation resources with an opportunity for impressive market growth as millions of people joined the information highway in the last decade. Its continued strength in interactivity with Net-delivered media is currently a key component of AOL-Time Warner's new growth-oriented strategy in 2004.

Cell 4 is the least favorable situation, with the firm facing major environmental threats from a weak resource position. This situation clearly calls for strategies that reduce or redirect involvement in the products or markets examined by means of SWOT analysis. Texas Instruments offers a good example of a Cell 4 firm. It was a sprawling maker of chips, calculators, laptop PCs, military electronics, and engineering software on a sickening slid toward oblivion just ten years ago. Its young CEO, Tom Engibous, reinvigorated the ailing electronics giant and turned it into one of the hottest plays in semiconductors by betting the company on an emerging class of chips known as digital signal processors (DSPs). The chips crunch vast streams of data for an array of digital gadgets, including modems and cellular phones. Engibous shed billions of dollars worth of assets to focus on DSPs, which he calls "the most important silicon technology of the next decade." TI now commands nearly half of the $4.4 billion global market for the most advanced DSPs, and it's the No. 1 chip supplier to the sizzling digital wireless phone market.

In Cell 2, a firm whose RBV has identified several key strengths faces an unfavorable environment. In this situation, strategies would seek to redeploy those strong resources and competencies to build long-term opportunities in more opportunistic product markets. IBM, a dominant manufacturer of mainframes, servers, and PCs worldwide, has nurtured many strengths in computer-related and software-related markets for many years. Increasingly, however, it has had to address major threats that include product commoditization, pricing pressures, accelerated pace of innovation, and the like. Fortunately, Sam Palmisano's determined development of ISSC, better known now as IBM Global Services, has allowed IBM to build a long-term opportunity in more profitable growing markets of the next decade. In the last ten years since Palmisano ran it, Global Services has become the fastest-growing division of the company, its largest employer, and the keystone of IBM's strategic future. The group does everything from running a customer's IT department to consulting on legacy system upgrades to building custom supply-chain management applications. As IBM's hardware divisions struggle against price wars and commoditization and its software units fight to gain share beyond mainframes, it is Global Services that drives the company's growth.

A firm in Cell 3 faces impressive market opportunity but is constrained by weak internal resources. The focus of strategy for such a firm is eliminating the internal weaknesses so as to more effectively pursue the market opportunity. The AOL-Time Warner merger may well have afforded both companies a way to overcome key weaknesses, keeping them from pursuing vast twenty-first-century, Internet-based opportunities. AOL lacks programming content and the ability to sell programming profitably over time. Time Warner is at a loss in managing the complexities of interactive media services.

SWOT analysis has been a framework of choice among many managers for a long time because of its simplicity and its portrayal of the essence of sound strategy formulation—matching a firm's opportunities and threats with its strengths and weaknesses. Central to making SWOT analysis effective is accurate internal analysis—the identification of specific strengths and weaknesses around which sound strategy can be built. One of the historical deficiencies of SWOT analysis was the tendency to rely on a very general, categorical assessment of internal capabilities. The resource-based view came to exist in part as a remedy to this void in the strategic management field. It is an excellent way to identify internal strengths and weaknesses and use that information to enhance the quality of a SWOT analysis. Similarly, value chain analysis identifies elements of a company's capabilities and operations that are useful in conducting a SWOT analysis.

Using RBV, value chain analysis, and SWOT analysis improves the quality of internal analysis. This is particularly the case when managers make meaningful comparisons. The next section examines how meaningful comparisons are accomplished.

INTERNAL ANALYSIS: MAKING MEANINGFUL COMPARISONS

Managers need objective standards to use when examining internal resources and value-building activities. Whether applying the RBV, value chain analysis, or the SWOT approach, strategists rely on four basic perspectives to evaluate where their firm stacks up on its internal capabilities. These four perspectives are discussed in this section.

Comparison with Past Performance

Strategists use the firm's historical experience as a basis for evaluating internal factors. Managers are most familiar with the internal capabilities and problems of their firm because they have been immersed in its financial, marketing, production, and R&D activities. Not surprisingly, a manager's assessment of whether a certain internal factor—such as production facilities, sales organization, financial capacity, control systems, or key personnel—is a strength or a weakness will be strongly influenced by his or her experience in connection with that factor. In the capital-intensive airline industry, for example, debt capacity is a strategic internal factor. Delta Airlines managers view Delta's debt-equity ratio of less than 1.9 brought on by its acquisition of PanAm's international operations as a real weakness limiting its flexibility to invest in facilities because it maintained a ratio less than 0.6 for over 20 years. Continental Airlines managers, on the other hand, view Continental's much higher 3.5 debt-equity ratio as a growing strength, because it is down 50 percent from its 7.0 level five years earlier.

Although historical experience can provide a relevant evaluation framework, strategists must avoid tunnel vision in making use of it. NEC, Japan's IBM, initially dominated Japan's PC market with a 70 percent market share using a proprietary hardware system, much higher screen resolution, powerful distribution channels, and a large software library from third-party vendors. Far from worried, Hajime Ikeda, manager of NEC's planning division at the time, was quoted as saying: "We don't hear complaints from our users." By 2001, IBM, Apple, and Compaq filled the shelves in Japan's famous consumer electronics district, Akihabara. Hiroki Kamata, president of a Japanese computer research firm, reported that Japan's PC market, worth over $25 billion in 2001, saw Apple and IBM compatibles each having more market share than NEC because of better technology, software, and the restrictions created by NEC's proprietary technology. Clearly, using only historical experience as a basis for identifying strengths and weaknesses can prove dangerously inaccurate.

Stages of Industry Evolution

The requirements for success in industry segments change over time. Strategists can use these changing requirements, which are associated with different stages of industry evolution, as a framework for identifying and evaluating the firm's strengths and weaknesses.

Exhibit 5–13 depicts four stages of industry evolution and the typical changes in functional capabilities that are often associated with business success at each of these stages. The early development of a product market, for example, entails minimal growth in sales,

EXHIBIT 5–13

Sources of Distinctive Competence at Different Stages of Industry Evolution

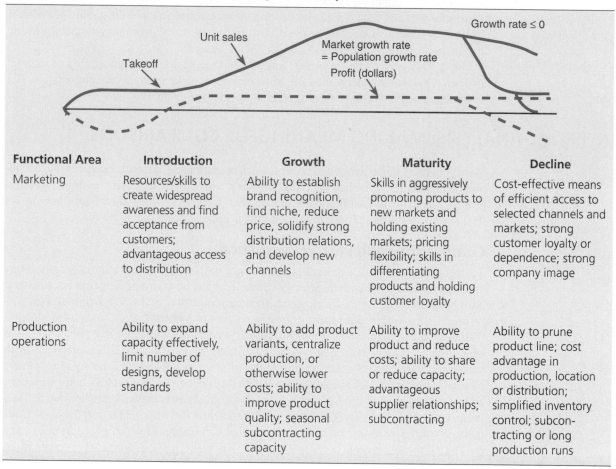

Functional Area	Introduction	Growth	Maturity	Decline
Marketing	Resources/skills to create widespread awareness and find acceptance from customers; advantageous access to distribution	Ability to establish brand recognition, find niche, reduce price, solidify strong distribution relations, and develop new channels	Skills in aggressively promoting products to new markets and holding existing markets; pricing flexibility; skills in differentiating products and holding customer loyalty	Cost-effective means of efficient access to selected channels and markets; strong customer loyalty or dependence; strong company image
Production operations	Ability to expand capacity effectively, limit number of designs, develop standards	Ability to add product variants, centralize production, or otherwise lower costs; ability to improve product quality; seasonal subcontracting capacity	Ability to improve product and reduce costs; ability to share or reduce capacity; advantageous supplier relationships; subcontracting	Ability to prune product line; cost advantage in production, location or distribution; simplified inventory control; subcontracting or long production runs

major R&D emphasis, rapid technological change in the product, operating losses, and a need for sufficient resources or slack to support a temporarily unprofitable operation. Success at this introduction stage may be associated with technical skill, with being first in new markets, or with having a marketing advantage that creates widespread awareness. Radio Shack's initial success with its TRS–80 home computer was based in part on its ability to gain widespread exposure and acceptance in the ill-defined home computer market via the large number of existing Radio Shack outlets throughout the country.

The strengths necessary for success change in the growth stage. Rapid growth brings new competitors into the product market. At this stage, such factors as brand recognition, product differentiation, and the financial resources to support both heavy marketing expenses and the effect of price competition on cash flow can be key strengths. IBM entered the personal computer market in the growth stage and was able to rapidly become the market leader with a strategy based on its key strengths in brand awareness and possession of the financial resources needed to support consumer advertising. Radio Shack discontinued its TRS–80 due to IBM's strength. Within a few years, however, IBM lost that lead in the next stage as speed in distribution and cost structures became the key success factors—strengths for Dell and several mail order–oriented computer assemblers.

EXHIBIT 5–13
(continued)

Functional Area	Introduction	Growth	Maturity	Decline
Finance	Resources to support high net cash overflow and initial losses; ability to use leverage effectively	Ability to finance rapid expansion, to have net cash outflows but increasing profits; resources to support product improvements	Ability to generate and redistribute increasing net cash inflows; effective cost control systems	Ability to reuse or liquidate unneeded equipment; advantage in cost of facilities; control system accuracy; streamlined management control
Personnel	Flexibility in staffing and training new management; existence of employees with key skills in new products or markets	Existence of an ability to add skilled personnel; motivated and loyal workforce	Ability to cost effectively, reduce workforce, increase efficiency	Capacity to reduce and reallocate personnel; cost advantage
Engineering and research and development	Ability to make engineering changes, have technical bugs in product and process resolved	Skill in quality and new feature development; ability to start developing successor product	Ability to reduce costs, develop variants, differentiate products	Ability to support other grown areas or to apply product to unique customer needs
Key functional area and strategy focus	Engineering: market penetration	Sales: consumer loyalty; market share	Production efficiency, successor products	Finance, maximum investment recovery

As the industry moves through a shakeout phase and into the maturity stage, industry growth continues, but at a decreasing rate. The number of industry segments expands, but technological change in product design slows considerably. As a result, competition usually becomes more intense, and promotional or pricing advantages and differentiation become key internal strengths. Technological change in process design becomes intense as the many competitors seek to provide the product in the most efficient manner. Where R&D was critical in the introduction stage, efficient production is now crucial to continued success in the broader industry segments. Ford's emphasis on quality control and modern, efficient production has helped it prosper in the maturing U.S. auto industry, while General Motors, which pays almost 50 percent more than Ford to produce a comparable car, continues to decline.

When the industry moves into the decline stage, strengths and weaknesses center on cost advantages, superior supplier or customer relationships, and financial control. Competitive advantage can exist at this stage, at least temporarily, if a firm serves gradually shrinking markets that competitors are choosing to leave.

Exhibit 5–13 is a rather simple model of the stages of industry evolution. These stages can and do vary from the model. What should be borne in mind is that the relative importance of various determinants of success differs across the stages of industry evolution. Thus, the state of that evolution must be considered in internal analysis. Exhibit 5–13 suggests dimensions that are particularly deserving of in-depth consideration when a company profile is being developed.

Benchmarking—Comparison with Competitors

A major focus in determining a firm's resources and competencies is comparison with existing (and potential) competitors. Firms in the same industry often have different marketing skills, financial resources, operating facilities and locations, technical know-how, brand images, levels of integration, managerial talent, and so on. These different internal resources can become relative strengths (or weaknesses) depending on the strategy a firm chooses. In choosing a strategy, managers should compare the firm's key internal capabilities with those of its rivals, thereby isolating its key strengths and weaknesses.

In the home appliance industry, for example, Sears and General Electric are major rivals. Sears's principal strength is its retail network. For GE, distribution—through independent franchised dealers—has traditionally been a relative weakness. GE's possession of the financial resources needed to support modernized mass production has enabled it to maintain both cost and technological advantages over its rivals, particularly Sears. This major strength for GE is a relative weakness for Sears, which depends solely on subcontracting to produce its Kenmore appliances. On the other hand, maintenance and repair service are important in the appliance industry. Historically, Sears has had strength in this area because it maintains fully staffed service components and spreads the costs of components over numerous departments at each retail location. GE, on the other hand, has had to depend on regional service centers and on local contracting with independent service firms by its independent local dealers. Among the internal factors that Sears and GE must consider in developing a strategy are distribution networks, technological capabilities, operating costs, and service facilities. Managers in both organizations have built successful strategies yet those strategies are quite different. Benchmarking each other, they have identified ways to build on relative strengths while avoiding dependence on capabilities at which the other firm excels.

Benchmarking, comparing the way "our" company performs a specific activity with a competitor or other company doing the same thing, has become a central concern of managers in quality commitment companies worldwide. Particularly as the value chain framework has taken hold in structuring internal analysis, managers seek to systematically benchmark the costs and results of the smallest value activities against relevant competitors or other useful standards because it has proven to be an effective way to continuously improve that activity. The ultimate objective in benchmarking is to identify the "best practices" in performing an activity, to learn how lower costs, fewer defects, or other outcomes linked to excellence are achieved. Companies committed to benchmarking attempt to isolate and identify where their costs or outcomes are out of line with what the best practicers of a particular activity experience (competitors and noncompetitors) and then attempt to change their activities to achieve the new best practices standard.

Comparison with key competitors can prove useful in ascertaining whether their internal capabilities on these and other factors are strengths or weaknesses. Significant favorable differences (existing or expected) from competitors are potential cornerstones of a firm's strategy. Moreover, through comparison with major competitors, a firm may avoid strategic commitments that it cannot competitively support. Exhibit 5–14, Strategy in Action, shows how UPS used competitor comparison to assess its strengths and weaknesses in the package transportation industry.

Comparison with Success Factors in the Industry

Industry analysis (see Chapter 3) involves identifying the factors associated with successful participation in a given industry. As was true for the evaluation methods discussed above,

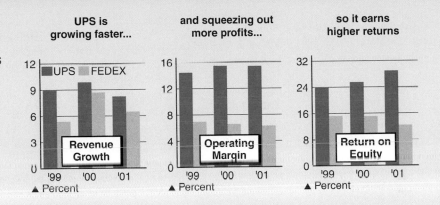

Success Begets Success Stacking UPS up against FedEx

UPS is growing faster... (Revenue Growth, Percent)

and squeezing out more profits... (Operating Margin, Percent)

so it earns higher returns (Return on Equity, Percent)

Data: Banc of America Securities ©BW

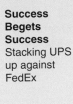

BusinessWeek Over the past two years, the company has quietly shed its image as the slowpoke of shipping. Be it e-tailing frenzy or dot-com crash, UPS has captured customers by bombarding them with choices: fast flights versus cheap ground delivery, simple shipping or a panoply of manufacturing, warehousing, and supply-chain services. In the United States and several foreign markets, UPS has grabbed a commanding lead over FedEx—and not just in everyday package delivery but in the New Economy services such as logistics. In North America, UPS has even snagged the distinction of preferred carrier to the Web generation: The company handles 36 percent of all online purchases, versus 13 percent for FedEx. "UPS is doing things in e-commerce that other companies are just starting to talk about," says Jack R. Staff, chief economist at Zona Research in Redwood City, Calif.

The ascent of UPS charts a reversal of fortune in one of the fiercest rivalries in Corporate America. It was FedEx, after all, that pioneered both overnight delivery of packages and the ability to track their journey using computers. These 1970s' era innovations rocked the shipping industry and helped set the stage for the Internet Revolution of the 1990s. Even now, FedEx rules in certain areas of air freight. Its carefully burnished brand still says "absolutely, positively" to thousands of loyal customers—and not without reason. FedEx is one of America's great success stories, extolled for its customer service.

In the view of many analysts and industry execs, however, UPS now has a pronounced advantage in several hotly contested areas. In addition to its overwhelming lead in ground shipping and its online triumphs, UPS can point to a logistics business that is growing by 40 percent a year. FedEx is struggling to reverse a decline in this area.

Even in sectors where FedEx still rules, UPS is catching up quickly. FedEx has a commanding lead in the profitable overnight service, for example, delivering more than 3 million such packages daily in 200-plus countries and accounting for 39 percent of the market. UPS is No. 2, with 2.2 million overnight packages—but its volume has been growing faster than FedEx's for at least three years. In 2000, UPS's overnight business grew at 8 percent, compared with FedEx's 3.6 percent. And UPS's operating margin on its domestic air-express service is higher—24 percent versus 6 percent—according to Gary H. Yablon, a transportation analyst at Credit Suisse First Boston.

So what accounts for UPS's growth in overnight? The company trumpets its decision in 1999 to integrate overnight delivery into its vast ground-transportation network. UPS, like FedEx, still uses planes to make most such deliveries. But in the past two years, its logisticians have also figured out how to make quick mid-distance deliveries—as far as 500 miles in one night—by truck, which is much less expensive than by air. As a result, UPS's overall cost per package is $6.65, compared with FedEx's $11.89, according to CSFB. Even though FedEx also uses trucks for short hauls, "UPS has a real cost advantage," says John D. Kasarda, director of the University of North Carolina's Frank Hawkins Kenan Institute of Private Enterprise and a former FedEx consultant.

UPS's core strength is its fleet of 152,000 brown trucks, which reach virtually every address in the United States—and increasingly, the world. FedEx has belatedly begun to build its own home-delivery system. But the cost of duplicating a system UPS has spent nearly 100 years building could prove prohibitive. And with $3 billion in cash on hand, UPS could easily wage a price war against FedEx, which isn't generating any spare cash. "This is a game FedEx can't win,"

(continued)

says Peter V. Coleman, a transportation analyst at Bank of America Securities. That leaves FedEx dependent on an air-delivery system that is increasingly expensive to operate.

	UPS	FedEx
Founded	1907	1971
Chairman	James P. Kelly	Frederick W. Smith
Headquarters	Atlanta, Ga.	Memphis, Tenn.
2000 Revenue	$29.77 billion	$18.3 billion
Net Income	$2.93 billion	$688 million
Employees	359,000	215,000
Daily Package Volume	13.2 million	5 million
Fleet	152,500 trucks, 560 planes	43,500 trucks, 662 planes

	Unit Cost	Unit Profit	Operating Margin	Avg Daily Volume
Air Deliveries, U.S.				
FedEx	$15.27	$0.93	6%	2,924,000
UPS	$14.60	$3.76	22%	2,162,000
Ground Deliveries, U.S.				
FedEx	$4.77	$0.68	13%	1,541,000
UPS	$4.95	$0.61	11%	10,945,000
Overall Average, including International				
FedEx	$11.89	$0.85	7%	4,788,000
UPS	$6.65	$1.17	15%	14,236,000

Data: Credit Suisse First Boston

Source: "UPS: Can It Keep Delivering?" *BusinessWeek*, 3/24/03.

the key determinants of success in an industry may be used to identify a firm's internal strengths and weaknesses. By scrutinizing industry competitors, as well as customer needs, vertical industry structure, channels of distribution, costs, barriers to entry, availability of substitutes, and suppliers, a strategist seeks to determine whether a firm's current internal capabilities represent strengths or weaknesses in new competitive arenas. The discussion in Chapter 3 provides a useful framework—five industry forces—against which to examine a firm's potential strengths and weaknesses. General Cinema Corporation, the largest U.S. movie theater operator, determined that its internal skills in marketing, site analysis, creative financing, and management of geographically dispersed operations were key strengths relative to major success factors in the soft-drink bottling industry. This assessment proved accurate. Within 10 years after it entered the soft-drink bottling industry, General Cinema became the largest franchised bottler of soft drinks in the United States, handling Pepsi, 7UP, Dr Pepper, and Sunkist. Exhibit 5–15, Strategy in Action, describes how Avery Dennison used industry evolution benchmarking versus 3M to create a new, successful strategy.

Summary

This chapter looked at several ways managers achieve greater objectivity and rigor as they analyze their company's internal capabilities. Managers often start their internal analysis with questions like: "How well is the current strategy working? What is our current situation? Or what are our strengths and weaknesses?" The resource-based view provides a key, fundamental framework for analyzing firm success based on the firm's internal resources and competencies. This chapter described how insightful managers look at their business as a chain of activities that add value creating the products or services they sell—this is called *value chain analysis.* Managers who use value chain analysis to understand the value structure within their firm's activities and look at the value system, which also includes upstream suppliers and downstream partners and buyers, often gain very meaningful insights into their company's strategic resources, competencies, and options. *SWOT analysis,* a widely used approach to internal analysis, provides a logical way to apply the results of an RBV and a value chain analysis. Managers frequently use RBV, value chain, and SWOT analysis to introduce realism and greater objectivity into their internal analysis.

Strategy in Action
Avery Dennison Uses Benchmarking and Stage of Industry Evaluation to Turn Weakness into Strength

BusinessWeek

Avery Dennison has long made adhesives and what it calls "sticky papers" for business customers. Ten years ago, AD decided to take on 3M with its own version of 3M's highly successful Post-It notes and Scotch transparent tape.

How frequently did you buy Avery Notes and Avery Tape? You probably have never heard of them, right? That is because Avery was beat up in that market by 3M and AD exited the business after just a few years. Key strengths, distribution and brand name, that 3M used to build those products were major weaknesses at AD. Plus, in President Charles Miller's way of viewing it, 3M remained aggressive and true to an innovative culture to back its products while AD had grown rusty and "me too" rather than being the innovator it had traditionally been with

pressure-sensitive papers. So faced with considerable weakness competing against a major threat, Miller refocused AD on getting innovative in areas of traditional technical strength.

Today, AD has 30 percent of its sales from products introduced in the past five years. It has half the market for adhesive paper stock and 40 percent of the market for coated paper films for package labels. Says Miller, "We believe in market evolution. The best way to control a market is to invent it. With innovative products, superstores aren't able to squeeze margins, as they can in commodity products." New products now pour out of AD labs to position AD strengths against early life cycle stage opportunities.

Source: "The Business Week 50," *BusinessWeek,* March 23, 2001.

Finally, this chapter covered four ways objectivity and realism are enhanced when managers use meaningful standards for comparison regardless of the particular analytical framework they employ in internal analysis. This chapter is followed by an appendix covering traditional financial analysis to serve as a refresher and reminder about this basic internal analysis tool.

When matched with management's environmental analyses and mission priorities, the process of internal analysis provides the critical foundation for strategy formulation. Armed with an accurate, thorough, and timely internal analysis, managers are in a better position to formulate effective strategies. The next chapter describes basic strategy alternatives that any firm may consider.

Questions for Discussion

1. Describe SWOT analysis as a way to guide internal analysis. How does this approach reflect the basic strategic management process?

2. What is the resource-based view of the firm? Give examples of three different types of resources.

3. What are three characteristics that make resources more, or less, valuable? Provide an example of each.

4. Why do you think value chain analysis has become a preferred approach to guide internal analysis? What are its strengths? Its weaknesses?

5. Apply SWOT analysis to yourself and your career aspirations. What are your major strengths and weaknesses? How might you use your knowledge of these strengths and weaknesses to develop your future career plans?

Chapter 5 Discussion Case

Can Dunkin' KO Krispy?

BusinessWeek

1 In the war of the doughnuts, the reigning champ has been getting hopped by the upstart. Now, Dunkin' Donuts is plotting a new offensive. For half a century, Krispy Kreme and Dunkin' Donuts have warily eyed each other from different sides of the Mason-Dixon line, Krispy Kreme Doughnuts ruled the Southeast with its hot, gooey glazed doughnuts, and Dunkin' blanketed New England with boxy outlets that served more cups of coffee than they did crullers.

2 Each chain built a cult following: Krispy Kreme combined a wholesome, 1950s image with an airy, sweet-beyond-imagination doughnut. Dunkin' was the dependable delight at the strip mall, a blue-collar joint that supplied cops and construction workers but also drew regular folks who shunned $3 lattes from Starbucks.

SUNKEN REPUTATION

3 Yet the doughnut détente is about to end as both chains race to expand nationwide. Krispy Kreme took a major step in June when it opened its first store in Massachusetts—Dunkin' Donuts' home turf. But the impact of KK's lone Bay State outlet on DD will be more symbolic than financial in the near term, Dunkin', a division of Allied Domecq based in Randolph, Mass., boasts 600 stores in the Boston area and 3,800 stores nationwide, versus Krispy Kreme's 292. Its $2.8 billion in annual revenue dwarfs Krispy Kreme's sales of $492 million in the year ending Feb. 2.

4 So why does Dunkin' Donuts seem like the underdog in this battle? Partly because Krispy Kreme has come on so strong since it went public in April, 2000. Since then, it has opened about 150 stores—more than it estimated in half the time it allotted. Krispy's stock price has quadrupled to more than $40, and same-store sales grew 11 percent last year, versus 6 percent for Dunkin' Donuts. Krispy Kreme spends nothing on advertising (except for handing out free doughnuts to local media outlets when it opens a new store), yet it boasts nearly as much brand buzz as megamarketing wonders like Nike or Coke.

5 For investors, the question is whether Krispy Kreme's run in the sun on Wall Street is threatened. Dunkin' Donuts is gearing up big-time to fight back even as it has had to combat negative images about its brand. Outlets that weren't doing enough housekeeping to meet the chain's standards became the butt of late-night jokes. Some franchisees were convicted of underreporting income and evading income taxes. Dunkin' sued hundreds of franchisees to help clean up the chain's reputation.

COFFEE AND KREME

6 Unlike Krispy Kreme, investors can't bet on just Dunkin' Donuts. It's just one part of the Quick Service Restaurant (QSR) division of the British-based Allied Domecq. Baskin Robbins and Togo's are the other two. QSR makes up 9.5 percent of sales and 13 percent of the parent's profit.

7 Still, Dunkin' has its work cut out for it. After 53 years of making doughnuts, the chain has yet to match its well-known brand name with a nationwide presence. "Dunkin' Donuts is the 800-pound gorilla that is only living in 40 percent of the forest," says Christopher Muller, an associate professor at the University of Florida's Rosen School of Hospitality. Nearly two-thirds of its stores are located in the Northeast and mid-Atlantic states, with very few west of the Mississippi.

8 Meanwhile, Krispy Kreme's blistering expansion has helped it pick up market share. In 2002, it owned 13.1 percent of the U.S. doughnut market, up from 4.8 percent in 1999. In the same period, Dunkin' Donuts' share has dropped 20 points, to 57 percent. Some of that has gone to mom-and-pop operations, but a huge chunk has gone to its main rival, according to Technomic Information Services.

MORNING RITUAL

9 Dunkin's numbers could erode further as Krispy Kreme borrows a move from its competitor's playbook. First, it's not stopping at doughnuts. It'll be building a bread business, and it's heating up its coffee offerings—just like Dunkin' Doughnuts. And Krispy plans to open smaller, cheaper satellite stores.

"They'll make Krispy Kreme much more convenient for customers," says Scott Livengood, the Southern chain's CEO.

10 Convenience is exactly what has made Dunkin' Donuts thrive. In the densest parts of its core New England market, it boasts one store per 6,750 people (Krispy Kreme until now has aimed for one store to serve 100,000). In some places, four or five Dunkin' outlets can be found within a half mile of each other, each with cars lined up through the parking lot and out onto the highway shoulder during morning rush hour. For Boston-area commuters, stopping at a Dunkin' Donuts outlet for coffee in the morning is about as routine as getting dressed.

11 "We're talking massive customer loyalty," says Nancy Koehn, professor of business administration at Harvard Business School. Even a Krispy Kreme manager at the Medford (Mass.) construction site had an orange-and-purple Dunkin' cup and bag on his desk.

MASSIVE BUILDOUT

12 Yet spreading that customer loyalty beyond the Northeast and getting existing customers to spend more each time they come in is a tall order. Jon Luther, who heads the chain as CEO of Allied Domecq's QSR unit, is trying to serve up solutions. To get more franchisees in new areas to sign on, he has offered to build doughnut-production facilities for them and run them for up to five years. In the past, franchisees in an area formed a co-op and shared the burden.

13 "Dunkin' Donuts' weakness is that it isn't national, but it will be," says Luther, the first outsider to run the company since founder Bill Rosenberg sold his first Dunkin' doughnut in 1950. The chain plans to open 342 new stores this year in the United States and 630 more in 2004—the equivalent of more than three entire Krispy Kreme chains.

14 Next, Luther will try to convince customers used to a regular cuppa joe to switch to pricier espresso and latte. But doesn't the upscale coffee clash with the chain's Joe Doughnut image? Not necessarily, say some marketing experts. The popularity of Starbucks and other specialty coffee stores has started to move once-elite espresso and cappuccino into the mainstream—where Dunkin' Donuts rules.

DUNKINIZATION

15 "Small luxuries [like premium coffee] have become more mass market," says Koehn of Harvard. "Core customers are considering trying a latte or cappuccino. It may seem more palatable or trustworthy in a Dunkin' Donuts cup." The trick for Dunkin' will be to serve them fast. The chain promises to deliver a cappuccino in less than a minute.

16 Dunkin' has never claimed to be a trendsetter. Quite the opposite, in fact. After Starbucks introduced frappuccino, Dunkin' came out with its Coolatta and saw beverage sales soar. When bagels took off in the mid '90s, Dunkin' jumped on that trend, too. Now it's the largest bagel retailer in the country. "We watch trends and then Dunkinize them," says Ken Kimmel, a vice-president of Dunkin' Donuts Concepts, the chain's marketing arm.

17 And at the pace Dunkin is going now, the pressure on Krispy Kreme to execute its strategy perfectly increases. It's something for investors to think about the next time they bite into a nice sugary donut.

Source: Faith Arner, "Can Dunkin' KO Krispy?" *Business Week*, July 3, 2003.

Appendix 5

Using Financial Analysis

One of the most important tools for assessing the strength of an organization within its industry is financial analysis. Managers, investors, and creditors all employ some form of this analysis as the beginning point for their financial decision making. Investors use financial analyses in making decisions about whether to buy or sell stock, and creditors use them in deciding whether or not to lend. They provide managers with a measurement of how the company is doing in comparison with its performance in past years and with the performance of competitors in the industry.

Although financial analysis is useful for decision making, some weaknesses should be noted. Any picture that it provides of the company is based on past data. Although trends may be noteworthy, this picture should not automatically be assumed to be applicable to the future. In addition, the analysis is only as good as the accounting procedures that have provided the information. When making comparisons between companies, one should keep in mind the variability of accounting procedures from firm to firm.

There are four basic groups of financial ratios: liquidity, leverage, activity, and profitability.

Depicted in Exhibit 5–A are the specific ratios calculated for each of the basic groups. Liquidity and leverage ratios represent an assessment of the risk of the firm. Activity and profitability ratios are measures of the return generated by the assets of the firm. The interaction between certain groups of ratios is indicated by arrows.

Typically, two common financial statements are used in financial analyses: the balance sheet and the income statement. Exhibit 5–B is a balance sheet and Exhibit 5–C an income statement for the ABC Company. These statements will be used to illustrate the financial analyses.

LIQUIDITY RATIOS

Liquidity ratios are used as indicators of a firm's ability to meet its short-term obligations. These obligations include any current liabilities, including currently maturing long-term debt. Current assets move through a normal cash cycle of inventories—sales—accounts receivable—cash. The firm then uses cash to pay off or reduce its current liabilities. The best-known liquidity ratio is the current ratio: current assets divided by current liabilities. For the ABC Company, the current ratio is calculated as follows:

$$\frac{\text{Current assets}}{\text{Current liabilities}} = \frac{\$4,125,000}{\$2,512,500} = 1.64 \,(2005)$$

$$= \frac{\$3,618,000}{\$2,242,250} = 1.161 \,(2004)$$

Most analysts suggest a current ratio of 2 to 3. A large current ratio is not necessarily a good sign; it may mean that an organization is not making the most efficient use of its assets. The optimum current ratio will vary from industry to industry, with the more volatile industries requiring higher ratios.

Source: Prepared by Elizabeth Gatewood, Indiana University. ©Elizabeth Gatewood, 2004. Reprinted by permission of Elizabeth Gatewood.

EXHIBIT 5–A   **Financial Ratios**

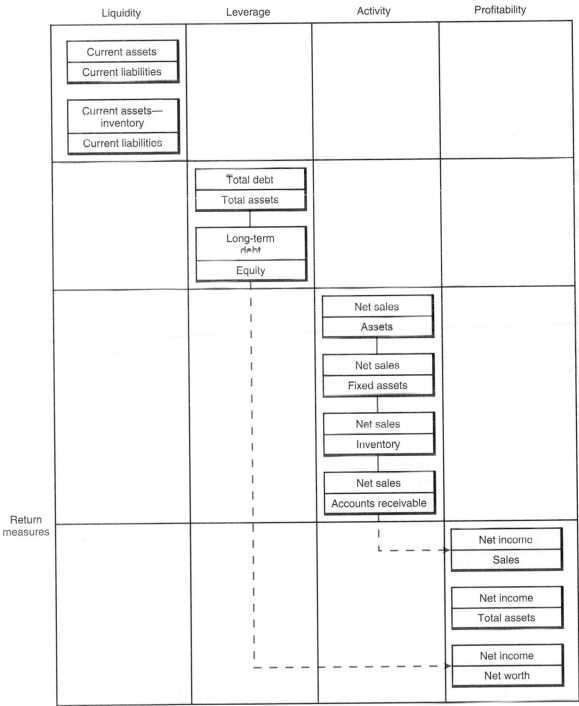

EXHIBIT 5–B
ABC Company Balance Sheet As of December 31, 2004, and 2005

		2005		2004
Assets				
Current assets:				
Cash		$ 140,000		$ 115,000
Accounts receivable		1,760,000		1,440,000
Inventory		2,175,000		2,000,000
Prepaid expenses		50,000		63,000
Total current assets		4,125,000		3,618,000
Fixed assets:				
Long-term receivable		1,255,000		1,090,000
Property and plant	$2,037,000		$2,015,000	
Less: Accumulated depreciation	862,000		860,000	
Net property and plant		1,175,000		1,155,000
Other fixed assets		550,000		530,000
Total fixed assets		2,980,000		2,775,000
Total assets		$7,105,000		$6,393,000
Liabilities and Stockholders' Equity				
Current liabilities:				
Accounts payable		$1,325,000		$1,225,000
Bank loans payable		475,000		550,000
Accrued federal taxes		675,000		425,000
Current maturities (long-term debt)		17,500		26,000
Dividends payable		20,000		16,250
Total current liabilities		2,512,500		2,242,250
Long-term liabilities		1,350,000		1,425,000
Total liabilities		3,862,000		3,667,250
Stockholders' equity:				
Common stock				
(104,046 shares outstanding in 1995;				
101,204 shares outstanding in 1994)		44,500		43,300
Additional paid-in-capital		568,000		372,450
Retained earnings		2,630,000		2,310,000
Total stockholders' equity		3,242,500		2,725,750
Total liabilities and stockholders' equity		$7,105,000		$6,393,000

Since slow-moving or obsolescent inventories could overstate a firm's ability to meet short-term demands, the quick ratio is sometimes preferred to assess a firm's liquidity. The quick ratio is current assets minus inventories, divided by current liabilities. The quick ratio for the ABC Company is calculated as follows:

$$\frac{\text{Current assets} - \text{Inventories}}{\text{Current liabilities}} = \frac{\$1,950,000}{\$2,512,500} = 0.78 \ (2005)$$

$$= \frac{\$1,618,000}{\$2,242,250} = 0.72 \ (2004)$$

EXHIBIT 5–C
ABC Company Income Statement For the Years Ending December 31, 2004, and 2005

	2005		2004	
Net sales		$8,250,000		$8,000,000
Cost of goods sold	$5,100,000		$5,000,000	
Administrative expenses	1,750,000		1,680,000	
Other expenses	420,000		390,000	
Total		7,270,000		7,070,000
Earnings before interest and taxes		980,000		930,000
Less: Interest expense		210,000		210,000
Earnings before taxes		770,000		720,000
Less: Federal income taxes		360,000		325,000
Earnings after taxes (net income)		$ 410,000		$ 395,000
Common stock cash dividends		$ 90,000		$ 84,000
Addition to retained earnings		$ 320,000		$ 311,000
Earnings per common share		$ 3.940		$ 3.90
Dividends per common share		$ 0.865		$ 0.83

A quick ratio of approximately 1 would be typical for American industries. Although there is less variability in the quick ratio than in the current ratio, stable industries would be able to operate safely with a lower ratio.

LEVERAGE RATIOS

Leverage ratios identify the source of a firm's capital — owners or outside creditors. The term *leverage* refers to the fact that using capital with a fixed interest charge will "amplify" either profits or losses in relation to the equity of holders of common stock. The most commonly used ratio is total debt divided by total assets. Total debt includes current liabilities and long-term liabilities. This ratio is a measure of the percentage of total funds provided by debt. A total debt–total assets ratio higher than 0.5 is usually considered safe only for firms in stable industries.

$$\frac{\text{Total debt}}{\text{Total assets}} = \frac{\$3,862,500}{\$7,105,000} = 0.54 \,(2005)$$

$$= \frac{\$3,667,250}{\$6,393,000} = 0.57 \,(2004)$$

The ratio of long-term debt to equity is a measure of the extent to which sources of long-term financing are provided by creditors. It is computed by dividing long-term debt by the stockholders' equity.

$$\frac{\text{Long-term debt}}{\text{Equity}} = \frac{\$1,350,000}{\$3,242,500} = 0.42 \,(2005)$$

$$= \frac{\$1,425,000}{\$2,725,750} = 0.52 \,(2004)$$

3. A net decrease in any liability.
4. A retirement or purchase of stock.
5. Payment of cash dividends.

We compute gross changes to depreciable fixed assets by adding depreciation from the income statement for the period to net fixed assets at the end of the period and then subtracting from the total net fixed assets at the beginning of the period. The residual represents the change in depreciable fixed assets for the period.

For the ABC Company, the following change would be calculated:

Net property and plant (2005)	$1,175,000
Depreciation for 2005	+ 80,000
	$1,255,000
Net property and plant (2004)	−1,155,000
	$ 100,000

To avoid double counting, the change in retained earnings is not shown directly in the funds statement. When the funds statement is prepared, this account is replaced by the earnings after taxes, or net income, as a source of funds, and dividends paid during the year as a use of funds. The difference between net income and the change in the retained earnings account will equal the amount of dividends paid during the year. The accompanying sources and uses of funds statement was prepared for the ABC Company.

A funds analysis is useful for determining trends in working-capital positions and for demonstrating how the firm has acquired and employed its funds during some period.

ABC Company
Sources and Uses of Funds Statement
for 2005

Sources

Prepaid expenses	$ 13,000
Accounts payable	100,000
Accrued federal taxes	250,000
Dividends payable	3,750
Common stock	1,200
Additional paid-in capital	195,000
Earnings after taxes (net income)	410,000
Depreciation	80,000
Total sources	$1,053,500

Uses

Cash	$ 25,000
Accounts receivable	320,000
Inventory	175,000
Long-term receivables	165,000
Property and plant	100,000
Other fixed assets	20,000
Bank loans payable	75,000
Current maturities of long-term debt	8,500
Long-term liabilities	75,000
Dividents paid	90,000
Total uses	$1,053,500

EXHIBIT 5–E
A Summary of the Financial Position of a Firm

Ratios and Working Capital	2001	2002	2003	2004	2005	Trend	Industry Average	Interpre- tation
Liquidity: Current								
Quick								
Leverage: Debt-assets								
Debt-equity								
Activity: Asset turnover								
Fixed asset ratio								
Inventory turnover								
Accounts receivable turnover								
Average collection period								
Profitability: ROS								
ROI								
ROE								
Working-capital position								

CONCLUSION

It is recommended that you prepare a chart, such as that shown in Exhibit 5–E, so you can develop a useful portrayal of these financial analyses. The chart allows a display of the ratios over time. The "Trend" column could be used to indicate your evaluation of the ratios over time (e.g., "favorable," "neutral," or "unfavorable"). The "Industry Average" column could include recent industry averages on these ratios or those of key competitors. These would provide information to aid interpretation of the analyses. The "Interpretation" column could be used to describe your interpretation of the ratios for this firm. Overall, this chart gives a basic display of the ratios that provides a convenient format for examining the firm's financial condition.

Finally, Exhibit 5–F is included to provide a quick reference summary of the calculations and meanings of the ratios discussed earlier.

EXHIBIT 5–F
A Summary of Key Financial Ratios

Ratio	Calculation	Meaning
Liquidity Ratios:		
Current ratio	$\dfrac{\text{Current assets}}{\text{Current liabilities}}$	The extent to which a firm can meet its short-term obligations.
Quick ratio	$\dfrac{\text{Current assets–Inventory}}{\text{Current liabilities}}$	The extent to which a firm can meet its short-term obligations without relying on the sale of inventories.
Leverage Ratios:		
Debt-to-total-assets ratio	$\dfrac{\text{Total debt}}{\text{Total assets}}$	The percentage of total funds that are provided by creditors.
Debt-to-equity ratio	$\dfrac{\text{Total debt}}{\text{Total stockholders' equity}}$	The percentage of total funds provided by creditors versus the percentage provided by owners.
Long-term-debt-to-equity ratio	$\dfrac{\text{Long-term debt}}{\text{Total stockholders' equity}}$	The balance between debt and equity in a firm's long-term capital structure.
Times-interest-earned ratio	$\dfrac{\text{Profits before interest and taxes}}{\text{Total interest charges}}$	The extent to which earnings can decline without the firm becoming unable to meet its annual interest costs.
Activity Ratios:		
Inventory turnover	$\dfrac{\text{Sales}}{\text{Inventory of finished goods}}$	Whether a firm holds excessive stocks of inventories and whether a firm is selling its inventories slowly compared to the industry average.
Fixed assets turnover	$\dfrac{\text{Sales}}{\text{Fixed assets}}$	Sales productivity and plant equipment utilization.
Total assets turnover	$\dfrac{\text{Sales}}{\text{Total assets}}$	Whether a firm is generating a sufficient volume of business for the size of its assets investment.
Accounts receivable turnover	$\dfrac{\text{Annual credit sales}}{\text{Account receivable}}$	In percentage terms, the average length of time it takes a firm to collect on credit sales.
Average collection period	$\dfrac{\text{Account receivable}}{\text{Total sales/365 days}}$	In days, the average length of time it takes a firm to collect on credit sales.

EXHIBIT 5–F
(continued)

Ratio	Calculation	Meaning
Profitability Ratios:		
Gross profit margin	$$\frac{\text{Sales} - \text{Cost of goods sold}}{\text{Sales}}$$	The total margin available to cover operating expenses and yield a profit.
Operating profit margin	$$\frac{\text{Earning before interest and taxes (EBIT)}}{\text{Sales}}$$	Profitability without concern for taxes and interest.
Net profit margin	$$\frac{\text{Net income}}{\text{Sales}}$$	After-tax profits per dollar of sales.
Return on total assets (ROA)	$$\frac{\text{Net income}}{\text{Total assets}}$$	After-tax profits per dollar of assets; this ratio is also called *return on investment* (ROI).
Return on stockholders' equity (ROE)	$$\frac{\text{Net Income}}{\text{Total stockholders' equity}}$$	After-tax profits per dollar of stockholders investment in the firm.
Earnings per share (EPS)	$$\frac{\text{Net income}}{\text{Number of shares of common stock outstanding}}$$	Earnings available to the owners of common stock.
Growth Ratio:		
Sales	Annual percentage growth in total sales	Firm's growth rate in sales.
Income	Annual percentage growth in profits	Firm's growth rate in profits.
Earnings per share	Annual percentage growth in EPS	Firm's growth rate in EPS.
Dividends per share	Annual percentage growth in dividends per share	Firm's growth rate in dividends per share.
Price-earnings ratio	$$\frac{\text{Market price per share}}{\text{Earnings per share}}$$	Faster-growing and less risky firms tend to have higher price-earnings ratios.

Chapter **Six**

Formulating Long-Term Objectives and Grand Strategies

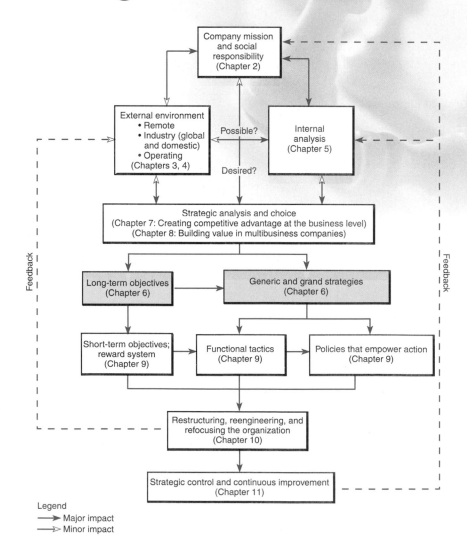

Legend
⟶ Major impact
⟶⟩ Minor impact

The company mission was described in Chapter 2 as encompassing the broad aims of the firm. The most specific statement of aims presented in that chapter appeared as the goals of the firm. However, these goals, which commonly dealt with profitability, growth, and survival, were stated without specific targets or time frames. They were always to be pursued but could never be fully attained. They gave a general sense of direction but were not intended to provide specific benchmarks for evaluating the firm's progress in achieving its aims. Providing such benchmarks is the function of objectives.[1]

The first part of this chapter will focus on long-term objectives. These are statements of the results a firm seeks to achieve over a specified period, typically three to five years. The second part will focus on the formulation of grand strategies. These provide a comprehensive general approach in guiding major actions designed to accomplish the firm's long-term objectives.

The chapter has two major aims: (1) to discuss in detail the concept of long-term objectives, the topics they cover, and the qualities they should exhibit; and (2) to discuss the concept of grand strategies and to describe the 15 principal grand strategy options that are available to firms singly or in combination, including three newly popularized options that are being used to provide the basis for global competitiveness.

LONG-TERM OBJECTIVES

Strategic managers recognize that short-run profit maximization is rarely the best approach to achieving sustained corporate growth and profitability. An often repeated adage states that if impoverished people are given food, they will eat it and remain impoverished; however, if they are given seeds and tools and shown how to grow crops, they will be able to improve their condition permanently. A parallel choice confronts strategic decision makers:

1. Should they eat the seeds to improve the near-term profit picture and make large dividend payments through cost-saving measures such as laying off workers during periods of slack demand, selling off inventories, or cutting back on research and development?

2. Or should they sow the seeds in the effort to reap long-term rewards by reinvesting profits in growth opportunities, committing resources to employee training, or increasing advertising expenditures?

For most strategic managers, the solution is clear—distribute a small amount of profit now but sow most of it to increase the likelihood of a long-term supply. This is the most frequently used rationale in selecting objectives.

To achieve long-term prosperity, strategic planners commonly establish long-term objectives in seven areas:

Profitability   The ability of any firm to operate in the long run depends on attaining an acceptable level of profits. Strategically managed firms characteristically have a profit objective, usually expressed in earnings per share or return on equity.

Productivity   Strategic managers constantly try to increase the productivity of their systems. Firms that can improve the input-output relationship normally increase profitability. Thus, firms almost always state an objective for productivity. Commonly used productivity objectives are the number of items produced or the number of services rendered per unit of

---

[1]The terms *goals* and *objectives* are each used to convey a special meaning, with goals being the less specific and more encompassing concept. Most authors follow this usage; however, some use the two words interchangeably, while others reverse the usage.

input. However, productivity objectives sometimes are stated in terms of desired cost decreases. For example, objectives may be set for reducing defective items, customer complaints leading to litigation, or overtime. Achieving such objectives increases profitability if unit output is maintained.

Competitive Position   One measure of corporate success is relative dominance in the marketplace. Larger firms commonly establish an objective in terms of competitive position, often using total sales or market share as measures of their competitive position. An objective with regard to competitive position may indicate a firm's long-term priorities. For example, Gulf Oil set a five-year objective of moving from third to second place as a producer of high-density polypropylene. Total sales were the measure.

Employee Development   Employees value education and training, in part because they lead to increased compensation and job security. Providing such opportunities often increases productivity and decreases turnover. Therefore, strategic decision makers frequently include an employee development objective in their long-range plans. For example, PPG has declared an objective of developing highly skilled and flexible employees and, thus, providing steady employment for a reduced number of workers.

Employee Relations   Whether or not they are bound by union contracts, firms actively seek good employee relations. In fact, proactive steps in anticipation of employee needs and expectations are characteristic of strategic managers. Strategic managers believe that productivity is linked to employee loyalty and to appreciation of managers' interest in employee welfare. They, therefore, set objectives to improve employee relations. Among the outgrowths of such objectives are safety programs, worker representation on management committees, and employee stock option plans.

Technological Leadership   Firms must decide whether to lead or follow in the marketplace. Either approach can be successful, but each requires a different strategic posture. Therefore, many firms state an objective with regard to technological leadership. For example, Caterpillar Tractor Company established its early reputation and dominant position in its industry by being in the forefront of technological innovation in the manufacture of large earthmovers. E-commerce technology officers will have more of a strategic role in the management hierarchy of the future, demonstrating that the Internet has become an integral aspect of corporate long-term objective setting. In offering an e-technology manager higher-level responsibilities, a firm is pursuing a leadership position in terms of innovation in computer networks and systems. Officers of e-commerce technology at GE and Delta Air have shown their ability to increase profits by driving down transaction-related costs with Web-based technologies that seamlessly integrate their firms' supply chains. These technologies have the potential to "lock in" certain suppliers and customers and heighten competitive position through supply chain efficiency.

Public Responsibility   Managers recognize their responsibilities to their customers and to society at large. In fact, many firms seek to exceed government requirements. They work not only to develop reputations for fairly priced products and services but also to establish themselves as responsible corporate citizens. For example, they may establish objectives for charitable and educational contributions, minority training, public or political activity, community welfare, or urban revitalization. In an attempt to exhibit their public responsibility in the United States, Japanese companies, such as Toyota, Hitachi, and Matsushita, contribute more than $500 million annually to American educational projects, charities, and nonprofit organizations.

Qualities of Long-Term Objectives

What distinguishes a good objective from a bad one? What qualities of an objective improve its chances of being attained? These questions are best answered in relation to seven criteria that should be used in preparing long-term objectives: acceptable, flexible, measurable over time, motivating, suitable, understandable, and achievable.

Acceptable   Managers are most likely to pursue objectives that are consistent with their preferences. They may ignore or even obstruct the achievement of objectives that offend them (e.g., promoting a high-sodium food product) or that they believe to be inappropriate or unfair (e.g., reducing spoilage to offset a disproportionate allocation of fixed overhead). In addition, long-term corporate objectives frequently are designed to be acceptable to groups external to the firm. An example is efforts to abate air pollution that are undertaken at the insistence of the Environmental Protection Agency.

Flexible   Objectives should be adaptable to unforeseen or extraordinary changes in the firm's competitive or environmental forecasts. Unfortunately, such flexibility usually is increased at the expense of specificity. One way of providing flexibility while minimizing its negative effects is to allow for adjustments in the level, rather than in the nature, of objectives. For example, the personnel department objective of providing managerial development training for 15 supervisors per year over the next five-year period might be adjusted by changing the number of people to be trained. In contrast, changing the personnel department's objective of "assisting production supervisors in reducing job-related injuries by 10 percent per year" after three months had gone by would understandably create dissatisfaction.

Measurable   Objectives must clearly and concretely state what will be achieved and when it will be achieved. Thus, objectives should be measurable over time. For example, the objective of "substantially improving our return on investment" would be better stated as "increasing the return on investment on our line of paper products by a minimum of 1 percent a year and a total of 5 percent over the next three years."

Motivating   People are most productive when objectives are set at a motivating level—one high enough to challenge but not so high as to frustrate or so low as to be easily attained. The problem is that individuals and groups differ in their perceptions of what is high enough. A broad objective that challenges one group frustrates another and minimally interests a third. One valuable recommendation is that objectives be tailored to specific groups. Developing such objectives requires time and effort, but objectives of this kind are more likely to motivate.

Suitable   Objectives must be suited to the broad aims of the firm, which are expressed in its mission statement. Each objective should be a step toward the attainment of overall goals. In fact, objectives that are inconsistent with the company mission can subvert the firm's aims. For example, if the mission is growth oriented, the objective of reducing the debt-to-equity ratio to 1.00 would probably be unsuitable and counterproductive.

Understandable   Strategic managers at all levels must understand what is to be achieved. They also must understand the major criteria by which their performance will be evaluated. Thus, objectives must be so stated that they are as understandable to the recipient as they are to the giver. Consider the misunderstandings that might arise over the objective of "increasing the productivity of the credit card department by 20 percent within two years." What does this objective mean? Increase the number of outstanding cards? Increase the use of outstanding cards? Increase the employee workload? Make productivity gains each year? Or hope that the new computer-assisted system, which should improve productivity, is approved by year 2? As this simple example illustrates, objectives must be clear, meaningful, and unambiguous.

Achievable Finally, objectives must be possible to achieve. This is easier said than done. Turbulence in the remote and operating environments affects a firm's internal operations, creating uncertainty and limiting the accuracy of the objectives set by strategic management. To illustrate, the rapidly declining U.S. economy in 2000–2003 made objective setting extremely difficult, particularly in such areas as sales projections.

The Balanced Scorecard

The Balanced Scorecard is a set of measures that are directly linked to the company's strategy. Developed by Robert S. Kaplan and David P. Norton, it directs a company to link its own long-term strategy with tangible goals and actions. The scorecard allows managers to evaluate the company from four perspectives: financial performance, customer knowledge, internal business processes, and learning and growth.

The Balanced Scorecard, as shown in Exhibit 6–1, contains a concise definition of the company's vision and strategy. Surrounding the vision and strategy are four additional boxes; each box contains the objectives, measures, targets, and initiatives for one of the four perspectives:

- The box at the top of Exhibit 6–1 represents the financial perspective, and answers the question "To succeed financially, how should we appear to our shareholders?"

- The box to the right represents the internal business process perspective and addresses the question "To satisfy our shareholders and customers, what business processes must we excel at?"

- The learning and growth box at the bottom of Exhibit 6–1 answers the question "To achieve our vision, how will we sustain our ability to change and improve?"

- The box at the left reflects the customer perspective, and responds to the question "To achieve our vision, how should we appear to our customers?"

EXHIBIT 6–1 **The Balanced Scorecard**

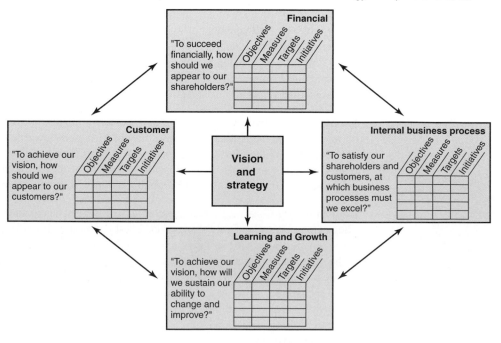

The balanced scorecard provides a framework to translate a strategy into operational terms

All of the boxes are connected by arrows to illustrate that the objectives and measures of the four perspectives are linked by cause-and-effect relationships that lead to the successful implementation of the strategy. Achieving one perspective's targets should lead to desired improvements in the next perspective, and so on, until the company's performance increases overall.

A properly constructed scorecard is balanced between short- and long-term measures; financial and nonfinancial measures; and internal and external performance perspectives.

The Balanced Scorecard is a management system that can be used as the central organizing framework for key managerial processes. Chemical Bank, Mobil Corporation's US Marketing and Refining Division, and CIGNA Property and Casualty Insurance have used the Balanced Scorecard approach to assist in individual and team goal setting, compensation, resource allocation, budgeting and planning, and strategic feedback and learning.

GENERIC STRATEGIES

Many planning experts believe that the general philosophy of doing business declared by the firm in the mission statement must be translated into a holistic statement of the firm's strategic orientation before it can be further defined in terms of a specific long-term strategy. In other words, a long-term or grand strategy must be based on a core idea about how the firm can best compete in the marketplace.

The popular term for this core idea is *generic strategy*. From a scheme developed by Michael Porter, many planners believe that any long-term strategy should derive from a firm's attempt to seek a competitive advantage based on one of three generic strategies:

1. Striving for overall low-cost leadership in the industry.

2. Striving to create and market unique products for varied customer groups through *differentiation*.

3. Striving to have special appeal to one or more groups of consumer or industrial buyers, *focusing* on their cost or differentiation concerns.

Advocates of generic strategies believe that each of these options can produce above-average returns for a firm in an industry. However, they are successful for very different reasons.

Low-cost leaders depend on some fairly unique capabilities to achieve and sustain their low-cost position. Examples of such capabilities are: having secured suppliers of scarce raw materials, being in a dominant market share position, or having a high degree of capitalization. Low-cost producers usually excel at cost reductions and efficiencies. They maximize economies of scale, implement cost-cutting technologies, stress reductions in overhead and in administrative expenses, and use volume sales techniques to propel themselves up the earning curve. The commonly accepted requirements for successful implementation of the low-cost and the other two generic strategies are overviewed in Exhibit 6–2.

A low-cost leader is able to use its cost advantage to charge lower prices or to enjoy higher profit margins. By so doing, the firm effectively can defend itself in price wars, attack competitors on price to gain market share, or, if already dominant in the industry, simply benefit from exceptional returns. As an extreme case, it has been argued that National Can Company, a corporation in an essentially stagnant industry, is able to generate attractive and improving profits by being the low-cost producer.

Strategies dependent on differentiation are designed to appeal to customers with a special sensitivity for a particular product attribute. By stressing the attribute above other product qualities, the firm attempts to build customer loyalty. Often such loyalty translates into

EXHIBIT 6–2
Requirements for Generic Competitive Strategies

Source: Free Press *Competitive Strategy: Techniques for Analyzing Industries and Competitors*, pp. 40–41. Reprinted with permission of the Free Press, a division of Simon & Schuster, from *Competitive Strategy: Techniques for Analyzing Industries and Competitors*, by Michael E. Porter. Copyright © 1980 by Michael E. Porter.

Generic Strategy	Commonly Required Skills and Resources	Common Organizational Requirements
Overall cost leadership	Sustained capital investment and access to capital. Process engineering skills. Intense supervision of labor. Products designed for ease in manufacture. Low-cost distribution system.	Tight cost control. Frequent, detailed control reports. Structured organization and responsibilities. Incentives based on meeting strict quantitative targets.
Differentiation	Strong marketing abilities. Product engineering. Creative flare. Strong capability in basic research. Corporate reputation for quality or technological leadership. Long tradition in the industry or unique combination of skills drawn from other businesses. Strong cooperation from channels.	Strong coordination among functions in R&D, product development, and marketing. Subjective measurement and incentives instead of quantitative measures. Amenities to attract highly skilled labor scientists, or creative people.
Focus	Combination of the above policies directed at the particular strategic target.	Combination of the above policies directed at the regular strategic target.

a firm's ability to charge a premium price for its product. Cross-brand pens, Brooks Brothers suits, Porsche automobiles, and Chivas Regal Scotch whiskey are all examples.

The product attribute also can be the marketing channels through which it is delivered, its image for excellence, the features it includes, and the service network that supports it. As a result of the importance of these attributes, competitors often face "perceptual" barriers to entry when customers of a successfully differentiated firm fail to see largely identical products as being interchangeable. For example, General Motors hopes that customers will accept "only genuine GM replacement parts."

A focus strategy, whether anchored in a low-cost base or a differentiation base, attempts to attend to the needs of a particular market segment. Likely segments are those that are ignored by marketing appeals to easily accessible markets, to the "typical" customer, or to customers with common applications for the product. A firm pursuing a focus strategy is willing to service isolated geographic areas; to satisfy the needs of customers with special financing, inventory, or servicing problems; or to tailor the product to the somewhat unique demands of the small- to medium-sized customer. The focusing firms profit from their willingness to serve otherwise ignored or underappreciated customer segments. The classic example is cable television. An entire industry was born because of a willingness of cable firms to serve isolated rural locations that were ignored by traditional television services. Brick producers that typically service a radius of less than 100 miles and commuter airlines that serve regional geographic areas are other examples of industries where a focus strategy frequently yields above-average industry profits.

While each of the generic strategies enables a firm to maximize certain competitive advantages, each one also exposes the firm to a number of competitive risks. For example, a low-cost leader fears a new low-cost technology that is being developed by a competitor; a differentiating firm fears imitators; and a focused firm fears invasion by a firm that largely targets customers. As Exhibit 6–3 suggests, each generic strategy presents the firm with a number of risks.

EXHIBIT 6–3
Risks of the Generic Strategies

Source: Free Press *Competitive Advantage: Creating and Sustaining Superior Performance*, p. 21. Adapted with the permission of the Free Press, a division of Simon & Schuster, from *Competitive Strategy: Creating and Sustaining Superior Performance*, by Michael E. Porter. Copyright © 1985 by Michael E. Porter.

Risks of Cost Leadership	Risks of Differentiation	Risks of Focus
Cost of leadership is not sustained: • Competitors imitate. • Technology changes. • Other bases for cost leadership erode.	Differentiation is not sustained: • Competitors imitate. • Bases for differentiation become less important to buyers.	The focus strategy is imitated. The target segment becomes structurally unattractive: • Structure erodes. • Demand disappears.
Proximity in differentiation is lost.	Cost proximity is lost.	Broadly targeted competitors overwhelm the segment: • The segment's differences from other segments narrow. • The advantages of a broad line increase.
Cost focusers achieve even lower cost in segments.	Differentiation focusers achieve even greater differentiation in segments.	New focusers subsegment the industry

THE VALUE DISCIPLINES

International management consultants Michael Treacy and Fred Wiersema propose an alternative approach to generic strategy that they call the value disciplines.[2] They believe that strategies must center on delivering superior customer value through one of three value disciplines: operational excellence, customer intimacy, or product leadership.

Operational excellence refers to providing customers with convenient and reliable products or services at competitive prices. Customer intimacy involves offerings tailored to match the demands of identified niches. Product leadership, the third discipline, involves offering customers leading-edge products and services that make rivals' goods obsolete.

Companies that specialize in one of these disciplines, while simultaneously meeting industry standards in the other two, gain a sustainable lead in their markets. This lead is derived from the firm's focus on one discipline, aligning all aspects of operations with it. Having decided on the value that must be conveyed to customers, firms understand more clearly what must be done to attain the desired results. After transforming their organizations to focus on one discipline, companies can concentrate on smaller adjustments to produce incremental value. To match this advantage, less focused companies require larger changes than the tweaking that discipline leaders need.

Operational Excellence

Operational excellence is a specific strategic approach to the production and delivery of products and services. A company that follows this strategy attempts to lead its industry in price and convenience by pursuing a focus on lean and efficient operations. Companies that employ operational excellence work to minimize costs by reducing overhead, eliminating intermediate production steps, reducing transaction costs, and optimizing business

[2]The ideas and examples in this section are drawn from Michael Treacy and Fred Wiersema, "Customer Intimacy and Other Value Disciplines," *Harvard Business Review*, 71(1): 84–94, 1993.

processes across functional and organizational boundaries. The focus is on delivering products or services to customers at competitive prices with minimal inconvenience.

Through its focus on operational excellence, Dell Computer has shown PC buyers that they do not have to sacrifice quality of state-of-the art technology in order to buy personal computers easily and inexpensively. Dell recognized the opportunity to cut retail dealers out of the industry's traditional distribution process. Through this approach—which includes direct sales, building to order, and creating a disciplined, extremely low-cost culture—Dell has been able to undercut other PC makers in price yet provide high-quality products and service.

Operational excellence is also the strategic focus of General Electric's large appliance business. Historically, the distribution strategy for large appliances was based on requiring that dealers maintain large inventories. Price breaks for dealers were based on order quantities. However, as the marketplace became more competitive, principally as a result of competition for multibrand dealers like Sears, GE recognized the need to adjust its production and distribution plans.

The GE system addresses the delivery of products. As a step toward organizational excellence, GE created a computer-based logistics system to replace its in-store inventories model. Retailers use this software to access a 24-hour on-line order processing system that guarantees GE's best price. This system allows dealers to better meet customer needs, with instantaneous access to a warehouse of goods and accurate shipping and production information. GE benefits from the deal as well. Efficiency is increased since manufacturing now occurs in response to customer sales. Additionally, warehousing and distribution systems have been streamlined to create the capability of delivering to 90 percent of destinations in the continental United States within one business day.

Firms that implement the strategy of operational excellence typically restructure their delivery processes to focus on efficiency and reliability, and use state-of-the art information systems that emphasize integration and low-cost transactions.

Customer Intimacy

Companies that implement a strategy of customer intimacy continually tailor and shape products and services to fit an increasingly refined definition of the customer. Companies excelling in customer intimacy combine detailed customer knowledge with operational flexibility. They respond quickly to almost any need, from customizing a product to fulfilling special requests to create customer loyalty.

Customer-intimate companies are willing to spend money now to build customer loyalty for the long term, considering each customer's lifetime value to the company, not the profit of any single transaction. Consequently, employees in customer-intimate companies go to great lengths to ensure customer satisfaction with low regard for initial cost.

Home Depot implements the discipline of customer intimacy. Home Depot clerks spend the necessary time with customers to determine the product that best suits their needs, because the company's business strategy is built around selling information and service in addition to home-repair and improvement items. Consequently, consumers concerned solely with price fall outside Home Depot's core market.

Companies engaged in customer intimacy understand the difference between the profitability of a single transaction and the profitability of a lifetime relationship with a single customer. The company's profitability depends in part on its maintaining a system that differentiates quickly and accurately the degree of service that customers require and the revenues their patronage is likely to generate. Firms using this approach recognize that not every customer is equally profitable. For example, a financial services company installed a telephone-computer system capable of recognizing individual clients by their telephone numbers when they call. The system routes customers with large accounts and frequent transactions to their own senior account representative. Other customers may be routed to a trainee or junior representative. In any case, the customer's file appears on the representative's screen before the phone is answered.

The new system allows the firm to segment its services with great efficiency. If the company has clients who are interested in trading in a particular financial instrument, it can group them under the one account representative who specializes in that instrument. This saves the firm the expense of training every representative in every facet of financial services. Additionally, the company can direct certain value-added services or products to a specific group of clients that would have interest in them.

Businesses that select a customer intimacy strategy have decided to stress flexibility and responsiveness. They collect and analyze data from many sources. Their organizational structure emphasizes empowerment of employees close to customers. Additionally, hiring and training programs stress the creative decision-making skills required to meet individual customer needs. Management systems recognize and utilize such concepts as customer lifetime value, and norms among employees are consistent with a "have it your way" mind set.

Product Leadership

Companies that pursue the discipline of product leadership strive to produce a continuous stream of state-of-the-art products and services. Three challenges must be met to attain that goal. Creativity is the first challenge. Creativity is recognizing and embracing ideas usually originating outside the company. Second, innovative companies must commercialize ideas quickly. Thus, their business and management processes need to be engineered for speed. Product leaders relentlessly pursue new solutions to problems. Finally, firms utilizing this discipline prefer to release their own improvements rather than wait for competitors to enter. Consequently, product leaders do not stop for self-congratulation; they focus on continual improvement.

For example, Johnson & Johnson's organizational design brings good ideas in, develops them quickly, and looks for ways to improve them. In 1983, the president of J&J's Vistakon, Inc., a maker of specialty contact lenses, received a tip concerning an ophthalmologist who had conceived of a method to manufacture disposable contact lenses inexpensively. Vistakon's president received this tip from a J&J employee from a different subsidiary whom he had never met. Rather than dismiss the tip, the executives purchased the rights to the technology, assembled a management team to oversee the product's development team to oversee the product's development, and built a state-of-the-art facility in Florida to manufacture disposable contact lenses called Acuvue. Vistakon and its parent, J&J, were willing to incur high manufacturing and inventory costs before a single lens was sold. A high-speed production facility helped give Vistakon a six-month head start over the competition that, taken off guard, never caught up.

Like other product leaders, J&J creates and maintains an environment that encourages employees to share ideas. Additionally, product leaders continually scan the environment for new product or service possibilities and rush to capitalize them. Product leaders also avoid bureaucracy because it slows commercialization of their ideas. In a product leadership company, a wrong decision often is less damaging than one made late. As a result, managers make decisions quickly, their companies encouraging them to decide today and implement tomorrow. Product leaders continually look for new methods to shorten their cycle times.

The strength of product leaders lies in reacting to situations as they occur. Shorter reaction times serve as an advantage in dealings with the unknown. For example, when competitors challenged the safety of Acuvue lenses, the firm responded quickly and distributed data combating the charges to eye-care professionals. This reaction created goodwill in the marketplace.

Product leaders act as their own competition. These firms continually make the products and services they have created obsolete. Product leaders believe that if they do not develop a successor, a competitor will. So, although Acuvue is successful in the marketplace, Vistakon continues to investigate new material that will extend the wearability of contact lenses and technologies that will make current lenses obsolete. J&J and other innovators recognize that the long-run profitability of an existing product or service is less important to the company's future than maintaining its product leadership edge and momentum.

GRAND STRATEGIES

While the need for firms to develop generic strategies remains an unresolved debate, designers of planning systems agree about the critical role of grand strategies. *Grand strategies,* often called master or business strategies, provide basic direction for strategic actions. They are the basis of coordinated and sustained efforts directed toward achieving long-term business objectives.

The purpose of this section is twofold: (1) to list, describe, and discuss 15 grand strategies that strategic managers should consider and (2) to present approaches to the selection of an optimal grand strategy from the available alternatives.

Grand strategies indicate the time period over which long-range objectives are to be achieved. Thus, a grand strategy can be defined as a comprehensive general approach that guides a firm's major actions.

The 15 principal grand strategies are: concentrated growth, market development, product development, innovation, horizontal integration, vertical integration, concentric diversification, conglomerate diversification, turnaround, divestiture, liquidation, bankruptcy, joint ventures, strategic alliances, and consortia. Any one of these strategies could serve as the basis for achieving the major long-term objectives of a single firm. But a firm involved with multiple industries, businesses, product lines, or customer groups—as many firms are—usually combines several grand strategies. For clarity, however, each of the principal grand strategies is described independently in this section, with examples to indicate some of its relative strengths and weaknesses.

Concentrated Growth

Many of the firms that fell victim to merger mania were once mistakenly convinced that the best way to achieve their objectives was to pursue unrelated diversification in the search for financial opportunity and synergy. By rejecting that "conventional wisdom," such firms as Martin-Marietta, KFC, Compaq, Avon, Hyatt Legal Services, and Tenant have demonstrated the advantages of what is increasingly proving to be sound business strategy. A firm that has enjoyed special success through a strategic emphasis on increasing market share through concentration is Chemlawn. With headquarters in Columbus, Ohio, Chemlawn is the North American leader in professional lawn care. Like others in the lawn-care industry, Chemlawn is experiencing a steadily declining customer base. Market analysis shows that the decline is fueled by negative environmental publicity, perceptions of poor customer service, and concern about the price versus the value of the company's services, given the wide array of do-it-yourself alternatives. Chemlawn's approach to increasing market share hinges on addressing quality, price, and value issues; discontinuing products that the public or environmental authorities perceive as unsafe; and improving the quality of its workforce.

These firms are just a few of the majority of American firms that pursue a concentrated growth strategy by focusing on a specific product and market combination. *Concentrated growth* is the strategy of the firm that directs its resources to the profitable growth of a single product, in a single market, with a single dominant technology. The main rationale for this approach, sometimes called a market penetration or concentration strategy, is that the firm thoroughly develops and exploits its expertise in a delimited competitive arena.

Rationale for Superior Performance

Concentrated growth strategies lead to enhanced performance. The ability to assess market needs, knowledge of buyer behavior, customer price sensitivity, and effectiveness of promotion are characteristics of a concentrated growth strategy. Such core capabilities are a more important determinant of competitive market success than are the environmental forces faced by the firm. The high success rates of new products also are tied to avoiding situations that require undeveloped skills, such as serving new customers and markets, acquiring new technology, building new channels, developing new promotional abilities, and facing new competition.

A major misconception about the concentrated growth strategy is that the firm practicing it will settle for little or no growth. This is certainly not true for a firm that correctly utilizes the strategy. A firm employing concentrated growth grows by building on its competences, and it achieves a competitive edge by concentrating in the product-market segment it knows best. A firm employing this strategy is aiming for the growth that results from increased productivity, better coverage of its actual product-market segment, and more efficient use of its technology.

Conditions That Favor Concentrated Growth

Specific conditions in the firm's environment are favorable to the concentrated growth strategy. The first is a condition in which the firm's industry is resistant to major technological advancements. This is usually the case in the late growth and maturity stages of the product life cycle and in product markets where product demand is stable and industry barriers, such as capitalization, are high. Machinery for the paper manufacturing industry, in which the basic technology has not changed for more than a century, is a good example.

An especially favorable condition is one in which the firm's targeted markets are not product saturated. Markets with competitive gaps leave the firm with alternatives for growth, other than taking market share away from competitors. The successful introduction of traveler services by Allstate and Amoco demonstrates that even an organization as entrenched and powerful as the AAA could not build a defensible presence in all segments of the automobile club market.

A third condition that favors concentrated growth exists when the firm's product markets are sufficiently distinctive to dissuade competitors in adjacent product markets from trying to invade the firm's segment. John Deere scrapped its plans for growth in the construction machinery business when mighty Caterpillar threatened to enter Deere's mainstay, the farm machinery business, in retaliation. Rather than risk a costly price war on its own turf, Deere scrapped these plans.

A fourth favorable condition exists when the firm's inputs are stable in price and quantity and are available in the amounts and at the times needed. Maryland-based Giant Foods is able to concentrate in the grocery business largely due to its stable long-term arrangements with suppliers of its private-label products. Most of these suppliers are makers of the national brands that compete against the Giant labels. With a high market share and aggressive retail distribution, Giant controls the access of these brands to the consumer. Consequently, its suppliers have considerable incentive to honor verbal agreements, called *bookings,* in which they commit themselves for a one-year period with regard to the price, quality, and timing of their shipments to Giant.

The pursuit of concentrated growth also is favored by a stable market—a market without the seasonal or cyclical swings that would encourage a firm to diversify. Night Owl Security, the District of Columbia market leader in home security services, commits its customers to initial four-year contracts. In a city where affluent consumers tend to be quite transient, the length of this relationship is remarkable. Night Owl's concentrated growth strategy has been reinforced by its success in getting subsequent owners of its customers' homes to extend and renew the security service contracts. In a similar way, Lands' End reinforced its growth strategy by asking customers for names and addresses of friends and relatives living overseas who would like to receive Lands' End catalogs.

A firm also can grow while concentrating, if it enjoys competitive advantages based on efficient production or distribution channels. These advantages enable the firm to formulate advantageous pricing policies. More efficient production methods and better handling of distribution also enable the firm to achieve greater economies of scale or, in conjunction with marketing, result in a product that is differentiated in the mind of the consumer. Graniteville Company, a large South Carolina textile manufacturer, enjoyed decades of growth and profitability by adopting a "follower" tactic as part of its concentrated growth strategy. By producing fabrics only after market demand had been well established, and by featuring products that reflected its expertise in adopting manufacturing innovations and in maintaining highly efficient long production runs, Graniteville prospered through concentrated growth.

Finally, the success of market generalists creates conditions favorable to concentrated growth. When generalists succeed by using universal appeals, they avoid making special appeals to particular groups of customers. The net result is that many small pockets are left open in the markets dominated by generalists, and that specialists emerge and thrive in these pockets. For example, hardware store chains, such as Home Depot, focus primarily on routine household repair problems and offer solutions that can be easily sold on a self-service, do-it-yourself basis. This approach leaves gaps at both the "semiprofessional" and "neophyte" ends of the market—in terms of the purchaser's skill at household repairs and the extent to which available merchandise matches the requirements of individual homeowners.

Risk and Rewards of Concentrated Growth

Under stable conditions, concentrated growth poses lower risk than any other grand strategy; but, in a changing environment, a firm committed to concentrated growth faces high risks. The greatest risk is that concentrating in a single product market makes a firm particularly vulnerable to changes in that segment. Slowed growth in the segment would jeopardize the firm because its investment, competitive edge, and technology are deeply entrenched in a specific offering. It is difficult for the firm to attempt sudden changes if its product is threatened by near-term obsolescence, a faltering market, new substitutes, or changes in technology or customer needs. For example, the manufacturers of IBM clones faced such a problem when IBM adopted the OS/2 operating system for its personal computer line. That change made existing clones out of date.

The concentrating firm's entrenchment in a specific industry makes it particularly susceptible to changes in the economic environment of that industry. For example, Mack Truck, the second-largest truck maker in America, lost $20 million as a result of an 18-month slump in the truck industry.

Entrenchment in a specific product market tends to make a concentrating firm more adept than competitors at detecting new trends. However, any failure of such a firm to properly forecast major changes in its industry can result in extraordinary losses. Numerous makers of inexpensive digital watches were forced to declare bankruptcy because they failed to anticipate the competition posed by Swatch, Guess, and other trendy watches that emerged from the fashion industry.

A firm pursuing a concentrated growth strategy is vulnerable also to the high opportunity costs that result from remaining in a specific product market and ignoring other options that could employ the firm's resources more profitably. Overcommitment to a specific technology and product market can hinder a firm's ability to enter a new or growing product market that offers more attractive cost-benefit trade-offs. Had Apple Computers maintained its policy of making equipment that did not interface with IBM equipment, it would have missed out on what have proved to be its most profitable strategic options.

Concentrated Growth Is Often the Most Viable Option

Examples abound of firms that have enjoyed exceptional returns on the concentrated growth strategy. Such firms as McDonald's, Goodyear, and Apple Computers have used firsthand knowledge and deep involvement with specific product segments to become powerful competitors in their markets. The strategy is associated even more often with successful smaller firms that have steadily and doggedly improved their market position.

The limited additional resources necessary to implement concentrated growth, coupled with the limited risk involved, also make this strategy desirable for a firm with limited funds. For example, through a carefully devised concentrated growth strategy, medium-sized John Deere & Company was able to become a major force in the agricultural machinery business even when competing with such firms as Ford Motor Company. While other firms were trying to exit or diversify from the farm machinery business, Deere spent $2 billion in upgrading its machinery, boosting its efficiency, and engaging in a program to strengthen its dealership system. This concentrated growth strategy enabled it to become the leader in the farm machinery business despite the fact that Ford was more than 10 times its size.

The firm that chooses a concentrated growth strategy directs its resources to the profitable growth of a narrowly defined product and market, focusing on a dominant technology. Firms that remain within their chosen product market are able to extract the most from their technology and market knowledge and, thus, are able to minimize the risk associated with unrelated diversification. The success of a concentration strategy is founded on the firm's use of superior insights into its technology, product, and customer to obtain a sustainable competitive advantage. Superior performance on these aspects of corporate strategy has been shown to have a substantial positive effect on market success.

A grand strategy of concentrated growth allows for a considerable range of action. Broadly speaking, the firm can attempt to capture a larger market share by increasing the usage rates of present customers, by attracting competitors' customers, or by selling to nonusers. In turn, each of these options suggests more specific options, some of which are listed in the top section of Exhibit 6–4.

When strategic managers forecast that their current products and their markets will not provide the basis for achieving the company mission, they have two options that involve moderate costs and risk: market development and product development.

Market Development

Market development commonly ranks second only to concentration as the least costly and least risky of the 15 grand strategies. It consists of marketing present products, often with only cosmetic modifications, to customers in related market areas by adding channels of distribution or by changing the content of advertising or promotion. Several specific market development approaches are listed in Exhibit 6–4. Thus, as suggested by the figure,

EXHIBIT 6–4

Specific Options under the Grand Strategies of Concentration, Market Development, and Product Development

Source: Adapted from Philip Kotler, *Marketing Management Analysis, Planning, and Control*, 11th ed., 2002. Reprinted by permission of Prentice Hall, Inc., Upper Saddle River, NJ.

Concentration (increasing use of present products in present markets):

1. Increasing present customers' rate of use:
   a. Increasing the size of purchase.
   b. Increasing the rate of product obsolescence.
   c. Advertising other uses.
   d. Giving price incentives for increased use.
2. Attracting competitors' customers:
   a. Establishing sharper brand differentiation.
   b. Increasing promotional effort.
   c. Initiating price cuts.
3. Attracting nonusers to buy the product:
   a. Inducing trial use through sampling, price incentives, and so on.
   b. Pricing up or down.
   c. Advertising new uses.

Market development (selling present products in new markets):

1. Opening additional geographic markets:
   a. Regional expansion.
   b. National expansion.
   c. International expansion.
2. Attracting other market segments:
   a. Developing product versions to appeal to other segments.
   b. Entering other channels of distribution.
   c. Advertising in other media.

Product development (developing new products for present markets):

1. Developing new product features:
   a. Adapt (to other ideas, developments).
   b. Modify (change color, motion, sound, odor, form, shape).
   c. Magnify (stronger, longer, thicker, extra value).
   d. Minify (smaller, shorter, lighter).
   e. Substitute (other ingredients, process, power).
   f. Rearrange (other patterns, layout, sequence, components).
   g. Reverse (inside out).
   h. Combine (blend, alloy, assortment, ensemble; combine units, purposes, appeals, ideas).
2. Developing quality variations.
3. Developing additional models and sizes (product proliferation).

firms that open branch offices in new cities, states, or countries are practicing market development. Likewise, firms are practicing market development if they switch from advertising in trade publications to advertising in newspapers or if they add jobbers to supplement their mail-order sales efforts. Kmart pursued market development with its recent emphasis on increasing market share among Hispanics as described in Strategy in Action Exhibit 6–5.

Market development allows firms to practice a form of concentrated growth by identifying new uses for existing products and new demographically, psychographically, or geographically defined markets. Frequently, changes in media selection, promotional appeals, and distribution are used to initiate this approach. Du Pont used market development when it found a new application for Kevlar, an organic material that police, security, and military personnel had used primarily for bulletproofing. Kevlar now is being used to

BusinessWeek Move over, Martha. Here comes Thalia. The sexy Mexico-born pop star is about to add some sizzle to Kmart Corp.'s tired image. Industry sources say the queen of Latin pop will lend her name to a new line of clothing, shoes, and cosmetics for Kmart. Although unknown to many English-speaking Americans, Thalia (pronounced Tah-lee-ah) has a big following among Hispanics in the United States. The exclusive apparel line is part of a new strategy to woo Hispanic shoppers that may be Kmart's best hope for reviving its flagging business.

For years, Kmart has struggled to find a niche between Wal-Mart's low prices and Target's cheap chic. Kmart's biggest failure, last year's price war with Wal-Mart, helped land the company in bankruptcy court. Now, in its bid to survive, Kmart is latching on to the one advantage it has over its discount rivals, stores in heavily populated urban areas. That means catering more to multicultural consumers, who already make up nearly 40 percent of Kmart's sales.

Thalia's line is just the start. Kmart says it hopes to announce a similar deal with an African American celebrity by year-end. Meanwhile, it is adding more Hispanic merchandise to its stores and reaching out to Hispanics with new Spanish-language ads and publications. "It's a very strong step Kmart is taking," says Kurt Barnard, publisher of *Barnard's Retail Trend Report*. "It's going to pay big dividends."

The strategy isn't risk-free. Kmart could alienate its existing customers if it swings too far toward the Hispanic market. And Wal-Mart, already targeting Hispanics, plans to open more urban stores. "There's a window of opportunity for Kmart," says Ira Kalish, chief economist at Columbus (Ohio) consultant Retail Forward, Inc., "But it's going to close quickly."

Kmart is coming late to this party. Wal-Mart and Sears, Roebuck & Co. several years ago began letting local managers buy products suited to their communities. Kmart's previous management thought it more efficient for buyers at headquarters to purchase for stores nationwide. But, says CEO James B. Adamson, who took over in March, "people sitting in Troy, Mich., can't understand the difference between stores in Los Angeles, New York, Texas, or Miami."

That's why Adamson is giving store managers more say over what goes on their shelves. For Frank Gonzales, manager of a San Jose (Calif.) Kmart, that means selling tortilla warmers, tamale pots, and such produce as avocados, mangoes, and cilantro. "We were missing a lot of those sales," says Gonzales.

Kmart knows its Hispanic focus must not be seen as pandering. "They've got to know you're not giving them lip service," says Adamson, who is credited with turning around the Denny's restaurant chain after complaints of racial discrimination tarnished its image. In an effort to build loyalty, Kmart is launching on Sept. 15 *La Vida*, a four-page weekly magazine in Spanish to go out with a new Spanish ad circular. It will feature celebrities and lifestyle articles.

With Hispanics expected to outnumber African Americans by 2009, this may be Kmart's best chance. But it will take more than Hispanic shoppers to save the company. Its problems—ranging from poor inventory controls to lousy distribution—are deep-seated and can't be fixed overnight. But getting shoppers back is a start. And Thalia may help.

Source: *By Joann Muller in Troy, Mich., with Wendy Zellner in Dallas. BusinessWeek, September 9, 2002, p. 46.*

refit and maintain wooden-hulled boats, since it is lighter and stronger than glass fibers and has 11 times the strength of steel.

The medical industry provides other examples of new markets for existing products. The National Institutes of Health's report of a study showing that the use of aspirin may lower the incidence of heart attacks was expected to boost sales in the $2.2 billion analgesic market. It was predicted that the expansion of this market would lower the market share of nonaspirin brands, such as industry leaders Tylenol and Advil. Product extensions currently planned include Bayer Calendar Pack, 28-day packaging to fit the once-a-day prescription for the prevention of a second heart attack.

Another example is Chesebrough-Ponds, a major producer of health and beauty aids, which decided several years ago to expand its market by repacking its Vaseline Petroleum Jelly in pocket size squeeze tubes as Vaseline "Lip Therapy." The corporation decided to place a strategic emphasis on market development, because it knew from market studies that its petroleum-jelly customers already were using the product to prevent chapped lips. Company leaders reasoned that their market could be expanded significantly if the product were repackaged to fit conveniently in consumers' pockets and purses.

BusinessWeek PepsiCo Corp. diverted some of its advertising attention away from its flagship cola toward newer and narrower brands like Sierra Mist and Pepsi Twist. It was the latest sign of how the soft-drink giant had reformulated its mission from bolstering core brands like Pepsi-Cola and Mountain Dew to peppering the market with niche products and brand extensions. Pepsi's market had splintered and big brands no longer had universal appeal. To attract a younger, less cohesive generation, Purchase (N.Y.)-based Pepsi had to rethink the way it developed and marketed its wares. "The era of the mass brand has been over for a long time," said David Burwick, chief marketing officer of Pepsi-Cola North America.

Pepsi's response had been a raft of new products, most bearing the Pepsi or Mountain Dew names. Its biggest hit had been cherry-flavored, caffeine-loaded Mountain Dew Code Red. Pepsi Twist and berry-flavored Pepsi Blue had developed more modest followings. Sierra Mist was a youth-skewed challenger to Cadbury Schweppes PLC's 7 Up.

Code Red, Twist, Blue, and Mist accounted for barely 5 percent of Pepsi's soft-drink sales. In the past, Pepsi might not have bothered with such small fry. In 2003, though, it was looking for products that could crack a hard-to-reach demographic group. Code Red, for example, had reeled in urbanites, women, and African Americans who had not previously shown any impulse to do the Dew. That could have helped offset flagship Pepsi's 2 percent volume sales decline in 2002.

Because these new drinks were more narrowly targeted, Pepsi had to refine its marketing techniques. To launch Code Red in 2001, the company handed out a million samples at youth magnets like the Winter X Games and the NCAA Final Four basketball tourney before the brand was available in stores. That helped create a buzz that got Code Red off to a brisk start. For teen-oriented Pepsi Blue last fall, Pepsi went beyond hiring rock stars to appear in ads. Instead, it worked out an innovative deal with Universal Music Group.

Source: Excerpted from Gerry Khermouch, "Call It the Pepsi Blue Generation." *BusinessWeek,* February 3, 2003, p. 96.

Product Development

Product development involves the substantial modification of existing products or the creation of new but related products that can be marketed to current customers through established channels. The product development strategy often is adopted either to prolong the life cycle of current products or to take advantage of a favorite reputation or brand name. The idea is to attract satisfied customers to new products as a result of their positive experience with the firm's initial offering. The bottom section in Exhibit 6–4 lists some of the options available to firms undertaking product development. A revised edition of a college textbook, a new car style, and a second formula of shampoo for oily hair are examples of the product development strategy.

A detailed example of Pepsi's product development activities is provided in Exhibit 6–6, Strategy in Action. In 2001, Pepsi changed its strategy on beverage products by creating new products to follow the industry movement away from mass branding. This new movement was designed to attract a younger, hipper customer segment. Pepsi's new products include a version of Mountain Dew, called Code Red, and new Pepsi brands, called Pepsi Twist and Pepsi Blue.

The product development strategy is based on the penetration of existing markets by incorporating product modifications into existing items or by developing new products with a clear connection to the existing product line. The telecommunications industry provides an example of product extension based on product modification. To increase its estimated 8 to 10 percent share of the $5 to $6 billion corporate user market, MCI Communication Corporation extended its direct-dial service to 146 countries, the same as those serviced by AT&T, at lower average rates than those of AT&T. MCI's addition of 79 countries to its network underscores its belief in this market, which it expects to grow 15 to 20 percent annually. Another example of expansions linked to existing lines is Gerber's decision to engage in general merchandise marketing. Gerber's recent introduction included 52 items that ranged from feeding accessories to toys and children's wear. Likewise, Nabisco Brands seeks competitive advantage by placing its strategic emphasis on product development.

With headquarters in Parsippany, New Jersey, the company is one of three operating units of RJR Nabisco. It is the leading producer of biscuits, confections, snacks, shredded cereals, and processed fruits and vegetables. To maintain its position as leader, Nabisco pursues a strategy of developing and introducing new products and expanding its existing product line. Spoon Size Shredded Wheat and Ritz Bits crackers are two examples of new products that are variations on existing products.

Innovation

In many industries, it has become increasingly risky not to innovate. Both consumer and industrial markets have come to expect periodic changes and improvements in the products offered. As a result, some firms find it profitable to make *innovation* their grand strategy. They seek to reap the initially high profits associated with customer acceptance of a new or greatly improved product. Then, rather than face stiffening competition as the basis of profitability shifts from innovation to production or marketing competence, they search for other original or novel ideas. The underlying rationale of the grand strategy of innovation is to create a new product life cycle and thereby make similar existing products obsolete. Thus, this strategy differs from the product development strategy of extending an existing product's life cycle. For example, Intel, a leader in the semiconductor industry, pursues expansion through a strategic emphasis on innovation. With headquarters in California, the company is a designer and manufacturer of semiconductor components and related computers, of microcomputer systems, and of software. Its Pentium microprocessor gives a desktop computer the capability of a mainframe.

While most growth-oriented firms appreciate the need to be innovative occasionally, a few firms use it as their fundamental way of relating to their markets. An outstanding example is Polaroid, which heavily promotes each of its new cameras until competitors are able to match its technological innovation; by this time, Polaroid normally is prepared to introduce a dramatically new or improved product. For example, it introduced consumers in quick succession to the Swinger, the SX-70, the One Step, and the Sun Camera 660.

Few innovative ideas prove profitable because the research, development, and premarketing costs of converting a promising idea into a profitable product are extremely high. A study by the Booz Allen & Hamilton management research department provides some understanding of the risks. As shown in Exhibit 6–7, Booz Allen & Hamilton found that less

EXHIBIT 6–7
Decay of New Product Ideas (51 Companies)

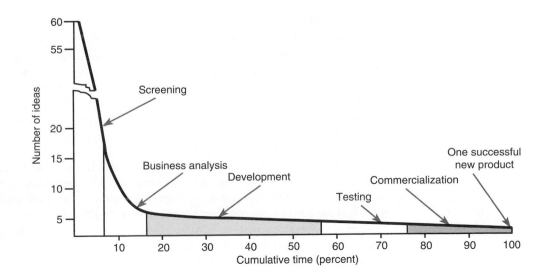

BusinessWeek Measured against the nation's wireless giants, VoiceStream Wireless Corp. has been a bit of a pipsqueak. So why would Germany's Deutsche Telekom pay an eye-popping $21,639 per subscriber for the little Bellevue, Washington, cell phone company? Simply put, Deutsche Telekom is not buying subscribers in the United States. It's buying potential—in this case, the potential to become a dominant player—not just in the United States, but globally. By the end of 2000, only about 32.5 percent of the U.S. population was using some form of wireless compared with 52 percent in Europe and 60 percent in Japan. Growth prospects in such a relatively undeveloped market, the German executives reckon, are so high that their company will emerge almost immediately as a formidable rival. U.S. telecom execs say a DT-VoiceStream link will force U.S. players to step up efforts to provide wireless Net service to a broader market, including overseas.

To gain this kind of sway over the lucrative U.S. market and the global market, Deutsche Telekom felt it was worth significantly besting the $4,390 per subscriber Britain's Vodafone paid for AirTouch in 1999 or the estimated $12,400 that the combined Vodafone-AirTouch paid for Mannesmann earlier this year. That has set off a torrent of criticism that it has wildly overpaid for its position. However, Deutsche Telekom's CEO Sommer is confident. Here's what he considered when he agreed to the price: VoiceStream owns licenses in 23 of the top 25 U.S. markets. In wireless lingo, its licenses cover areas with a 220 million subscriber base. Though it has relatively few subscribers signed up and currently does not actually provide service to many of the locales where it holds licenses, it is adding subscribers at a sizzling pace—an 18.5 percent growth rate that is among the top in the industry.

Wireless companies across the country are taking note, given DT's deep pockets and promise to make a starting investment of at least $5 billion in VoiceStream. With the $5 billion, VoiceStream can accelerate construction of wireless systems in places like California and Ohio. Stanton estimates that the cash infusion will help him push up the roll-out of his service by 6 to 18 months. Also, Deutsche Telekom's cash is expected to allow VoiceStream to participate in a major way in the upcoming auction of more spectrum licenses by the FCC.

Source: Excerpted from R. O. Crockett and D. Fairlamb, August 7, 2000, "Deutsche Telekom's Wireless Wager," *BusinessWeek* (3693), pp. 30–32.

than 2 percent of the innovative projects initially considered by 51 companies eventually reached the marketplace. Specifically, out of every 58 new product ideas, only 12 pass an initial screening test that finds them compatible with the firm's mission and long-term objectives, only 7 remain after an evaluation of their potential, and only 3 survive development attempts. Of the three survivors, two appear to have profit potential after test marketing and only one is commercially successful.

Horizontal Integration

When a firm's long-term strategy is based on growth through the acquisition of one or more similar firms operating at the same stage of the production-marketing chain, its grand strategy is called *horizontal integration*. Such acquisitions eliminate competitors and provide the acquiring firm with access to new markets. One example is Warner-Lambert's acquisition of Parke Davis, which reduced competition in the ethical drugs field for Chilcott Laboratories, a firm that Warner-Lambert previously had acquired. Another example is the long-range acquisition pattern of White Consolidated Industries, which expanded in the refrigerator and freezer market through a grand strategy of horizontal integration, by acquiring Kelvinator Appliance, the Refrigerator Products Division of Bendix Westinghouse Automotive Air Brake, and Frigidaire Appliance from General Motors. Nike's acquisition in the dress shoes business and N. V. Homes's purchase of Ryan Homes have vividly exemplified the success that horizontal integration strategies can bring.

Exhibit 6–8, Global Strategy in Action, describes Deutsche Telekom growth strategy of horizontal acquisition. Deutsche Telekom was a dominant player in the European wireless services market, but without a presence in the fast-growing U.S. market. To correct this limitation, Deutsche Telekom horizontally integrated by purchasing the American firm Voice-Stream Wireless, a company that was growing faster than most domestic rivals and that owned spectrum licenses providing access to 220 million potential customers.

Vertical Integration

When a firm's grand strategy is to acquire firms that supply it with inputs (such as raw materials) or are customers for its outputs (such as warehousers for finished products), *vertical integration* is involved. To illustrate, if a shirt manufacturer acquires a textile producer—by purchasing its common stock, buying its assets, or exchanging ownership interests—the strategy is vertical integration. In this case, it is *backward* vertical integration, since the acquired firm operates at an earlier stage of the production-marketing process. If the shirt manufacturer had merged with a clothing store, it would have been *forward* vertical integration—the acquisition of a firm nearer to the ultimate consumer.

Amoco emerged as North America's leader in natural gas reserves and products as a result of its acquisition of Dome Petroleum. This backward integration by Amoco was made in support of its downstream businesses in refining and in gas stations, whose profits made the acquisition possible.

Exhibit 6–9 depicts both horizontal and vertical integration. The principal attractions of a horizontal integration grand strategy are readily apparent. The acquiring firm is able to greatly expand its operations, thereby achieving greater market share, improving economies of scale, and increasing the efficiency of capital use. In addition, these benefits are achieved with only moderately increased risk, since the success of the expansion is principally dependent on proven abilities.

The reasons for choosing a vertical integration grand strategy are more varied and sometimes less obvious. The main reason for backward integration is the desire to increase the dependability of the supply or quality of the raw materials used as production inputs. That desire is particularly great when the number of suppliers is small and the number of competitors is large. In this situation, the vertically integrating firm can better control its costs and, thereby, improve the profit margin of the expanded production-marketing system. Forward integration is a preferred grand strategy if great advantages accrue to stable production. A firm can increase the predictability of demand for its output through forward integration; that is, through ownership of the next stage of its production-marketing chain.

EXHIBIT 6–9
Vertical and Horizontal Integrations

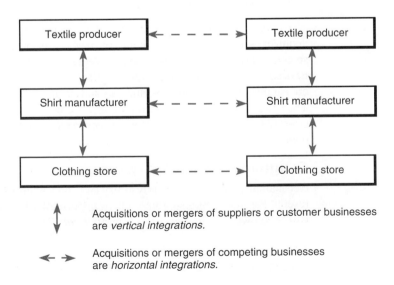

Acquisitions or mergers of suppliers or customer businesses are *vertical integrations*.

Acquisitions or mergers of competing businesses are *horizontal integrations*.

Some increased risks are associated with both types of integration. For horizontally integrated firms, the risks stem from increased commitment to one type of business. For vertically integrated firms, the risks result from the firm's expansion into areas requiring strategic managers to broaden the base of their competences and to assume additional responsibilities.

Concentric Diversification

Grand strategies involving diversification represent distinctive departures from a firm's existing base of operations, typically the acquisition or internal generation (spin-off) of a separate business with synergistic possibilities counterbalancing the strengths and weaknesses of the two businesses. For example, Head Ski initially sought to diversify into summer sporting goods and clothing to offset the seasonality of its "snow" business. However, diversifications occasionally are undertaken as unrelated investments, because of their high profit potential and their otherwise minimal resource demands.

Regardless of the approach taken, the motivations of the acquiring firms are the same:

- Increase the firm's stock value. In the past, mergers often have led to increases in the stock price or the price-earnings ratio.

- Increase the growth rate of the firm.

- Make an investment that represents better use of funds than plowing them into internal growth.

- Improve the stability of earnings and sales by acquiring firms whose earnings and sales complement the firm's peaks and valleys.

- Balance or fill out the product line.

- Diversify the product line when the life cycle of current products has peaked.

- Acquire a needed resource quickly (e.g., high-quality technology or highly innovative management).

- Achieve tax savings by purchasing a firm whose tax losses will offset current or future earnings.

- Increase efficiency and profitability, especially if there is synergy between the acquiring firm and the acquired firm.[3]

Concentric diversification involves the acquisition of businesses that are related to the acquiring firm in terms of technology, markets, or products. With this grand strategy, the selected new businesses possess a high degree of compatibility with the firm's current businesses. The ideal concentric diversification occurs when the combined company profits increase the strengths and opportunities and decrease the weaknesses and exposure to risk. Thus, the acquiring firm searches for new businesses whose products, markets, distribution channels, technologies, and resource requirements are similar to but not identical with its own, whose acquisition results in synergies but not complete interdependence.

Conglomerate Diversification

Occasionally a firm, particularly a very large one, plans to acquire a business because it represents the most promising investment opportunity available. This grand strategy is commonly known as *conglomerate diversification*. The principal concern, and often the sole

---

[3]Godfrey Devlin and Mark Bleackley, "Strategic Alliances—Guidelines for Success," *Long Range Planning,* October 1988, pp. 18–23.

1. *The wrong target.*

The first step to avoid such a mistake is for the acquiror and its financial advisors to determine the strategic goals and identify the mission. The product of this strategic review will be specifically identified criteria for the target.

The second step required to identify the right target is to design and carry out an effective due diligence process to ascertain whether the target indeed has the identified set of qualities selected in the strategic review.

2. *The wrong price.*

The key to avoiding this problem lies in the acquiror's valuation model. The model will incorporate assumptions concerning industry trends and growth patterns developed in the strategic review.

3. *The wrong structure.*

The two principal aspects of the acquisition process that can prevent this problem are a comprehensive regulatory compliance review and tax and legal analysis.

4. *The lost deal.*

The letter of intent must spell out not only the price to be paid but also many of the relational aspects that will make the strategic acquisition successful. Although an acquiror may justifiably focus on expenses, indemnification, and other logical concerns in the letter of intent, relationship and operational concerns are also important.

5. *Management difficulties.*

The remedy for this problem must be extracted from the initial strategic review. The management compensation structure must be designed with legal and business advisors to help achieve those goals. The financial rewards to management must depend upon the financial and strategic success of the combined entity.

6. *The closing crisis.*

Closing crises may stem from unavoidable changed conditions, but most often they result from poor communication. Negotiators sometimes believe that problems swept under the table maintain a deal's momentum and ultimately allow for its consummation. They are sometimes right—and often wrong. Charting a course through an acquisition requires carefully developed skills for every kind of professional—business, accounting, and legal.

7. *The operating transition crisis.*

Even the best conceived and executed acquisition will prevent significant transition and postclosing operation issues. Strategic goals cannot be achieved by quick asset sales or other accelerated exit strategies. Management time and energy must be spent to ensure that the benefits identified in the strategic review are achieved.

Source: From Academy of Management Review by D.A. Tanner. Copyright © 1991 by Academy of Management. Reproduced with permission of Academy of Management via Copyright Clearance Center.

concern, of the acquiring firm is the profit pattern of the venture. Unlike concentric diversification, conglomerate diversification gives little concern to creating product-market synergy with existing businesses. What such conglomerate diversifiers as ITT, Textron, American Brands, Litton, U.S. Industries, Fuqua, and I. C. Industries seek is financial synergy. For example, they may seek a balance in their portfolios between current businesses with cyclical sales and acquired businesses with countercyclical sales, between high-cash/low-opportunity and low-cash/high-opportunity businesses, or between debt-free and highly leveraged businesses.

The principal difference between the two types of diversification is that concentric diversification emphasizes some commonality in markets, products, or technology, whereas conglomerate diversification is based principally on profit considerations.

Several of the grand strategies discussed above, including concentric and conglomerate diversification and horizontal and vertical integration, often involve the purchase or acquisition of one firm by another. It is important to know that the majority of such acquisitions fail to produce the desired results for the companies involved. Exhibit 6–10, Strategy in Action, provides seven guidelines that can improve a company's chances of a successful acquisition.

Turnaround

For any one of a large number of reasons, a firm can find itself with declining profits. Among these reasons are economic recessions, production inefficiencies, and innovative break-throughs by competitors. In many cases, strategic managers believe that such a firm can survive and eventually recover if a concerted effort is made over a period of a few years to fortify its distinctive competences. This grand strategy is known as *turnaround*. It typically is begun through one of two forms of retrenchment, employed singly or in combination:

1. *Cost reduction.* Examples include decreasing the workforce through employee attrition, leasing rather than purchasing equipment, extending the life of machinery, eliminating elaborate promotional activities, laying off employees, dropping items from a production line, and discontinuing low-margin customers.

2. *Asset reduction.* Examples include the sale of land, buildings, and equipment not essential to the basic activity of the firm and the elimination of "perks," such as the company airplane and executives' cars.

Interestingly, the turnaround most commonly associated with this approach is in management positions. In a study of 58 large firms, researchers Shendel, Patton, and Riggs found that turnaround almost always was associated with changes in top management.[4] Bringing in new managers was believed to introduce needed new perspectives on the firm's situation, to raise employee morale, and to facilitate drastic actions, such as deep budgetary cuts in established programs.

Strategic management research provides evidence that the firms that have used a *turnaround strategy* have successfully confronted decline. The research findings have been assimilated and used as the building blocks for a model of the turnaround process shown in Exhibit 6–11.

The model begins with a depiction of external and internal factors as causes of a firm's performance downturn. When these factors continue to detrimentally impact the firm, its financial health is threatened. Unchecked decline places the firm in a turnaround situation.

A *turnaround situation* represents absolute and relative-to-industry declining performance of a sufficient magnitude to warrant explicit turnaround actions. Turnaround situations may be the result of years of gradual slowdown or months of sharp decline. In either case, the recovery phase of the turnaround process is likely to be more successful in accomplishing turnaround when it is preceded by planned retrenchment that results in the achievement of near-term financial stabilization. For a declining firm, stabilizing operations and restoring profitability almost always entail strict cost reduction followed by a shrinking back to those segments of the business that have the best prospects of attractive profit margins. The need for retrenchment was reflected in unemployment figures during the 2000–2003 recession. More layoffs of American workers were announced in 2001 than in any of the previous eight years when U.S. companies announced nearly 2 million layoffs as the economy sunk into its first recession in a decade.

The immediacy of the resulting threat to company survival posed by the turnaround situation is known as *situation severity*. Severity is the governing factor in estimating the speed with which the retrenchment response will be formulated and activated. When severity is low, a firm has some financial cushion. Stability may be achieved through cost retrenchment alone. When turnaround situation severity is high, a firm must immediately stabilize the decline or bankruptcy is imminent. Cost reductions must be supplemented with more drastic

---

[4]Other forms of joint ventures (such as leasing, contract manufacturing, and management contracting) offer valuable support strategies. They are not included in the categorization, however, because they seldom are employed as grand strategies.

EXHIBIT 6–11   A Model of the Turnaround Process

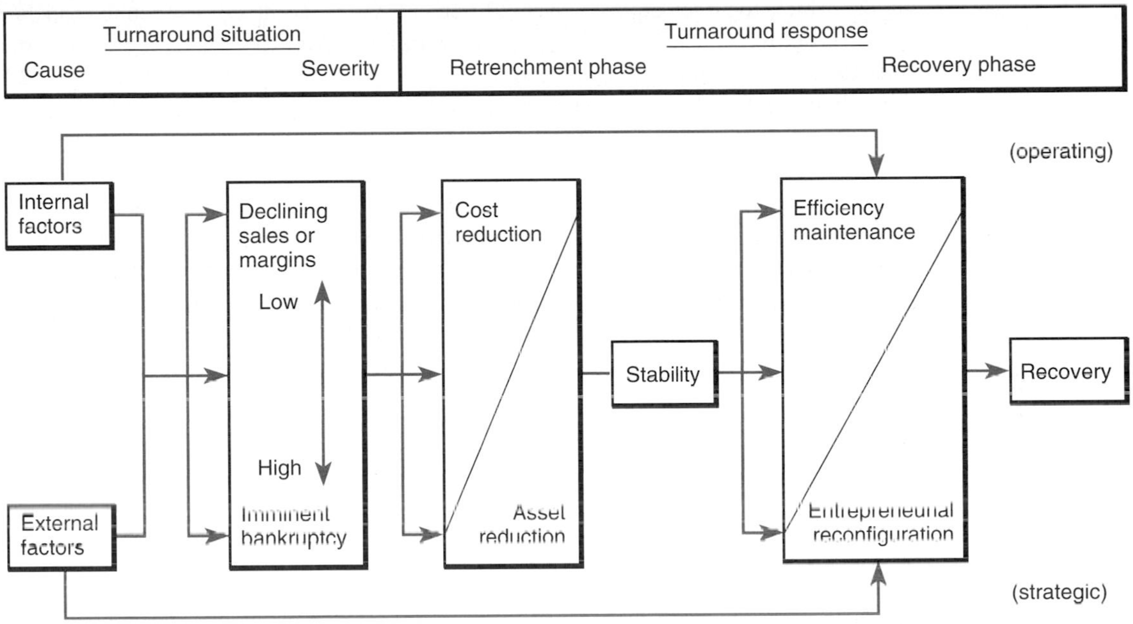

asset reduction measures. Assets targeted for divestiture are those determined to be under-productive. In contrast, more productive resources are protected from cuts and represent critical elements of the future core business plan of the company (i.e., the intended recovery response).

Turnaround responses among successful firms typically include two stages of strategic activities: retrenchment and the recovery response. *Retrenchment* consists of cost-cutting and asset-reducing activities. The primary objective of the retrenchment phase is to stabilize the firm's financial condition. Situation severity has been associated with retrenchment responses among successful turnaround firms. Firms in danger of bankruptcy or failure (i.e., severe situations) attempt to halt decline through cost and asset reductions. Firms in less severe situations have achieved stability merely through cost retrenchment. However, in either case, for firms facing declining financial performance, the key to successful turnaround rests in the effective and efficient management of the retrenchment process.

The primary causes of the turnaround situation have been associated with the second phase of the turnaround process, the *recovery response*. For firms that declined primarily as a result of external problems, turnaround most often has been achieved through creative new entrepreneurial strategies. For firms that declined primarily as a result of internal problems, turnaround has been most frequently achieved through efficiency strategies. *Recovery* is achieved when economic measures indicate that the firm has regained its predownturn levels of performance.

Divestiture

A *divestiture strategy* involves the sale of a firm or a major component of a firm. Sara Lee Corp. (SLE) provides a good example. It sells everything from Wonderbras and Kiwi shoe polish to Endust furniture polish and Chock full o'Nuts coffee. The company used a conglomerate diversification strategy to build Sara Lee into a huge portfolio of disparate brands. A new president, C. Steven McMillan, faced stagnant revenues and earnings. So he consolidated, streamlined, and focused the company on its core categories—food, underwear, and household products. He divested 15 businesses, including Coach leather goods, which together equaled over 20 percent of the company's revenue, and laid off 13,200 employees, nearly 10 percent of the workforce. McMillan used the cash from asset sales to snap up brands that enhanced Sara Lee's clout in key categories, like the $2.8 billion purchase of St. Louis-based breadmaker Earthgrains Co. to quadruple Sara Lee's bakery operations.

When retrenchment fails to accomplish the desired turnaround, as in the Goodyear situation, or when a nonintegrated business activity achieves an unusually high market value, strategic managers often decide to sell the firm. However, because the intent is to find a buyer willing to pay a premium above the value of a going concern's fixed assets, the term *marketing for sale* is often more appropriate. Prospective buyers must be convinced that because of their skills and resources or because of the firm's synergy with their existing businesses, they will be able to profit from the acquisition.

As discussed in Exhibit 6–12, Strategy in Action, Corning undertook a turnaround that followed retrenchment with divestitures. In 2001, Corning found itself in a declining market for its core product of fiber optic cable. The company needed to develop a strategy that would allow it to turnaround its falling sales and begin to grow once more. It began with retrenchment. Corning laid off 12,000 workers in 2001 and another 4,000 in 2002. Corning also began the divestiture of its non-core assets, such as its non-telecom businesses, and its money-losing photonics operation to stabilize its financial situation so that it could begin its recovery.

The reasons for divestiture vary. They often arise because of partial mismatches between the acquired firm and the parent corporation. Some of the mismatched parts cannot be integrated into the corporation's mainstream activities and, thus, must be spun off. A second reason is corporate financial needs. Sometimes the cash flow or financial stability of the corporation as a whole can be greatly improved if businesses with high market value can be sacrificed. The result can be a balancing of equity with long-term risks or of long-term debt payments to optimize the cost of capital. A third, less frequent reason for divestiture is government antitrust action when a firm is believed to monopolize or unfairly dominate a particular market.

Although examples of the divestiture grand strategy are numerous, CBS, Inc., provides an outstanding example. In a two-year period, the once diverse entertainment and publishing giant sold its Records Division to Sony, its magazine publishing business to Diamandis Communications, its book publishing operations to Harcourt Brace Jovanovich, and its music publishing operations to SBK Entertainment World. Other firms that have pursued this type of grand strategy include Esmark, which divested Swift & Company, and White Motors, which divested White Farm.

Liquidation

When liquidation is the grand strategy, the firm typically is sold in parts, only occasionally as a whole—but for its tangible asset value and not as a going concern. In selecting liquidation, the owners and strategic managers of a firm are admitting failure and recognize that this action is likely to result in great hardships to themselves and their employees. For these reasons, liquidation usually is seen as the least attractive of the grand strategies. As a long-term strategy, however, it minimizes the losses of all the firm's stockholders. Faced with bankruptcy, the liquidating firm usually tries to develop a planned and orderly system that will result in the greatest possible return and cash conversion as the firm slowly relinquishes its market share.

Planned liquidation can be worthwhile. For example, Columbia Corporation, a $130 million diversified firm, liquidated its assets for more cash per share than the market value of its stock.

BusinessWeek The year is 2002. Corning, the deeply weakened fiber-optic powerhouse, is trying to navigate between the telecom meltdown and a looming liquidity squeeze.

When James Houghton left retirement to retake the reins at Corning (GLW) in June, 2001, the world's largest fiber-optic cable maker clearly had lost its footing. Its customers were cutting their capital budgets as their own customers demanded lower prices. Corning's revenues were beginning to drop precipitously. Houghton, who joined Corning in 1962 and became its chairman and CEO before retiring in 1996, was returning just as his glass empire was starting to crack.

Things haven't improved much so far in 2002. Corning's sales, at $2 billion in the fourth quarter of 2000, reached only $896 million in the second quarter of 2002. That's down 52 percent from year ago levels and slightly down from the first quarter. Corning had already laid off 12,000 workers in 2001 at its Corning (N.Y.) headquarters. But on July 23, it announced an additional 4,000 layoffs, bringing its workforce down to 28,000. Its stock, trading at $340 per share in 2000, before a split, hit a new low of $1.50 on Aug. 1. Analysts say a $2 billion credit line could be in jeopardy. And Corning might not reach profitability in 2003, as promised. It might even have difficulty paying off $2.1 billion zero-coupon, convertible bonds due in 2005. Ironically, no one is saying that Corning's products are substandard. Just the opposite, in fact. But that might not be enough to get it over a very tough financial patch.

Liquidity remains a key concern. At the end of its most recent quarter, Corning had $940 million in cash and $383 million in short-term investments. But the funds are needed for day-to-day operations, restructuring, and debt payments, so by the end of 2003, Corning will go through most of that stash. Standard & Poor's has downgraded Corning's credit rating to below investment grade, meaning the company could have trouble raising additional funds—which are exactly what Corning might need for operations if some of its short-term investments aren't sellable, says Kingston. As of June 30, Corning had $4.76 billion in property, plants, and equipment. Its four fiber plants—two in North Carolina, one in Germany, and one in Australia—are running at 40 percent capacity. The larger, U.S.-based plants cost about $450 million each to build, and Corning could, potentially, write off half of the capacity, or about $1 billion.

Goodwill write-offs could be massive as well. Most of the value in the $2 billion goodwill account comes from Corning's optical-components business. Considering that several companies currently trying to sell similar businesses are having a hard time getting even a few cents on the dollar, the write-off could be huge.

Corning could raise money by issuing more equity—and diluting the interests of existing shareholders. Recently, it sold $575 million of three-year mandatory convertible preferred stock, with a coupon rate of 7 percent. Of course, Corning could sell some of its businesses for cash. Though it's known mainly for its optical cable, Corning also makes glass for flat-panel monitors, funnels for large-screen TVs, and frequency controls for electronics. These businesses account for half of its revenues, and many are growing and are profitable.

Barring some unprecedented telecom turnaround, without more cost cuts Corning is unlikely to reach profitability in 2003. That's a long time to ask investors to hang tough in this kind of market. And demand for fiber could remain weak for three more years, says Russ McGuire, chief strategist at telecom consultancy TeleChoice. Even when it does turn up, demand likely won't soar. All of the major telecom networks are already built out, and the stretches that remain will require less capacity—and less fiber, says Patrick Fay, an analyst at fiber-consultancy KMI.

Source: Excerpted from Olga Kharif, "Corning's 'Very Narrow Straits.' " *BusinessWeek Online*, August 30, 2002.

Bankruptcy

Business failures are playing an increasingly important role in the American economy. In an average week, more than 300 companies fail. More than 75 percent of these financially desperate firms file for a *liquidation bankruptcy*—they agree to a complete distribution of their assets to creditors, most of whom receive a small fraction of the amount they are owed. Liquidation is what the layperson views as bankruptcy: The business cannot pay its debts, so it must close its doors. Investors lose their money, employees lose their jobs, and managers lose their credibility. In owner-managed firms, company and personal bankruptcy commonly go hand in hand.

The other 25 percent of these firms refuse to surrender until one final option is exhausted. Choosing a strategy to recapture its viability, such a company asks the courts for a *reorganization bankruptcy*. The firm attempts to persuade its creditors to temporarily freeze their claims while it undertakes to reorganize and rebuild the company's operations more profitably. The appeal of a reorganization bankruptcy is based on the company's ability to convince creditors that it can succeed in the marketplace by implementing a new strategic plan, and that when the plan produces profits, the firm will be able to repay its creditors, perhaps in full. In other words, the company offers its creditors a carefully designed alternative to forcing an immediate, but fractional, repayment of its financial obligations. The option of reorganization bankruptcy offers maximum repayment of debt at some specified future time if a new strategic plan is successful.

The Bankruptcy Situation

Imagine that your firm's financial reports have shown an unabated decline in revenue for seven quarters. Expenses have increased rapidly, and it is becoming difficult, and at times not possible, to pay bills as they become due. Suppliers are concerned about shipping goods without first receiving payment, and some have refused to ship without advanced payment in cash. Customers are requiring assurances that future orders will be delivered and some are beginning to buy from competitors. Employees are listening seriously to rumors of financial problems and a higher than normal number have accepted other employment. What can be done? What strategy can be initiated to protect the company and resolve the financial problems in the short term?

The Harshest Resolution

If the judgment of the owners of a business is that its decline cannot be reversed, and the business cannot be sold as a going concern, then the alternative that is in the best interest of all may be a liquidation bankruptcy, also known as Chapter 7 of the Bankruptcy Code. The court appoints a trustee, who collects the property of the company, reduces it to cash, and distributes the proceeds proportionally to creditors on a pro rata basis as expeditiously as possible. Since all assets are sold to pay outstanding debt, a liquidation bankruptcy terminates a business. This type of filing is critically important to sole proprietors or partnerships. Their owners are personally liable for all business debts not covered by the sale of the business assets unless they can secure a Chapter 7 bankruptcy, which will allow them to cancel any debt in excess of exempt assets. Although they will be left with little personal property, the liquidated debtor is discharged from paying the remaining debt.

The shareholders of corporations are not liable for corporate debt and any debt existing after corporate assets are liquidated is absorbed by creditors. Corporate shareholders may simply terminate operations and walk away without liability to remaining creditors. However, filing a Chapter 7 proceeding will provide for an orderly and fair distribution of assets to creditors and thereby may reduce the negative impact of the business failure.

A Conditional Second Chance

A proactive alternative for the endangered company is reorganization bankruptcy. Chosen for the right reasons, and implemented in the right way, reorganization bankruptcy can provide a financially, strategically, and ethically sound basis on which to advance the interests of all of the firm's stakeholders.

A thorough and objective analysis of the company may support the idea of its continuing operations if excessive debt can be reduced and new strategic initiatives can be undertaken. If the realistic possibility of long-term survival exists, a reorganization under Chapter 11 of the Bankruptcy Code can provide the opportunity. Reorganization allows a business debtor to restructure its debts and, with the agreement of creditors and approval of the court, to continue as a viable business. Creditors involved in Chapter 11 actions often receive less than the total debt due to them but far more than would be available from liquidation.

A Chapter 11 bankruptcy can provide time and protection to the debtor firm (which we will call the *Company*) to reorganize and use future earnings to pay creditors. The Company may restructure debts, close unprofitable divisions or stores, renegotiate labor contracts, reduce its workforce, or propose other actions that could create a profitable business. If the plan is accepted by creditors, the Company will be given another chance to avoid liquidation and emerge from the bankruptcy proceedings rehabilitated.

Seeking Protection of the Bankruptcy Court

If creditors file lawsuits or schedule judicial sales to enforce liens, the Company will need to seek the protection of the Bankruptcy Court. Filing a bankruptcy petition will invoke the protection of the court to provide sufficient time to work out a reorganization that was not achievable voluntarily. If reorganization is not possible, a Chapter 7 proceeding will allow for the fair and orderly dissolution of the business.

If a Chapter 11 proceeding is the required course of action, the Company must determine what the reorganized business will look like, if such a structure can be achieved, and how it will be accomplished while maintaining operations during the bankruptcy proceeding. Will sufficient cash be available to pay for the proceedings and reorganization? Will customers continue to do business with the Company or seek other more secure businesses with which to deal? Will key personnel stay on or look for more secure employment? Which operations should be discontinued or reduced?

Emerging from Bankruptcy

Bankruptcy is only the first step toward recovery for a firm. Many questions should be answered: How did the business get to the point at which the extreme action of bankruptcy was necessary? Were warning signs overlooked? Was the competitive environment understood? Did pride or fear prevent objective analysis? Did the business have the people and resources to succeed? Was the strategic plan well designed and implemented? Did financial problems result from unforeseen and unforeseeable problems or from bad management decisions?

Commitments to "try harder," "listen more carefully to the customer," and "be more efficient" are important but insufficient grounds to inspire stakeholder confidence. A recovery strategy must be developed to delineate how the company will compete more successfully in the future.

An assessment of the bankruptcy situation requires executives to consider the causes of the Company's decline and the severity of the problem it now faces. Investors must decide whether the management team that governed the company's operations during the downturn can return the firm to a position of success. Creditors must believe that the company's managers have learned how to prevent a recurrence of the observed and similar problems. Alternatively, they must have faith that the company's competencies can be sufficiently augmented by key substitutions to the management team, with strong support in decision making from a board of directors and consultants, to restore the firm's competitive strength.

CORPORATE COMBINATIONS

The 15 grand strategies discussed above, used singly and much more often in combinations, represent the traditional alternatives used by firms in the United States. Recently, three new grand types have gained in popularity; all fit under the broad category of corporate combinations. Although they do not fit the criterion by which executives retain a high degree of control over their operations, these grand strategies deserve special attention and consideration especially by companies that operate in global, dynamic, and technologically driven industries. These three newly popularized grand strategies are joint ventures, strategic alliances, and consortia.

Joint Ventures

Occasionally two or more capable firms lack a necessary component for success in a particular competitive environment. For example, no single petroleum firm controlled sufficient resources to construct the Alaskan pipeline. Nor was any single firm capable of processing and marketing all of the oil that would flow through the pipeline. The solution was a set of *joint ventures,* which are commercial companies (children) created and operated for the benefit of the co-owners (parents). These cooperative arrangements provided both the funds needed to build the pipeline and the processing and marketing capacities needed to profitably handle the oil flow.

The particular form of joint ventures discussed above is *joint ownership.* In recent years, it has become increasingly appealing for domestic firms to join foreign firms by means of this form. For example, Diamond-Star Motors is the result of a joint venture between a U.S. company, Chrysler Corporation, and Japan's Mitsubishi Motors corporation. Located in Normal, Illinois, Diamond-Star was launched because it offered Chrysler and Mitsubishi a chance to expand on their long-standing relationship in which subcompact cars (as well as Mitsubishi engines and other automotive parts) are imported to the United States and sold under the Dodge and Plymouth names.

The joint venture extends the supplier-consumer relationship and has strategic advantages for both partners. For Chrysler, it presents an opportunity to produce a high-quality car using expertise brought to the venture by Mitsubishi. It also gives Chrysler the chance to try new production techniques and to realize efficiencies by using the workforce that was not included under Chrysler's collective bargaining agreement with the United Auto Workers. The agreement offers Mitsubishi the opportunity to produce cars for sale in the United States without being subjected to the tariffs and restrictions placed on Japanese imports.

As a second example, Bethlehem Steel acquired an interest in a Brazilian mining venture to secure a raw material source. The stimulus for this joint ownership venture was grand strategy, but such is not always the case. Certain countries virtually mandate that foreign firms entering their markets do so on a joint ownership basis. India and Mexico are good examples. The rationale of these countries is that joint ventures minimize the threat of foreign domination and enhance the skills, employment, growth, and profits of local firms.

It should be noted that strategic managers understandably are wary of joint ventures. Admittedly, joint ventures present new opportunities with risks that can be shared. On the other hand, joint ventures often limit the discretion, control, and profit potential of partners, while demanding managerial attention and other resources that might be directed toward the firm's mainstream activities. Nevertheless, increasing globalization in many industries may require greater consideration of the joint venture approach, if historically national firms are to remain viable.

Strategic Alliances

Strategic alliances are distinguished from joint ventures because the companies involved do not take an equity position in one another. In many instances, strategic alliances are partnerships that exist for a defined period during which partners contribute their skills and expertise to a cooperative project. For example, one partner provides manufacturing capabilities while a second partner provides marketing expertise. Many times, such alliances are undertaken because the partners want to learn from one another with the intention to be able to develop in-house capabilities to supplant the partner when the contractual arrangement between them reaches its termination date. Such relationships are tricky since in a sense the partners are attempting to "steal" each other's know-how. Exhibit 6–13, Global Strategy in Action, lists many important

Objective	Major Questions
1. Assess and value partner knowledge.	• What were the strategic objectives in forming the alliance? • What are the core competencies of our alliance partner? • What specific knowledge does the partner have that could enhance our competitive strategy? • What are the core partner skills relevant for our product/markets?
2. Determine knowledge accessibility.	• How have key alliance responsibilities been allocated to the partners? • Which partner controls key managerial responsibilities? • Does the alliance agreement specify restrictions on our access to the alliance operations?
3. Evaluate knowledge tacitness and ease of transfer.	• Is our learning objective focused on explicit operational knowledge? • Where in the alliance does the knowledge reside? • Is the knowledge strategic or operational? • Do we understand what we are trying to learn and how we can use the knowledge?
4. Establish knowledge connections between the alliance and the partner.	• Are parent managers in regular contact with senior alliance managers? • Has the alliance been incorporated into parent strategic plans and do alliance managers participate in parent strategic planning discussions? • What is the level of trust between parent and alliance managers? • Do alliance financial issues dominate meetings between alliance and parent managers?
5. Draw on existing knowledge to facilitate learning.	• In the learning process, have efforts been made to involve managers with prior experience in either/both alliance management and partner ties? • Are experiences with other alliances being used as the basis for managing the current alliance? • Are we realistic about our partner's learning objectives? • Are we open-minded about knowledge without immediate short-term applicability?
6. Ensure that partner and alliance managerial cultures are in alignment.	• Is the alliance viewed as a threat or an asset by parent managers? • In the parent, is there agreement on the strategic rationale for the alliance? • In the alliance, do managers understand the importance of the parent's learning objective?

Source: From Academy of Management Executive: The Thinking Manager's Source by Andrew C. Inkpen. Copyright 1998 by Academy of Management. Reproduced with permission of Academy of Management via Copyright Clearance Center.

questions about their learning intentions that prospective partners should ask themselves before entering into a strategic alliance.

In other instances, strategic alliances are synonymous with licensing agreements. Licensing involves the transfer of some industrial property right from the U.S. licensor to a motivated licensee in a foreign country. Most tend to be patents, trademarks, or technical know-how that are granted to the licensee for a specified time in return for a royalty and for avoiding tariffs or import quotas. Bell South and U.S. West, with various marketing and service competitive advantages valuable to Europe, have extended a number of licenses to create personal computer networks in the United Kingdom (U.K.).

Another licensing strategy open to U.S. firms is to contract the manufacturing of its product line to a foreign company to exploit local comparative advantages in technology, materials, or labor. For example, MIPS Computer Systems has licensed Digital Equipment Corporation, Texas Instruments, Cypress Semiconductor, and Bipolar Integrated Technology in the United States, and Fujitsu, NEC, and Kubota in Japan to market computers based on its designs in the partner's country.

Service and franchise-based firms—including Anheuser-Busch, Avis, Coca-Cola, Hilton, Hyatt, Holiday Inns, Kentucky Fried Chicken, McDonald's, and Pepsi—have long engaged in licensing arrangements with foreign distributors as a way to enter new markets with standardized products that can benefit from marketing economies.

Outsourcing is a rudimentary approach to strategic alliances that enables firms to gain a competitive advantage. Significant changes within many segments of American business continue to encourage the use of outsourcing practices. Within the health care arena, an industry survey recorded 67 percent of hospitals using provider outsourcing for at least one department within their organization. Services such as information systems, reimbursement, and risk and physician practice management are outsourced by 51 percent of the hospitals that use outsourcing.

Another successful application of outsourcing is found in human resources. A survey of human resource executives revealed 85 percent have personal experience leading an outsourcing effort within their organization. In addition, it was found that two-thirds of pension departments have outsourced at least one human resource function.

Within customer service and sales departments, outsourcing increased productivity in such areas as product information, sales and order taking, sample fulfillment, and complaint handling. Exhibit 6–14 presents the top five strategic and tactical reasons for exploiting the benefits of outsourcing.

EXHIBIT 6–14
The Top Five Strategic Reasons for Outsourcing

Source: Material prepared for a paid advertising section which appeared in the October 16, 1995, issue of *Fortune* © 1995, Time, Inc. All rights reserved.

1. **Improve Business Focus.**
   For many companies, the single most compelling reason for outsourcing is that several "how" issues are siphoning off huge amounts of management's resources and attention.
2. **Access to World-Class Capabilities.**
   By the very nature of their specialization, outsourcing providers bring extensive worldwide, world-class resources to meeting the needs of their customers. Partnering with an organization with world-class capabilities can offer access to new technology, tools, and techniques that the organization may not currently possess; better career opportunities for personnel who transition to the outsourcing provider; more structured methodologies, procedures, and documentation; and competitive advantage through expanded skills.
3. **Accelerated Reengineering Benefits.**
   Outsourcing is often a byproduct of another powerful management tool—business process reengineering. It allows an organization to immediately realize the anticipated benefits of reengineering by having an outside organization—one that is already reengineered to world-class standards—take over the process.
4. **Shared Risks.**
   When companies outsource they become more flexible, more dynamic, and better able to adapt to changing opportunities.
5. **Free Resources for Other Purposes.**
   Outsourcing permits an organization to redirect its resources from noncore activities toward activities that have the greater return in serving the customer.

Consortia, Keiretsus, and Chaebols

Consortia are defined as large interlocking relationships between businesses of an industry. In Japan such consortia are known as *keiretsus,* in South Korea as *chaebols.*

In Europe, consortia projects are increasing in number and in success rates. Examples include the Junior Engineers' and Scientists' Summer Institute, which underwrites cooperative learning and research; the European Strategic Program for Research and Development in Information Technologies, which seeks to enhance European competitiveness in fields related to computer electronics and component manufacturing; and EUREKA, which is a joint program involving scientists and engineers from several European countries to coordinate joint research projects.

A Japanese *keiretsu* is an undertaking involving up to 50 different firms that are joined around a large trading company or bank and are coordinated through interlocking directories and stock exchanges. It is designed to use industry coordination to minimize risks of competition, in part through cost sharing and increased economies of scale. Examples include Sumitomo, Mitsubishi, Mitsui, and Sanwa. Exhibit 6–15, Global Strategy in Action, presents a new side to *keiretsus,* namely, that they are adding global partners, including several from the United States. Their cooperative nature is growing in evidence as is their market success.

A South Korean chaebol resembles a consortium or keiretsu except that they are typically financed through government banking groups and largely are run by professional managers trained by participating firms expressly for the job.

SELECTION OF LONG-TERM OBJECTIVES AND GRAND STRATEGY SETS

At first glance, the strategic management model, which provides the framework for study throughout this book, seems to suggest that strategic choice decision making leads to the sequential selection of long-term objectives and grand strategies. In fact, however, strategic choice is the simultaneous selection of long-range objectives and grand strategies. When strategic planners study their opportunities, they try to determine which are most likely to result in achieving various long-range objectives. Almost simultaneously, they try to forecast whether an available grand strategy can take advantage of preferred opportunities so the tentative objectives can be met. In essence, then, three distinct but highly interdependent choices are being made at one time. Several triads, or sets, of possible decisions are usually considered.

A simplified example of this process is shown in Exhibit 6–16. In this example, the firm has determined that six strategic choice options are available. These options stem from three interactive opportunities (e.g., West Coast markets that present little competition). Because each of these interactive opportunities can be approached through different grand strategies—for options 1 and 2, the grand strategies are horizontal integration and market development—each offers the potential for achieving long-range objectives to varying degrees. Thus, a firm rarely can make a strategic choice only on the basis of its preferred opportunities, long-range objectives, or grand strategy. Instead, these three elements must be considered simultaneously, because only in combination do they constitute a strategic choice.

In an actual decision situation, the strategic choice would be complicated by a wider variety of interactive opportunities, feasible company objectives, promising grand strategy options, and evaluative criteria. Nevertheless, Exhibit 6–16 does partially reflect the nature and complexity of the process by which long-term objectives and grand strategies are selected.

In the next chapter, the strategic choice process will be fully explained. However, knowledge of long-term objectives and grand strategies is essential to understanding that process.

BusinessWeek Amid rolling hills outside Nagoya, Toshiba Corp. recently took the wraps off a new $1 billion chipmaking facility that uses ultraviolet lithography to etch circuits less than one micron wide—a tiny fraction of the width of a human hair.

The Toshiba chip site owes much to a strategic alliance with IBM and Siemens of Germany. In fact, IBM's know-how in chemical mechanical polishing, essential to smoothing the tiny surfaces of multilayered chips, played a critical role. "We had little expertise here," concedes Toshiba's Koichi Suzuki.

QUIET CHANGE

What's more, about 20 IBM engineers will show up shortly to transfer the technology back to an IBM-Toshiba facility in Manassas, Virginia. In addition to the semiconductor cooperation, IBM and Toshiba jointly make liquid-crystal display panels—even though they use the LCDs in their fiercely competitive lines of laptop computers. "It's no longer considered a loss of corporate manhood to let others help out," says IBM Asia Pacific President Robert C. Timpson.

For years, many U.S. tie-ups with Japanese companies tended to be defensive in nature, poorly managed, and far removed from core businesses. Now, the alliances are deepening, taking on increasingly important products, and expanding their geographic reach in terms of sales. U.S.-Japanese partnerships are, for example, popping up in Asia's emerging but tricky markets, reducing the risks each company faces.

This deepening web of relationships reflects a quiet change in thinking by Japanese and U.S. multinationals in an era when keeping pace with technological change and competing globally have stretched the resources of even the richest companies. "The scale and technology are so great that neither can do it alone," says Jordan D. Lewis, author of *The Connected Corporation.*

Overall, instances of joint investments in research, products, and distribution by Japanese companies and foreign counterparts, mostly American, jumped 26 percent, to 155, in the first quarter of 1996—on top of a 33 percent increase between 1993 and 1995—according to the Sakura Institute of Research.

ENVY

And while Uncle Sam and U.S. companies with grievances have attacked Japan's system of big industrial groups, called keiretsu, as exclusionary, other chieftains of Corporate America have quietly become *stakeholders* of sorts. The list includes companies as diverse as IBM, General Motors, TRW, Boeing, and Caterpillar.

Many American executives who established these alliances say they appreciate the attributes of Japan's big industrial groups. U.S. managers have always envied the keiretsu edge in spreading risk over a cluster of companies when betting on a new technology or blitzing emerging markets.

In one industry after another, U.S. and Japanese partners are breaking new ground in their level of cooperation. The impact is felt far beyond the U.S. and Japanese home markets. Take the 50–50 venture between Caterpillar Inc. and Mitsubishi Heavy Industries LTD., part of Japan's $200 billion keiretsu of the same name. Early on, Cat wanted a way to sell its construction equipment in Japan and compete with rival Komatsu Ltd. on its home turf. Mitsubishi wanted to play catch-up with Komatsu, too, and expand its export markets.

Their alliance played a key role in taming Komatsu. But the partners have broader ambitions. Since Cat shifted all design work for its "300" series of excavators to the partnership back in 1987, the venture's two Japanese factories have emerged as Cat's primary source of production for sales to fast-growing Asia. The alliance's products reach the world market through Cat's network of 186 independent dealers in 197 countries.

Source: Brian Bemner in Tokyo, with Zachary Schiller in Cleveland, Tim Smart in Fairfield, William J. Holstein in New York, and bureau reports, "Keiretsu Connections," *BusinessWeek,* July 22, 1996.

SEQUENCE OF OBJECTIVES AND STRATEGY SELECTION

The selection of long-range objectives and grand strategies involves simultaneous, rather than sequential, decisions. While it is true that objectives are needed to prevent the firm's direction and progress from being determined by random forces, it is equally true that objectives can be achieved only if strategies are implemented. In fact, long-term objectives and grand strategies are so interdependent that some business consultants do not distinguish between them. Long-term objectives and grand strategies are still combined under the heading of company strategy in most of the popular business literature and in the thinking of most practicing executives.

EXHIBIT 6–16

A Profile of Strategic Choice Options

	Six Strategic Choice Options					
	1	**2**	**3**	**4**	**5**	**6**
Interactive opportunities	West Coast markets present little competition		Current markets sensitive to price competition		Current industry product lines offer too narrow a range of markets	
Appropriate long-range objectives (limited sample): Average 5-year ROI. Company sales by year 5. Risk of negative profits.	15% + 50% .30	19% + 40% .25	13% + 20% .10	17% + 0% .15	23% + 35% .20	15% + 25% .05
Grand strategies	Horizontal integration	Market development	Concentration	Selective retrenchment	Product development	Concentration

However, the distinction has merit. Objectives indicate what strategic managers want but provide few insights about how they will be achieved. Conversely, strategies indicate what types of actions will be taken but do not define what ends will be pursued or what criteria will serve as constraints in refining the strategic plan.

Does it matter whether strategic decisions are made to achieve objectives or to satisfy constraints? No, because constraints are themselves objectives. The constraint of increased inventory capacity is a desire (an objective), not a certainty. Likewise, the constraint of an increase in the sales force does not ensure that the increase will be achieved, given such factors as other company priorities, labor market conditions, and the firm's profit performance.

Summary

Before we learn how strategic decisions are made, it is important to understand the two principal components of any strategic choice; namely, long-term objectives and the grand strategy. The purpose of this chapter was to convey that understanding.

Long-term objectives were defined as the results a firm seeks to achieve over a specified period, typically five years. Seven common long-term objectives were discussed: profitability, productivity, competitive position, employee development, employee relations, technological leadership, and public responsibility. These, or any other long-term objectives, should be acceptable, flexible, measurable over time, motivating, suitable, understandable, and achievable.

Grand strategies were defined as comprehensive approaches guiding the major actions designed to achieve long-term objectives. Fifteen grand strategy options were discussed: concentrated growth, market development, product development, innovation, horizontal integration, vertical integration, concentric diversification, conglomerate diversification, turnaround, divestiture, liquidation, bankruptcy, joint ventures, strategic alliances, and consortia.

Questions
for Discussion

1. Identify firms in the business community nearest to your college or university that you believe are using each of the 15 grand strategies discussed in this chapter.

2. Identify firms in your business community that appear to rely principally on 1 of the 15 grand strategies. What kind of information did you use to classify the firms?

3. Write a long-term objective for your school of business that exhibits the seven qualities of long-term objectives described in this chapter.

4. Distinguish between the following pairs of grand strategies:

   a. Horizontal and vertical integration.
   b. Conglomerate and concentric diversification.
   c. Product development and innovation.
   d. Joint venture and strategic alliance.

5. Rank each of the 15 grand strategy options discussed in this chapter on the following three scales:

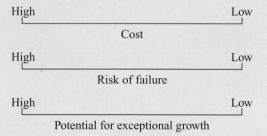

6. Identify firms that use one of the eight specific options shown in Exhibit 6–4 under the grand strategies of concentration, market development, and product development.

Chapter 6 Discussion Case

Novartis

BusinessWeek

1 Novartis (NVS) Chairman and CEO Daniel L. Vasella doesn't take no for an answer. The head of the world's sixth-largest drugmaker (by sales) goes after what he wants and, more often than not, gets it. When the Swiss company began work on a $4 billion research facility in Cambridge, Mass., last year, Vasella decided to draft a world-famous scientist to run it. But his candidate, Dr. Mark C. Fishman, a renowned geneticist and cardiologist at Harvard Medical School, flatly refused, saying he was happy in his current job. "It has been years since that happened to me," Vasella recalls with a laugh. But Vasella wore him down. After six months of persistent wooing on two continents, the Cambridge center was up and running by the end of March with Fishman in charge.

2 Hiring Fishman—and turning the Cambridge center into a leader in the discovery of cardiovascular, cancer, antiviral, and diabetes drugs—are the latest elements of a grand plan that the courteous, soft-spoken Swiss has developed with a mixture of patience and quiet ferocity. The first stage was to generate some respect for Novartis, a product of the 1996 merger of two Swiss companies, Sandoz Ltd. and Ciba-Geigy. That was the hard part. Until two years ago, the industry dismissed Novartis as a sleepy European giant without the marketing and sales firepower to compete in the United States, the world's most lucrative market for prescription drugs. There, Novartis was a midtier player—certainly no match for Merck (MRK) & Co. or Pfizer (PFE) Inc. But Vasella, a physician himself, devoted every penny he could find to marketing and research and took the world by surprise in May 2001 with Glivec, one of the most effective new cancer therapies going. "Novartis is emerging as one of the premier powerhouses in the global pharmaceuticals industry," says Richard R. Stover, senior analyst with brokerage Natexis Bleichroeder Inc. in New York.

3 Glivec's success set the stage for the next phase of the plan: creating a profit machine. On April 15, Novartis reported a 24 percent jump in first-quarter operating earnings, to $1.4 billion, on sales of $5.7 billion. That news was better than expected, thanks partially to Novartis' decision to begin reporting results in dollars rather than in Swiss francs. A currency switch isn't the whole story, though. Despite higher spending on research and development, pharmaceutical margins at the Swiss drugmaker powered ahead, to 30.5 percent from 28.1 percent year on year. The stock has climbed 15 percent since mid-March and continues to outperform the industry (charts).

4 Now for stage three, elevating Novartis to the pantheon of the truly great global pharmaceutical giants. Novartis' No. 6 ranking is good, but more blockbusters such as Glivec would make it better. That's where hugely ambitious projects like the Cambridge research center come in. "Personally, I'd simply like to beat the competition," says Vasella.

5 That means building a portfolio of superior drugs. Making them in your own labs is one way to do that; buying them from rivals is another. Novartis certainly has money to spend. The Swiss company is sitting on $7 billion in net cash, more than any other drugmaker in Europe—more even than the money-spinning GlaxoSmithKline (GSK) PLC. And that figure is set to rise to $10 billion by yearend, estimates Marc Booty, European pharmaceuticals analyst at Commerzbank Securities in London.

6 Vasella has been carefully laying the groundwork for acquisitions. That's one reason he switched the company's financial reporting to dollars. It makes a deal with a U.S. company much easier for American investors to figure out (and signals to Pfizer and Merck that Novartis thinks it's in the same league). Takeover candidates? Schering-Plough (SGP) Corp., for one. Vasella and Schering's newly appointed CEO, Fred Hassan, go way back, plus Schering has the exclusive rights to sell Novartis' Foradil for asthma in the United States. Another possibility is Wyeth, whose pipeline would complement Novartis' own.

7 Big transatlantic deals are notoriously tough due to regulatory hurdles, so Vasella is not waiting around. In March, Novartis paid $225 million in cash for a majority stake in Cambridge (Mass.)–based Idenix Pharmaceuticals Inc. The acquisition gives Novartis access to a promising line of new drugs to treat hepatitis B and C.

8 Certainly, a play for a top American drugmaker would vastly strengthen Novartis' hand in the United States, where all of the European pharmaceuticals get the bulk of their profits, thanks to higher prices for prescription drugs and doctors' willingness to prescribe innovative treatments, regardless of the cost. But Vasella is already working on a deal closer to home

that could, in a stroke, turn Novartis into the second-biggest pharmaceutical company on the planet, behind Pfizer. This is a target Vasella can practically see from his office window: Roche Group, also based in Basel.

9   A union between the crosstown rivals would have repercussions far beyond this picturesque city on the Rhine. The merged company would have sales of more than $45 billion, a nearly 7 percent share of the global market, a powerful cancer franchise, and one of the best biotech research facilities around, thanks to Roche's ownership of U.S. biotech Genentech (DNA) Inc. Novartis already owns 32.7 percent of Roche, just under the one-third stake that would require the company to make a formal bid under Swiss stock exchange rules.

10   There's just one hitch: Roche CEO Franz B. Humer is staunchly opposed to any deal. "We are better off as an independent company, and a megamerger with Novartis or anyone else is not an answer," he says. And for now, at least, Humer has the backing of the descendants of founder Fritz Hoffman-La Roche, who control the majority of the company's voting rights despite owning less than 10 percent of the equity. André Hoffman, the family spokesman, vows Roche will elude takeover.

11   Vasella is equally determined to make it happen. "There has been value destruction [at Roche], and as a shareholder, one can't be happy with that," he says. "Roche's management and board need to do the right thing for all [of] their shareholders." Roche shares have declined 16 percent in the last 12 months. The company posted a $3 billion loss in 2002 due mainly to the poor performance of its investment portfolio.

12   Vasella can afford to bide his time. Novartis' pipeline is full, a rarity in the industry. The company has launched 10 drugs since 2000, three times more than its nearest rival. Another 15 are expected to debut by 2006. Among the current crop are Zelmac, a drug for irritable-bowel syndrome; eczema treatment Elidel; and Zometa, a treatment for bone metastases. What's more, none of Novartis' major moneymakers is set to go off-patent soon. Earnings should rise almost 10 percent this year; they would go higher were it not for Vasella's insistence on ramping up the research budget to $3.5 billion in 2003, equal to 17.5 percent of sales, well above the industry average.

13   Then there's Glivec, the first treatment ever proven to cause certain types of tumors to disappear. While other cancer drugs work indiscriminately, killing off healthy cells along with sick ones, Glivec is part of a new class of drugs that interfere with the proteins that cause tumors to grow. Initially approved for the treatment of chronic myeloid leukemia,

Glivec also is used to treat other rare types of cancer such as gastrointestinal stromal tumors (GIST) and is now being tested in combination with other drugs in fighting prostate cancer. "Novartis shows other drugmakers that these little niches can be extraordinarily valuable scientifically, as well as commercially feasible," says Dr. George D. Demetri, director of the sarcoma center at Harvard Medical School's Dana-Farber Cancer Institute in Boston. Other drugmakers already are developing targeted drugs, such as AstraZenecas (AZN) Iressa for lung cancer, and ImClone (IMCLE) Erbitux, for colorectal cancer.

14   Glivec, introduced in the United States in 2001 under the brand name Gleevec, was worth every penny that Novartis invested. Sales rose more than 300 percent in 2002, and could hit the $1 billion mark by the end of this year, according to Commerzbank's Booty. Although an annual course of Glivec can cost as much as $25,000, demand for the drug took off so quickly that Novartis was forced to run its production line around the clock. One of the first patients to have access to the medicine was Anita Scherzer of Little Falls, N.J. In 1994, the then 52-year-old Scherzer was diagnosed with gastrointestinal stromal tumors. She underwent countless surgeries to remove tumors in her stomach and liver, followed by chemotherapy, but the cancer kept spreading. She enrolled in a small clinical trial for Glivec in August 2000. Just 10 days after taking her first dose of the drug, doctors were astonished to discover that a tumor in Anita's liver had shrunk. Just a month after starting treatment, she was in remission. "I knew I was getting better when I went for a biopsy and the doctor couldn't find the tumor," Scherzer says. Glivec is not a magic bullet, though. Some patients have developed resistance to the drug.

15   Glivec's success stems from Novartis' stress on science. Under the leadership of Joerg Reinhardt, a 20-year company veteran who heads global development, the company has shaved nearly two years off the time it takes to bring a drug from clinic to market. Novartis now needs just over 7 years—18 months less than the industry average.

16   He did it partly by running discovery-and-development projects in parallel instead of sequentially. That means a potential drug being tested for colon cancer might simultaneously be screened for effectiveness against lung cancer or even schizophrenia. Before the mapping of the human genome, scientists made such discoveries by chance. Today, technologies such as functional genomics, in which Novartis invests approximately $150 million a year, have given scientists a bet-

ter understanding of the molecular causes of some diseases. Vasella wants the Cambridge center to be at the forefront of this type of research.

17 Reinhardt's breakthrough is due in part to the constant pressure Vasella puts on employees to beat industry benchmarks. Employees describe him as a demanding boss with exceptionally high standards. When Vasella saw the early clinical results on Glivec, he gave the development team just two years to bring the drug to market. "When I think something needs to be done," says Vasella, "I generally think it needs to be done quickly."

18 Novartis' boss is an unusual mix, an aggressive manager who still keeps something of the gentle bedside manner he developed as a general practitioner. Although Vasella recognizes his first loyalty is to his shareholders, he never loses sight of the patients. It's an attitude that grows out of his own admiration for the doctors who treated him as a child, when he contracted tuberculosis and meningitis. Vasella is also an unbuttoned type who likes roaring around the Swiss countryside on his BMW bike.

19 Vasella's rivals underestimated him at first, especially when he embarked on the merger of Sandoz and Ciba. The companies were old-style conglomerates with roots in the agrichemicals industry, but with very different corporate cultures. Sandoz was autocratic and hierarchical, while at Ciba a collegial and informal atmosphere bred better morale but little accountability among the staff. "It was a difficult marriage to make work," says Natexis' Stover. Vasella's appointment to the top job at the newly merged company in March, 1996, fueled accusations of nepotism (his high-school sweetheart and wife of 25 years, Anne-Laurence, is the niece of Sandoz' former chairman) and grumblings that he was in over his head.

20 Determined to prove critics wrong, the new boss promptly set about cleaning house. After much-touted synergies failed to materialize, he dumped the company's ailing agrochemicals unit to focus on higher-margin pharmaceuticals. He also rapidly boosted R&D spending.

21 But one of Vasella's shrewdest moves was to sharpen marketing in the United States, one of Novartis' big weaknesses. So in 1999 he hired Paulo Costa, a former Johnson & Johnson (JNJ) exec, to head Novartis' stateside pharmaceutical business. Costa doubled the size of the U.S. sales force to 6,200 and this year tripled spending on direct-to-consumer advertising to $120 million. So far, it seems to be working: Launched in March 2002 with massive marketing support, Elidel became the No. 1 branded eczema product in the United States after just four months on the market. "They've changed the market's perception about how well a European company can compete in the United States," says Commerzbank's Booty. Today, U.S. sales account for 43 percent of overall revenues. Credit also goes to Thomas Ebeling, a marketing whiz from PepsiCo (PEP) Inc., who was promoted in July, 2001, to head Novartis global pharmaceutical business. In a quest to create global brands, Ebeling decided to devote more than 50 percent of the Novartis' marketing budget to a handful of drugs, such as hypertension medicine Diovan, Lotrel, Glivec, and Zometa.

22 Vasella increasingly sees the United States as vital to the company's destiny (a merger with Roche, which relies so much on California-based Genentech for its pipeline and profits, would reinforce Novartis' American position). That's why he has been shifting more and more of the company's R&D to the United States, a country which he says has a much better regulatory and scientific environment for drugmakers than Europe. This year alone, spending on R&D is set to rise by 20 percent, to $3.5 billion, to cover the development of new drugs such as Prexige, a treatment for osteoarthritis and acute pain, and Xolair, for severe asthma.

23 Still, there are considerable risks. Vasella concedes that the big boost in R&D spending will put pressure on margins and earnings. But he contends that this is inevitable if Novartis wants to keep innovating. "It's not an option to stand still," he says. His biggest challenge will be revving up sales of new drugs to offset the large increases in investment. It won't be easy. Many of Novartis' newer drugs are in either crowded or immature markets. Prexige, slated for launch in mid-2004, will be the fifth entrant into a large field dominated by Pharmacia's Celebrex. To make a dent, analysts estimate Novartis may have to spend as much as $1 billion in the first three years after launch.

24 Costly stuff. But Vasella has deep pockets. In March, Novartis acquired the rights to Pfizer's incontinence drug Enablex for $255 million, beating out bigger players such as GlaxoSmithKline. The drug, which Pfizer was forced to sell as part of an antitrust agreement before it could take over Pharmacia, is considered a potential billion-dollar blockbuster. One way or another, the doctor is determined to build his powerhouse.

Source: Kerry Capell, "Novartis," *BusinessWeek,* May 26, 2003

Chapter **Seven**

Strategic Analysis and Choice in Single- or Dominant-Product Businesses: Building Sustainable Competitive Advantages

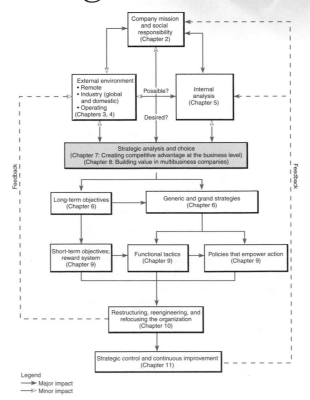

Company mission and social responsibility (Chapter 2)

External environment
• Remote
• Industry (global and domestic)
• Operating (Chapters 3, 4)

Possible?

Internal analysis (Chapter 5)

Desired?

Strategic analysis and choice
(Chapter 7: Creating competitive advantage at the business level)
(Chapter 8: Building value in multibusiness companies)

Long-term objectives (Chapter 6)

Generic and grand strategies (Chapter 6)

Short-term objectives; reward system (Chapter 9)

Functional tactics (Chapter 9)

Policies that empower action (Chapter 9)

Restructuring, reengineering, and refocusing the organization (Chapter 10)

Strategic control and continuous improvement (Chapter 11)

Feedback

Feedback

Legend
→ Major impact
⇢ Minor impact

Strategic analysis and choice is the phase of the strategic management process when business managers examine and choose a business strategy that allows their business to maintain or create a sustainable competitive advantage. Their starting point is to evaluate and determine which value chain activities provide the basis for distinguishing the firm in the customer's mind from other reasonable alternatives. Businesses with a dominant product or service line must also choose among alternate grand strategies to guide the firm's activities, particularly when they are trying to decide about broadening the scope of the firm's activities beyond its core business.

This chapter examines strategic analysis and choice in single- or dominant-product/service businesses by addressing two basic issues:

1. **What strategies are most effective at building sustainable competitive advantages for single business units?** What competitive strategy positions a business most effectively in its industry? For example, Scania, the most productive truck manufacturer in the world, joins its major rival Volvo as two anchors of Sweden's economy. Scania's return on sales of 9.9 percent far exceeds Mercedes (2.6 percent) and Volvo (2.5 percent), a level it has achieved most of the last 60 years. Scania has built a sustainable competitive advantage with a strategy of focusing solely on heavy trucks, in a limited geographic area—Europe—and by providing customized trucks with standardized components (20,000 components per truck versus 25,000 for Volvo and 40,000 for Mercedes). Scania is a low-cost producer of a differentiated truck that can be custom-manufactured quickly and sold to a regionally focused market.

2. **Should dominant-product/service businesses diversify** to build value and competitive advantage? What grand strategies are most appropriate? For example, Compaq Computers and Coca-Cola managers have examined the question of diversification and apparently concluded that continued concentration on their core products and services and development of new markets for those same core products and services are best. IBM and Pepsi examined the same question and concluded that concentric diversification and vertical integration were best. Why?

EVALUATING AND CHOOSING BUSINESS STRATEGIES: SEEKING SUSTAINED COMPETITIVE ADVANTAGE

Business managers evaluate and choose strategies that they think will make their business successful. Businesses become successful because they possess some advantage relative to their competitors. The two most prominent sources of competitive advantage can be found in the business's cost structure and its ability to differentiate the business from competitors. Disney World in Orlando offers theme park patrons several unique, distinct features that differentiate it from other entertainment options. Wal-Mart offers retail customers the lowest prices on popular consumer items because they have created a low-cost structure resulting in a competitive advantage over most competitors.

Businesses that create competitive advantages from one or both of these sources usually experience above-average profitability within their industry. Businesses that lack a cost or differentiation advantage usually experience average or below-average profitability. Two recent studies found that businesses that do not have either form of competitive advantage perform the poorest among their peers while businesses that possess both forms of competitive advantage enjoy the highest levels of profitability within their industry.[1]

[1] R. B. Robinson and J. A. Pearce, "Planned Patterns of Strategic Behavior and Their Relationship to Business Unit Performance," *Strategic Management Journal* 9, no. 1 (1988), pp. 43–60; G. G. Dess and G. T. Lumpkin, "Emerging Issues in Strategy Process Research," in *Handbook of Strategic Management*, Hitt et al., 2002.

The average return on investment for over 2,500 businesses across seven industries looked as follows:

Differentiation Advantage	Cost Advantage	Overall Average ROI across Seven Industries
High	High	35.0%
Low	High	26.0
High	Low	22.0
Low	Low	9.5

Initially, managers were advised to evaluate and choose strategies that emphasized one type of competitive advantage. Often referred to as *generic strategies,* firms were encouraged to become either a differentiation-oriented or low-cost–oriented company. In so doing, it was logical that organizational members would develop a clear understanding of company priorities and, as these studies suggest, likely experience profitability superior to competitors without either a differentiation or low-cost orientation.

The studies mentioned above, and the experience of many other businesses, indicate that the highest profitability levels are found in businesses that possess both types of competitive advantage at the same time. In other words, businesses that have one or more value chain activities that truly differentiate them from key competitors and also have value chain activities that let them operate at a lower cost will consistently outperform their rivals that don't. So the challenge for today's business managers is to evaluate and choose business strategies based on core competencies and value chain activities that sustain both types of competitive advantage simultaneously. Exhibit 7–1, Global Strategy in Action, shows Honda Motor Company attempting to do just this in Europe.

Evaluating Cost Leadership Opportunities

Business success built on cost leadership requires the business to be able to provide its product or service at a cost below what its competitors can achieve. And it must be a sustainable cost advantage. Through the skills and resources identified in Exhibit 7–2, a business must be able to accomplish one or more activities in its value chain activities—procuring materials, processing them into products, marketing the products, and distributing the products or support activities—in a more cost-effective manner than that of its competitors or it must be able to reconfigure its value chain so as to achieve a cost advantage. Exhibit 7–2 provides examples of ways this might be done.

Strategists examining their business's value chain for low-cost leadership advantages evaluate the sustainability of those advantages by *benchmarking* (refer to Chapter 5 for a discussion of this comparison technique) their business against key competitors and by considering the impact of any cost advantage on the five forces in their business's competitive environment. Low-cost activities that are sustainable and that provide one or more of these advantages relative to key industry forces should become the basis for the business's competitive strategy.

Low-Cost Advantages That Reduce the Likelihood of Pricing Pressure from Buyers When key competitors cannot match prices from the low-cost leader, customers pressuring the leader risk establishing a price level that drives alternate sources out of business.

Truly Sustained Low-Cost Advantages May Push Rivals into Other Areas, Lessening Price Competition Intense, continued price competition may be ruinous for all rivals, as seen occasionally in the airline industry.

BusinessWeek Honda is hot. In the United States, the Tokyo company can barely keep up with demand for models like the Acura MDX sport utility vehicle and the Odyssey minivan. North American sales have grown 60 percent in the last decade and its cost leadership is legendary: Honda earned $1,581 on every car sold in North America last year, versus $701 for General Motors.

But the road is not entirely smooth for the Japanese carmaker. Honda Motor Co. has suffered a serious breakdown in Europe. Honda's operations in the Old World reported a loss of nearly a billion dollars in Britain and the Continent for 2002. "A big worry for us is weak sales in Europe," says CEO Takeo Fukui.

So Honda managers have gone into overdrive to repair the European business. Their game plan includes cost leadership initiatives: boosting capacity at two plants in Britain, heeding European calls for cars with diesel engines, and implementing a hard-nosed cost-cutting program that targets parts suppliers . . . and differentiation opportunities: launching an all-new car for the subcompact market.

Honda has a reputation for tackling all of its challenges head-on. But the European problem, even against the background of record results in the United States, underscores Honda's fragility. Although less than 10 percent of Honda's global volume—and far less revenue—comes from Europe, the region has outsized importance to Fukui and his deputies. Why? Because Honda has no safe harbor if its sales in the United States begin to flag, as some analysts expect. The company earns some 90 percent of its profits in America, a far higher percentage than other Japanese carmakers. "Honda is the least globally diverse Japanese automobile manufacturer," says Chris Redl, director of equity research at UBS Warburg's office in Tokyo. "It's a minor problem for now, but with the U.S. market heading down, it could become a major problem." So a closer look at the cost leadership and differentiation approach at Honda Europe, their confident answer, is as follows:

COST LEADERSHIP

Honda's struggles in Europe today are partly the result of a key strategic error it made when it started making cars in Britain 10 years ago. Company officials didn't foresee the huge runup in the value of the British pound against Europe's single currency, the euro, which made its cars more expensive than competing models manufactured on the Continent. Subpar sales cut output in Britain last year to levels near 50 percent of capacity: It's impossible to make money at that production level. "Europe is definitely an Achilles' heel for Honda," says Toru Shimano, an analyst at Okasan Securities Co. in Tokyo.

So Honda is increasing purchases of cheaper parts from suppliers outside Britain and moving swiftly to freshen its lineup. Earlier this year, a remodeled and roomier five-door Civic hatchback with improved fuel efficiency rolled off production lines in Britain. To goose output at its British operations, Honda will start exporting perky three-door Civic sedans built at its newest plant to the United States and Japan this year. It also plans to export its British-made CR-V compact SUV to America to augment the Japan-made CR-Vs now being sold there.

DIFFERENTIATION

All of that will help, but Honda's big issue is the hole in its lineup: subcompacts. While 1-liter-engine cars sell poorly in the United States, Europeans and Japanese can't get enough of them. "Honda does not have a product for Europe yet," says UBS Warburg's Redl. It missed out with its 1-liter Logo. "It didn't stand out from the crowd," Yoshino admits.

So the Logo is history, and Honda's new salvation in Europe is a five-door hatchback called the Fit. At 1.3 liters, its engine outpowers Toyota's competing Vitz-class line of cars. Honda says the sporty Fit also boasts a number of nifty features. The only one it would confirm, however, is that owners will be able to flatten all four seats, including the driver's, at the flick of a switch—a selling point for youths keen to load bikes or sleep in it on long road trips.

Source: "Honda is Ready for a Tune Up," *BusinessWeek,* July 7, 2003; and "Honda's Weak Spot: Europe," *BusinessWeek,* June 11, 2001.

New Entrants Competing on Price Must Face an Entrenched Cost Leader without the Experience to Replicate Every Cost Advantage EasyJet, a British startup with a Southwest Airlines copycat strategy, entered the European airline market with much fanfare and low priced, city-to-city, no-frills flights.

Analysts caution that by the time you read this, British Airways, KLM's no-frills offshoot, Buzz, and Virgin Express will simply match fares on EasyJet's key routes and let high landing fees and flight delays take their toll on the British upstart.

EXHIBIT 7–2
Evaluating a Business's Cost Leadership Opportunities

Source: Based on Michael Porter, On Competition, 1998, Harvard Business School Press.

A. Skills and Resources That Foster Cost Leadership

Sustained capital investment and access to capital.
Process engineering skills.
Intense supervision of labor or core technical operations.
Products or services designed for ease of manufacture or delivery.
Low-cost distribution system.

B. Organizational Requirements to Support and Sustain Cost Leadership Activities

Tight cost control.
Frequent, detailed control reports.
Continuous improvement and benchmarking orientation.
Structured organization and responsibilities.
Incentives based on meeting strict, usually quantitative targets.

C. Examples of Ways Businesses Achieve Competitive Advantage via Cost Leadership

Technology Development	Process innovations that lower production costs.		Product redesign to reduce the number of components.		
Human Resource Management	Safety training for all employees reduces absenteeism, downtime, and accidents.				
General Administration	Reduced levels of management cuts corporate overhead.		Computerized, integrated information system reduces errors and administrative costs.		
Procurement	Favorable long-term contracts; captive suppliers or key customer for supplier.				
	Global, online suppliers provide automatic restocking of orders based on our sales.	Economy of scale in plant reduces equipment costs and depreciation.	Computerized routing lowers transportation expense.	Cooperative advertising with distributors creates local cost advantage in buying media space and time.	Subcontracted service technicians repair product correctly the first time or they bear all costs.
	Inbound logistics	Operations	Outbound logistics	Marketing and Sales	Service

Profit margin

Low-Cost Advantages Should Lessen the Attractiveness of Substitute Products   A serious concern of any business is the threat of a substitute product in which buyers can meet their original need. Low-cost advantages allow the holder to resist this happening because it allows them to remain competitive even against desirable substitutes and it allows them to lessen concerns about price facing an inferior, lower-priced substitute.

Higher Margins Allow Low-Cost Producers to Withstand Supplier Cost Increases and Often Gain Supplier Loyalty over Time   Sudden, particularly uncontrollable increases in the costs suppliers face can be more easily absorbed by low-cost, higher-margin producers. Severe droughts in California quadrupled the price of lettuce—a key restaurant demand. Some chains absorbed the cost; others had to confuse customers with a "lettuce tax." Furthermore, chains that worked well with produce suppliers gained a loyal, cooperative "partner" for possible assistance in a future, competitive situation.

Once managers identify opportunities to create cost advantage–based strategies, they must consider whether key risks inherent in cost leadership are present in a way that may mediate sustained success. The key risks with which they must be concerned are discussed next.

Many Cost-Saving Activities Are Easily Duplicated Computerizing certain order entry functions among hazardous waste companies gave early adopters lower sales costs and better customer service for a brief time. Rivals quickly adapted, adding similar capabilities with similar impacts on their costs.

Exclusive Cost Leadership Can Become a Trap Firms that emphasize lowest price and can offer it via cost advantages where product differentiation is increasingly not considered must truly be convinced of the sustainability of those advantages. Particularly with commodity-type products, the low-cost leader seeking to sustain a margin superior to lesser rivals may encounter increasing customer pressure for lower prices with great damage to both leader and lesser players.

Obsessive Cost Cutting Can Shrink Other Competitive Advantages Involving Key Product Attributes Intense cost scrutiny can build margin, but it can reduce opportunities for or investment in innovation, processes, and products. Similarly, such scrutiny can lead to the use of inferior raw materials, processes, or activities that were previously viewed by customers as a key attribute of the original products. Some mail-order computer companies that sought to maintain or enhance cost advantages found reductions in telephone service personnel and automation of that function backfiring with a drop in demand for their products even though their low prices were maintained.

Cost Differences Often Decline over Time As products age, competitors learn how to match cost advantages. Absolute volumes sold often decline. Market channels and suppliers mature. Buyers become more knowledgeable. All of these factors present opportunities to lessen the value or presence of earlier cost advantages. Said another way, cost advantages that are not sustainable over a period of time are risky.

Once business managers have evaluated the cost structure of their value chain, determined activities that provide competitive cost advantages, and considered their inherent risks, they start choosing the business's strategy. Those managers concerned with differentiation-based strategies, or those seeking optimum performance incorporating both sources of competitive advantage, move to evaluating their business's sources of differentiation.

Evaluating Differentiation Opportunities

Differentiation requires that the business have sustainable advantages that allow it to provide buyers with something uniquely valuable to them. A successful differentiation strategy allows the business to provide a product or service of perceived higher value to buyers at a "differentiation cost" below the "value premium" to the buyers. In other words, the buyer feels the additional cost to buy the product or service is well below what the product or service is worth compared to other available alternatives.

Differentiation usually arises from one or more activities in the value chain that create a unique value important to buyers. Perrier's control of a carbonated water spring in France, Stouffer's frozen food packaging and sauce technology, Apple's highly integrated chip designs in its Mac computers, American Greeting Card's automated inventory system for retailers, and Federal Express's customer service capabilities are all examples of sustainable advantages around which successful differentiation strategies have been built. A business

EXHIBIT 7–3
Evaluating a Business's Differentiation Opportunities

Source: Based on Michael Porter, On Competition, 1998, Harvard Business School Press.

A. Skills and Resources That Foster Differentiation

Strong marketing abilities.
Product engineering.
Creative talent and flair.
Strong capabilities in basic research.
Corporate reputation for quality or technical leadership.
Long tradition in an industry or unique combination of skills drawn from other businesses.
Strong cooperation from channels.
Strong cooperation from suppliers of major components of the product or service.

B. Organizational Requirements to Support and Sustain Differentiation Activities

Strong coordination among functions in R&D, product development, and marketing.
Subjective measurement and incentives instead of quantitative measures.
Amenities to attract highly skilled labor, scientists, and creative people.
Tradition of closeness to key customers.
Some personnel skilled in sales and operations—technical and marketing.

C. Examples of Ways Businesses Achieve Competitive Advantage via Differentiation

Technology Development	Cutting-edge production technology and product features to maintain a "distinct" image and actual product.
Human Resource Management	Programs to ensure technical competence of sales staff and a marketing orientation of service personnel.
General Administration	Comprehensive, personalized database to build knowledge of groups of customers and individual buyers to be used in "customizing" how products are sold, serviced, and replaced.
Procurement	Quality control presence at key supplier facilities; work with suppliers' new product development activities

Inbound logistics	Operations	Outbound logistics	Marketing and Sales	Service
Purchase superior quality, well-known components, raising the quality and image of final products.	Careful inspection of products at each step in production to improve product performance and lower defect rate.	JIT coordination with buyers; use of own or captive transportation service to ensure timeliness.	Expensive, informative advertising and promotion to build brand image.	Allowing service personnel considerable discretion to credit customers for repairs.

Profit margin

can achieve differentiation by performing its existing value activities or reconfiguring in some unique way. And the sustainability of that differentiation will depend on two things—a continuation of its high perceived value to buyers and a lack of imitation by competitors.

Exhibit 7–3 suggests key skills that managers should ensure are present to support an emphasis on differentiation. Examples of value chain activities that provide a differentiation advantage are also provided.

Strategists examining their business's value chain for differentiation advantages evaluate the sustainability of those advantages by *benchmarking* (refer to Chapter 5 for a discussion of this comparison technique) their business against key competitors and by considering the impact of any differentiation advantage on the five forces in their business's competitive environment. Sustainable activities that provide one or more of the following opportunities relative to key industry forces should become the basis for differentiation aspects of the business's competitive strategy:

Rivalry Is Reduced When a Business Successfully Differentiates Itself   BMW's new Z23, made in Greer, South Carolina, does not compete with Saturns made in central Tennessee. A Harvard education does not compete with an education from a local technical school. Both situations involve the same basic needs, transportation or education. However, one rival has clearly differentiated itself from others in the minds of certain buyers. In so doing, they do not have to respond competitively to that competitor.

Buyers Are Less Sensitive to Prices for Effectively Differentiated Products   The Highlands Inn in Carmel, California, and the Ventana Inn along the Big Sur charge a minimum of $600 and $900, respectively, per night for a room with a kitchen, fireplace, hot tub, and view. Other places are available along this beautiful stretch of California's spectacular coastline, but occupancy rates at these two locations remain over 90 percent. Why? You can't get a better view and a more relaxed, spectacular setting to spend a few days on the Pacific Coast. Similarly, buyers of differentiated products tolerate price increases low-cost–oriented buyers would not accept. The former become very loyal to certain brands.

Brand Loyalty Is Hard for New Entrants to Overcome   Many new beers are brought to market in the United States, but Budweiser continues to gain market share. Why? Brand loyalty is hard to overcome! And Anheuser-Busch has been clever to extend its brand loyalty from its core brand into newer niches, like nonalcohol brews, that other potential entrants have pioneered.

Managers examining differentiation-based advantages must take potential risks into account as they commit their business to these advantages. Some of the more common ways risks arise are discussed next.

Imitation Narrows Perceived Differentiation, Rendering Differentiation Meaningless   AMC pioneered the Jeep passenger version of a truck 40 years ago. Ford created the Explorer, or luxury utility vehicle, in 1990. It took luxury car features and put them inside a jeep. Ford's payoff was substantial. The Explorer has become Ford's most popular domestic vehicle. However, virtually every vehicle manufacturer offered a luxury utility in 2003, with customers beginning to be hard pressed to identify clear distinctions between lead models. Ford's Explorer managers were looking for a new business strategy for the next decade that relied on new sources of differentiation and placed greater emphasis on low-cost components in their value chain.

Technological Changes That Nullify Past Investments or Learning   The Swiss controlled over 95 percent of the world's watch market into the 1970s. The bulk of the craftspeople, technology, and infrastructure resided in Switzerland. U.S.-based Texas Instruments decided to experiment with the use of its digital technology in watches. Swiss producers were not interested, but Japan's SEIKO and others were. In 2005, the Swiss will make less than 5 percent of the world's watches.

The Cost Difference between Low-Cost Competitors and the Differentiated Business Becomes Too Great for Differentiation to Hold Brand Loyalty   Buyers may begin to choose to sacrifice some of the features, services, or image possessed by the differentiated business for large cost savings. The rising cost of a college education, particularly at several "premier" institutions, has caused many students to opt for lower-cost destinations that offer very similar courses without image, frills, and professors that seldom teach undergraduate students anyway.

Evaluating Speed as a Competitive Advantage

While most telecommunication companies have used the last decade to leap aboard the information superhighway, GTE continued its impressive turnaround focusing on its core business—providing local telephone services. Long lagging behind the Baby Bells in profitability and efficiency, GTE has emphasized improving its poor customer service throughout the decade. The service was so bad in Santa Monica, California, that officials once tried to remove GTE as the local phone company. Candidly saying "we were the pits," new CEO Chuck Lee largely did away with its old system of taking customer service requests by writing them down and passing them along for resolution. Now, using personal communication services and specially designed software, service reps can solve 70 percent of all problems on the initial call—triple the success rate at the beginning of the last decade. Repair workers meanwhile plan their schedules on laptops, cutting down-time and speeding responses. CEO Lee has spent $1.5 billion on reengineering that slashed 17,000 jobs, replaced people with technology, and prioritized *speed* as the defining feature of GTE's business practices.

Speed, or rapid response to customer requests or market and technological changes, has become a major source of competitive advantage for numerous firms in today's intensely competitive global economy. Speed is certainly a form of differentiation, but it is more than that. Speed involves the *availability of a rapid response* to a customer by providing current products quicker, accelerating new product development or improvement, quickly adjusting production processes, and making decisions quickly. While low cost and differentiation may provide important competitive advantages, managers in tomorrow's successful companies will base their strategies on creating speed-based competitive advantages. Exhibit 7–4 describes and illustrates key skills and organizational requirements that are associated with speed-based competitive advantage. Jack Welch, now retired, the CEO who transformed General Electric from a fading company into one of Wall Street's best performers over the last 20 years, had this to say about speed:

> Speed is really the driving force that everyone is after. Faster products, faster product cycles to market. Better response time to customers. . . . Satisfying customers, getting faster communications, moving with more agility, all these things are easier when one is small. And these are all characteristics one needs in a fast-moving global environment.[2]

Speed-based competitive advantages can be created around several activities:

Customer Responsiveness All consumers have encountered hassles, delays, and frustration dealing with various businesses from time to time. The same holds true when dealing business to business. Quick response with answers, information, and solutions to mistakes can become the basis for competitive advantage . . . one that builds customer loyalty quickly.

Product Development Cycles Japanese car makers have focused intensely on the time it takes to create a new model because several experienced disappointing sales growth in the last decade in Europe and North America competing against new vehicles like Ford's Explorer and Renault's Megane. VW had recently conceived, prototyped, produced, and marketed a totally new 4-wheel-drive car in Europe within 12 months. Honda, Toyota, and Nissan lowered their product development cycle from 24 months to 9 months from con-

---

[2] "Jack Welch: A CEO Who Can't Be Cloned," *BusinessWeek*, September 17, 2001.

EXHIBIT 7–4
Evaluating a Business's Rapid Response (Speed) Opportunities

A. Skills and Resources That Foster Speed

Process engineering skills.
Excellent inbound and outbound logistics.
Technical people in sales and customer service.
High levels of automation.
Corporate reputation for quality or technical leadership.
Flexible manufacturing capabilities.
Strong downstream partners.
Strong cooperation from suppliers of major components of the product or service.

B. Organizational Requirements to Support and Sustain Rapid Response Activities

Strong coordination among functions in R&D, product development, and marketing.
Major emphasis on customer satisfaction in incentive programs.
Strong delegation to operating personnel.
Tradition of closeness to key customers.
Some personnel skilled in sales and operations—technical and marketing.
Empowered customer service personnel.

C. Examples of Ways Businesses Achieve Competitive Advantage via Speed

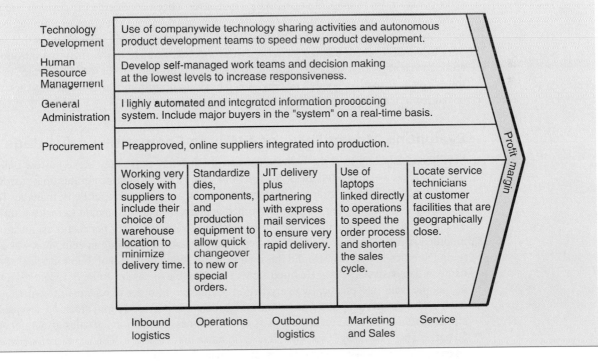

Technology Development	Use of companywide technology sharing activities and autonomous product development teams to speed new product development.			
Human Resource Management	Develop self-managed work teams and decision making at the lowest levels to increase responsiveness.			
General Administration	Highly automated and integrated information processing system. Include major buyers in the "system" on a real-time basis.			
Procurement	Preapproved, online suppliers integrated into production.			
Working very closely with suppliers to include their choice of warehouse location to minimize delivery time.	Standardize dies, components, and production equipment to allow quick changeover to new or special orders.	JIT delivery plus partnering with express mail services to ensure very rapid delivery.	Use of laptops linked directly to operations to speed the order process and shorten the sales cycle.	Locate service technicians at customer facilities that are geographically close.
Inbound logistics	Operations	Outbound logistics	Marketing and Sales	Service

Profit margin

ception to production. This capability is old hat to 3M Corporation, which is so successful at speedy product development that one-fourth of its sales and profits each year are from products that didn't exist five years earlier.

Product or Service Improvements   Like development time, companies that can rapidly adapt their products or services and do so in a way that benefits their customers or creates new customers have a major competitive advantage over rivals that cannot do this.

Speed in Delivery or Distribution   Firms that can get you what you need when you need it, even when that is tomorrow, realize that buyers have come to expect that level of responsiveness. Federal Express's success reflects the importance customers place on speed in inbound and outbound logistics.

Information Sharing and Technology   Speed in sharing information that becomes the basis for decisions, actions, or other important activities taken by a customer, supplier, or partner has become a major source of competitive advantage for many businesses. Telecommunications, the Internet, and networks are but a part of a vast infrastructure that is being used by knowledgeable managers to rebuild or create value in their businesses via information sharing.

These rapid response capabilities create competitive advantages in several ways. They create a way to lessen rivalry because they have *availability* of something that a rival may not have. It can allow the business to charge buyers more, engender loyalty, or otherwise enhance the business's position relative to its buyers. Particularly where impressive customer response is involved, businesses can generate supplier cooperation and concessions since their business ultimately benefits from increased revenue. Finally, substitute products and new entrants find themselves trying to keep up with the rapid changes rather than introducing them. Exhibit 7–5, Strategy in Action, provides examples of how "speed" has become a source of competitive advantage for several well-known companies around the world.

While the notion of speed-based competitive advantage is exciting, it has risks managers must consider. First, speeding up activities that haven't been conducted in a fashion that prioritizes rapid response should only be done after considerable attention to training, reorganization, and/or reengineering. Second, some industries—stable, mature ones that have very minimal levels of change—may not offer much advantage to the firm that introduces some forms of rapid response. Customers in such settings may prefer the slower pace or the lower costs currently available or they may have long time frames in purchasing such that speed is not that important to them.

Evaluating Market Focus as a Way to Competitive Advantage

Small companies, at least the better ones, usually thrive because they serve narrow market niches. This is usually called *focus,* the extent to which a business concentrates on a narrowly defined market. Take the example of Soho Beverages, a business former Pepsi manager Tom Cox bought from Seagram after Seagram had acquired it and was unable to make it thrive. The tiny brand, once a healthy niche product in New York and a few other east coast locations, muddled within Seagrams because its sales force was unused to selling in delis. Cox was able to double sales in one year. He did this on a lean marketing budget that didn't include advertising or database marketing. He hired Korean- and Arabic-speaking college students and had his people walk into practically every deli in Manhattan in order to reacquaint owners with the brand, spot consumption trends, and take orders. He provided rapid stocking services to all Manhattan-area delis, regardless of size. The business has continued sales growth at over 50 percent per year. Why? Cox says "It is attributable to focusing on a niche market, delis; differentiating the product and its sales force; achieving low costs in promotion and delivery; and making rapid, immediate response to any deli owner request its normal practice."

Two things are important in this example. First, this business focused on a narrow niche market in which to build a strong competitive advantage. But focus alone was not enough to build competitive advantage. Rather, Cox created several value chain activities that achieved differentiation, low-cost, and rapid response competitive advantages within this niche market that would be hard for other firms, particularly mass market-oriented firms, to replicate.

Strategy in Action
Examples of SPEED as a Source of Competitive Advantage

Exhibit 7–5

BusinessWeek | SPEED IN DISTRIBUTION AND DELIVERY

Clad in a blue lab coat, a technician in Singapore waves a scanner like a wand over a box of newly minted computer chips. With that simple act, he sets in motion a delivery process that is efficient and automated, almost to the point of magic. This cavernous National Semiconductor Corp. (NSM) warehouse was designed and built by shipping wizards at United Parcel Service Inc. (UPS). It is UPS's computers that speed the box of chips to a loading dock, then to truck, to plane, and to truck once again. In just 12 hours, the chips will reach one of National's customers, a PC maker half a world away in Silicon Valley. Throughout the journey, electronic tags embedded in the chips will let the customer track the order with accuracy down to about three feet. In the two years since UPS and National starting this relationship, the team in brown has slashed National Semiconductor's inventory and shipment costs by 15 percent while reducing the time from factory floor to customer site by 60 percent.

INFORMATION SHARING AND TECHNOLOGY

Meanwhile, in the Old Economy, UPS is winning giant customers such as Ford Motor Co., which uses UPS's computerized logistics to route cars more efficiently to its dealerships. In a year, Ford has reduced delivery times by 26 percent and saved $240 million, says Frank M. Taylor, Ford's vice president for material planning and logistics. "Speed is the mindset at UPS. They'll meet a deadline at any cost," Taylor says. UPS Chairman James P. Kelly chalks it up to the company's slow-and-steady work ethic. "We've spent the past seven years studying where we should be long-term," he says.

While FedEx backpedals in logistics, UPS is in growth mode. And it has figured out how to manage distribution for many companies at one central location—a massive warehouse in Louisville, Ky. Here, UPS handles storage, tracking, repair, and shipping for clients such as Sprint, Hewlett-Packard (HWP), and Nike (NKE) using a mix of high- and low-tech methods. Computerized forklifts scan in new inventory while people in sneakers dash across the vast warehouse to pluck products, box them, and ship them out. In short, UPS uses expensive technology only where it cuts costs.

SPEED IN NEW PRODUCT DEVELOPMENT AND MANAGEMENT DECISION MAKING

Recently retired Volkswagen CEO Ferdinand Piëch has every reason to feel satisfied. The Austrian engineer and scion of one of Europe's most noted automotive dynasties can boast of one of the great turnarounds in automotive history, based on his attention to new product development combined with speed of decision making. Unlike many other auto chiefs, he called the shots on product design and engineering. And if you worked for Dr. Piëch, you had better get it right. In Wolfsburg, executives used to joke that PEP, the acronym for the product development process (Produkt entwicklungsprozess) really stood for Piëch entscheidet personlich—Piëch decides himself. And he did it fast. He is said to have sketched out the Audi's all-wheel-drive system on the back of an envelope.

Obsession with detail and speed are key reasons VW has succeeded so brilliantly reviving its fortunes in the United States, where the VW brand was road kill a decade ago. Last year, VW and Audi sales in the United States jumped 14 percent, to 437,000 units, for a combined 2.5 percent market share. That's up from a microscopic 0.5 percent five years earlier. Although VW trails its Japanese rivals, it's the only European mass-market carmaker in the United States. Volkswagen's four main brands—VW (VLKAY), Audi, Seat, and Skoda—have taken 19 percent of the European auto market, a gain of some three points in eight years, mostly at the expense of General Motors Corp. (GM) and Ford. Not bad for a company that eight years ago suffered from quality problems and a paucity of hit models. In South America, VW vehicles account for one quarter of car sales, and in China, one-half.

SPEED IN CUSTOMER RESPONSIVENESS

Stuart Klaskin's flight on Delta Air Lines was leaving in just 20 minutes. Although he raced through New York's LaGuardia Airport, the behind-schedule aviation consultant suspected he would make it. Why? He bypassed the long check-in lines, stopping instead at one of Delta's 670 self-service kiosks, where all he did was insert his frequent-flier card to get a boarding pass. Not only did Klaskin make his flight but, he says, "I even had time to grab a cup of coffee."

Kiosks are just the start. Delta is using everything from high-definition screens providing real-time info to direct phone access to reservation agents to speed up travel. While its rivals use similar technologies, Delta is the first airline to package it all as a comprehensive, hassle-free system. "We are pioneering significant changes in the way passengers will move through airports," says Richard W. Cordell, Delta's senior vice-president for airport customer service. "In two years, 80 percent of our passengers will check in somewhere other than the old counter."

Source: "Delta's Flight to Self-Service," *BusinessWeek,* July 7, 2003; "UPS: Can It Keep Delivering," *BusinessWeek,* March 24 2003; "VW Needs a Jump," *BusinessWeek,* May 12, 2003.

Focus allows some businesses to compete on the basis of low cost, differentiation, and rapid response against much larger businesses with greater resources. Focus lets a business "learn" its target customers—their needs, special considerations they want accommodated—and establish personal relationships in ways that "differentiate" the smaller firm or make it more valuable to the target customer. Low costs can also be achieved filling niche needs in a buyer's operations that larger rivals either do not want to bother with or cannot do as cost effectively. Cost advantage often centers around the high level of customized service the focused, smaller business can provide. And perhaps the greatest competitive weapon that can arise is rapid response. With enhanced knowledge of its customers and intricacies of their operations, the small, focused company builds up organizational knowledge about timing sensitive ways to work with a customer. Often the needs of that narrow set of customers represent a large part of the small, focused business's revenues. Exhibit 7–6, Global Strategy in Action, illustrates how Ireland's Ryanair has become the European leader in discount air travel via the focused application of low cost, differentiation, and speed.

The risk of focus is that you attract major competitors that have waited for your business to "prove" the market. Domino's proved that a huge market for pizza delivery existed and now faces serious challenges. Likewise, publicly traded focused companies become takeover targets for large firms seeking to fill out a product portfolio. And perhaps the greatest risk of all is slipping into the illusion that it is focus itself, and not some special form of low cost, differentiation, or rapid response, that is creating the business's success.

Managers evaluating opportunities to build competitive advantage should link strategies to value chain activities that exploit low cost, differentiation, and rapid response competitive advantages. When advantageous, they should consider ways to use focus to leverage these advantages. One way business managers can enhance their likelihood of identifying these opportunities is to consider several different "generic" industry environments from the perspective of the typical value chain activities most often linked to sustained competitive advantages in those unique industry situations. The next section discusses five key generic industry environments and the value chain activities most associated with success.

SELECTED INDUSTRY ENVIRONMENTS AND BUSINESS STRATEGY CHOICES

The analysis and choice of the ways a business will seek to build competitive advantage can be enhanced when managers take industry conditions into account. Chapter 3 discussed ways to examine industry conditions, so we do not repeat that here. Likewise, Chapter 5 showed how the market life cycle concept can be used to examine business strengths. What is important to recognize as managers evaluate opportunities to emphasize a narrow set of core competencies and potential competitive advantages is that different sets appear to be more useful in different, unique industry environments. We examine five "typical" industry settings and opportunities for generating competitive advantages that strategists should look for in their deliberations. Three of these five settings relate to industry life cycle. Managers use these as ways to evaluate their value chain activities and then select the ones around which it is most critical to build competitive advantage.[3]

---

[3] These industry characterizations draw heavily on the work of Michael E. Porter, *Competitive Advantage: Creating and Sustaining Superior Performance* (New York: Free Press, 1985).

BusinessWeek It was vintage Michael O'Leary. The 42-year-old CEO of Dublin-based discount airline Ryanair outfitted his staff in full combat gear, drove an old World War II tank to England's Luton airport, an hour north of London, then demanded access to the base of archrival easy Jet Airline Co. With the theme to the old television series *The A-Team* blaring, O'Leary declared he was "liberating the public from easy Jet's high fares." When security—surprise!—refused to let the Ryanair armor roll in, O'Leary led the troops in his own rendition of a platoon march song. "I've been told and it's no lie. easy Jet's fares are way too high!"

Buffoonery? Of course. But O'Leary can get away with it. Ryanair's 31 percent operating margin dwarfs British Airways 3.8 percent, easy Jet's 8.7 percent, and the 8.6 percent of the granddaddy of discount carriers, Dallas-based Southwest Airlines. Ryanair has built up $1 billion in cash. Its $5 billion market capitalization exceeds that of British Air, Lufthansa, and Air France. Ryanair, meanwhile, is expected to post pretax profits of $308 million for the year ended Mar. 31, up 53 percent from 2002 on sales of close to $1 billion. "O'Leary and his management team are absolutely the best at adopting a focus strategy and sticking to it relentlessly," says Ryanair's Chairman David Bonderman.

Ryanair's Focus Strategy has key differentiation, low cost, and speed elements allowing it to far outpace direct and indirect European airline competitors. They are as follows:

DIFFERENTIATION

Ryanair flies to small, secondary airports outside major European cities. Often former military bases are attractive access points to European tourists, which the airports and small towns encourage. Virtually all of its rivals, including discount rival easy Jet, focus on business travelers and major international airports in Europe's largest cities. Its fares average 30 percent less than rival easy Jet, and are far lower than major European airlines. And Ryanair vows to lower its fares 5 percent a year for the foreseeable future, further differentiating itself from others, much like Southwest in the United States. It also offers one of Europe's leading e-tailers, Ryanair.com which sells more than 90 percent of its tickets online, and has hooked up with hotel chains, car rentals, life insurers and mobile phone companies to offer one-stop shopping to the European leisure traveler.

LOW COST

Ryanair ordered 100 new Boeing 737-800s to facilitate the company's rapid European growth plans, less than a year after placing an order for 150 next-generation 737s. Analysts estimate Boeing offered Ryanair 40 percent off list price, significantly lowering Ryanair's cost of capital, maintenance costs, and operating expenses. Ryanair's differentiation choice of flying mainly to small, secondary airports outside major European cities has led to sweetheart deals on everything from landing and handling fees to marketing support. Less congestion lets Ryanair significantly lower personnel costs and the time a plane stays on the ground compared with rivals. Ryanair grows by acquiring small, recent entrants into the discount segment that are losing money at bargain basement prices—like Buzz, the loss-making discount carrier of KLM Royal Dutch Airlines—and then reducing routes, personnel, and bloated costs by 80 percent or more. Ryanair sells snacks and rents the back of seats and overhead storage to advertisers. Its use of less congested airports allows Ryanair to get its planes back in the air in 25 minutes—half the time it takes competitors at major airports.

SPEED

Ryanair's Ryanair.com sells over 90 percent of its tickets quickly and conveniently for customers seeking simplicity, speed, and convenience. Its large purchases from Boeing allow it to grow to additional airports at a rate of about 30 percent annually. Airport turnaround time that is half the industry average allows Ryanair to provide significantly more frequent flights which simplifies and adds time-saving convenience for the leisure traveler and business traveler.

FOCUS

O'Leary continues to focus like a light beam on small outlying airports and leisure travelers with speedy, low-cost services.

O'Leary's currently talking to 40 new European airports and scouting out future options in Eastern Europe. When he's not travelling in Europe, he's back at headquarters at Dublin Airport, where he joins in the company's Thursday football match. He recently acquired a Mercedes taxi and driver, enabling him to speed through Dublin's notorious traffic in the bus and taxi lane. "I've always been a transport innovator," he jokes. Millions of Europeans flying Ryanair planes would agree.

Source: "Ryanair Rising," *BusinessWeek*, June 2, 2003.

Competitive Advantage in Emerging Industries

Emerging industries are newly formed or re-formed industries that typically are created by technological innovation, newly emerging customer needs, or other economic or sociological changes. Emerging industries of the last decade have been the Internet browser, fiber optics, solar heating, cellular telephone, and on-line services industries.

From the standpoint of strategy formulation, the essential characteristic of an emerging industry is that there are no "rules of the game." The absence of rules presents both a risk and an opportunity—a wise strategy positions the firm to favorably shape the emerging industry's rules.

Business strategies must be shaped to accommodate the following characteristics of markets in emerging industries.

Technologies that are mostly proprietary to the pioneering firms and technological uncertainty about how product standardization will unfold.

Competitor uncertainty because of inadequate information about competitors, buyers, and the timing of demand.

High initial costs but steep cost declines as the experience curve takes effect.

Few entry barriers, which often spurs the formation of many new firms.

First-time buyers requiring initial inducement to purchase and customers confused by the availability of a number of nonstandard products.

Inability to obtain raw materials and components until suppliers gear up to meet the industry's needs.

Need for high-risk capital because of the industry's uncertainty prospects.

For success in this industry setting, business strategies require one or more of these features:

1. The ability to *shape the industry's structure* based on the timing of entry, reputation, success in related industries or technologies, and role in industry associations.

2. The ability to *rapidly improve product quality* and performance features.

3. *Advantageous relationships* with key suppliers and promising distribution channels.

4. The ability to *establish the firm's technology as the dominant one* before technological uncertainty decreases.

5. The early acquisition of *a core group of loyal customers* and then the expansion of that customer base through model changes, alternative pricing, and advertising.

6. The ability to *forecast future competitors* and the strategies they are likely to employ.

A firm that has had repeated successes with business in emerging industries is 3M Corporation. In each of the last 20 years, over 25 percent of 3M's annual sales have come from products that did not exist 5 years earlier. Start-up companies enhance their success by having experienced entrepreneurs at the helm, a knowledgeable management team and board of directors, and patient sources of venture capital. Steven Jobs' dramatic unveiling of Apple's iChat technology in 2003 was seen by some as the catalyst for a revolution in long-distance telephone service—perhaps an emerging niche industry. Jobs is certainly an experienced entrepreneur. So read Exhibit 7–7 and see if an emerging industry was born and if Apple's strategy foretells success.

BusinessWeek Read this *BusinessWeek* account of Apple's iChat innovation and see if it spawned a new industry niche along with positioning Apple with a strategy to succeed in that emerging industry niche.

Give Steve Jobs credit. For a man who heads a comparatively small technology company, he sure knows how to alter the tech landscape. The exuberant and often exasperating CEO of Apple Computer gave the music industry its groove back in April when he introduced a powerful one-two punch of iTunes and the online Apple Music Store. With 99-cent downloads, Jobs also handed music lovers what they wanted: high-quality downloads, a fair price, a good selection, and the right to do what they see fit with their music. With 5 million paid downloads in two months and a version for Microsoft Windows users on the way, it's easy to see why music industry execs are dancing in their boardrooms. While the record labels have been a lucky benefactor of Jobsian innovation, the phone companies are about to get whacked by Jobs's quest to give Apple users something else they want. All you need is a Mac running OS X, a decent external microphone, and a connection of 28 kilobits per second or so.

Best of all, iChat lets me bypass the phone company. For the few people on my instant-messaging buddy list who have iChat, I don't pick up the phone anymore to talk to them. I simply look to see if they're available and, if they are, I click on the voice connection button in iChat. A few seconds later, I have the equivalent of a phone line. If everyone on my IM list had the new version of iChat, I would think very seriously about dumping my wireline phone service. Just give me a cordless headset to connect to my Mac, and my IM will supplant the phone almost entirely.

Take this one step further, and it's not so farfetched to imagine that the various IM systems from America Online (AOL), Microsoft (MSFT) and Yahoo! (YHOO), among others, will quickly morph into major competitors against the lumbering telecoms. And it will hasten the day when Internet users can set up their own phone service, or at least something that functions as phone service does today. All they'll need is a dumb pipe connected to the Internet with no costly bells and whistles attached.

Everyone agrees that communications using packets of data typified by the Internet will ultimately replace the circuit-based system used by the legacy phone network. All the big telecom providers are busily switching from networks built largely to handle dedicated circuits for voice calls to vastly more efficient and flexible networks that handle voice traffic in bits and bytes, just like data. But their efforts presuppose a paradigm where they'll continue their role as the middlemen who route all calls.

Already the Baby Bells and long-distance companies are seeking to consolidate their hold on that role with fierce lobbying efforts aimed at regulating so-called voice-over-IP communications, like iChart. Upstart companies, such as New Jersey–based Vonage, have the audacity to tap into the phone system the cheap way. Rather than pay stiff interconnection fees to complete long-distance calls or costly tariffs to rent high-capacity local circuits, Vonage and others sell specially equipped phones that can turn any home broadband connection into a phone hook-up. The voice traffic flowing over these users' broadband connections is virtually indistinguishable from data traffic. On the Net, surfing to Amazon.com and phoning Grandma can be one and the same.

Still, all of this presupposes a phone network and a system designed specifically to move voice traffic. Now, though, there's no longer any need for someone to sell voice service. Consumers can piece together their own phone networks over the Internet, thanks to the rising tide of iChat-like technology. Since most Internet traffic still travels over dial up connections, that part of the phone network will still be necessary, and users will continue paying for connections to the Net. But there would be no reason to pay special fees, such as long-distance charges, for antiquated, dedicated voice phone service.

Let's do the numbers. America Online (AOL) alone has 350 million users on its two IM services, AOL Instant Messenger and ICQ. Several technologists have told me that what Apple has done, while technologically sophisticated, wouldn't be hard for other IM services to replicate. In fact, iChat and AOL IM are already compatible. iChat users show up on the buddy lists of AOL IM users and vice versa. Give all those users an iChat-like voice capability, and all of a sudden you have a phone network with more than 350 million users.

These number don't include Yahoo and MSN's IM customers. If at some point those two interconnect with AOL's dominant IM network, the tally would likely eclipse 500 million. And once word gets out that you can have free phone service simply by signing up for IM, I guarantee millions more people will come aboard.

AN INDUSTRY REBIRTH?

The net effect on the telecoms would be nothing short of catastrophic. The rise of IM as a viable mechanism for voice communication would undermine the pricing power of flat-rate voice plans by virtue of being even cheaper than Vonage, which mails out phones that it sells below cost. A desktop microphone suitable for iChat costs $15.

It will also eliminate the need for a middleman to mind the huge chunk of the phone networks used for interconnecting

(continued)

dedicated voice calls and the services associated with those calls. Everyone will be able to connect directly. That would hasten the decrease in the value and utility of legacy phone networks, which rely on massive penetration and use to make money.

Granted, none of this could happen overnight. Big shifts in technology take shape over years, not months. Although Apple is making a big splash, it remains a bit player in the grand scheme, without enough users to shift markets.

Further, traditional phone service carries all sorts of regulatory baggage that makes replacing it with IM tricky. For example, voice-over-IP won't work if someone can't afford to buy a computer. Likewise, the phone goes down if power or the Internet connection goes down. That would be a serious problem because the legacy phone system remains a lifeline, although cell phones are a potential replacement here, too. After all, most users find their cell phones as reliable as local

phone connections because no one buys a cell with a coverage plan that doesn't work in their own home and neighborhood. Further, cell networks have proven more resilient. Witness the aftermath of September 11, when mobile networks held up while Lower Manhattan's wireline circuits remained dark for days.

In the past, Apple has contributed to big technological shifts such as introducing the graphical user interface to consumers and, more recently, creating a viable platform for digital music sales online. If past is prologue, then Jobs's latest innovation could hasten a coming age when anyone who wants to can use their PC to bypass traditional phone services and spawn a new industry in the process . . . like dropping a phone book on the Baby Bells' heads.

Source: "With iChat, Who Needs A Phone?" *BusinessWeek,* July 9, 2003.

Competitive Advantage in the Transition to Industry Maturity

As an industry evolves, its rate of growth eventually declines. This "transition to maturity" is accompanied by several changes in its competitive environment:

Competition for market share becomes more intense as firms in the industry are forced to achieve sales growth at one another's expense.

Firms in the industry sell increasingly to experienced, repeat buyers that are now making choices among known alternatives.

Competition becomes more oriented to cost and service as knowledgeable buyers expect similar price and product features.

Industry capacity "tops out" as sales growth ceases to cover up poorly planned expansions.

New products and new applications are harder to come by.

International competition increases as cost pressures lead to overseas production advantages.

Profitability falls, often permanently, as a result of pressure to lower prices and the increased costs of holding or building market share.

These changes necessitate a fundamental strategic reassessment. Strategy elements of successful firms in maturing industries often include:

1. *Pruning the product line* by dropping unprofitable product models, sizes, and options from the firm's product mix.

2. *Emphasis on process innovation* that permits low-cost product design, manufacturing methods, and distribution synergy.

3. *Emphasis on cost reduction* through exerting pressure on suppliers for lower prices, switching to cheaper components, introducing operational efficiencies, and lowering administrative and sales overhead.

4. *Careful buyer selection* to focus on buyers that are less aggressive, more closely tied to the firm, and able to buy more from the firm.

5. *Horizontal integration* to acquire rival firms whose weaknesses can be used to gain a bargain price and are correctable by the acquiring firms.

6. *International expansion* to markets where attractive growth and limited competition still exist and the opportunity for lower-cost manufacturing can influence both domestic and international costs.

Business strategists in maturing industries must avoid several pitfalls. First, they must make a clear choice among the three generic strategies and avoid a middle-ground approach, which would confuse both knowledgeable buyers and the firm's personnel. Second, they must avoid sacrificing market share too quickly for short-term profit. Finally, they must avoid waiting too long to respond to price reductions, retaining unneeded excess capacity, engaging in sporadic or irrational efforts to boost sales, and placing their hopes on "new" products, rather than aggressively selling existing products.

Competitive Advantage in Mature and Declining Industries

Declining industries are those that make products or services for which demand is growing slower than demand in the economy as a whole or is actually declining. This slow growth or decline in demand is caused by technological substitution (such as the substitution of electronic calculators for slide rules), demographic shifts (such as the increase in the number of older people and the decrease in the number of children), and shifts in needs (such as the decreased need for red meat).

Firms in a declining industry should choose strategies that emphasize one or more of the following themes:

1. *Focus* on segments within the industry that offer a chance for higher growth or a higher return.

2. *Emphasize product innovation and quality improvement,* where this can be done cost effectively, to differentiate the firm from rivals and to spur growth.

3. *Emphasize production and distribution efficiency* by streamlining production, closing marginal productions facilities and costly distribution outlets, and adding effective new facilities and outlets.

4. *Gradually harvest the business*—generate cash by cutting down on maintenance, reducing models, and shrinking channels and make no new investment.

Strategists who incorporate one or more of these themes into the strategy of their business can anticipate relative success, particularly where the industry's decline is slow and smooth and some profitable niches remain. Penn Tennis, the nations' number one maker of tennis balls, watched industrywide sales steadily decline the last decade. In response it started marketing tennis balls as "dog toys" in the rapidly growing pet products industry. It secondly made Penn balls the official ball at major tournaments. Third, it created three different quality levels, then, as sales revived, Penn Sports sold its tennis ball business to Head Sports.

Competitive Advantage in Fragmented Industries

A fragmented industry is one in which no firm has a significant market share and can strongly influence industry outcomes. Fragmented industries are found in many areas of the economy and are common in such areas as professional services, retailing, distribution, wood and metal fabrication, and agricultural products. The funeral industry is an example of a highly fragmented industry. Business strategists in fragmented industries pursue low-cost, differentiation, or focus competitive advantages in one of five ways.

Tightly Managed Decentralization

Fragmented industries are characterized by a need for intense local coordination, a local management orientation, high personal service, and local autonomy. Recently, however, successful firms in such industries have introduced a high degree of professionalism into the operations of local managers.

"Formula" Facilities

This alternative, related to the previous one, introduces standardized, efficient, low-cost facilities at multiple locations. Thus, the firm gradually builds a low-cost advantage over localized competitors. Fast-food and motel chains have applied this approach with considerable success.

Increased Value-Added

The products or services of some fragmented industries are difficult to differentiate. In this case, an effective strategy may be to add value by providing more service with the sale or by engaging in some product assembly that is of additional value to the customer.

Specialization

Focus strategies that creatively segment the market can enable firms to cope with fragmentation. Specialization can be pursued by:

1. *Product type.* The firm builds expertise focusing on a narrow range of products or services.

2. *Customer type.* The firm becomes intimately familiar with and serves the needs of a narrow customer segment.

3. *Type of order.* The firm handles only certain kinds of orders, such as small orders, custom orders, or quick turnaround orders.

4. *Geographic area.* The firm blankets or concentrates on a single area.

Although specialization in one or more of these ways can be the basis for a sound focus strategy in a fragmented industry, each of these types of specialization risks limiting the firm's potential sales volume.

Bare Bones/No Frills

Given the intense competition and low margins in fragmented industries, a "bare bones" posture—low overhead, minimum wage employees, tight cost control—may build a sustainable cost advantage in such industries.

Competitive Advantage in Global Industries

A global industry is one that comprises firms whose competitive positions in major geographic or national markets are fundamentally affected by their overall global competitive positions. To avoid strategic disadvantages, firms in global industries are virtually required to compete on a worldwide basis. Oil, steel, automobiles, apparel, motorcycles, televisions, and computers are examples of global industries.

Global industries have four unique strategy-shaping features:

Differences in prices and costs from country to country due to currency exchange fluctuations, differences in wage and inflation rates, and other economic factors.

Differences in buyer needs across different countries.

Differences in competitors and ways of competing from country to country.

Differences in trade rules and governmental regulations across different countries.

These unique features and the global competition of global industries require that two fundamental components be addressed in the business strategy: (1) the approach used to gain global market coverage and (2) the generic competitive strategy.

Three basic options can be used to pursue global market coverage:

1. *License* foreign firms to produce and distribute the firm's products.

2. *Maintain a domestic production base* and export products to foreign countries.

3. *Establish foreign-based plants and distribution* to compete directly in the markets of one or more foreign countries.

Along with the market coverage decision, strategists must scrutinize the condition of the global industry features identified earlier to choose among four generic global competitive strategies:

1. *Broad-line global competition*—directed at competing worldwide in the full product line of the industry, often with plants in many countries, to achieve differentiation or an overall low-cost position.

2. *Global focus* strategy—targeting a particular segment of the industry for competition on a worldwide basis.

3. *National focus* strategy—taking advantage of differences in national markets that give the firm an edge over global competitors on a nation-by-nation basis.

4. *Protected niche* strategy—seeking out countries in which governmental restraints exclude or inhibit global competitors or allow concessions, or both, that are advantageous to localized firms.

Competing in global industries is an increasing reality for many U.S. firms. Strategists must carefully match their skills and resources with global industry structure and conditions in selecting the most appropriate strategy option.

In conclusion, the analysis and choice of business strategy involves three basic considerations. First, strategists must recognize that their overall choice revolves around three sources of competitive advantage that require total, consistent commitment. Second, strategists must carefully weigh the skills, resources, organizational requirements, and risks associated with each source of competitive advantage. Finally, strategists must consider the unique influence that the generic industry environment most similar to the firm's situation will have on the set of value chain activities they choose to build competitive advantage.

DOMINANT PRODUCT/SERVICE BUSINESSES: EVALUATING AND CHOOSING TO DIVERSIFY TO BUILD VALUE

McDonald's has frequently looked at numerous opportunities to diversify into related businesses or to acquire key suppliers. Its decision has consistently been to focus on its core business using the grand strategies of concentration, market development, and product development. Rival Pepsi, on the other hand, has chosen to diversify into related businesses and vertical integration as the best grand strategies for it to build long-term value. Both firms experienced unprecedented success during the last 20 years.

Many dominant product businesses face this question as their core business proves successful: What grand strategies are best suited to continue to build value? Under what circumstances should they choose an expanded focus (diversification, vertical integration); steady continued focus (concentration, market or product development); or a narrowed focus (turnaround or divestiture)? This section examines two ways you can analyze a dominant product company's situation and choose among the 15 grand strategies identified in Chapter 6.

Grand Strategy Selection Matrix

One valuable guide to the selection of a promising grand strategy is the matrix shown in Exhibit 7–8. The basic idea underlying the matrix is that two variables are of central concern in the selection process: (1) the principal purpose of the grand strategy and (2) the choice of an internal or external emphasis for growth or profitability.

In the past, planners were advised to follow certain rules or prescriptions in their choice of strategies. Now, most experts agree that strategy selection is better guided by the conditions of the planning period and by the company strengths and weaknesses. It should be noted, however, that even the early approaches to strategy selection sought to match a concern over internal versus external growth with a desire to overcome weaknesses or maximize strengths.

EXHIBIT 7–8
Grand Strategy
Selection Matrix

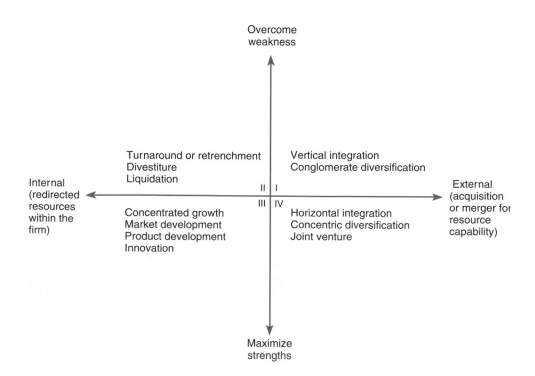

The same considerations led to the development of the grand strategy selection matrix. A firm in quadrant I, with "all its eggs in one basket," often views itself as over-committed to a particular business with limited growth opportunities or high risks. One reasonable solution is *vertical integration,* which enables the firm to reduce risk by reducing uncertainty about inputs or access to customers. Another is *conglomerate diversification,* which provides a profitable investment alternative with diverting management attention from the original business. However, the external approaches to overcoming weaknesses usually result in the most costly grand strategies. Acquiring a second business demands large investments of time and sizable financial resources. Thus, strategic managers considering these approaches must guard against exchanging one set of weaknesses for another.

More conservative approaches to overcoming weaknesses are found in quadrant II. Firms often choose to redirect resources from one internal business activity to another. This approach maintains the firm's commitment to its basic mission, rewards success, and enables further development of proven competitive advantages. The least disruptive of the quadrant II strategies is *retrenchment,* pruning the current activities of a business. If the weaknesses of the business arose from inefficiencies, retrenchment can actually serve as a *turnaround* strategy—that is, the business gains new strength from the streamlining of its operations and the elimination of waste. However, if those weaknesses are a major obstruction to success in the industry and the costs of overcoming them are unaffordable or are not justified by a cost-benefit analysis, then eliminating the business must be considered. *Divestiture* offers the best possibility for recouping the firm's investment, but even *liquidation* can be an attractive option if the alternatives are bankruptcy or an unwarranted drain on the firm's resources.

A common business adage states that a firm should build from strength. The premise of this adage is that growth and survival depend on an ability to capture a market share that is large enough for essential economies of scale. If a firm believes that this approach will be profitable and prefers an internal emphasis for maximizing strengths, four grand strategies hold considerable promise. As shown in quadrant III, the most common approach is *concentrated growth,* that is, market penetration. The firm that selects this strategy is strongly committed to its current products and markets. It strives to solidify its position by reinvesting resources to fortify its strengths.

Two alternative approaches are *market development* and *product development.* With these strategies, the firm attempts to broaden its operations. Market development is chosen if the firm's strategic managers feel that its existing products would be well received by new customer groups. Product development is chosen if they feel that the firm's existing customers would be interested in products related to its current lines. Product development also may be based on technological or other competitive advantages. The final alternative for quadrant III firms is *innovation.* When the firm's strengths are in creative product design or unique production technologies, sales can be stimulated by accelerating perceived obsolescence. This is the principle underlying the innovative grand strategy.

Maximizing a firm's strengths by aggressively expanding its base of operations usually requires an external emphasis. The preferred options in such cases are shown in quadrant IV. *Horizontal integration* is attractive because it makes possible a quick increase in output capability. Moreover, in horizontal integration, the skills of the managers of the original business often are critical in converting newly acquired facilities into profitable contributors to the parent firm; this expands a fundamental competitive advantage of the firm—its management.

Concentric diversification is a good second choice for similar reasons. Because the original and newly acquired businesses are related, the distinctive competencies of the diversifying firm are likely to facilitate a smooth, synergistic, and profitable expansion.

The final alternative for increasing resource capability through external emphasis is a *joint venture* or *strategic alliance.* This alternative allows a firm to extend its strengths into

EXHIBIT 7–9
**Model of Grand
Strategy Clusters**

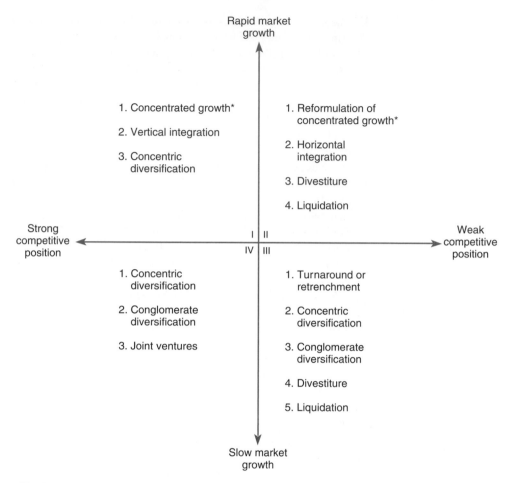

*This is usually via market development, product development, or a combination of both.

competitive arenas that it would be hesitant to enter alone. A partner's production, techno-logical, financial, or marketing capabilities can reduce the firm's financial investment sig-nificantly and increase its probability of success.

Model of Grand Strategy Clusters

A second guide to selecting a promising grand strategy is shown in Exhibit 7–9. The figure is based on the idea that the situation of a business is defined in terms of the growth rate of the general market and the firm's competitive position in that market. When these factors are considered simultaneously, a business can be broadly categorized in one of four quad-rants: (I) strong competitive position in a rapidly growing market, (II) weak position in a rapidly growing market, (III) weak position in a slow-growth market, or (IV) strong posi-tion in a slow-growth market. Each of these quadrants suggests a set of promising possi-bilities for the selection of a grand strategy.

Firms in quadrant I are in an excellent strategic position. One obvious grand strategy for such firms is continued concentration on their current business as it is currently defined. Be-cause consumers seem satisfied with the firm's current strategy, shifting notably from it would endanger the firm's established competitive advantages. McDonald's Corporation has followed this approach for 25 years. However, if the firm has resources that exceed the demands of a concentrated growth strategy, it should consider vertical integration. Either forward or backward integration helps a firm protect its profit margins and market share by ensuring better access to consumers or material inputs. Finally, to diminish the risks associated with a narrow product or service line, a quadrant I firm might be wise to consider concentric diversification; with this strategy, the firm continues to invest heavily in its basic area of proven ability.

Firms in quadrant II must seriously evaluate their present approach to the marketplace. If a firm has competed long enough to accurately assess the merits of its current grand strategy, it must determine (1) why that strategy is ineffectual and (2) whether it is capable of competing effectively. Depending on the answers to these questions, the firm should choose one of four grand strategy options: formulation or reformulation of a concentrated growth strategy, horizontal integration, divestiture, or liquidation.

In a rapidly growing market, even a small or relatively weak business often is able to find a profitable niche. Thus, formulation or reformulation of a concentrated growth strategy is usually the first option that should be considered. However, if the firm lacks either a critical competitive element or sufficient economies of scale to achieve competitive cost efficiencies, then a grand strategy that directs its efforts toward horizontal integration is often a desirable alternative. A final pair of options involve deciding to stop competing in the market or product area of the business. A multiproduct firm may conclude that it is most likely to achieve the goals of its mission if the business is dropped through divestiture. This grand strategy not only eliminates a drain on resources but also may provide funds to promote other business activities. As an option of last resort, a firm may decide to liquidate the business. This means that the business cannot be sold as a going concern and is at best worth only the value of its tangible assets. The decision to liquidate is an undeniable admission of failure by a firm's strategic management and, thus, often is delayed—to the further detriment of the firm.

Strategic managers tend to resist divestiture because it is likely to jeopardize their control of the firm and perhaps even their jobs. Thus, by the time the desirability of divestiture is acknowledged, businesses often deteriorate to the point of failing to attract potential buyers. The consequences of such delays are financially disastrous for firm owners because the value of a going concern is many times greater than the value of its assets.

Strategic managers who have a business in quadrant III and expect a continuation of slow market growth and a relatively weak competitive position will usually attempt to decrease their resource commitment to that business. Minimal withdrawal is accomplished through retrenchment; this strategy has the side benefits of making resources available for other investments and of motivating employees to increase their operating efficiency. An alternative approach is to divert resources for expansion through investment in other businesses. This approach typically involves either concentric or conglomerate diversification because the firm usually wants to enter more promising arenas of competition than integration or concentrated growth strategies would allow. The final options for quadrant III businesses are divestiture, if an optimistic buyer can be found, and liquidation.

Quadrant IV businesses (strong competitive position in a slow-growth market) have a basis of strength from which to diversify into more promising growth areas. These businesses have characteristically high cash flow levels and limited internal growth needs. Thus, they are in an excellent position for concentric diversification into ventures that utilize their proven acumen. A previous example in this chapter described how the number-one tennis ball maker, Penn Racquet Sports, chose concentric diversification from humans to dogs as their best option. A second option is conglomerate diversification, which spreads investment risk and does not divert managerial attention from the present business. The final option is joint ventures, which are especially attractive to multinational firms. Through joint ventures, a domestic business can gain competitive advantages in promising new fields while exposing itself to limited risks.

Opportunities for Building Value as a Basis for Choosing Diversification or Integration

The grand strategy selection matrix and model of grand strategy clusters are useful tools to help dominant product company managers evaluate and narrow their choices among alternative grand strategies. When considering grand strategies that would broaden the scope of their company's business activities through integration, diversification, or joint venture strategies, managers must examine whether opportunities to build value are present. Opportunities to build value via diversification, integration, or joint venture strategies are usually found in market-related, operating-related, and management activities. Such opportunities center around reducing costs, improving margins, or providing access to new revenue sources more cost effectively than traditional internal growth options via concentration, market development, or product development. Major opportunities for sharing and value building as well as ways to capitalize on core competencies are outlined in the next chapter, which covers strategic analysis and choice in diversified companies.

Dominant product company managers who choose diversification or integration eventually create another management challenge. That challenge is charting the future of a company that becomes a collection of several distinct businesses. These distinct businesses often encounter different competitive environments, challenges, and opportunities. The next chapter examines ways managers of such diversified companies attempt to evaluate and choose corporate strategy. Central to their challenge is the continued desire to build value, particularly shareholder value.

Summary

This chapter examined how managers in businesses that have a single or dominant product or service evaluate and choose their company's strategy. Two critical areas deserve their attention: first, their business's value chain; second, the appropriateness of 12 different grand strategies based on matching environmental factors with internal capabilities.

Managers in single-product-line business units examine their business's value chain to identify existing or potential activities around which they can create sustainable competitive advantages. As managers scrutinize their value chain activities, they are looking for three sources of competitive advantage: low cost, differentiation, and rapid response capabilities. They also examine whether focusing on a narrow market niche provides a more effective, sustainable way to build or leverage these three sources of competitive advantage.

Managers in single or dominant product/service businesses face two interrelated issues. First, they must choose which grand strategies make best use of their competitive advantages. Second, they must ultimately decide whether to diversify their business activity. Twelve grand strategies were identified in this chapter along with three frameworks that aid managers in choosing which grand strategies should work best and when diversification or integration should be the best strategy for the business. The next chapter expands the coverage of diversification to look at how multibusiness companies evaluate continued diversification and how they construct corporate strategy.

Questions for Discussion

1. What are three activities or capabilities a firm should possess to support a low-cost leadership strategy? Use Exhibit 7–2 to help you answer this question. Can you give an example of a company that has done this?

2. What are three activities or capabilities a firm should possess to support a differentiation-based strategy? Use Exhibit 7–3 to help you answer this question. Can you give an example of a company that has done this?

3. What are three ways a firm can incorporate the advantage of speed in its business? Use Exhibit 7–4 to help you answer this question. Can you give an example of a company that has done this?

4. Do you think is it better to concentrate on one source of competitive advantage (cost versus differentiation versus speed) or to nurture all three in a firm's operation?

5. How does market focus help a business create competitive advantage? What risks accompany such a posture?

6. Using Exhibits 7–8 and 7–9, describe situations or conditions under which horizontal integration and concentric diversification would be preferred strategic choices.

Chapter 7 Discussion Case

Strategic Analysis and Choice at Korea's Samsung Electronics

The Samsung Way

BusinessWeek

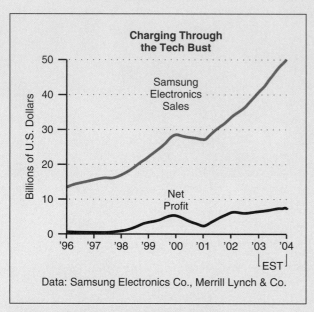

Charging Through the Tech Bust

Samsung Electronics Sales

Net Profit

Billions of U.S. Dollars

'96 '97 '98 '99 '00 '01 '02 '03 '04
⌊EST⌋

Data: Samsung Electronics Co., Merrill Lynch & Co.

It thrives in low-margin consumer electronics. It favors hardware over software. It's still a conglomerate that makes everything itself. Can Samsung keep defying conventional wisdom?

1   A black-suited Agent Smith sprints down a city street. As he is felled by an acrobatic kung fu kick from Trinity, the camera pulls back to show the action taking place inside a giant, floating Samsung TV. The screen rotates, revealing that the set is just three inches thick. "You cannot escape the Samsung 40-inch LCD flat-panel TV," intones the baritone voice of actor Laurence Fishburne. "Welcome to the new dimension."

2   The ad, which appeared in many U.S. theaters showing *The Matrix: Reloaded,* had an element of truth: Whether you're a consumer in America, Europe, or Asia, it's getting pretty darn hard to escape anything made by Samsung Electronics Co. Take the United States alone. Stroll the aisles of Best Buy Co. (BBY) electronics stores, and stylish Samsung high-definition TVs, phones, plasma displays, and digital music and video players are everywhere. Log on to the home pages of *USA Today* (GCI) CNN (AOL) and other heavily trafficked sites, and Samsung's ads are first to pop out. You see its blue elliptical logo emblazoned on Olympic scoreboards. And expect more Matrix tie-ins: Samsung is selling a wireless phone just like the one Keanu Reeves uses to transport himself in the movie. Samsung was even more visible in the fall 2003 sequel, *The Matrix: Revolutions.*

STRATEGIC ANALYSIS AT SAMSUNG

3   Samsung's Matrix moment was just one of its latest steps in its reincarnation as one of the world's coolest brands. Its success in a blizzard of digital gadgets and in chips has wowed consumers and scared rivals around the world. The achievement is all the more remarkable considering that just six years earlier, Samsung was financially crippled, its brand associated with cheap, me-too TVs and microwaves.

4   Samsung Electronics' ascent is an unlikely tale. The company was left with huge debt following the 1997 Korean financial crisis, a crash in memory-chip prices, and a $700 million write-off after an ill-advised takeover of AST Technologies, a U.S. maker of PCs. Its subsidiaries paid little heed to profits and focused on breaking production and sales records—even if much of the output ended up unsold in warehouses.

5   A jovial toastmaster at company dinners but a tough-as-nails boss when he wants results, CEO Yun Jong Yong shuttered Samsung's TV factories for two months until old inventory cleared. Yun also decreed Samsung would sell only high-end goods. Many cellular operators resisted. "Carriers didn't buy our story," says telecom exec Park. "They wanted lower prices all the time. At some point, we had to say no to them."

6   A top priority was straightening out the business in the United States, where "we were in a desperate position," recalls Samsung America chief Oh, appointed in early 2001. "We had a lot of gadgets. But they had nowhere to go." Samsung lured Peter

Skaryznski from AT&T (T) to run handset sales, and Peter Weedfald, who worked at ViewSonic Corp. and *Computer World* magazine, to head marketing.

7   Yun brought new blood to Seoul, too. One recruit was Eric B. Kim, 48, who moved to the United States from Korea at age 13 and worked at various tech companies. Kim was named executive vice-president of global marketing in 2000. With his Korean rusty, Kim made his first big presentation to 400 managers in English. Sensing Kim would be resented, Yun declared: "Some of you may want to put Mr. Kim on top of a tree and then shake him down. If anybody tries that, I will kill you!"

8   The first coup in the United States came in 1997 when Sprint PCS Group began selling Samsung handsets. Sprint's service was based on CDMA, and Samsung had an early lead in the standard due to an alliance in Korea with Qualcomm (QCOM) Inc. Samsung's SCH-3500, a silver, clamshell-shaped model priced at $149, was an instant hit. Soon, Samsung was world leader in CDMA phones. Under Weedfald, Samsung also pulled its appliances off the shelves of Wal-Mart and Target and negotiated deals with higher-end chains like Best Buy and Circuit City.

9   Samsung's status in chips and displays, which can make up 90 percent of the cost of most digital devices, gives it an edge in handsets and other products. Besides dominating DRAM chips, Samsung leads in static random access memory and controls 55 percent of the $2 billion market for NAND flash memory, a technology mainly used in removable cards that store large music and color-image files. With portable digital appliances expected to skyrocket, analysts predict NAND flash sales will soar to $7 billion by 2005, overtaking the more established market for NOR flash, which is embedded onto PCs, dominated by Intel and Advanced Micro Devices (AMD).

10   The company's breadth in displays gives it a similar advantage. It leads in thin-film LCDs, which are becoming the favored format for PCs, normal-size TVs, and all mobile devices. Samsung predicts a factory being built in Tangjung, Korea, that will produce LCD sheets as big as a queen-size mattress and will help to halve prices of large-screen LCD TVs by 2005. Samsung also aims to be No. 1 in plasma and projection displays.

11   If Samsung has a major flaw, it may be its lack of software and content. Samsung has no plans to branch out into music, movies, and games, as Sony and Apple have done. Sony figures that subscription-to-content will provide a more lucrative source of revenue. Samsung's execs remain convinced they're better off collaborating with content and software providers. They say this strategy offers customers more choices than Nokia, which uses its own software.

12   Can the good times last? That's a serious question, since Samsung is challenging basic New Economy dogma. In high tech, the assumption is that developing proprietary software and content gives you higher margins and a long lead time over rivals. Yet Samsung defiantly refuses to enter the software business. It's wedded to hardware and betting it can thrive in a period of relentless deflation for the industry. Rather than outsource manufacturing, the company sinks billions into huge new factories. Instead of bearing down on a few "core competencies," Samsung remains diversified and vertically integrated—Samsung chips and displays go into its own digital products. "If we get out of manufacturing," says CEO and Vice Chairman Yun Jong Yong, "we will lose."

13   Yet the industrial history of the past two decades suggests that this model does not work in the long run. The hazard—as many Japanese, U.S., and European companies learned in the 1980s and '90s—is that Samsung must keep investing heavily in R&D and new factories across numerous product lines. Samsung has sunk $19 billion over five years into new chip facilities. Rivals can buy similar technologies from other vendors without tying up capital or making long-term commitments. What's more, the life cycle of much hardware is brutally short and subject to relentless commoditization. The average price of a TV set has dropped 30 percent in five years; a DVD player goes for less than a quarter. The Chinese keep driving prices ever lower, leveraging supercheap wages and engineering talent. Meanwhile, the Japanese are building their own Chinese factories to lower costs. No wonder Samsung exited the low-margin market for TV sets 27 inches and under.

14   Faced with these perils, Samsung needs a constant stream of well-timed hits to stay on top. Even Sony has stumbled in this race: It now depends on PlayStation to support a consumer-electronics business whose glory days seem behind it. Other legendary hardware makers—Apple, Motorola, Ericsson (ERICY)—have learned the perils of the hardware way.

15   Investors got a sharp reminder of the risks Samsung is running when the company announced first-quarter results. In a tough environment, Samsung

racked up the biggest market-share gain of any company in handsets, from 9.3 percent to 10.5 percent. Yet it had to lower prices to get there, and memory-chip prices also hit the bottom line. The result was a drop in first-quarter profits of 41 percent, to $942 million, on sales of $8 billion. Second-quarter profits could drop further, analysts say, hurt by lower sales in Korea's slumping economy—and in China and other Asian countries struck by the 2003 SARS epidemic. Controversy also flared in 2003 when Samsung Electronics agreed to invest a further $93 million in a troubled credit-card affiliate. Many critics believe Samsung should divest the unit but that it is propping it up under orders of its parent, Samsung Group. Concern over corporate governance is the big reason Samsung continues to trade at a discount to its global peers. Even though it's regarded as one of the most transparent emerging-market companies anywhere, Korea's history of corporate scandals means many foreigners will always suspect its numbers.

16   If the earnings continue to soften, plenty of investors around the world will stand to lose. Samsung is the most widely held emerging-market stock, with $41 billion in market capitalization, and foreigners hold more than half its shares. Over the past five years, the shares have risen more than tenfold, to a recent $273. But concerns over recent earnings have driven the shares off their recent high this year.

17   The challenges are huge, but so are Samsung's strengths. It is used to big swings: Nearly half its profits come from memory chips, a notoriously cyclical business. Even in the weak first quarter, Samsung earned more than any U.S. tech company other than Microsoft, IBM, and Cisco. Meanwhile, Sony lost $940 million in this year's first three months and chip rivals Micron, Infineon, and Hynix lost a combined $1.88 billion. In cell phones, Samsung has kept its average selling price at $191, compared with $154 for Nokia (NOK) and $147 for Motorola, according to Technology Business Research. What's more, since 1997 its debt has shrunk from an unsustainable $10.8 billion to $1.4 billion, leaving Samsung in a healthy net cash position. And its net margins have risen from 0.4 percent to 12 percent.

18   Driving this success is CEO Yun, a career company man who took over in the dark days of 1997. Yun and his boss, Samsung Group Chairman Lee Kun Hee, grasped that the electronics industry's shift from analog to digital, making many technologies accessible, would leave industry leadership up for grabs. "In the analog era, it was difficult for a latecomer to catch up," Yun says. But in the digital era, "if you are two months late, you're dead. So speed and intelligence are what matter, and the winners haven't yet been determined."

SAMSUNG'S STRATEGIC CHOICE: FOCUSED DIFFERENTIATION, LOW COST, AND SPEED

DIFFERENTIATION: FOCUS ON HIGH-END CONSUMER ELECTRONIC ITEMS

19   Now the company seems to be entering a new dimension. Its feature-jammed gadgets are racking up design awards, and the company is rapidly muscling its way to the top of consumer-brand awareness surveys. Samsung thinks the moment is fast arriving when it can unseat Sony Corp. as the most valuable electronics brand and the most important shaper of digital trends. "We believe we can be No. 1," says Samsung America Chief Executive Oh Dong Jin. Its rivals are taking the challenge seriously. "I ask for a report on what Samsung is doing every week," says Sony President Kunitake Ando.

20   The next step is to customize as much as possible. Even in memory chips, the ultimate commodity, Samsung commands prices that are 17 percent above the industry average. A key reason is that 60 percent of its memory devices are custom-made for products like Dell servers, Microsoft Xbox game consoles, and even Nokia's cell phones. "Samsung is one of a handful of companies you can count on to bridge the technical and consumer experiences and bring them successfully to market," says Will Poole, Senior Vice President at Microsoft's Windows Client Business, which works with the Koreans.

21   A few measures of Samsung's progress: It has become the biggest maker of digital mobile phones using code division multiple access (CDMA) technology—and while it still lags No. 2 Motorola (MOT) Inc. in handsets sold, it has just passed it in overall global revenues. A year ago, you'd have been hard pressed to find a Samsung high-definition TV in the United States. Now, Samsung is the best-selling brand in TVs priced at $3,000 and above—a mantle long held by Sony and Mitsubishi Corp. In the new market for digital music players, Samsung's three-year-old Yepp is behind only the Rio of Japan's D&M Holdings Inc. and Apple Computer (AAPI) Inc.'s

iPod. Samsung has blown past Micron Technology (MU), Infineon Technologies (IFX), and Hynix Semiconductor in dynamic random-access memory (DRAM) chips—used in all PCs—and is gaining on Intel (INTC) in the market for flash memory, used in digital cameras, music players, and handsets. In 2002, with most of techdom reeling, Samsung earned $5.9 billion on sales of $33.8 billion.

LOWER COSTS

22 Samsung's strategy to win is pretty basic, but it's executing it with ferocious drive over a remarkably broad conglomerate. To streamline, Yun cut 24,000 workers and sold $2 billion in noncore businesses when he took over. Second, Samsung often forces its own units to compete with outsiders to get the best solution. In the liquid-crystal-display business, Samsung buys half of its color filters from Sumitomo Chemical Co. of Japan and sources the other half internally, pitting the two teams against each other. "They really press these departments to compete," says Sumitomo President Hiromasa Yonekura. Third, Samsung makes its own semiconductors, thereby internalizing limited margins plus, perhaps more importantly, customizing their semiconductors in a way that cost-effectively enhances Samsung's end products as well as the products of customers Dell, Microsoft, and Nokia.

SPEED

23 The final ingredient is speed. Samsung says it takes an average of five months to go from new product concept to rollout, compared with 14 months six years ago. After Samsung persuaded T-Mobile, the German–U.S. cell-phone carrier, to market a new camera-phone last April, for example, it quickly assembled 80 designers and engineers from its chip, telecom, display, computing, and manufacturing operations. In four months, they had a prototype for the V205, which has an innovative lens that swivels 270 degrees and transmits photos wirelessly. Then Samsung flew 30 engineers to Seattle to field-test the phone on T-Mobile's servers and networks. By November, the phones were rolling out of the Korean plant. Since then, Samsung has sold 300,000 V205s a month at $350 each. Park Sang Jin, executive vice-president for mobile communications, estimates the turnaround time is half what Japanese rivals would require. "Samsung has managed to get all its best companies globally to pull in the same direction, something Toshiba, Motorola, and Sony have faced

big challenges in doing," says Allen Delattre, director of Accenture Ltd. (ACN) high-tech practice.

24 Samsung can also use South Korea as a test market. Some 70 percent of the country's homes are wired for broadband. Twenty percent of the population buys a new cell phone every seven months. Samsung already sells a phone in Korea that allows users to download and view up to 30 minutes of video and watch live TV for a fixed monthly fee. Samsung is selling 100,000 video-on-demand phones a month in Korea at $583 each. Verizon plans to introduce them in three U.S. cities this fall.

25 Samsung managers who have worked for big competitors say they go through far fewer layers of bureaucracy to win approval for new products, budgets, and marketing plans, speeding up their ability to seize opportunities. In a recent speech, Sony Chairman Nobuyuki Idei noted Samsung's "aggressive restructuring" and said: "To survive as a global player, we too have to change."

26 This year alone, Samsung will launch 95 new products in the United States, including 42 new TVs. Motorola plans to introduce a dozen new cell-phone models, says Technology Business Research Inc. analyst Chris Foster. Samsung will launch 20. Nokia also is a whiz at snapping out new models. But most are based on two or three platforms, or basic designs. The 130 models Samsung will introduce globally this year are based on 78 platforms. Whereas Motorola completely changes its product line every 12 to 18 months, Foster says, Samsung refreshes its lineup every nine months. Samsung has already introduced the first voice-activated phones, handsets with MP3 players, and digital camera phones that send photos over global system for mobile (GSM) communications networks.

27 Samsung has been just as fast in digital TVs. It became the first to market projection TVs using new chips from Texas Instruments Inc. (TXN) that employed digital-light processing (DLP). DLP chips contain 1.3 million micromirrors that flip at high speeds to create a sharper picture. TI had given Japanese companies the technology early in 1999, but they never figured out how to make the sets economically. Samsung entered the scene in late 2001, and already has seven DLP projection sets starting at $3,400 that have become the hottest-selling sets in their price range. "They'll get a product to market a lot faster than their counterparts," says George Danko, Best Buy's senior vice-president for consumer electronics.

28 Samsung hopes all this is just a warm-up for its bid to dominate the digital home. For years, Philips,

Sony, and Apple have been developing home appliances, from handheld computers to intelligent refrigerators, that talk to each other and adapt to consumers' personal needs. Infrastructure bottlenecks and a lack of uniform standards got in the way.

29   Now, many analysts predict that digital appliances will take off within five years. By then, as many as 40 percent of U.S. households should be wired for high-speed Internet access, and digital TVs, home appliances, and networking devices will be much more affordable. Samsung is showing a version of its networked home in Seoul's Tower Palace apartment complex, where 2,400 families can operate appliances from washing machines to air conditioners by tapping on a wireless "Web pad" device, which doubles as a portable flat-screen TV.

30   It's a grandiose dream. But if the digital home becomes reality, Samsung has a chance. "They've got the products, a growing reputation as the innovator, and production lines to back that up," says In-Stat/MDR consumer-electronics analyst Cindy Wolf. With nearly $7 billion in cash, Samsung has plenty to spend on R&D, factories, and marketing.

31   Yun has heard tech gurus, publications, and even Samsung execs warn him to forsake the vertical model. His response: Samsung needs it all. "Everyone can get the same technology now," he says. "But that doesn't mean they can make an advanced product." Stay at the forefront of core technologies and master the manufacturing, Yun believes, and you control your future. Many tech companies have tried that strategy and failed. Samsung is betting billions it can overcome the odds.

Source: Cliff Edwards in Ridgefield Park, NJ, Moon Ihlwan in Seoul, and Pete Engardio in Suwon. "The Samsung Way," *BusinessWeek,* June 16, 2003.

Chapter **Eight**

Strategic Analysis and Choice in the Multibusiness Company: Rationalizing Diversification and Building Shareholder Value

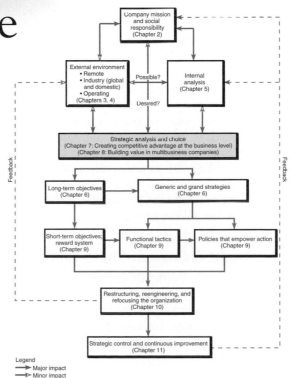

Company mission and social responsibility (Chapter 2)

External environment
• Remote
• Industry (global and domestic)
• Operating (Chapters 3, 4)

Possible?

Internal analysis (Chapter 5)

Desired?

Strategic analysis and choice
(Chapter 7: Creating competitive advantage at the business level)
(Chapter 8: Building value in multibusiness companies)

Long-term objectives (Chapter 6)

Generic and grand strategies (Chapter 6)

Short-term objectives; reward system (Chapter 9)

Functional tactics (Chapter 9)

Policies that empower action (Chapter 9)

Restructuring, reengineering, and refocusing the organization (Chapter 10)

Strategic control and continuous improvement (Chapter 11)

Feedback

Feedback

Legend
→ Major impact
⇢ Minor impact

Strategic analysis and choice is more complicated for corporate-level managers because they must create a strategy to guide a company that contains numerous businesses. They must examine and choose which businesses to own and which ones to forgo or divest. They must consider business managers' plans to capture and exploit competitive advantage in each business, and then decide how to allocate resources among those businesses. This chapter covers ways managers in multibusiness companies analyze and choose what businesses to be in and how to allocate resources across those businesses.

The portfolio approach was one of the early approaches to chart strategy and allocate resources in multibusiness companies. While many companies have moved on to use other approaches, the portfolio approach remains a useful technique for many as well. At the heart of effective diversification is the identification of core competencies in a business or set of businesses to then leverage as the basis for competitive advantage in the growth of those businesses and the entry in or divestiture of other businesses. This notion of leveraging core competencies as a basis for strategic choice in multibusiness companies has been a popular one for the last 20 years.

Recent evolution of strategic analysis and choice in this setting has expanded on the core competency notion to focus on a series of fundamental questions that multibusiness companies should address in order to make diversification work. With both the accelerated rates of change in most global markets and trying economic conditions, multibusiness companies have adapted the fundamental questions into an approach called "patching" to map and remap their business units swiftly against changing market opportunities. Finally, as companies have embraced lean organizational structures, strategic analysis in multibusiness companies has included careful assessment of the corporate parent, its role, and value or lack thereof in contributing to the stand-alone performance of their business units.

THE PORTFOLIO APPROACH

The last 30 years we have seen a virtual explosion in the extent to which businesses seek to acquire other businesses to grow and to diversify. Several rationales gave rise to this trend years ago—to enter businesses with greater growth potential, businesses with different cyclical considerations, to diversify inherent risks, to increase vertical integration, to capture value added, to instantly have a market presence rather than slower internal growth—to name just a few. As corporate strategists jumped on the diversification bandwagon, they soon found a challenge in managing the resource needs of diverse businesses and their respective strategic missions, particularly in times of limited resources. Responding to this challenge, the Boston Consulting Group pioneered an approach called *portfolio techniques* that attempted to help managers "balance" the flow of cash resources among their various businesses while also identifying their basic strategic purpose within the overall portfolio. Three of these techniques are reviewed here. Once reviewed, we will identify some of the problems with the portfolio approach that you should keep in mind when considering its use.

The BCG Growth-Share Matrix

Managers using the BCG matrix plotted each of the company's businesses according to market growth rate and relative competitive position. *Market growth rate* is the projected rate of sales growth for the market being served by a particular business. Usually measured as the percentage increase in a market's sales or unit volume over the two most recent years, this rate serves as an indicator of the relative attractiveness of the markets served by each

EXHIBIT 8–1 **The BCG Growth-Share Matrix**

Source: The growth-share matrix was originally developed by the Boston Consulting Group.

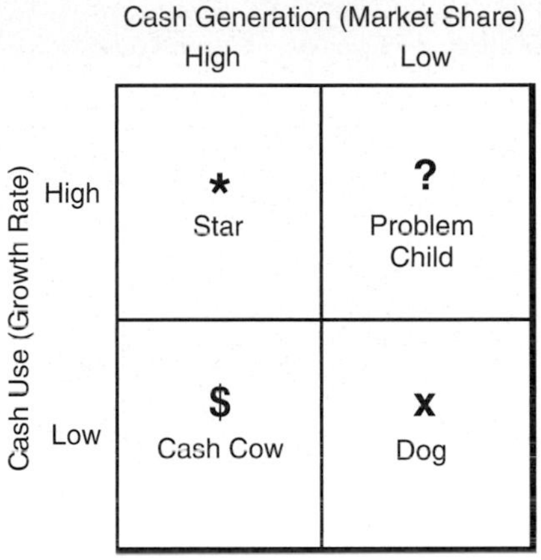

Cash Generation (Market Share)

	High	Low
High	＊ Star	？ Problem Child
Low	$ Cash Cow	X Dog

Cash Use (Growth Rate)

Description of Dimensions

Market Share: Sales relative to those of other competitors in the market (dividing point is usually selected to have only the two–three largest competitors in any market fall into the high market share region)

Growth Rate: Industry growth rate in constant dollars (dividing point is typically the GNP's growth rate)

---

business in the firm's portfolio of businesses. *Relative competitive position* usually is expressed as the market share of a business divided by the market share of its largest competitor. Thus, relative competitive position provides a basis for comparing the relative strengths of the businesses in the firm's portfolio in terms of their positions in their respective markets. Exhibit 8–1 illustrates the growth-share matrix.

The *stars* are businesses in rapidly growing markets with large market shares. These businesses represent the best long-run opportunities (growth and profitability) in the firm's portfolio. They require substantial investment to maintain (and expand) their dominant position in a growing market. This investment requirement is often in excess of the funds that they can generate internally. Therefore, these businesses are often short-term, priority consumers of corporate resources.

Cash cows are businesses with a high market share in low-growth markets or industries. Because of their strong positions and their minimal reinvestment requirements, these businesses often generate cash in excess of their needs. Therefore, they are selectively "milked" as a source of corporate resources for deployment elsewhere (to stars and question marks). Cash cows are yesterday's stars and the current foundation of corporate portfolios. They provide the cash needed to pay corporate overhead and dividends and provide debt capacity. They are managed to maintain their strong market share while generating excess resources for corporatewide use. Strategy in Action Exhibit 8–2 summarizes *BusinessWeek's* 2003 assessment of Hewlett-Packard's "cash cow," its printer business.

Low market share and low market growth businesses are the *dogs* in the firm's portfolio. Facing mature markets with intense competition and low profit margins, they are managed for short-term cash flow (through ruthless cost cutting, for example) to supplement corporate-level resource needs. According to the original BCG prescription, they are divested or liquidated once this short-term harvesting has been maximized.

BusinessWeek	HP's $20 billion printing division contributed 28% of 2002 sales and 105% of operating profits. The company boasts nearly 40% of the worldwide printer market and over half of the lucrative U.S. ink market. But it faces a growing number of challenges.

Challenge	Response	Bottom Line
THE DELL FACTOR Last September, Dell Computer began selling printers, suggesting that one day it will apply its margin-busting business model to this market.	**INNOVATION MATTERS** By spending $1 billion in annual printer R&D (more than Dell's entire R&D budget), HP is betting it can prevent printers from becoming commodities.	**NOT A BIG THREAT** Dell's direct-sales model doesn't fit the printer biz well: Consumers are used to buying ink in stores, and printer components aren't as standardized as PC components.
NEW MARKETS Customers are migrating away from black-and-white printers, where HP is most dominant, to color printers and all-in-one print, copy, fax, and scan units.	**NEW-PRODUCT BLITZ** HP is uncorking 100 new printer products this fall, in a move internally dubbed "Big Bang II," The idea: Offer the most complete range of products in these growth markets.	**NOT TO WORRY** Already a leader in many of these strengthening printer markets, HP should solidify its standing by the end of this year.
INK SPILL The EU's Parliament has passed legislation that could force printer makers to eliminate by 2006 chips embedded in ink cartridges that make them hard to refill and reuse.	**DEFUSE THE ISSUE** Increasingly, HP and its competitors are marketing cartridges for which only the ink needs to be replaced when it runs out–not the entire cartridge.	**A FUTURE THREAT** While not an imminent concern, the EU ruling is a symptom of a growing backlash over the cost and environmental Impact of printer supplies that could one day hurt HP.

Source: "What's Ahead for HP's Cash Cow," *BusinessWeek*, July 19, 2003.

Question marks are businesses whose high growth rate gives them considerable appeal but whose low market share makes their profit potential uncertain. Question marks are cash guzzlers because their rapid growth results in high cash needs, while their small market share results in low cash generation. At the corporate level, the concern is to identify the question marks that would increase their market share and move into the star group if extra corporate resources were devoted to them. Where this long-run shift from question mark to star is unlikely, the BCG matrix suggests divesting the question mark and repositioning its resources more effectively in the remainder of the corporate portfolio.

The Industry Attractiveness–Business Strength Matrix

Corporate strategists found the growth-share matrix's singular axes limiting in their ability to reflect the complexity of a business's situation. Therefore, some companies adopted a matrix with a much broader focus. This matrix, developed by McKinsey & Company at General Electric, is called the Industry Attractiveness–Business Strength Matrix. This matrix uses multiple factors to assess industry attractiveness and business strength rather than the single measures (market share and market growth, respectively) employed in the BCG matrix. It also has nine cells as opposed to four—replacing the high/low axes with high/medium/low axes to make finer distinctions among business portfolio positions.

EXHIBIT 8–3

Factors Considered in Constructing an Industry Attractiveness–Business Strength Matrix

Industry Attractiveness

Nature of Competitive Rivalry
Number of competitors
Size of competitors
Strength of competitors' corporate parents
Price wars
Competition on multiple dimensions

Bargaining Power of Suppliers/Customers
Relative size of typical players
Numbers of each
Importance of purchases from or sales to
Ability to vertically integrate

Threat of Substitute Products/New Entrants
Technological maturity/stability
Diversity of the market
Barriers to entry
Flexibility of distribution system

Economic Factors
Sales volatility
Cyclicality of demand
Market growth
Capital intensity

Financial Norms
Average profitability
Typical leverage
Credit practices

Sociopolitical Considerations
Government regulation
Community support
Ethical standards

Business Strength

Cost Position
Economies of scale
Manufacturing costs
Overhead
Scrap/waste/rework
Experience effects
Labor rates
Proprietary processes

Level of Differentiation
Promotion effectiveness
Product quality
Company image
Patented products
Brand awareness

Response Time
Manufacturing flexibility
Time needed to introduce new products
Delivery times
Organizational flexibility

Financial Strength
Solvency
Liquidity
Break-even point
Cash flows
Profitability
Growth in revenues

Human Assets
Turnover
Skill level
Relative wage/salary
Morale
Managerial commitment
Unionization

Public Approval
Goodwill
Reputation
Image

The company's businesses are rated on multiple strategic factors within each axis, such as the factors described in Exhibit 8–3. The position of a business is then calculated by "subjectively" quantifying its rating along the two dimensions of the matrix. Depending on the location of a business within the matrix as shown in Exhibit 8–4, one of the following strategic approaches is suggested: (1) invest to grow, (2) invest selectively and manage for earnings, or (3) harvest or divest for resources. The resource allocation decisions remain quite similar to those of the BCG approach.

EXHIBIT 8–4

**The Industry
Attractiveness–
Business Strength
Matrix**

Source: McKinsey & Company
and General Electric.

Industry Attractiveness

	High	**Medium**	**Low**
High	Invest	Selective Growth	Grow or Let Go
Medium	Selective Growth	Grow or Let Go	Harvest
Low	Grow or Let Go	Harvest	Divest

(Business Strength)

Description of Dimensions

Industry Attractiveness: Subjective assessment based on broadest possible range of external opportunities and threats beyond the strict control of management

Business Strength: Subjective assessment of how strong a competitive advantage is created by a broad range of the firm's internal strengths and weaknesses

Although the strategic recommendations generated by the Industry Attractiveness–Business Strength Matrix are similar to those generated by the BCG matrix, the Industry Attractiveness–Business Strength Matrix improves on the BCG matrix in three fundamental ways. First, the terminology associated with the Industry Attractiveness–Business Strength Matrix is preferable because it is less offensive and more understandable. Second, the multiple measures associated with each dimension of the business strength matrix tap many factors relevant to business strength and market attractiveness besides market share and market growth. And this, in turn, makes for broader assessment during the planning process, bringing to light considerations of importance in both strategy formulation and strategy implementation.

The Life Cycle–Competitive Strength Matrix

One criticism of the first two portfolio methods was their static quality—their portrayal of businesses as they exist at one point in time, rather than as they evolve over time. A third portfolio approach was introduced that attempted to overcome these deficiencies and better identify "developing winners" or potential "losers."[1] This approach uses the multiple-

[1]Attributed to Arthur D. Little, a consulting firm, and to Charles W. Hofer in "Conceptual Constructs for Formulating Corporate and Business Strategies" (Boston: Harvard Case Services, #9-378-754, 1977).

EXHIBIT 8–5
The Market Life Cycle–Competitive Strength Matrix

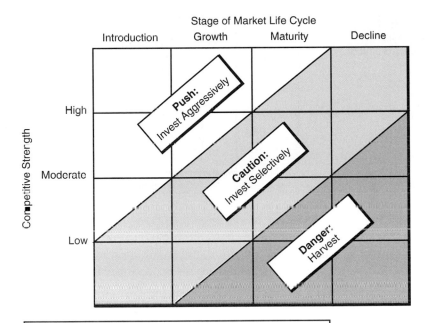

Description of Dimensions

Stage of Market Life Cycle: See Exhibit 5–13 on pages 170–171 for a description of each stage of the market life cycle.

Competitive Strength: Overall subjective rating, based on a wide range of factors regarding the likelihood of gaining and maintaining a competitive advantage

factor approach to assess competitive strength as one dimension and stage of the market life cycle as the other dimension.

The life cycle dimension allows users to consider multiple strategic issues associated with each life cycle stage (refer to the discussion in Chapter 5), thereby enriching the discussion of strategic options. It also gives a "moving indication" of both issues—those strategy needs to address currently and those that could arise next. Exhibit 8–5 provides an illustration of this matrix. It includes basic strategic investment parameters recommended for different positions in the matrix. While this approach seems valuable, its recommendations are virtually identical to the previous two portfolio matrices.

BCG's Strategic Environments Matrix

BCG's latest matrix offering (see Exhibit 8–6) took a different approach using the idea that it was the nature of competitive advantage in an industry that determined the strategies available to a companies businesses, which in turn determined the structure of the industry. Their idea was that such a framework could help ensure that individual business' strategies were consistent with strategies appropriate to their strategic environment. Furthermore, for corporate managers in multiple business companies, this matrix offered one way to rationalize which businesses they are in—businesses that share core competencies and associated competitive advantages because of similar strategic environments.

The matrix has two dimensions. The number of sources of competitive advantage could be many with complex products and services (e.g. automobiles, financial services) and few with commodities (chemicals, microprocessors). Complex products offer

EXHIBIT 8–6
BCG's Strategic
Environments Matrix

Source: R. M. Grant,
Contemporary Strategy
Analysis (Oxford: Blackwell,
2002), p. 327.

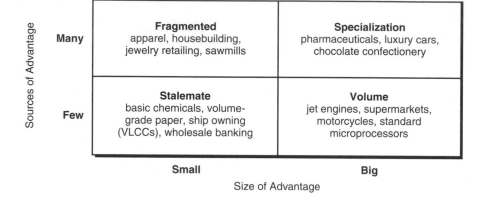

multiple opportunities for differentiation as well as cost, while commodities must seek opportunities for cost advantages to survive.

The second dimension is size of competitive advantage. How big is the advantage available to the industry leader? The two dimensions then define four industry environments as follows:

Volume businesses are those that have few sources of advantage, but the size is large—typically the result of scale economies. Advantages established in one such business may be transferable to another as Honda has done with its scale and expertise with small gasoline engines.

Stalemate businesses have few sources of advantage, with most of those small. This results in very competitive situations. Skills in operational efficiency, low overhead, and cost management are critical to profitability.

Fragmented businesses have many sources of advantage, but they are all small. This typically involves differentiated products with low brand loyalty, easily replicated technology, and minimal scale economies. Skills in focused market segments, typically geographic, the ability to respond quickly to changes, and low costs are critical in this environment.

Specialization businesses have many sources of advantage, and find those advantages potentially sizable. Skills in achieving differentiation—product design, branding expertise, innovation, first-mover, and perhaps scale—characterize winners here.

BCG viewed this matrix as providing guidance to multibusiness managers to determine whether they possessed the sources and size of advantage associated with the type of industry facing each business; and allow them a framework to realistically explore the nature of the strategic environments in which they competed or were interested in entering.

Limitations of Portfolio Approaches

Portfolio approaches made several contributions to strategic analysis by corporate managers convinced of their ability to transfer the competitive advantage of professional management across a broad array of businesses. They helped convey large amounts of information about diverse business units and corporate plans in a greatly simplified format. They illuminated similarities and differences between business units and helped convey the logic behind corporate strategies for each business with a common vocabulary. They simplified priorities for sharing corporate resources across diverse business units that generated and used those resources. They provided a simple prescription that gave corporate managers a sense of what they should accomplish—a balanced portfolio of businesses—and a way to control and allocate resources among them. While these approaches offered meaningful contributions, they had several critical limitations and shortcomings:

- A key problem with the portfolio matrix was that it did not address how value was being created across business units—the only relationship between them was cash. Addressing each business unit as a stand-alone entity ignores common core competencies and internal synergies among operating units.

- Truly accurate measurement for matrix classification was not as easy as the matrices portrayed. Identifying individual businesses, or distinct markets, was not often as precise as underlying assumptions required. Comparing business units on only two fundamental dimensions can lead to the conclusion that these are the only factors that really matter, and that every unit can be compared fairly on those bases.

- The underlying assumption about the relationship between market share and profitability—the experience curve effect—varied across different industries and market segments. Some have no such link. Some find that firms with low market share can generate superior profitability with differentiation advantages.

- The limited strategic options, intended to describe the flow of resources in a company, came to be seen more as basic strategic missions. Doing this creates a false sense of what strategies were when none really existed. This becomes more acute when attempting to use the matrices to conceive strategies for average businesses in average growth markets.

- The portfolio approach portrayed the notion that firms needed to be self-sufficient in capital. This ignored capital raised in capital markets.

- The portfolio approach typically failed to compare the competitive advantage a business received from being owned by a particular company with the costs of owning it. The 1980s saw many companies build enormous corporate infrastructures that created only small gains at the business level. The reengineering and deconstruction of numerous global conglomerates in the last ten years reflects this important omission. We will examine this consideration in greater detail later in this chapter.

Constructing business portfolio matrices must be undertaken with these limitations in mind. Perhaps it is best to say that they provide one form of input to corporate managers seeking to balance financial resources and to provide a basis for further discussion of corporate strategy and the allocation of corporate resources, and to provide a picture of the "balance" of resource generators and users to test underlying assumptions about these issues in more involved corporate planning efforts to leverage core competencies to build sustained competitive advantages. Indeed the next major approach in the evolution of multibusiness strategic analysis was to leverage shared capabilities and core competencies.

THE SYNERGY APPROACH: LEVERAGING CAPABILITIES AND CORE COMPETENCIES

Opportunities to build value via diversification, integration, or joint venture strategies are usually found in market-related, operating-related, and management activities. Each business's basic value chain activities or infrastructure becomes a source of potential synergy and competitive advantage for another business in the corporate portfolio. Morrison's Cafeteria, long a mainstay in U.S. food services markets, rapidly accelerated its diversification into other restaurant concepts like Ruby Tuesdays. Numerous opportunities for shared operating capabilities and management capabilities drove this decision and, upon repeated strategic analysis, accelerated corporate managers' decision to move Morrison's totally out of the cafeteria segment by 2000. Some of the more common opportunities to share value chain activities and build value are identified in Exhibit 8–7.

EXHIBIT 8–7 Value Building in Multibusiness Companies

Source: Based on Michael Porter, On Competition, 1998, Harvard Business School Press.

Opportunities to Build Value or Sharing	Potential Competitive Advantage	Impediments to Achieving Enhanced Value
Market-Related Opportunities:		
Shared sales force activities or shared sales office, or both.	Lower selling costs. Better market coverage. Stronger technical advice to buyers. Enhanced convenience for buyers (can buy from single source). Improved access to buyers (have more products to sell).	• Buyers have different purchasing habits toward the products. • Different salespersons are more effective in representing the product. • Some products get more attention than others. • Buyers prefer to multiple-source rather than single-source their purchases.
Shared after-sale service and repair work.	Lower servicing costs. Better utilization of service personnel (less idle time). Faster servicing of customer calls.	• Different equipment or different labor skills, or both, are needed to handle repairs. • Buyers may do some in-house repairs.
Shared brand name.	Stronger brand image and company reputation. Increased buyer confidence in the brand.	• Company reputation is hurt if quality of one product is lower.
Shared advertising and promotional activities.	Lower costs. Greater clout in purchasing ads.	• Appropriate forms of messages are different. • Appropriate timing of promotions is different.
Common distribution channels.	Lower distribution costs. Enhanced bargaining power with distributors and retailers to gain shelf space, shelf positioning, stronger push and more dealer attention, and better profit margins.	• Dealers resist being dominated by a single supplier and turn to multiple sources and lines. • Heavy use of the shared channel erodes willingness of other channels to carry or push the firm's products.
Shared order processing.	Lower order processing costs. One-stop shopping for buyer enhances service and, thus, differentiation.	• Differences in ordering cycles disrupt order processing economies.
Operating Opportunities:		
Joint procurement of purchased inputs.	Lower input costs. Improved input quality. Improved service from suppliers.	• Input needs are different in terms of quality or other specifications. • Inputs are needed at different plant locations, and centralized purchasing is not responsive to separate needs of each plant.

EXHIBIT 8–7
continued

Opportunities to Build Value or Sharing	Potential Competitive Advantage	Impediments to Achieving Enhanced Value
Operating Opportunities: (continued)		
Shared manufacturing and assembly facilities.	Lower manufacturing/assembly costs. Better capacity utilization, because peak demand for one product correlates with valley demand for other. Bigger scale of operation improves access to better technology and results in better quality.	• Higher changeover costs in shifting from one product to another. • High-cost special tooling or equipment is required to accommodate quality differences or design differences.
Shared inbound or outbound shipping and materials handling.	Lower freight and handling costs. Better delivery reliability. More frequent deliveries, such that inventory costs are reduced.	• Input sources or plant locations, or both, are in different geographic areas. • Needs for frequency and reliability of inbound/outbound delivery differ among the business units.
Shared product and process technologies or technology development or both.	Lower product or process design costs, or both, because of shorter design times and transfers of knowledge from area to area. More innovative ability, owing to scale of effort and attraction of better R&D personnel.	• Technologies are the same, but the applications in different business units are different enough to prevent much sharing of real value.
Shared administrative support activities.	Lower administrative and operating overhead costs.	• Support activities are not a large proportion of cost, and sharing has little cost impact (and virtually no differentiation impact).
Management Opportunities:		
Shared management know-how, operating skills, and proprietary information.	Efficient transfer of a distinctive competence—can create cost savings or enhance differentiation. More effective management as concerns strategy formulation, strategy implementation, and understanding of key success factors.	• Actual transfer of know-how is costly or stretches the key skill personnel too thinly, or both. • Increased risks that proprietary information will leak out.

Strategic analysis is concerned with whether or not the potential competitive advantages expected to arise from each value opportunity have materialized. Where advantage has not materialized, corporate strategists must take care to scrutinize possible impediments to achieving the synergy or competitive advantage. We have identified in Exhibit 8–7 several impediments associated with each opportunity, which strategists are well advised to examine. Good strategists assure themselves that their organization has ways to avoid or minimize the impact of any impediments or they recommend against further integration or diversification and consider divestiture options.

Two elements are critical in meaningful shared opportunities. First, the shared opportunities must be a significant portion of the value chain of the businesses involved. Returning to Morrison's Cafeteria, its purchasing and inbound logistics infrastructure give Ruby Tuesday's operators an immediate cost-effective purchasing and inventory management capability that lowered its cost in a significant cost activity. Second, the businesses involved must truly have shared needs—need for the same activity—or there is no basis for synergy in the first place. Novell, the U.S.-based networking software giant, paid $900 million for Word-Perfect, envisioning numerous synergies serving offices globally not to mention 15 million WordPerfect users. Little more than a year later, Novell would sell WordPerfect for less than $300 million, because, as CEO Bob Frankenberg said, "It is not because WordPerfect is not a business without a future, but for Novell it represented a distraction from our strategy." Corporate strategies have repeatedly rushed into diversification only to find perceived opportunities for sharing were nonexistent because the businesses did not really have shared needs.

Capitalize on Core Competencies

Perhaps the most compelling reason companies should diversify can be found in situations where core competencies—key value-building skills—can be leveraged with other products or into markets that are not a part of where they were created. Where this works well, extraordinary value can be built. Managers undertaking diversification strategies should dedicate a significant portion of their strategic analysis to this question.

General Cinema was a company that grew from drive-in theaters to eventually dominate the multicinema, movie exhibition industry. Next, they entered soft-drink bottling and became the largest bottler of soft drinks (Pepsi) in North America. Their stock value rose 2,000 percent in 10 years. They found that core competencies in movie exhibition—managing many small, localized businesses; dealing with a few large suppliers; applying central marketing skills locally; and acquiring or crafting a "franchise"—were virtually the same in soft-drink bottling. On the other hand, Disney and ABC are still searching for the shared core competencies they thought would be central to their success in today's global entertainment industry (see Strategy in Action Exhibit 8–8). These and many more companies look to three basic considerations to evaluate whether they are capitalizing on core competencies.

Each Core Competency Should Provide a Relevant Competitive Advantage to the Intended Businesses

The core competency must assist the intended business in creating strength relative to key competition. This could occur at any step in the business's value chain. But it must represent a major source of value to be a basis for competitive advantage—and the core competence must be transferrable. Honda of Japan viewed itself as having a core competence in manufacturing small, internal combustion engines. It diversified into small garden tools, perceiving that traditional electric tools would be much more attractive if powered by a lightweight, mobile, gas combustion motor. Their core competency created a major competitive advantage in a market void of gas-driven hand tools. When Coca-Cola added bottled water to its portfolio of products, it expected its extraordinary core competencies in marketing and distribution to rapidly build value in this business. Ten years later, Coke sold its water assets, concluding that the product did not have enough margin to interest its franchised bottlers and that marketing was not a significant value-building activity among many small suppliers competing primarily on the cost of "producing" and shipping water. In the last few years, however, Coke has reversed its decision and added the Dasani water

BusinessWeek Hit movies have boosted earnings. However, from the theme parks to ABC to Pixar, Mouse House problems are stifling. Shared infrastructure, core competencies, and overall synergies expected in the ABC merger remain elusive or nonexistent.

In *Finding Nemo,* 2003's animated blockbuster from Walt Disney, a timid clownfish searching for his son struggles against all odds. Disney can relate. Hammered by falling ratings at its ABC network, a prolonged travel slump that savaged its theme-park business, and an economic slowdown that crimped sales of Mickey and Minnie merchandise, Disney has been looking to sprinkle some magic on its balance sheet. Virtually a decade after its merger with ABC, Disney is still in search of synergies in TV and movie production, advertising, and shared broad media access that diversification was supposed to bring.

Disney's movie studio is hitting on all cylinders, with *Finding Nemo* swimming past $320 million at the box office and the Jerry Bruckheimer–produced action film *Pirates of the Caribbean* closing in on $220 million. But Disney is still hampered by lackluster performance at its giant theme-park unit, which, in better times, contributed about half of operating income. Theme-park earnings were down 22 percent in 2003.

VANISHED VISITORS

Analysts would like to see the return of free-spending international travelers to Walt Disney World in Orlando, which gets nearly one-third of its visitors from overseas, or to the trio of Disneyland Resort hotels in Anaheim, Calif. Instead, attendance at Disney World this summer has been off by 8 percent. And while Disneyland—which relies less heavily on foreign tourists—saw attendance rise by 7 percent, many of those visitors hailed from close by. Such patrons tend to spend less on food and lengthy hotel stays, further cutting into the parks' operating earnings.

When will they come back? Disney executives don't sound terribly optimistic. "A dramatic uptick in visitation is unlikely in the near term," admits President Robert Iger. Indeed, SG Cowen analyst Lowell Singer figures it may take until mid-2004 before European travelers return to the United States in sufficient numbers to help Disney.

In the meantime, the Mouse House is heavily discounting travel packages and ticket prices to generate what business it can from those markets. Travelers can get seven-day Disney World packages for the price of a four-day trip. And in California, a four-day pass to Disneyland and the adjacent Disney California Adventure in Anaheim is going for 50 percent off the daily ticket price.

STUCK IN PARK

Result? The promotional cost has taken its toll. Theme-park earnings will likely decline to $166 million in the fourth quarter, down 29 percent from the $235 million in for the year-ago quarter. While Disney awaits the tourists' return, it's struggling on other fronts. Ratings at ABC stubbornly refuse to rise. So, Disney is slashing program costs by relying less on expensive, one-hour dramas and leaning more toward sitcoms, which bring the added benefit of selling better as reruns. Also, the network has reduced what it pays to buy shows from other studios. ABC was expected to reduce losses to $420 million in 2004, down from the $540 million in 2003. An advertising upturn will help ABC, its wholly owned and network-affiliated TV stations, and Disney's ESPN cable sports channel, all of which are writing contracts with double-digit price hikes. Overall, analysts see earnings at Disney's TV operations rising by 30 percent in 2004.

THE PIXAR WRANGLE

Disney is also overhauling some of its less profitable units. It has hired investment bankers to sell off its 500-outlet Disney Store chain, which loses about $100 million a year. Also, it has trimmed the number of products it licenses, focusing on higher-end wares and reducing its reliance on movie-driven products that don't sell as well.

Another gambit is beefing up products based on Disney Channel TV shows like *Kim Possible* and *Lizzie McGuire.* To improve earnings at its studio operation, CEO Michael Eisner says Disney has cut back on the number of expensive films it produces and is churning out more lower-budget films like the Queen Latifah comedy *Bringing Down the House* and remakes like the recently opened *Freaky Friday.*

Disney is locked in negotiations to extend its contract with Pixar Animation Studios, which made such Disney blockbusters as *Monsters, Inc.,* the *Toy Story* movies, and *Nemo.* Pixar, controlled by Apple Chairman Steve Jobs, wants to reduce Disney's 50 percent stake in films Pixar makes, starting in 2006. The studio wants to finance its own films and give Disney a much lower percentage, perhaps as little as 6 percent to distribute its films.

FRENCH CONNECTION

"During a recent conference call with analysts, Eisner refused to answer questions on the talks, saying that Disney would sign a contract with Pixar only "if there is a deal that makes sense for both Disney and Pixar shareholders." Pixar remains under contract to deliver two more films to Disney, *The Incredibles* next year, and *Cars* in 2005 or 2006, Eisner added.

(continued)

Another hot spot: Disney may have to provide funding to its 39 percent-owned Euro Disney theme park in France. Staggered by a slowdown in European travel, Disney says it has already agreed not to charge royalties and management fees to the separately traded company. On top of that, Disney may be required to take a noncash writedown of its $522 million loan to the park if its management can't restructure debt and violates covenant agreements. Disney CFO Tom Staggs says he's confident Euro Disney can restructure, as its executives have done in the past.

Disney, which long relished its reputation as the Happiest Place on Earth for shareholders, still has plenty of remodeling to do. It could use a lift in worldwide travel, some hits at ABC, and a diplomatic coup that would keep Jobs's Pixar in the family. A turnaround could have more twists and curves than Disneyland's Matterhorn ride—but it sure won't be as fast. So, it seems, Disney's search for multiple synergies in its blockbuster merger with ABC and other entertainment diversification remain where it all started—an intriguing yet elusive strategic assumption.

Source: "Disney's Hunt for a Happy Ending," *BusinessWeek,* August 8, 2003.

brand because a rapidly increasing consumer demand has made the value of its extensive distribution network a relevant competitive advantage to the Dasani water product line.

Businesses in the Portfolio Should be Related in Ways That Make the Company's Core Competencies Beneficial

Related versus unrelated diversification is an important distinction to understand as you evaluate the diversification question. "Related" businesses are those that rely on the same or similar capabilities to be successful and attain competitive advantage in their respective product markets. Earlier, we described General Cinema's spectacular success in both movie exhibition and soft-drink bottling. Seemingly unrelated, they were actually very related businesses in terms of key core competencies that shaped success—managing a network of diverse business locations, localized competition, reliance on a few large suppliers, and centralized marketing advantages. Thus, the products of various businesses do not necessarily have to be similar to leverage core competencies. While their products may not be related, it is essential that some activities in their value chains require similar skills to create competitive advantage if the company is going to leverage its core competence(s) in a value-creating way.

Situations that involve "unrelated" diversification occur when no real overlapping capabilities or products exist other than financial resources. We refer to this as *conglomerate diversification* in Chapter 6. Recent research indicates that the most profitable firms are those that have diversified around a set of resources and capabilities that are specialized enough to confer a meaningful competitive advantage in an attractive industry, yet adaptable enough to be advantageously applied across several others. The least profitable are broadly diversified firms whose strategies are built around very general resources (e.g., money) that are applied in a wide variety of industries, but are seldom instrumental to competitive advantage in those settings.[2]

Any Combination of Competencies Must be Unique or Difficult to Re-create

Skills that corporate strategists expect to transfer from one business to another, or from corporate to various businesses, may be transferrable. They may also be easily replicated by competitors. When this is the case, no sustainable competitive advantage is created. Sometimes

[2]David J. Collis and Cynthia A. Montgomery, *Corporate Strategy* (Chicago: Irwin), 1997, p. 88. "Why Mergers Fail," *McKinsey Quarterly Report,* 2001, vol. 4. "Deals That Create Value," *McKinsey Quarterly Report,* 2001, vol. 1.

WHAT CAN OUR COMPANY DO BETTER THAN ANY OF ITS COMPETITORS IN ITS CURRENT MARKET(S)?

Managers often diversify on the basis of vague definitions of their business rather than on a systematic analysis of what sets their company apart from its competitors. By determining what they can do better than their existing competitors, companies will have a better chance of succeeding in new markets.

WHAT CORE COMPETENCIES DO WE NEED IN ORDER TO SUCCEED IN THE NEW MARKET?

Excelling in one market does not guarantee success in a new and related one. Managers considering diversification must ask whether their company has every core competency necessary to establish a competitive advantage in the territory it hopes to conquer.

CAN WE CATCH UP TO OR LEAPFROG COMPETITORS AT THEIR OWN GAME?

All is not necessarily lost if managers find that they lack a critical core competency. There is always the potential to buy what is missing, develop it in-house, or render it unnecessary by changing the competitive rules of the game.

WILL DIVERSIFICATION BREAK UP CORE COMPETENCIES THAT NEED TO BE KEPT TOGETHER?

Many companies introduce their time-tested core competencies and capabilities in a new market and still fail. That is because they have separated core competencies and capabilities that rely on one another for their effectiveness and hence are not able to function alone.

WILL WE BE SIMPLY A PLAYER IN THE NEW MARKET OR WILL WE EMERGE A WINNER?

Diversifying companies are often quickly outmaneuvered by their new competitors. Why? In many cases, they have failed to consider whether their strategic assets can be easily imitated, purchased on the open market, or replaced.

WHAT CAN OUR COMPANY LEARN BY DIVERSIFYING, AND ARE WE SUFFICIENTLY ORGANIZED TO LEARN IT?

Savvy companies know how to make diversification a learning experience. They see how new businesses can help improve existing ones, act as stepping-stones to industries previously out of reach, or improve organizational efficiency.

Source: Reprinted by permission of Harvard Business Review. Exhibit from "To Diversify or Not to Diversify," by C. C. Markides, Nov.–Dec. 1997. Copyright © 1997 by the Harvard Business School Publishing Corporation, all rights reserved.

strategists look for a combination of competencies, a package of various interrelated skills, as another way to create a situation where seemingly easily replicated competencies become unique, sustainable competitive advantages. 3M Corporation has the enviable record of having 25 percent of its earnings always coming from products introduced within the last five years. 3M has been able to "bundle" the skills necessary to accelerate the introduction of new products so that it consistently extracts early life cycle value from adhesive-related products that hundreds of competitors with similar technical or marketing competencies cannot touch.

All too often companies envision a combination of competencies that make sense conceptually. This vision of synergy develops an energy of its own leading CEOs to relentlessly push the merger of the firms involved. But what makes sense conceptually and is seen as difficult for competitors to re-create often proves difficult if not impossible to create in the first place. Exhibit 8–9, Strategy in Action, summaries six key questions managers should answer in order to identify the strategic risks and opportunities that diversification presents.

STRATEGIC ANALYSIS AND CHOICE IN MULTIBUSINESS COMPANIES: THE CORPORATE PARENT ROLE

Realizing synergies from shared capabilities and core competencies is a key way value is added in multibusiness companies. Research suggests that figuring out if the synergies are real and, if so, how to capture those synergies is most effectively accomplished by business unit managers, not the corporate parent.[3] How then can the corporate parent add value to its businesses in a multibusiness company? We want to acquaint you with two perspectives to use in attempting to answer this question: the parenting framework, and the patching approach.

The Parenting Framework

This perspective sees multibusiness companies as creating value by influencing—or parenting—the businesses they own. The best parent companies create more value than any of their rivals do or would if they owned the same businesses. To add value, a parent must improve its businesses. Obviously there must be room for improvement. Advocates of this perspective call the potential for improvement within a business "a parenting opportunity." They identify ten places to look for parenting opportunities which become the focus of strategic analysis and choice across multiple businesses and their interface with the parent organization.[4] Let's look at each briefly.

Size and Age   Old, large, successful businesses frequently engender entrenched bureaucracies and overhead structures that are hard to dismantle from inside the business. Doing so may add value, and getting it done may be best done by an external catalyst, the parent. Small, young businesses may lack some key functional skills, or outgrow their top managers' capabilities, or lack capital to deal with a temporary downturn or accelerated growth opportunity. Where these are relevant issues within one or more businesses, a parenting opportunity to add value may exist.

Management   Does the business employ managers superior in comparison with its competitors? Is the business' success dependent on attracting and keeping people with specialized skills? Are key managers focused on the right objectives? Ensuring that these issues are addressed, objectively assessed, and assisting in any resolution may be a parenting opportunity that could add value.

Business Definition   Business unit managers may have a myopic or erroneous vision of what their business should be, which, in turn, has them targeting a market that is too narrow or broad. They may employ too much vertical integration, or not enough. Accelerated trends toward outsourcing and strategic alliances are changing the definitions of many businesses. All of this creates a parenting opportunity to help redefine a business unit in a way that creates greater value.

Predictable Errors   The nature of a business and its unique situation can lead managers to make predictable mistakes. Managers responsible for previous strategic decisions are vested in the success of those decisions, which may prevent openness to new alternatives. Older, mature businesses often accumulate a variety of products and markets, which becomes excessive diversification within a particular business. Cyclical markets can lead to underinvestment during downturns and overinvestment during the upswing. Lengthy product life cycles can lead to overreliance on old products. All of these are predictable errors a parent can monitor and attempt to avoid creating, in turn, adding value.

---

[3]Michael Goold, Andrew Campbell, and Marcus Alexander, "The Quest For Parenting Advantage," *Harvard Business Review,* March–April, 1995; Michael Goold, Andrew Campbell, and Marcus Alexander, "How Corporate Parents Add Value to the Stand-Alone Performance of Their Businesses," *Business Strategy Review,* Winter, 1994.
[4]*Ibid,* page 126. These ten areas of opportunity are taken from an insert entitled "Ten places to look for parenting opportunities" on this page of the *Harvard Business Review* article.

Linkages   Business units may be able to improve market position or efficiency by linking with other businesses that are not readily apparent to the management of the business unit in question. Whether apparent or not, linkages among business units within or outside the parent company may be complex or difficult to establish without parent company help. In either case, an opportunity to add value may exist.

Common Capabilities   Fundamental to successful diversification, as we have discussed earlier, is the notion of sharing capabilities and competencies needed by multiple business units. Parenting opportunities to add value may arise from time-to-time through regular scrutiny of opportunities to share capabilities or add shared capabilities that would otherwise go unnoticed by business unit managers closer to daily business operations.

Specialized Expertise   There may be situations where the parent company possesses specialized or rare expertise that may benefit a business unit and add value in the process. Unique legal, technical, or administrative expertise critical in a particular situation or decision point, which is quickly and easily available, can prove very valuable.

External Relations   Does the business have external stakeholders—governments, regulators, unions, suppliers, shareholders—which the parent company could manage more effectively than individual business units? If so, a natural parenting opportunity exists that should add value.

Major Decisions   A business unit may face difficult decisions in areas which it lacks expertise—for example, making an acquisition, entering China, a major capacity expansion, divesting and outsourcing a major part of the business' operations. Obtaining capital externally to fund a major investment may be much more difficult than doing so through the parent company—GE proved this could be a major parenting advantage in the way it developed GE Capital into a major source of capital for its other business units as well as to finance major capital purchases by customers of its own business units.

Major Changes   Sometimes a business needs to make major changes in ways critical to the business' future success yet which involve areas or considerations in which the business unit's management has little or no experience. A complete revamping of a business unit's information management process, outsourcing all that capability to India, or shifting all of a business units' production operations to another business unit in another part of the world—these are just a few examples of major changes in which the parent may have extensive experience with that feels like unknown territory to the business' management team.

Overlap in some of these ten sources of parenting opportunities may exist. For example, specialized expertise in China and a major decision to locate or outsource operations there may be the same source of added value. And that decision would involve a major change. The fact that overlap, or redundancy may exist in classifying sources of parenting opportunity is a minor consideration, however, relative to the value of the parenting framework for strategic analysis in multibusiness companies. The portfolio approaches focus on how businesses' cash, profit, and growth potential create a balance within the portfolio. The core competence approach concentrates on how business units are related and can share technical and operating know-how and capacity. The parenting framework adds to these approaches and the strategic analysis in a multibusiness company because it focuses on competencies of the parent organization and on the value created from the relationship between the parent and its businesses.

The Patching Approach

Another approach that focuses on the role and ability of corporate managers to create value in the management of multibusiness companies is called "patching."[5] *Patching* is the process by which corporate executives routinely remap businesses to match rapidly changing market opportunities. It can take the form of adding, splitting, transferring, exiting, or combining chunks of businesses. Patching is not seen as critical in stable, unchanging markets. When markets are turbulent and rapidly changing, patching is seen as critical to the creation of economic value in a multibusiness company.

Proponents of this perspective on the strategic decision-making function of corporate executives say it is the critical and arguably only way corporate executives can add value beyond the sum of the businesses within the company. They view traditional corporate strategy as creating defensible strategic positions for business units by acquiring or building valuable assets, wisely allocating resources to them, and weaving synergies among them. In volatile markets, they argue, this traditional approach results in business units with strategies that are quickly outdated and competitive advantages rarely sustained beyond a few years.[6] As a result, they say, strategic analysis should center on *strategic processes* more than *strategic positioning*. In these volatile markets, patchers' strategic analysis focuses on making quick, small frequent changes in parts of businesses and organizational processes that enable dynamic strategic repositioning rather than building long-term defensible positions. Exhibit 8–10 compares differences between traditional approaches to shaping corporate strategy with the patching approach.

To be successful with a patching approach to corporate strategic analysis and choice in turbulent markets, Eisenhardt and Sull suggest that managers should flexibly seize opportunities—as long as that flexibility is disciplined. Effective corporate strategists, they argue, focus on key processes and *simple rules*. The following example at Miramax helps illustrate the notion of strategy as simple rules:

> Miramax—well known for artistically innovative movies such as *The Crying Game, Life is Beautiful,* and *Pulp Fiction*—has boundary rules that guide the all-important movie-picking process: first, every movie must revolve around a central human condition, such as love (*The Crying Game*) or envy (*The Talented Mr. Ripley*). Second, a movie's main character must be appealing but deeply flawed—the hero of *Shakespeare in Love* is gifted and charming but steals ideas from friends and betrays his wife. Third, movies must have a very clear story line with a beginning, middle, and end (although in *Pulp Fiction* the end comes first). Finally, there is a firm cap on production costs. Within the rules, there is flexibility to move quickly when a writer or director shows up with a great script. The result is an enormously creative and even surprising flow of movies and enough discipline to produce superior, consistent financial results. *The English Patient,* for example, cost $27 million to make, grossed more than $200 million, and grabbed nine Oscars.[7]

Different types of rules help managers and strategists manage different aspects of seizing opportunities. Exhibit 8–11 explains and illustrates five such types of rules. These rules are called "simple" rules because they need to be brief, axiomatic, and convey fundamental guidelines to decisions or actions. They need to provide just enough structure to allow managers to move quickly to capture opportunities with confidence that the judgments and

[5]Kathleen M. Eisenhardt and Shona L. Brown, "Patching: Restitching Business Portfolios in Dynamic Markets," *Harvard Business Review,* May–June, 1999, pp. 72–82.
[6]*Ibid,* p. 76; K. M. Eisenhardt and D. N. Sull, "Strategy as Simple Rules," *Harvard Business Review,* January, 2001.
[7]*Ibid,* Eisenhardt and Sull, 2001, p. 111.

EXHIBIT 8–10
Three Approaches to Strategy

Managers competing in business can choose among three distinct ways to fight. They can build a fortress and defend it; they can nurture and leverage unique resources; or they can flexibly pursue fleeting opportunities within simple rules. Each approach requires different skill sets and works best under different circumstances.

	Position	Resources	Simple Rules
Strategic logic	Establish position	Leverage resources	Pursue opportunities
Strategic steps	Identify an attractive market Locate a defensible position Fortify and defend	Establish a vision Build resources Leverage across markets	Jump into the confusion Keep moving Seize opportunities Finish strong
Strategic question	Where should we be?	What should we be?	How should we proceed?
Source of advantage	Unique, valuable position with tightly integrated activity system	Unique, valuable, inimitable resources	Key processes and unique simple rules
Works best in	Slowly changing, well structured markets	Moderately changing, well structured markets	Rapidly changing, ambiguous markets
Duration of advantage	Sustained	Sustained	Unpredictable
Risk	It will be too difficult to alter position as conditions change	Company will be too slow to build new resources as conditions change	Managers will be too tentative in executing on promising opportunities
Performance goal	Profitability	Long-term dominance	Growth

commitments they make are consistent with corporate intent. At the same time, while they set parameters on actions and decisions, they are not thick manuals or rules and policies which managers in turbulent environments may find paralyze any efforts to quickly capitalize on opportunities. Strategy in Action Exhibit 8–12 helps explain the simple rules idea behind the patching approach to corporate strategic decision making by explaining what simple rules are not.

The patching approach then relies on simple rules unique to a particular parent company that exist to guide managers in the corporate organization and its business units in making rapid decisions about quickly reshaping parts of the company and allocating time as well as money to capitalize on rapidly shifting market opportunities. The fundamental argument of this approach is that no one can predict how long a competitive advantage will last, particularly in turbulent, rapidly changing markets. While managers in stable markets may be able to rely on complex strategies built on detailed predictions of future trends, managers in complex, fast-moving markets where significant growth and wealth creation may occur face constant unpredictability; hence, strategy must be simple, responsive, and dynamic to encourage success.

EXHIBIT 8–11
Simple Rules, Summarized

In turbulent markets, managers should flexibly seize opportunities—but flexibility must be disciplined. Smart companies focus on key processes and simple rules. Different types of rules help executives manage different aspects of seizing opportunities.

Type	Purpose	Example
How-to rules	They spell out key features of how a process is executed—"What makes our process unique?"	Akamai's rules for the customer service process: staff must consist of technical gurus, every question must be answered on the first call or e-mail, and R&D staff must rotate through customer service.
Boundary rules	They focus managers on which opportunities can be pursued and which are outside the pale.	Cisco's early acquisitions rule: companies to be acquired must have no more than 75 employees, 75 percent of whom are engineers.
Priority rules	They help managers rank the accepted opportunities.	Intel's rule for allocating manufacturing capacity: allocation is based on a product's gross margin.
Timing rules	They synchronize managers with the pace of emerging opportunities and other parts of the company.	Nortel's rules for product development: project teams must know when a product has to be delivered to the leading customer to win, and product development time must be less than 18 months.
Exit rules	They help managers decide when to pull out of yesterday's opportunities.	Oticon's rule for pulling the plug on projects in development: if a key team member—manager or not—chooses to leave the project for another within the company, the project is killed.

Summary

This chapter examined how managers make strategic decisions in multibusiness companies. One of the earliest approaches was to look at the company as a portfolio of businesses. This portfolio was then examined and evaluated based on each business' growth potential, market position, and need for and ability to generate cash. Corporate strategists then allocated resources, divested, and acquired businesses based on the balance across this portfolio of businesses or possible businesses.

The notion of synergy across business units, sharing capabilities, and leveraging core competencies, has been another very widely adopted approach to making strategic decisions in multibusiness companies. Sharing capabilities allows for greater efficiencies, enhanced expertise, and competitive advantage. Core competencies that generate competitive advantage can often be leveraged across multiple businesses, thereby expanding the impact and value added from that competitive advantage.

Globalization, rapid change, outsourcing, and other major forces shaping today's economic landscape have ushered in multibusiness strategic decision making that also focuses on the role and value-added contributions, if any, of the parent company itself. Does the parent company add or could it add value beyond the sum of the businesses it owns? Two perspectives that have gained popularity in multibusiness companies' strategic decision making are the *parenting framework* and the *patching approach*. The parenting framework focuses on ten areas of opportunity managers should carefully explore to find ways the parent organization might add value to one or more businesses and the overall company. The patching approach concentrates on multibusiness companies in turbulent markets of the twenty-first century where managers need to make quick, small shifts and adjustments in processes, markets, and products and offers five types of "simple rules" which managers use as guidelines to structure quick decisions throughout a multibusiness company on a continuous basis.

It is impossible to dictate exactly what a company's simple rules should be. It is possible, however, to say what they should *not* be.

BROAD

Managers often confuse a company's guiding principles with simple rules. The celebrated "HP way," for example, consists of principles like "we focus on a high level of achievement and contribution" and "we encourage flexibility and innovation." The principles are designed to apply to every activity within the company, from purchasing to product innovation. They may create a productive culture, but they provide little concrete guidance for employees trying to evaluate a partner or decide whether to enter a new market. The most effective simple rules, in contrast, are tailored to a single process.

VAGUE

Some rules cover a single process but are too vague to provide real guidance. One Western bank operating in Russia, for example, provided the following guideline for screening investment proposals: all investments must be currently undervalued and have potential for long-term capital appreciation. Imagine the plight of a newly hired associate who turns to that rule for guidance!

A simple screen can help managers test whether their rules are too vague. Ask: could any reasonable person argue the exact opposite of the rule? In the case of the bank in Russia, it is hard to imagine anyone suggesting that the company target overvalued companies with no potential for long-term capital appreciation. If your rules flunk this test, they are not effective.

MINDLESS

Companies whose simple rules have remained implicit may find upon examining them that these rules destroy rather than create value. In one company, managers listed their recent partnership relationships and then tried to figure out what rules could have produced the list. To their chagrin, they found that one rule seemed to be: always form partnerships with small, weak companies that we can control. Another was: always form partnerships with companies that are not as successful as they once were. Again, use a simple test—reverse-engineer your processes to determine your implicit simple rules. Throw out the ones that are embarrassing.

STALE

In high-velocity markets, rules can linger beyond their sell-by dates. Consider Banc One. The Columbus, Ohio-based bank grew to be the seventh-largest bank in the United States by acquiring more than 100 regional banks. Banc One's acquisitions followed a set of simple rules that were based on experience: Banc One must never pay so much that earnings are diluted, it must only buy successful banks with established management teams, it must never acquire a bank with assets greater than one-third of Banc One's, and it must allow acquired banks to run as autonomous affiliates. The rules worked well until others in the banking industry consolidated operations to lower their costs substantially. Then Banc One's loose confederation of banks was burdened with redundant operations, and it got clobbered by efficient competitors.

How do you figure out if your rules are stale? Slowing growth is a good indicator. Stock price is even better. Investors obsess about the future, while your own financials report the past. So if your share price is dropping relative to your competitors' share prices, or if your percentage of the industry's market value is declining, or if growth is slipping, your rules may need to be refreshed.

Questions for Discussion

1. How does strategic analysis at the corporate level differ from strategic analysis at the business unit level? How are they related?

2. When would multi-industry companies find the portfolio approach to strategic analysis and choice useful?

3. What are three types of opportunities for sharing that form a sound basis for diversification or vertical integration? Give an example of each from companies you have read about.

4. Describe three types of opportunities through which a corporate parent could add value beyond the sum of its separate businesses.

5. What does "patching" refer to and describe and illustrate two rules that might guide managers to build value in their businesses.

Chapter 8   Discussion Case

Quanta Group—Is Diversification Wise?

One of the exciting entrepreneurial success stories in the computer industry over the last ten years has been Taiwan's Quanta Computer, recently renamed Quanta Group. Started just 15 years ago by a former calculator salesman, Quanta became the largest maker of notebook computers in the world in 2003. It became number two on *BusinessWeek's* list of the top IT companies worldwide in 2003.

What follows is a short *BusinessWeek* article about Quanta's founder and CEO making the decision to pursue a diversification strategy at Quanta. Since it is occurring just as we write this chapter, we are also including some additional articles about two Asian companies that are focused competitors of Quanta. Once you read these articles, discuss whether CEO Lam appears to be making a sound decision diversifying Quanta. Then conduct current research through www.BusinessWeek.com and other sources to see where Quanta stands on its diversification strategy as you read this discussion case.

ONLINE EXTRA: QUANTA'S NEW LEAP

THE TAIWANESE PRIVATE-LABEL COMPUTER MAKER PLANS TO EXPAND BEYOND NOTEBOOKS AND INTO HIGHER-MARGIN DISPLAYS AND SERVERS

1   If you want to see where Barry Lam is taking his business, consider the new name that he uses for it. Today, he calls his suburban Taipei-based company Quanta Group (2382 TW). It's a slight but significant change from the name he had been using since founding the company back in 1988: Quanta Computer. (The Quanta name in Chinese translates into "vast, wide, extensive.")

2   As its original moniker suggests, Quanta focused zealously on computers, in particular notebook PCs. Like many other Taiwanese computer makers, it was an anonymous producer of notebooks on a contract basis for some of the world's biggest brand-name players.

3   There's no question that former calculator salesman Lam has succeeded as a computer maker. Quanta last year produced 16 percent of the world's note-books, designing and manufacturing machines for the likes of Hewlett-Packard (HPO) and Gateway (GTW).

BIG BACKING

4   This year, Lam is likely to see his company's market share increase to 20 percent, thanks to the addition of several new customers such as NEC (NIPNY) and Acer and increases in orders from old ones like Dell (DELL) and Apple (AAPL). Such results helped catapult Quanta near the top of the world's information-technology mountain, landing at number two in this year's *BusinessWeek* IT 100.

5   Lam isn't content to be the number one producer of outsourced notebook PCs, though. He wants to make the company as synonymous with products like servers and flat-panel displays as it is now with laptops. So Quanta has diversified, with one subsidiary—Quanta Display—making TFT-LCDs (the thin liquid crystal display screens used in notebook PCs and, increasingly, desktops). A joint venture with Sharp and several Taiwanese investors, Quanta Display has already received $1 billion in investment from Quanta and is due to receive another $1 billion in the coming 18 months, Lam says.

6   Another subsidiary—Quanta Storage—will have an initial public offering this year in Taiwan, Lam says. A few other subsidiaries are less capital-intensive. For instance, Quanta Network Systems develops set-top boxes. And Quanta has also developed a venture-capital arm to help fund startups that can provide technology to support these businesses.

7   Why branch out like this? "This strategy will make Quanta grow bigger," says Lam. "It's a big market with much bigger value and a much bigger product range. This is something that makes Quanta valuable to customers."

"SWEET SPOT"

8   Lam figures this diversification can help Quanta escape becoming a victim of its own success. As it wins more outsourcing customers thanks to the need for multinationals to reduce costs, the ability to grow becomes more limited. After all, Taiwanese notebook makers already control 60 percent of the market. It won't be long before there are no new outsourcing orders to win.

9 Moreover, the merger of Hewlett Packard with Compaq means that Taiwanese are feeling even more pressure to lower prices. So Quanta needs to find businesses with fatter margins.

10 "The notebook PC is continuously replacing the desktop, so the market will further expand," says Lam. But when it comes to flat panels, servers, and storage devices, "the margins are much higher," he adds. "More than two times higher." Hence Quanta's move into new products that are "value-added and involve a lot of R&D," he says. "This kind of business is really a sweet spot for Quanta."

11 This strategy isn't unique to Quanta. At the big Computex electronics trade show in Taipei in early June, most of the big Taiwanese players were touting their ability to diversify. Analysts say their chances are good, as Taiwanese manufacturers relying on outsourcing orders have a big advantage as they pursue these new businesses. Unlike North American-based contract manufacturers like Celestica (CLS) or Flextronics (FLEX), which stick largely to manufacturing, many Taiwanese have engineers who do much of the design work for their customers.

BARGAIN TIME?

12 That should help Taiwan's outsourcers as they seek to expand into new types of products, says Sean Debow, Asia tech strategist at UBS Warburg in Hong Kong. Design experience means "they bring more to the table," he says. "That's a big value-added. It's the right place to be in a difficult tech market—being able to cut costs and increase design innovation."

13 Investors focused on the short term, though, might want to be wary about the Taiwanese players such as Quanta. While most of the island's electronics stocks soared in the months after September 11, they have been struggling recently. Quanta's stock closed June 12 at T$90 (that's $2.65), down from a high of T$146 ($4.29) on Jan. 11. That's partially because of growing doubts about when U.S. demand will recover. Indeed, citing worries about weakness in the PC industry, Salomon Smith Barney on June 12 downgraded Quanta shares from a buy to a hold.

14 Taiwan's computer makers are now trading at an average price-earnings ratio of 16 times next year's earnings, at the low end of the long-term range. That's because many investors are downbeat about the chances of American corporate buyers splurging for new computers in the months ahead. On the other hand, that also means the stocks are now relatively cheap. That could be good news for investors who believe in Quanta's diversification strategy.

MEET THE LATEST TECH ALL-STAR FROM TAIWAN

HTC IS GROWING FAST, THANKS TO PDAs AND SMART PHONES

15 For years, big U.S. tech companies such as Dell Computer (DELL), Motorola (MOT), and Hewlett-Packard (HPO) have relied on nimble Taiwanese manufacturers to make PCs, cell phones, and chips for them. This outsourcing has turned the likes of Quanta Computer, Compal Electronics, and Taiwan Semiconductor Manufacturing (TSM) into billion-dollar players in the global electronics industry. Now, it may be time to add a new name to this all-star list: High Tech Computer Corp., based near Taipei. "HTC knocks the leather off the ball," raves Brian Burns, vice-president of Asia Pacific Ventures, a venture-capital and consulting firm in Palo Alto, Calif.

16 Part of HTC's success can be attributed to heavyweight friends. HTC produces the successful iPAQ handheld PC for Hewlett-Packard. Taiwanese chip-design house Via Technologies is the biggest shareholder. HTC's chairwoman is Cher Wang, daughter of one of Taiwan's richest men, petrochemicals billionaire Y. C. Wang. Cellular-technology giant Qualcomm (QCOM) is an investor, and Texas Instruments and Intel help HTC design new products.

17 Oh—and then there's Microsoft Corp. (MSFT). Two years ago, when HTC was showing off its first "smart phone"—a cellular handset that can double as a personal digital assistant—the little-known Taiwanese manufacturer got a boost when Microsoft Chief Executive Steven A. Ballmer demonstrated the gizmo at a big trade show in Orlando. After that high-profile debut, HTC worked with the U.S. software giant on a Windows-based handset that would go far beyond simple voice calls and allow users to view photos, listen to music, watch videos, manage appointments, and more.

18 Those devices are now hitting the streets. Last year, British cellular carrier Orange started selling HTC's $300 SPV phone, one of the first to use Microsoft's new Smartphone 2002 software. This year, German operator T-Mobile, Smart Communications of the Philippines, and U.S. carrier AT&T Wireless (AWE) all plan to introduce HTC-made phones. That's helping HTC reduce its dangerous dependence on sales of the iPAQ, which accounted for 85 percent of HTC's revenues in

2001. This year, brokerage Morgan Stanley estimates the iPAQ will represent just a third of HTC's sales.

19   All the new business is firing up HTC's results. Revenues last year grew by 32 percent, to $592 million, while profits jumped by 45 percent, to $40 million, according to the company's unaudited results. For 2003, Morgan Stanley expects sales to grow by 27 percent and earnings to soar by 83 percent. HTC's share price has shot up by 50 percent since September. "No one expected this little Taiwanese company to come along so fast," says Julian Snelder, a Morgan Stanley banker.

20   So is this Taiwan's answer to Nokia (NOK)? Well, not yet. HTC's bright light is attracting some unwanted attention. On the Internet, message boards are hopping with comments from British consumers who have purchased the SPV from Orange. Some are rapturous, but others gripe about bugs and slow performance. On Feb. 24, the companies released new software that's intended to address the problems. Perhaps even more worrisome for HTC, British phonemaker Sendo has sued Microsoft, claiming that the U.S. giant gave Sendo's intellectual property to HTC. Microsoft denies the claim. It's possible that HTC will be the next target for Sendo's lawyers, but neither company would comment.

21   HTC faces growing competition at home, too. Computer maker Wistron, a subsidiary of Acer, is branching out from the slumping PC business last year with contracts to make handhelds for Dell and a smart phone with Microsoft and Intel (INTC). Compal Electronics in late December unveiled its own Microsoft-powered phone. And on Feb. 12, Symbian Ltd., the British rival to Microsoft, announced it would help Taipei-based BenQ Corp. launch a similar device this year.

22   HTC CEO H. T. Cho says he won't get burned by rivals. He plans to trim costs by moving some production to China as early as next year. More important, he'll concentrate on "slimmer and lighter and more attractive" machines with wireless links. He says Taiwanese newcomers to the handheld industry are more accustomed to operating in the high-volume, low-innovation PC business. Cho figures these would-be rivals aren't up to the complicated work of producing wireless devices. "We are only working on PDAs and smart phones, and the whole company's engineering and manufacturing is focused on this area," Cho says. If Cho's confidence is justified, then the world will be hearing a lot more from this Taiwan hotshot.

THE UNDERDOG NIPPING AT QUANTA'S HEELS

NOTEBOOK MAKER COMPAL IS CLOSING THE SALES GAP WITH ITS ARCHRIVAL

23   In the ultracompetitive Taiwanese tech industry, few rivalries match that of Quanta Computer Inc. and Compal Electronics Inc. Both have the same focus: designing and manufacturing notebook PCs for other companies. The two compete for business from major laptop makers and count Dell Computer Corp. (DELL) as their leading customer. And they're both diversifying into new markets such as cell phones and handhelds. To top it off, Quanta Chairman Barry Lam used to run Compal: He quit to launch Quanta in 1988, when Compal was reeling from a factory fire. "The company almost collapsed—and he left," says Compal President Ray Chen, still angry at the departure of his old boss.

24   The competition is about to get even fiercer. Since founding Quanta, Lam has built it into Taiwan's biggest producer of notebook PCs, while Compal has had to settle for second place. But now, Compal is coming on strong: Taipei brokerage KGI Securities PLC expects Compal to boost laptop sales by 70 percent this year, to 3.9 million units, compared with a 20 percent increase, to 5.2 million, for Quanta. KGI says Compal will see overall sales of $2.8 billion for 2002, up 30 percent, while it expects Quanta's sales to grow by 27 percent, to $4.1 billion.

25   Better yet, Compal's share price is surging. It's up by 10.4 percent since July, compared with a 24.9 percent fall for Quanta. Now, Chen isn't going to settle for also-ran status anymore. "We believe we are the best," he boasts. Lam isn't losing sleep. "Compal makes a lot of noise," he says. "It doesn't mean a lot."

26   The biggest driver of Compal's success has been Dell. In early October, the Texas dynamo announced its third-quarter revenue would grow 22 percent from last year. While that's good news for both Taiwanese rivals—Dell accounts for about half of sales at each—Compal has benefited more, says UBS Warburg analyst Sharon Su. The reason: Dell has made a strong push into consumer PCs this year, and the bulk of Compal's sales to Dell are consumer machines. Quanta concentrates on corporate laptops, a sector that remains weak.

27   Another competitive edge for Compal is its expansion into China. Since early last year, Compal has been making computers on the mainland, where costs

are about one-third what they are in Taiwan. Now, Compal makes 60 percent of its notebooks in China. Quanta, meanwhile, leased a small Chinese plant last year but didn't open a big factory until July.

28   Still, Compal has a way to go before it can topple Quanta. KGI analyst Angela Hsiang points out that Quanta serves 9 of the 10 biggest notebook makers. Compal, in comparison, focuses largely on Dell, Toshiba, Hewlett-Packard, and Apple. And, she says, with Quanta's new plant coming on line, Compal can't rely on its head start on the mainland much longer. "Quanta will catch up in China," she says.

29   The Quanta-Compal competition now extends beyond laptops. Compal makes handsets for Motorola Inc. (MOT) as well as up-and-coming Chinese players such as Eastcom Corp. and Haier Corp. By next year, Chen says, phones will account for 25 percent of sales, up from 10 percent today. And like Quanta, Compal has diversified into liquid crystal displays. It has a $1.1 billion venture with Taiwanese foodmaker Uni-President Enterprises Corp. to produce the tiny screens used in next-generation cell phones and handheld computers.

30   It's a risky move, given the volatility of the phone business, but Chen is convinced the bet will pay off once the industry's funk lifts. "Next year, when there's a shortage in the market, [LCDs] will be a very strong advantage," he says. And nothing gives Chen more pleasure than gaining an advantage over Barry Lam.

Source: "Meet the Latest Tech All-Star From Taiwan," *BusinessWeek,* March 10, 2003; "The Underdog Nipping at Quanta's Heels," *BusinessWeek,* October 21, 2002; "Quanta's New Leap," *BusinessWeek,* June 24, 2002.

Part **Three**

Strategy Implementation

The last section of this book examines what is often called the action phase of the strategic management process: implementation of the chosen strategy. Up to this point, three phases of that process have been covered—strategy formulation, analysis of alternative strategies, and strategic choice. Although important, these phases alone cannot ensure success. To ensure success, the strategy must be translated into carefully implemented action. This means that:

1. The strategy must be translated into guidelines for the daily activities of the firm's members.

2. The strategy and the firm must become one—that is, the strategy must be reflected in the way the firm organizes its activities and in the firm's values, beliefs, and tone

3. In implementing the strategy, the firm's managers must direct and control actions and outcomes and adjust to change.

Chapter 9 explains how organizational action is successfully initiated in four inter-related steps:

1. Creation of clear *short-term objectives* and *action plans*.

2. Development of specific *functional tactics* that create competitive advantage.

3. Empowerment of operating personnel through *policies* to guide decisions.

4. Implementation of effective *reward system*.

Short-term objectives and action plans guide implementation by converting long-term objectives into short-term actions and targets. Functional tactics translate the business strategy into activities that build advantage. Policies empower operating personnel by defining guidelines for making decisions. Reward systems encourage effective results.

Today's competitive environment often necessitates restructuring and reengineering the organization to sustain competitive advantage. Chapter 10 examines how restructuring and reengineering are pursued in three organizational elements that provide fundamental, long-term means for institutionalizing the firm's strategy:

1. The firm's *structure*.
2. The *leadership* provided by the firm's CEO and key managers.
3. The fit between the strategy and the firm's *culture*.

Since the firm's strategy is implemented in a changing environment, successful implementation requires that execution be controlled and continuously improved. The control and improvement process must include at least these dimensions:

1. *Strategic controls* that "steer" execution of the strategy.
2. *Operations control systems* that monitor performance, evaluate deviations, and initiate corrective action.
3. *Continuous improvement* through total quality initiatives of a balanced scorecard perspective.

Chapter 11 examines the dimensions of the control and improvement process. It explains the essence of change as an ever-present force driving the need for strategic control. The chapter concludes with a look at the global "quality imperative," which is redefining the essence of control into the twenty-first century.

Implementation is "where the action is." It is the arena that most students enter at the start of their business careers. It is the strategic phase in which staying close to the customer, achieving competitive advantage, and pursuing excellence become realities. The chapters in this part will help you understand how this is done.

Chapter Nine

Implementing Strategy through Short-Term Objectives, Functional Tactics, Reward System, and Employee Empowerment

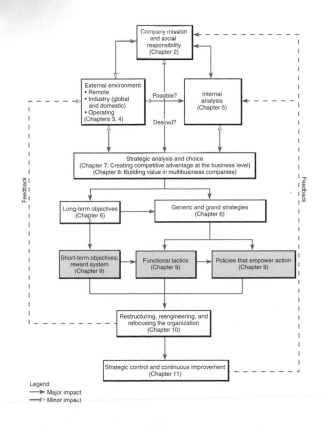

Company mission and social responsibility (Chapter 2)

External environment
• Remote
• Industry (global and domestic)
• Operating (Chapters 3, 4)

Possible?

Internal analysis (Chapter 5)

Desired?

Strategic analysis and choice
(Chapter 7: Creating competitive advantage at the business level)
(Chapter 8: Building value in multibusiness companies)

Long-term objectives (Chapter 6)

Generic and grand strategies (Chapter 6)

Short-term objectives; reward system (Chapter 9)

Functional tactics (Chapter 9)

Policies that empower action (Chapter 9)

Restructuring, reengineering, and refocusing the organization (Chapter 10)

Strategic control and continuous improvement (Chapter 11)

Feedback

Feedback

Legend
—→ Major impact
--→ Minor impact

Once corporate and business strategies have been agreed upon and long-term objectives set, the strategic management process moves into a critical new phase—translating strategic thought into organizational action. In the words of two well-worn phrases, they move from "planning their work" to "working their plan" as they shift their focus from strategy formulation to strategy implementation. Managers successfully make this shift when they do four things well:

1. Identify short-term objectives.

2. Initiate specific functional tactics.

3. Communicate policies that empower people in the organization.

4. Design effective rewards.

Short-term objectives translate long-range aspirations into this year's targets for action. If well developed, these objectives provide clarity, a powerful motivator and facilitator of effective strategy implementation.

Functional tactics translate business strategy into daily activities people need to execute. Functional managers participate in the development of these tactics, and their participation, in turn, helps clarify what their units are expected to do in implementing the business's strategy.

Policies are empowerment tools that simplify decision making by empowering operating managers and their subordinates. Policies can empower the "doers" in an organization by reducing the time required to decide and act.

A powerful part of getting things done in any organization can be found in the way its reward system rewards desired action and results. Rewards that align manager and employee priorities with organizational objectives and shareholder value provide very effective direction in strategy implementation.

SHORT-TERM OBJECTIVES

Chapter 6 described business strategies, grand strategies, and long-term objectives that are critically important in crafting a successful future. To make them become a reality, however, the people in an organization that actually "do the work" of the business need guidance in exactly what needs to be done today and tomorrow to make those long-term strategies become reality. Short-term objectives help do this. They provide much more specific guidance for what is to be done, a clear delineation of impending actions needed, which helps translate vision into action.

Short-term objectives help implement strategy in at least three ways. First, short-term objectives "operationalize" long-term objectives. If we commit to a 20 percent gain in revenue over five years, what is our specific target or objective in revenue during the current year, month, or week to indicate we are making appropriate progress? Second, discussion about and agreement on short-term objectives help raise issues and potential conflicts within an organization that usually require coordination to avoid otherwise dysfunctional consequences. Exhibit 9–1 illustrates how objectives within marketing, manufacturing, and accounting units within the same firm can be very different even when created to pursue the same firm objective (e.g., increased sales, lower costs). The third way short-term objectives assist strategy implementation is to identify measurable outcomes of action plans or functional activities, which can be used to make feedback, correction, and evaluation more relevant and acceptable.

Short-term objectives are usually accompanied by action plans, which enhance these objectives in three ways. First, action plans usually identify functional tactics and activities

EXHIBIT 9–1
Potential Conflicting Objectives and Priorities

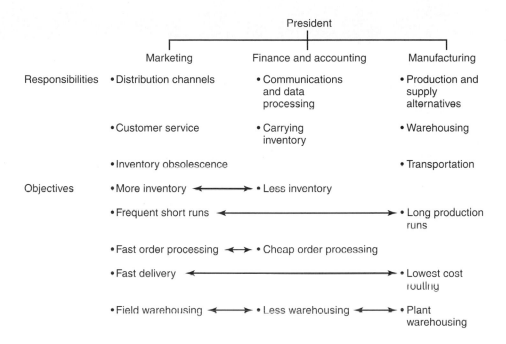

that will be undertaken in the next week, month, or quarter as part of the business's effort to build competitive advantage. The important point here is *specificity*—what exactly is to be done. We will examine functional tactics in a subsequent section of this chapter. The second element of an action plan is a clear *time frame for completion*—when the effort will begin and when its results will be accomplished. A third element action plans contain is identification of *who is responsible* for each action in the plan. This accountability is very important to ensure action plans are acted upon.

Because of the particular importance of short-term objectives in strategy implementation, the next section addresses how to develop meaningful short-term objectives. Exhibit 9–2 provides a *BusinessWeek* interview with Symantec CEO John Thompson about the nature and importance of short-term objectives to Symantec's success.

Qualities of Effective Short-Term Objectives

Measurable

Short-term objectives are more consistent when they clearly state *what* is to be accomplished, *when* it will be accomplished, and *how* its accomplishment will be *measured.* Such objectives can be used to monitor both the effectiveness of each activity and the collective progress across several interrelated activities. Exhibit 9–3 illustrates several effective and ineffective short-term objectives. Measurable objectives make misunderstanding less likely among interdependent managers who must implement action plans. It is far easier to quantify the objectives of *line* units (e.g., production) than of certain *staff* areas (e.g., personnel). Difficulties in quantifying objectives often can be overcome by initially focusing on *measurable activity* and then identifying *measurable outcomes.*

Priorities

Although all annual objectives are important, some deserve priority because of a timing consideration or their particular impact on a strategy's success. If such priorities are not established, conflicting assumptions about the relative importance of annual objectives may inhibit progress toward strategic effectiveness. Facing the most rapid, dramatic decline in

BusinessWeek "You can't manage what you don't measure," says Symantec CEO John Thompson, who explains why objectives are vital in implementing strategy.

"If you could only monitor five objectives to run/steer your business, what would they be and why?" is a question *BusinessWeek* posed Thompson, chairman and CEO of Symantec, a Cupertino (Calif)-based Internet security outfit that makes antivirus and firewall technology. In the four years since Thompson joined Symantec as top exec, revenues have more than doubled, from $632 million $1,407 billion in 2003. The company has not missed an earnings projection in the last two years.

Q: So what would be your critical objectives, and why?

A: Let's define what objectives are: They are vectors for how you are performing now, but also indicators for how you will do in the future. Here are five critical objectives I use to manage Symantec. Our most critical objectives are customer satisfaction and market share.

Customer satisfaction

We use an outside firm to poll customers on a continuous basis to determine their satisfaction with our products and services. This needs to be an anonymous relationship—a conversation between our pollster and our customers. Polling is done by product area: firewall, antivirus, services, and other product lines.

Market share

There are a couple of ways we look at this. We have our own views based on relevant markets. Then we use industry analysts such as Gartner, IDC, and Giga as benchmarks for annualized results on market share. On a quarterly basis, we look at our revenue performance and growth rates, and that of our competitors. We compare against actual realized growth rates, as compared to growth rates of relevant competitors in similar segments.

The purpose is to get trending data. That gives us a sense of market changes and market growth. We also use a blended (rating) of analyst companies in the same space. Each industry-analyst firm counts things a bit differently, based on its methodology. The numbers don't have to be spot on or Six Sigma precise.

Revenue growth

You have to consider if revenue is growing at a rate equal to or greater than the market rate. If you look at the antivirus market, for example, industry analysts projected growth in the high teens while our enterprise antivirus sector grew at a rate of 32 percent. This indicates that we are gaining market share faster than the market growth rate for the industry.

We can then assess how we had planned to grow. Did we plan to grow at 32 percent or less—or more? You have to gauge your growth relative to the market for your product or service and your own internal expectations of your performance.

Expenses

It is important to always plan for how much money will have to be spent to generate a certain level of revenue. This enables you to monitor funds flow in the company. Did I plan to spend $10 or $12, and what did I get for that expense in return? The purpose is to keep expenses in equilibrium to revenue generation.

Earnings

Two keys to watch here—operating margins and earnings per share (EPS). A business running efficiently is improving its operating margins. If you are efficient in your operating margins, this should produce a strong EPS, which is a strong objective that Wall Street looks at all the time.

Q: What problems do tracking objectives solve for a corporation? How does maintaining objectives help you manage and steer the direction of the corporation?

A: I am a little old-fashioned—I don't believe you can manage what you don't measure. The importance of objectives becomes more important as the enterprise grows in size and scale. Objectives also serve as an indication for the team about what you are paying attention

profitability of any major computer manufacturer as it confronted relentless lower pricing by Dell Computer and AST, Compaq Computer formulated a retrenchment strategy with several important annual objectives in pricing, product design, distribution, and financial condition. But its highest priority was to dramatically lower overhead and production costs so as to satisfy the difficult challenge of dramatically lowering prices while also restoring profitability.

Priorities are established in various ways. A simple *ranking* may be based on discussion and negotiation during the planning process. However, this does not necessarily communicate the real difference in the importance of objectives, so such terms as *primary, top,* and *secondary* may be used to indicate priority. Some firms assign *weights* (e.g., 0 to 100 per-to. If employees know you are measuring market growth and customer satisfaction, they will pay attention to those considerations and will behave based on indicators that you, as the leader, provide to the organization. Objectives helps the team focus on what's important for an organization.

Q: To what degree is maintaining objectives also about managing expectations of different audiences: investors, Wall Street analysts, and other parties? How do you manage the expectations of these third parties and other constituent groups?

A: The one that is the most interesting group to try to manage today is the expectation that investors have in our company and its performance. Our chief financial officer and I spend a lot of time on that topic. The ones investors watch most closely are revenue growth and EPS. We set expectations realistically and deliver against those expectations consistently. These considerations are at the core of how Wall Street fundamentally values a company. You have to properly set expectations and cascade those objectives down through the organization.

I wouldn't want to say to Wall Street that we have revenue growth rate projections of 18 percent and not internalize communication of that objective to the 4,500 people that are part of the company. It would be a huge mistake if you set up different expectations for what you communicate externally and how you manage internally. You can't have a disconnect between the two.

Q: How should companies consider industry-specific objectives versus broad financial objectives: P/E ratio, etc?

A: This is an issue for all of us. I am on the board of a utility company. The company has achieved modest single-digit revenue growth. They are quite proud of that, while I would be quite concerned if that were to be the growth rate for a software firm. For example: An important

consideration may be what you are spending in R&D in comparison to your peer group. Or, for a software firm, what is the license revenue mix?

I couldn't care less about the performance of Symantec relative to that of a financial-services company. But I would care about the performance of Symantec in comparison with an enterprise software company or with another securities software firm. Whatever measures you choose should give you the ability to measure your performance against like-industry companies.

Q: What do other CEOs need to keep in mind as they consider/reevaluate the use of objectives for their companies?

A: Live by the adage that you can't manage what you can't measure. The best objectives are simple to understand, simple to communicate, and relatively easy for everyone to get access to the data that represents the results. That makes your objectives an effective management tool. If you make your objectives difficult to gather, manage, or communicate, they won't be effective. Simplicity is key.

My experience has proven to me the importance of picking the few objectives that are the most critical for the running of the business. Stick with them—and communicate them to both internal and external audiences.

You don't change these objectives regardless of the whimsical views of Wall Street or the problem du jour. You have to pick the most important objectives and manage to this set standard. At the same time, you have to continually evaluate as the business changes over time to ensure that your objectives remain relevant. I would argue that all good leaders do this.

Source: "The Key to Success? Go Figure," *BusinessWeek,* July 21, 2003.

cent) to establish and communicate the relative priority of objectives. Whatever the method, recognizing priorities is an important dimension in the implementation value of short-term objectives.

Linked to Long-Term Objectives

Short-term objectives can add breadth and specificity in identifying *what* must be accomplished to achieve long-term objectives. For example, Wal-Mart's top management recently set out "to obtain 45 percent market share in five years" as a long-term objective. Achieving that objective can be greatly enhanced if a series of specific short-term objectives identify what must be accomplished each year in order to do so. If Wal-Mart's market share is

EXHIBIT 9–3
Creating Measurable
Objectives

Examples of Deficient Objectives	Examples of Objectives with Measurable Criteria for Performance
To improve morale in the division (plant, department, etc.)	To reduce turnover (absenteeism, number of rejects, etc.) among sales managers by 10 percent by January 1, 2004. *Assumption:* Morale is related to measurable outcomes (i.e., high and low morale are associated with different results).
To improve support of the sales effort	To reduce the time lapse between order data and delivery by 8 percent (two days) by June 1, 2004.
	To reduce the cost of goods produced by 6 percent to support a product price decrease of 2 percent by December 1, 2004.
	To increase the rate of before- or on-schedule delivery by 5 percent by June 1, 2004.
To improve the firm's image	To conduct a public opinion poll using random samples in the five largest U.S. metropolitan markets to determine average scores on 10 dimensions of corporate responsibility by May 15, 2004. To increase our score on those dimensions by an average of 7.5 percent by May 1, 2005.

now 25 percent, then one likely annual objective might be "to have each regional office achieve a minimum 4 percent increase in market share in the next year." "Open two regional distribution centers in the Southwest in 2005" might be an annual objective that Wal-Mart's marketing and distribution managers consider essential if the firm is to achieve a 45 percent market share in five years. "Conclude arrangements for a $1 billion line of credit at 0.25 percent above prime in 2004" might be an annual objective of Wal-Mart's financial managers to support the operation of new distribution centers and the purchase of increased inventory in reaching the firm's long-term objective.

The link between short-term and long-term objectives should resemble cascades through the firm from basic long-term objectives to specific short-term objectives in key operation areas. The cascading effect has the added advantage of providing a clear reference for communication and negotiation, which may be necessary to integrate and coordinate objectives and activities at the operating level.

The qualities of good objectives discussed in Chapter 6—acceptable, flexible, suitable, motivating, understandable, and achievable—also apply to short-term objectives. They will not be discussed again here, but you should review the discussion in Chapter 6 to appreciate these qualities, common to all good objectives.

The Value-Added Benefits of Short-Term Objectives and Action Plans

One benefit of short-term objectives and action plans is that they give operating personnel a better understanding of their role in the firm's mission. "Achieve $2.5 million in 2005 sales in the Chicago territory," "Develop an OSHA-approved safety program for handling acids at all Georgia Pacific plants in 2005," and "Reduce Ryder Truck's average age of accounts receivable to 31 days by the end of 2005" are examples of how short-term objectives clarify the role of particular personnel in their firm's broader mission. Such *clarity of purpose* can be a major force in helping use a firm's "people assets" more effectively, which may add tangible value.

A second benefit of short-term objectives and action plans comes from the process of developing them. If the managers responsible for this accomplishment have participated in their development, short-term objectives and action plans provide valid bases for addressing and accommodating conflicting concerns that might interfere with strategic effectiveness (see Exhibit 9–1). Meetings to set short-term objectives and action plans become the forum for raising and resolving conflicts between strategic intentions and operating realities.

A third benefit of short-term objectives and action plans is that they provide a *basis for strategic control.* The control of strategy will be examined in detail in Chapter 11. However, it is important to recognize here that short-term objectives and action plans provide a clear, measurable basis for developing budgets, schedules, trigger points, and other mechanisms for controlling the implementation of strategy. Exhibit 9–2, Strategy in Action, describes how new Symantec CEO John Thompson used short-term objectives as a key basis for strategic control.

A fourth benefit is often a *motivational payoff.* Short-term objectives and action plans that clarify personal and group roles in a firm's strategies and are also measurable, realistic, and challenging can be powerful motivators of managerial performance—particularly when these objectives are linked to the firm's reward structure.

FUNCTIONAL TACTICS THAT IMPLEMENT BUSINESS STRATEGIES

Functional tactics are the key, routine activities that must be undertaken in each functional area—marketing, finance, production/operations, R&D, and human resource management—to provide the business's products and services. In a sense, functional tactics translate thought (grand strategy) into action designed to accomplish specific short-term objectives. Every value chain activity in a company executes functional tactics that support the business's strategy and help accomplish strategic objectives.

Exhibit 9–4 illustrates the difference between functional tactics and corporate and business strategy. It also shows that functional tactics are essential to implement business strategy. The corporate strategy defined General Cinema Corporation's general posture in the broad economy. The business strategy outlined the competitive posture of its operations in the movie theater industry. To increase the likelihood that these strategies would be successful, specific functional tactics were needed for the firm's operating components. These functional tactics clarified the business strategy, giving specific, short-term guidance to operating managers in the areas of marketing, operations, and finance.

Differences between Business Strategies and Functional Tactics

Functional tactics are different from business or corporate strategies in three fundamental ways:

1. Time horizon.

2. Specificity.

3. Participants who develop them.

Time Horizon

Functional tactics identify activities to be undertaken "now" or in the immediate future. Business strategies focus on the firm's posture three to five years out. Delta Air lines is committed to a concentration/market development business strategy that seeks competitive advantage via differentiation in its level of service and focus on the business traveler. Its pricing tactics are often to price above industry averages, but it often lowers fares on selected routes to thwart low-cost competition. Its business strategy is focused 10 years out; its pricing tactics change weekly.

EXHIBIT 9–4
Functional Tactics at General Cinema Corporation

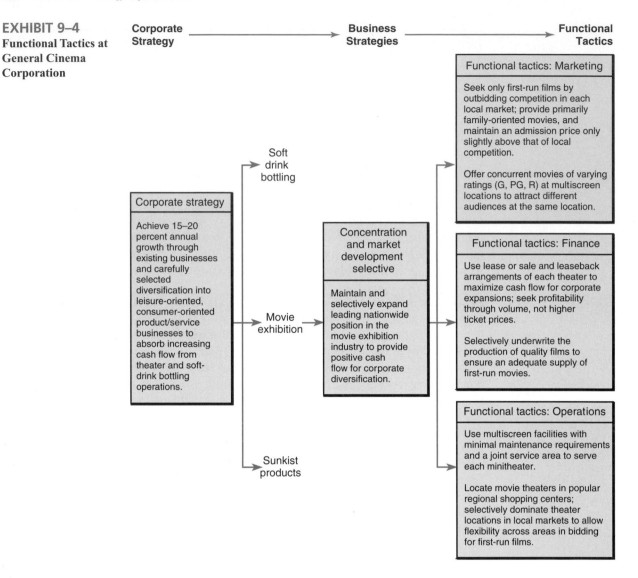

Corporate Strategy ⟶ Business Strategies ⟶ Functional Tactics

Corporate strategy

Achieve 15–20 percent annual growth through existing businesses and carefully selected diversification into leisure-oriented, consumer-oriented product/service businesses to absorb increasing cash flow from theater and soft-drink bottling operations.

Soft drink bottling

Movie exhibition

Sunkist products

Concentration and market development selective

Maintain and selectively expand leading nationwide position in the movie exhibition industry to provide positive cash flow for corporate diversification.

Functional tactics: Marketing

Seek only first-run films by outbidding competition in each local market; provide primarily family-oriented movies, and maintain an admission price only slightly above that of local competition.

Offer concurrent movies of varying ratings (G, PG, R) at multiscreen locations to attract different audiences at the same location.

Functional tactics: Finance

Use lease or sale and leaseback arrangements of each theater to maximize cash flow for corporate expansions; seek profitability through volume, not higher ticket prices.

Selectively underwrite the production of quality films to ensure an adequate supply of first-run movies.

Functional tactics: Operations

Use multiscreen facilities with minimal maintenance requirements and a joint service area to serve each minitheater.

Locate movie theaters in popular regional shopping centers; selectively dominate theater locations in local markets to allow flexibility across areas in bidding for first-run films.

The shorter time horizon of functional tactics is critical to the successful implementation of a business strategy for two reasons. First, it focuses the attention of functional managers on what needs to be done *now* to make the business strategy work. Second, it allows functional managers like those at Delta to adjust to changing current conditions.

Specificity

Functional tactics are more specific than business strategies. Business strategies provide general direction. Functional tactics identify the specific activities that are to be undertaken in each functional area and thus allow operating managers to work out *how* their unit is expected to pursue short-term objectives. General Cinema's business strategy gave its movie theater division broad direction on how to pursue a concentration and selective market development strategy. Two functional tactics in the marketing area gave managers specific direction on what types of movies (first-run, primarily family-oriented, G, PG, R) should be shown and what pricing strategy (competitive in the local area) should be followed.

Specificity in functional tactics contributes to successful implementation by:

- Helping ensure that functional managers know what needs to be done and can focus on accomplishing results.

- Clarifying for top management how functional managers intend to accomplish the business strategy, which increases top management's confidence in and sense of control over the business strategy.

- Facilitating coordination among operating units *within* the firm by clarifying areas of interdependence and potential conflict.

Exhibit 9–5, Strategy in Action, illustrates the nature and value of specificity in functional tactics versus business strategy in an upscale pizza restaurant chain.

Participants

Different people participate in strategy development at the functional and business levels. Business strategy is the responsibility of the general manager of a business unit. That manager typically delegates the development of functional tactics to subordinates charged with running the operating areas of the business. The manager of a business unit must establish long-term objectives and a strategy that corporate management feels contributes to corporate-level goals. Similarly, key operating managers must establish short-term objectives and operating strategies that contribute to business-level goals. Just as business strategies and objectives are approved through negotiation between corporate managers and business managers, so, too, are short-term objectives and functional tactics approved through negotiation between business managers and operating managers.

Involving operating managers in the development of functional tactics improves their understanding of what must be done to achieve long-term objectives and, thus, contributes to successful implementation. It also helps ensure that functional tactics reflect the reality of the day-to-day operating situation. And perhaps most important, it can increase the commitment of operating managers to the strategies developed.

EMPOWERING OPERATING PERSONNEL: THE ROLE OF POLICIES

Specific functional tactics provide guidance and initiate action implementing a business's strategy, but more is needed. Supervisors and personnel in the field have been charged in today's competitive environment with being responsible for customer value—for being the "front line" of the company's effort to truly meet customers' needs. Meeting customer needs, becoming obsessed with quality service, was the buzzword that started organizational revolutions in the 1980s. Efforts to do so often failed because employees that were the real contact point between the business and its customers were not *empowered* to make decisions or act to fulfill customer needs. One solution has been to empower operating personnel by pushing down decision making to their level. General Electric allows appliance repair personnel to decide about warranty credits on the spot, a decision that used to take several days and multiple organizational levels. Delta Air Lines allows customer service personnel and their supervisors wide range in resolving customer ticket pricing decisions. Federal Express couriers make decisions and handle package routing information that involves five management levels in the U.S. Postal Service.

Empowerment is being created in many ways. Training, self-managed work groups, eliminating whole levels of management in organizations, and aggressive use of automation are some of the ways and ramifications of this fundamental change in the way business organizations function. At the heart of the effort is the need to ensure that decision making

Strategy in Action
The Nature and Value of Specificity in Functional Tactics versus Business Strategy

Exhibit 9–5

BusinessWeek A restaurant business was encountering problems. Although its management had agreed unanimously that it was committed to a business strategy to differentiate itself from other competitors based on concept and customer service rather than price, it continued to encounter inconsistencies across different store locations in how well it did this. Consultants indicated that the customer experience varied greatly from store to store. The conclusion was that while the management understood the "business strategy," and the employees did too in general terms, the implementation was inadequate because of a lack of specificity in the functional tactics—what everyone should do every day in the restaurant—to make the vision a reality in terms of the customers' dining experience. The following breakdown of part of their business strategy into specific functional tactics just in the area of customer service helps illustrate the value specificity in functional tactics brings to strategy implementation.

Source: Adapted from "California Pizza Kitchen: Say Cheese!," *BusinessWeek,* July 15, 2003; and A. Campbell and K. Luchs, *Strategic Synergy* (London: Butterworth-Heineman, 1992).

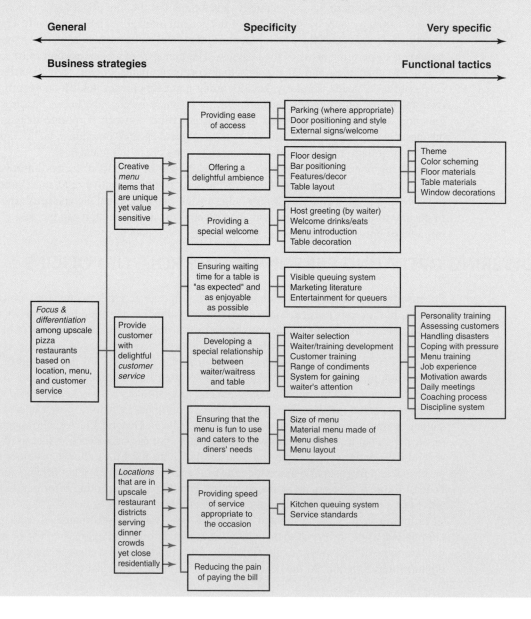

is consistent with the mission, strategy, and tactics of the business while at the same time allowing considerable latitude to operating personnel. One way operating managers do this is through the use of policies.

Policies are directives designed to guide the thinking, decisions, and actions of managers and their subordinates in implementing a firm's strategy. Previously referred to as *standard operating procedures,* policies increase managerial effectiveness by standardizing many routine decisions and clarifying the discretion managers and subordinates can exercise in implementing functional tactics. Logically, policies should be derived from functional tactics (and, in some instances, from corporate or business strategies) with the key purpose of aiding strategy execution.[1] Exhibit 9–6, Strategy in Action, illustrates selected policies of several well-known firms.

Creating Policies That Empower

Policies communicate guidelines to decisions. They are designed to control decisions while defining allowable discretion within which operational personnel can execute business activities. They do this in several ways:

1. *Policies establish indirect control over independent action* by clearly stating how things are to be done *now.* By defining discretion, policies in effect control decisions yet empower employees to conduct activities without direct intervention by top management.

2. *Policies promote uniform handling of similar activities.* This facilitates the coordination of work tasks and helps reduce friction arising from favoritism, discrimination, and the disparate handling of common functions—something that often hampers operating personnel.

3. *Policies ensure quicker decisions* by standardizing answers to previously answered questions that otherwise would recur and be pushed up the management hierarchy again and again—something that required unnecessary levels of management between senior decision makers and field personnel.

4. *Policies institutionalize basic aspects of organization behavior.* This minimizes conflicting practices and establishes consistent patterns of action in attempts to make the strategy work—again, freeing operating personnel to act.

5. *Policies reduce uncertainty in repetitive and day-to-day decision making,* thereby providing a necessary foundation for coordinated, efficient efforts and freeing operating personnel to act.

6. *Policies counteract resistance to or rejection of chosen strategies by organization members.* When major strategic change is undertaken, unambiguous operating policies clarify what is expected and facilitate acceptance, particularly when operating managers participate in policy development.

[1] The term *policy* has various definitions in management literature. Some authors and practitioners equate policy with strategy. Others do this inadvertently by using *policy* as a synonym for company mission, purpose, or culture. Still other authors and practitioners differentiate policy in terms of "levels" associated respectively with purpose, mission, and strategy. "Our policy is to make a positive contribution to the communities and societies we live in" and "our policy is not to diversify out of the hamburger business" are two examples of the breadth of what some call policies. This book defines *policy* much more narrowly as specific guides to managerial action and decisions in the implementation of strategy. This definition permits a sharper distinction between the formulation and implementation of functional strategies. And, of even greater importance, it focuses the tangible value of the policy concept where it can be most useful—as a key administrative tool to enhance effective implementation and execution of strategy.

3M Corporation has a *personnel policy,* called the *15 percent rule,* that allows virtually any employee to spend up to 15 percent of the workweek on anything that he or she wants to, as long as it's product related.

(This policy supports 3M's corporate strategy of being a highly innovative manufacturer, with each division required to have a quarter of its annual sales come from products introduced within the past five years.)

Wendy's has a *purchasing policy* that gives local store managers the authority to buy fresh meat and produce locally, rather than from regionally designated or company-owned sources.

(This policy supports Wendy's functional strategy of having fresh, unfrozen hamburgers daily.)

General Cinema has a *financial policy* that requires annual capital investment in movie theaters not to exceed annual depreciation.

(By seeing that capital investment is no greater than depreciation, this policy supports General Cinema's financial strategy of maximizing cash flow—in this case, all profit—to its growth areas. The policy also reinforces General Cinema's financial strategy of leasing as much as possible.)

IBM had a *marketing policy* of not giving free IBM personal computers (PCs) to any person or organization.

(This policy attempted to support IBM's image strategy by maintaining its image as a professional, high-value, service business as it sought to dominate the PC market.)

Crown, Cork, and Seal Company has an *R&D policy* of not investing any financial or people resources in basic research.

(This policy supports Crown, Cork, and Seal's functional strategy, which emphasizes customer services, not technical leadership.)

Bank of America has an *operating policy* that requires annual renewal of the financial statement of all personal borrowers.

(This policy supports Bank of America's financial strategy, which seeks to maintain a loan-to-loss ratio below the industry norm.)

---

7. *Policies offer predetermined answers to routine problems.* This greatly expedites dealing with both ordinary and extraordinary problems—with the former, by referring to these answers; with the latter, by giving operating personnel more time to cope with them.

8. *Policies afford managers a mechanism for avoiding hasty and ill-conceived decisions in changing operations.* Prevailing policy can always be used as a reason for not yielding to emotion-based, expedient, or temporarily valid arguments for altering procedures and practices.

Policies may be written and formal or unwritten and informal. Informal, unwritten policies are usually associated with a strategic need for competitive secrecy. Some policies of this kind, such as promotion from within, are widely known (or expected) by employees and implicitly sanctioned by management. Managers and employees often like the latitude granted by unwritten and informal policies. However, such policies may detract from the long-term success of a strategy. Formal, written policies have at least seven advantages:

1. They require managers to think through the policy's meaning, content, and intended use.

2. They reduce misunderstanding.

3. They make equitable and consistent treatment of problems more likely.

4. They ensure unalterable transmission of policies.

5. They communicate the authorization or sanction of policies more clearly.

6. They supply a convenient and authoritative reference.

7. They systematically enhance indirect control and organizationwide coordination of the key purposes of policies.

EXHIBIT 9–7
Make Sure Policies Aren't Used To Drive Away Customers

Every Year *Inc. Magazine* sponsors a conference for the 500 fastest growing companies in the United States to share ideas, hear speakers, and network. A recent conference included a talk by Martha Rogers, coauther of *The One to One Future*. Here is an interesting anecdote about policies she used in her talk:

"The story was about a distinguished-looking gentleman in blue jeans who walked into a bank and asked a teller to complete a transaction. The teller said she was sorry, but the person responsible was out for the day. The man would have to come back. He then asked to have his parking receipt validated. Again, she said she was sorry, but under bank policy she could not validate a parking receipt unless the customer completed a transaction. The man pressed her. She did not waver. "That's our policy," she said.

So the man completed a transaction. He withdrew all $1.5 million from his account. It turned out he was John Akers, then chairman of IBM.

The moral: Give employees information about the value of customers, not mindless policies."

The strategic significance of policies can vary. At one extreme are such policies as travel reimbursement procedures, which are really work rules and may not have an obvious link to the implementation of a strategy. Exhibit 9–7 provides an interesting example of how the link between a simple policy and strategy implementation regarding customer service can have serious negative consequences when it is neither obvious to operating personnel nor well thought out by bank managers. At the other extreme are organizationwide policies that are virtually functional strategies, such as Wendy's requirement that every location invest 1 percent of its gross revenue in local advertising.

Policies can be externally imposed or internally derived. Policies regarding equal employment practices are often developed in compliance with external (government) requirements, and policies regarding leasing or depreciation may be strongly influenced by current tax regulations.

Regardless of the origin, formality, and nature of policies, the key point to bear in mind is that they can play an important role in strategy implementation. Communicating specific policies will help overcome resistance to strategic change, empower people to act, and foster commitment to successful strategy implementation.

Policies empower people to act. Compensation, at least theoretically, rewards their action. The last decade has seen many firms realize that the link between compensation, particularly executive management compensation, and value-building strategic outcomes within their firms was uncertain. The recognition of this uncertainty has brought about increased recognition of the need to link management compensation with the successful implementation of strategies that build long-term shareholder value. The next section examines this development and major types of executive bonus compensation plans.

EXECUTIVE BONUS COMPENSATION PLANS[2]

Major Plan Types

The goal of an executive bonus compensation plan is to motivate executives to achieve maximization of shareholder wealth—the underlying goal of most firms. Since shareholders are both owners and investors of the firm, they desire a reasonable return on their investment. Because they are absentee landlords, shareholders want the decision-making logic of their firm's executives to be concurrent with their own primary motivation.

---

[2] We wish to thank Roy Hossler for his assistance on this section.

However, agency theory instructs us that the goal of shareholder wealth maximization is not the only goal that executives may pursue. Alternatively, executives may choose actions that increase their personal compensation, power, and control. Therefore, an executive compensation plan that contains a bonus component can be used to orient management's decision making toward the owners' goals. The success of bonus compensation as an incentive hinges on a proper match between an executive bonus plan and the firm's strategic objectives. As one author has written: "Companies can succeed by clarifying their business vision or strategy and aligning company pay programs with its strategic direction."[3]

Stock Options

A common measure of shareholder wealth creation is appreciation of company stock price. Therefore, a popular form of bonus compensation is stock options. Stock options have typically represented over 50 percent of a chief executive officer's average pay package.[4] Stock options provide the executive with the right to purchase company stock at a fixed price in the future. The precise amount of compensation is based on the difference, or "spread," between the option's initial price and its selling, or exercised, price. As a result, the executive receives a bonus only if the firm's share price appreciates. If the share price drops below the option price, the options become worthless. The largest single option sale of all time occurred on December 3, 1997. Disney Chief Executive Officer Michael D. Eisner exercised more than 7 million options on Disney stock that he had been given in 1989 as part of his bonus plan. Eisner sold his shares for more than $400 million.

Stock options were the source of extraordinary wealth creation for executives, managers, and rank-and-file employees in the technology boom of the last decade. Behind using options as compensation incentives was the notion that they were essentially free. Although they dilute shareholders' equity when they're exercised, taking the cost of stock options as an expense against earnings was not required. That, in turn, helped keep earnings higher than actual costs to the company and its shareholders. The bear market and corporate scandals of the last few years brought increased scrutiny on the use of and accounting for stock options. As of this writing there is increased pressure to begin expensing stock options to more accurately reflect company performance. The table below shows the effect expensing stocks options would have on the net earnings of the S&P 500 firms in recent years. "Stock options were a free resource, and because of that, they were used freely," said BankOne CEO James Dimon, who voluntarily began to expense stock options in 2003. "But now," he said, "when you have to expense options, you start to think" 'Is it an effective cost?' Is there a better way?" The Financial Accounting Standards Board was preparing a new ruling in 2004 that would require expensing of stock options.

A Big Hit To Earnings

If options had been expensed, earnings would have been whacked as their popularity grew

Options Expense As a Percent of Net Earnings for S&P 500 Companies

1996	1998	2000	2002
2%	5%	8%	23%

Data: The Analysis Accounting Observer R. G. Associates Inc.

---

[3] James E. Nelson, "Linking Compensation to Business Strategy," *The Journal of Business Strategy* 19, no. 2 (1998), pp. 25–27.
[4] Louis Lavelle, Frederick Jespersen, and Spencer Ante, "Executive Pay," *BusinessWeek*, April 21, 2003.

Microsoft shocked the business world in 2003 by announcing it would discontinue stock options, eliminating a form of pay that made thousands of Microsoft employees millionaires and helped define the culture of the tech industry. Starting in September, 2003, the company began paying its 54,000 employees with restricted stock, a move that will let employees make money even if the company's share price declines. Like options, the restricted stock will vest gradually over a five-year period and grants of restricted stock counted as expenses and charged against earnings. Said CEO Steven Ballmer, "We asked: Is there a smarter way to compensate our people, a way that would make them feel even more excited about their financial deal at Microsoft and at the same time be something that was at least as good for the shareholders as today's compensation package?" At the time of Ballmer's announcement, over 20,000 employees that had joined Microsoft in the past three years held millions of stock options that were "under water," meaning the market value of Microsoft stock was far below the stock price of their stock options.

Restricted stock has the advantage of offering employees more certainty, even if there is less potential for a big win. It also means shareholders don't have to worry about massive dilution after employees exercise big stock gains, as happened in the 1990s. Another advantage is that grants of restricted stock are much easier to value than options since restricted stock is equivalent to a stock transfer at the market price. That improves the transparency of corporate accounting.[5] At the same time, while several tech companies started downsizing their options programs in recent years, several old-line companies have been beefing their options programs up as shown in the box below.

Late to The Party
As many technology companies have downsized their options programs, old-line companies have been beefing theirs up.

	2002 Options Grant Millions	Change In Shares From 2001		2002 Options Grant Millions	Change In Shares From 2001
Lucent	14	−96%	Conoco Philips	29	+600%
Siebel Systems	6	−95	Sysco	31	+560
Aplied Materials	9	−91	Southwest Airlines	53	+435
Microsoft	41	−82	Safeco	3	+326
AOL Time Warner	115	−41	Campbell Soup	15	+301

Data: The Analyst's Accounting Observer, R.G. Associates Inc.

Research suggests that stock option plans lack the benefits of plans that include true stock ownership. Stock option plans provide unlimited upside potential for executives, but limited downside risk since executives incur only opportunity costs. Because of the tremendous advantages to the executive of stock price appreciation, there is an incentive for the executive to take undue risk. Thus, supporters of stock ownership plans argue that direct ownership instills a much stronger behavioral commitment, even when the stock price falls, since it binds

---

[5] Many argue that stock options are critical to start-up firms as a way to motivate and retain talented employees with the promise of getting rich should the new venture succeed. Among them appear to be FASB chairman Robert Herz, who favors sentiment to make special exceptions in the expensing of options in pre-IPO firms.

executives to their firms more than do options.[6] Additionally, "Executive stock options may be an efficient means to induce management to undertake more risky projects."[7]

Options may have been overused in the last bull market, but evidence suggests that the smart use of options and other incentive compensation does boost performance. Companies that spread ownership throughout a large portion of their workforce deliver higher returns than similar companies with more concentrated ownership. If options seemed for a time to be the route that enriched CEOs, employees, and investors alike, it still appears they will be used although with less emphasis than a mix of options, restricted stock, and cash bonuses. Whatever the exact mix, they are likely to be more closely tied to achieving specific operating goals. The next section examines restricted stock and cash bonuses in greater detail.

Restricted Stock

A restricted stock plan is designed to provide benefits of direct executive stock ownership. In a typical restricted stock plan, an executive is given a specific number of company stock shares. The executive is prohibited from selling the shares for a specified time period. Should the executive leave the firm voluntarily before the restricted period ends, the shares are forfeited. Therefore, restricted stock plans are a form of deferred compensation that promotes longer executive tenure than other types of plans.

In addition to being contingent on a vesting period, restricted stock plans may also require the achievement of predetermined performance goals. Price-vesting restricted stock plans tie vesting to the firm's stock price in comparison to an index, or to reaching a predetermined goal or annual growth rate. If the executive falls short on some of the restrictions, a certain amount of shares are forfeited. The design of these plans motivates the executive to increase shareholder wealth while promoting a long-term commitment to stay with the firm.

If the restricted stock plan lacks performance goal provisions, the executive needs only to remain employed with the firm over the vesting period to cash in on the stock. Performance provisions make sure executives are not compensated without achieving some level of shareholder wealth creation. Like stock options, restricted stock plans offer no downside risk to executives, since the shares were initially gifted to the executive. Unlike options, the stock retains value tied to its market value once ownership is fully vested. Shareholders, on the other hand, do suffer a loss in personal wealth resulting from a share price drop.

Investment bank Lehman Brothers has a restricted stock plan in place for hundreds of managing directors and senior vice presidents. The plan vests with time and does not include stock price performance provisions. It is a two-tiered plan consisting of a principal stock grant and a discounted share plan. For managing directors, the discount is 30 percent. For senior vice presidents, the discount is 25 percent. The principal stock grant is a block of shares given to the executive. The discounted share plan allows executives to purchase shares with their own money at a discount to current market prices.

Managing directors at Lehman are able to cash in on one-half the principal portion of their stock grant three years after the grant is awarded. The rest of the principal and any shares bought at a discount must vest for five years. Senior vice presidents receive the entire principal after two years and any discounted shares after five years. Provisions also exist for resignation. If managing directors leave Lehman for a competitor within three years

[6] Jeffrey Pfeffer, "Seven Practices of Successful Organizations," *California Management Review*, Winter 1998.

[7] Richard A. DeFusco, Robert R. Johnson, and Thomas S. Zorn, "The Effect of Executive Stock Option Plans on Stockholders and Bondholders," *Journal of Finance* 45, no. 2 (1990), pp. 617–35.

of the award, all stock compensation is forfeited. For senior vice presidents, the period is two years, and the penalties for jumping to a noncompetitor of Lehman's are not as severe.

Golden Handcuffs

The rationale behind plans that defer compensation forms the basis for another type of executive compensation called *golden handcuffs*. Golden handcuffs refer to either a restricted stock plan, where the stock compensation is deferred until vesting time provisions are met, or to bonus income deferred in a series of annual installments. This type of plan may also involve compensating an executive a significant amount upon retirement or at some predetermined age. In most cases, compensation is forfeited if the executive voluntarily resigns or is discharged before certain time restrictions.

Many boards consider their executives' skills and talents to be their firm's most valuable assets. These "assets" create and sustain the professional relationships that generate revenue and control expenses for the firm. Research suggests that the departure of key executives is unsettling for companies and often disrupts long-range plans when new key executives adopt a different management strategy.[8] Thus, the golden handcuffs approach to executive compensation is more congruent with long-term strategies than short-term performance plans, which offer little staying-power incentive.

Firms may turn to golden handcuffs if they believe stability of management is critical to sustain growth. Jupiter Asset Management recently tied 10 fund managers to the firm with golden handcuffs. The compensation scheme calls for a cash payment in addition to base salaries if the managers remain at the firm for five years. In the first year of the plan, the firm's pretax profits more than doubled, and their assets under management increased 85 percent. The firm's chairman has also signed a new incentive deal that will keep him at Jupiter for four years.

Deferred compensation is worrisome to some executives. In cases where the compensation is payable when the executives are retired and no longer in control, as when the firm is acquired by another firm or a new management hierarchy is installed, the golden handcuff plans are considerably less attractive to executives.

Golden handcuffs may promote risk averseness in executive decision making due to the huge downside risk borne by executives. This risk averseness could lead to mediocre performance results from executives' decisions. When executives lose deferred compensation if the firm discharges them voluntarily or involuntarily, the executive is less likely to make bold and aggressive decisions. Rather, the executive will choose safe, conservative decisions to reduce the downside risk of bold decision making.

Golden Parachutes

Golden parachutes are a form of bonus compensation that is designed to retain talented executives. A *golden parachute* is an executive perquisite that calls for a substantial cash payment if the executive quits, is fired, or simply retires. In addition, the golden parachute may also contain covenants that allow the executive to cash in on noninvested stock compensation.

The popularity of golden parachutes grew during the last decade, when abundant hostile takeovers would often oust the acquired firm's top executives. In these cases, the golden parachutes encouraged executives to take an objective look at takeover offers. The executives could decide which move was in the best interests of the shareholders, having been

---

[8] William E. Hall, Brian J. Lake, Charles T. Morse, and Charles T. Morse, Jr., "More Than Golden Handcuffs," *Journal of Accountancy* 184, no. 5 (1997), pp. 37–42.

personally protected in the event of a merger. The "parachute" helps soften the fall of the ousted executive. It is "golden" because the size of the cash payment often varies from several to tens of millions of dollars.

AMP Incorporated, the world's largest producer of electronic connectors, had golden parachutes for several executives. When Allied Signal proclaimed itself an unsolicited suitor for AMP, the action focused attention on the AMP parachutes for its three top executives. Robert Ripp became AMP's chief executive officer during this time. If Allied Signal ousted him, he stood to receive a cash payment of three times the amount of his salary as well as his highest annual bonus from the previous three years. His salary at the time was $600,000 and his previous year's bonus was $200,000. The cash payment to Ripp would therefore exceed $2 million. Parachutes would also open for the former chief executive officer and the former chairman who were slated to officially retire a year later. They stood to receive their parachutes if they were ousted before their respective retirement dates with each parachute valued at more than $1 million.

In addition to cash payments, these three executives' parachutes also protect existing blocks of restricted stock grants and nonvested stock options. The restricted stock grants were scheduled to become available within three years. Should the takeover come to fruition, the executives would receive the total value of the restricted stock even if it was not yet vested. The stock options would also become available immediately. Some of the restricted stock was performance restricted. Under normal conditions this stock would not be available without the firm reaching certain performance levels. However, the golden parachutes allow the executives to receive double the value of the performance-restricted stock.

Golden parachutes are designed in part to anticipate hostile takeovers like this. In AMP's case, Ripp's position is to lead the firm's board of directors in deciding if Allied Signal's offer is in the long-term interests of shareholders. Since Ripp is compensated heavily whether AMP is taken over or not, the golden parachute has helped remove the temptation that Ripp could have of not acting in the best interests of shareholders.

By design, golden parachutes benefit top executives whether or not there is evidence that value is created for shareholders. In fact, research has suggested that since high-performing firms are rarely taken over, golden parachutes often compensate top executives for abysmal performance.[9] Recent stockholder reactions to excessive executive compensation regardless of company performance are seen in Exhibit 9–8.

Cash

Executive bonus compensation plans that focus on accounting measures of performance are designed to offset the limitations of market-based measures of performance. This type of plan is most usually associated with the payment of periodic (quarterly or annual) cash bonuses. Market factors beyond the control of management, such as pending legislation, can keep a firm's share price repressed even though a top executive is exceeding the performance expectations of the board. In this situation, a highly performing executive loses bonus compensation due to the undervalued stock. However, accounting measures of performance correct for this problem by tying executive bonuses to improvements in internally measured performance.

Traditional accounting measures, such as net income, earnings per share, return on equity, and return on assets, are used because they are easily understood, are familiar to senior management, and are already tracked by firm data systems.[10] Sears bases annual bonus

[9] Graef S. Crystal, *In Search of Excess* (New York: W. W. Norton & Company, 1991).
[10] Francine C. McKenzie and Matthew D. Shilling, "Avoiding Performance Measurement Traps: Ensuring Effective Incentive Design and Implementation," *Compensation and Benefits Review,* July–August 1998, pp. 57–65.

FED-UP SHAREHOLDERS

Unions and public pension funds have racked up more than two dozen majority votes for shareholder resolutions opposing high executive pay

GOLDEN PARACHUTES
At Alcoa, 65% of shareholders voted for a union resolution calling for stockholder approval of lavish executive severance packages. Similar proposals won majorities at Delta and Raytheon.

CUSHY RETIREMENT DEALS
A proposal at U.S. Bancorp seeking shareholder votes on special executive pension benefits passed by 52%. Labor pulled resolutions at GE, Coke, and Exelon after they agreed to reforms.

EXPENSING STOCK OPTIONS
Labor resolutions demanding that companies deduct option costs from earnings have garnered majorities at 15 companies, including Apple and Capital One.

Source: "Executive Pay: Labor Strikes Back," *BusinessWeek*, May 26, 2003.

payments on such performance criteria, given an executive's business unit and level with the firm. The measures used by Sears include return on equity, revenue growth, net sales growth, and profit growth.

Critics argue that due to inherent flaws in accounting systems, basing compensation on these figures may not result in an accurate gauge of managerial performance. Return on equity estimates, for example, are skewed by inflation distortions and arbitrary cost allocations. Accounting measures are also subject to manipulation by firm personnel to artificially inflate key performance figures. Firm performance schemes, critics believe, need to be based on a financial measure that has a true link to shareholder value creation.[11] This issue led to the creation of the Balanced Scorecard, which emphasizes not only financial measures, but also such measures as new product development, market share, and safety as discussed in Chapters 6 and 11 of this book.

Matching Bonus Plans and Corporate Goals

Exhibit 9–9 provides a summary of the five types of executive bonus compensation plans. The figure includes a brief description, a rationale for implementation, and the identification of possible shortcomings for each of the compensation plans. Not only do compensation plans differ in the method through which compensation is rewarded to the executive, but they also provide the executive with different incentives.

[11] William Franklin, "Making the Fat Cats Earn Their Cream," *Accountancy*, July 1998, pp. 38–39.

EXHIBIT 9–9

Types of Executive Bonus Compensation

Bonus Type	Description	Rationale	Shortcomings
Stock option grants	Right to purchase stock in the future at a price set now. Compensation is determined by "spread" between option price and exercise price.	Provides incentive for executive to create wealth for shareholders as measured by increase in firm's share price.	Movement in share price does not explain all dimensions of managerial performance.
Restricted stock plan	Shares given to executive who is prohibited from selling them for a specific time period. May also include performance restrictions.	Promotes longer executive tenure than other forms of compensation.	No downside risk to executive, who always profits unlike other shareholders.
Golden handcuffs	Bonus income deferred in a series of annual installments. Deferred amounts not yet paid are forfeited with executive resignation.	Offers an incentive for executive to remain with the firm.	May promote risk-averse decision making due to downside risk borne by executive.
Golden parachute	Executives have right to collect the bonus if they lose position due to takeover, firing, retirement, or resignation.	Offers an incentive for executive to remain with the firm.	Compensation is achieved whether or not wealth is created for shareholders. Rewards either success or failure.
Cash based on internal business performance using financial measures	Bonus compensation based on accounting performance measures such as return on equity.	Offsets the limitations of focusing on market-based measures of performance.	Weak correlation between earnings measures and shareholder wealth creation. Annual earnings do not capture future impact of current decisions.

Exhibit 9–10 matches a company's strategic goal with the most likely compensation plan. On the vertical axis are common strategic goals. The horizontal axis lists the main compensation types that serve as incentives for executives to reach the firm's goals. A rationale is provided to explain the logic behind the connection between the firm's goal and the suggested method of executive compensation.

Researchers emphasize that fundamental to these relationships is the importance of incorporating the level of strategic risk of the firm into the design of the executive's compensation plan. Incorporating an appropriate level of executive risk can create a desired behavioral change commensurate with the risk level of strategies shareholders and their firms want.[12] To help motivate an executive to pursue goals of a certain risk-return level, the compensation plan can quantify that risk-return level and reward the executive accordingly.

The links we show between bonus compensation plans and strategic goals were derived from the results of prior research. The basic principle underlying Exhibit 9–10 is that different types of bonus compensation plans are intended to accomplish different purposes; one element

[12] "Executive Pay," *Business Week,* April 21, 2003.

EXHIBIT 9–10
Compensation Plan Selection Matrix

Strategic Goal	Type of Bonus Compensation					Rationale
	Cash	Golden Handcuffs	Golden Parachutes	Restricted Stock Plans	Stock Options	
Achieve corporate turnaround					X	Executive profits only if turnaround is successful in returning wealth to shareholders.
Create and support growth opportunities					X	Risk associated with growth strategies warrants the use of this high-reward incentive.
Defend against unfriendly takeover			X			Parachute helps remove temptation for executive to evaluate takeover based on personal benefits.
Evaluate suitors objectively			X			Parachute compensates executive if job is lost due to a merger favorable to the firm.
Globalize operations					X	Risk of expanding overseas requires a plan that compensates only for achieved success.
Grow share price incrementally	X					Accounting measures can identify periodic performance benchmarks.
Improve operational efficiency	X					Accounting measures represent observable and agreed-upon measures of performance.
Increase assets under management				X		Executive profits proportionally as asset growth leads to long-term growth in share price.
Reduce executive turnover		X				Handcuffs provide executive tenure incentive.
Restructure organization					X	Risk associated with major change in firm's assets warrant the use of this high-reward incentive.
Streamline operations				X		Rewards long-term focus on efficiency and cost control

may serve to attract and retain executives, another may serve as an incentive to encourage behavior that accomplishes firm goals.[13] Although every strategy option has probably been linked to each compensation plan at some time, experience shows that there may be scenarios where a plan type best fits a strategy option. Exhibit 9–10 attempts to display the "best matches."

Once the firm has identified strategic goals that will best serve shareholders' interests, an executive bonus compensation plan can be structured in such a way as to provide the executive with an incentive to work toward achieving these goals.

Summary

The first concern in the implementation of business strategy is to translate that strategy into action throughout the organization. This chapter discussed four important tools for accomplishing this.

Short-term objectives are derived from long-term objectives, which are then translated into current actions and targets. They differ from long-term objectives in time frame, specificity, and measurement. To be effective in strategy implementation, they must be integrated and coordinated. They also must be consistent, measurable, and prioritized.

Functional tactics are derived from the business strategy. They identify the specific, immediate actions that must be taken in key functional areas to implement the business strategy.

Employee empowerment through policies provides another means for guiding behavior, decisions, and actions at the firm's operating levels in a manner consistent with its business and functional strategies. Policies empower operating personnel to make decisions and take action quickly.

Compensation rewards action and results. Once the firm has identified strategic objectives that will best serve stockholder interests, there are five bonus compensation plans that can be structured to provide the executive with an incentive to work toward achieving those goals.

Objectives, functional tactics, policies, and compensation represent only the start of the strategy implementation. The strategy must be institutionalized—it must permeate the firm. The next chapter examines this phase of strategy implementation.

Questions for Discussion

1. How does the concept "translate thought into action" bear on the relationship between business strategy and operating strategy? Between long-term and short-term objectives?

2. How do functional tactics differ from corporate and business strategies?

3. What key concerns must functional tactics address in marketing? Finance? POM? Personnel?

4. How do policies aid strategy implementation? Illustrate your answer.

5. Use Exhibits 9–9 and 9–10 to explain five executive bonus compensation plans.

6. Illustrate a policy, an objective, and a functional tactic in your personal career strategy.

7. Why are short-term objectives needed when long-term objectives are already available?

[13] James E. Nelson, "Linking Compensation to Business Strategy," *The Journal of Business Strategy* 19, no. 2 (1998), pp. 25–27.

Chapter 9 Discussion Case A

BusinessWeek

Thinking outside the Cereal Box

General Mills' Far-flung Search for Efficiency Ideas

General Mills' CEO searches for short-term objectives, functional tactics, and operating policies in unusual ways and places so he can translate a 10-year goal into tactical actions and results. Read this story about what he is doing and then see if you detect ways he is doing so!

1 As the economy has unraveled over the past three years, managers desperate to prop up profits have been beating the bushes for new ways to cut costs. Few, however, have wandered further afield in pursuit of smart ideas than General Mills (GIS), Inc. chief technical officer Randy G. Darcy. He has participated in predawn raids with a U.S. Marshals Service SWAT team, hung out with a NASCAR pit crew, and watched Air Force mechanics fix Stealth bombers. Darcy's unlikely goal: to make his operation "the best supply chain in the world."

2 It's more than just a theoretical ambition. CEO Stephen W. Sanger has given Darcy an epic challenge: cut $1 billion out of General Mills' supply chain in 10 years. By getting the company into fighting trim, Sanger hopes he'll be able to dig out from under a staggering $8.9 billion in debt from his $10.1 billion acquisition of Pillsbury from Diageo PLC in 2001. That's no small task for a company with $10.5 billion in sales that has already cut hundreds of millions of dollars over the last decade.

3 Slashing costs is just one of many challenges General Mills faces. It needs to regain market share that it ceded to archrival Kellogg Co., which became the number one U.S. cereal maker last year. And it's fighting off fierce competition from Campbell Soup Co. and ConAgra Foods Inc. in canned soups and ready-to-eat meals. Says Sanger: "We can't get by doing what we did yesterday."

4 Darcy is confident that he can save $800 million of the $1 billion target by adapting lessons in efficiency learned elsewhere. But money-saving ideas from pit crews and SWAT teams? Don't laugh: He has already made considerable progress. Darcy targets groups that routinely take performance to the extreme, studying them for efficiency secrets that might benefit General Mills—either by applying those secrets directly or by jolting employees into thinking of new ways of doing their jobs. By observing how a NASCAR pit crew was able to work with blinding speed simply through better organization, General Mills was able to cut the time it took workers to change a production line at a Lodi (Calif.) factory from one Betty Crocker product to another from 4.5 hours to just 12 minutes. And by watching the way that Stealth bomber pilots and maintenance crews cooperated, the company was able to improve its own teamwork, helping to cut cereal production costs by 25 percent at a plant in Buffalo.

5 Such gains, while impressive, may represent only a fraction of what's possible for General Mills, the maker of Cheerios cereal, Betty Crocker cake mixes, and Hamburger Helper. Anand Sharma, the CEO of TBM Consulting Group Inc. in Durham, N.C., who specializes in efficiency, says the company should be able to triple its cost-cutting goals—aiming for annual productivity improvements of 15 percent and profit gains of an additional 4 percent by aggressively applying what it learns. Moreover, experts say that seeking inspiration outside one's industry, as General Mills is doing, is the only way to leapfrog ahead of rivals. "Given how efficient many organizations have become, the next big idea won't come from internal thinking," says Ravin Jesuthasan, principal at Towers Perrin's reward and performance management consulting practice in Chicago. "It has got to come from revolutionary, outside-the-box thinking."

6 But even with all of General Mills' efforts to borrow management ideas from the unlikeliest of places, reaching the $1 billion savings goal won't be easy. Companies like General Mills, which has been cutting costs for years, may find future efficiency gains harder to come by.

7 And while Darcy believes the benefits from his excursions outside the cereal biz are real, some are impossible to measure. For example, the SWAT team's cooperative approach to nabbing fugitives inspired General Mills to replace separate performance goals for engineering, purchasing, and production with a single set of goals for all departments, eliminating the incentive for one department to cut corners at another's expense. Darcy cites a purchasing manager who met

cost-cutting goals under the old system by buying thinner cartons—even though they jammed up the production lines, raising manufacturing costs. Gross margins have improved in the four years since the new incentives were implemented—from 44 percent to 47 percent—but it's unclear how much of the improvement can be attributed to the change.

8   Finally, not all the efficiency lessons that Darcy brings back from the field can be adapted throughout General Mills. While the company was able to use the NASCAR lessons to transform the Betty Crocker plant—by replacing standard bolts with those requiring only a quarter turn and stocking toolboxes with the specific gear needed to switch product lines—efforts to duplicate much of that success elsewhere failed because many plant functions were unique.

9   Darcy isn't giving up, though. Lately, he's been working with Erik Weihenmayer, a blind mountaineer who has scaled the seven greatest summits. The goal: to understand his method for assembling expedition teams based on personality traits, instead of climbing skill, insights that Darcy says will prove critical to the success of the Pillsbury integration. "The only way to cross a glacier is on a rope to which your entire team is tied," says Weihenmayer. "You either all plunge together or succeed together." Darcy and his team are betting they won't be falling into the abyss any time soon.

Source: "Thinking Outside the Box," *BusinessWeek,* July 28, 2003.

Chapter 9 Discussion Case B

BusinessWeek

Is Kohl's Coming Unbuttoned?

Slovenly Stores and Shrewd Competition Have Hurt Sales

1 Shopping recently at a Kohl's (KSS) store in Niles, Ill., Kimberly Rellinger can't find any boys' shorts as she digs through a jumble of misplaced items. And she gives up on the shorts idea altogether when she sees the five-person checkout line. Instead, she heads to a nearby Old Navy (GPS) where she finds what she wants with no wait. "Now I will go there first," says the 36-year-old mother of two boys.

2 Plenty of Kohl's shoppers seem to be making the same call these days. On July 10, the apparel discounter reported a 2.4 percent decline in June sales at stores open at least a year. Worse, it warned that for the first time since going public in 1992, second-quarter earnings would decline. In part, the disappointing numbers reflect growing competition from department and specialty-apparel stores. But Kohl's Corp. execs may also have lost their Midas touch: Distracted by a big expansion into California, they have misjudged inventories and relaxed once-tight control of existing operations.

3 It's quite a reversal for this '90s retail star. Until recently, it seemed the Menomonee Falls (Wis,) chain could do no wrong. Kohl's has posted 35 percent compounded annual earnings growth over the past five years. It did so with the simplest of strategies: selling casual brands at low prices. By locating its stores in strip centers, Kohl's draws shoppers who find malls inconvenient. Now, having missed sales targets for 7 of the past 9 months, Kohl's heady days may be over. "It's the first crack in the growth story," says Deutsche Bank Securities Inc. analyst Bill Dreher.

4 Nonsense, says Kohl's CEO R. Lawrence Montgomery. He attributes the weak sales to a sluggish market for apparel, which affects Kohl's more than department-store rivals because clothing makes up a higher percentage of its sales. But, he admits, the competition has "narrowed a little bit."

5 Indeed, rivals ranging from JCPenney (JCP) and Sears, Roebuck to Federated Department Stores (FD) Macy's unit have borrowed from Kohl's playbook. Like Kohl's, they made their stores easier to navigate and beefed up casual brands. Most of all, they have cut prices to counter the advantage of Kohl's locations, says Marshall Cohen, chief analyst at market-research firm NPD Group Inc. As a result, Penney, Sears, and Federated all posted better sales results than Kohl's in June. "The consumer is going back to the mall because they can get a better price with a wider variety," Cohen says.

6 Department stores aren't the only ones playing better defense. Gap (GPS) Inc.'s Old Navy unit, whose shops are often based in strip centers with Kohl's, has recently shifted from trendy teenage fashion toward clothing that appeals to mothers with children, one of Kohl's targets. On the low end, Kohl's is facing more pressure from Wal-Mart (WMT) Stores Inc., which is upping the quality of its apparel and adding national brands like Levi's. "Wal-Mart is also after the same middle-level shopper," says Patrick McKeever, an analyst at Sun Trust Robinson Humphrey Capital Markets.

7 Meanwhile, Kohl's expansion into California seems to be distracting management. The chain has opened 28 stores this year in the greater Los Angeles area, where it is encountering fierce resistance from entrenched players such as Mervyn's and Macy's West. Some analysts say the challenging expansion helps explain recent stumbles at Kohl's existing stores. While the retailer has always loaded up on inventory, this year it misjudged demand and wound up having to discount heavily, which dented profits. Shoppers also complain that stores are less well-kept and check-out lines longer than they were.

8 Most troubling, perhaps, is that sales have slipped at Kohl's most mature outlets. That raises questions about the chain's growth prospects as older stores become a larger percentage of Kohl's locations. Deutsche Bank estimates that same-store sales at outlets five years old or more have declined for the past three years. In June, Kohl's worst-performing stores were in the Midwest, home to the bulk of its older shops. Montgomery blames a weak Midwest economy and lousy weather. If he's wrong, Kohl's days of rapid growth may be behind it.

Source: "Is Kohl's Coming Unbuttoned?" *BusinessWeek*, July 28, 2003.

Appendix 9

Functional Tactics

FUNCTIONAL TACTICS THAT IMPLEMENT BUSINESS STRATEGIES

Functional tactics are the key, routine activities that must be undertaken in each functional area—marketing, finance, production/operations, R&D, and human resource management—to provide the business's products and services. In a sense, functional tactics translate thought (grand strategy) into action designed to accomplish specific short-term objectives. Every value chain activity in a company executes functional tactics that support the business's strategy and help accomplish strategic objectives.

The next several sections will highlight key tactics around which managers can build competitive advantage and add value in each of the various functional areas.

FUNCTIONAL TACTICS IN PRODUCTION/OPERATIONS

Basic Issues

Production/operations management (POM) is the core function of any organization. That function converts inputs (raw materials, supplies, machines, and people) into value-enhanced output. The POM function is most easily associated with manufacturing firms, but it also applies to all other types of businesses (service and retail firms, for example). POM tactics must guide decisions regarding (1) the basic nature of the firm's POM system, seeking an optimum balance between investment input and production/operations output and (2) location, facilities design, and process planning on a short-term basis. Exhibit 9–A highlights key decision areas in which the POM tactics should provide guidance to functional personnel.

POM facility and equipment tactics involve decisions regarding plant location, size, equipment replacement, and facilities utilization that should be consistent with grand strategy and other operating strategies. In the mobile home industry, for example, the facilities and equipment tactic of Winnebago was to locate one large centralized, highly integrated production center (in Iowa) near its raw materials. On the other extreme, Fleetwood, Inc., a California-based competitor, located dispersed, decentralized production facilities near markets and emphasized maximum equipment life and less-integrated, labor-intensive production processes. Both firms are leaders in the mobile home industry, but have taken very different tactical approaches.

The interplay between computers and rapid technological advancement has made flexible manufacturing systems (FMS) a major consideration for today's POM tacticians. FMS allows managers to automatically and rapidly shift production systems to retool for different products or other steps in a manufacturing process. Changes that previously took hours or days can be done in minutes. The result is decreased labor cost, greater efficiency, and increased quality associated with computer-based precision.

Sourcing has become an increasingly important component in the POM area. Many companies now accord sourcing a separate status like any other functional area. Sourcing tactics provide guidelines about questions such as: Are the cost advantages of using only a few suppliers outweighed by the risk of overdependence? What criteria (e.g., payment requirements) should be used in selecting vendors? Which vendors can provide "just-in-time" inventory and how can the business provide it to our customers? How can operations be supported by the volume and delivery requirements of purchases?

EXHIBIT 9–A
Key Functional Tactics in POM

Functional Tactic	Typical Questions That the Functional Tactic Should Answer
Facilities and equipment	How centralized should the facilities be? (One big facility or several small facilities?)
	How integrated should the separate processes be?
	To what extent should further mechanization or automation be pursued?
	Should size and capacity be oriented toward peak or normal operating levels?
Sourcing	How many sources are needed?
	How should suppliers be selected, and how should relationships with suppliers be managed over time?
	What level of forward buying (hedging) is appropriate?
Operations planning and control	Should work be scheduled to order or to stock?
	What level of inventory is appropriate?
	How should inventory be used (HIFO/LIFO), controlled, and replenished?
	What are the key foci for control efforts (quality, labor cost, downtime, product use, other)?
	Should maintenance efforts be oriented to prevention or to breakdown?
	What emphasis should be placed on job specialization? Plant safety? The use of standards?

POM planning and control tactics involve approaches to the management of ongoing production operations and are intended to match production/operations resources with longer range, overall demand. These tactical decisions usually determine whether production/operations will be demand oriented, inventory oriented, or outsourcing oriented to seek a balance between the two extremes. Tactics in this component also address how issues like maintenance, safety, and work organization are handled. Quality control procedures are yet another focus of tactical priorities in this area.

Just-in-time (JIT) delivery, outsourcing, and statistical process control (SPC) have become prominent aspects of the way today's POM managers create tactics that build greater value and quality in their POM system. JIT delivery was initially a way to coordinate with suppliers to reduce inventory carrying costs of items needed to make products. It also became a quality control tactic because smaller inventories made quality checking easier on smaller, frequent deliveries. It has become an important aspect of supplier-customer relationships in today's best businesses.

Outsourcing, or the use of a source other than internal capacity to accomplish some task or process, has become a major operational tactic in today's downsizing-oriented firms. Outsourcing is based on the notion that strategies should be built around core competencies that add the most value in the value chain, and functions or activities that add little value or that cannot be done cost effectively should be done outside the firm—outsourced. When done well, the firm gains a supplier that provides superior quality at lower cost than it could provide itself. JIT and outsourcing have increased the strategic importance of the purchasing function. Outsourcing must include intense quality control by the buyer. ValuJet's tragic 1996 crash in the Everglades was caused by poor quality control over its outsourced maintenance providers.

The Internet and "E-commerce" have begun to revolutionize functional tactics in operations and marketing. How we sell, where we make things, how we logistically coordinate what we do, all of these basic business functions and questions have new perspectives and ways of being addressed because of the technological impact of the globally emerging ways we link together electronically, quickly, and accurately.

FUNCTIONAL TACTICS IN MARKETING

The role of the marketing function is to achieve the firm's objectives by bringing about the profitable sale of the business's products/services in target markets. Marketing tactics should guide sales and marketing managers in determining who will sell what, where, to whom, in what quantity, and how. Marketing tactics at a minimum should address four fundamental areas: products, price, place, and promotion. Exhibit 9–B highlights typical questions marketing tactics should address.

In addition to the basic issues raised in Exhibit 9–B, marketing tactics today must guide managers addressing the impact of the *communication revolution* and the *increased diversity* among market niches worldwide. The Internet and the accelerating blend of computers and telecommunications has facilitated instantaneous access to several places around the world. A producer of plastic kayaks in Easley, South Carolina, receives orders from somewhere in the world about every 30 minutes over the Internet without any traditional distribution structure or global advertising. It fills the order within five days without any transportation capability. Speed linked to the ability to communicate instantaneously is causing marketing tacticians to radically rethink what they need to do to remain competitive and maximize value.

Diversity has accelerated because of communication technology, logistical capability worldwide, and advancements in flexible manufacturing systems. The diversity that has resulted is a

EXHIBIT 9–B
Key Functional Tactics in Marketing

Functional Tactic	Typical Questions That the Functional Tactic Should Answer
Product (or service)	Which products do we emphasize? Which products/services contribute most to profitability? What product/service image do we seek to project? What consumer needs does the product/service seek to meet? What changes should be influencing our customer orientation?
Price	Are we competing primarily on price? Can we offer discounts or other pricing modifications? Are our pricing policies standard nationally, or is there regional control? What price segments are we targeting (high, medium, low, and so on)? What is the gross profit margin? Do we emphasize cost/demand or competition-oriented pricing?
Place	What level of market coverage is necessary? Are there priority geographic areas? What are the key channels of distribution? What are the channel objectives, structure, and management? Should the marketing managers change their degree of reliance on distributors, sales reps, and direct selling? What sales organization do we want? Is the sales force organized around territory, market, or product?
Promotion	What are the key promotion priorities and approaches? Which advertising/communication priorities and approaches are linked to different products, markets, and territories? Which media would be most consistent with the total marketing strategy?

virtual explosion of market niches, adaptations of products to serve hundreds of distinct and diverse customer segments that would previously have been served with more mass-market, generic products or services. Where firms used to rely on volume associated with mass markets to lower costs, they now encounter smaller niche players carving out subsegments they can serve more timely *and* more cost effectively. These new, smaller players lack the bureaucracy and committee approach that burdens the larger firms. They make decisions, outsource, incorporate product modifications, and make other agile adjustments to niche market needs before their larger competitors get through the first phase of committee-based decision making. Jack Welch, the CEO of General Electric, commented on this recently with the editors of *BusinessWeek:*

> Size is no longer the trump card it once was in today's brutally competitive world marketplace— a marketplace that is unimpressed with logos and sales numbers but demands, instead, value and performance. At GE we're trying to get that small-company soul — and small company speed inside our big-company body. Faster products, faster product cycles to market. Better response time. New niches, Satisfying customers, getting faster communications, moving with more agility, all these are easier when one is small. All these are essential to succeed in the diverse, fast-moving global environment.

FUNCTIONAL TACTICS IN ACCOUNTING AND FINANCE

While most functional tactics guide implementation in the immediate future, the time frame for functional tactics in the area of finance varies, because these tactics direct the use of financial resources in support of the business strategy, long-term goals, and annual objectives. Financial tactics with longer time perspectives guide financial managers in long-term capital investment, debt financing, dividend allocation, and leveraging. Financial tactics designed to manage working capital and short-term assets have a more immediate focus. Exhibit 9–C highlights some key questions that financial tactics must answer.

EXHIBIT 9–C
Key Functional Tactics in Finance and Accounting

Source: From Terence P. Pare, "A New Tool for Managing Costs," Fortune, June 14, 1993, pp. 124–129. Copyright © 1993 Time Inc. All rights reserved.

Functional Tactic	Typical Questions That the Functional Tactics Should Answer
Capital acquisition	What is an acceptable cost of capital?
	What is the desired proportion of short- and long-term debt? Preferred and common equity?
	What balance is desired between internal and external funding?
	What risk and ownership restrictions are appropriate?
	What level and forms of leasing should be used?
Capital allocation	What are the priorities for capital allocation projects?
	On what basis should the final selection of projects be made?
	What level of capital allocation can be made by operating managers without higher approval?
Dividend and working capital management	What portion of earnings should be paid out as dividends?
	How important is dividend stability?
	Are things other than cash appropriate as dividends?
	What are the cash flow requirements? The minimum and maximum cash balances?
	How liberal/conservative should the credit policies be?
	What limits, payment terms, and collection procedures are necessary?
	What payment timing and procedure should be followed?

Accounting managers have seen their need to contribute value increasingly scrutinized. Traditional expectations centered around financial accounting; reporting requirements from bank and SEC entities and tax law compliance remain areas in which actions are dictated by outside governance. Managerial accounting, where managers are responsible for keeping records of costs and the use of funds within their company, has taken on increased strategic significance in the last decade. This change has involved two tactical areas: (1) how to account for costs of creating and providing their business's products and services, and (2) valuing the business, particularly among publicly traded companies.

Managerial cost accounting has traditionally provided information for managers using cost categories like those shown on the left side below. However, value chain advocates have been increasingly successful getting managers to seek activity-based cost accounting information like that shown on the right side below. In so doing, accounting is becoming a more critical, relevant source of information that truly benefits strategic management.

Traditional Cost Accounting In a Purchasing Department		Activity-Based Cost Accounting in the Same Purchasing Department	
Wages and salaries	$350,000	Evaluate supplier capabilities	$135,750
Employee benefits	115,000	Process purchase orders	82,100
Supplies	6,500	Expedite supplier deliveries	23,500
Travel	2,400	Expedite internal processing	15,840
Depreciation	17,000	Check quality of items purchased	94,300
Other fixed charges	124,000	Check incoming deliveries against purchase orders	48,450
Miscellaneous operating expenses	25,250	Resolve problems	110,000
		Internal administration	130,210
	$640,150		$640,150

Source: Adapted from information in Terence P. Paré, "A New Tool for Managing Costs," *Fortune*, June 14, 1993, pp. 124–29. *Fortune*, © 1993, Time, Inc. All rights reserved.

FUNCTIONAL TACTICS IN RESEARCH AND DEVELOPMENT

With the increasing rate of technological change in most competitive industries, research and development (R&D) has assumed a key strategic role in many firms. In the technology-intensive computer and pharmaceutical industries, for example, firms typically spend between 4 and 6 percent of their sales dollars on R&D. In other industries, such as the hotel/motel and construction industries, R&D spending is less than 1 percent of sales. Thus, functional R&D tactics may be more critical instruments of the business strategy in some industries than in others.

Exhibit 9–D illustrates the types of questions addressed by R&D tactics. First, R&D tactics should clarify whether basic research or product development research will be emphasized. Several major oil companies now have solar energy subsidiaries in which basic research is emphasized, while the smaller oil companies emphasize product development research.

The choice of emphasis between basic research and product development also involves the time horizon for R&D efforts. Should these efforts be focused on the near term or the long term? The solar energy subsidiaries of the major oil companies have long-term per-

EXHIBIT 9–D
Key Functional Tactics in R&D

R&D Decision Area	Typical Questions That the Functional Tactics Should Answer
Basic research versus product and process development	To what extent should innovation and breakthrough research be emphasized? In relation to the emphasis on product development, refinement, and modification?
	What critical operating processes need R&D attention?
	What new projects are necessary to support growth?
Time horizon	Is the emphasis short term or long term?
	Which orientation best supports the business strategy? The marketing and production strategy?
Organizational fit	Should R&D be done in-house or contracted out?
	Should R&D be centralized or decentralized?
	What should be the relationship between the R&D units and product managers? Marketing managers? Production managers?
Basic R&D posture	Should the firm maintain an offensive posture, seeking to lead innovation in its industry?
	Should the firm adopt a defensive posture, responding to the innovations of its competitors?

spectives, while the smaller oil companies focus on creating products now in order to establish a competitive niche in the growing solar industry.

R&D tactics also involve organization of the R&D function. For example, should R&D work be conducted solely within the firm, or should portions of that work be contracted out? A closely related issue is whether R&D should be centralized or decentralized. What emphasis should be placed on process R&D versus product R&D?

Decisions on all of the above questions are influenced by the firm's R&D posture, which can be offensive or defensive, or both. If that posture is offensive, as is true for small high-technology firms, the firm will emphasize technological innovation and new product development as the basis for its future success. This orientation entails high risks (and high payoffs) and demands considerable technological skill, forecasting expertise, and the ability to quickly transform innovations into commercial products.

A defensive R&D posture emphasizes product modification and the ability to copy or acquire new technology. Converse Shoes is a good example of a firm with such an R&D posture. Faced with the massive R&D budgets of Nike and Reebok, Converse placed R&D emphasis on bolstering the product life cycle of its prime products (particularly canvas shoes).

Large companies with some degree of technological leadership often use a combination of offensive and defensive R&D strategy. GE in the electrical industry, IBM in the computer industry, and Du Pont in the chemical industry all have a defensive R&D posture for currently available products *and* an offensive R&D posture in basic, long-term research.

FUNCTIONAL TACTICS IN HUMAN RESOURCE MANAGEMENT (HRM)

The strategic importance of HRM tactics received widespread endorsement in the 1990s. HRM tactics aid long-term success in the development of managerial talent and competent employees; the creation of systems to manage compensation or regulatory concerns; and

EXHIBIT 9–E
Key Functional Tactics in HRM

Functional Tactic	Typical Questions That HRM Tactics Should Answer
Recruitment, selection, and orientation	What key human resources are needed to support the chosen strategy?
	How do we recruit these human resources?
	How sophisticated should our selection process be?
	How should we introduce new employees to the organization?
Career development and training	What are our future human resource needs?
	How can we prepare our people to meet these needs?
	How can we help our people develop?
Compensation	What levels of pay are appropriate for the tasks we require?
	How can we motivate and retain good people?
	How should we interpret our payment, incentive, benefit, and seniority policies?
Evaluation, discipline, and control	How often should we evaluate our people? Formally or informally?
	What disciplinary steps should we take to deal with poor performance or inappropriate behavior?
	In what ways should we "control" individual and group performance?
Labor relations and equal opportunity requirements	How can we maximize labor-management cooperation?
	How do our personnel practices affect women/minorities? Should we have hiring policies?

guiding the effective utilization of human resources to achieve both the firm's short-term objectives and employees' satisfaction and development. HRM tactics are helpful in the areas shown in Exhibit 9–E. The recruitment, selection, and orientation should establish the basic parameters for bringing new people into a firm and adapting them to "the way things are done" in the firm. The career development and training component should guide the action that personnel takes to meet the future human resources needs of the overall business strategy. Merrill Lynch, a major brokerage firm whose long-term corporate strategy is to become a diversified financial service institution, has moved into such areas as investment banking, consumer credit, and venture capital. In support of its long-term objectives, it has incorporated extensive early-career training and ongoing career development programs to meet its expanding need for personnel with multiple competencies. Larger organizations need HRM tactics that guide decisions regarding labor relations; EEOC requirements; and employee compensation, discipline, and control.

Current trends in HRM parallel the reorientation of managerial accounting by looking at their cost structure anew. HRM's "paradigm shift" involves looking at people expense as an investment in human capital. This involves looking at the business's value chain and the "value" of human resource components along the various links in that chain. One of the results of this shift in perspective has been the downsizing and outsourcing phenomena of the last quarter century. While this has been traumatic for millions of employees in companies worldwide, its underlying basis involves an effort to examine the use of "human capital" to create value in ways that maximize the human contribution. This scrutiny continues to challenge the HRM area to include recent major trends to outsource some or all HRM activities not regarded as part of a firm's core competence. The emerging implications for human resource management tactics may be a value-oriented perspective on the role of human resources in a business's value chain as suggested below.

Traditional HRM Ideas	Emerging HRM Ideas
Emphasis solely on physical skills	Emphasis on total contribution to the firm
Expectation of predictable, repetitious behavior	Expectation of innovative and creative behavior
Comfort with stability and conformity	Tolerance of ambiguity and change
Avoidance of responsibility and decision making	Accepting responsibility for making decisions
Training covering only specific tasks	Open-ended commitment; broad continuous development
Emphasis placed on outcomes and results	Emphasis placed on processes and means
High concern for quantity and throughput	High concern for total customer value
Concern for individual efficiency	Concern for overall effectiveness
Functional and subfunctional specialization	Cross-functional integration
Labor force seen as unnecessary expense	Labor force seen as critical investment
Workforce is management's adversary	Management and workforce are partners

Source: A. Miller, *Strategic Management*, p. 400. © 2002 by McGraw-Hill, Inc. Reproduced with the permission of The McGraw-Hill Companies.

To summarize, functional tactics reflect how each major activity of a firm contributes to the implementation of the business strategy. The specificity of functional tactics and the involvement of operating managers in their development help ensure understanding of and commitment to the chosen strategy. A related step in implementation is the development of policies that empower operating managers and their subordinates to make decisions and to act autonomously.

Chapter **Ten**

Implementing Strategy: Structure, Leadership, and Culture

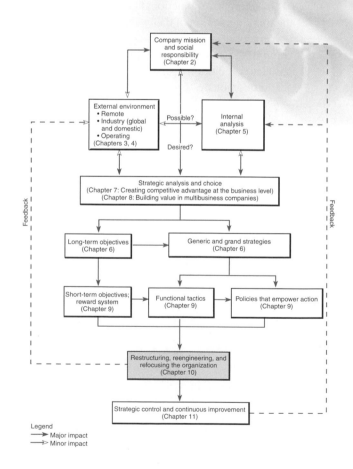

Company mission and social responsibility (Chapter 2)

External environment
• Remote
• Industry (global and domestic)
• Operating
(Chapters 3, 4)

Possible?

Desired?

Internal analysis (Chapter 5)

Strategic analysis and choice
(Chapter 7: Creating competitive advantage at the business level)
(Chapter 8: Building value in multibusiness companies)

Long-term objectives (Chapter 6)

Generic and grand strategies (Chapter 6)

Short-term objectives; reward system (Chapter 9)

Functional tactics (Chapter 9)

Policies that empower action (Chapter 9)

Restructuring, reengineering, and refocusing the organization (Chapter 10)

Strategic control and continuous improvement (Chapter 11)

Feedback

Feedback

Legend
→ Major impact
⇢ Minor impact

Until this point in the strategic management process, managers have maintained a decidedly market-oriented focus as they formulate strategies and begin implementation through action plans detailing the tactics and actions that will be taken in each functional activity. Now the process takes an organizational focus—getting the work of the business done efficiently and effectively so as to make the strategy work. What is the best way to organize ourselves to accomplish the mission? Where should leadership come from? What values should guide our activities each day? What should this organization and its people be like? These are some of the fundamental issues managers face as they turn to the heart of strategy implementation.

While the focus is internal, the firm must still consider external factors as well. The intense competition in today's global marketplace has led most companies to consider their structure, or how the activities within their business are conducted, with an unprecedented attentiveness to what that marketplace—customers, competitors, suppliers, distribution partners—suggests or needs from the "internal" organization. This chapter explores three basic "levers" through which managers can implement strategy. The first lever is structure—the basic way the firm's different activities are organized. Second is leadership, encompassing the need to establish direction, embrace change and build a team to execute the strategy. The third lever is culture—the shared values that create the norms of individual behavior and the tone of the organization.

Consider the situation new CEO Carly Fiorina faced at Hewlett Packard in the midst of a global recession. The unfortunate reality for her: HP's lumbering organization was losing touch with its global customers. Her response: As illustrated in Exhibit 10–1, Strategy in Action, Fiorina immediately dismantled the decentralized structure honed throughout HP's 64-year history. Pre-Fiorina, HP was a collection of 83 independently run units, each focused on a product such as scanners or security software. Fiorina collapsed those into four sprawling organizations. One so-called back-end unit develops and builds computers, and another focuses on printers and imaging equipment. The back-end divisions hand products off to two "front-end" sales and marketing groups that peddle the wares—one to consumers, the other to corporations. The theory: The new structure would boost collaboration, giving sales and marketing execs a direct pipeline to engineers so products are developed from the ground up to solve customer problems. This was the first time a company with thousands of product lines and scores of businesses attempted a front-back approach, a structure that requires laser focus and superb coordination.

Fiorina believed she had little choice lest the company experience a near-death experience like Xerox or, ten years earlier, IBM. The conundrum: how to put the full force of the company behind winning in its immediate fiercely competitive technology business when they must also cook up brand-new megamarkets? It's a riddle Fiorina said she could solve only by sweeping structural change that would ready HP for the next stage of the technology revolution, when companies latch on to the Internet to transform their operations. At its core lay a conviction that HP must become "ambidextrous" excelling at short-term execution while pursuing long-term visions that create new markets. In addition to changing HP's structure, Fiorina also sought to revamp its culture of creativity. Her plan for unleashing a new culture of creativity was what she called "inventing at the intersection." Until 2001, HP made stand-alone products and innovations from $20 ink cartridges to $3 million servers. To revolutionize HP's culture and approach, she launched three "cross-company initiatives"—wireless services, digital imaging, and printing—the first formal effort to get all of HP's separate and sometimes warring "tribes" working together.

Will it work? You are in the position of using hindsight to find out. Regardless, she earned high marks for zeroing in on HP's core problems and for having the courage to tackle them head-on. And, if it did, the then 46-year-old CEO would become a twenty-first century management hero for a reinvigorated HP becoming a blueprint for others trying to transform major technology companies into twenty-first century dynamos. Said Stanford

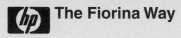 ## The Fiorina Way

When Fiorina arrived at HP, the company was a confederation of 83 autonomous product units reporting through four groups. She radically revamped the structure into two "back-end" divisions—one developing printers, scanners, and the like, and the other computers. These report to "front-end" groups that market and sell HP's wares. Here's how the overhaul stacks up:

The Old HP
Each product unit was responsible for its own profit/loss performance

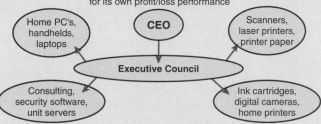

- Home PC's, handhelds, laptops
- CEO
- Scanners, laser printers, printer paper
- Executive Council
- Consulting, security software, unit servers
- Ink cartridges, digital cameras, home printers

The New HP

Carly Fiorina

➤ Authority
➤ Recommendations
➤ Ideas & innovations
➤ Products and information

Strategy Council
Nine fast-rising managers who advise the executive council on allocating money and people to growth initiatives.

Executive Council
Eight top lieutenants, including heads of the four front- and back-end groups.

Front end

Corporate Sales
$34 billion in annual revenues

Job Meet near-term financial targets by selling technology solutions to corporate clients. Keep back-end units abreast of what's hot.

Front end

Consumer Sales
$15 billion in annual revenues

Job Sell consumer gear with focus on meeting current year earnings and revenue goals. Let back end know of must-have products and features.

Back end

Printers
43% of annual production

Job Build new printing and imaging products to ensure HP's long-term growth. Track trends with help from front-end units.

Back end

Computers
57% of annual production

Job Focus on future success by making computers that companies and consumers want, with sales input from front-end.

Cross-Company Initiatives

Personnel from the front- and back-end groups collaborate on projects aimed at sniffing out new markets that will create growth.

Digital Imaging Make photos, drawings, and videos as easy to create, store, and send as e-mail.

Wireless Services Develop wireless technologies that will fuel sales of HP-made devices, ranging from handhelds to servers.

Commercial Printing Divert printing jobs from offset presses to Net-linked HP printers.

The Assessment

Benefits

Happier Customers Clients should find HP easier to deal with, since they'll work with just one account team.

Sales Boost HP should maximize its selling opportunities because account reps will sell all HP products, not just those from one division.

Real Solutions HP can sell its products in combination as "solutions"—instead of just PCs or printers—to companies facing e-business problems.

Financial Flexibility With all corporate sales under one roof, HP can measure the total value of a customer, allowing reps to discount some products and still maximize profits on the overall contract.

Risks

Overwhelmed with duties With so many products being made and sold by just four units, HP execs have more on their plates and could miss the details that keep products competitive

Poorer Execution When product managers oversaw everything from manufacturing to sales, they could respond quickly to changes. That will be harder with front- and back-end groups synching their plans only every few weeks.

Less Accountability Profit-and-loss responsibility is shared between the front- and back-end groups so no one person is on the hot seat. Finger-pointing and foot-dragging could replace HP's collegial cooperation.

Fewer Spending Controls With powerful division chiefs keeping a tight rein on the purse strings, spending rarely got out of hand in the old HP. In the fourth quarter, expenses soared as those lines of command broke down.

EXHIBIT 10–2
What a Difference a
Century Can Make

Source: "21st Century
Corporation," *BusinessWeek,*
August 28, 2000.

Contrasting views of the corporation:

Characteristic	20th Century	21st Century
ORGANIZATION	The Pyramid	The Web or Network
FOCUS	Internal	External
STYLE	Structured	Flexible
SOURCE OF STRENGTH	Stability	Change
STRUCTURE	Self-sufficiency	Interdependencies
RESOURCES	Atoms—physical assets	Bits—information
OPERATIONS	Vertical integration	Virtual integration
PRODUCTS	Mass production	Mass customization
REACH	Domestic	Global
FINANCIALS	Quarterly	Real-time
INVENTORIES	Months	Hours
STRATEGY	Top-down	Bottom-up
LEADERSHIP	Dogmatic	Inspirational
WORKERS	Employees	Employees and free agents
JOB EXPECTATIONS	Security	Personal growth
MOTIVATION	To compete	To build
IMPROVEMENTS	Incremental	Revolutionary
QUALITY	Affordable best	No compromise

professor Robert Burgelman at the time, "there isn't a major technology company in the world that has solved the problem she's trying to address, and we're all going to learn from her experience."[1]

What CEO Fiorina faced, and Professor Burgelman recognizes, is the vast difference between business organizations of the twentieth century and those of today. Exhibit 10–2 compares both on 18 different characteristics. The contrasts are striking, perhaps most so for leaders and managers faced with implementing strategies within them.

Fiorina offers a courageous example of a leader who recognized these compelling differences in the HP of the twentieth century and what the HP of the twenty-first century needed to be. And her decision to adopt a laserlike focus on three key "levers" within HP to attempt to make HP's strategy successful are reflected in the focus of this chapter. Her first lever was HP's *organizational structure,* which was so important from her point of view that, without major change, would mean a partial or complete failure of HP. Her second concern was *leadership,* both from herself and key managers throughout HP. Finally, she knew that the HP *culture,* in this case birth of a new one, was the third critical lever with which to make the new HP vision and strategy have a chance for success.

STRUCTURING AN EFFECTIVE ORGANIZATION

Exhibit 10–2 offers a useful starting point in examining effective organizational structure. In contrasting twentieth century and twenty-first century corporations on different characteristics, it offers a historical or evolutionary perspective on organizational attributes associated with successful strategy execution today and just a few years ago. Successful organization once required an internal focus, structured interaction, self-sufficiency, a top-down approach. Today and tomorrow, organizational structure reflects an external focus,

[1] "The Radical," *BusinessWeek,* February 19, 2001.

flexible interaction, interdependency, and a bottom-up approach, just to mention a few characteristics associated with strategy execution and success. Three fundamental trends are driving decisions about effective organizational structures in the twenty-first century: globalization, the Internet, and speed of decision making.

Globalization   The earlier example at Hewlett-Packard showed CEO Fiorina facing a desperate truth: HP's cumbersome organization was losing touch with its global customers. So she radically reorganized HP in part so multinational clients could go to just one sales and marketing group to buy everything from ink cartridges to supercomputers, in Buffalo or Bangkok. Over two-thirds of all industry either operates globally (e.g., computers, aerospace) or will soon do so. In the last ten years, the percentage of sales from outside the home market for these five companies grew dramatically:

	1995	2000	2005
General Electric	16.5%	35.1%	41.7%
Wal-Mart	0.0	18.8	32.2
McDonald's	46.9	65.5	71.8
Nokia	85.0	98.6	99.1
Toyota	44.6	53.5	61.2

The need for global coordination and innovation is forcing constant experimentation and adjustment to get the right mix of local initiative, information flow, leadership, and corporate culture. At Swedish-based Ericsson, top managers scrutinize compensation schemes to make managers pay attention to global performance and avoid turf battles, while also attending to their local operations. Companies like Dutch electronics giant Philips regularly move headquarters for different businesses to the hottest regions for new trends—the "high voltage" markets. Its digital set-top box is now in California, its audio business moved from Europe to Hong Kong.[2]

Global once meant selling goods in overseas markets. Next was locating operations in numerous countries. Today it will call on talents and resources wherever they can be found around the globe, just as it now sells worldwide. It may be based in the United States, do its software programming in New Delhi, its engineering in Germany, and its manufacturing in Indonesia. The ramifications for organizational structures are revolutionary.

The Internet   The Net gives everyone in the organization, or working with it, from the lowest clerk to the CEO to any supplier or customer, the ability to access a vast array of information—instantaneously, from anywhere. Ideas, requests, instructions zap around the globe in the blink of an eye. It allows the global enterprise with different functions, offices, and activities dispersed around the world to be seamlessly connected so that far-flung customers, employees, and suppliers can work together in real time. The result—coordination, communication and decision-making functions accomplished through and the purpose for traditional organizational structures become slow, inefficient, noncompetitive weights on today's organization.

Speed   Technology, or digitization, means removing human minds and hands from an organization's most routine tasks and replacing them with computers and networks. Digitizing everything from employee benefits to accounts receivable to product design cuts cost,

[2] "See the World, Erase Its Borders," *BusinessWeek,* August 28, 2000.

time, and payroll resulting in cost savings and vast improvements in speed. "Combined with the Internet, the speed of actions, deliberations, and information will increase dramatically," says Intel's Andy Grove. "You are going to see unbelievable speed and efficiencies," says Cisco's John Chambers, "with many companies about to increase productivity 20 percent to 40 percent per year." Leading-edge technologies will enable employees throughout the organization to seize opportunity as it arises. These technologies will allow employees, suppliers, and freelancers anywhere in the world to converse in numerous languages online without need for a translator to develop markets, new products, new processes. Again, the ramifications for organizational structures are revolutionary.

Whether technology assisted or not, globalization of business activity creates a potential sheer velocity of decisions that must be made which challenges traditional hierarchial organizational structures. A company like Cisco, for example, may be negotiating 50–60 alliances at one time due to the nature of its diverse operations. The speed at which these negotiations must be conducted and decisions made require a simple and accommodating organizational structure lest the opportunities may be lost.

Faced with these and other major trends, how should managers structure effective organizations? Consider these recent observations by *BusinessWeek* editors at the end of a year long research effort asking just the same question:

> The management of multinationals used to be a neat discipline with comforting rules and knowable best practices. But globalization and the arrival of the information economy have rapidly demolished all the old precepts. The management of global companies, which must innovate simultaneously and speed information through horizontal, global-spanning networks, has become a daunting challenge. Old, rigid hierarchies are out—and flat, speedy, virtual organizations are in. Teamwork is a must and compensation schemes have to be redesigned to reward team players. But aside from that bit of wisdom, you can throw out the textbooks.
>
> CEOs will have to custom-design their organizations based on their industry, their own corporate legacy, and their key global customers—and they may have to revamp more than once to get it right. Highly admired companies such as General Electric, Hewlett-Packard, ABB Ltd., and Ericsson have already been through several organizational reincarnations in the past decade to boost global competitiveness.[3]

Our research concurs with these findings by *BusinessWeek* editors—there is no one best organizational structure. At the same time, there are several useful guidelines and approaches that help answer this question which we will now cover in the next several sections.

Match Structure to Strategy

The recent changes at Hewlett-Packard in Exhibit 10–1, Strategy in Action, illustrate this fundamental guideline. CEO Fiorina adopted the difficult, career-risking path of creating a major new structure at HP because that new structure reflected the needs of HP's strategy for the twenty-first century. An easier alternative would have been to create a strategy compatible with the existing decentralized structure of 83 semiautonomous business units that had been in place for over half a century. While easier, however, the result would have been damaging to HP in the long run, perhaps even fatal, because strategic priorities and initiatives would have been guided by structural considerations, rather than the other way around.

[3] "The 21st Century Corporation," *BusinessWeek*, August 28, 2000.

The origins of this maxim come from a historical body of strategic management research[4] that examined how the evolution of a business over time and the degree of diversification from a firm's core business affected its choice of organizational structure. The primary organizational structures associated with this important research are still prevalent today—simple functional structures, geographical structures, multidivisional structures, and strategic business units.[5] Four basic conclusions were derived from this research:

1. *A single-product firm or single dominant business firm should employ a functional structure.* This structure allows for strong task focus through an emphasis on specialization and efficiency, while providing opportunity for adequate controls through centralized review and decision making.

2. *A firm in several lines of business that are somehow related should employ a multidivisional structure.* Closely related divisions should be combined into groups within this structure. When synergies (i.e., shared or linked activities) are possible within such a group, the appropriate location for staff influence and decision making is at the group level, with a lesser role for corporate-level staff. The greater the degree of diversity across the firm's businesses, the greater should be the extent to which the power of staff and decision-making authority is lodged within the divisions.

3. *A firm in several unrelated lines of business should be organized into strategic business units.* Although the strategic business unit structure resembles the multidivisional structure, there are significant differences between the two. With a strategic business unit structure, finance, accounting, planning, legal, and related activities should be centralized at the corporate office. Since there are no synergies across the firm's businesses, the corporate office serves largely as a capital allocation and control mechanism. Otherwise, its major decisions involve acquisitions and diverstitures. All operational and business-level strategic plans are delegated to the strategic business units.

4. *Early achievement of a strategy-structure fit can be a competitive advantage.* A competitive advantage is obtained by the first firm among competitors to achieve appropriate strategy-structure fit. That advantage will disappear as the firm's competitors also attain such a fit. Moreover, if the firm alters its strategy, its structure must obviously change as well. Otherwise, a loss of fit will lead to a competitive disadvantage for the firm.

These research-based guidelines were derived from twentieth century companies not yet facing the complex, dynamically changing environments we see today. So an easy conclusion would be to consider them of little use. That is not the case, however. First, the admonition to let strategy guide structure rather than the other way around is very im-

---

[4] Alfred D. Chandler, *Strategy and Structure* (Cambridge: MIT Press, 1962); Larry Wrigley, *Divisional Autonomy and Diversification,* doctoral dissertation, Harvard Business School, 1970; Richard Rumelt, "Diversification Strategy and Performance," *Strategic Management Journal* 3 (January–February 1982), pp. 359–69; Richard Rumelt, *Strategy, Structure and Economic Performance* (Boston: HBS Press, 1986). Rumelt used a similar, but more detailed classification scheme; D. A. Nathanson and J. S. Cassano, "Organization, Diversity, and Performance," *Wharton's Magazine* 6 (1982), pp. 19–26; and Christopher A. Bartlett and Sumantra Ghoshal, "Matrix Management: Not a Structure, a Frame of Mind," *Harvard Business Review* 68, no. 4 (1990), pp. 138–45; V. R. Galbraith and R. K. Kazanjian, *Strategy Implementation: Structure, Systems & Processes* (St. Paul, MN: West Publishing, 1986).
[5] Each primary structure is diagrammed and described in detail along with the advantages and disadvantages historically associated with each in an appendix to this chapter.

portant today. While seemingly simple and obvious, resistance to changing existing structures—"the way we do things around here"—continues to be a major challenge to new strategies in many organizations even today as HP again illustrates. Second, the notion that firms evolve over time from a single product/service focus to multiple products/services and markets requiring different structures is an important reality to accommodate when implementing growth strategies. Finally, many firms today have found value in multiple structures operating simultaneously in their company. People may be assigned within the company as part of a functional structure, but they work on teams or other groupings that operate outside the primary functional structure. We will explore this practice in a subsequent section, but the important point here is that while new and important hybrid organizational structures have proven essential to strategy implementation in the twenty-first century, these same "innovative" firms incorporate these "older" primary organizational structures in the fabric of their contemporary organizational structure.

Balance the Demands for Control/Differentiation with the Need for Coordination/Integration

Specialization of work and effort allows a unit to develop greater expertise, focus, and efficiency. So it is that some organizations adopt functional, or similar structures. Their strategy depends on dividing different activities within the firm into logical, common groupings—sales, operations, administration, or geography—so that each set of activity can be done most efficiently. Control of sets of activities is at a premium. Dividing activities in this manner, sometimes called "differentiation," is an important structural decision. At the same time, these separate activities, however they are differentiated, need to be coordinated and integrated back together as a whole so the business functions effectively. Demands for control and the coordination needs differ across different types of businesses and strategic situations.

The rise of a consumer culture around the world has led brand marketers to realize they need to take a multidomestic approach to be more responsive to local preferences. Coca-Cola, for example, used to control its products rigidly from its Atlanta headquarters. But managers have found in some markets consumers thirst for more than Coke, Diet Coke, and Sprite. So Coke has altered its structure to reduce the need for control in favor of greater coordination/integration in local markets where local managers independently launch new flavored drinks. At the same time, GE, the paragon of new age organization, had altered its GE Medical Systems organization structure to allow local product managers to handle everything from product design to marketing. This emphasis on local coordination and reduced central control of product design led managers obsessed with local rivalries to design and manufacture similar products for different markets—a costly and wasteful duplication of effort. So GE reintroduced centralized control of product design, with input from a worldwide base of global managers, and their customers, resulting in the design of several single global products produced quite cost competitively to sell worldwide. GE's need for control of product design outweighed the coordination needs of locally focused product managers.[6] At the same time, GE obtained input from virtually every customer or potential customer worldwide before finalizing the product design of several initial products, suggesting that it rebalanced in favor of more control, but organizationally coordinated input from global managers and customers so as to ensure a better potential series of medical scanner for hospitals worldwide.

[6] See the World, Erase Its Borders," *BusinessWeek,* August 28, 2000.

Restructure to Emphasize and Support Strategically Critical Activities

Restructuring has been the buzzword of global enterprise for the last 10 years. Its contemporary meaning is multifaceted. At the heart of the restructuring trend is the notion that some activities within a business's value chain are more critical to the success of the business's strategy than others. Wal-Mart's organizational structure is designed to ensure that its impressive logistics and purchasing competitive advantages operate flawlessly. Coordinating daily logistical and purchasing efficiencies among separate stores lets Wal-Mart lead the industry in profitability yet sell retail for less than many competitors buy the same merchandise at wholesale. Motorola's organizational structure is designed to protect and nurture its legendary R&D and new product development capabilities—spending over twice the industry average in R&D alone each year. Motorola's R&D emphasis continually spawns proprietary technologies that support its technology-based competitive advantage. Coca-Cola emphasizes the importance of distribution activities, advertising, and retail support to its bottlers in its organizational structure. All three of these companies emphasize very different parts of the value chain process, but they are extraordinarily successful in part because they have designed their organizational structures to emphasize and support strategically critical activities. Exhibit 10–3, Strategy in Action, provides some guidelines that should influence how an organization is structured, depending on which among five different sources of competitive advantage are emphasized in its strategy.

Two critical considerations arise when restructuring the organization to emphasize and support strategically critical activities. First, managers need to make the strategically critical activities the central building blocks for designing organization structure. Those activities should be identified and separated as much as possible into self-contained parts of the organization. Then the remaining structure must be designed so as to ensure timely integration with other parts of the organization.

While this is easily proposed, managers need to recognize that strategically relevant activities may still reside in different parts of the organization, particularly in functionally organized structures. Support activities like finance, engineering, or information processing are usually self-contained units, often outside the unit around which core competencies are built. This often results in an emphasis on departments obsessed with performing their own tasks more than emphasizing the key results (customer satisfaction, differentiation, low costs, speed) the business as a whole seeks. So the second consideration is to design the organizational structure so that it helps coordinate and integrate these support activities to (1) maximize their support of strategy-critical primary activities in the firm's value chain and (2) does so in a way to minimize the costs for support activities and the time spent on internal coordination. Managerial efforts to do this in the 1990s have placed reengineering, downsizing, and outsourcing as prominent tools for strategists restructuring their organizations.

Reengineer Strategic Business Processes

Business process reengineering (BPR), popularized by consultants Michael Hammer and James Champy,[7] is one of the more popular methods by which organizations worldwide are undergoing restructuring efforts to remain competitive in the twenty-first century. BPR is intended to place the decision-making authority that is most relevant to the customer closer to the customer, in order to make the firm more responsive to the needs of the customer. This is accomplished through a form of empowerment, facilitated revamping organizational structure.

Business reengineering reduces fragmentation by crossing traditional departmental lines and reducing overhead to compress formerly separate steps and tasks that are strategically intertwined in the process of meeting customer needs. This "process orientation," rather than a traditional functional orientation, becomes the perspective around which various activities

---

[7] Michael Hammer and James Champy, *Reengineering the Corporation* (New York: HarperBusiness, 1993).

One of the key things business managers should keep in mind when restructuring their organizations is to devise the new structure so that it emphasizes strategically critical activities within the business's value chain. This means that the structure should allow those activities to have considerable autonomy over issues that influence their operating excellence and timeliness; they should be in a position to easily coordinate with other parts of the business—to get decisions made fast.

Below are five different types of critical activities that may be at the heart of a business's effort to build and sustain competitive advantage. Beside each one are typical conditions that will affect and shape the nature of the organization's structure:

Potential Strategic Priority and Critical Activities	Concomitant Conditions That May Affect or Place Demands on the Organizational Structure and Operating Activities to Build Competitive Advantage
1. Compete as low-cost provider of goods or services.	Broadens market. Requires longer production runs and fewer product changes. Requires special-purpose equipment and facilities.
2. Compete as high-quality provider.	Often possible to obtain more profit per unit, and perhaps more total profit from a smaller volume of sales. Requires more quality-assurance effort and higher operating cost. Requires more precise equipment, which is more expensive. Requires highly skilled workers, necessitating higher wages and greater training efforts.
3. Stress customer service.	Requires broader development of servicepeople and service parts and equipment. Requires rapid response to customer needs or changes in customer tastes, rapid and accurate information system, careful coordination. Requires a higher inventory investment.
4. Provide rapid and frequent introduction of new products.	Requires versatile equipment and people. Has higher research and development costs. Has high retraining costs and high tooling and changeover costs. Provides lower volumes for each product and fewer opportunities for improvements due to the learning curve.
5. Seek vertical integration.	Enables firm to control more of the process. May not have economies of scale at some stages of process. May require high capital investment as well as technology and skills beyond those currently available within the firm.

and tasks are then grouped to create the building blocks of the organization's structure. This is usually accomplished by assembling a multifunctional, multilevel team that begins by identifying customer needs and how the customer wants to deal with the firm. Customer focus must permeate all phases. Companies that have successfully reengineered their operations around strategically critical business processes have pursued the following steps:[8]

- Develop a flowchart of the total business process, including its interfaces with other value chain activities.

[8] Judy Wade, "How to Make Reengineering Really Work," *Harvard Business Review* 71, no. 6 (November–December 1993), pp. 119–31.

- Try to simplify the process first, eliminating tasks and steps where possible and analyzing how to streamline the performance of what remains.

- Determine which parts of the process can be automated (usually those that are repetitive, time-consuming, and require little thought or decision); consider introducing advanced technologies that can be upgraded to achieve next-generation capability and provide a basis for further productivity gains down the road.

- Evaluate each activity in the process to determine whether it is strategy-critical or not. Strategy-critical activities are candidates for benchmarking to achieve best-in-industry or best-in-world performance status.

- Weigh the pros and cons of outsourcing activities that are noncritical or that contribute little to organizational capabilities and core competencies.

- Design a structure for performing the activities that remain; reorganize the personnel and groups who perform these activities into the new structure.

When asked about his networking-oriented structure that helped revitalize IBM, former IBM CEO Gerstner responded: "It's called *reengineering.* It's called *getting competitive.* It's called *reducing cycle time and cost, flattening organizations, increasing customer responsiveness.* All of these require a collaboration with the customer and with suppliers and with vendors."

Downsize and Self-Manage: Force Decisions to Operating Level

Reengineering and a value orientation have led managers to scrutinize even further the way their organizational structures are crucial to strategy implementation. That scrutiny has led to downsizing, outsourcing, and self-management as three important themes influencing the organizational structures into the twenty-first century. *Downsizing* is eliminating the number of employees, particularly middle management, in a company. The arrival of a global marketplace, information technology, and intense competition caused many companies to reevaluate middle management activities to determine just what value was really being added to the company's products and services. The result of this scrutiny, along with continuous improvements in information processing technology, has been widespread downsizing in the number of management personnel in thousands of companies worldwide. These companies often eliminate whole levels of management. General Electric went from 400,000 to 280,000 employees in the last decade while its sales tripled and its profit rose fivefold. Former CEO Jack Welch's observations about GE's downsizing and the results of *BusinessWeek*'s survey of companies worldwide that have been actively downsizing (which attempts to extract guidelines for downsizing) are shown in Strategy in Action Exhibit 10–4.

One of the outcomes of downsizing was increased *self-management* at operating levels of the company. Cutbacks in the number of management people left those that remained with more work to do. The result was that they had to give up a good measure of control to workers, and they had to rely on those workers to help out. Spans of control, traditionally thought to maximize under 10 people, have become much larger due to information technology, running "lean and mean," and delegation to lower levels. Ameritech, one of the Baby Bells, has seen its spans of control rise to as much as 30 to 1 in some divisions because most of the people that did staff work—financial analysts, assistant managers, and so on—have disappeared. This delegation, also known as empowerment, is accomplished through concepts like self-managed work groups, reengineering, and automation. It is also seen through efforts to create distinct businesses within a business—conceiving a business

BusinessWeek GE used to have things like department managers, subsection managers, unit managers, supervisors. We're driving those titles out . . . We used to go from the CEO to sectors, to groups, to businesses. We now go from the CEO to businesses. Nothing else.

—Jack Welch

It's hard to find a major corporation that hasn't downsized in recent years. But simple reductions in staffing don't make for lean management. Here's a checklist, developed by *BusinessWeek* from interviews with executives and consultants, that may tell you if your company needs a diet.

Company Characteristic	Analysis
1. Layers of management between CEO and the shop floor.	Some companies, such as Ameritech, now have as few as four or five where as many as 12 had been common. More than six is most likely too many.
2. Number of employees managed by the typical executive.	At lean companies, spans of control range up to one manager to 30 staffers. A ratio of lower than 1:10 is a warning of arterial sclerosis.
3. Amount of work cut out by your downsizing.	Eliminating jobs without cutting out work can bring disaster. A downsizing should be accompanied by at least a 25 percent reduction in the number of tasks performed. Some lean companies have hit 50 percent.
4. Skill levels of the surviving management group.	Managers must learn to accept more responsibility and to eliminate unneeded work. Have you taught them how?
5. Size of your largest profit center by number of employees.	Break down large operating units into smaller profit centers—less than 500 employees is a popular cutoff to gain the economies of entrepreneurship and offset the burdens of scale.
6. Post-downsizing size of staff at corporate headquarters.	The largest layoffs, on a percentage basis, should be at corporate headquarters. It is often the most overstaffed—and the most removed from customers.

Source: "The 21st Century Corporation," *BusinessWeek,* August 28, 2000.

as a confederation of many "small" businesses, rather than one large, interconnected business. Whatever the terminology, the idea is to push decision making down in the organization by allowing major management decisions to be made at operating levels. The result is often the elimination of up to half the levels of management previously existing in an organizational structure.

Allow Multiple Structures to Operate Simultaneously within the Organization to Accommodate Products, Geography, Innovation and Customers

The *matrix organization* described in this chapter's Appendix was one of the early structural attempts to do this so that skills and resources could be better assigned and used within a large company. People typically had a permanent assignment to a certain organizational unit, usually a functional or staff department, yet they were also frequently assigned to work in another project or activity at the same time. For example, a product development project

EXHIBIT 10–5
The Product-Team
Structure

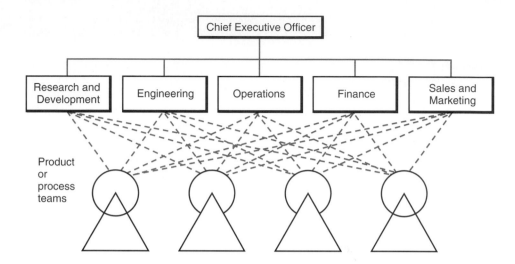

may need a market research specialist for several months and a financial analyst for a week. It was tried by many companies, and is still in use today. The dual chains of command, particularly given a temporary assignment approach, proved problematic for some organizations, particularly in an international context complicated by distance, language, time, and culture.

The *product-team structure* emerged as an alternative to the matrix approach to simplify and amplify the focus of resources on a narrow but strategically important product, project, market, customer or innovation. Exhibit 10–5 illustrates how the product-team structure looks.

The product-team structure assigns functional managers and specialists (e.g., engineering, marketing, financial, R&D, operations) to a new product, project, or process team that is empowered to make major decisions about their product. The team is usually created at the inception of the new product idea, and they stay with it indefinitely if it becomes a viable business. Instead of being assigned on a temporary basis, as in the matrix structure, team members are assigned permanently to that team in most cases. This results in much lower coordination costs and, since every function is represented, usually reduces the number of management levels above the team level needed to approve team decisions.

It appears that product teams formed at the beginning of product-development processes generate cross-functional understanding that irons out early product or process design problems. They also reduce costs associated with design, manufacturing, and marketing, while typically speeding up innovation and customer responsiveness because authority rests with the team allowing decisions to be made more quickly. That ability to make speedier, cost-saving decisions has the added advantage of eliminating the need for one or more management layers above the team level, which would traditionally have been in place to review and control these types of decisions. While seemingly obvious, it has only recently become apparent that those additional management layers were also making these decisions with less firsthand understanding of the issues involved than the cross-functional team members brought to the product or process in the first place. Exhibit 10–6, Strategy in Action, gives examples of a product-team approach at several well-known companies and some of the advantages that appear to have accrued.

Take Advantage of Being a Virtual Organization

True twenty-first century corporations will increasingly see their structure become an elaborate network of external and internal relationships. This organizational phenomenon has been termed the *virtual organization,* which is defined as a temporary network of inde-

BusinessWeek Building teams is a new organization art form for Corporate America. Getting people to work together successfully has become a critical managerial skill. Those companies that learn the secrets of creating cross-functional teams are winning the battle for global market share and profits. Those that don't are losing out.

One of the most effective uses of the cross-functional teams in in the area of product development—everything from designing cars to developing new prescription drugs. This kind of teamwork not only increases efficiency but boosts innovation—the holy grail of companies hoping to produce the Next Big Thing in their industry. General Motors, for one, chalked up big wins since setting up a collaborative engineering system in 2000 that allows GM employees and external auto parts suppliers to share product design information. Previously, GM had no way of coordinating its complex designs across its 14 engineering sites scattered across the world, plus the dozens of partners who design subsystems. Now, GM's collaboration system serves as a centralized clearinghouse for all the design data. More than 16,000 designers and other workers use the new Web system from Electronic Data Systems Corp. to share 3-D designs and keep track of parts and subassemblies. The system automatically updates the master design when changes are finalized so everyone is on the same page. The result: GM has slashed the time it takes to complete a full mock-up of a car from 12 weeks to two. The time saved by online collaboration frees up workers to think more creatively—mocking up three or four more alternative designs per car.

Consider Modicon Inc., a North Andover (Massachusetts) maker of automation-control equipment with annual revenues of $300 million. Instead of viewing product development as a task of the engineering function, President Paul White defined it more broadly as a process that would involve a team of 15 managers from engineering, manufacturing, marketing, sales, and finance. By working together, Modicon's team avoided costly delays from disagreements and misunderstandings. "In the past," says White, "an engineering team would have worked on this alone with some dialogue from marketing. Manufacturing wouldn't get involved until the design was brought into the factory. Now, all the business issues are right on the table from the beginning." The change allowed Modicon to bring six software products to market in one-third the time it would normally take. The company still has a management structure organized by function. But many of the company's 900 employees are involved in up to 30 teams that span several functions and departments. Predicts White: "In five years, we'll still have some formal functional structure, but people will probably feel free enough to spend the majority of their time outside their functions."

Eastman Chemical Co., the $3.5 billion unit of Eastman Kodak Co. recently spun off as a stand-alone company, replaced several of its senior vice-presidents in charge of the key functions with "self-directed work teams." Instead of having a head of manufacturing, for example, the company uses a team consisting of all its plant managers. "It was the most dramatic change in the company's 70-year history," maintains Ernest W. Deavenport Jr., president of Eastman Chemical. "It makes people take off their organizational hats and put on their team hats. It gives people a much broader perspective and forces decision-making down at least another level." In creating the new organization, the 500 senior managers agreed that the primary role of the functions was to support Eastman's business in chemicals, plastics, fibers, and polymers. "A function does not and should not have a mission of its own," insists Deavenport. Common sense? Of course. But over the years, the functional departments had grown strong and powerful, as they have in many organizations, often at the expense of the overall company as they fought to protect and build turf. Now, virtually all of the company's managers work on at least one cross-functional team, and most work on two or more on a daily basis. For example, Tom O. Nethery, a group vice-president, runs an industrial-business group. But he also serves on three other teams that deal with such diverse issues as human resources, cellulose technology, and product-support services.

Source: "The New Teamwork," *BusinessWeek,* Feb. 18, 2002.

pendent companies—suppliers, customers, subcontractors, even competitors—linked primarily by information technology to share skills, access to markets, and costs.[9] Outsourcing along with strategic alliances are integral in making a virtual organization work. Globalization has accelerated the use of and need for the virtual organization.

Outsourcing was an early driving force for the virtual organization trend. Dell does not make PCs. Cisco doesn't make its world renowned routers. Motorola doesn't make cell phones. Sony makes Apple's low-end PowerBook computers. *Outsourcing* is simply obtaining

[9] W. H. Davidow and M. S. Malone, *The Virtual Corporation* (New York: Harper, 1992).

EXHIBIT 10–7
General Motors: Alliances with Competitors

Source: General Motors Corporation Annual Reports; "Carmakers Take Two Routes to Global Growth," *Financial Times* (July 11, 2000), p. 19.

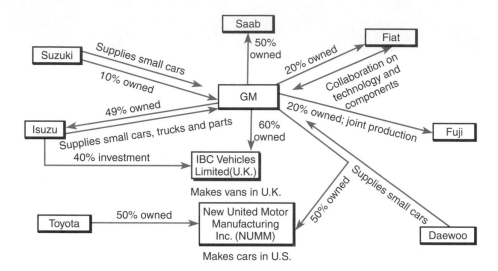

work previously done by employees inside the companies from sources outside the company. Managers have found that as they attempt to restructure their organizations, particularly if they do so from a business process orientation, numerous activities can often be found in their company that are not "strategically critical activities." This has particularly been the case of numerous staff activities and administrative control processes previously the domain of various middle management levels in an organization. But it can also refer to primary activities that are steps in their business's value chain—purchasing, shipping, making certain parts, and so on. Further scrutiny has led managers to conclude that these activities not only add little or no value to the product or services, but that they can be done much more cost effectively (and competently) by other businesses specializing in these activities. If this is so, then the business can enhance its competitive advantage by outsourcing the activities. Many organizations have outsourced information processing, various personnel activities, and production of parts that can be done better outside the company. Outsourcing, then, can be a source of competitive advantage and result in a leaner, flatter organizational structure.

Strategic alliances, some long-term and others for very short periods, with suppliers, partners, contractors, and other providers of world class capabilities allow partners to the alliance to focus on what they do best, farm out everything else, and quickly provide value to the customer. Engaging in alliances, whether long term or one time, lets each participant take advantage of fleeting opportunities quickly, usually without tying up vast amounts of capital. FedEx and the U.S. Postal Service have formed an alliance—FedEx planes carry USPS next-day letters and USPS delivers FedEx ground packages—to allow both to challenge their common rival, UPS. Exhibit 10–7 shows how General Motors, in its effort to become more competitive globally, has entered into numerous alliances with competitors. Cisco owns only two of 34 plants that produce its routers, and over 50 percent of all orders fulfilled by Cisco are done without a Cisco employee being involved.

Web-Based Organizations   As we noted at the beginning of this section, globalization has accelerated many changes in the way organizations are structured, and that is certainly the case in driving the need to become part of a virtual organization or make use of one. Technology, particularly driven by the Internet, has and will be a major driver of the virtual organization. Commenting on technology's impact on Cisco, John Chambers observed that with all its outsourcing and strategic alliances, roughly 90 percent of all orders come into Cisco without ever being touched by human hands. "To my customers, it looks like one big virtual plant where my suppliers and inventory systems are directly tied into our virtual or-

EXHIBIT 10–8
From Traditional Structure to B-Web Structure

Source: Adapted and reprinted by permission of Harvard Business School Press. From *Digital Capital: Harnessing the Power of Business Webs* by Don Tapscott, David Ticoll, and Alex Lowy, Boston, MA 1993, p. 18. Copyright © 1993 by Don Tapscott, David Ticoll, and Alex Lowy; all rights reserved.

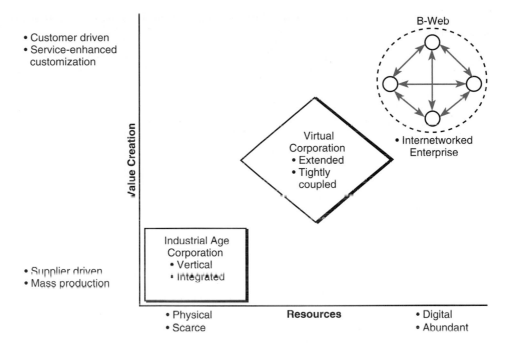

ganization," he said. "That will be the norm in the future. Everything will be completely connected, both within a company and between companies. The people who get that will have a huge competitive advantage."

The Web's contribution electronically has simultaneously become the best analogy in explaining the future virtual organization. So it is not just the Web as in the Internet, but a web-like shape of successful organizational structures in the future. If there are a pair of images that symbolize the vast changes at work, they are the pyramid and the web. The organizational chart of large-scale enterprise had long been defined as a pyramid of ever-shrinking layers leading to an omnipotent CEO at its apex. The twenty-first century corporation, in contrast, is far more likely to look like a web: a flat, intricately woven form that links partners, employees, external contractors, suppliers, and customers in various collaborations. The players will grow more and more interdependent. Fewer companies will try to master all the disciplines necessary to produce and market their goods but will instead outsource skills—from research and development to manufacturing—to outsiders who can perform those functions with greater efficiency.[10] Exhibit 10–8 illustrates this evolution in organization structure to what it calls the B-Web, a truly Internet-driven form of organization designed to deliver speed, customized service-enhanced products to savvy customers from an integrated virtual B-Web organization pulling together abundant, world-class resources digitally.

Managing this intricate network of partners, spin-off enterprises, contractors, and free-lancers will be as important as managing internal operations. Indeed, it will be hard to tell the difference. All of these constituents will be directly linked in ways that will make it nearly impossible for outsiders to know where an individual firm begins and where it ends. "Companies will be much more molecular and fluid," predicts Don Tapscott, co-author of *Digital Capital*. "They will be autonomous business units connected not necessarily by a big building but across geographies all based on networks. The boundaries of the firm will be not only fluid or blurred but in some cases hard to define."[11]

[10] "The 21st Century Organization," *BusinessWeek,* August 28, 2000.
[11] Ibid.

Remove Structural Barriers and Create a Boundaryless, Ambidextrous Learning Organization

The evolution of the virtual organizational structure as an integral mechanism managers use to implement strategy has brought with it recognition of the central role knowledge plays in this process. *Knowledge* may be in terms of operating know-how, relationships with and knowledge of customer networks, technical knowledge upon which products or processes are based or will be, relationships with key people or a certain person than can get things done quickly, and so forth. Exhibit 10–9, Strategy in Action, shares how McKinsey organizational expert Lowell Bryan sees this shaping future organizational structure with managers becoming knowledge "nodes" through which intricate networks of personal relationships—inside and outside the formal organization—are constantly coordinated to bring together relevant know-how and successful action.

Management icon Jack Welch coined the term *boundaryless* organization, to characterize what he attempted to make GE become in order for it to be able to generate knowledge, share knowledge and get knowledge to the places it could be best used to provide superior value. A key component of this concept was erasing internal divisions so the people in GE could work across functional, business, and geographic boundaries to achieve an integrated diversity—the ability to transfer the best ideas, the most developed knowledge, and the most valuable people quickly, easily, and freely throughout GE. Here is his description:

> Boundaryless behavior is the soul of today's GE . . . Simply put, people seem compelled to build layers and walls between themselves and others, and that human tendency tends to be magnified in large, old institutions like ours. These walls cramp people, inhibit creativity, waste time, restrict vision, smother dreams and above all, slow things down . . . Boundaryless behavior shows up in actions of a woman from our Appliances Business in Hong Kong helping NBC with contacts needed to develop satellite television service in Asia . . . And finally, boundaryless behavior means exploiting one of the unmatchable advantages a multibusiness GE has over almost any other company in the world. Boundaryless behavior combines 12 huge global businesses—each number one or number two in its markets—into a vast laboratory whose principal product is new ideas, coupled with a common commitment to spread them throughout the Company.

> —Letter to Shareholders, Jack Welch
> Chairman, General Electric Company, 1981–2001

A shift from what Subramanian Rangan calls *exploitation to exploration* indicates the growing importance of organizational structures that enable a *learning organization* to allow global companies the chance to build competitive advantage.[12] Rather than going to markets to exploit brands or for inexpensive resources, in Rangan's view, the smart ones are going global to learn. This shift in the intent of the structure, then, is to seek information, to create new competences. Demand in another part of the world could be a new product trendsetter at home. So a firm's structure needs to be organized to enable learning, to share knowledge, to create opportunities to create it. Others look to companies like 3M or Procter & Gamble that allow slack time, new product champions, manager mentors—all put in place in the structure to provide resources, support, and advocacy for cross-functional collaboration leading to innovation in new product development, the generation and use of new ideas. This perspective is similar to the boundaryless notion—accommodate the speed of change and therefore opportunity by freeing up historical constraints found in traditional organizational approaches. So having structures that emphasize coordination over control, that allow flexibility (are *ambidextrous*), that emphasize the value and importance of informal relationships

[12] Subramanian Rangan, *A Prism on Globalization* (Fountainebleau, FR.: INSEAD, 1999).

BusinessWeek Lowell Bryan, a senior partner and director at consultancy McKinsey & Co., leads McKinsey's global industries practice and is the author of *Race for the World: Strategies to Build a Great Global Firm* and *Market Unbound: Unleashing Global Capitalism*.

Q: How will global companies be managed in the twenty-first century?

A: Describing it is hard because the language of management is based on command-and-control structures and "who reports to whom." Now, the manager is more of a network operator. He is part of a country team and part of a business unit. Some companies don't even have country managers anymore.

Q: What is the toughest challenge in managing global companies today?

A: Management structures are now three-dimensional. You have to manage by geography, products, and global customers. The real issue is building networked structures between those three dimensions. That is the state of the art. It's getting away from classic power issues. Managers are becoming nodes, which are part of geographical structures and part of a business unit.

Q: What are the telltale questions that reflect whether a company is truly global?

A: CEOs should ask themselves four questions: First, how do people interact with each other: Do employees around the world know each other and communicate regularly? Second, do management processes reflect a network or an old-style hierarchy? Third, is information provided to everyone simultaneously? And fourth, is the company led from the bottom up, not the top down?

Q: Why do multinationals that have operated for decades in foreign markets need to overhaul their management structures?

A: The sheer velocity of decisions that must be made is impossible in a company depending on an old-style vertical hierarchy. Think of a company [like] Cisco that is negotiating 50 to 60 alliances at one time. The old corporate structures [can't] integrate these decisions fast enough. The CEO used to be involved in every acquisition, every alliance. Now, the role of the corporate center is different. Real business decisions move down to the level of business units.

Q: If there is not clear hierarchy, and managers have conflicting opinions, how does top management know when to take a decision? Doesn't that raise the risk of delay and inaction?

A: In the old centralized model, there was no communication. If you have multiple minds at work on a problem, the feedback is much quicker. If five managers or "nodes" in the network say something is not working right, management better sit up and take notice.

Q: Are there any secrets to designing a new management architecture?

A: Many structures will work. [H]aving the talent and capabilities you need to make a more fluid structure work [is key]. [But] it's much harder to do. The key is to create horizontal flow across silos to meet customers needs. The question is how you network across these silos. [G]etting people to work together [is paramount]. That's the revolution that is going on now.

Q: What is the role of the CEO?

A: The CEO is the architect. He puts in place the conditions to let the organization innovate. No one is smart enough to do it alone anymore. Corporate restructuring should liberate the company from the past. As you break down old formal structures, knowledge workers are the nodes or the glue that hold different parts of the company together. They are the network. Nodes are what it is all about.

Q: How do you evaluate performance in such a squishy system?

A: The role of the corporate center is to worry about talent and how people do relative to each other. Workers build a set of intangibles around who they are. If they are not compensated for their value-added, they will go somewhere else.

Source: *BusinessWeek,* August 28, 2000.

and interaction over formal systems, techniques, and controls are all characteristics associated with what are seen as effective structures for the twenty-first century.

Redefine the Role of Corporate Headquarters from Control to Support and Coordination

The role of corporate management is multibusiness, and multinational companies increasingly face a common dilemma—how can the resource advantages of a large company be exploited, while ensuring the responsiveness and creativity found in the small companies against which each of their businesses compete? This dilemma constantly presents managers with conflicting priorities or adjustments as corporate managers:[13]

- Rigorous financial controls and reporting enable cost efficiency, resource deployment, and autonomy across different units; flexible controls are conductive to responsiveness, innovation and "boundary spanning."

- Multibusiness companies historically gain advantage by exploiting resources and capabilities across different business and markets, yet competitive advantage in the future increasingly depends on the creation of new resources and capabilities.

- Aggressive portfolio management seeking maximum shareholder value is often best achieved through independent businesses; the creation of competitive advantage increasingly requires the management—recognition and coordination—of business interdependencies.

Increasingly, globally engaged multibusiness companies are changing the role of corporate headquarters from one of control, resource allocation, and performance monitoring to one of coordinator of linkages across multiple business, supporter and enabler of innovation and synergy. One way this has been done is to create an executive council comprised of top managers from each business, usually including four to five of their key managers, with the council then serving as the critical forum for corporate decision, discussions, and analysis. Exhibit 10–1, Strategy in Action, at the beginning of this chapter showed this type of forum as central to HP's radical restructuring. GE created this approach over 20 years ago in its rise to top corporate success. These councils replace the traditional corporate staff function of overseeing and evaluating various business units, replacing it instead with a forum to share business unit plans, to discuss problems and issues, to seek assistance and expertise, and to foster cooperation and innovation.

Welch's experience at GE provides a useful example. Upon becoming chairman, he viewed GE headquarters as interfering too much in GE's various businesses, generating too much paperwork, and offering minimal value added. He sought to "turn their role 180 degrees from checker, inquisitor, and authority figure to facilitator, helper, and supporter of GE's 13 businesses." He said, "What we do here at headquarters . . . is to multiply the resources we have, the human resources, the financial resources, and the best practices . . . Our job is to help, it's to assist, it's to make these businesses stronger, to help them grow and be more powerful." GE's Corporate Executive Council was reconstituted from predominantly a corporate level group of sector managers (which was eliminated) into a group comprised of the leaders of GE's 13 businesses and a few corporate executives. They met formally two days each quarter to discuss problems and issues and to enable cooperation and resource sharing. This has expanded to other councils throughout GE intent on greater coordination, synergy, and idea sharing.

---

[13] Robert M. Grant, *Contemporary Strategy Analysis* (Oxford: Blackwell, 2001), p. 503.

ORGANIZATIONAL LEADERSHIP

The job of leading a company has never been more demanding, and it will only get tougher in the twenty-first century. The CEO will retain ultimate authority, but the corporation will depend increasingly on the skills of the CEO and a host of subordinate leaders. The accelerated pace and complexity of business will continue to force corporations to push authority down through increasingly horizontal management structures. In the future, every line manager will have to exercise leadership's prerogatives—and bear its burdens—to an extent unthinkable 20 years ago.[14]

John Kotter, a widely recognized leadership expert, predicted this evolving role of leadership in an organization when he distinguished between management and leadership:[15]

> Management is about coping with complexity. Its practices and procedures are largely a response to one of the most significant developments of the twentieth century: the emergence of large organizations. Without good management, complex enterprises tend to become chaotic in ways that threaten their very existence. Good management brings a degree of order and consistency to key dimensions like the quality and profitability of products.
>
> Leadership, by contrast, is about coping with change. Part of the reason it has become so important in recent years is that the business world has become more competitive and more volatile. . . . The net result is that doing what was done yesterday, or doing it 5 percent better, is no longer a formula for success. Major changes are more and more necessary to survive and compete effectively in this new environment. More change always demands more leadership.

Organizational leadership, then, involves action on two fronts. The first is in guiding the organization to deal with constant change. This requires CEOs that embrace change, and that do so by clarifying strategic intent, that build their organization and shape their culture to fit with opportunities and challenges change affords. *BusinessWeek* Strategy in Action, Exhibit 10–10, provides an interview with P&G CEO Alan Lafley, who *BusinessWeek* calls "a catalyst and encourager of change," to explore Lafley's thoughts on doing these very things. The second front is in providing the management skill to cope with the ramifications of constant change. This means identifying and supplying the organization with operating managers prepared to provide operational leadership and vision as never before. Let's explore each of these five aspects to organizational leadership.

Strategic Leadership: Embracing Change

The blending of telecommunications, computers, the Internet, and one global marketplace has increased the pace of change exponentially during the last 10 years. All business organizations are affected. Change has become an integral part of what leaders and managers deal with daily.

The leadership challenge is to galvanize commitment among people within an organization as well as stakeholders outside the organization to embrace change and implement strategies intended to position the organization to do so. Leaders galvanize commitment to embrace change through three interrelated activities: clarifying strategic intent, building an organization, and shaping organizational culture.

Clarifying Strategic Intent

Leaders help stakeholders embrace change by setting forth a clear vision of where the business's strategy needs to take the organization. Traditionally, the concept of vision has been

---

[14] Anthony Bianco, "The New Leadership," *BusinessWeek,* August 28, 2000.
[15] John P. Kotter, "What Leaders Really Do," *Harvard Business Review,* May–June, 1990, p. 104.

BusinessWeek Chief Exec. A. G. Lafley says he shares his predecessor's zeal to revamp P&G. The difference is the approach. Since becoming Procter & Gamble's chief executive in June 2000, Alan G. "A.G." Lafley has led a turnaround that has defied expectations. In 2003 P&G posted a 13 percent increase in net income on 8 percent higher sales. That would bring P&G's annual compounded earnings growth rate under the three years of Lafley's leadership to 15 percent—a rate well above rivals. During that period, P&G's stock price has climbed by 58 percent, while the Standard & Poor's 500-stock index fell by 32 percent.

Less obvious than his turnaround success, however, is how Lafley is changing P&G. He's undertaking the company's most sweeping remake since it was founded in 1837. Nothing is sacred any longer at the Cincinnati-based maker of Tide, Pampers, and Crest.

Lafley has inverted the invent-it-here mentality by turning outwards for innovation. He's broadening P&G's definition of brands and how it prices goods. He's moving P&G deep into the beauty-care business with its two largest acquisitions ever, Clairol in 2001 and Wella in 2003. And he's redefining P&G's core business by outsourcing operations—like information technology and bar-soap manufacturing.

What's surprising is that at the start, Lafley was perceived as a tame pair of hands—far from a person who would conduct a radical makeover. He followed a forceful change agent, Durk Jager, who had tried to jump-start internal innovation, launching a host of new brands. Jager also criticized P&G's insular culture, which he sought to shake up. In the end, though, he overreached, as P&G missed earnings forecasts and employees bucked under his leadership.

Lafley answered some questions recently about his views on leading **change** at P&G:

Q: When you started, you weren't perceived as a forceful change agent like your predecessor. Yet you're making more dramatic changes. Can you discuss that?

A: Durk and I had believed very strongly that the company had to change and make fundamental changes in a lot of the same directions. There are two simple differences: One is I'm very externally focused. I expressed the change in the context of how we're going to serve consumers better, how we're going to win with the retailer, and how we're going to defeat the competitor in the marketplace.

The most important thing—I didn't attack. I avoided saying P&G people are bad. I thought that was a big mistake [on Jager's part]. The difference is, I preserved the core of the culture and pulled people where I wanted to go. I enrolled them in change. I didn't tell them.

Q: Why did you both see a need for change?

A: We were looking at slow growth. An inability to move quickly, to commercialize on innovation and get full advantage out of it. We were looking at new technologies that were changing competition in our industry, retailers, and the supply base. We were looking at a world that all of a sudden was going to go 24/7, and we weren't ready for that kind of world.

Q: Was the view on the need for change widely held within P&G?

A: It depends on who you ask. Without a doubt, Durk and I and a few others were in the camp of "We need a much bigger change."

a description or picture of what the company could be that accommodates the needs of all its stakeholders. The intensely competitive, rapidly changing global marketplace has refined this to be targeting a very narrowly defined strategic intent—*an articulation of a simple criterion or characterization of what the company must become to establish and sustain global leadership.* Former IBM CEO Lou Gerstner is a good example of a leader in the middle of trying to shape strategic intent. "One of the great things about this industry is that every decade or so, you get a chance to redefine the playing field," said Gerstner. "We're in that phase of redefinition right now, and winners or losers are going to emerge from it. We've got to become *the leader in 'network-centric computing.'* " It's an opportunity brought about by telecommunications-based change that will change IBM more than semiconductors did in the last decade. Said Gerstner, "I sensed there were too many people inside IBM who wanted to fight the war we lost," referring to PCs and PC software, so he aggressively instilled network-centric computing as the strategic intent for IBM in the next decade.

Q: Jager says he tried to change P&G too fast. What do you think about that?

A: I think he's right.

Q: Are you concerned about the same thing?

A: I'm worried that I will ask the organization to change ahead of its understanding, capability, and commitment, because that's a problem. I have been a catalyst of change and encourager of change and a coach of change management. And I've tried not to drive change for a sake of change.

Q: How do you pace change?

A: I have tremendous trust in my management team. I let them be the brake. I am the accelerator. I help with direction and let them make the business strategic choices.

Q: Did the fact that P&G was in crisis when you came in help you implement change?

A: It was easier. I was lucky. When you have a mess, you have a chance to make more changes.

Q: Jager tried to drive innovation from within. You would like P&G to ultimately get 50 percent of its ideas from outside. Why?

A: Durk and I both wanted more innovation. We both felt we absolutely, positively had to get more innovation. We had to get more innovation commercialized and more innovation globalized. So we were totally together.

He tried to drive it all internally. He tried to rev the R&D organization, supercharge them, and hoped that enough would come out of there that we would achieve the goals of commercializing more of it and globalizing more of it.

We got in trouble cause we pulled stuff out that was half-baked or that was never going to be successful. We hadn't developed it far enough.

The difference is that my hypothesis is that innovation and discovery are likely to come from anywhere. What P&G is really good at is developing innovations and commercializing them. So what I said is, "We need an open marketplace."

We're probably as good as the next guy at inventing. But we are not absolutely and positively better than everybody else at inventing. There are a lot of good inventors out there.

Q: How hard will it be to shift P&G's R&D focus outwards, given that it has historically focused inwards?

A: It will be a challenge, but I think we'll get there. It's like a flywheel. That first turn is really difficult. Then the second turn is a little bit easier. This has been like turning a flywheel. We will have failures. We will have to celebrate that failure.

Q: When you couple your outward focus on innovation with your moves toward outsourcing, it seems you're making P&G a less vertically integrated company.

A: I don't believe in vertical integration. I think it's a trap. I believe in horizontal networked organizations.

Our core capability is to develop and commercialize. Branding is a core capability. Customer business development is a core capability. We concluded in a lot of areas that manufacturing isn't. Therefore, I let the businesses go do more outsourcing. We concluded that running a back room wasn't a core capability. You do what you do best and can do world-class.

Source: "P&G: New & Improved," *BusinessWeek*, July 7, 2003.

Clarifying strategic intent can come in many different forms. Coca-Cola's legendary former CEO and Chairman Roberto Goizueta said, "Our company is a global business system for which we raise capital to make concentrate and sell it at an operating profit. Then we pay the cost of that capital. Shareholders pocket the difference." Coke averaged 27 percent annual return on stockholder equity for 18 years under his leadership.

Exhibit 10–10 shows how CEO Alan Lafley articulates a radically different strategic intent for the *new* P&G that involves P&G's legendary R&D focusing outward, instead of inward and outsourcing noncore activities in a historically vertically integrated firm. While Coke and P&G are very different situations, their leaders were both very effective in shaping and clarifying strategic intent in a way that helped stakeholders understand what needed to be done.

Building an Organization

The previous section examined alternative structures to use in designing the organization necessary to implement strategy. Leaders spend considerable time shaping and refining their organizational structure and making it function effectively to accomplish strategic intent. Since leaders are attempting to embrace change, they are often rebuilding or remaking their organization to align it with the ever-changing environment and needs of the strategy. And since embracing change often involves overcoming resistance to change, leaders find themselves addressing problems like the following as they attempt to build or rebuild their organization:

- Ensuring a common understanding about organizational priorities.

- Clarifying responsibilities among managers and organizational units.

- Empowering newer managers and pushing authority lower in the organization.

- Uncovering and remedying problems in coordination and communication across the organization.

- Gaining the personal commitment to a shared vision from managers throughout the organization.

- Keeping closely connected with "what's going on in the organization and with its customers."

Leaders do this in many ways. Larry Bossidy, Chairman of Honeywell and co-author of the best seller, *Execution*, spends 50 percent of his time each year flying to Allied Signal's various operations around the world meeting with managers and discussing decisions, results, and progress. Bill Gates at Microsoft reportedly spent two hours each day reading and sending E-mail to any of Microsoft's 36,000 employees that want to contact him. All managers adapt structures, create teams, implement systems, and otherwise generate ways to coordinate, integrate, and share information about what their organization is doing and might do. Others create customer advisory groups, supplier partnerships, R&D joint ventures, and other adjustments to build an adaptable, learning organization that embraces the leader's vision and strategic intent and the change driving the future opportunities facing the business. These, in addition to the fundamental structural guidelines described in the previous section for restructuring to support strategically critical activities, are the issues leaders constantly address as they attempt to build a supportive organization.

Shaping Organization Culture

Leaders know well that the values and beliefs shared throughout their organization will shape how the work of the organization is done. And when attempting to embrace accelerated change, reshaping their organization's culture is an activity that occupies considerable time for most leaders. Listen to these observations by and about Ryanair CEO Michael O'Leary about competing in the increasingly competitive European airline industry and arch-rival easyJet:

> It was vintage Michael O'Leary. On May 13, the 42-year-old CEO of Dublin-based discount airline Ryanair outfitted his staff in full combat gear, drove an old World War II tank to England's Luton airport, an hour north of London, then demanded access to the base of archrival easyJet Airline Co. With the theme to the old television series The A-Team blaring, O'Leary declared he was "liberating the public from easyJet's high fares." When security—surprise!—refused to let the Ryanair armor roll in, O'Leary led the troops in his own rendition of a platoon march song: "I've been told and it's no lie. EasyJet's fares are way too high!" So it is that there are new rivals for O'Leary to conquer. "When we were a much smaller company, we compared ourselves to British Airways. But they are such a mess, most people just feel sorry for them," O'Leary says. "Now we're turning the guns on easyJet."[16]

It appears that Ryanair CEO O'Leary wanted an organizational culture that was aggressive, competitive and somewhat free-wheeling in order to take advantage of change in the

[16] "Ryanair Rising," *BusinessWeek,* June 2, 2003.

BusinessWeek

EXPERIENCE

- Multinational Corp.—Worked with top-notch mentors in an established company with global operations. Managed a talented and fickle staff and helped tap new markets.

- Foreign Operation LLC—A stint at a subsidiary of a U.S. company, or at a foreign operation in a local market. Exposure to different cultures, conditions, and ways of doing business.

- Startup Inc.—Helped to build a business from the ground up, assisting with everything from product development to market research. Honed entrepreneurial skills.

- Major Competitor Ltd.—Scooped up by the competition and exposed to more than one corporate culture.

EDUCATION

- Liberal Arts University—Majored in economics, but took courses in psychology (how to motivate customers and employees), foreign language (the world is a lot bigger than the 50 states), and philosophy (to seek vision and meaning in your work).

- Graduate Studies—The subject almost doesn't matter, so long as you developed your thinking and analytical skills.

EXTRACURRICULAR

- Debating (where you learned to market ideas and think on your feet).

- Sports (where you learned discipline and teamwork).

- Volunteer work (where you learned to step outside your own narrow world to help others).

- Travel (where you learned about different cultures).

Source: "A Résumé for the 21st Century," *BusinessWeek*, August 28, 2000.

European airline industry. He did this by example, by expectations felt by his managers, and in the way decision making is approached within Ryanair.

Leaders use reward systems, symbols, and structure among other means to shape the organization's culture. Travelers' Insurance Co.'s notable turnaround was accomplished in part by changing its "hidebound" culture through a change in its agent reward system. Employees previously on salary with occasional bonuses were given rewards that involved substantial cash bonuses and stock options. Observed a customer and risk management director at drugmaker Becton Dickinson, "They're hungrier now. They want to make deals. They're different than the old, hidebound Travelers' culture."

As leaders clarify strategic intent, build an organization, and shape their organization's culture, they look to one key element to help—their management team throughout their organization. As Honeywell's Chairman Larry Bossidy candidly observed when asked about how after 42 years at General Electric, Allied Signal and now Honeywell with seemingly drab businesses he could expect exciting growth: "There's no such thing as a mature market. What we need is mature executives who can find ways to grow." Leaders look to managers they need to execute strategy as another source of leadership to accept risk and cope with the complexity that change brings about. So assignment of key managers becomes a leadership tool.

Recruiting and Developing Talented Operational Leadership

As we noted at the beginning of this section on Organizational Leadership, the accelerated pace and complexity of business will increase pressure on corporations to push authority down in their organizations ultimately meaning that every line manager will have to exercise leadership's prerogatives to an extent unthinkable a generation earlier. They will each be global managers, change agents, strategists, motivators, strategic decision-makers, innovators, and collaborators if the business is to survive and prosper. Exhibit 10–11, Strategy in

EXHIBIT 10–12
**What Competencies
Should Managers
Possess?**

Source: From Ruth L. Williams
and Joseph P. Cothrel,
"Building Tomorrow's Leaders
Today," *Strategy and Leader-
ship,* Vol. 26, October 1997,
Reprinted with permission of
Emerald Group Publishing
Limited.

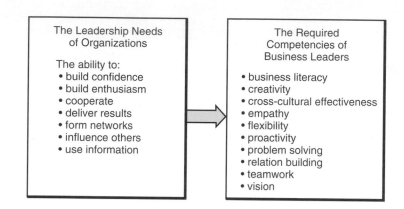

The Leadership Needs
of Organizations

The ability to:
- build confidence
- build enthusiasm
- cooperate
- deliver results
- form networks
- influence others
- use information

The Required
Competencies of
Business Leaders

- business literacy
- creativity
- cross-cultural effectiveness
- empathy
- flexibility
- proactivity
- problem solving
- relation building
- teamwork
- vision

Action, provides an interesting perspective on this reality showing *BusinessWeek*'s version of a résumé for the typical twenty-first century operating manager every company will be looking for in today's fast-paced, global marketplace.

Today's need for fluid, learning organizations capable of rapid response, sharing, and cross-cultural synergy place incredible demands on young managers to bring important competencies to the organization. Exhibit 10–12 describes the needs organizations look to managers to meet, and then identifies the corresponding competencies managers would need to do so. Ruth Williams and Joseph Cothrel drew this conclusion in their research about competencies needed from managers in today's fast-changing business environment:[17]

> Today's competitive environment requires a different set of management competencies than we traditionally associate with the role. The balance has clearly shifted from attributes traditionally thought of as masculine (strong decision making, leading the troops, driving strategy, waging competitive battle) to more feminine qualities (listening, relationship-building, and nurturing). The model today is not so much "take it on your shoulders" as it is to "create the environment that will enable others to carry part of the burden." The focus is on unlocking the organization's human asset potential.

Researcher David Goleman addressed the question of what types of personality attributes generate the type of competencies described in Exhibit 10–12. His research suggested that a set of four characteristics commonly referred to as emotional intelligence play a key role in bringing the competencies needed from today's desirable manager:[18]

- *Self-awareness* in terms of the ability to read and understand one's emotions and assess one's strengths and weaknesses, underlain by the confidence that stems from positive self-worth.

- *Self-management* in terms of control, integrity, conscientiousness, initiative, and achievement orientation.

- *Social awareness* in relation to sensing others' emotions (empathy), reading the organization (organizational awareness), and recognizing customers' needs (service orientation).

- *Social skills* in relation to influencing and inspiring others; communicating, collaborating, and building relationships with others; and managing change and conflict.

---

[17] Ruth Williams and Joseph Cothrel, "Building Tomorrow's Leaders Today," *Strategy and Leadership* 26 (September–October 1997), p. 21.
[18] D. Goleman, "What Makes a Leader?," *Harvard Business Review* (November–December 1998), pp. 93–102.

EXHIBIT 10–13
Management Processes and Levels of Management

Source: C. A. Bartlett and S. Ghoshal, "The Myth of the General Manager: New Personal Competencies for New Management Roles," *California Management Review* 40 (Fall 1997): R. M. Grant, *Contemporary Strategy Analysis* (Oxford: Blackwell, 2001), p. 529.

	RENEWAL PROCESS	
Attracting resources and capabilities and developing the business	Developing operating managers and supporting their activities. Maintaining organizational trust	Providing institutional leadership through shaping and embedding corporate purpose and challenging embedded assumptions
Managing operational interdependencies and personal networks	INTEGRATION PROCESS Linking skills, knowledge, and resources across units. Reconciling short-term performance and long-term ambition	Creating corporate direction. Developing and nurturing organizational values
Creating and pursuing opportunities. Managing continuous performance improvement	ENTREPRENEURIAL PROCESS Reviewing, developing, and supporting initiatives	Establishing performance standards
Front-Line Management	Middle Management	Top Management

One additional perspective on the role of organizational leadership and management selection is found in the work of Bartlett and Ghoshal. Their study of several of the most successful global companies in the last decade suggests that combining flexible responsiveness with integration and innovation requires rethinking the management role and the distribution of management roles within a twenty-first century company. They see three critical management roles: the *entrepreneurial process* (decisions about opportunities to pursue and resource deployment), the *integration process* (building and deploying organizational capabilities), and the *renewal process* (shaping organizational purpose and enabling change). Traditionally viewed as the domain of top management, their research suggests that these functions need to be shared and distributed across three management levels as suggested in Exhibit 10–13.[19]

ORGANIZATIONAL CULTURE

Organizational culture is the set of important assumptions (often unstated) that members of an organization share in common. Every organization has its own culture. An organization's culture is similar to an individual's personality—an intangible yet ever-present theme that provides meaning, direction, and the basis for action. In much the same way as personality influences the behavior of an individual, the shared assumptions (beliefs and values) among a firm's members influence opinions and actions within that firm.

A member of an organization can simply be aware of the organization's beliefs and values without sharing them in a personally significant way. Those beliefs and values have more personal meaning if the member views them as a guide to appropriate behavior in the organization and, therefore, complies with them. The member becomes fundamentally committed to the beliefs and values when he or she internalizes them; that is, comes to

---

[19]C. A. Barlett and S. Ghoshal, "The Myth of the General Manager: New Personal Competencies for New Management Roles," *California Management Review* 40 (Fall 1997), pp. 92–116; and "Beyond Structure to Process," *Harvard Business Review* (January–February 1995).

hold them as personal beliefs and values. In this case, the corresponding behavior is *intrinsically rewarding* for the member—the member derives personal satisfaction from his or her actions in the organization because those actions are congruent with corresponding personal beliefs and values. *Assumptions become shared assumptions through internalization among an organization's individual members.* And those shared, internalized beliefs and values shape the content and account for the strength of an organization's culture.

Leaders typically attempt to manage and create distinct cultures through a variety of ways. Some of the most common ways are as follows:

Emphasize Key Themes or Dominant Values Businesses build strategies around distinct competitive advantages they possess or seek. Quality, differentiation, cost advantages, and speed are four key sources of competitive advantage. So insightful leaders nurture key themes or dominant values within their organization that reinforce competitive advantages they seek to maintain or build. Key themes or dominant values may center around wording in an advertisement. They are often found in internal company communications. They are most often found as a new vocabulary used by company personnel to explain "who we are." At Xerox, the key themes include respect for the individual and services to the customer. At Procter & Gamble (P&G), the overarching value is product quality; McDonald's uncompromising emphasis on QSCV—quality, service, cleanliness, and value—through meticulous attention to detail is legendary; Delta Airlines is driven by the "family feeling" theme, which builds a team spirit and nurtures each employee's cooperative attitude toward others, cheerful outlook toward life, and pride in a job well done. Du Pont's safety orientation—a report of every accident must be on the chairman's desk within 24 hours—has resulted in a safety record that was 17 times better than the chemical industry average and 68 times better than the all-manufacturing average.

Encourage Dissemination of Stories and Legends about Core Values Companies with strong cultures are enthusiastic collectors and tellers of stories, anecdotes, and legends in support of basic beliefs. Frito-Lay's zealous emphasis on customer service is reflected in frequent stories about potato chip route salespeople who have slogged through sleet, mud, hail, snow, and rain to uphold the 99.5 percent service level to customers in which the entire company takes great pride. Milliken (a textile leader) holds "sharing" rallies once every quarter at which teams from all over the company swap success stories and ideas. Typically, more than 100 teams make five-minute presentations over a two-day period. Every rally is designed around a major theme, such as quality, cost reduction, or customer service. No criticisms are allowed, and awards are given to reinforce this institutionalized approach to storytelling. L. L. Bean tells customer service stories; 3M tells innovation stories; P&G, Johnson & Johnson, IBM, and Maytag tell quality stories. These stories are very important in developing an organizational culture, because organization members identify strongly with them and come to share the beliefs and values they support.

Institutionalize Practices That Systematically Reinforce Desired Beliefs and Values Companies with strong cultures are clear on what their beliefs and values need to be and take the process of shaping those beliefs and values very seriously. Most important, the values these companies espouse undergird the strategies they employ. For example, McDonald's has a yearly contest to determine the best hamburger cooker in its chain. First, there is a competition to determine the best hamburger cooker in each store; next, the store winners compete in regional championships; finally, the regional winners compete in the "All-American" contest. The winners, who are widely publicized throughout the company, get trophies and All-American patches to wear on their McDonald's uniforms.

Adapt Some Very Common Themes in Their Own Unique Ways The most typical beliefs that shape organizational culture include (1) a belief in being the best (or, as at GE, "better than the best"); (2) a belief in superior quality and service; (3) a belief in the importance of people as individuals and a faith in their ability to make a strong contribution; (4) a belief in the importance of the details of execution, the nuts and bolts of doing the job well; (5) a belief that customers should reign supreme; (6) a belief in inspiring people to do their best, whatever their ability; (7) a belief in the importance of informal communication; and (8) a belief that growth and profits are essential to a company's well-being. Every company implements these beliefs differently (to fit its particular situation), and every company's values are the handiwork of one or two legendary figures in leadership positions. Accordingly, every company has a distinct culture that it believes no other company can copy successfully. And in companies with strong cultures, managers and workers either accept the norms of the culture or opt out from the culture and leave the company.

The stronger a company's culture and the more that culture is directed toward customers and markets, the less the company uses policy manuals, organization charts, and detailed rules and procedures to enforce discipline and norms. The reason is that the guiding values inherent in the culture convey in crystal-clear fashion what everybody is supposed to do in most situations. Poorly performing companies often have strong cultures. However, their cultures are dysfunctional, being focused on internal politics or operating by the numbers as opposed to emphasizing customers and the people who make and sell the product.

Managing Organizational Culture in a Global Organization[20]

The reality of today's global organizations is that organizational culture must recognize cultural diversity. *Social norms* create differences across national boundaries that influence how people interact, read personal cues, and otherwise interrelate socially. *Values* and *attitudes* about similar circumstances also vary from country to country. Where individualism is central to a North American's value structure, the needs of the group dominate the value structure of their Japanese counterparts. *Religion* is yet another source of cultural differences. Holidays, practices, and belief structures differ in very fundamental ways that must be taken into account as one attempts to shape organizational culture in a global setting. Finally, *education,* or ways people are accustomed to learning, differ across national borders. Formal classroom learning in the United States may teach things that are only learned via apprenticeship in other cultures. Since the process of shaping an organizational culture often involves considerable "education," leaders should be sensitive to global differences in approaches to education to make sure their cultural education efforts are effective. The discussion case on Procter & Gamble at the end of this chapter provides some relevant examples of how CEO Alan Lafley is trying to radically alter P&G's organization's culture.

Managing the Strategy-Culture Relationship

Managers find it difficult to think through the relationship between a firm's culture and the critical factors on which strategy depends. They quickly recognize, however, that key components of the firm—structure, staff, systems, people, style—influence the ways in which key managerial tasks are executed and how critical management relationships are formed. And implementation of a new strategy is largely concerned with adjustments in these components to accommodate the perceived needs of the strategy. Consequently,

[20] Differing backgrounds, often referred to as *cultural diversity,* is something that most managers will certainly see more of, both because of the growing cultural diversity domestically and the obvious diversification of cultural backgrounds that result from global acquisitions and mergers. For example, Harold Epps, manager of DEC's computer keyboard plant in Boston, manages 350 employees representing 44 countries of origin and 19 languages.

EXHIBIT 10–14
Managing the Strategy-Culture Relationship

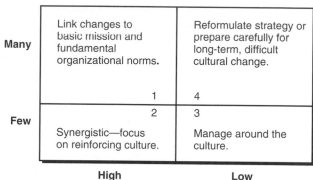

Changes in key organizational factors that are necessary to implement the new strategy

	High	Low
Many	Link changes to basic mission and fundamental organizational norms. 1	Reformulate strategy or prepare carefully for long-term, difficult cultural change. 4
Few	2 Synergistic—focus on reinforcing culture.	3 Manage around the culture.

Potential compatibility of changes with existing culture

managing the strategy-culture relationship requires sensitivity to the interaction between the changes necessary to implement the new strategy and the compatibility or "fit" between those changes and the firm's culture. Exhibit 10–14 provides a simple framework for managing the strategy-culture relationship by identifying four basic situations a firm might face.

Link to Mission

A firm in cell 1 is faced with a situation in which implementing a new strategy requires several changes in structure, systems, managerial assignments, operating procedures, or other fundamental aspects of the firm. However, most of the changes are potentially compatible with the existing organizational culture. Firms in this situation usually have a tradition of effective performance and are either seeking to take advantage of a major opportunity or are attempting to redirect major product-market operations consistent with proven core capabilities. Such firms are in a very promising position: They can pursue a strategy requiring major changes but still benefit from the power of cultural reinforcement.

Four basic considerations should be emphasized by firms seeking to manage a strategy-culture relationship in this context. First, *key changes should be visibly linked to the basic company mission.* Since the company mission provides a broad official foundation for the organizational culture, top executives should use all available internal and external forums to reinforce the message that the changes are inextricably linked to it. Second, *emphasis should be placed on the use of existing personnel* where possible to fill positions created to implement the new strategy. Existing personnel embody the shared values and norms that help ensure cultural compatibility as major changes are implemented. Third, *care should be taken if adjustments in the reward system are needed.* These adjustments should be consistent with the current reward system. If, for example, a new product-market thrust requires significant changes in the way sales are made, and, therefore, in incentive compensation, common themes (e.g., incentive oriented) should be emphasized. In this way, current and future reward approaches are related and the changes in the reward system are justified (encourage development of less familiar markets). Fourth, *key attention should be paid to the changes that are least compatible with the current culture,* so current norms are not disrupted. For example, a firm may choose to subcontract an important step in a production process because that step would be incompatible with the current culture.

IBM's strategy in entering the Internet-based market is an illustration. Serving this radically different market required numerous organizational changes. To maintain maximum compatibility with its existing culture while doing so, IBM went to considerable public and internal effort to link its new Internet focus with its long-standing mission. Numerous messages relating the network-centric computing to IBM's tradition of top-quality service appeared on television and in magazines, and every IBM manager was encouraged to go online. Where feasible, IBM personnel were used to fill the new positions created to implement the strategy. But because the software requirements were not compatible with IBM's current operations, virtually all of its initial efforts were linked to newly acquired Lotus Notes Software.

Maximize Synergy

A firm in cell 2 needs only a few organizational changes to implement its new strategy, and those changes are potentially quite compatible with its current culture. A firm in this situation should emphasize two broad themes: (1) *take advantage of the situation to reinforce and solidify the current culture* and (2) *use this time of relative stability to remove organizational roadblocks to the desired culture.* Holiday Inns' move into casino gambling required a few major organizational changes. Holiday Inns saw casinos as resort locations requiring lodging, dining, and gambling/entertainment services. It only had to incorporate gambling/entertainment expertise into its management team, which was already capable of managing the lodging and dining requirements of casino (or any other) resort locations. It successfully inculcated this single major change by selling the change internally as completely compatible with its mission of providing high-quality accommodations for business and leisure travelers. The resignation of Roy Clymer, its CEO, removed an organizational roadblock, legitimizing a culture that placed its highest priority on quality service to the middle-to-upper-income business traveler, rather than a culture that placed its highest priority on family-oriented service. The latter priority was fast disappearing from Holiday Inns' culture, with the encouragement of most of the firm's top management, but its disappearance had not yet been fully sanctioned because of Clymer's personal beliefs. His voluntary departure helped solidify the new values that top management wanted.

Manage around the Culture

A firm in cell 3 must make a few major organizational changes to implement its new strategy, but these changes are potentially inconsistent with the firm's current organizational culture. The critical question for a firm in this situation is whether it can make the changes with a reasonable chance of success.

A firm can manage around the culture in various ways: create a separate firm or division; use task forces, teams, or program coordinators; subcontract; bring in an outsider; or sell out. These are a few of the available options, but the key idea is to create a method of achieving the change desired that avoids confronting the incompatible cultural norms. As cultural resistance diminishes, the change may be absorbed into the firm.

In the Southeast, Rich's was a highly successful, quality-oriented department store chain that served higher income customers in several southeastern locations. With Wal-Mart and Kmart experiencing rapid growth in the sale of mid- to low-priced merchandise, Rich's decided to serve this market as well. Finding such merchandise inconsistent with the successful values and norms of its traditional business, it created a separate business called Richway to tap this growth area in retailing. Through a new store network, it was able to *manage around its culture.* Both Rich's and Richway experienced solid regional success, though their cultures are radically different in some respects.

Reformulate the Strategy or Culture

A firm in cell 4 faces the most difficult challenge in managing the strategy-culture relationship. To implement its new strategy, such a firm must make organizational changes

Thomas Charlton, president and CEO of software outfit TIDAL, fits the latter category. As he tells it, the company was going nowhere when he stepped up from his former job as vice-president for sales to helm the entire business, which is based in Mountain View, Calif., and produces job-scheduling software that manages business processes in large corporate data systems. BusinessWeek Online invited Charlton to explain the challenges he faced, the steps he took to meet them, and the end result: the fastest-growing independent software vendor in the job-scheduling market.

The date was May 15, 2000. I was the 33-year-old vice-president of sales for a privately held software company in Silicon Valley. The company had received an initial round of funding and I'd been hired to substantially increase revenues after 17 years of flat growth, and expand the sales organization from a staff of four tele-salespeople. Within 18 months of overhauling sales, our team had grown to almost two-dozen presales and account executives, and five regional offices. Revenues for the company more than doubled.

While my task had been accomplished I saw significant challenges ahead for TIDAL Software. The marketing department erroneously positioned the core product for a niche market, eliminating a huge source of prospects. The vice-president of development was reluctant to make simple changes to the product, even though it would result in winning large competitive deals. The CEO was not providing direction, and TIDAL's board of directors had lost confidence in the management team. And, although revenues had doubled, the infrastructure was growing faster than product sales. TIDAL was losing approximately $800,000 per quarter. We were in desperate need of cash to survive.

STAY OR GO?

Moreover, the dot-com explosion was in full swing and sales-executive positions were plentiful. I was left with a few options: resign, grab one of the dot-com "dangling carrots" and retire in six months—or remain at TIDAL and watch a sinking ship.

The third choice was to make a radical proposal to the board that, if they turned control of the company over to me, we would grow revenues in record time. My recommendation came with one proviso: jettison the executive staff.

By my observation, TIDAL employees had a tremendous commitment to see the company succeed: Our flagship product could easily compete among the larger vendors. Our developers were capable of programming new features in record time and expanding the product line. The intrepid sales reps were unwilling to take "no" for an answer. Senior management, however, wasn't providing the proper mentoring to train and mobilize their teams and sustain the company's growth.

The problem was overwhelmingly a cultural one.

HEADS ROLL

So, on that Monday in May, after receiving board support for taking operational control of the company and initiating a growth plan, the management team was removed . . . all managers in every department, with the exception of sales.

That afternoon, I faced the 40 remaining employees, who had invested a lot of time and energy in the company. I told them that it was up to us as a group of individuals to pull together as a team if we wanted to enjoy some of the Silicon Valley dream. I asked for their commitment over the next 12 months, with the option of evaluating my performance every 30 days. Except for one unplanned turnover no one left the entire year.

Once the foundation was laid, I chose an employee from each department to represent the company and meet with me to create and execute a turn-around plan. Together we engendered a renewed sense of pride for TIDAL. As the new president and CEO, I established the following rules of engagement for fostering a new culture and growing the company:

- Build trust upon reorganizing the company.

- Enlist the support and alignment of remaining employees, and prove my ability to lead.

- Establish a new performance-based culture.

- Instill in each employee that their value to the company is measured by their individual contribution to the organization. Personal relationships are secondary to the needs of the team's objective.

- Get employees very busy with projects that focus on the future and don't give them time to bemoan the past.

that are incompatible with its current, usually entrenched, values and norms. A firm in this situation faces the complex, expensive, and often long-term challenge of changing its culture; it is a challenge that borders on impossible. Exhibit 10–15, Strategy in Action, describes how 33-year-old Thomas Charlton transformed a 17-year-old Silicon Valley software vendor into the fastest-growing job-scheduling software vendor by radically changing its culture.

- Pick team leaders from each department and get them engaged with their teams in the success and growth of TIDAL.

- Have each employee set individual goals and objectives for his or her department that contributes to the overall revenue goals.

- Make sure each and every employee knows what the quarterly revenue goals are and knows what his or her specific role is in achieving those goals.

- Instill the belief that the entire company closes the sale—in other words, deals get done because every employee contributes his or her specific, measurable value to the sales process. Even tech-support personnel bring in sales leads.

- Learn more from direct interactions, rather than through hearsay, by inviting people to communicate openly and honestly with their managers and the executive team.

- Get employees to focus on the big picture by creating a safe structure where they have permission to communicate grievances, suggestions, etc. to their managers, with impunity.

- Encourage employees to take risks.

- Be a student and a teacher. Accept the wisdom of others, including frontline staff.

- Treat every employee as a solid contributor and encourage feedback, knowing they can see what the CEO can't always see. They may know what the CEO doesn't.

- Challenge employees and give them the opportunity to show conviction and commitment to the company's success. Test their mettle and turn employees into warriors who fight for the company.

- Understand how management style affects the bottom line.

- Put managers through rigorous training with quarterly training updates and evaluations.

- As employees helped TIDAL grow and become successful, they developed and grew themselves.

- By establishing a culture where people are encouraged to take risks in support of the company's success they experience their own personal growth and development.

- Find out why you're struggling. Don't just look to your own brain for the answer.

- Speak to Board members, employees and managers, and read the words of successful business leaders, don't just rely on your own intuition.

As the new culture supplanted the old, we set and achieved our business goals and were able to generate a second round of funding. Some of the results below include:

- TIDAL went from losing $800,000 per quarter to breaking even in three quarters. Instead of raising capital at a low valuation, the company sold its way out of debt.

- Revenues grew from $9.6 million to $14.7 million in the year following the restructuring, an increase of 67 percent.

- Overall, TIDAL revenues have increased 400 percent over the last three years.

- TIDAL raised $12 million in second-round funding from JP Morgan Partners.

- TIDAL moved from ranking one of 29 vendors to being a "Visionary" in [tech research outfit] Gartner's Magic Quadrant. It was also ranked the fastest-growing independent software vendor, and fourth by Gartner behind industry behemoths IBM, Computer Associates, and BMC.

- TIDAL is one of the only vendors to innovate in this space, with a whole-product strategy built around a new automation paradigm—event-driven scheduling.

These results were made possible by the 100 employees at TIDAL who embraced the new vision, direction, and culture, which they brought forth as a team. As CEO, I set the stage for them to perform.

Source: "To Fix a Business, Change the Culture," *BusinessWeek Online,* June 18, 2002.

When a strategy requires massive organizational change and engenders cultural resistance, a firm should determine whether reformulation of the strategy is appropriate. Are all of the organizational changes really necessary? Is there any real expectation that the changes will be acceptable and successful? If these answers are yes, then massive changes in management personnel are often necessary. AT&T offered early retirement to over 20,000 managers as part of a massive recreation of its culture to go along with major strategic changes in recent years. If the answer to these questions is no, the firm might reformulate its strategic plan so as to make it more consistent with established organizational norms and practices.

Merrill Lynch faced the challenge of strategy-culture incompatibility in the last decade. Seeking to remain number one in the newly deregulated financial services industry, it chose to pursue a product development strategy in its brokerage business. Under this strategy, Merrill Lynch would sell a broader range of investment products to a more diverse customer base and would integrate other financial services, such as real estate sales, into the Merrill Lynch organization. The new strategy could succeed only if Merrill Lynch's traditionally service-oriented brokerage network became sales and marketing oriented. Initial efforts to implement the strategy generated substantial resistance from Merrill Lynch's highly successful brokerage network. The strategy was fundamentally inconsistent with long-standing cultural norms at Merrill Lynch that emphasized personalized service and very close broker-client relationships. Merrill Lynch ultimately divested its real estate operation, reintroduced specialists that supported broker/retailers, and refocused its brokers more narrowly on basic client investment needs.

Summary

This chapter examined the idea that a key aspect of implementing a strategy is the *institutionalization* of the strategy so it permeates daily decisions and actions in a manner consistent with long-term strategic success. The "recipe" that binds strategy and organization involves three key ingredients: *organizational structure, leadership,* and *culture.*

Five fundamental organizational structures were examined, and the advantages and disadvantages of each were identified. Institutionalizing a strategy requires a good strategy-structure fit. This chapter dealt with how this requirement often is overlooked until performance becomes inadequate and then indicated the conditions under which the various structures would be appropriate.

Organizational leadership is essential to effective strategy implementation. The CEO plays a critical role in this regard. Assignment of key managers, particularly within the top-management team, is an important aspect of organizational leadership. Deciding whether to promote insiders or hire outsiders is often a central leadership issue in strategy implementation. This chapter showed how this decision could be made in a manner that would best institutionalize the new strategy.

Organizational culture has been recognized as a pervasive influence on organizational life. Organizational culture, which is the shared beliefs and values of an organization's members, may be a major help or hindrance to strategy implementation. This chapter discussed an approach to managing the strategy-culture fit. It identified four fundamentally different strategy-culture situations and provided recommendations for managing the strategy-culture fit in each of these situations.

The chapter concluded with an examination of structure, leadership, and culture for twenty-first century companies. Networked organizations, with intense customer focus, and alliances are keys to success. Talent-focused acquisitions, success sharing, and leaders as coaches round out the future success scenario.

Questions for Discussion

1. What key structural considerations must be incorporated into strategy implementation? Why does structural change often lag behind a change in strategy?

2. Which organizational structure is most appropriate for successful strategy implementation? Explain how state of development affects your answer.

3. Why is leadership an important element in strategy implementation? Find an example in a major business periodical of the CEO's key role in strategy implementation.

4. Under what conditions would it be more appropriate to fill a key management position with someone from outside the firm when a qualified insider is available?

5. What is organizational culture? Why is it important? Explain two different situations a firm might face in managing the strategy-culture relationship.

Chapter 10 Discussion Case

P&G: New and Improved

BusinessWeek

How A. G. Lafley Is Revolutionizing a Bastion of Corporate Conservatism

1 It's Mother's Day, and Alan G. "A.G." Lafley, chief executive of Procter & Gamble Co., is meeting with the person he shares time with every Sunday evening—Richard L. Antoine, the company's head of human resources. Lafley doesn't invite the chief financial officer of the $43 billion business, nor does he ask the executive in charge of marketing at the world's largest consumer-products company. He doesn't invite friends over to watch *The Sopranos,* either. No, on most Sunday nights it's just Lafley, Antoine, and stacks of reports on the performance of the company's 200 most senior executives. This is the boss's signature gesture. It shows his determination to nurture talent and serves notice that little escapes his attention. If you worked for P&G, you would have to be both impressed and slightly intimidated by that kind of diligence.

2 On this May evening, the two executives sit at the dining-room table in Antoine's Cincinnati home hashing over the work of a manager who distinguished himself on one major assignment but hasn't quite lived up to that since. "We need to get him in a position where we can stretch him," Lafley says. Then he rises from his chair and stands next to Antoine to peer more closely at a spreadsheet detailing P&G's seven management layers. Lafley points to one group while tapping an empty water bottle against his leg. "It's not being felt strongly enough in the middle of the company," he says in his slightly high-pitched voice. "They don't feel the hot breath of the consumer."

3 If they don't feel it yet, they will. Lafley, who took over when Durk I. Jager was pressured to resign in June, 2000, is in the midst of engineering a remarkable turnaround. The first thing Lafley told his managers when he took the job was just what they wanted to hear: Focus on what you do well—selling the company's major brands such as Tide, Pampers, and Crest—instead of trying to develop the next big thing.

4 Now, those old reliable products have gained so much market share that they are again the envy of the industry. So is the company's stock price, which has climbed 58 percent, to $92 a share, since Lafley started, while the Standard & Poor's 500-stock index has declined 32 percent. Banc of America analyst William H. Steele forecasts that P&G's profits for its current fiscal year, which ended June 30, will rise by 13 percent, to $5.57 billion, on an 8 percent increase in sales, to $43.23 billion. That exceeds most rivals. Volume growth has averaged 7 percent over the past six quarters, excluding acquisitions, well above Lafley's goal and the industry average.

5 The conventional thinking is that the soft-spoken Lafley was exactly the antidote P&G needed after Jager. After all, Jager had charged into office determined to rip apart P&G's insular culture and remake it from the bottom up. Instead of pushing P&G to excel, however, the torrent of proclamations and initiatives during Jager's 17-month reign nearly brought the venerable company to a grinding halt.

6 Enter Lafley. A 23-year P&G veteran, he wasn't supposed to bring fundamental change; he was asked simply to restore the company's equilibrium. In fact, he came in warning that Jager had tried to implement too many changes too quickly (which Jager readily admits now). Since then, the mild-mannered 56-year-old chief executive has worked to revive both urgency and hope: urgency because, in the previous 15 years, P&G had developed exactly one successful new brand, the Swiffer dust mop; and hope because, after Jager, employees needed reassurance that the old ways still had value. Clearly, Lafley has undone the damage at P&G.

7 What's less obvious is that, in his quiet way, Lafley has proved to be even more of a revolutionary than the flamboyant Jager. Lafley is leading the most sweeping transformation of the company since it was founded by William Procter and James Gamble in 1837 as a maker of soap and candles. Long before he became CEO, Lafley had been pondering how to make P&G relevant in the twenty-first century, when speed and agility would matter more than heft. As president of North American operations, he even spoke with Jager about the need to remake the company.

8 So how has Lafley succeeded where Jager so spectacularly failed? In a word, style. Where Jager was gruff, Lafley is soothing. Where Jager bullied, Lafley persuades. He listens more than he talks. He is living proof that the messenger is just as important as the message. As he says, "I'm not a screamer, not a yeller. But don't get confused by my style. I am very

decisive." Or as Robert A. McDonald, president of P&G's global fabric and home-care division, says, "people want to follow him. I frankly love him like my brother."

9   Indeed, Lafley's charm offensive has so disarmed most P&Gers that he has been able to change the company profoundly. He is responsible for P&G's largest acquisitions ever, buying Clairol in 2001 for $5 billion and agreeing to purchase Germany's Wella in March for a price that now reaches $7 billion. He has replaced more than half of the company's top 30 officers, more than any P&G boss in memory, and cut 9,600 jobs. And he has moved more women into senior positions. Lafley skipped over 78 general managers with more seniority to name 42-year-old Deborah A. Henretta to head P&G's then-troubled North American baby-care division. "The speed at which A. G. has gotten results is five years ahead of the time I expected," says Scott Cook, founder of software maker Intuit (INTU) Inc., who joined P&G's board shortly after Lafley's appointment.

10   Still, the Lafley revolution is far from over. Precisely because of his achievements, Lafley is now under enormous pressure to return P&G to what it considers its rightful place in Corporate America: a company that is admired, imitated, and uncommonly profitable. Nowhere are those expectations more apparent than on the second floor of headquarters, where three former chief executives still keep offices. John Pepper, a popular former boss who returned briefly as chairman when Jager left but gave up the post to Lafley last year, leans forward in his chair as he says: "It's now clear to me that A. G. is going to be one of the great CEOs in this company's history."

OUTSOURCING If it's not a core function, the new P&G won't do it. Info tech and bar-soap manufacturing have already been contracted out. Other jobs will follow.

ACQUISITIONS Not everything has to be invented in company labs. Lafley wants half of all new-product ideas to come from the outside.

BUILDING STAFF Managers are under much closer scrutiny, as Lafley scans the ranks for the best and the brightest and singles them out for development.

BRAND EXPANSION The Crest line now includes an electric toothbrush and tooth-whitening products along with toothpaste. Lafley is making similar moves elsewhere.

PRICING P&G isn't just the premium-priced brand. It will go to the lower end if that's where opportunity lies.

---

11   But here's the rub: What Lafley envisions may be far more radical than what Pepper has in mind. Consider a confidential memo that circulated among P&G's top brass in late 2001 and angered Pepper for its audacity. It argued that P&G could be cut to 25,000 employees, a quarter of its current size. Acknowledging the memo, Lafley admits: "It terrified our organization."

12   Lafley didn't write the infamous memo, but he may as well have. It reflects the central tenet of his vision—that P&G should do only what it does best, nothing more. Lafley wants a more outwardly focused, flexible company. That has implications for every facet of the business, from manufacturing to innovation. For example, in April he turned over all bar-soap manufacturing, including Ivory, P&G's oldest surviving brand, to a Canadian contractor. In May, he outsourced P&G's information-technology operation to Hewlett-Packard Co.

13   No bastion has been more challenged than P&G's research and development operations. Lafley has confronted head-on the stubbornly held notion that everything must be invented within P&G, asserting that half of its new products should come from the outside. (P&G now gets about 20 percent of its ideas externally—up from about 10 percent when he took over.) "He's absolutely breaking many well-set molds at P&G," says eBay (EBAY) Inc.'s CEO, Margaret C. "Meg" Whitman, whom Lafley appointed to the board.

14   Lafley's quest to remake P&G could still come to grief. As any scientist will attest, buying innovation is tricky. Picking the winners from other labs is notoriously difficult and often expensive. And P&G will remain uncomfortably reliant on Wal-Mart (WMT) Stores Inc., which accounts for nearly a fifth of its sales. Lafley is looking to pharmaceuticals and beauty care for growth, where the margins are high but where P&G has considerably less experience than rivals.

15   The biggest risk, though, is that Lafley will lose the P&Gers themselves. Theirs is a culture famously resistant to new ideas. To call the company insular may not do it justice. Employees aren't kidding when they say they're a family. They often start out there and grow up together at P&G, which only promotes from within. Cincinnati itself is a small town: Employees live near one another, they go to the same health clubs and restaurants. They are today's company men and women—and proud of it.

16   Lafley is well aware of his predicament. On a June evening, as he sits on the patio behind his home, he

muses about just that. The house, which resembles a Tuscan villa and overlooks the Ohio River and downtown Cincinnati, is infused with P&G history. Lafley bought it from former CEO John G. Smale three years before he was named chief executive. A black-and-gold stray cat the family feeds sits a few feet away and watches Lafley as he sips a Beck's beer. The clouds threaten rain. "I am worried that I will ask the organization to change ahead of its understanding, capability, and commitment," Lafley admits.

17   For most of its 166 years, P&G was one of America's preeminent companies. Its brands are icons: It launched Tide in 1946 and Pampers, the first disposable diaper, in 1961. Its marketing was innovative: In the 1880s, P&G was one of the first companies to advertise nationally. Fifty years later, P&G invented the soap opera by sponsoring the *Ma Perkins* radio show and, later, *Guiding Light.*

P&G Famous Firsts

1931

Promotion department manager and future CEO Neil McElroy creates modern theory of **brand management.**

1960

P&G wins **American Dental Assn.** approval of Crest as an effective cavity fighter.

1961

The company launches Pampers, **the first disposable diaper.**

1986

Pert Plus, **the first shampoo conditioner combination**, is unveiled.

18   Its management techniques, meanwhile, became the gold standard: In the 1930s, P&G developed the idea of brand management—setting up marketing teams for each brand and urging them to compete against each other. P&G has long been the business world's finest training ground. General Electric (GE) Co.'s Jeffrey R. Immelt and 3M (MMM) W. James McNerney Jr. both started out on Ivory. Meg Whitman and Steven M. Case were in toilet goods, while Steven A. Ballmer was an assistant product manager for Duncan Hines cake mix, among other goods. They, of course, went on to lead eBay, AOL Time Warner (AOL), and Microsoft.

19   But by the 1990s, P&G was in danger of becoming another Eastman Kodak (EK) Co. or Xerox (XRX) Corp., a once-great company that had lost its way. Sales on most of its 18 top brands were slowing; the company was being outhustled by more focused rivals such as Kimberly-Clark (KMB) Corp. and Colgate-Palmolive (CL) Co. The only way P&G kept profits growing was by cutting costs, hardly a strategy for the long term. At the same time, the dynamics of the industry were changing as power shifted from manufacturers to massive retailers. Through all of this, much of senior management was in denial. "Nobody wanted to talk about it," Lafley says. "Without a doubt, Durk and I and a few others were in the camp of 'We need a much bigger change.' "

20   When Jager took over in January, 1999, he was hell-bent on providing just that—with disastrous results. He introduced expensive new products that never caught on while letting existing brands drift. He wanted to buy two huge pharmaceutical companies, a plan that threatened P&G's identity but never was carried out. And he put in place a companywide reorganization that left many employees perplexed and preoccupied. Soaring commodity prices, unfavorable currency trends, and a tech-crazed stock market didn't help either. At a company prized for consistent earnings, Jager missed forecasts twice in six months. In his first and last full fiscal year, earnings per share rose by just 3.5 percent instead of an estimated 13 percent. And during that time, the share price slid 52 percent, cutting P&G's total market capitalization by $85 billion. Employees and retirees hold about 20 percent of the stock. The family began to turn against its leader.

21   But Jager's greatest failing was his scorn for the family. Jager, a Dutchman who had joined P&G overseas and worked his way to corporate headquarters, pitted himself against the P&G culture, contending that it was burdensome and insufferable, says Susan E. Arnold, president of P&G's beauty and feminine care division. Some go-ahead employees even wore buttons that read "Old World/New World" to express disdain for P&G's past. "I never wore one," Arnold sneers. " 'The old Procter is bad, and the new world is good.' That didn't work."

22   On June 6, 2000, his thirtieth wedding anniversary, Lafley was in San Francisco when he received a call from Pepper, then a board member: Would he become CEO? Back in Cincinnati, a boardroom coup unprecedented in P&G's history had taken place.

23   As Lafley steps into the small study in his house three years later, a Japanese drawing on the wall

reminds him of what it was like to become CEO. The room, with its painting of a samurai warrior and red elephant-motif wallpaper, alludes to his stint running P&G's Asian operations. Bookshelves hold leather-bound volumes of Joseph Conrad and Mark Twain. A simple wooden desk faces the window. Lafley focuses on the drawing, which depicts a man caught in a spider's web; it was given to him by the elder of his two sons, Patrick. "In the first few days, you are just trying to figure out what kind of web it is," he says.

24   In a sense, Lafley had been preparing for this job his entire adult life. He never hid the fact that he wanted to run P&G one day. Or if not the company, then a company. That itself is unusual since, like almost all P&Gers, Lafley has never worked anywhere else. After graduating from Hamilton College in 1969, Lafley decided to pursue a doctorate in medieval and Renaissance history at the University of Virginia. But he dropped out in his first year to join the Navy (and avoid being drafted into the Army). He served in Japan, where he got his first experience as a merchandiser, supplying Navy retail stores. When his tour of duty ended in 1975, he enrolled in the MBA program at Harvard Business School. And from there, he went directly to Cincinnati.

25   When he was hired as a brand assistant for Joy dish detergent in 1977 at age 29; he was older than most of his colleagues and he worried that his late start might hinder his rise at P&G. Twice within a year in the early 1980s, Lafley quit. "Each time, I talked him back in only after drinking vast amounts of Drambuie," says Thomas A. Moore, his boss at the time, who now runs biotech company Biopure (BPUR) Corp. On the second occasion, then-CEO John Smale met with Lafley, who had accepted a job as a consultant in Connecticut (NIPNY). Without making any promises, Smale says he told Lafley that "we thought there was no limit on where he was going to go."

26   Sure enough, Lafley climbed quickly to head P&G's soap and detergent business, where he introduced Liquid Tide in 1984. A decade later, he was promoted to head the Asian division. Lafley returned from Kobe, Japan, to Cincinnati in 1998 to run the company's entire North American operations. To ease the transition home, he and his younger son, Alex, who was then 12, studied guitar together. Two years later, Lafley was named CEO.

27   Along the way, he developed a reputation as a boss who stepped back to give his staff plenty of responsibility and helped shape decisions by asking a series of keen questions—a process he calls "peeling the onion." And he retained a certain humility. He still collects baseball cards, comic books, and rock 'n' roll 45s. Whereas some executives might have a garage full of antique cars or Harley-Davidsons (HDI); Lafley keeps two Vespa motor scooters. "People wanted him to succeed," says Virginia Lee, a former P&Ger who worked for Lafley at headquarters and overseas.

28   As CEO, Lafley hasn't made grand pronouncements on the future of P&G. Instead, he has spent an inordinate amount of time patiently communicating how he wants P&G to change. In a company famed for requiring employees to describe every new course of action in a one-page memo, Lafley's preferred approach is the slogan. For example, he felt that P&G was letting technology rather than consumer needs dictate new products. Ergo: "The consumer is boss." P&G wasn't working closely enough with retailers, the place where consumers first see the product on the shelf: "The first moment of truth." P&G wasn't concerned enough with the consumer's experience at home: "The second moment of truth."

29   Lafley uses these phrases constantly, and they are echoed throughout the organization. At the end of a three-day leadership seminar, 30 young marketing managers from around the world present what they have learned to Lafley. First on the list: "We are the voice of the consumer within P&G, and they are the heart of all we do." Lafley, dressed in a suit, sits on a stool in front of the group and beams. "I love the first one," he laughs as the room erupts in applause.

30   When he talks about his choice of words later, Lafley is a tad self-conscious. "It's *Sesame Street* language—I admit that," he says. "A lot of what we have done is make things simple because the difficulty is making sure everybody knows what the goal is and how to get there."

31   Lafley has also mastered the art of the symbolic gesture. The eleventh floor at corporate headquarters had been the redoubt of senior executives since the 1950s. Lafley did away with it, moving all five division presidents to the same floors as their staff. Then he turned some of the space into a leadership training center. On the rest of the floor, he knocked down the walls so that the remaining executives, including himself, share open offices. Lafley sits next to the two people he talks to the most, which, in true P&G style, was officially established by a flow study: HR head Antoine and Vice-Chairman Bruce Byrnes. As

if the Sunday night meetings with Antoine weren't proof enough of Lafley's determination to make sure the best people rise to the top. And Byrnes, whom Lafley refers to as "Yoda"—the sage-like *Star Wars* character—gets a lot of face time because of his marketing expertise. As Lafley says, "the assets at P&G are what? Our people and our brands."

32   Just as emblematic of the Lafley era is the floor's new conference room, where he and P&G's 12 other top executives meet every Monday at 8 A.M. to review results, plan strategy, and set the drumbeat for the week. The table used to be rectangular; now it's round. The execs used to sit where they were told; now they sit where they like. At one of those meetings, an outsider might have trouble distinguishing the CEO: He occasionally joins in the discussion, but most of the time the executives talk as much to each other as to Lafley. "I am more like a coach," Lafley says afterward. "I am always looking for different combinations that will get better results." Jeff Immelt, who asked Lafley to join GE's board in 2002, describes him as "an excellent listener. He's a sponge."

33   And now, Lafley is carefully using this information to reshape the company's approach to just about everything it does. When Lafley describes the P&G of the future, he says: "We're in the business of creating and building brands." Notice, as P&Gers certainly have, that he makes no mention of manufacturing. While Lafley shies away from saying just how much of the company's factory and back-office operations he may hand over to someone else, he does admit that facing up to the realities of the marketplace "won't always be fun." Of P&G's 102,000 employees, nearly one-half work in its plants. So far, "Lafley has deftly handled the outsourcing deals, which has lessened fear within P&G," says Roger Martin, a close adviser of Lafley's who is dean of the University of Toronto's Joseph L. Rotman School of Management. All 2,000 of the information-technology workers were moved over to HP. At the bar-soap operations, based entirely in Cincinnati, 200 of the 250 employees went to work for the Canadian contractor.

34   Lafley's approach to selling P&G products is unprecedented at the company, too: He argues that P&G doesn't have to produce just premium-priced goods. So now there's a cheaper formulation for Crest in China. The Clairol deal gave P&G bargain shampoos such as Daily Defense. And with Lafley's encouragement, managers have looked at their most expensive products to make sure they aren't too costly. In many cases, they've actually lowered the prices.

35   And Lafley is pushing P&G to approach its brands more creatively. Crest, for example, isn't just about toothpaste anymore: There's also an electric toothbrush, SpinBrush, which P&G acquired in January, 2001. P&G is also willing to license its own technologies to get them to the marketplace faster. It joined with Clorox Co., maker of Glad Bags, last October to share a food-wrap technology it had developed. It was unprecedented for P&G to work with a competitor, says licensing head Jeffrey Weedman. The overall effect is undeniable. "Lafley has made P&G far more flexible," says Banc of America's Steele.

36   But Lafley still faces daunting challenges. Keeping up the earnings growth, for example, will get tougher as competitors fight back and as P&G winds down a large restructuring program—started under Jager but accelerated under Lafley. Furthermore, some of the gains in profit have resulted from cuts in capital and R&D spending, which Lafley has pared back to the levels of the company's rivals. And already, P&G has missed a big opportunity: It passed up the chance to buy water-soluble strips that contain mouthwash. Now, Listerine is making a bundle on the product.

37   Nor are all investors comfortable with growth through acquisitions. The deals make it harder for investors to decipher earnings growth from existing operations. Then there's the risk of fumbling the integration, notes Arthur B. Cecil, an analyst at T. Rowe Price Group (TROW) Inc., which holds 1.74 million P&G shares. "I would prefer they not make acquisitions," he says. Already, Clairol hair color, the most important product in P&G's recent purchase, has lost five points of market share to L'Oréal in the United States, according to ACNeilsen Corp.

38   Making deals, however, could be the only way to balance P&G's growing reliance on Wal-Mart. Former and current P&G employees say the discounter could account for one-third of P&G's global sales by the end of the decade. Meanwhile, the pressure from consumers and competitors to keep prices low will only increase. "P&G has improved its ability to take on those challenges, but those challenges are still there," says Lehman analyst Ann Gillin.

39   Still, Lafley may be uniquely suited to creating a new and improved P&G. Even Jager agrees that

P&G Turning the Tide

	Sales	Operating Profit Margin	Outlook
Baby and Family Care	23%	17%	GOOD

P&G now vies with Kimberly-Clark to dominate the disposable-diaper market. But competition has pushed prices down, which is why this division has the slowest profit-margin growth.

Fabric and Home Care	29%	25%	VERY GOOD

Lafley has aggressively cut costs in the company's largest division. But Tide in particular faces intense competition from lower-priced rivals. To compensate, Lafley is introducing high-margin products, such as the Swiffer Duster.

Beauty Care	28%	23%	GOOD

Lafley has quickly expanded this business by acquiring Clairol and Wella. But the company has less expertise here and still has to prove it can grow internally.

Health Care	13%	18%	MIXED

With its SpinBrush and tooth-whitening products, P&G has regained the lead in oral care from Colgate. The division will get a lift from distributing heart-burn drug Prilosec over the counter. But the pharmaceutical business depends on one big seller, Actonel for osteoporosis.

Snacks and Beverages	7%	15%	WEAK

Because the division generates the company's lowest profit margins, many expect Lafley to continue to extricate P&G from these businesses. He has already sold Crisco and Jiff to J. M. Smuckers.

*Share of total sales. Estimates for fiscal year ending June 30, 2003
Data: Banc America Securities

Lafley was just what the company needed. "He has calmed down the confusion that happened while I was there," says the former CEO. Jager left a letter on Lafley's desk the day he resigned telling his successor not to feel responsible for his fall. "You earned it," he recalls writing. "Don't start out with guilt."

40 Lafley says he learned from Jager's biggest mistake. "I avoided saying P&G people were bad," he says. "I enrolled them in change." Lafley, a company man through and through, just can't resist trying out a new slogan.

Source: "P&G: New and Improved," *BusinessWeek,* July 7, 2003.

Primary Organizational Structures and Their Strategy-Related Pros and Cons

Matching the structure to the strategy is a fundamental task of company strategists. To understand how that task is handled, we first must review the five basic primary structures. We will then turn to guidelines for matching structure to strategy.

The five basic primary structures are: (1) functional, (2) geographic, (3) divisional, or strategic business unit, (4) matrix, and (5) product team. Each structure has advantages and disadvantages that strategists must consider when choosing an organization form.

FUNCTIONAL ORGANIZATIONAL STRUCTURE

Functional structures predominate in firms with a single or narrow product focus. Such firms require well-defined skills and areas of specialization to build competitive advantages in providing their products or services. Dividing tasks into functional specialties enables the personnel of these firms to concentrate on only one aspect of the necessary work. This allows use of the latest technical skills and develops a high level of efficiency.

Product, customer, or technology considerations determine the identity of the parts in a functional structure. A hotel business might be organized around housekeeping (maids), the front desk, maintenance, restaurant operations, reservations and sales, accounting, and personnel. An equipment manufacturer might be organized around production, engineering/quality control, purchasing, marketing, personnel, and finance/accounting. Two examples of functional organizations are illustrated in Exhibit 10–A.

The strategic challenge presented by the functional structure is effective coordination of the functional units. The narrow technical expertise achieved through specialization can lead to limited perspectives and to differences in the priorities of the functional units. Specialists may see the firm's strategic issues primarily as "marketing" problems or "production" problems. The potential conflict among functional units makes the coordinating role of the chief executive critical. Integrating devices (such as project teams or planning committees) are frequently used in functionally organized firms to enhance coordination and to facilitate understanding across functional areas.

GEOGRAPHIC ORGANIZATIONAL STRUCTURE

Firms often grow by expanding the sale of their products or services to new geographic areas. In these areas, they frequently encounter differences that necessitate different approaches in producing, providing, or selling their products or services. Structuring by geographic areas is usually required to accommodate these differences. Thus, Holiday Inns is organized by regions of the world because of differences among nations in the laws, customs, and economies affecting the lodging industry. And even within its U.S. organization, Holiday Inns is organized geographically because of regional differences in traveling requirements, lodging regulations, and customer mix.

EXHIBIT 10–A
Functional Organization Structures

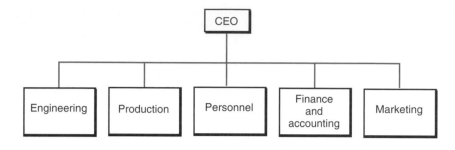

A process-oriented functional structure (an electronics distributor):

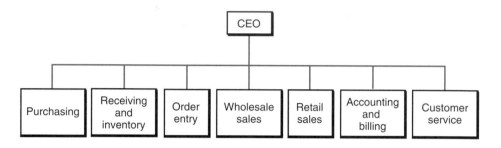

Strategic Advantages	Strategic Disadvantages
1. Achieves efficiency through specialization.	1. Promotes narrow specialization and functional rivalry or conflict.
2. Develops functional expertise.	2. Creates difficulties in functional coordination and interfunctional decision making.
3. Differentiates and delegates day-to-day operating decisions.	3. Limits development of general managers.
4. Retains centralized control of strategic decisions.	4. Has a strong potential for interfunctional conflict—priority placed on functional areas, not the entire business.
5. Tightly links structure to strategy by designating key activities as separate units.	

The key strategic advantage of geographic organizational structures is responsiveness to local market conditions. Exhibit 10–B illustrates a typical geographic organizational structure and itemizes the strategic advantages and disadvantages of such structures.

DIVISIONAL OR STRATEGIC BUSINESS UNIT STRUCTURE

When a firm diversifies its product/service lines, utilizes unrelated market channels, or begins to serve heterogeneous customer groups, a functional structure rapidly becomes inadequate. If a functional structure is retained under these circumstances, production managers may have to oversee the production of numerous and varied products or services, marketing managers may have to create sales programs for vastly different products or sell through vastly different distribution channels, and top management may be confronted with excessive coordination

EXHIBIT 10–B
A Geographic Organizational Structure

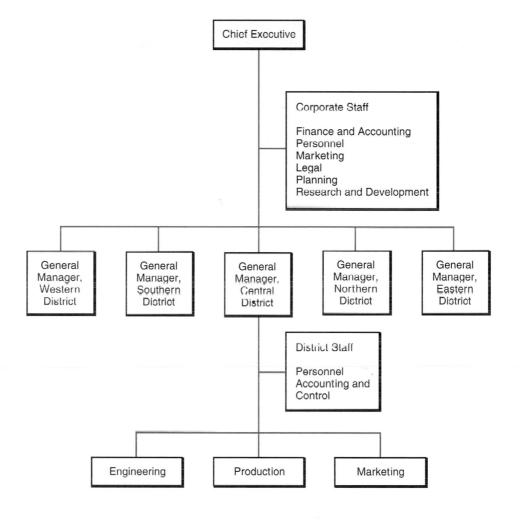

Strategic Advantages	Strategic Disadvantages
1. Allows tailoring of strategy to needs of each geographic market.	1. Poses problem of deciding whether headquarters should impose geographic uniformity or geographic diversity should be allowed.
2. Delegates profit/loss responsibility to lowest strategic level.	2. Makes it more difficult to maintain consistent company image/reputation from area to area.
3. Improves functional coordination within the target market.	3. Adds layer of management to run the geographic units.
4. Takes advantage of economies of local operations.	4. Can result in duplication of staff services at headquarters and district levels.
5. Provides excellent training grounds for higher level general managers.	

demands. A new organizational structure is often necessary to meet the increased coordination and decision-making requirements that result from increased diversity and size, and the divisional or strategic business unit (SBU) organizational structure is the form often chosen.

For many years, Ford and General Motors have used divisional/SBU structures organized by product groups. Manufacturers often organize sales into divisions based on differences in distribution channels.

A divisional/SBU structure allows corporate management to delegate authority for the strategic management of distinct business entities—the division/SBU. This expedites decision making in response to varied competitive environments and enables corporate management to concentrate on corporate-level strategic decisions. The division/SBU usually is given profit responsibility, which facilitates accurate assessment of profit and loss.

Exhibit 10–C illustrates a divisional/SBU organizational structure and specifies the strategic advantages and disadvantages of such structures.

MATRIX ORGANIZATIONAL STRUCTURE

In large companies, increased diversity leads to numerous product and project efforts of major strategic significance. The result is a need for an organizational form that provides skills and resources where and when they are most vital. For example, a product development project needs a market research specialist for two months and a financial analyst one day per week. A customer site application needs a software engineer for one month and a customer service trainer one day per month for six weeks. Each of these situations is an example of a matrix organization that has been used to temporarily put people and resources where they are most needed. Among the firms that now use some form of matrix organization are Citicorp, Matsushita, DaimlerChrysler, Microsoft, Dow Chemical, and Texas Instruments.

The matrix organization provides dual channels of authority, performance responsibility, evaluation, and control, as shown in Exhibit 10–D. Essentially, subordinates are assigned both to a basic functional area and to a project or product manager. The matrix form is intended to make the best use of talented people within a firm by combining the advantages of functional specialization and product-project specialization.

The matrix structure also increases the number of middle managers who exercise general management responsibilities (through the project manager role) and, thus, broaden their exposure to organizationwide strategic concerns. In this way, the matrix structure overcomes a key deficiency of functional organizations while retaining the advantages of functional specialization.

Although the matrix structure is easy to design, it is difficult to implement. Dual chains of command challenge fundamental organizational orientations. Negotiating shared responsibilities, the use of resources, and priorities can create misunderstanding or confusion among subordinates. These problems are heightened in an international context with the complications introduced by distance, language, time, and culture.

To avoid the deficiencies that might arise from a permanent matrix structure, some firms are accomplishing particular strategic tasks, by means of a "temporary" or "flexible" *overlay structure*. This approach, used recently by such firms as NEC, Matsushita, Philips, and Unilever, is meant to take *temporary* advantage of a matrix-type team while preserving an underlying divisional structure. Thus, the basic idea of the matrix structure—*to simplify and amplify the focus of resources on a narrow but strategically important product, project, or market*—appears to be an important structural alternative for large, diverse organizations.

EXHIBIT 10–C
Divisional or
Strategic Business
Unit Structure

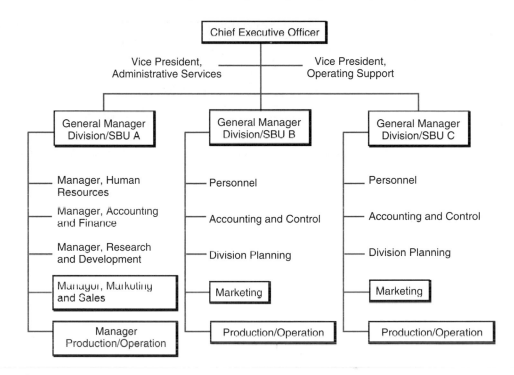

Strategic Advantages	Strategic Disadvantages
1. Forces coordination and necessary authority down to the appropriate level for rapid response.	1. Fosters potentially dysfunctional competition for corporate-level resources.
2. Places strategy development and implementation in closer proximity to the unique environments of the divisions/SBUs.	2. Presents the problem of determining how much authority should be given to division/SBU managers.
3. Frees chief executive officer for broader strategic decision making.	3. Creates a potential for policy inconsistencies among divisions/SBUs.
4. Sharply focuses accountability for performance.	4. Presents the problem of distributing corporate overhead costs in a way that's acceptable to division managers with profit responsibility.
5. Retains functional specialization within each division/SBU.	5. Increases costs incurred through duplication of functions.
6. Provides good training grounds for strategic managers.	6. Creates difficulty maintaining overall corporate image.
7. Increases focus on products, markets, and quick response to change.	

EXHIBIT 10–D
Matrix
Organizational
Structure

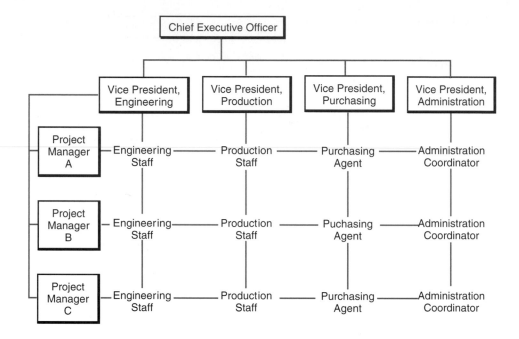

Strategic Advantages

1. Accommodates a wide variety of project-oriented business activity.
2. Provides good training grounds for strategic managers.
3. Maximizes efficient use of functional managers.
4. Fosters creativity and multiple sources of diversity.
5. Gives middle management broader exposure to strategic issues.

Strategic Disadvantages

1. May result in confusion and contradictory policies.
2. Necessitates tremendous horizontal and vertical coordination.
3. Can proliferate information logjams and excess reporting.
4. Can trigger turf battles and loss of accountability.

Chapter **Eleven**

Strategic Control and Continuous Improvement

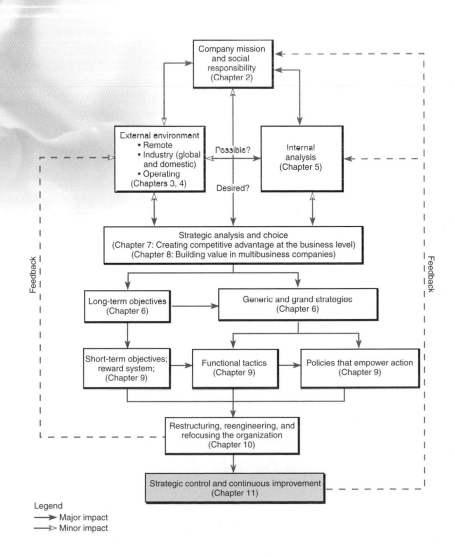

Company mission and social responsibility (Chapter 2)

External environment
• Remote
• Industry (global and domestic)
• Operating
(Chapters 3, 4)

Possible?

Desired?

Internal analysis (Chapter 5)

Strategic analysis and choice
(Chapter 7: Creating competitive advantage at the business level)
(Chapter 8: Building value in multibusiness companies)

Long-term objectives (Chapter 6)

Generic and grand strategies (Chapter 6)

Short-term objectives; reward system; (Chapter 9)

Functional tactics (Chapter 9)

Policies that empower action (Chapter 9)

Restructuring, reengineering, and refocusing the organization (Chapter 10)

Strategic control and continuous improvement (Chapter 11)

Feedback

Feedback

Legend
⟶ Major impact
⟶▷ Minor impact

Strategies are forward looking, designed to be accomplished several years into the future, and based on management assumptions about numerous events that have not yet occurred. How should managers control a strategy?

Strategic control is concerned with tracking a strategy as it is being implemented, detecting problems or changes in its underlying premises, and making necessary adjustments. In contrast to postaction control, strategic control is concerned with guiding action in behalf of the strategy as that action is taking place and when the end result is still several years off. Managers responsible for the success of a strategy typically are concerned with two sets of questions:

1. Are we moving in the proper direction? Are key things falling into place? Are our assumptions about major trends and changes correct? Are we doing the critical things that need to be done? Should we adjust or abort the strategy?

2. How are we performing? Are objectives and schedules being met? Are costs, revenues, and cash flows matching projections? Do we need to make operational changes?

The rapid, accelerating change of the global marketplace has made *continuous improvement* another aspect of strategic control in many business organizations. Synonymous with the total quality movement, continuous improvement provides a way for organizations to provide strategic control that allows an organization to respond more proactively and timely to rapid developments in hundreds of areas that influence a business's success. This chapter discusses traditional strategic controls and then explains ways that the *continuous improvement quality imperative* and the balanced scoreboard methodology can be key vehicles for strategic control.

ESTABLISHING STRATEGIC CONTROLS

The control of strategy can be characterized as a form of "steering control." Ordinarily, a good deal of time elapses between the initial implementation of a strategy and achievement of its intended results. During that time, investments are made and numerous projects and actions are undertaken to implement the strategy. Also, during that time, changes are taking place in both the environmental situation and the firm's internal situation. Strategic controls are necessary to steer the firm through these events. They must provide the basis for adapting the firm's strategic actions and directions in response to these developments and changes.

The four basic types of strategic control are:

1. Premise control.
2. Special alert control.
3. Strategic surveillance.
4. Implementation control.

The nature of these four types is summarized in Exhibit 11–1.

Premise Control

Every strategy is based on certain planning premises—assumptions or predictions. *Premise control is designed to check systematically and continuously whether the premises on which the strategy is based are still valid.* If a vital premise is no longer valid, the strategy may have to be changed. The sooner an invalid premise can be recognized and rejected, the bet-

EXHIBIT 11–1 **Four Types of Strategic Control**

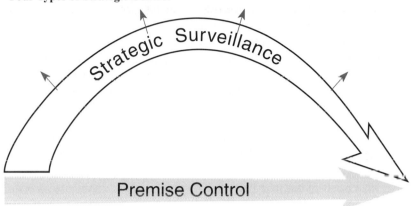

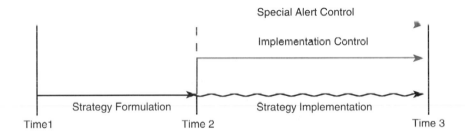

Characteristics of the Four Types of Strategic Control

| Basic Characteristics | Types of Strategic Control | | | |
	Premise Control	Implementation Control	Strategic Surveillance	Special Alert Control
Objects of control	Planning premises and projections	Key strategic thrusts and milestones	Potential threats and opportunities related to the strategy	Occurrence of recognizable but unlikely events
Degree of focusing	High	High	Low	High
Data acquisition:				
Formalization	Medium	High	Low	High
Centralization	Low	Medium	Low	High
Use with:				
Environmental factors	Yes	Seldom	Yes	Yes
Industry factors	Yes	Seldom	Yes	Yes
Strategy-specific factors	No	Yes	Seldom	Yes
Company-specific factors	No	Yes	Seldom	Seldom

Source: From Academy of Management Review by G. Schreyogg and H. Steinmann. Copyright © 1987 by Academy of Management. Reproduced with permission of Academy of Management via Copyright Clearance Center.

ter are the chances that an acceptable shift in the strategy can be devised. Planning premises are primarily concerned with environmental and industry factors.

Environmental Factors

Although a firm has little or no control over environmental factors, these factors exercise considerable influence over the success of its strategy, and strategies usually are based on key premises about them. Inflation, technology, interest rates, regulation, and demographic/social changes are examples of such factors.

EPA regulations and federal laws concerning the handling, use, and disposal of toxic chemicals have a major effect on the strategy of Velsicol Chemical Company, a market leader in pesticide chemicals sold to farmers and exterminators. So Velsicol's management makes and constantly updates premises about future regulatory actions.

Industry Factors

The performance of the firms in a given industry is affected by industry factors. These differ among industries, and a firm should be aware of the factors that influence success in its particular industry. Competitors, suppliers, product substitutes, and barriers to entry are a few of the industry factors about which strategic assumptions are made.

Rubbermaid has long been held up as a model of predictable growth, creative management, and rapid innovation in the plastic housewares and toy industry. Its premise going into the twenty-first century was that large retail chains would continue to prefer its products over competitors' because of this core competence. This premise included continued receptivity to regular price increases when necessitated by raw materials costs. Retailers, most notably Wal-Mart, recently balked at Rubbermaid's attempt to raise prices to offset the doubling of resin costs. Furthermore, traditionally overlooked competitors have begun to make inroads with computerized stocking services. Rubbermaid is moving aggressively to adjust its strategy because of the response of Wal-Mart and other key retailers.

Strategies are often based on numerous premises, some major and some minor, about environmental and industry variables. Tracking all of these premises is unnecessarily expensive and time consuming. Managers must select premises whose change (1) is likely and (2) would have a major impact on the firm and its strategy.

Strategic Surveillance

By their nature, premise controls are focused controls; strategic surveillance, however, is unfocused. *Strategic surveillance is designed to monitor a broad range of events inside and outside the firm that are likely to affect the course of its strategy.*[1] The basic idea behind strategic surveillance is that important yet unanticipated information may be uncovered by a general monitoring of multiple information sources.

Strategic surveillance must be kept as unfocused as possible. It should be a loose "environmental scanning" activity. Trade magazines, *The Wall Street Journal,* trade conferences, conversations, and intended and unintended observations are all subjects of strategic surveillance. Despite its looseness, strategic surveillance provides an ongoing, broad-based vigilance in all daily operations that may uncover information relevant to the firm's strategy. Citicorp benefited significantly from a Brazilian manager's strategic surveillance of political speeches by Lula Da Silva, Brazil's new president, as discussed in Exhibit 11–2, Strategy in Action.

Special Alert Control

Another type of strategic control, really a subset of the other three, is special alert control. *A special alert control is the thorough, and often rapid, reconsideration of the firm's strategy because of a sudden, unexpected event.* The tragic events of September 11, 2001, an outside firm's sudden acquisition of a leading competitor, an unexpected product difficulty, such as the poisoned Tylenol capsules—events of these kinds can drastically alter the firm's strategy.

---

[1] G. Schreyogg and H. Steinmann, "Strategic Control: A New Perspective," *Academy of Management Review* 12, no. 1 (1987), p. 101.

BusinessWeek

IMPLEMENTATION CONTROL AT DAYS INN

When Days Inn pioneered the budget segment of the lodging industry, its strategy placed primary emphasis on company-owned facilities and it insisted on maintaining a roughly 3-to-1 company-owned/franchise ratio. This ratio ensured the parent company's total control over standards, rates, and so forth.

As other firms moved into the budget segment, Days Inn saw the need to expand rapidly throughout the United States and, therefore, reversed its conservative franchise posture. This reversal would rapidly accelerate its ability to open new locations. Longtime executives, concerned about potential loss of control over local standards, instituted *implementation controls* requiring both franchise evaluation and annual milestone reviews. Two years into the program, Days Inn executives were convinced that a high franchise-to-company ratio was manageable, and so they accelerated the growth of franchising by doubling the franchise sales department.

STRATEGIC SURVEILLANCE AT CITICORP

Citicorp has been pursuing an aggressive product development strategy intended to achieve an annual earnings growth of 15 percent while it becomes an institution capable of supplying clients with any kind of financial service anywhere in the world. A major obstacle to the achievement of this earnings growth is Citicorp's exposure to default because of its extensive earlier loans to troubled developing countries. Citicorp is sensitive to the wide variety of predictions about impending defaults.

Citicorp's long-range plan assumes an annual 10 percent default on its developing economy loans over any five-year period.

Yet it maintains active *strategic surveillance control* by having each of its international branches monitor daily announcements from key governments and from inside contacts for signs of changes in a host country's financial environment. When that surveillance detects a potential problem, management attempts to adjust Citicorp's posture. For example, when Brazil's President-elect Lula Da Silva stated that his country may not pay interest on its debt as scheduled, Citicorp raised its annual default charge to 20 percent of its $2.5 billon Brazillian exposure.

SPECIAL ALERT CONTROL AT UNITED AIRLINES

The sudden impact of an airline crash can be devastating to a major airline. United Airlines has made elaborate preparations to deal with this contingency. Its executive vice president, James M. Guyette, heads a crisis team that is permanently prepared to respond. Members of the team carry beepers and are always on call. When United's Chicago headquarters received word of the September 11th hijacking and crash, they were in a "war room" within an hour to direct the response. Beds are set up nearby so team members can catch a few winks; while they sleep, alternates take their places.

Members of the team have been carefully screened through simulated crisis drills. "The point is to weed out those who don't hold up well under stress," says Guyette. Although the team was established to handle flight disasters, it has since assumed an expanded role. The crisis team was activated when American Airlines launched a fare war. And according to Guyette, "We're brainstorming about how we would be affected by everything from a competitor who had a serious problem to a crisis involving a hijacking or taking a United employee hostage."

Such an event should trigger an immediate and intense reassessment of the firm's strategy and its current strategic situation. In many firms, crisis teams handle the firm's initial response to unforeseen events that may have an immediate effect on its strategy. Increasingly, firms have developed contingency plans along with crisis teams to respond to circumstances such as United Airlines did on September 11, 2001, as summarized in Strategy in Action 11–2.

Implementation Control

Strategy implementation takes place as series of steps, programs, investments, and moves that occur over an extended time. Special programs are undertaken. Functional areas initiate strategy-related activities. Key people are added or reassigned. Resources are mobilized. In other words, managers implement strategy by converting broad plans into the concrete, incremental actions and results of specific units and individuals.

Implementation control is the type of strategic control that must be exercised as those events unfold. *Implementation control is designed to assess whether the overall strategy should be changed in light of the results associated with the incremental actions that implement the overall strategy.* The two basic types of implementation control are (1) monitoring strategic thrusts and (2) milestone reviews.

Monitoring Strategic Thrusts or Projects

As a means of implementing broad strategies, narrow strategic projects often are undertaken—projects that represent part of what needs to be done if the overall strategy is to be accomplished. These strategic thrusts provide managers with information that helps them determine whether the overall strategy is progressing as planned or needs to be adjusted.

Although the utility of strategic thrusts seems readily apparent, it is not always easy to use them for control purposes. It may be difficult to interpret early experience or to evaluate the overall strategy in light of such experience. One approach is to agree early in the planning process on which thrusts or which phases of thrusts are critical factors in the success of the strategy. Managers responsible for these implementation controls will single them out from other activities and observe them frequently. Another approach is to use stop/go assessments that are linked to a series of meaningful thresholds (time, costs, research and development, success, and so forth) associated with particular thrusts. A program of regional development via company-owned inns in the Rocky Mountain area was a monitoring thrust that Days Inn used to test its strategy of becoming a nationwide motel chain. Problems in meeting time targets and unexpectedly large capital needs led Days Inn's executives to abandon the overall strategy and eventually sell the firm.

Milestone Reviews

Managers often attempt to identify significant milestones that will be reached during strategy implementation. These milestones may be critical events, major resource allocations, or simply the passage of a certain amount of time. The milestone reviews that then take place usually involve a full-scale reassessment of the strategy and of the advisability of continuing or refocusing the firm's direction.

A useful example of implementation control based on milestone review is offered by Boeing's product-development strategy of entering the supersonic transport (SST) airplane market. Boeing had invested millions of dollars and years of scarce engineering talent during the first phase of its SST venture, and competition from the British/French Concorde effort was intense. Since the next phase represented a billion-dollar decision, Boeing's management established the initiation of the phase as a milestone. The milestone reviews greatly increased the estimates of production costs; predicted relatively few passengers and rising fuel costs, thus raising the estimated operating costs; and noted that the Concorde, unlike Boeing, had the benefit of massive government subsidies. These factors led Boeing's management to scrap its SST strategy in spite of high sunk costs, pride, and patriotism. Only an objective, full-scale strategy reassessment could have led to such a decision.

In this example, a milestone review occurred at a major resource allocation decision point. Milestone reviews may also occur concurrently when a major step in a strategy's implementation is being taken or when a key uncertainty is resolved. Managers even may set an arbitrary period, say two years, as a milestone review point. Whatever the basis for selecting that point, the critical purpose of a milestone review is to thoroughly scrutinize the firm's strategy so as to control the strategy's future.

Implementation control is also enabled through operational control systems like budgets, schedules and key success factors. While strategic controls attempt to steer the company over an extended period (usually five years of more), operational controls provide postaction evaluation and control over short periods—usually from one month to one year. To be effective, operational control systems must take four steps common to all postaction controls:

1. Set standards of performance.

2. Measure actual performance.

3. Identify deviations from standards set.

4. Initiate corrective action.

EXHIBIT 11–3 **Monitoring and Evaluating Performance Deviations**

Key Success Factors	Objective, Assumption, or Budget	Forecast Performance at This Time	Current Performance	Current Deviation	Analysis
Cost control: Ratio of indirect overhead cost to direct field and labor costs	10%	15%	12%	+3 (ahead)	Are we moving too fast, or is there more unnecessary overhead than was originally thought?
Gross profit	39%	40%	40%	0%	
Customer service: Installation cycle in days	2.5 days	3.2 days	2.7 days	+0.5 (ahead)	Can this progress be maintained?
Ratio of service to sales personnel	3.2	2.7	2.1	−0.6 (behind)	Why are we behind here? How can we maintain the installation-cycle progress?
Product quality: Percentage of products returned	1.0%	2.0%	2.1%	−0.1% (behind)	Why are we behind here? What are the ramifications for other operations?
Product performance versus specification	100%	92%	80%	−12% (behind)	
Marketing: Monthly sales per employee	$12,500	$11,500	$12,100	+$600 (ahead)	Good progress. Is it creating any problems to support?
Expansion of product line	6	3	5	+2 products (ahead)	Are the products ready? Are the perfect standards met?
Employee morale in service area: Absenteeism rate	2.5%	3.0%	3.0%	(on target)	
Turnover rate	5%	10%	15%	−8% (behind)	Looks like a problem! Why are we so far behind?
Competition: New product introductions (average number)	6	3	6	−3 (behind)	Did we underestimate timing? What are the implications for our basic assumptions?

Exhibit 11–3 illustrates a typical operational control system. These indicators represent progress after two years of a five-year strategy intended to differentiate the firm as a customer-service–oriented provider of high-quality products. Management's concern is to compare *progress to date* with *expected progress*. The *current deviation* is of particular interest, because it provides a basis for examining *suggested actions* (usually suggested by subordinate managers) and for finalizing decisions on changes or adjustments in the firm's operations.

From Exhibit 11–3, it appears that the firm is maintaining control of its cost structure. Indeed, it is ahead of schedule on reducing overhead. The firm is well ahead of its delivery cycle target, while slightly below its target service-to-sales personnel ratio. Its product returns look OK, although product performance versus specification is below standard. Sales per employee and expansion of the product line are ahead of schedule. The absenteeism rate in the service area is on target, but the turnover rate is higher than that targeted. Competitors appear to be introducing products more rapidly than expected.

After deviations and their causes have been identified, the implications of the deviations for the ultimate success of the strategy must be considered. For example, the rapid product-line expansion indicated in Exhibit 11–3 may have been a response to the increased rate of competitors' product expansion. At the same time, product performance is still low; and, while the installation cycle is slightly above standard (improving customer service), the ratio of service to sales personnel is below the targeted ratio. Contributing to this substandard ratio (and perhaps reflecting a lack of organizational commitment to customer service) is the exceptionally high turnover in customer service personnel. The rapid reduction in indirect overhead costs might mean that administration integration of customer service and product development requirements has been cut back too quickly.

This information presents operations managers with several options. They may attribute the deviations primarily to internal discrepancies. In that case, they can scale priorities up or down. For example, they might place more emphasis on retaining customer service personnel and less emphasis on overhead reduction and new product development. On the other hand, they might decide to continue as planned in the face of increasing competition and to accept or gradually improve the customer service situation. Another possibility is reformulating the strategy or a component of the strategy in the face of rapidly increasing competition. For example, the firm might decide to emphasize more standardized or lower-priced products to overcome customer service problems and take advantage of an apparently ambitious sales force.

This is but one of many possible interpretations of Exhibit 11–3. The important point here is the critical need to monitor progress against standards and to give serious in-depth attention to both the causes of observed deviations and the most appropriate responses to them. After the deviations have been evaluated, slight adjustments may be made to keep progress, expenditure, or other factors in line with the strategy's programmed needs. In the unusual event of extreme deviations—generally because of unforeseen changes—management is alerted to the possible need for revising the budget, reconsidering certain functional plans related to budgeted expenditures, or examining the units concerned and the effectiveness of their managers.

Correcting deviations in performance brings the entire management task into focus. Managers can correct such deviations by changing measures or plans. They also can eliminate poor performance by changing how things are done, by hiring or retraining workers, by changing job assignments, and so on. Correcting deviations, therefore, can involve all of the functions, tasks, and responsibilities of operations managers. Managers in other cultures, most notably Japan, have for some time achieved operational control by seeking their unit's continuous improvement. Companies worldwide have adapted this point of view that operational control is best achieved through a pervasive commitment to quality, originally called *total quality management* (TQM), which is seen as essential to strategic success in the twenty-first century.

THE QUALITY IMPERATIVE: CONTINUOUS IMPROVEMENT TO BUILD CUSTOMER VALUE

The initials TQM have become the most popular abbreviation in business management literature since MBO (management by objectives). TQM Stands for *total quality management,* an umbrella term for the quality programs that have been implemented in many businesses worldwide in the last two decades. TQM was first implemented in several large U.S. manufacturers in the face of the overwhelming success of Japanese and German competitors. Japanese manufacturers embraced the quality messages of Americans W. Edwards Deming and J. M. Juran following World War II, and by the 1970s Japanese products had acquired unquestioned reputations for superior high quality.

Growing numbers of U.S. manufacturers have attempted to change this imbalance with their own quality programs, and the practice has spread to large retail and service companies as well. Increasingly, smaller companies that supply big TQM companies have adopted quality programs, often because big companies have required small suppliers to adopt quality programs of their own. Exhibit 11–4, Strategy in Action, describes the aggressive quality imperative thrust on Detroit automakers today.

TQM is viewed as virtually a new organizational culture and way of thinking. It is built around an intense focus on customer satisfaction; on accurate measurement of every critical variable in a business's operation; on continuous improvement of products, services, and processes; and on work relationships based on trust and teamwork. One useful explanation of the quality imperative suggests 10 essential elements of implementing total quality management, as follows:

1. **Define *quality* and *customer value*.** Rather than be left to individual interpretation, company personnel should have a clear definition of what *quality* means in the job, department, and throughout the company. It should be developed from your customer's perspective and communicated as a written policy.

Thinking in terms of customer value broadens the definition of *quality* to include efficiency and responsiveness. Said another way, quality to your customer often means that the product performs well; that it is priced competitively (efficiency); and that you provide it quickly and adapt it when needed (responsiveness). Customer value is found in the combination of all three—quality, price, and speed.

2. **Develop a customer orientation.** Customer value is what the customer says it is. Don't rely on secondary information—talk to your customers directly. Also recognize your "internal" customers. Usually less than 20 percent of company employees come into contact with external customers, while the other 80 percent serve internal customers—other units with real performance expectations.

The value chain provides an important way to think about customer orientation, particularly to recognize *internal* as well as external (ultimate) customers. Operating personnel are *internal* customers of the accounting department for useful information and also the purchasing department for quality, timely supplies. When they are "served" with quality, efficiency, and responsiveness, value is added to their efforts, and is passed on to their internal customers and, eventually, external (ultimate) customers.

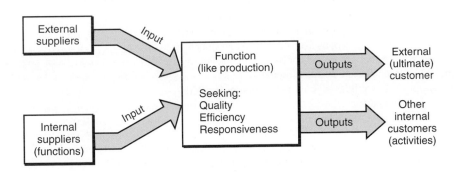

BusinessWeek When J. D. Power & Associates Inc. released its all-important Initial Quality Study of new cars recently, domestic auto makers again crowed that they had narrowed the gap with Japanese vehicles and beat some of the pricey European makes. For four years, U.S. carmakers have been showing signs that they're getting quality right, and here, finally, was the proof. Domestic brands took three of the top six slots as once-moribund names such as Mercury and Buick—yes, Buick—jumped ahead of BMW and Toyota. General Motors Corp.'s resurgent Cadillac division trailed only Lexus.

But will Detroit be able to exploit its quality gains? Unfortunately, many consumers still have doubts, and for good reason. Scores for the entire GM, Ford Motor, and Daimler-Chrysler lineups are still below the industry average. Worse, Detroit has yet to make a convincing case that its cars hold up over time as well as Japanese models.

That's the acid test for most consumers. As it is, buyers still remember the bad old days, as recently as the early '90s, when U.S.-made vehicles were unreliable. Michael Austill, a Vestal (N.Y.) aerospace manager, suffered a 1980 Ford Fairmont, a clunky 1984 Pontiac 6000, and a 1995 Oldsmobile Aurora that was in the shop 18 times. He gave up on Detroit and has been happily driving Japanese and European cars since. "I have not [set] foot in a U.S. car showroom," says Austill.

The latest round of quality ratings probably won't convince buyers to abandon their skepticism. Although GM and Ford score well on initial quality—measured by problems per vehicle in the first three months of ownership—their cars still register as subpar over longer periods. In a recent issue of *Consumer Reports,* a survey of defects in three-year-old cars finds that all of the big-selling domestic names finished below the industry average. That will only change if Detroit is able to continue pushing tight controls that would allow better-built cars—such as Lincoln's Town Car, which gets high marks for reliability on the *Consumer Reports* survey—to work their way through the market. Says J. D. Power product research director Brian Walters: "It will take years of good performance for the domestic reputation to change."

The Big Three have worked hard over the past decade to adopt many of the quality initiatives of their Japanese rivals—and have come up with some of their own. All have tightened up inspections at their plants. They are working with suppliers to use proven reliable parts from existing vehicles in future models instead of engineering new parts from scratch. When launching some models, Ford keeps thousands of vehicles in holding yards for months of testing before shipping them to dealers.

To demonstrate confidence in its cars, Chrysler is offering extended warranties that can be transferred to subsequent owners. Says Chrysler marketing boss James C. Schroer: "We need to convince customers that the new vehicles being produced are reliable, and that when they go to trade them in, they'll get a good value." GM plans to launch an ad campaign in June called "Road to Redemption" that fesses up to years of inferior quality—and points to its Power ratings as evidence of a turnaround.

If only it were that simple. Detroit still has far to go. Imports have built a durable image for quality by focusing much more on the parts of a car that drivers actually feel. Japanese and European autos have plusher interiors and better knobs, switches, and gauges. Consumers have had such a dim view of domestic cars that they regard some foreign cars as better built even when they aren't. They believe European luxury cars made by Mercedes-Benz Audi, and Volkswagen are among the industry's best, says Power. But in actual studies measuring problems, none of them ranks near the top. All were topped in the Power survey by Cadillac, whose sales are up 17 percent thanks to its new CTS sedan.

There's only one way to change that perception: Keep improving. Power's Walters says strong results in initial quality eventually pay off in long-term studies. So while GM is eager to play up its gains, North America President Gary L. Cowger knows the company still has plenty of work to do. "We want to become the best in quality, bar none," he says. If the Big Three can pull that off, buyers may actually start to listen.

A Discouraging Look Down the Pike
American buyers won't abandon their skepticism until the Big Three's cars perform better over time

Initial Quality*	Long-Term Quality**
1 Lexus	1 Acura
2 Cadillac ▲	2 Toyota
3 Infiniti	3 Lexus
4 Acura	4 Honda
5 Buick	5 Mazda
6 Mercury	6 Subaru
7 Porsche	7 Saab
8 BMW	8 Nissan
9 Toyota	9 Mitsubishi
10 Jaguar	10 Lincoln ▶

*Problems in the first 90 days of ownership.

**Problems after three years of ownership.

Data: J. D. Power & Associates 2003 Initial Quality

Survey: *Consumer Reports* 2003 Reliability Survey for long-term quality.

Source: "Way to Go, Detroit—Now Go a Lot Further," *BusinessWeek,* May 26, 2003.

3. **Focus on the company's business processes.** Break down every minute step in the process of providing the company's product or service and look at ways to improve it, rather than focusing simply on the finished product or service. Each process contributes value in some way, which can be improved or adapted to help other processes (internal customers) improve. Examples of ways customer value is enhanced across business processes in several functions are:

	Quality	**Efficiency**	**Responsiveness**
Marketing	Provides accurate assessment of customer's product preferences to R&D	Targets advertising campaign at customers, using cost-effective medium	Quickly uncovers and reacts to changing market trends
Operations	Consistently produces goods matching engineering design	Minimizes scrap and rework through high-production yield	Quickly adapts to latest demands with production flexibility
Research and development	Designs products that combine customer demand and production capabilities	Uses computers to test feasibility of idea before going to more expensive full-scale prototype	Carries out parallel product/process designs to speed up overall innovation
Accounting	Provides the information that managers in other functions need to make decisions	Simplifies and computerizes to decrease the cost of gathering information	Provides information in "real time" (as the events described are still happening)
Purchasing	Selects vendors for their ability to join in an effective "partnership"	Given the required vendor quality, negotiates prices to provide good value	Schedules inbound deliveries efficiently, avoiding both extensive inventories and stock-outs
Personnel	Trains workforce to perform required tasks	Minimizes employee turnover, reducing hiring and training expenses	In response to strong growth in sales, finds large numbers of employees and quickly teaches needed skills

4. **Develop customer and supplier partnerships.** Organizations have a destructive tendency to view suppliers and even customers adversarily. It is better to understand the horizontal flow of a business—outside suppliers to internal suppliers/customers (a company's various departments) to external customers. This view suggests suppliers are partners in meeting customer needs, and customers are partners by providing input so the company and suppliers can meet and exceed those expectations.

Ford Motor Company's Dearborn, Michigan, plant is linked electronically with supplier Allied Signal's Kansas City, Missouri, plant. A Ford computer recently sent the design for a car's connecting rod to an Allied Signal factory computer, which transformed the design into instructions that it fed to a machine tool on the shop floor. The result: quality, efficiency, and responsiveness.

5. **Take a preventive approach.** Many organizations reward "fire fighters," not "fire preventers," and identify errors after the work is done. Management, instead, should be rewarded for being prevention oriented and seeking to eliminate nonvalue-added work.

6. **Adopt an error-free attitude.** Instill an attitude that "good enough" is not good enough anymore. "Error free" should become each individual's performance standard, with managers taking every opportunity to demonstrate and communicate the importance of this imperative.

7. **Get the facts first.** Continuous improvement–oriented companies make decisions based on facts, not on opinions. Accurate measurement, often using readily available statistical techniques, of every critical variable in a business's operation—and using those measurements to trace problems to their roots and eliminate their causes—is a better way.

8. **Encourage every manager and employee to participate.** Employee participation, empowerment, participative decision making, and extensive training in quality techniques, in statistical techniques, and in measurement tools are the ingredients continuous improvement companies employ to support and instill a commitment to customer value.

9. **Create an atmosphere of total involvement.** Quality management cannot be the job of a few managers or of one department. Maximum customer value cannot be achieved unless all areas of the organization apply quality concepts simultaneously.

10. **Strive for continuous improvement.** Stephen Yearout, director of Ernst & Young's Quality Management Center, recently observed that "Historically, meeting your customers' expectations would distinguish you from your competitors. The twenty-first century will require you to anticipate customer expectations and deliver quality service faster than the competition." Quality, efficiency, and responsiveness are not one-time programs of competitive response, for they create a new standard to measure up to. Organizations quickly find that continually improving quality, efficiency, and responsiveness in their processes, products, and services is not just good business; it's a necessity for long-term survival.

Six-Sigma Approach to Continuous Improvement

Sometimes referred to as the "new TQM," Six-Sigma is a highly rigorous and analytical approach to quality and continuous improvement with an objective to improve profits through defect reduction, yield improvement, improved consumer satisfaction and best-in-class performance. Six-Sigma complements TQM philosophies such as management leadership, continuous education and customer focus while deploying a disciplined and structured approach of hard-nosed statistics. Critics of TQM see key success factors differentiating Six-Sigma from TQM.

- Acute understanding of customers and the product or service provided

- Emphasis on the science of statistics and measurement

- Meticulous and structured training development

- Strict and project-focused methodologies

- Reinforcement of the doctrine advocated by Juran such as top management support and continuous education

Companies such as Honeywell (1994), Motorola (1987), GE (1995), Polaroid (1998) and Texas Instruments (1988) have adopted the Six-Sigma discipline as a major business initiative. Many of these companies invested heavily in and pursued this model initially in order to create products and services that were of equal and higher quality than those of its competitors and to improve relationships with customers. Much like TQM, the technique implies a whole culture of strategies, tools, and statistical methodologies to improve the bottom line resulting in tremendous savings, subsequent improvement initiatives, and management action.

A Six-Sigma program at many organizations simply means a measure of quality that strives for near perfection in every facet of the business including every product, process, and transaction. The approach was introduced and established at Motorola in 1987, becoming the key factor in Motorola winning the 1988 Malcolm Baldrige Award for Quality, and has had impressive and undisputed results for many companies who have undertaken it. Allied Signal reported an estimated savings of $1.5 billion in its 1997 annual report while GE's savings in a 1998 annual letter to its shareholders reported benefits exceeding $750 million a year.

How the Six-Sigma Statistical Concept Works

Six-Sigma means a failure rate of 3.4 parts per million or 99.9997%. At the six standard deviation from the mean under a normal distribution, 99.9996% of the population is under the curve with not more than 3.4 parts per million defective. The higher the sigma value, the less likely a process will produce defects as excellence is approached.

If you played 100 rounds of golf per year and played at:
2 Sigma: You'd miss 6 putts per round.
3 Sigma: You'd miss 1 putt per round.
4 Sigma: You'd miss 1 putt every 9 rounds.
5 Sigma: You'd miss 1 putt every 2.33 years.
6 Sigma: You'd miss 1 putt every 163 years!

Source: From John Petty, "When Near Enough is Not Good Enough," Australian CPA, May 2000, pp. 34–35. Reprinted with permission of CPA Australia.

Many frameworks, management philosophies, and specific statistical tools exist for implementing the Six-Sigma methodology and its objective to create a near perfect process or service. One such method for improving a system for existing processes falling below specification while looking for incremental improvement is the DMAIC process (define, measure, analyze, improve, control).

Define

- Project Definition
- Project Charter
- Gathering Voice of the Customer
- Translating Customer Needs into Specific Requirements

Measure

- Process Mapping (As-Is Process)
- Data Attributes (Continuous vs. Discrete)
- Measurement System Analysis
- Gage Repeatability and Reproducibility
- Measuring Process Capability
- Calculating Process Sigma Level
- Visually Displaying Baseline Performance

Analyze

- Visually Displaying Data (Histogram, Run Chart, Pareto Chart, Scatter Diagram)
- Value-Added Analysis
- Cause and Effect Analysis (a.k.a. Fishbone, Ishikawa)
- Verification of Root Causes
- Determining Opportunity (Defects and Financial) for Improvement
- Project Charter Review and Revision

Improve

- Brainstorming
- Quality Function Deployment (House of Quality)
- Failure Modes and Effects Analysis (FMEA)
- Piloting Your Solution
- Implementation Planning
- Culture Modification Planning for Your Organization

Control

- Statistical Process Control (SPC) Overview
- Developing a Process Control Plan
- Documenting the Process

Six-Sigma programs promote an uncompromising orientation of all business processes toward the customer. The first step is always achieving an understanding of customer expectations so that suitable tools can be employed to improve both the internal and external processes. This program does not come fast and cheap; however, management commitment is crucial to the success, and employees must be trained in Six-Sigma methodologies. Exhibit 11–5, Strategy in Action, describes the use of Six-Sigma at Citibank.

ISO 9004 and the Era of International Standards

The ISO 9004 quality management system standard, introduced in 1987, is international in both scope and impact. In early 2003 there were almost 400,000 firms registered in over 153 countries, almost 35,000 of those registered firms in the United States. The trend towards ISO 9004 registration and the creation of additional management system standards such as ISO 14004 (environmental), ISO 18004 (health and safety) and sector-specific standards such as QS-9004 (automotive) and AS-9004 (aerospace) has continued to grow and develop internationally. The standards are voluntary and apply to many kinds of businesses including manufacturers, distributors, services, software developers, public utilities, government agencies, and financial and educational institutions.

The *ISO 9004 standard* focuses on achieving customer satisfaction through continuous measurement, documentation, assessment, and adjustment. A diagram of the approach is provided below. The standard specifies requirements for a quality management system where an organization:

1. Needs to demonstrate its ability to consistently provide product and services that meet customer requirements, and

THE BIG PICTURE

In 1997 Citibank set about to apply this technique to its nonmanufacturing environment by contracting with Motorola University Consulting and Training Services for extensive Six-Sigma training. The goal was to improve Citibank operations globally through defect reduction and process timeline improvement while increasing customer loyalty and satisfaction.

Citibank's mission focused on becoming the premier international financial company in the next millennium requiring excellence in every facet of the business and action on the part of every Citibank employee. This quality initiative began with training 650 senior managers by October 1997 and over 92,000 employees trained worldwide by early 1999.

SIX-SIGMA TO THE RESCUE

The initial phase of the Six-Sigma process involved Motorola University training Citibank employees on both Cycle Time Reduction (CTR) and Cross Functional Process Mapping (CFPM). These methodologies essentially set the stage for Six-Sigma by mapping and eliminating wasteful and nonvalue-added processing steps from the business. In a nonmanufacturing company, 90 percent of activities may fall into this category. A sigma is a statistical term which measures to what degree a process varies from perfection. A rating of three sigma equals 66,807 defects per million opportunities; a rating of Six-Sigma equals 3.4 defects per million opportunities, or virtual perfection.

Six-Sigma is accomplished using simple tools, including the Pareto chart. The data on the chart identify which problems occur with the greatest frequency or incur the highest cost. It provides the direct evidence of what would be analyzed and corrected first. Typically 20 percent of the possible causes are responsible for 80 percent of any problem.

Citibank undertook the Six-Sigma process to investigate why it was not achieving complete customer satisfaction with a goal to have 10 times reduction in defects and cycle time by December 2000 and 10 times again every two years. Six-Sigma classifies a defect as anything that results in customer dissatisfaction and unhappiness. Indicators of less than optimal status are customer opinions such as:

- You're difficult to do business with;

- You don't fix my problems;

- You're not staying innovative and your systems are not state-of-the-art;

- You are slow and complicated.

TEAM APPROACH

A team composed of bankers and operations people identified the entire funds transfer process, tabulating defects and analyzing them using Pareto charts. Highest on the list of defects for this process was the internal callback procedure, which required a staffer to phone back the requester to make sure that the instructions were correct, or had not been altered. "We cut monthly callbacks from 8,000 to 1,000 and we eliminated callbacks for 73 percent of the transactions coming in," says Cherylann Munoz, compliance director of Citibank's Private Bank in the United States and Western Hemisphere.

In Citibank's Global Cash and Trade Organization (GCTO), MU's Six-Sigma methodology helped track defects and documented the results by teaching team members to identify appropriate metrics, determine a baseline, establish appropriate standards, and monitor execution. The employees formed teams to solve any issues they discovered during this analysis.

To reduce the time for opening an account, Citibank formed a cross-functional global team of 80 people. The team first identified sponsors and formed a steering committee to champion the effort. Employees were invited to participate based on their subject matter know-how and ability to assist with the solution. The biggest hurdle for Citibank employees was allocating the time to participate while juggling their daily job responsibilities. Sue Andros, a global process owner in the GCTO responsible for the end-to-end customer experience says process mapping "lets people get to know one another."

"Team members worked well together, since achieving the objectives would make their professional responsibilities easier and would benefit their customers—a win/win situation for everyone," Andros says. "The focus on cycle time and deficiencies has made an impact on how we serve customers. It's not just a matter of doing things faster, it's doing things better. This means eliminating redundancy, minimizing hand-offs, and establishing metrics that reflect performance in the eyes of the customer."

Dipak Rastogi, executive vice president for Citibank's Eastern European/Central Asia and Africa region headquartered in London, agrees with those sentiments. "Introducing quality as a core strategy was viewed as a unique opportunity and differentiating feature not only with regard to our customers, but also our employees," says Rastogi. "When implemented correctly, quality increases customer satisfaction and leads to shorter reaction time and faster introduction of new products—providing a sustainable competitive advantage."

(continued)

MANAGEMENT COMMITMENT

Teams involved in the Citibank quality initiative needed to have full autonomy to make decisions about changes to the established processes. Senior management sponsored these initiatives or served on steering committees to champion the work and there was an "open door" policy so that teams could gain access to them as needed. According to Peter Klimes, quality director for Citibank in the Czech Republic, the involvement of senior support is a continuous process all the way from setting critical business issues and objectives, to the final improvement implementation. "We have had a well-balanced split between projects initiated by senior management and those initiated by employees," Klimes says. "Our senior operations officer and our corporate bank head were our most active supporters of Six-Sigma projects. Their commitment helps balance back and front office aspects of projects."

Source: "Citibank Increases Loyalty with Defect-Free Processes," *The Journal for Quality & Participation,* Fall 2000, pp. 32–36.

2. Aims to enhance customer satisfaction through the effective application of the system, including processes for continual improvement of the system and the ensurance of conformity to customer requirements.

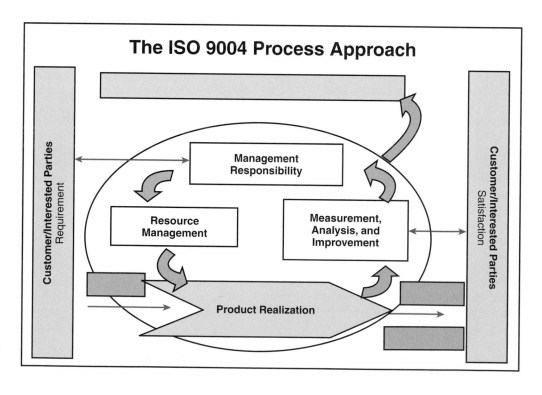

ISO 9004 has strong commonalities with other quality schemes such as Mil-Q, Deming's 14 points, TQM and the Malcolm Baldrige National Quality Award Criteria. The four focus areas of the ISO 9004 process approach are (1) management responsibility, (2) resource management, (3) product realization, and (4) measurement, analysis, and improvement. ISO 9004 differs from other quality approaches in that it involves formal certification by a sanctioned ISO certification source before a company can claim to meet the standard. Exhibit 11–6, Strategy in Action, describes how well-known golf club maker Ping chose to become ISO 9004 certified.

When John Solheim took the helm at golf equipment maker Ping in 1995, he had a legacy to protect and improve—that of his father, Karsten Solheim. When the employee handbook was written in 1993, Karsten wrote: "It is the customer who keeps us in business, and we must always be sure to give each one first-class treatment. The role of each employee is also very important because dedication to quality assures the success of the company."

The family business was founded over 42 years ago and is based in Phoenix. Today Ping is best known for its custom fit, custom-built golf clubs and competes in a highly innovative and competitive $4 billion golf equipment industry. John wasn't satisfied with the existing standard of quality and set about to find a way to measure the company business against an internationally accepted standard, ISO 9004. "By embarking on this journey, we hoped to measure ourselves against recognized criteria that would reassure us we were doing business appropriately," says Solheim. "We also believed such an accomplishment might help identify areas where we could advance." Both of Solheim's hopes were fulfilled.

THE IMPLEMENTATION AND REGISTRATION PROCESS

After conducting some research, John Solheim decided to pursue registration to both ISO 9004 (quality management system standard) and ISO 14004 (environmental management system standard). This decision was based on several factors:

1. The ISO (International Organization for Standardization) standards are internationally recognized.

2. Attaining registration would provide Ping with a competitive advantage in the marketplace. Ping would be the first competitor in the golf industry to be registered to both ISO 9004 and ISO 14004 standards.

3. Ping wanted the benefits of implementing the management systems such as improved quality, increased environmental awareness, customer satisfaction, and continuous improvement.

Ping began the implementation process in November 1999. The first step was to develop documentation, identify and improve processes, and provide training to all personnel involved in the implementation. A preassessment audit acted as a dress rehearsal for employees and heightened their understanding of the requirements as well as identified opportunities for improvement in the existing system.

During this process Ping faced many challenges. First, its workforce consisted of over 1,000 employees who spoke at least six different languages. Additionally, company processes, documentation, and policies were very informal. Many hours were spent training and developing valuable manuals that are used as reference resources. "The registration process helped me see how everything in the company ties together and our processes really interrelate," said Solheim. "I thought I was fairly well-organized, but the registration audit taught me to dot my I's and cross my T's."

BENEFITS

Ping's steering committee identified many benefits of the ISO 9004 and ISO 14004 registration.

1. Enhanced internal communication and increased focus on customer requirements throughout the organization.

2. The generation of useful information to allow more strategic decision making by all levels of management.

3. Better measurement of the processes that are responsible for quality and the ability to continually improve product quality.

4. Improved customer satisfaction and the continued reputation for quality, innovation, and service in the golf equipment market.

5. Development of a new customer service call system that improved customer response time.

6. Improved environmental performance resulting in reduced emissions.

7. Improved cycle times to meet our customers' demands.

Ping officially achieved registration on October 17, 2000. Ping is now in the process of implementing ISO 9004 and ISO 14004 in its sister company, Ping Europe Ltd., in Gainsborough, United Kingdom. This registration will include the Gainsborough Golf Club, a private 36-hole facility with a driving range and modern clubhouse. Ping believes this will be the first country club to ever be registered to international standards.

Now registered, the company is continuing to focus intensely on continuous improvement of the quality of its systems, operations, service, and products in a highly competitive worldwide market. "We continuously hone our ISO 9004 and 14004 systems, strengthening our quality and environmental objectives while looking for improvement opportunities. No one asked us to become ISO registered," Solheim says. "We raised our standards because golfers ultimately decide the fate of our products. Customer satisfaction will be the program's greatest benefit."

Upon introduction of the ISO 9004 series of standards, many American and multinational firms not only foresaw the competitive advantage possible by adopting ISO 9004, but also saw the value of quality management system implementation in achieving customer satisfaction. As a result, many of these larger firms subsequently imposed the requirements of ISO 9004 on suppliers as a condition to do business and as a way to reduce the supply base to only those suppliers committed to quality and service. It is believed by many that eventually ISO 9004 would reduce and possibly eliminate the need for customer-sponsored audits. In the ISO 9004 registration scheme, third-party auditors employed by registrars conduct ISO 9004 registration audits. National and international accreditation bodies accredit the registrars to certify and publish that the company has met the requirements of ISO 9004.

Customer mandates initially served as an incentive for suppliers desiring to retain existing levels of business with their customers to jump on the ISO 9004 bandwagon and pursue registration. In many cases registration to ISO 9004 gave these suppliers a clear competitive advantage in the marketplace. However, as many companies continue to pursue and maintain registration, ISO 9004 functions as a way of life for many companies and has become ingrained in daily processes, no longer thought of as a unique or identifiable program. Other companies, who were not pressured to implement ISO 9004, chose to put it into practice as a methodology by which to systematize their operations and to focus on and improve both daily operations and quality levels throughout their organizations.

Nevertheless, along with the establishment of ISO 9004 standards came many misperceptions. Here are just a few of the criticisms targeted at ISO 9004.

- *ISO 9004 is a European standard and cannot be applicable to American firms.* ISO 9004 has traceable American ancestry to military quality systems. The United States is a member of International Organization for Standardization (ISO) and participates in the formulation and continuing committee reviews of ISO 9004.

- *Implementing ISO 9004 is mandatory if you plan to do business in Europe.* This is true for a small number of firms manufacturing a relative handful of products—a list that may continue to grow in the coming years. But the doors to Europe did not slam shut on non-ISO 9004 registered companies in January 2003. Rather, ISO 9004 registration has increasingly become desired, expected and even required in certain markets and industries (i.e., Automotive QS-9004), but growth was driven primarily by customer requirements and competitive pressures.

- *ISO 9004 is all about paperwork.* Ironically, ISO 9004 had in most cases reduced the redundancy and massive manuals and shelves of procedures and books that already exist. Documentation is central to ISO 9004 requirements for the purposes of planning, controlling, training, and providing objective evidence of conformance. The goal is to make the documentation support the value-added activity clearly and concisely, eliminating redundancy while supporting usefulness. The standard does not prescribe specific solutions, tactics, strategies, or procedures which gives ISO 9004 enormous flexibility.

- *ISO 9004 is inspection-based as opposed to prevention-based.* ISO 9004 requires the quality management system monitor conformance to requirements. This is just one part of the measurement, analysis, and continuous improvement cycle at the heart of the standard. Implementation of the standard alone will not guarantee quality. Management commitment and employee involvement are instrumental in the implementation process.

Since its introduction, international participation in ISO 9004 continues to climb and offers organizations a framework for quality system management. It is no longer new or radical, yet it provides a common language for quality that is easily translatable and applicable across many countries, cultures, and businesses. The focus is not on products and services but rather on the organization's network of activities designed and operated to ensure that output meets the ultimate business objective: satisfying the customer.

The Balanced Scorecard Methodology

A new approach to strategic control was developed in the last decade by Harvard Business School professors Robert Kaplan and David Norton. They named this system the *balanced scorecard.* Recognizing some of the weaknesses and vagueness of previous implementation and control approaches, the balanced scorecard approach was intended to provide a clear prescription as to what companies should measure in order to "balance" the financial perspective in implementation and control of strategic plans.[2]

The balanced scorecard was viewed as a *management system* (not only a measurement system) that enables companies to clarify their strategies, translate them into action, and provide meaningful feedback. It provides feedback around both the internal business processes and external outcomes in order to continuously improve strategic performance and results. When fully deployed, the balanced scorecard is intended to transform strategic planning from a separate top management exercise into the nerve center of an enterprise. Kaplan and Norton describe the innovation of the balanced scorecard as follows:

> The balanced scorecard retains traditional financial measures. But financial measures tell the story of past events, an adequate story for industrial age companies for which investments in long-term capabilities and customer relationships were not critical for success. These financial measures are inadequate, however, for guiding and evaluating the journey that information age companies must make to create future value through investment in customers, suppliers, employees, processes, technology, and innovation.[3]

The balanced scorecard methodology adapts the TQM ideas of customer-defined quality, continuous improvement, employee empowerment, and measurement-based management/feedback into an expanded methodology that includes traditional financial data and results. The balanced scorecard incorporates feedback around internal business process *outputs,* as in TQM, but also adds a feedback loop around the *outcomes* of business strategies. This creates a "double-loop feedback" process in the balanced scorecard. In doing so, it links together two areas of concern in strategy execution—quality operations and financial outcomes—that are typically addressed separately yet are obviously critically intertwined as any company executes its strategy. A system that links shareholder interests in return on capital with a system of performance management that is linked to ongoing, operational activities and processes within the company is what the balanced scorecard attempts to achieve.

Exhibit 11–7 illustrates the balanced scorecard approach drawing on the traditional DuPont formula discussed in Chapter 5 and historically used to examine drivers of stockholder-related financial performance across different company activities. The balanced scorecard seeks to "balance" shareholder goals with customer goals and operational performance goals, and Exhibit 11–7 shows that they are interconnected—shareholder value creation is linked to divisional concerns for return on capital employed, which, in turn, is driven by functional outcomes in sales, inventory, capacity utilization, that, in turn, come

[2] This methodology is covered in great detail in a number of books and articles by R. S. Kaplan and D. P. Norton. It is also the subject of frequent special publications by the *Harvard Business Review* that provided updated treatment of uses and improvements in the balanced scorecard methodology. Some useful books include *Balanced Scorecard: Translating Strategies into Action* (Boston: Harvard Business School Press, 1996); *The Strategy-Focused Organization* (Boston: Harvard Business School Press, 2001). And, in HBR, "Using the Balanced Scorecard as a Strategic Management System," *Harvard Business Review* (January–February, 1996). Numerous useful websites also exist such as www.bscol.com.
[3] Another useful treatment of various aspects of the Balanced Scoreboard to include further learning opportunities you may wish to explore, especially with regard to the use of this approach with governmental organizations, may be found at www.balancedscorecard.org. Chapter 6 in this book describes how the Balanced Scorecard approach is used to help create measurable objectives linked directly to the company's strategy.

EXHIBIT 11–7
Integrating Shareholder Value and Organizational Activities across Organizational Levels

Source: R. M. Grant, *Contemporary Strategy Analysis* (Oxford, UK: Blackwell, 2002), p. 56).

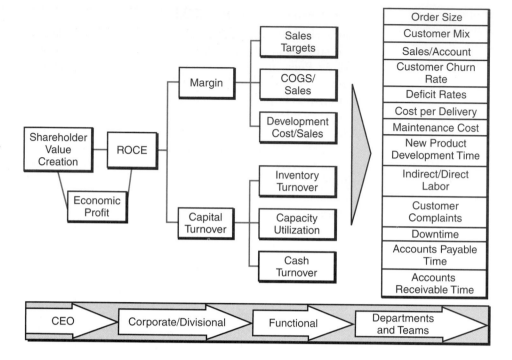

about through the results of departments and teams daily activities throughtout the company. The balanced scorecard suggests that we view the organization from *four* perspectives, and to develop metrics, collect data, and analyze it relative to each of these perspectives:

1. *The Learning and Growth Perspective: How well are we continuously improving and creating value?* The scorecard insists on measures related to innovation and organizational learning to gauge performance on this dimension—technological leadership, product development cycle times, operational process improvement, and so on.

2. *The Business Process Perspective: What are our core competencies and areas of operational excellence?* Internal business processes and their effective execution as measured by productivity, cycle time, quality measures, downtime, various cost measures among others provide scorecard input here.

3. *The Customer Perspective: How satisfied are our customers?* A customer satisfaction perspective typically adds measures related to defect levels, on-time delivery, warranty support, product development among others that come from direct customer input and are linked to specific company activities.

4. *The Financial Perspective: How are we doing for our shareholders?* A financial perspective typically using measures like cash flow, return on equity, sales and income growth.

Through the integration of goals from each of these four perspectives, the balanced scorecard approach enables the strategy of the business to be linked with shareholder value creation while providing several measurable short-term outcomes that guide and monitor strategy implementation. Kaplan and Norton provide this account of the use of the balanced scorecard at FMC:

> Strategists came up with 5- and 10-year plans, controllers with one-year budgets and near-term forecasts. Little interplay occurred between the two groups. But the [balanced] scorecard now bridges the two. The financial perspective builds on the traditional function

EXHIBIT 11–8

Balanced Scorecard for Mobil Corporation's NAM&R

		Strategic Objectives	Strategic Measures
Financially Strong	**Financial**	F1 Return on Capital Employed F2 Cash Flow F3 Profitability F4 Lowest Cost F5 Profitable Growth F6 Manage Risk	• ROCE • Cash Flow • Net Margin • Full cost per gallon delivered to customer • Volume growth rate vs. industry • Risk index
Delight the Consumer Win–Win Relationship	**Customer**	C1 Continually delight the targeted consumer C2 Improve dealer/distributor profitability	• Share of segment in key markets • Mystery shopper rating • Dealer/distributor margin on gasoline • Dealer/distributor survey

Safe and Reliable
 	
Competitive Supplier
 	
Good Neighbor
 	
On Spec On Time
	Internal	I1 Marketing
		  1. Innovative products and services
		  2. Dealer/distributor quality
		
		I2 Manufacturing
		  1. Lower manufacturing costs
		  2. Improve hardware and performance
		
		I3 Supply, Trading, Logistics
		  1. Reducing delivered cost
		  2. Trading organization
		  3. Inventory management
		
		I4 Improve health, safety, and environmental performance
		I5 Quality
			• Non-gasoline revenue and margin per square foot
			• Dealer/distributor acceptance rate of new programs
			• Dealer/distributor quality ratings
			• ROCE on refinery
			• Total expenses (per gallon) vs. competition
			• Profitability index
			• Yield index
			Delivered cost per gallon vs. competitors
			• Trading margin
			• Inventory level compared to plan and to output rate
			• Number of incidents
			• Days away from work
			• Quality index

Motivated and Prepared	**Learning and growth**	L1 Organization involvement L2 Core competencies and skills L3 Access to strategic information	• Employee survey • Strategic competitive availability • Strategic information availabiilty

performed by controllers. The other three perspectives make the division's long-term objectives measurable.[4]

Another example that helps you understand the integrating power of the balanced scorecard can be seen at Mobil Corporation's North American Marketing and Refining business (NAM&R). NAM&R's scorecard is shown in Exhibit 11–8. Assisted by Kaplan and Norton,

---

[4] R. Kaplan and D. Norton, "Putting the Balanced Scorecard to Work," *Harvard Business Review* (September–October, 1993), p. 147.

an unprofitable NAM&R adopted the scorecard methodology to better link its strategy with financial objectives and to translate these into operating performance targets tailored to outcomes in each business unit, functional departments, and operating processes within them. They included measures developed with key customers from their perspective. The result was an integrated system where scorecards provided measurable outcomes through which the performance of each department and operating unit, team or activity within NAM&R was monitored, adjusted, and used to determine performance-related pay bonuses.[5]

The balanced scorecard reflects continuous improvement in management thought about how to better manage organizations. Our coverage of the concept is brief, and you are encouraged to seek additional information and resources suggested in various footnotes or through your own current Web search. Strategic control, continuous improvement, specific measurable feedback and inclusion of everyone in some way responsible for customer satisfaction and organizational success are important developments in the art of strategic management and the science of its succesful application.

Summary

Three fundamental perspectives—strategic control, continuous improvement, and the balanced scoreboard—provide the basis for designing strategy control systems. Strategic controls are intended to steer the company toward its long-term strategic goals. Premise controls, implementation controls, strategic surveillance, and special alert controls are types of strategic control. All four types are designed to meet top management's needs to track the strategy as it is being implemented, to detect underlying problems, and to make necessary adjustments. These strategic controls are linked to the environmental assumptions and the key operating requirements necessary for successful strategy implementation. Ever-present forces of change fuel the need for and focus of strategic control.

Operational control systems require systematic evaluation of performance against predetermined standards or targets. A critical concern here is identification and evaluation of performance deviations, with careful attention paid to determining the underlying reasons for and strategic implications of observed deviations before management reacts. Some firms use trigger points and contingency plans in this process.

The "quality imperative" of the last 20 years has redefined global competitiveness to include reshaping the way many businesses approach strategic and operational control. What has emerged is a commitment to continuous improvement in which personnel across all levels in an organization define customer value, identify ways every process within the business influences customer value, and seek continuously to enhance the quality, efficiency, and responsiveness with which the processes, products, and services are created and supplied. This includes attending to internal as well as external customers. The "balanced scorecard" is a control system that integrates strategic goals, operating outcomes, customer satisfaction, and continuous improvement into an ongoing strategic management system.

Questions for Discussion

1. Distinguish strategic control from operating control. Give an example of each.

2. Select a business whose strategy is familiar to you. Identify what you think are the key premises of the strategy. Then select the key indicators that you would use to monitor each of these premises.

3. Explain the differences between implementation controls, strategic surveillance, and special alert controls. Give an example of each.

---

[5] "How Mobil Became a Strategy-Focused Organization," Chapter 2 in R. Kaplan and D. Norton, *The Strategy-Focused Organization* (Boston: Harvard Business School Press, 2001). For an online version of the Mobil NAM&R case study, see www.bscol.com.

4. Why are budgets, schedules, and key success factors essential to operations control and evaluation?

5. What are key considerations in monitoring deviations from performance standards?

6. What are five key elements of quality management? How are quality imperative and continuous improvement related to strategic and operational control?

7. How might customer value be linked to quality, efficiency, and responsiveness?

8. Is it realistic that a commitment to continuous improvement could actually replace operational controls? Strategic controls?

9. How is the balanced scorecard approach similar to continuous improvement? How is it different?

Chapter 11 Discussion Case A

Strategic Control at Xerox under Ann Mulcahy's Watch

BusinessWeek

1   Anne Mulcahy likes to tell the story of the business acquaintance who compared her to a farmer with a cow stuck in a ditch. The cow, of course, was copying and printing giant Xerox, of which Mulcahy became president in 2000 and CEO in August, 2001. It was no doubt the toughest assignment in her 27 years at the company: As she took charge, Xerox was experiencing its second consecutive year of steep losses amid rising rumors of bankruptcy. Mulcahy's job was to pull Xerox out of that ditch—and keep it out.

2   Mulcahy became the first woman CEO in Xerox's history, thanks in large part to her performance as its first female president and chief operating officer, a job she got after a succession of men had failed.

3   Mulcahy's turnaround strategy focused first on cash generation and cost reduction. Let's look at some of the basic controls that she used.

IMPLEMENTATION CONTROL

4   Monitoring key strategic thrusts to raise cash along with setting short-term milestone reviews on cost-cutting measures were Mulcahy's main means of implementation control. She had a preference early-on for close person monitoring and involvement in these controls.

5   Early in her strategy, Mulcahy, president and CEO-in-waiting at the time, flew from headquarters in Stamford, Conn., to Rochester, N.Y., the home of Xerox's big operations, to deliver devastating news. The company was killing its entire line of desktop inkjet printers—a one-year-old business that employed 1,500 people worldwide and had been championed by Mulcahy herself. The division would not turn a profit for at least two years, though, and Xerox needed cash now. "In a year of tough decisions, this one was toughest," Mulcahy says.

6   Tough hardly does justice to that year. Xerox's directors suddenly promoted Mulcahy to president in May 2000, after ousting G. Richard Thoman, who lasted all of 13 months, and reinstalling Chairman Paul A. Allaire as CEO. The company was close to foundering after years of weak sales and high costs; employees were as disgruntled as customers.

7   Then, when Xerox's financial situation worsened later that year, the company was forced to take drastic action. With Allaire fixated on repairing the balance sheet, Mulcahy focused on operations, promising to slash $1 billion from Xerox's annual costs in two years. She set specific milestone targets as a roadmap to accomplishing those targets, including major decreases in personnel costs and manufacturing costs. 11,500 middle managers and factory workers later, and with a combination of significant outsourcing and manufacturing facility consolidation, she accomplished her objective in 18 months. Notably, her penchant for personal involvement was seen in this difficult task—she tried to make the announcements in person whenever jobs were cut or facilities shut down.

8   Her aggressive cost-cutting exceeded her original goal and helped generate a respectable $1.9 billion in operating cash flow and $91 million in net income on $15.8 billion in revenues by year-end, 2002. Worries over Xerox's ability to pay off $21.3 billion in liabilities—$9.2 billion of them long-term—have also been put to rest. At the end of 2003, it raised $3.6 billion with offerings of stock and bonds, and through bank financing, enough to earn itself a credit upgrade—from BB− to BB—from ratings agency Fitch.

9   The next milestone investors will want to examine and which are part of Mulcahy's implementation control involve steady improvements in earnings on a quarterly basis. In late 2003 as we write this book, Wall Street analysts expect $89 million, or 12 cents a share, on quarterly revenues of $3.9 billion. While that's a penny less than the first quarter's adjusted earnings, when it rang up $3.76 billion in sales, Xerox has proved that it can cut fat. The big challenge now will be whether it increase revenues. And it is the top line that Mulcahy's implementation control now turns toward.

10   Analyst Shannon Cross of equity research boutique Cross Research thinks overall sales will be down slightly in 2003, from $15.7 billion last year. To

meet analysts' 2004 expectations, Xerox would have to expand sales by about 7 percent next year—or further reduce expenses. The problem with the second option: Not much is left to cut.

STRATEGIC ALERT CONTROL

11   As she sought to consolidate her operational control as the new president and COO of Xerox in early 2000, things went from bad to worse for Mulcahy. Not only did Xerox report its first quarterly loss in 16 years and see its debt load piling up, but three months into her new position the Securities & Exchange Commission began investigating whether Xerox used accounting tricks to boost income in the five previous years.

12   This startling announcement sent shock waves not only throughout Xerox and the investment community but, perhaps more critically, Xerox's customer base and their faith in Xerox's ability to survive. Bankruptcy rumors started.

13   Mulcahy had a management group set up a strategic alert control team to monitor every aspect of this issue—the SEC investigators, where the admonition from Mulcahy was full and complete cooperation; key customers; the business press—with the key concern being to try to quickly and responsively handle subsequent negative publicity combined with immediate efforts by herself and anyone needed to assure key customers and, most importantly, to get a settlement resolved quickly yet fairly so as to not jeopardize Xerox's fragile cash situation.

14   Finally, almost 20 months later, the Securities & Exchange Commission issued suspension orders against two former Xerox accounting officers, apparently closing the books on a scandal that last year forced the company to restate five years of sales revenues and pay a $10 million fine.

PREMISE CONTROL

15   Mulcahy's second phase in turning around Xerox centers on revenue growth and product innovation. Expectations for their success in this regard are built on several premises which her management team will closely monitor.

16   Xerox's growth should approach 7 percent if some key premises hold out. Premise number one is that recent product price cuts and added focus on services should help Xerox grow faster than other printer-and-copier makers. Premise number two is that Xerox's strong presence overseas—which represents a big chunk of the 40 percent of its overseas revenue—will benefit from the weak dollar. Premise number three, Xerox sales are closely tied to the U.S. economy, which is recovering.

17   Premise number four is that price-cutting could grab it an additional 2 percent to 3 percent share of the printer market, where it now holds 18 percent, estimates Peter Grant, an analyst with market consultancy Gartner. In the past, Xerox sold its printers and copiers at a premium of 10 percent to 15 percent over rivals' products. Xerox introduced 21 new models in 2003 and cut prices to the most competitive levels in its history. As a result, Xerox wares now sell at or below the cost of competitors like Sharp, says Andy Slawetsky, a vice president with imaging consultancy Industry Analysts. Independent tests already show that Xerox equipment makes copies faster than virtually all rivals, and customers consider its salesforce among the best-trained, adds Slawetsky. Also, Xerox software is considered an industry benchmark.

STRATEGIC SURVEILLANCE CONTROL

18   Perhaps most critical to Mulcahy's strategy at Xerox are expectations or premises that a major trend is underway where companies are switching from black and white to color printers and copiers. So Mulcahy's long-term success is heavily dependent on this trend unfolding as a basis for major growth at Xerox. Xerox plans to capitalize on customers' transition from black-and-white copying and printing to color. Overall revenues from monochrome printers are declining, but the U.S. market for color printers will grow from $1.2 billion this year to $1.8 billion in three years according to some estimates. As corporations switch to color, revenues could grow dramatically, since Xerox receives about 9 cents per page on color copying, versus about 1.5 cents for black-and-white prints. Xerox also has increased its focus on services, already a $3 billion-plus part of its business. Strategic surveillance of developments in all industry sectors that use copiers and printers is a critical control priority at Xerox to maximize its chances to take advantage of the switch to color trend and the need for services in doing so.

19   Also the subject of strategic surveillance are possible challenges: With Xerox dropping its prices, the competition will likely follow suit. In fact, Grant predicts that average selling prices for color printers will fall by more than 20 percent this year. That's less than last year's 25 percent decline, but Xerox would likely be obliged to respond with yet another cut. And its margins could drop from the current 42 percent to 40 percent, say analysts. In both products and services, Xerox will hit stiff competition. Hewlett-Packard (HPQ) is expected to come out with a new color printer-copier within the next 12 months. HP declined to comment on new-product introductions, but it's working to make its pricing easier to understand in the hope of appealing to small and midsize businesses, says Chris Morgan, vice-president for imaging and printing sales and marketing at HP. Both it and IBM (IBM) are pushing package deals for smaller companies, offerings that go beyond information-technology network services tied in with printers and copiers.

20   Xerox insists it isn't worried. "We expect that [rivals] don't have a lot of room in which to cut prices," says a spokesperson. "At the same time, we're confident that Xerox has the right business model to drive profitable revenue from these products while remaining competitive in this aggressive industry." Again, this is a sure premise to be monitored and a candidate for strategic surveillance control.

Source: "That Heartbeat You Hear Is Xerox," *BusinessWeek*, July 16, 2003.

Chapter 11 Discussion Case B

BusinessWeek

The Web of Quality: Worldwide Links Mean Better Products

1 Just a decade ago, U.S. businesses were crowing about the promise of new quality-improvement programs. Since then, the U.S. quality movement has altered and improved business practices, and many American companies have matched Japan's vaunted quality benchmarks. Industrial offices buzzed with phrases such as "total quality management (TQM)" and "Six-Sigma accuracy." Such catchphrases are heard less frequently because they've been replaced by Internet jargon. And that raises a question: Where does quality stand in the Internet age?

2 Concerns about quality have by no means disappeared. Rather, at most successful companies, quality has become internalized, says quality consultant Joseph A. DeFeo, CEO of Juran Institute Inc. in Wilton, Conn. The special software and management practices associated with the movement are now in everyday use, he says, so quality has become less self-conscious. But it has reemerged as a critical issue because of the rapid development of Internet links among companies. Quality is no longer the concern of just a single factory but of whole supply chains. As companies outsource more of their work, they need to take increasing care to make sure their partners measure up on quality, says Michael J. Burkett, a senior analyst at Boston's AMR Research Inc., a manufacturing consultant.

3 This report explores the role of quality in today's increasingly networked world. The first section looks at how a unit of General Electric Co. is blazing new quality trails in a field it helped pioneer. The second lifts the lid on efforts by Mexico's manufacturers to meet the quality demands of customers in North America and overseas.

GE: ZERO TO 60, NO SKID MARKS

4 Never before has General Electric Co. cranked out gas-powered turbines in such quantities. Given the growing preference for gas-powered generating plants over their much dirtier coal-burning cousins, demand is booming—with no sign of slowing. In May, GE's Power Systems unit installed five times the number of turbines it did a year earlier. Yet despite the problems of grappling with such a huge increase in production, GE has become progressively better at making good on de-

livery date promises. Indeed, the company has actually delivered many units ahead of schedule (see chart on p. 392). GE Power's success at managing its huge runup in output is a much-discussed success story among GE insiders—and a major reason they view Power Systems head Robert L. Nardelli as a top contender for GE's CEO job when Jack Welch retires.

5 While GE is hardly complaining about this upturn, executives realized that the runup would pose huge risks. In particular, they worried about maintaining their grip on quality, continuing to fill orders on time, and keeping customers happy. The last thing they wanted was to become another example of a company that lost control when it tried to goose production quickly after getting bombarded by orders. The production snafus at Boeing Co. in 1997 offered an ominous example of how things can go wrong in a big rampup. And when GE execs began taking notice in 1998 of industry numbers showing that electrical-power reserves in the United States were shrinking to alarming levels, Boeing's difficulties were painfully fresh.

6 OUTSIDE RISKS. To prepare for the projected hike in orders, GE Power Systems' managers visited companies that had lived through similar explosions in their businesses. They made a point of flying to Seattle to glean insights from Boeing officials. One thing became evident right away: The biggest risk to GE was outside the company. Suppliers that lacked GE's financial resources might not be able to expand production rapidly enough. At Boeing and other casualties of too-fast growth, most breakdowns occurred when suppliers overestimated their production capacity. Since more than 50 percent of a turbine's components are purchased from outside vendors, GE wasted no time shoring up its supply chain. In 1998, GE Power Systems launched an exhaustive study of the suppliers that provide key components for the gas turbines. After first screening 250 of its suppliers, it intensively audited 85 that posed the greatest risk. Teams consisting of specialists in supply sourcing, research and development, finance, and management spent up to two weeks at supplier facilities across the United States and around the world.

7 Since the last major rampup in production at Power Systems in the late 80s, GE had two new tools to help

it avoid supply-chain problems, says Victor R. Abate, general manager of fulfillment at Power Systems. One was the Internet. But more important was the company's vaunted Six-Sigma program, adopted in 1996. Six sigma is statistics-speak for 99.9999976 percent. Applied to manufacturing, it means a quality level of no more than 3.4 defects per million products. At GE, the Six-Sigma program also includes guidelines and tools for boosting productivity and wringing inefficiencies out of its manufacturing and service processes. Mark M. Little, a vice-president at GE Power Systems, says that with Six-Sigma's tools, GE no longer has to rely on bludgeoning suppliers to deliver. Instead, GE's auditors have the wherewithal to determine whether suppliers can hand over parts in time.

8 GE's vendor-checkers scrutinize myriad details right down to the individual machine tools that suppliers use to produce turbine parts. GE also evaluates the supplier's suppliers—their production capacity, shipping and delivery systems, and how rigorous their quality programs are. And the exam doesn't end there. Because a supplier might need to boost hiring, GE checks to see whether the company keeps a stack of résumés on hand. In the end, GE eliminated some suppliers and found backups for suppliers with obvious weaknesses. And they tagged some 350 potential problems that continued to be monitored until fixed by the suppliers.

9 INVALUABLE ASSET. Perhaps most important, the initial evaluation allowed GE to establish a framework for ensuring the quality of its supply chain as production rolled forward. Says analyst Nicholas P. Heymann of Prudential Securities Inc., who formerly worked as a GE auditor: "How many companies today have guys that can go into another company and fully assess where the flaws are—and not only that but also fix them? They've executed Six-Sigma all the way through the supplier chain."

10 That was an invaluable asset as orders flowed in and the stress on production systems mounted, both internally and among suppliers. With its new predictive tools, deep knowledge of its suppliers, and the ability to share information quickly via the Internet, GE could identify problems earlier and avoid potentially costly bottlenecks. "Whenever we see variation, we just attack it," Abate says.

11 Example: GE last year realized that a supplier of a core turbine component was poised to fall behind. Although the company was consistently delivering to GE on time, GE's Six-Sigma audit had found the supplier would be unable to keep up as GE went from producing 25 turbines to 45 per quarter in late 1999. GE sent a team to the company, and a settlement was

reached: The supplier would lease additional equipment to keep up with GE's production track. "With these very rigorous tools," says Little, "we now know what the leading indicators are, and we can act fast."

12 The Internet has made a big difference, too. When GE engineers are in the field, checking on deliveries at customers sites anywhere in the world, they can report on a problem on their laptops, and this information is available instantly throughout GE Power Systems. Before the Net, the field engineers would typically resolve each problem at the plant site—but GE managers would remain blissfully unaware of the solution, which would have to be engineered all over again the next time.

13 So what's the customer's view of how well GE is coping with its production surges? Duke Energy North America (DENA, a unit of Charlotte-based Duke Energy Corp.) is clearly satisfied. It placed a huge order with GE in the fall of 1998 to outfit nearly two dozen generating plants with gas turbines, four of which will be on line by month's end. Including service agreements, it was a $4 billion order. So far, everything has gone according to schedule or slightly ahead of it, says James M. Donnell, CEO of DENA. For Duke, there's a lot at stake. With summer already starting to stroke demand for electricity, each day that a gas-turbine plant isn't producing means a huge revenue loss. A 640-megawatt plant running at maximum capacity for 16 hours on a summer day, for example, translates into $1.75 million in gross revenues.

14 For GE the stakes are high, too. The company boasts that it has grabbed a 75 percent share of current turbine orders. With the power industry relying so heavily on one supplier, more eyes than ever will be watching to see if Power Systems can keep managing the boom.

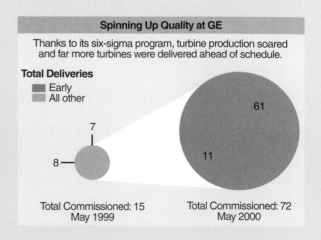

Spinning Up Quality at GE

Thanks to its six-sigma program, turbine production soared and far more turbines were delivered ahead of schedule.

Total Deliveries
- ■ Early
- ■ All other

7
8

61
11

Total Commissioned: 15
May 1999

Total Commissioned: 72
May 2000

Source: Petty, John, "When Near Enough is Not Good Enough," *Australian CPA,* May 2000, pp. 34–35.

Index